THE INDO-EUROPEAN LANGUAGES

D1388501

Other works in the series

The Romance Languages
The Celtic Languages
The Slavonic Languages
The Germanic Languages
The Dravidian Languages
The Uralic Languages
The Semitic Languages
The Bantu Languages
The Austronesian Languages of Asia and Madagascar
The Oceanic Languages
The Mongolic Languages
The Indo-Aryan Languages
The Sino-Tibetan Languages
The Indo-European Languages
The Turkic Languages

Forthcoming works in the series

The Tai-Kadai Languages
The Iranian Languages

THE
INDO-EUROPEAN
LANGUAGES

EDITED BY
Anna Giacalone Ramat
and
Paolo Ramat

LONDON AND NEW YORK

First published 1993 as *Le Lingue Indoeuropee*
© Società editrice Il Mulino, Bologna

Published 1998
by Routledge
2 Park Square, Milton Park, Abingdon, Oxon, OX14 4RN
270 Madison Ave, New York NY 10016

© 1998 This translation Routledge

Reprinted 2006

Routledge is an imprint of the Taylor & Francis Group, an informa business

Typeset in 10.5/12 Times by Solidus (Bristol) Ltd, Bristol
Printed and bound in Great Britain by
The Cromwell Press, Trowbridge, Wiltshire

British Library Cataloguing in Publication Data

A catalogue record for this book is available from the British Library

Library of Congress Cataloging-in-Publication Data

Lingue Indo europee.   English
        The Indo-European languages / edited by Anna Giacalone Ramat and
Paolo Ramat.
        (Routledge language family descriptions)
        Includes bibliographical references and index.
        1. Indo-European languages.   I. Giacalone Ramat, Anna
II. Ramat, Paolo.   III. Title.   IV. Series.
P561.L56   1997
410—dc2l   96–40341
                                                                        CIP

ISBN10: 0-415-41263-3
ISBN13: 978-0-415-41263-6

Contents

List of Maps with Acknowledgements

List of Figures

List of Tables

List of Contributors

Consultant Editors
J. H. W. Penney, Wolfson College, University of Oxford, UK.
Nigel Vincent, University of Manchester, UK.

Translators
R. Nigel Smith.
Adam Ledgeway (Preface and chapter 10, Latin).

Contributors
Roberto Ajello, Professor of Linguistics, University of Pisa, Italy.
Henning Andersen, University of California, Los Angeles, USA.
†Enrico Campanile
Bernard Comrie, Professor of Linguistics, University of Southern California, Los Angeles, USA.
Shaban Demiraj, Tirana, Albania.
Henry M. Hoenigswald, Professor Emeritus of Linguistics, University of Pennsylvania, USA.
Romano Lazzeroni, Professor of Linguistics, University of Pisa, Italy.
Silvia Luraghi, Professor of Linguistics, University of Rome III, Italy.
Paolo Ramat, Professor of Linguistics, University of Pavia, Italy.
William R. Schmalstieg, Edwin Erle Sparks Professor of Slavic Languages, Pennsylvania State University, USA.
Domenico Silvestri, Department of the Study of the Classical World, Istituto Universitario Orientale, Naples, Italy.
Nicholas Sims-Williams, Professor of Iranian and Central Asian Studies, School of Oriental and African Studies, University of London, UK.
Patrick Sims-Williams, Chair of Celtic Studies, University of Wales, Aberystwyth, UK.
Edoardo Vineis, Professor of Linguistics, Department of Modern Languages, University of Bologna, Italy.
Calvert Watkins, Harvard University, Cambridge, Massachusetts, USA.
Werner Winter, Professor Emeritus of Linguistics, University of Kiel, Germany.

Preface

The idea for the present volume grew from a combination of both practical concerns and the present editors' personal teaching experience, during the course of which the idea developed to write a book which would present an overview of current research in each of the individual languages and language families of Indo-European.

In an increasingly complex discipline such as linguistics, currently characterized by a wide variety of areas of interest, there is a clear need for scientifically tested tools which can present the latest research in a concise and clear manner, as witnessed by a number of recent volumes such as M. Harris and N. Vincent, *The Romance Languages* (Beckenham: Croom Helm 1988), B. Comrie and G. C. Corbett, *The Slavonic Languages* (London: Routledge 1993). Even within the field of IE linguistics, the degree of specialization today is such that it proves increasingly difficult to be an authority on the entire language family, as had still been possible for scholars such as Meillet. Indeed, the ambitious project of producing a modern version of K. Brugmann and B. Delbrück's *Vergleichende Grammatik*, namely the *Indogermanische Grammatik*, undertaken by J. Kuryłowicz in 1968, and subsequently continued by C. Watkins, W. Cowgill and M. Mayrhofer, sets out to bring together the expertise of several specialists in one volume (although, unfortunately, still far from completion at present). We too have recognized the necessity of such a collaborative approach.

It is our intention that this book will not only be of use to students specializing within the field of IE linguistics, who want to check out basic points of information on the various members of the family, but will also serve all those, students and scholars alike, interested in the problems of historical linguistics, language change and the methods of comparison and reconstruction more generally. With this aim in view, we have endeavoured to produce a book which presents the data in a clear and accessible manner, such that it may be used as both a general reference work and a text book for university students on undergraduate and graduate courses.

Needless to say the approach adopted in the present volume focuses on comparison and reconstruction within the IE family and on the differences encountered within the individual languages in relation to the common 'parent language'. Consequently, the subsequent developments of the individual languages and subgroups are not, except for very occasional references, treated in the present volume.

The general layout of the individual chapters adheres more or less to a common expository model, which includes a brief historical synthesis, followed by a definition of the position of each language within the IE family and a description of the most salient phonetic, morphological and syntactic features. Obviously, some of these topics are treated in greater depth in some chapters than in others, a decision which reflects the varying interests of the individual authors. However, the identical presentation of core topics in all chapters will aid the reader to draw comparisons across the individual languages, as well as serving to stimulate new research and a deeper understanding of the relevant issues.

In order to get this more or less common expository model the decision has also been taken not to deal with the so-called *Restsprachen*, i.e. languages which are scarcely and fragmentarily attested, such as Messapic, Thracian or Phrygian. The problems these languages raise are firstly of philological/epigraphic nature. At any rate any approach to them has necessarily to be very different from the approaches used in describing the languages dealt with in this volume (on Phrygian and Thracian see *Langues indo-européennes*, edited by Fr. Bader, CNRS, Paris 1994).

Some reviewers of the Italian edition of the present book have complained about the 'noninterventionist editorial policy' of the editors, which has led to inconsistencies among different chapters, concerning, e.g., the laryngeal phonemes and the glottalic obstruents.[1]

Yet, we still believe that it does not fall within the scope of the editors' duties to try to smooth out, where apparent, differences of opinion or of theoretical stance among the individual authors, which undeniably characterize a number of unresolved issues in present research within IE linguistics. We do not believe, however, that such differences will cause the reader to meet with difficulty when consulting the present volume, if, for example in the case of laryngeals and glottals, the correspondences between 'old' and 'new' systems are borne in mind. In any case, a number of cross-references have been introduced into individual chapters in order to aid the reader. None the less, it must be understood that each chapter forms an autonomous piece of research, concluding with a substantial bibliography, and may therefore be used independently.

Some differences in the presentation of facts are at any rate more conspicuous, particularly in the field of phonetics and phonology already alluded to where, after years of heated debate, the laryngealist theory appears, however, to have gained general acceptance in some form or other (cf. Th. Vennemann, *The New Sound of Indo-European: Essays in Phonological Reconstruction*, Mouton de Gruyter, 1989). The reader will observe that in the following chapters some authors, especially Italian contributors, prefer to use *sch(ə)wa* <ə> in reconstructed forms, whereas others favour the use of the three laryngeal symbols H_1, H_2, H_3. However, passing from one system of notation to the other proves relatively straightforward and in the vast majority of cases does not lead to alternative reconstructions of original forms (see Watkins, pp. 40–4 in this volume).

By contrast, T. Gamkrelidze and V. Ivanov's proposals regarding the reconstruction of the IE consonantal system (*Indoevropejskij jazyk i Indoevropejcy*, Tbilisi, Izdatel'stvo Tbilisskogo Universiteta, 1984; English translation by Johanna Nichols, *Indo-European and the Indo-Europeans*, Berlin: Mouton de Gruyter, 1995) have given rise to an impassioned debate in current research. However, the authors of the present volume have, on the whole, confined themselves to presenting the old reconstructed system *à la* Brugmann alongside the new system with glottalized consonants, e.g. $p = p^h$, $b = p'$, etc. Even in this instance, in the description of the IE languages the use of one or the other systems of reconstruction does not entail, in real terms, any substantial differences: 'the theory is essentially concerned with phonetic interpretation rather than with modification of the phonological system. Under the theory there are still three manners of articulation, and the same oppositions as for the traditional triad exemplified by *t d dh*' (Lehmann, *Theoretical Bases of Indo-European Linguistics*, London: Routledge, 1993; p. 100). In essence, differences are limited to notational practices which are more or less plausible from a typological perspective (see however the discussion of 'Germanic consonant shifts' in Chapter 13, §§ 5.2.1 and 5.2.2). Needless to say that from a theoretical perspective this represents a limitation of the method of comparative reconstruction and of its results, the latter derived from the sum of information that can be inductively established from an analysis of the historically attested languages of the family.

In a more in-depth theoretical discussion, the various proposals concerning the phonological system of Indo-European, both in terms of laryngeals and glottals, have a bearing on one of the crucial aspects of reconstruction, namely the reality or otherwise of the forms induced by the method of comparative reconstruction. It may be that the reconstructed consonantal systems with laryngeals and glottals are phonetically more plausible than the traditional system. However, in terms of phonemic structure, the reconstructed systems do not alter the relationships of correspondences which form the basis of comparison among the IE languages, the description of which is the principal aim of the present volume. Traditionally, there has been a split in the field of IE linguistics between those supporters of a method of 'realistic' reconstruction and those who adhere to a method of 'symbolic' reconstruction (cf. «Incontri linguistici» 9/1984, in particular Ramat, Lazzeroni, Campanile).

Although deliberately simplifying the problem, the method of symbolic reconstruction, it may be said, involves establishing a system of interlinguistic phonetic correspondences which can all be subsumed and captured by a single symbol. By way of example, Lat. *frater*, Goth. *broþar*, etc. can be traced back to the same original initial sound, which we can symbolize as $*b^h$ (or as $*b^{[h]}$

in the glottalist theory). As proposed by Benveniste, such a symbol could ultimately be represented by a number, rather than by a letter of the alphabet, although, as observed by Roman Jakobson in his distinguished contribution to the VIII International Congress of Linguists (Oslo, 1957), such an approach risks producing reconstructed forms which, from a typological perspective, are extremely improbable. Yet, we need not concern ourselves with an in-depth discussion of this issue in an introductory discussion of this type. Rather, the above remarks will suffice to clarify the reasons for the discrepancies between the various chapters in their treatment of the reconstructed forms of identical lexemes and morphemes.

It is not by chance that much of the current debate among specialists in IE linguistics centres around phonetics. This is due in part to the more rigidly structured nature of phonetic systems, in contrast to morphosyntactic and lexical systems: it would appear possible for the former to establish a more 'ordered' and strictly regulated phenomenal reality. In part this emphasis is also due to the fact that, from a typological perspective, both the vocalic and consonantal systems of Proto-Indo-European seem to exhibit, as noted above, features unusual and less common in the world's languages (cf. Chapter 3), which require explanation.

As the reader can verify by comparing the various chapters of this volume, agreement among linguists is greater in matters of morphology: witness the identical recognition of parts of speech and their formal markings, which clearly betray a common ancestry and typological homology.

Still little studied, by contrast, is the area of IE syntax, in spite of a small number of important general works (W. P. Lehmann, *Proto-Indo-European Syntax*, University of Texas Press, 1974; P. Ramat *et al.* (eds), *Linguistic Reconstruction and Indo-European Syntax*, Amsterdam: Benjamins, 1980). The reason why syntax had received only scant attention from specialists until quite recently, though not forgetting the distinguished precedents set by such scholars as Delbrück, Miklosič, Wackernagel and Hirt, is a result of external factors, namely the fragmentary nature of extant written records and the difficulty involved in comparing similar textual structures across languages. This, in turn, accounts for the limited number of pages given over to syntax in the individual chapters, though some contributors (cf. Watkins, Luraghi, Ramat, Andersen), adopting, of course, a typological approach, do address a number of phenomena, particularly word order in simple sentences and aspects of subordination.

The typological approach, one of the innovations of the present volume, is dealt with in particular detail by Comrie, although it equally recurs as a common feature of the other contributions. Comrie adopts an approach which compares Proto-Indo-European with other language families with which it was probably in contact and to which it is possibly genetically related. Such comparisons lend support to the plausibility of proposals regarding reconstructed forms (for example, cf. the discussion above concerning the consonantal system in relation to the theory of glottals) and account for the apparent typological anomalies of Indo-European.

Even if the concept of Indo-European is chiefly a linguistic designation, as irrefutably confirmed by the typological approach, it seemed necessary to complete the picture with a separate chapter on the reconstruction of IE culture, even in view of the recent flurry of studies in this area (see *Is there a Prehistory of Linguistics?* with contributions from C. Renfrew, T. Bynon, M. Ruhlen, A. Dolgopolsky and P. Bellwood, Cambridge Archaeological Journal 5, 2 (1995): 257–75). The late lamented E. Campanile (Chapter 1) provides both a concise and balanced outline of a 'vocabulary of the IE institutions', clearly drawing on the model presented in E. Benveniste's classic book and on G. Dumézil's studies of 'the religion of the Indo-Europeans'. Subsequently, Campanile discusses the most reliable methodological criteria for uncovering cultural evidence when faced with particularly difficult conditions, namely the absence of any direct texts and reliable archaeological evidence. Recently, thanks especially to work by archaeologists such as M. Gimbutas, C. Renfrew and J. P. Mallory, there has been a revival of interest in the issue of the *Urheimat*, the original homeland of the Indo-European people. Campanile expresses methodological doubts about the naive assumptions on which hypotheses on the original homeland of the Indo-Europeans are based. The real problem lies in how to bring together the archaeological evidence and the linguistic data, even though it is probably unanimously agreed that languages do not develop within a vacuum, but rather within the context of social groups. According to Gamkrelidze and Ivanov, the original homeland of the IE people is to be traced back to Eastern Anatolia, whereas M. Gimbutas, in contrast, favours the steppes of southern Russia to the north of the Black Sea. The reader is referred to the debate fuelled by Renfrew's book, *Archeology and Language, the Puzzle of Indo-European Origins* (London: Jonathan Cape, 1987). Renfrew holds that the ancient IE languages were already being spoken in eastern Anatolia in the seventh millennium AD; and that the expansion of the IE people towards the west would have followed the parallel expansion of farming from the Middle East. We cannot fail to mention, in this respect, the data from research carried out in the field of genetics (cf. A. J. Ammermann and L. Cavalli-Sforza, *The Neolithic Transition and the Genetics of Populations in Europe*, Princeton: Princeton University Press, 1984), which have revealed a mutation of genes in the human fossils scattered throughout Europe, a fact which directly betrays a change in dietary habits. Indeed, such a change points to the transformation of a civilization of non-cultivating pickers and hunters into a civilization of farmers. None the less, the problem of associating the speakers of different western IE languages with the subsequent waves of agricultural expansion still remains unsolved. For further discussion of the relationship between linguistic and archaeological data, the reader is referred to W. Meid, *Archäologie und Sprachwissenschaft. Kritisches zu neueren Hypothesen der*

Ausbreitung der Indogermanen (Innsbrucker Beiträge zur Sprachwissen-schaft, Vorträge 43, 1989); Edgar C. Polomé, 'Linguistics and archaeology: differences in perspective in the study of prehistoric cultures', in W. P. Lehmann and Helen-Jo Jakusz Hewitt (eds), *Language Typology 1988* (Amsterdam and Philadelphia: Benjamins, 1991, pp. 111–34); and W. P. Lehmann, *Theoretical Bases of Indo-European Linguistics*, ch. 12.

The editors would like to thank Davide Ricca and especially Pierluigi Cuzzolin for their valuable cooperation in the production of the present volume.

A.G.R. and P.R.

Note
1 However, we have adopted in all chapters the notation ‹bʰ, dʰ› etc., replacing the traditional *bh, dh* etc., which better represents the monophonemic value of the IE aspirates. We have also adopted the notation ‹j, w› instead of the traditional ‹i̯, u̯›, to conform transcriptions to the IPA system and to indicate the probably non-full vocalic value of [i, u], both in rising and falling diphthongs.

List of Linguistic Abbreviations

A	adjective	dat.	dative
abl.	ablative	dem.	demonstrative
acc.	accusative	dir.	directive
act.	active	Dor.	Doric
Ad	Adposition	EBalt.	East Baltic
adv. gen.	adverbial genitive	encl.	enclitic
adj.	adjective	Eng.	English
Aeol.	Aeolic	ESlav.	East Slavic
Alb.	Albanian	f.	feminine
Anat.	Anatolian	Fal.	Faliscan
aor.	aorist	Finn.	Finnish
Arc. Cypr.	Arcado-Cypriot	Fr.	French
arch.	archaic	fut.	future
Arm.	Armenian	G	genitive
Att.	Attic	Gaul.	Gaulish
aux.	auxiliary	gen.	genitive
Avest.	Avestan	Ger.	German
Balt.	Baltic	Gk	Greek
Bel.	Belorussian	Gmc	Germanic
Bret.	Breton	Goth.	Gothic
Bulg.	Bulgarian	Hitt.	Hittite
C	consonant	HLuw	Hieroglyphic Luwian
CC	Common Celtic	Hom.	Homeric Greek
CGmc	Common Germanic	I	indirect object
Ch.S	Church Slavonic	Icel.	Icelandic
CI	Celtiberian	IE	Indo-European
CLuw	Cuneiform Luwian	II	Indo-Iranian
comp.	comparative	Ill.	Illyrian
conn.	connective	imp.	imperative
CS	Common Slavic	impf.	imperfect
CToch.	Common Tocharian	ind.	indicative
Cz.	Czech	inf.	infinitive
Dan.	Danish	instr.	instrumental

intrans.	intransitive	perf.	perfect
Ion.	Ionian	Pers.	Persian
ipfr.	imperfective	pfv.	perfective
Ir.	Irish	PGmc	Proto-Germanic
Iran.	Iranian	PIE	Proto-Indo-European
It.	Italian	pl.	plural
Khot.	Khotanese	pluperf.	pluperfect
Kurd.	Kurdish	PN	personal name
Lat.	Latin	Pol.	Polish
Latv.	Latvian	Postpos.	postposition
LCS	Late Common Slavic	pple.	past participle
Lep.	Lepontic	Pr.	Prussian
Lith.	Lithuanian	pres.	present
loc.	locative	pret.	preterite
LS	Lower Sorbian	PPP	preterite participle
Luv.	Luvian	prev.	preverb
Luw.	Luwian	pron.	pronoun
Lyc.	Lycian	Pr.W etc.	Primitive Welsh etc.
Lyd.	Lydian	PS	Proto-Slavic
m.	masculine	ptc.	particle
Mac.	Macedonian	R	root
mid.	middle	refl.	reflexive
Mil.	Milyan	rel.	relative
MPers. etc.	Middle Persian etc.	Rum.	Rumanian
Myc.	Mycenaean	Russ.	Russian
n.	neuter	RV	RigVeda
N	Norse, noun	S	suffix
nom.	nominative	S. Pic.	South Picene
Norw.	Norwegian	Sax.	Saxon
obl.	oblique	SC	Serbo-Croatian
OCS	Old Church Slavonic	sc.	scilicet
OHG	Old High German	Serb.	Serbian
OI	Old Icelandic (or Norse)	sg.	singular
		Sk	Slovak
OIr. etc.	Old Irish etc.	Skt	Sanskrit
opt.	optative	Slav.	Slavic
Osc.	Oscan	Slov.	Slovincian
Oss.	Ossetic	Sn	Slovenian
Pael.	Paelignian	Sogd.	Sogdian
Pal.	Palaic	SSlav.	South Slavic
part.	participle	subj.	subject
Parth.	Parthian	suff.	suffix
Pb.	Polabian	SVO etc.	subject-verb-object etc.
Paelign.	Paelignian		

Swed.	Swedish	Ved.	Vedic
Toch.	Tocharian	Ven.	Venetic
trans.	transitive	voc.	vocative
trisyll.	trisyllabic	W	Welsh
U	Ukrainian	WCB	Welsh, Cornish and
Umbr.	Umbrian		Breton
US	Upper Sorbian	WSlav.	West Slavic
V	vowel	YAV	Young Avestan

List of Periodical Abbreviations

AArmL *Annual of Armenian Linguistics.* Cleveland, Ohio
AGI *Archivio Glottologico Italiano.* Florence
AIΩN *Annali dell'Istituto Orientale di Napoli.* Naples
ArchL *Archivum Linguisticum.* Edinburgh
ASNSP *Annali della Scuola Normale Superiore di Pisa.* Pisa
BBCS *Bwletin y Bwrdd Gwybodau Celtaidd. The Bulletin of the Board of Celtic Studies.* Cardiff
BSL *Bulletin de la Société Linguistique de Paris.* Paris
HA *Handes Amsorya. Zeitschrift für armenische Philologie.* Vienna
IF *Indogermanische Forschungen. Zeitschrift für Indogermanistik und allgemeine Sprachwissenschaft.* Berlin
IFŽ *Istoriko-filologičeskij žurnal Akademii nauk Armjanskoj SSR.* Erevan
JAOS *Journal of the American Oriental Society.* New Haven, Conn.
JIES *The Journal of Indo-European Studies.* Hattiesburg, Miss.
KZ *Zeitschrift für vergleichende Sprachforschung.* Göttingen. [Oggi Historische Sprachforschung/Historical linguistics (abbr. HS)]
Lg *Language. Journal of the Linguistic Society of America.* Baltimore
MSS *Münchener Studien zur Sprachwissenschaft.* Munich
NTS *New Testament Studies.* Cambridge
RALinc *Atti della Accademia Nazionale dei Lincei, Rendiconti della Classe di scienze morali, storiche e filologiche.* Serie VIII. Rome
REArm *Revue des Études Arméniennes.* Paris
RhM *Rheinisches Museum für Philologie. Neue Folge.* Frankfurt am Main
RIL *Rendiconti dell'Istituto Lombardo di Scienze e Lettere, Classe di lettere e scienze morali e storiche.* Milan
RL *Recherches Linguistiques de Vincennes.* Saint-Denis
SCO *Studi Classici e Orientali.* Pisa
SE *Studi Etruschi.* Florence
SLSal *Studi Linguistici Salentini.* Galatina
SSL *Studi e saggi linguistici.* Supplement to the journal *L'Italia dialettale.* Pisa
TPhS *Transactions of the Philological Society.* Oxford
VJ *Voprosy Jazykoznanija.* Moscow

The International Phonetic Alphabet

CONSONANTS

	Bilabial	Labiodental	Dental	Alveolar	Postalveolar	Retroflex	Palatal	Velar	Uvular	Pharyngeal	Glottal
Plosive	p b			t d		ʈ ɖ	c ɟ	k ɡ	q ɢ		ʔ
Nasal	m	ɱ		n		ɳ	ɲ	ŋ	N		
Trill	B			r					R		
Tap or Flap				ɾ		ɽ					
Fricative	ɸ β	f v	θ ð	s z	ʃ ʒ	ʂ ʐ	ç ʝ	x ɣ	χ ʁ	ħ ʕ	h ɦ
Lateral fricative				ɬ ɮ							
Approximant		ʋ		ɹ		ɻ	j	ɰ			
Lateral approximant				l		ɭ	ʎ	L			
Ejective stop	p’			t’		ʈ’	c’	k’	q’		
Implosive	ɓ ɓ			ɗ ɗ			ʄ ʄ	ɠ ɠ	ʠ ʛ		

Where symbols appear in pairs, the one to the right represents a voiced consonant. Shaded areas denote articulations judged impossible.

DIACRITICS

̥ Voiceless	n̥ d̥	̹ More rounded	ɔ̹	ʷ Labialized	tʷ dʷ	̃ Nasalized	ẽ
̬ Voiced	s̬ t̬	̜ Less rounded	ɔ̜	ʲ Palatalized	tʲ dʲ	ⁿ Nasal release	dⁿ
ʰ Aspirated	tʰ dʰ	̟ Advanced	u̟	ˠ Velarized	tˠ dˠ	ˡ Lateral release	dˡ
̤ Breathy voiced	b̤ a̤	̠ Retracted	i̠	ˤ Pharyngealized	tˤ dˤ	̚ No audible release	d̚
̰ Creaky voiced	b̰ a̰	̈ Centralized	ë	̴ Velarized or pharyngealized	ɫ		
̼ Linguolabial	t̼ d̼	̽ Mid centralized	ě	̝ Raised	e̝ (ɹ̝ = voiced alveolar fricative)		
̪ Dental	t̪ d̪	̩ Syllabic	n̩	̞ Lowered	e̞ (β̞ = voiced bilabial approximant)		
̺ Apical	t̺ d̺	̯ Non-syllabic	e̯	̘ Advanced Tongue Root	e̘		
̻ Laminal	t̻ d̻	˞ Rhoticity	ɚ	̙ Retracted Tongue Root	e̙		

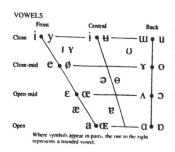

VOWELS

Front Central Back

Close: i y — ɨ ʉ — ɯ u
ɪ ʏ ʊ
Close-mid: e ø — ɘ ɵ — ɤ o
ə
Open-mid: ɛ œ — ɜ ɞ — ʌ ɔ
æ ɐ
Open: a ɶ — ɑ ɒ

Where symbols appear in pairs, the one to the right represents a rounded vowel.

OTHER SYMBOLS

ʍ Voiceless labial-velar fricative	ʘ Bilabial click		
w Voiced labial-velar approximant	ǀ Dental click		
ɥ Voiced labial-palatal approximant	ǃ (Post)alveolar click		
ʜ Voiceless epiglottal fricative	ǂ Palatoalveolar click		
ʢ Voiced epiglottal fricative	ǁ Alveolar lateral click		
ʡ Epiglottal plosive	ꞎ Alveolar lateral flap		
ɕ ʑ Alveolo-palatal fricatives	ʃ Simultaneous ʃ and X		
ɜ Additional mid central vowel			

Affricates and double articulations can be represented by two symbols joined by a ligature/tie bar if necessary. k͡p t͡s

SUPRASEGMENTALS

ˈ Primary stress
ˌ Secondary stress   ˌfoʊnəˈtɪʃən

ː Long	eː
ˑ Half-long	eˑ
̆ Extra-short	ĕ
. Syllable break	ɹi.ækt
ǀ Minor (foot) group	
‖ Major (intonation) group	
‿ Linking (absence of a break)	
↗ Global rise	
↘ Global fall	

TONES AND WORD ACCENTS

LEVEL			CONTOUR		
e̋ or ˥	Extra-high		ě or ˄	Rising	
é ˦	High		ê ˅	Falling	
ē ˧	Mid		e᷄ ˀ	High rising	
è ˨	Low		e᷅ ˀ	Low rising	
ȅ ˩	Extra-low		e᷈ ˀ	Rising-falling etc.	

↓ Downstep
↑ Upstep

xxiii

1 The Indo-Europeans: Origins and Culture

Enrico Campanile

The Reconstruction of Indo-European Culture

Although the concept of Indo-European is primarily a linguistic one, it is none the less clear that merely by postulating the existence of this language we have also to postulate the existence of a homogeneous group of speakers characterized by a particular culture, as is the case with any natural language. Indo-European formed an essential part of that culture and was to some extent a faithful reflection of it. This observation has many repercussions from historical and sociological perspectives.

In other words, it was natural that almost as soon as comparative linguistics had established the concept of Indo-European (no easy feat, since it was by no means obvious that an unattested language could be posited as the basis of a language family) and had fruitfully set out to reconstruct it, linguists also began to wonder about the material and intellectual culture of the unknown peoples who had at one time spoken Indo-European. This was the origin of research into the origins and culture of the Indo-Europeans.

Normally historians reconstruct history (including cultural history) using written or archaeological evidence. However, in the case of the Indo-Europeans this is not possible, since no texts or archaeological remains have survived: scholars can study only their language, or rather only those isolated linguistic fragments offered us by reconstruction.

The Lexicalist Method

It is understandable, then, that the first attempts to recover IE culture (those made by Adalbert Kuhn in the mid-nineteenth century) employed what we may term the 'lexicalist' method: an IE word was reconstructed, and from the existence of this lexeme it was deduced that the object denoted must have existed in IE culture. Thus, for example, from the existence of the lexeme *$r\bar{e}\hat{g}$-s* 'king' (cf. Ved. *rāj-*, Lat. *rēx*, Gaul. *-rīx*) it was deduced that the IE peoples were ruled by kings; from the existence of *$*owis$* 'sheep' (Lat. *ovis*, Ved. *avi-*, etc.) that they practised sheep rearing, and so on.

Kuhn used this technique in a series of studies published between 1845 and 1873 to produce an initial outline reconstruction of the culture of the Indo-

1

Europeans, portraying them as farmers and breeders of livestock, with a stable social structure and a monarchic system of government, religious, and with a strong sense of family.

Given the rather elementary nature of this methodology, it is not difficult to identify some of Kuhn's precursors. As early as 1828, for example, K.O. Müller, a great classical philologist with wide interests in history and language, had used lexical arguments to trace the origin of the Latin and Italic peoples back to a mixture of indigenous peoples and Grecian invaders (the concept of Indo-European did not then exist). Continuing with this type of analysis, he succeeded in attributing to the first group a considerable capability in the military sphere, and to the second a gentle farming culture. The jump from lexical information to deductions about culture was made by means of the following sort of logic: Lat. *ensis* 'sword' has no corresponding forms outside Italy and must therefore come from the vocabulary of the indigenous peoples, who, consequently, must have been a population of warriors; on the other hand, *bos* 'ox' is found in Greek and must therefore be a word brought in by the invaders who are thus shown to be breeders of livestock. In passing we may note that this argument is not only extremely simplistic, but also technically wrong, since *ensis* has an exact cognate in Ved. *asi-* 'sword', so that by Müller's own reasoning it would have to be attributed to the vocabulary of the invaders: but at that time, scientific knowledge of Indic was still in its infancy.

It is undeniable, then, that the credit for using the lexicalist method to trace the first basic outline of IE culture, solidly based on excellent etymologies, must go to Kuhn.

A comprehensive arrangement of all the results obtained from the reconstruction of IE culture appeared almost immediately with A. Pictet's work *Les Origines indo-européennes ou les Aryas primitifs. Essai de paléontologie linguistique* (2 vols, 1859–63), a title which, significantly, was to be taken up again by Pisani ('Paleontologia linguistica', 1938) and in a volume by Devoto (*Origini indeuropee*, 1962).

However, the lexicalist method has very serious limitations. Above all, it is simply not true that the existence of a word necessarily implies that the object denoted existed within the same linguistic area: almost all the languages in Europe share the same term for the word 'lion' (these are direct or indirect reflexes of Lat. *leonem*), even though lions are not in fact found in Europe.

Second, while the reconstruction of the *signifiant*, where possible, is unambiguous, this is much less true of the reconstruction of the *signifié*, which often points in a certain direction, but not without some ambiguity. Consider, for example, Ved. *siṁha-* and Arm. *inj*, which both go back to an IE form, *$sing^hos$*, which had a restricted geographical distribution. (It is irrelevant that the form may in turn have been borrowed from an oriental or African language, because the loan must have taken place during the IE period.) However, the problem is that *simha-* means 'lion', while *inj* refers to the leopard: which meaning are we then to assign to IE **singhos*? In cases of this sort Indo-Europeanists have tried to take refuge in the use of generic terms, reconstructing *signifiés* broad enough to include all the meanings of the words used in the comparison (which are, of course, the only real meanings): so in the above case, **singʰos* might be assigned the meaning 'large wild animal'. But is it reasonable to attribute to a language lexemes with a constantly generic, colourless meaning? On the contrary, we may be sure that the reality was very different: **singʰos* must have had a precise meaning which was either retained or changed in the passage to Vedic and Armenian, but we are no longer in a position to judge which language preserved the old state of affairs and which innovated.

It is worse still when we assume with *a priori* certainty that a given word has a particular meaning and then use that assumption to draw important conclusions for the reconstruction of culture. This is more or less what happened in the case of the so-called 'beech-tree argument', which was used to demonstrate that the original homeland of the Indo-Europeans was approximately in what is now western Poland.

The starting point is the analysis of the lexical series formed by Lat. *fāgus* 'beech-tree', OHG *buohha* (*id.*), Gk, *phēgós* 'oak', (Kurd. *būz* 'elm'),[1] Russ. *buziná* 'elder' (all from **bʰāwĝ-*). Now, since the beech tree does not naturally grow east of the Königsberg–Crimea line, it is deduced that the original meaning of 'beech tree' has only survived in Latin and Germanic, while elsewhere the term in question was used to denote other trees which grew locally. Since 'beech tree' was the original meaning, this proves both that this tree was a typical feature of the IE homeland and, obviously, that this homeland must have been situated within the area where the tree grows naturally, that is, either in Italy or the Germanic-speaking area (since the areas which are now Polish historically were German). Having eliminated Italy for obvious reasons (even at the beginning of the historical period it was still full of non-IE peoples), only the Germanic-speaking area remains and must therefore have been the original homeland of the Indo-Europeans.

It is clear that this 'beech tree argument' is based totally on the unproven – and unprovable – assumption that the meaning of IE **bʰāwĝ-* is 'beech tree', whereas the attested languages show a variety of meanings which diverge and vary to an extent which prevents any degree of certainty in the reconstruction.

However, even when we succeed in establishing a meaning with any degree of reliability, the lexicalist method does not necessarily help us towards a true reconstruction of IE culture. Consider again the case of IE **rēĝ-s* 'king'. Kuhn drew from this the obvious conclusion that the Indo-Europeans were familiar with a 'king' figure. But this observation does not in fact give us any more information about the world of the Indo-Europeans and its history, since the historian is interested not in the label but in the reality behind it: what the functions were of this 'king'; what powers he had; how he was chosen, and so on. A mere label cannot answer any of these questions.

The Textual Method

If culture is an organic entity where everything is internally coherent (*tout se tient*) but not everything is on the same plane, then the reconstruction of a culture should also be presented in an organic form, comprehensively and hierarchically. However, this is in fact virtually impossible if the basic working material is made up of a collection of lexemes whose meanings are now often extremely vague and where there are frequently irremediable gaps as a result of words which cannot be reconstructed.

After these initial attempts at reconstruction, carried out in broad sweeps and with pioneering boldness, the lexicalist method consequently split into two different approaches. On the one hand, scholars attempted to reconstruct anything they could, forgoing any attempt to adhere to organic structure. The culmination of this approach was reached in Schrader's *Reallexikon* of 1901, where the individual stems are listed in alphabetical order. The second approach investigates very specific areas with broad and compact lexical evidence, allowing an organic perspective on the facts considered, even if the argument remains of necessity isolated from all the other elements of IE culture. A model of this type of study is the monograph by Delbrück (1889) on kinship among the Indo-Europeans, where he demonstrates the existence both of a patriarchal structure and of a model of organization analogous to that of the 'extended family' which survived in the Slavic area until very recent times.

The lexicalist method contrasts with the 'textual' method. This starts off from the premise that the Indo-Europeans handed down to their descendants not only a language but also a culture, and that this culture can be reconstructed by comparing identical or analogous cultural features in different IE cultures, as long as these are not innovative in character and are not loan elements. We therefore speak of the 'textual method', in so far as the elements to be used in the reconstruction are in fact preserved for us in old written texts, even although in principle we cannot actually exclude the use of contemporary information not yet recorded in writing. This method is therefore based on the analysis of content and may range from the semantic content of a single word to the structure of an entire body of literature. Consequently, it is clear that in no case is it necessary to have lexical identity of the elements which express the content. We offer here a simple example involving IE metaphor.

In ancient Ireland a stranger would be termed 'blue wolf', not as an occasional metaphor, but as an institutional term. In the Germanic world a criminal expelled from his tribe would be referred to as a 'wolf'. In the Hittite laws, someone who loses the protection of the law for ravishing a woman is declared a 'wolf'. In Vedic India, 'wolf' denotes a hostile stranger.

The perfect overlap of these uses can only be explained if we accept that within IE culture there was already a metaphorical use of 'wolf' with the meaning 'person who is, or has become, estranged from the tribe and is hostile to it'. However, what has been preserved from Indo-European is only the content, the cultural rather than the linguistic information, since for 'wolf' in this sense each language uses its own term: OIr. *cú*, Gmc **wargaz*, Ved. *vṛka-* (Hittite has the ideogram UR.BAR.RA, perhaps to be read *uetna*). That is, each language has innovated freely at the linguistic level, but not at the level of cultural content. Moreover, this cultural content is also susceptible of variation, without the original information thus being lost. An example is furnished in this case by Old Irish, which does not simply say 'wolf', but rather 'blue wolf'. What is the origin of the use of this adjective? It originates in a typical historical experience of the Irish, for whom the hostile foreigner was identified above all with the British. Now the British, as we know from Caesar and Pliny, dyed their bodies blue in war and in religious ceremonies. The use of the adjective 'blue' originates in these practices, which were foreign to Irish culture.

The Tripartite Ideology

However, much more than an isolated IE metaphor can be recovered by means of the textual method. The essential starting point, in the area of culture, is the identification of the ideology, that is of the categories of analysis and judgement used to perceive and create reality. The identification and definition of IE ideology is the achievement of a great French scholar, G. Dumézil, who dedicated a lifetime of research to these problems.

Indo-European culture incorporated every aspect of reality, whether present or future, into one of three functions, namely: the sacred; the military; and the economic (the last to be understood both as production of goods and the enjoyment of anything that adds pleasure and security to life). The whole picture is composed of the coexistence of these three functions.

This 'tripartite' ideology survived the splitting up of the IE community by many millennia and went on to become the pattern according to which the individual peoples set up their cults, their legends and their mythologies. The oldest Roman history furnishes excellent examples of this.

When, at a very early stage, the Romans wanted to reconstruct and pass on the origins of their city, they were well aware of the need to set up a unified whole, without any imbalance in favour of one function or another. This need was met by the figures of the first three kings, each clearly expressing one of the three functions of IE ideology. Numa Pompilius, the indefatigable creator of religious cults and priestly colleges, represents the sacred aspect. Tullus Hostilius, the crude, brutal warrior, embodies the second function, the military aspect. Finally, Romulus, who protected the shepherds from robbers, founded the city and obtained wives and offspring for his men, is an expression of the economic function. In this way the foundation of Rome was laid on a perfectly complete basis, which was a guarantee of strength and duration.

More or less at the same time as the legend of the origins of Rome was being created, King Darius the Great of Persia placed an inscription at Persepolis, in which he prayed to Ahuramazda to ward off all evils from his people. These evils are expressed by three specific elements, each an expression of one of the three functions: famine (the third function); the enemy army (the second); and the cult of false gods (the first).

It would be impossible to understand the culture of the Indo-Europeans, and that of the individual IE peoples in antiquity, without constantly bearing in mind this 'tripartite ideology'. We know, for example, that at Rome, at a time preceding written records, Jove, Mars and Quirinus (the so-called 'pre-Capitoline triad', earlier than that formed by Jove, Juno and Minerva) were worshipped in the Capitoline temple. Why this choice? Clearly because Jove, father of the gods and of men, expressed the first function; Mars, god of war, the second; and Quirinus, god of fertility, the third. This temple was thus the only one that united all of the functions and so it came to represent the religious and moral centre of the city, unlike the other temples, which were dedicated to individual deities and thus expressed only one of the functions.

However, it is necessary to stress the fact that, contrary to what Dumézil himself once claimed and to what some scholars still try to maintain, this tripartite structure did not actually imply the existence of three separate castes (priests, warriors, farmers/breeders of livestock), since the trifunctionalism is only a category of the perception and interpretation of reality, not a division of a social kind. Only at a relatively late stage and only in a few areas of the IE world (India, and to a much lesser extent, Iran) did the three-caste system come to develop, a system to which a fourth, highly disdained, caste must be added, made up of subdued and impoverished natives. But this is an independent, secondary development, which plays no part in the framework of IE culture.

Indo-European Institutions

For the sake of clarity and brevity, an analytical outline of several individual but essential elements of IE culture is presented below: it should constantly be borne in mind that these were never considered to be independent elements and that the task of scholars, rather than continually attempting to isolate new elements, consists in recovering the organic structure of IE culture; isolating the links which, within the framework of a unitary system, relate the individual elements to each other; and recovering the depth and function of each of these in relation to that cultural system.

Religion

Symptomatic of the problems is the fact that, despite the attempts of many scholars, we have so far been able to reconstruct the name of only one deity:

Gk. *Zeús*, Ved. *Dyau-*, Lat. *Iu(ppiter)*, Hitt. *šiuš* (however, this is not a proper name, but means 'god'), which all suggest an IE form **Djēws*.

The reason for this gap in reconstruction lies in the fact that in this religion what was important was not the specific figure of the individual god, but rather the function which he represented, so the IE peoples were able continually to create or appropriate new deities from outside (thus forgetting the old ones), the only condition being that each one of them should clearly fulfil the function of the god whom he had just replaced. This attitude, where it is not the name but the function that counts, is also shown in historical times in the so-called *interpretatio Romana* of foreign pantheons: each time the Romans came into contact with the religion of a 'barbarian' people, they gave to each of its gods the name of the Roman deity who in their opinion fulfilled the same function. Thus in Tacitus, for example, Gmc **Wodanaz*, **Dunaraz* and **Teiwaz* become Jove, Hercules and Mars respectively.

Moreover, the inherent limit of the lexicalist method in cultural reconstruction becomes apparent in the case of the reconstructed form **Djēws*, as has already been made clear. In fact, even if the *significants* correspond perfectly, the religious elements referred to do not correspond. In Rome and Greece, Jupiter and Zeus are the supreme deities, the perfect expression of the first function; but Hitt. *šiuš* has become a generic term for any god and even in the oldest texts Ved. *Dyau-* appears as a cultural relic, whose sex even was not known.

The identical nature of the old religious systems of the IE peoples is thus not a matter of worshipping the same gods, but rather of dividing the members of their pantheon into the same tripartite schema: gods of the sacred, gods of war, gods of well-being. From this point of view, then, Mitra and Varuṇa, the Vedic gods expressing the first function, are perfectly comparable with the Roman Jupiter and with the Germanic Wodanaz who in their respective pantheons fulfil the same function.

The world of the gods represents a purely objective element in IE culture, a world to which man stands in a utilitarian relationship rather than one of love or emotion. A typically Christian concept such as 'the love of God' would have been incomprehensible to an Indo-European: man did not love the gods and the gods did not love man. Between them, however, transactions of mutual benefit might be conducted: man would offer up a sacrifice to a god, who in his turn would grant what had been requested. It should be noted that these requests were never of a metaphysical nature, but always concerned goods and benefits in life: health, abundant livestock, obedient and sturdy sons, victory in war, and so on.

In other words, the sacrifice was really a full legal contract which represented a sort of 'payment in advance', a *do ut des* from which the god could not withdraw. The extreme formalism which characterized the sacrifice and the related prayer is also typical of legal contracts. Everything would become null and void, for example, if the person praying did not use the correct name of the god or pronounced the prayer wrongly. In the oldest Vedic and Avestan texts the person praying specifies that he is using 'words pronounced correctly' and in Rome and Greece we find frequent precautionary formulae in which, after the invocation of the god by name, there follows the phrase 'or any other name by which you wish to be called'.

Sacrifice

The Vedic world records the sacrifice of Primordial Man, the first, exemplary victim, from whose severed limbs all physical and social reality originated; the liturgical texts, in their turn, recognize man as the best and most acceptable of victims. The Indic world was thus permeated at the level of myth and theological doctrine by reminders of human sacrifice, which certainly existed in the IE period. Moreover, it is difficult to find any IE peoples who were not still practising it in historical times. We have certain evidence of it with reference to the Celts, the *Germani*, the Slavs and the Scythians: this 'barbaric' custom that scandalized the Greeks and the Romans was in fact only the continuation of an IE custom which, as such, must also have been practised at some time by the Greeks and Romans. And there too, in fact, we find fairly clear evidence of human sacrifices.

In Greece this evidence exists at the level of the myth: in order to ensure the safe departure of the fleet heading for Ilium, Agamemnon promises to sacrifice his daughter Iphigenia. Naturally, the matter has a happy and civilized ending (Iphigenia escapes and a deer is sacrificed instead), because Greek culture could not attribute so terrible a custom to such an illustrious person. But it is clear that a promise of this sort would have made no sense unless it were formulated within the limits of contemporary customs.

At Rome, both Livy and Plutarch mention that in the third century human sacrifices were still made when the city found itself in situations of extreme peril; moreover, Plutarch adds that this custom still survived, but was veiled in state secrecy.

Human sacrifices were thus a very real part of life in the IE world, which gave them up reluctantly, at a late stage. Alongside these there must also have been animal sacrifices made according to precise rules, although we are no longer able to reconstruct these. Not all animals, for example, were suitable for sacrifice: it is probable that only domestic animals were suitable, which suggests a connection with the types of animal rearing which were practised. Consequently, the pig could be sacrificed in Rome (remember the *suovetaurilia*), but not in India, where it was not reared.

An essential point as far as both sacrifice and, in more general terms, IE religion are concerned, is that the deities were thought of exclusively as male. This androcentric conception of the gods is preserved in its purest state in India, where all the great deities are male, and female deities appear only as personifications of natural phenomena which are grammatically feminine in gender (e.g. Night, Dawn) or as the wives of the males, in which case they are such insignificant figures that they do not even have names of their own, but take the name of their husbands: the wife of Varuṇa is Varuṇānī, the wife of Indra is Indrānī, and so on.

The great female deities only begin to appear when the IE tribes come into contact with cultures where the woman had a relevant position: figures such as Juno or Aphrodite or the Great Mother of Uppsala are certainly not Indo-European in origin. This male-based structure of the original IE pantheon obviously reflects the social and family structure of that society, to which we shall return later.

The Afterlife

As we have seen, IE religion aimed only to guarantee worldly goods in this life and did not pose metaphysical questions. It was therefore neither in a position to respond to man's deepest existential needs nor to foretell what awaited him after death. Alongside the official religion, but not in opposition to it, there developed theories and faiths which placed the relationship between men and gods on a different basis and tried to perceive man's ultimate destiny.

In this area the cult of the Mothers is of relevance. This cult is attested in the Celtic, Germanic, Baltic and Vedic worlds: the Mothers are loving deities who protect their faithful, bestowing salvation and plenty on them. The anomalous character of this cult with respect to the official religion is clear from the very fact that they are female deities.

Some answers to the problem of the afterlife were also put forward. We cannot, for example, exclude the possibility of the existence as early as the IE stage of some form of faith in metempsychosis, which is widespread among the Celts and of which there would also appear to be traces in the oldest Indian culture.

There also existed a hope of a happy eternal life, a passing over to fertile and pleasant places, which in Greece were termed 'Elysian Fields' or 'Islands of the Blessed' and which the Irish called 'Land of the Living' and conceived of as distant islands in the west, where a hero could come by ship after overcoming infinite difficulties.

But this vision is only apparently optimistic, since both in Greece and in Ireland this happy destiny did not await all men, but only a small, select number of the privileged. On the contrary, it appears that a very unhappy fate awaited most men after death. They would survive, certainly, but in a horrible dark world where they were deprived of physical concreteness, degraded and devoid of hope. This is the world that Homer portrays in the *Nékyia*, where the most courageous Greek hero, Achilles, comes to declare that he should prefer to labour for a miserable peasant on earth rather than be king of all the dead in the afterlife.

There is certainly a close connection between this uncertain and pessimistic view of the afterlife and the yearning for 'immortal glory', the only form of survival that was really possible and desirable, which was typical of the methods of the IE warrior and which we shall go on to discuss further (see pp. 18–19).

The Family

As was demonstrated by Delbrück, the IE family had a structure similar to the 'extended family' which survives to this day among the southern Slavs and which consisted of all the descendants of a common progenitor. Its stable members were basically only the males, since the women, by marrying, would move across into their husband's family: links of friendship and alliance would thus be created between the two families.

From an examination of kinship terms, attempts have been made to determine what the internal structure of the family was, since we know from anthropology that the individualization of levels of kinship is not in fact universal or unequivocal: to us, for example, the distinction between 'father' and 'mother' appears obvious and necessary, but in Hawaiian society there is no such distinction; the two stand on an equal footing and are referred to by one term expressing only the fact that they are direct ancestors of the first degree. Attempts have thus been made to relate the internal structure of the IE family to models already noted by anthropology, ranging from the ancient Chinese model to that of the modern Omaha tribe (a Native American tribe situated along the Ohio river). The method used for this identification was in fact the analysis of the meanings of kinship terms both in the individual languages and at the level of reconstructed Indo-European.

The data certainly merit at least some consideration. Lat. *nepos*, for example, indicates two forms of kinship which are objectively different, in that it denotes both 'grandson' and 'nephew' (this double meaning is retained in modern Italian *nipote*). On the other hand, OIr. *niae*, which corresponds etymologically to Lat. *nepos*, has a much more restricted meaning, since it indicates only the sister's son. In addition, Lat. *avus* is the grandfather, but its diminutive form (*avunculus*) denotes the paternal uncle. Facts of this sort might allow us to draw general conclusions in the reconstruction of the internal structure of the IE family, if we were not faced with two major obstacles, as is often the case with lexical methods. The first is that it is difficult to establish a precise, unequivocal meaning at the IE level for certain terms which have different meanings in the historically attested languages: the second is that kinship terms are also subject to semantic and formal innovations. While Latin *cognatus* 'blood relative' does survive in the Romance languages, it has acquired a new meaning 'brother-in-law' (a case of semantic innovation); in various modern Celtic languages relationships established as a result of marriage are expressed according to French or English models, for example, Bret. *tad-kaer* 'father-in-law', a calque on Fr. *beau-père*, and Welsh *tad-yng-nghyfraith*, a calque on Eng. *father-in-law* (which in turn are innovations in relation to Lat. *socer* and OEng. *swéor* which continue IE **sweḱuros*).

These difficulties at the semantic level led one of the great Indo-Europeanists, O. Szemerényi (1978), to abandon the analysis of the internal structure of the IE family and to try instead to recover, by means of the etymological analysis of individual lexemes, the practical function and the social and affective position of its members. This attempt was not totally new, since for some time there had been scholars who, for example, would analyse **pH-tēr* 'father' as the *nomen agentis* of the same root which appears in Lat. *pasco*: the father, that is, was functionally identified as the provider of food. This theory is attractive but almost certainly unfounded, since it starts from the identification of the segment *-tēr* with the *nomina agentis* suffix *-tēr*, whereas nouns such as **dajwēr* 'brother-in-law' and **swesōr* 'sister' would seem to suggest, rather, the segmentation **pHt-ēr*.

Szemerényi's investigation, although conducted with great scholarship, comes up against the fact that most of the kinship terms are obscure from the point of view of etymology because of the very fact that they belong to the oldest stage of the language; this can lead Szemerényi to propose untenable etymologies. This may be shown by recalling the fact that, for example, **bʰrātēr* 'brother' is analysed as a compound **bʰr-ātēr* 'bearer of fire' (in family life, that is, his task would have been to keep the fire alight during moves). However, such a compound does not seem convincing from the point of view of the formal rules of IE nominal composition: what we should expect for 'bearer of fire' is something more like **ātr̥-bʰr̥t* (or **ātr̥-bʰoros*). The identification of the name for 'sister-in-law' (husband's sister), Gk *gálōs*, with the name for 'marten' (Skt *giri-*) is no more than an extremely vague theory, suggesting that the young, nimble little sister-in-law may have been denoted metaphorically in this way.

Otherwise, the serious limitation of this method consists in the fact that it does not take account of the fact that kinship terms are relative (the 'father' is such relative to the sons, the 'uncle' is such relative to the nephews, etc.), while Szemerényi's etymological analysis centres around absolute rather than relative meanings. Even if we accept, as a hypothesis, that a young member of the family was called 'bearer of fire', the development to 'brother' requires, as a necessary condition, that this term was used only relative to the other brothers; if it had been used, for example, relative to the father, then it would have developed into 'son' according to the same process.

It is thus better to give up this illusory reconstructional examination and to analyse, by means of the textual method, the real relationships which existed within the IE family.

The undisputed master (**potis*) of the IE family was the father (clearly to be understood not in the sense of physical father but in the sense of the Roman *paterfamiliās*). His authority was so unlimited that the title of 'father' was also conferred on the gods, with reference not to creation, a concept which did not yet exist, but to their absolute power over men. The feminine *potniH*, which in historical times comes to mean 'mistress (of a household)', should not lead us to assume an equal authority on the part of the wife, since the term originally had purely a possessive value, 'she who specifically belongs to the *potis*'. In fact, it is the emancipation of the members of the family from the despotic authority of the father which constitutes one of the essential, non-IE, features of modern Western civilisation, although its origins lie as far back as Greek and Roman times.

The house – not in an architectural sense, but as a social unit, the 'household' (Benveniste 1969: 296) – was termed *dom-*, and the 'master of the house' was therefore the *doms-potis/*dems-potis* (Ved. *dampati-*, Avest. *dǝ̄ng paiti-*, Gk. *despótēs*).

Marriage
The Indo-Europeans certainly practised forms of marriage, which we can reconstruct easily thanks to the surprising correspondences in the rules laid down in the old Indian, Irish and Welsh legal texts: these correspondences are confirmed, moreover, by some of the legendary elements of the oldest Roman history (such as the rape of the Sabine women or the story of Dido and Aeneas).

The most basic form of marriage simply consisted of two young people living together in amorous pursuits. But alongside this form of marriage, which we may also interpret as a judicious concession to youthful excess, there existed a more brutal form, marriage by rape. The memory of this survived in Rome in the myth of the rape of the Sabine women, but it also represented a fully recognized form of marriage, one which was particularly recommended for warriors. Finally, there also existed a form of marriage by purchase: the father of the young man would acquire a wife for him by giving specified goods to her father or her tribe. This was the only type of marriage which was sanctified by special religious ceremonies; Indian ethics justified the payment itself by adducing the great expenses which the father of the bride had to face for the matrimonial rites.

However, the economic situation was much less simple than it might appear, since although the girl's father received her price on the one hand, on the other he had to provide her with dowry and presents. In actual fact, it is probable that the situation was resolved by means of an exchange of goods between the two families, partly because the alliance between them resulting from the marriage essentially prevented the impoverishment of one in favour of the other.

There is no doubt that polygamy was widely practised, at least at the level of the richest and most powerful families (as a general practice it would be objectively impossible if only because of the fact that in any human grouping the number of women is more or less equal to the number of men). Polygamy is well attested not only in the eastern area of the IE world, but also in the western area. We know from a valuable comment by Caesar (*De bello Gallico* 6,19) that it was practised by the Gaulish nobility: indeed, whenever a nobleman died in suspicious circumstances, his wives (note the plural) would be subjected to torture. Moreover, we know from legal texts that it also existed in ancient Ireland, where the different wives were not placed on an equal footing but according to a hierarchical scale at the apex of which was the *prímben* 'wife of the first rank'.

In Greek culture there is a sure reference to polygamy in the *Iliad*, where Priam has two wives, old Hecuba, by whom he has had nineteen sons, and young Laothoe, who has provided him with another two. Laothoe is the daughter of the king of the Leleges and has brought him a large dowry; we may therefore exclude the possibility that she was simply a concubine.

The recognition of the new-born son was conducted formally and solemnly: the father would place him on his knees and the child would thus assume the status of legitimate son. This IE custom is preserved in the Sogdian phrase *z'nwk z'tk* 'legitimate heir' (lit. 'son of the knees'), to which the OIr. compound *glún-daltae* 'adoptive son' (lit. 'child of the knee') corresponds; the Latin adjective *genuinus* 'authentic, true' presupposes the same usage (Benveniste 1926). In Homer (*Odyssey* 19.400ff.), finally, there is a detailed portrayal of this custom: the nurse Eurycleia places the young Odysseus on the knees of his grandfather Autolycus and invites the latter to give the child a name. In other words, Autolycus legitimizes him and, as the first fruit of this legitimization, gives him his name; incidentally, we note that this act is carried out not by the father, Laertes, but by the figure who has most authority in the family, which leads us to assume that originally the legitimization was carried out by the **dems-potis*, the head of the household.

Tribal Organization

The **dom-*, as we have seen, is the smallest social unit, since within IE society the individual has no reality outside the group to which he belongs, to the extent that being expelled from this group is the punishment for the most serious crimes.

A group of **dom-* (i.e. of households, 'extended families') made up a **wiḱ-*, which we may translate as 'clan'; and just as the **dom-* had as its master the **doms-potis*, the **wiḱ-* had the **wiḱ-potis* (Ved. *viśpati-*, Lith. *viẽšpats*). In its meaning of 'tribal division', the element **wiḱ-* appears in Greek in the adjective *trikháikes* '(the Dorians) divided into three tribes' and, perhaps, if Szemerényi is right, in Homeric *hippóta*, an epithet used of illustrious warriors, which was traditionally interpreted as 'horseman, knight', but which may be better interpreted as reflecting an older **wiḱ-potēs* 'clan chief'.

Less certain is the reconstruction of the unit or units larger than the **wiḱ-*. It is probable that the only unit larger than the **wiḱ-* was the tribe in its entirety and that it was termed **toutā* (OIr. *túath* 'tribe', OHG *diot* 'people',

Osc. *touto* 'state, community of citizens, *civitas*', Lith. *tautà* 'people, country', Pers. *tōda* 'heap, pile, crowd'). At the head of the **toutā* there is a figure of fundamental importance in IE, the **rēĝ-s* 'king', a term which survives in only a few, but important, areas (Ved. *rāj-*, Lat. *rex*, Gaul. *-rīx*) and which elsewhere is formed either by a derivative of **teutā* (Goth. *þiudans*, Ill. *Teutana* 'queen') or by a variety of different innovations (Gk *basileús*, for example, is almost certainly borrowed from a non-IE language); but it would be gratuitous (not because the question is of no interest, but because we lack the material to resolve it on an objective basis) to speculate about the reasons for such substitutions.

In this section we have basically listed terms; but it would be methodologically wrong to deduce cultural information from mere lists of words. The aim of the investigation and reconstruction must therefore be to elucidate the actual content of these lexemes, and this can only be done by means of textual comparison. In fact, given the current state of research, this appears to be possible only in the case of the 'king', i.e. the tribal chief. As far as the rest is concerned, only a brief comment is possible: the clan and the 'family unit' should not be taken absolutely in the sense of administrative subdivisions of the tribe, nor their chiefs as functionaries; this is true, to some extent, only in the historical period and only in some areas. But the IE tribe is certainly not to be conceived of as a unitary, centralized state.

The King

The detailed reconstruction of this fundamental figure is one of the greatest successes of historical linguistics in the field of cultural reconstruction.

Contrary to what a simplistic use of the lexical method might lead us to assume, there is no military dimension to the IE king. He has a different, much more important function: positioned somewhere between men and gods, he is an instrument who presents the needs of his people to the gods and through whom the gods convey their gifts. In other words, the king is a sacramental figure, the priest *par excellence*. This was still quite clear at the beginning of the republican period in Rome: at the very moment when the kings were driven out, the new priest-figure of the *rex sacrificulus* was created, specifically to avoid a religious vacuum and in order not to leave unfulfilled those essential sacramental functions which could only be carried out by a *rex*.

Irish, Greek and Indian texts agree to a great extent in outlining the functions of the king. Basically, the well-being and the very life of the tribe depended on him, not because of any wise laws or provisions on his part, but rather thanks to his superhuman ability to obtain everything necessary from the gods. If the king is a true king, these texts say, the harvest will be good, animals prolific, the rivers full of fish, honey easy to find (remember that honey was used to make an alcoholic drink, **medʰu*), fine healthy children will be born, and the enemy will remain outside the tribal boundaries. If this does not happen, it means that the king is not a true king, and unfortunate measures then have to be taken.

To these textual agreements, themselves already more than sufficient, there may be added the concrete portrayal of the king in other IE cultures, a portrayal which fully conforms to this theoretical framework.

Consider again the legend of the origin of Rome. Writing about the encounter with the Sabines, Livy records that Romulus and Tatius were the kings of the two peoples; but, at the time of the battle, we see that these two kings are not commanding their armies, since the Roman commander is Hostius Hostilius, and the Sabine commander Mettius Curtius. So the kings do not have a military function; in other words, the legend is fully in keeping with the IE cultural information. But Romulus, though not fighting, is on the battlefield. His function is revealed when the Romans are put to flight: he raises his arms to the sky and calls for the aid of Jupiter Stator: a miracle ensues. The Romans stop fleeing, start fighting again and win easily. Obtaining miracles: this was the function of the king, even on the battlefield.

The king is a human and, at the same time, a divine figure. The way in which he could rise above the level of men and enter, at least partially, the level of the gods happened by means of a rite of enthronement which essentially consisted of his marriage to an indigenous goddess. The most archaic form of this rite is recorded for us by an English scholar of the Middle Ages, Giraldus Cambrensis, who observed it in an Irish tribe and relates it with some distaste, but with the honesty of a true historian: in the presence of his people, the man designated king would be united physically with a mare, an incarnation of the local goddess. After this rite had been performed, he was king.

The Irish (including noted scholars) have always maintained that this story is a scandalous English lie, invented to defame and ridicule them. However, fifty years ago it was shown that in India, too, there existed a similar rite of enthronement (which survived almost to the present day), so we may clearly conclude that Giraldus was not lying and also that the affinity between the two rites proves their common IE origin.

The fact that the accession to the throne took place, according to IE ideology, by means of a sacred marriage allows us to explain, among other things, the traditions and legends of peoples who, unlike the Indians and the Irish, had relinquished these practices in the historical period. Once again, we turn to the origins of Rome.

Numa Pompilius, the wise and pious man *par excellence*, had a strange relationship with the goddess Egeria; this relationship certainly took a matrimonial form (Livy uses the term *coniux*). All of this rather puzzled the historians of antiquity, partly because they knew that Numa was already conventionally married to Tatia (Plutarch avoids any difficulty by claiming that Numa's legitimate wife was already dead at the time of the relationship with Egeria). The reality is much simpler, even if the historians of antiquity could not recognize it: the matrimonial link between Numa and Egeria is a memory of the 'sacred marriage' which was necessary to become king (and which, obviously, had no relevance in connection with authentic human marriage).

This quasi-divine character of the king made him the religious centre of the tribe, but as a result left a considerable amount of free rein to the people, who in practical matters had to recognize as their true leaders the chiefs of the families and clans. It is therefore probable that as far back as the IE period there existed basic forms of democracy, represented by assemblies of 'elders' or 'seniors', which are variously attested in the ancient IE cultures (the senate at Rome, the *gerousía* in Greece, the *daranϑoa* among the Messapians, the Germanic *þinga-*, etc.). We thus have the impression of a society which is not yet differentiated into classes, even if imbalances from family to family have begun to become evident within it, presumably in connection with the acquisition of lands and wealth (and, therefore, also of men and arms) as a result of military expeditions.

Did slavery exist among the Indo-Europeans? The answer of scholars to this has always been an unqualified affirmative, clearly because slavery is attested among all the IE peoples in the historical period. However, a different view might be taken. First, we note, for what it is worth, that there is no trace of slavery in the reconstructed lexicon of Indo-European. The isogloss represented by Lat. *servus*, Gk *eíreron* 'slavery' and Avest. *haurva-* 'overseer' is totally spurious (Benveniste 1969). At the textual level, which is much more relevant, there is complete silence even in areas where we should expect slaves to be mentioned. One example will suffice.

We have seen that the Vedic liturgical texts continued to view man as the supreme sacrificial victim. But this refers to the free man, the successor to Primordial Man. Moreover, the same texts give us the hierarchy of the victims, and after man (by this time a victim in theory only) they place the horse, the ox and the sheep. There is no mention of the slave. This is a significant absence because respect for human life could not have included that of the slave (who was not thought of as a man among men: Varro defined the slave as an *instrumentum vocale* 'tool with the ability to speak'); if there had ever been a sacrifice of slaves, this would have been recorded in the liturgical list which preserves the very ancient tradition. This, it would seem, demonstrates that slavery did not exist in pre-Indian (i.e. Indo-European) culture.

This claim may appear to be at odds with what we shall say about the military and conquering activities of the Indo-Europeans, since victory for one side ought to imply slavery of the other side. But this is true only to a very minor degree. In fact, the transformation of men into slaves brought with it great dangers which only a strong, compact state could risk (as in Rome, for example, where even so the revolt of Spartacus took place); a very frequent practice was therefore to kill the males and reduce the women to slavery. The claim that slavery was originally a typically female institution is proved by various facts. In Ireland the pre-monetary unit of currency was the *cumal* (female slave), not the *mug* (male slave); again in Ireland, and almost certainly in Homeric Greece, the hardest task, that of milling the grain, was carried out by the female slaves; when Troy was conquered by the Greeks, the women (Andromache, Cassandra, etc.) became slaves, but the men (even children such as Astyanax) were killed.

The women of the conquered, therefore, entered the family of the conquerors not just to work but also, inevitably, as concubines. Yet it is not stated that the son of a female slave also had the status of slave. In Homer we find numerous illegitimate children (Teucer, Isus, Cebriones, Megapenthes, etc.) who have the position of freemen.

To sum up: rather than slavery in the classical sense of the word, the Indo-Europeans presumably practised systematic appropriation of the women of the conquered; the absence of any rights for these women captives was not so much a characteristic specific to them as the normal condition of all women.

The Common Man

It is not surprising that we know so little about this subject, since traditions, myths and legends deal at length with princes and heroes, but very rarely with the common man. However, some hypotheses can be formulated.

In the first reconstructions of IE culture it was already noted that the Indo-Europeans practised agriculture and the raising of livestock, a conclusion reached from the existence of IE lexemes pertaining to these areas of activity. In this case, however, the conclusion goes beyond the premise, since these lexemes can tell us at most that certain objects – plants and animals – were known, but not what importance they had in the IE economy.

Here, too, therefore, it is better to resort to the textual method, but taking care not to make deductions about the IE economy merely from correspondences in the economies of the historical periods as they are presented in our texts (since this could depend on similar lines of development), but rather on certain ancient locutions and metaphors which demonstrate the high incidence of agriculture and the raising of livestock in IE culture. Here we give only a couple of examples.

In the Irish, Greek and Vedic worlds there existed a coherent system of metaphor according to which the members of a family were referred to as the corresponding members of the bovine family: the man as the bull, the woman as the cow, the girl as the heifer and the boy as the bull-calf. In Pindar (*Pyth.* 4, 142) we read: 'Cretheus and proud Salmoneus had the same cow as mother'; and the old classical philologists, who did not know the venerable antiquity of this metaphor, were shocked by it (see for example the commentary by Boeckh). But, in the same way, in Ireland a girl who chose to lie with an over-timid young man would justify her own behaviour thus:

'The heifers have to be bold when the bulls are not.' Facts of this sort – and we could recount many others – prove the importance of the rearing of livestock in the IE world.

As far as agriculture is concerned, let us consider the metaphor where the sexual act is seen in terms of ploughing and sowing. An old womanizer is described thus in Plautus (*As.* 873): 'He returns late at night, tired with working outside: he ploughs the farm of others, and leaves his own uncultivated'; in Aeschylus (*Sept.* 738) Oedipus 'sowed in the sacred field of his mother, where he himself had been nurtured'. Nor are these occasional metaphors: in an Attic nuptial formula it is said that the man takes the wife 'for the *sowing* of legitimate sons'. The same phrases are used in the Indian legal texts: 'Where seed has been scattered in a field (= woman) with the consent of the owner of the field (= the husband), the result is considered to belong to both the owner of the seed (= the natural father) and to the owner of the field' (cf. Pisani 1942–5).

It is therefore not the existence of IE lexemes pertaining to the rearing of livestock and agriculture that conveys the importance of these activities in IE society, but rather the vitality and the persistence of a metaphorical use of language that suggests an economy of the agricultural, pastoral type.

This basic character of IE society should not be seen as incompatible with the warfaring and conquering characteristics of these tribes, which succeeded in subduing a territory extending from Chinese Turkestan to Ireland. The victorious migratory movement of the Indo-Europeans, in fact, should not be conceived of in continuous form, but as a collection of successive desultory episodes, punctuated by long periods of stability, during which peaceful and normal economic activities went on and in which the inevitable disagreements with neighbouring peoples were not necessarily realized in terms of territorial conquest and new settlement. This framework, moreover, is fully confirmed by the so-called 'barbarian invasions', which represent, in the historical period, the final major movement of IE peoples westwards (this time to the disadvantage of other IE peoples). The Goths, for example, probably left southern Sweden and arrived in North Africa; but this journey took place over the space of about a millennium and was punctuated by extremely long stays in Moesia, Italy, France and Spain.

However, it seems right to emphasize the fact that the IE colonization was a military phenomenon; that is, we cannot accept the hypothesis of Renfrew (1987), according to which the colonization was carried out by small, peaceful groups of farmers progressively advancing further in search of new lands to exploit. Indeed, this vision is in total contrast to the 'heroic' values present in IE culture.

The Warrior

In a society which was not subdivided into castes or classes of activity, the common man and the warrior were one and the same person, but at different times and in different situations. Just as the mild, pious Roman peasant of peacetime was transformed into a soldier of great skill in times of war, we can hypothesize that this was also the case in IE times.

However, in this area too the nature of our texts tells us much about the military ideology of the chiefs and very little about that of the common man. On the other hand, the extremely long, uninterrupted series of military successes which characterizes the history of the Indo-Europeans allows us to assume that the ideology of the élite was largely shared at all levels, especially since the fruits of victory, through the generosity of the chiefs, fell to all the people: new lands to exploit, women, plundered animals, valuables, reserves of food, and so on.

However, the ideal of the great warrior did not consist in this acquisition of material goods; on the contrary, it had a rigorously abstract and individualistic character and consisted in his achieving 'immortal glory' for himself. This is a fundamental concept which is an equally predominant force in the Vedic, Greek and Welsh texts. The basic alternative available to the warrior is that which Achilles (*Iliad* 9. 412ff.) puts to himself: 'If I remain here and fight the city of the Trojans, I shall never return home, but I shall have immortal glory; but if I go back to my homeland, there will never be immortal glory for me'; the warrior would always choose in favour of the latter. But what form did this 'immortal glory' take?

Essentially it consisted in the survival of a name, which in IE culture represented not a mere label, as it does today, but rather a basic constituent of every human being. However, a name could only survive if it was linked with glorious memories which were transmitted from generation to generation: hence the necessity for the warrior to commit a heroic, memorable deed through which, giving up his own life, he would enter into the eternal memory of his people.

It is completely natural to relate this heroic ideal very closely to what we have already noted in connection with IE religion. Faced with a religion which did not offer any hope of life after death and compared with vague suggestions of eternal unhappiness after death, 'immortal glory' offered the certainty of the indefinite survival of an essential part of oneself.

The Question of the Original Indo-European Homeland

Since we have mentioned the expansion of the Indo-Europeans, let us now outline in passing a long-debated question among linguists and archaeologists, that of the original homeland (Ger. *Urheimat*) of the Indo-Europeans.

In this area linguists have proceeded according to the lexicalist method, attempting to single out those IE lexemes which might be regarded as pointers to a particular geographical area. We have already mentioned the so-called 'beech-tree argument'; we might mention the analogous 'salmon argument', which also situates the Indo-Europeans on the shores of the Baltic. These arguments are worthless, not only because they become ensnared in the vicious circle of establishing a meaning already implicit in the premise, but also, more specifically, because the problem is never viewed in the light of popular taxonomy. In other words, there is no justification for thinking that the only fish which the Indo-Europeans called 'salmon' was *Salmo salar*, which lives on the shores of the Baltic; on the contrary, we may assume that, as happens at the popular level, the same name was also applied to other varieties of salmon (which also live elsewhere) or used for different species (for example the trout family); clearly, the same reservation applies in the case of the beech tree. In other words, we should not presume that the Indo-Europeans worked as rigorously or as systematically as a modern specialist (Cardona 1988).

The argument of the 'war chariot' does not appear to be much more convincing. We know that the Indo-Europeans reared horses, but used them not as saddle animals (even Homer pretends to be unaware of the existence of cavalry), but rather to pull their war chariots. Now, it has been argued, these chariots could only function in flat, forest-free areas; reasoning by a process of elimination, it was concluded that southern Russia should be viewed as the place where the Indo-Europeans, still as one people, used war chariots.

Of course, we have no definite knowledge of this IE chariot; however, it is certain that the Greeks of the Mycenean period made frequent use of war chariots, and Greece is not exactly flat. Equally, in Roman times they were used by the Celts of Gaul and Britain, both of which were much more wooded than nowadays. In other words, we have the distinct impression that the conditions under which war chariots could operate have been set artificially high in order to come up with a precise geographical location.

The archaeologists, for their part, proceeded in an essentially similar manner and, using the lexicalist analysis at second hand, went in search of archaeological remains whose discovery would tally with the material culture of the Indo-Europeans as reconstructed by lexical methods. Using this method, a noted American archaeologist, Marija Gimbutas (1982), localized the original homelands of the Indo-Europeans in southern Russia because material remains were found there of a culture which, like the IE culture, practised war and worshipped gods. To this suggestion it was rightly objected that an infinite number of other cultures could also exhibit these same characteristics. Another archaeologist, Renfrew (1987), localizes the original homeland of the Indo-Europeans in present-day Turkey because it was there, in his opinion, that the cultivation of grain began, which was of such importance for the Indo-Europeans. This is rather like saying that the Germans must have originated in Peru because they eat a lot of potatoes (a plant which, as is known, comes from the Andes region).

In fact it would be more appropriate to consider the actual validity of such a problem. To talk of 'original homelands' is in fact tantamount to presuming that up to about 4000 or 5000 BC the Indo-Europeans were a sedentary people, firmly fixed in a particular territory, and that at a certain moment they suddenly became nomadic conquerors. There is no documentary basis for such a hypothesis and it is unconsciously prompted only by a desire to provide the history of the Indo-Europeans with a beginning: from earliest times until 5000 BC the Indo-Europeans remained rooted in one place, like natural elements; after that date, they began to move, hence the beginning of their history.

This is an ingenuous assumption. History has no beginning other than an arbitrary point chosen by the historian as a place to begin, and the presence of documents, direct or indirect, on which it can be based. In the case of the Indo-Europeans there is no evidence of the existence of an 'original homeland': we could equally imagine them as nomadic peoples as far back as the oldest periods. Like all false problems, more than one solution is possible.

The Poet
Let us return, after this digression, to the problem of 'immortal glory'.

The survival of the name is linked to the persistence of the memory of heroic deeds; here that character fundamental to IE culture whom we may conventionally call 'the poet' enters the scene. In reality the poet was a professional dealing with words and everything which is realized in words was part of his sphere of competence. He was thus a priest (in that he knew the precatory formulae with which to address the gods during sacrifices and prayer), a doctor (in that he knew the magic formulae to cure all illnesses), a lawyer (in that he knew the formulae of customary law), a historian (in that he knew and told the story, more or less legendary, of his tribe); and, finally, moved by divine inspiration, he celebrated in poetry the glorious exploits of princes and heroes present and past.

This person, who seems so important to us because of his role in preserving and transmitting to future generations the whole intellectual culture of his people, did not in fact have a particularly elevated status among his own people: he was placed on the same level as highly specialized artisans, such as the smith or the chariot-maker. His last descendants survived into the modern period in the most conservative areas: the Yugoslavian *guslars* improvised lyrics in recent times in honour of Tito.

This great intellectual patrimony was acquired by means of a rigorously scholarly oral training at the side of an older poet. Caesar records that in Gaul this took as long as twenty years; in medieval Ireland it took at least twelve, and we still have the programmes and teaching methods. The same 'poet' figure survives and is known to us in other ancient IE cultures, albeit in less detail than is the case with Ireland. We have already mentioned the Slavic *guslar*, but the same figure was present in Greece, Rome, Iran and India.

This 'poet' would perform his various activities moving from place to place, in search of anyone who needed his services. His payment was often poor: it is significant that an Irish itinerant poet had composed an ode in honour of a young noblewoman who had offered him a 'good draught of beer'.

But the political chiefs soon realized the usefulness of the 'poet' as a propagator of the dominant ideology and celebrator of their own persons and their families. There thus arose the figure of the court poet, a poet who was permanently resident in the prince's household and whose primary function was to entertain the prince with the countless stories he knew and to exalt in poetry his exploits and those of his great ancestors. Naturally, this pre-supposes a situation of economic prosperity which allowed the prince not only to maintain the poet and associated entourage (wives, children, servants, pupils), but also to present him with those outstanding gifts which were the concrete realization of the prince's great generosity.

In Homer both of these types of poet are mentioned. Alcinous, preparing a banquet in honour of Odysseus, immediately sends for the minstrel Demodocus, an essential trapping of the feast: in other words, Demodocus was an itinerant poet who went wherever his work was required. On the other hand, when Agamemnon is leaving for Troy, he entrusts his wife to a poet; this is clearly the court poet, who was also used as a counsellor and man to be trusted; this frequently happens elsewhere as well.

What kind of verse did the IE poet use in his compositions? This is a question which linguists and philologists have asked since the middle of the nineteenth century, and which inspired a specific area of research going by the name of 'Indo-European metrics'. Obviously the approach taken was the usual one of comparing verse in different languages in order to reconstruct the IE archetype.

However, it appears rather more probable that the IE poets never used either quantity- or syllable-based verse. We should rather consider that the defining characteristic of IE poetry was purely linguistic in nature: take, as a very approximate example, the language of the Homeric poems, a language which was never really spoken by anyone, but which is immediately characterized by the presence of archaisms, pseudo-archaisms, analogical innovations, forms from different dialects, set formulae, metaphors, fixed locutions, and so on. The language of IE poetry must have been typologically something like this.

It is certainly not possible to reconstruct an IE poetic text; but we do at least know how the king Labraid Longsech Moen, the illustrious ancestor of the sovereign who successfully ruled over Leinster, was celebrated in an extremely conservative culture, that of Ireland (and we can also imagine that the recitation took place at the end of a rich banquet, where much beer and expensive wine of French origin had been poured out):

The exceptional Moen, when still a boy – in the manner of the great princes – killed the king, a princely act, Labraid, the descendant of Lorc.   1

The warriors of the Gailiain took up their spears (*láigne*); from this, the active troop took on the name of Laigin.   2
They won battles as far as the shores of the Lands of Éremon; after the exile the flame of the troops held sway over the Irish.   3
Higher than the shining sun the exceptional Moen, son of Aine, stood out over worlds of men and a god among gods is he, the exceptional king.   4

(Campanile 1988b)

A rather obscure text, it might be said (although the original Irish is much more obscure); in reality, the text is intentionally obscure, because the poet did not intend to say anything new or definite, but rather to create a musical atmosphere evoking a great past. We know, moreover, that when the King of Oriel had listened to the ode composed in his honour by Dallán, he exclaimed enthusiastically: 'Wonderful. What a pity I understood none of it.'

Note
1 However, the Kurdish form should be excluded from the comparison: cf. Henning 1963.

References
The bibliography on Indo-European origins and culture is very extensive. This list, prepared by M. P. Bologna, contains only those works explicitly or implicitly mentioned in the text.

Benveniste, Emile (1927) 'Un emploi du nom du "genou" en viel-irlandais et en sogdien', *Bulletin de la Société Linguistique de Paris* 27: 51–3.
—— (1969) *Le Vocabulaire des institutions indo-européennes*, Paris: Les Editions de Minuit.
Bettini, Maurizio (1986) *Antropologia e cultura romana: Parentela, tempo, immagini dell'anima*, Rome: NIS.
Campanile, Enrico (1974) 'I.E. metaphors and non-I.E. metaphors', *Journal of Indo-European Studies* 2: 247–58.
—— (1977) *Ricerche di cultura poetica indoeuropea*, Pisa: Giardini.
—— (1981) *Studi di cultura celtica e indoeuropea*, Pisa: Giardini.
—— (1983) 'Sulla struttura del matrimonio indoeuropeo', *Studi Classici e Orientali* 33: 273–86.
—— (1987) 'Indogermanische Dichtersprache', in Meid 1987: 21–8.
—— (1988a) 'Tradizione storiografica romana e ideologia indoeuropea', in E. Campanile (ed.), *Alle origini di Roma*, Pisa: Giardini, pp. 9–16.
—— (1988b), *Die älteste Hofdichtung von Leinster*, Vienna: Österreichische Akademie der Wissenschaften.
—— (1990) *La ricostruzione della cultura indoeuropea*, Pisa: Giardini.
Cardona, Giorgio R. (1988) 'Dati linguistici e modelli antropologici', *Annali dell'Istituto Orientale di Napoli* 10: 97–115.
Delbrück, Berthold (1889) *Die indogermanischen Verwandtschaftsnamen*, Leipzig.
Devoto, Giacomo (1962) *Origini indeuropee*, Florence: Sansoni.
Dumézil, George (1958) *L'Idéologie tripartie des Indo-Européens*, Brussels.
—— (1969) *Heur et malheur du guerrier: Aspects mythiques de la fonction*

guerrière chez les Indo-Européens, Paris: PUF.

—— (1977) *Les Dieux souverains des Indo-Européens*, 2nd edn, Paris: Gallimard, 1980.

—— (1979) *Mariages indo-européens*, Paris: Payot.

Gimbutas, Marija (1982) *The Goddesses and Gods of Old Europe (6500–3500 BC): Myths and Cult Images*, London.

Henning, W. B. (1963) 'The Kurdish Elm', *Asia Major* 10: 76–86.

Kuhn, Adalbert (1845) 'Zur ältesten Geschichte der indogermanischen Völker'. *Program des Kölnischen Realgymnasiums*, Berlin; expanded version in *Indische Studien* 1 (1850): 321ff.

—— (1855) 'Die Sprachvergleichung und die Urgeschichte der indogermanischen Völker', *Zeitschrift für vergleichende Sprachforschung* 4: 81ff.

—— (1873) 'Ueber Entwicklungsstufen der Mythenbildung', *Abh. Kön. Ak. Wiss. Berlin, Hist.-Phil. Kl.*: 123ff.

Leist, Burkard W. (1889) *Alt-Arisches Jus Gentium*, repr. Innsbruck: Innsbrucker Beiträge zur Sprachwissenschaft, 1978.

Meid, Wolfgang (ed.) (1987) *Studien zum indogermanischen Wortschatz*, Innsbruck: Innsbrucker Beiträge zur Sprachwissenschaft.

Müller, Karl O. (1828) *Die Etrusker*, Breslau; 2nd edn Stuttgart, 1877.

Pictet, Adolphe (1859–63) *Les Origines indo-européennes ou les Aryas primitifs: Essai de paléontologie linguistique*, 2 vols, Paris: Cherbulier (2nd edn 1877).

Pisani, Vittore (1938) 'Paleontologia linguistica', *Annali della Fac. di Lett. e Filos. della R. Univ. di Cagliari* 9: 54ff.

—— (1942–5) 'La donna e la terra', *Anthropos* 37–40: 241–53.

—— (1948) 'Aspetti della religione presso gli antichi Indoeuropei', *Acme* 1: 241–53.

Polomé, Edgar (1987a) 'Der indogermanische Wortschatz auf dem Gebiete der Religion', in Meid 1987: 201–17.

—— (1987b) 'Muttergottheiten im alten Westeuropa', in *Matronen und verwandte Gottheiten: Ergebnisse eines Kolloquiums veranstaltet von der Göttinger Akademiekommission für die Altertumskunde Mittel- und Nordeuropas*, Cologne: Rheinland-Verlag, pp. 201–12.

Renfrew, Colin (1987) *Archaeology and Language*, London: Cape.

Schmitt, Rüdiger (1967) *Dichtung und Dichtersprache in indogermanischer Zeit*, Wiesbaden: Harrassowitz.

Schrader, Otto (1901) *Reallexikon der indogermanischen Altertumskunde*, Strasburg; 2nd edn ed. A. Nehring, Berlin/Leipzig, 1917–29.

Szemerényi, Oswald (1978) 'Studies in the kinship terminology of the Indo-European languages', *Acta Iranica* 16: 1–240.

2 Proto-Indo-European: Comparison and Reconstruction

Calvert Watkins

Indo-European is the name given for geographic reasons to the large and well-defined genetic family including most of the languages of Europe, past and present, and extending across Iran and Afghanistan to the northern half of the Indian subcontinent.

A curious by-product of the age of colonialism and mercantilism was the introduction of Sanskrit in the eighteenth century to European intellectual and scholars long familiar with Latin and Greek, and with the European languages of culture, Romance, Germanic and Slavic. This new third member of the comparison, in addition to the two classical languages, revolutionized the perception of linguistic relationships. The English jurist and orientalist Sir William Jones (1746–94), speaking to the Asiatick Society in Calcutta on 2 February 1786, uttered his now famous pronouncement:

> The Sanscrit language, whatever be its antiquity, is of a wonderful structure, more perfect than the Greek, more copious than the Latin, and more exquisitely refined than either, yet bearing to both of them a stronger affinity, both in the roots of verbs and in the forms of grammar, than could possibly have been produced by accident; so strong indeed, that no philologer could examine them all three, without believing them to have sprung from some common source, which, perhaps, no longer exists. There is a similar reason, though not quite so forcible, for supposing that both the Gothick and the Celtick, though blended with a very different idiom, had the same origin with the Sanscrit, and the old Persian might be added to the same family, if this were the place for discussing any question concerning the antiquities of Persia.

Jones was content with the assertion of the common origin of these languages; it remained for others to explore systematically the true nature of their linguistic relationship in the first decades of the nineteenth century. The new science of comparative grammar was founded in 1816 by the young German Franz Bopp (1791–1867), after four years of study of oriental languages in Paris, with the appearance of his work *Ueber das Conjugationssystem der Sanskritsprache, in Vergleichung mit jenem der griechischen, lateinischen, persischen, und germanischen Sprachen, nebst Episoden des Ramajan und Mahabharat in genauen metrischen Uebersetzungen aus dem Originaltexte und einigen Abschnitten aus den Veda's.* To Bopp and his near contemporary the Dane Rasmus Rask (1787–1832) must go the principal credit for first correctly seeing the relationships and systematically evaluating the similarities of the Indo-European family. The publication of the manuals of Lithuanian, with its strikingly archaic appearance, and the development of Slavic philology enabled Bopp to add the Baltic and Slavic branch to the growing Indo-European family. The Celtic languages, with their apparently idiosyncratic initial consonant mutations were the first real challenge to the emergent comparative method. That they too were Indo-European was asserted by Rask and others, and conclusively demonstrated by Bopp in 1838, with an elegant historical explanation of the troublesome initial mutations. Albanian was later added to the family, and in 1875 Hübschmann showed that Armenian was an independent branch rather than an aberrant form of Iranian. Representatives of all eight of these branches survive to the present day; Celtic is the only one threatened with extinction. Two new branches, both now extinct, were added early in the twentieth century, thanks to the discovery of new documents: Anatolian (including Hittite and others) and Tocharian.

The similarities among these languages, attested over nearly four millennia, require us to assume they are the continuation of a single prehistoric common language, spoken perhaps some seven thousand years ago, called *Indo-European* or *Proto-Indo-European*. The systematic investigation of the resemblances among these languages, by the comparative method, enables us to reconstruct the principal features of the grammar and lexicon of this proto-language. The reconstruction in turn (as with any proto-language) provides us with an initial stage starting from which we can describe the history of the individually attested daughter languages, which is the ultimate goal of historical linguistics.

Principal Branches

The principal branches of the Indo-European family are given below, in the order of their earliest historical attestation, focusing on the principal languages and the character of their documentation in the earlier periods.

Three branches are attested in the second millennium BC.

Anatolian. Excavations in central Turkey at Hattusas, the capital city of the Hittite Empire (near the village of Boğazköy, now Boğazkale), have unearthed extensive documents in *Hittite* written on clay tablets in a cuneiform script. Philologically we can distinguish *Old Hittite* (*c.* 1700–1500 BC), *Middle Hittite*

(1500–1350 BC) and *Neo-Hittite* (1350–1200 BC). Fragmentary remains of two other related languages are found in the same cuneiform Hittite sources: *Palaic*, in texts contemporary with Old Hittite and spoken to the north-west of Hattusas, and *Cuneiform Luvian*, in texts contemporary with Old and Middle Hittite and spoken over much of southern and western Anatolia (a form of Luvian in the north-west may have been the language of the Trojans). The preponderance of Luvian personal names and the loan words in neo-Hittite texts would indicate widespread use of the Luvian language in Hittite context as well. A very closely related dialect is *Hieroglyphic Luvian* (formerly called Hieroglyphic Hittite), written in an autochthonous pictographic syllabary, attested on seals and isolated rock inscriptions from Middle and neo-Hittite times, and from a number of monumental and other inscriptions from the region of northern Syria, 1000–750 BC. In classical times in south-western Anatolia we have sepulchral and administrative inscriptions (some quite extensive) in *Lycian* (5th to 4th century BC), and further north in the west, short inscriptions in *Lydian* (6th to 4th century BC), both written in epichoric alphabets. Lycian is clearly developed from a variety of Luvian; the other Anatolian languages cannot yet be organized in subgroups.

Archaeological excavations in Turkey are ongoing, and continue to yield new texts and fragments of texts in Hittite and the other cuneiform languages, in Hieroglyphic Luvian, and in the alphabetic languages of the first millennium. Each discovery brings new additions and new precision to our understanding of these languages, and the process may be expected to continue.

Indo-Iranian consists of two large and ancient groups, *Indic* (or Indo-Aryan) and *Iranian*, and a third, *Nuristani* (formerly called *Kafiri*, and sometimes improperly *Dardic*), attested from modern times in remotest North Afghanistan and neighbouring Pakistan and India. The earliest Indic consists of words and names in Anatolian texts (fifteenth century BC).

Extended Indic texts in *Vedic Sanskrit* begin with the RigVeda, whose earliest parts were probably composed in the Punjab in the second half of the second millennium BC, and continue through the other Vedas, Brāhmanas, Sūtras, etc. By c. 500 BC the language was codified in the grammar of Pāṇini as *Classical Sanskrit*, used to the present day as a learned literary language. From the fifth century BC on we have extensive *Middle Indic* documents (Pali, Prakrits; the very numerous *Modern Indo-Aryan* languages begin to be attested around AD 1000 (see Map 2.2).

Iranian, once spoken over vast stretches of south-eastern Eurasia, is first attested in *Old (Gathic) Avestan*, the hymns (*gāthās*) composed by Zarathustra, of uncertain date, but significantly older than the *Younger Avestan* of the middle of the first millennium BC. *Old Persian* is known from the monumental inscriptions of the Achaemenid kings of the sixth to fourth centuries BC; it is the ancestor of *Middle (Pahlavi)* and *Modern Persian (Farsi)*. Several other *Middle Iranian* languages, known only from twentieth-century discoveries are attested from Seleucid, Arsacid and Sassanian times, like *Parthian*, *Sogdian* and *Saka*, descended from the language of the ancient Scythians. By Islamic times we find the first attestations of some of the numerous *Modern Iranian* languages (see Figure 2.2).

Greek. First attested in documents is *Mycenean* Greek, on the mainland and in Crete from the thirteenth century BC, written in the Linear B syllabary, and deciphered only in 1952. Greek was written on the island of Cyprus in the Cypriot syllabary, clearly of common origin with the Linear B syllabary. The oldest inscription is a single name from the eleventh century BC; the rest date from the eighth century BC to Hellenistic times. Alphabetic Greek is attested continuously from *c.* 800 BC, beginning with the Homeric poems and continuing through the *Classical* and *Hellenistic* (*koinē*) periods, to *medieval* (Byzantine) and *modern* times. A striking historical fact about Greek is that over this long period of virtually continuous documentation this branch maintained its identity as a single language (with different dialects at different times) down to the present day. Greek shares this feature with Armenian, and it is perhaps significant that some scholars posit an intermediary common Graeco-Armenian language.

Two substantial branches and several fragmentary languages are attested in the first millennium BC.

Italic. *Old Latin* and the closely related *Faliscan* are attested in short inscriptions from the sixth to the third century BC; from then on we have extensive documentation of *Classical Latin*. The main other Italic dialects *South Picene*, *Oscan* and *Umbrian* (together constituting the *Sabellic* group) are attested in inscriptions from the seventh or sixth to the first century BC. The affinity of the *Venetic* language to the Italic branch is controversial; the very recently reported Venetic inscriptions said to be found in southern Hungary seem to be imaginary. The Italic affinity of the various ancient languages of Sicily, *Siculan* (*Sikel*), *Sicanian* and *Elymian* is likewise uncertain due to the scarcity of evidence. Latin spread by conquest, replacing the other Italic dialects, and ultimately prevailed over large areas of southern and central Europe; the descendants of the spoken language are the medieval and modern *Romance* languages from Portugal to Romania (see Map 2.2), whose differentiation can be documented from the seventh and eighth century AD.

Celtic languages were in the first millennium BC spoken over large areas of Europe from the Iberian peninsula through southern Germany, the Po valley and Austria to the Danube plains, and as far as Galatia in central Anatolia. In our documentation we distinguish geographically between *Continental Celtic* (third century BC to third century AD, extinct; inscriptions in *Gaulish*, *Celtiberian*, *Lepontic* and others) and *Insular Celtic*, the languages spoken now or formerly in the British Isles. These form two groups, *Goidelic* (Gaelic) in Ireland and *Brythonic* (British) in Britain. The former comprise *Irish* (Primitive or *Ogam* AD 400–600, *Old Irish* AD 600–900,

Middle AD 900–1200, and *Modern* 1200 +); *Scottish Gaelic* (1200 +) and the extinct *Manx*. Brythonic includes *Welsh* (*Old* eighth to twelfth century AD; *Middle* twelfth to fifteenth century, *Modern*), *Breton* (*Old* and *Modern*) and the extinct *Cornish*.

Other fragmentarily attested languages, clearly Indo-European but of disputed origin, are *Phrygian* (western central Anatolia, short inscriptions eighth to fifth century BC, first to second century AD), and *Messapic* (the 'heel' of Italy, short inscriptions fifth to first century BC). Both are sometimes, but for geographic reasons only, grouped with the (poorly understood) ancient Balkan languages. (See Map 2.1.)

The remaining five branches of the family are first attested in the Christian era.

Germanic. The earliest extensive representative is *Gothic* (extinct), known from the Bible translation of the fourth century, which together with the other language remnants (Vandalic, Burgundian, etc.) form East Germanic. *North Germanic* is attested from a few runic inscriptions (third century AD +) and principally from *Old Norse* (ninth to sixteenth century) and the later West (Norwegian, Icelandic) and East (Danish, Swedish) Scandanavian languages. The principal earliest *West Germanic* monuments are in *Old English* (*c.* AD 700 +), *Old Saxon* (*c.* AD 850 +), and *Old High German* (*c.* AD 750 +), with the later medieval and modern forms of English, Frisian, Dutch, Low German and High German.

Armenian. Known from the Bible translation of the fifth century and subsequent literature is *Classical Armenian*, with its medieval and modern descendants spoken in several dialects, notably the Eastern (Russian) and the Western (Turkish and post-diaspora).

Tocharian. Two languages, now extinct, found in documents (mostly Buddhist translation literature) from the eastern (*Toch. A*) and western (*Toch. B*) parts of the Tarim basin in Chinese Turkestan (Xinjiang), dating from sixth to eighth century AD.

Balto-Slavic. The Slavic and Baltic languages appear to form a single subgroup within Indo-European, though some scholars would keep them apart. *Slavic* is first attested in the Bible translation of the ninth century in *Old Church Slavonic*. The dialect division into *East Slavic* (Russian, Ukrainian, Belorussian), *West Slavic* (Polish, Czech, Slovak, etc.), and *South Slavic* (Slovene, Serbo-Croatian, Macedonian, Bulgarian) is probably not much older than the middle of the first millennium AD. Old Church Slavonic is basically Common Slavic with some South Slavic dialect features.

Of the *Baltic* languages, the earliest attested is the extinct Old Prussian (fourteenth to seventeenth century) followed by the two flourishing *East Baltic* languages Lithuanian and Latvian (sixteenth century). Despite this late attestation Baltic and Slavic languages are in phonology and morphology remarkably conservative.

Albanian is known only from the fifteenth century on, in two dialects, a

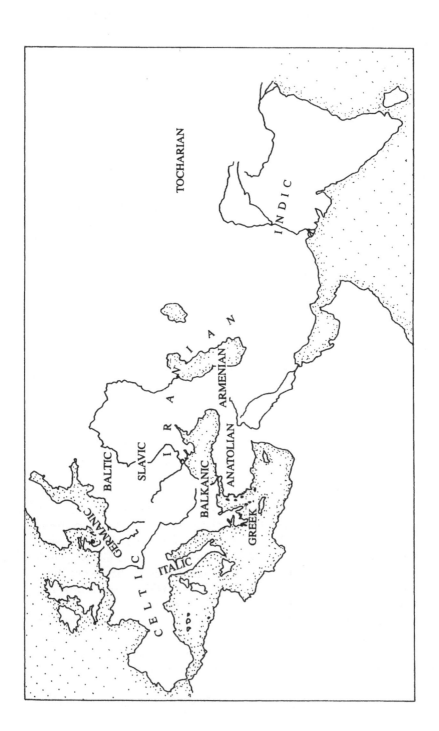

Map 2.1   Indo-European languages in the first millennium BC
Used with permission of C. Watkins

northern (Geg) and a southern (Tosk). Some scholars are now inclined to see Albanian as the descendant of Daco-Mysian, a reconstructed language of the Eastern Balkan area.

Subgrouping

The ten or eleven attested branches can be arranged in larger subgroups, constituting dialectal divisions within Proto-Indo-European which go back to a period long before the speakers arrived in their historical areas of attestation. It is clear from the archaeological record that the Indo-European languages were brought into the areas they historically occupied in Europe and south-western Asia by a series of movements of people, small or large, over many millennia. A number of archaic features in morphology and phonology set Anatolian apart from the other branches, and indicate that it was the earliest to hive off. But Anatolian remains derivable from Proto-Indo-European, and periodic efforts to situate Anatolian as a sister language to Indo-European, both deriving from a putative 'Indo-Hittite', have not found a following.

On the basis of a number of shared innovations and other common features we may schematically display the dialectal affinities among the remaining ten branches in four quadrants; corresponding to the points of the compass (Figure 2.1). Each branch shares certain features with the nearest branch in the adjacent quadrants, the closest affinities of Anatolian are with the western group.

The Homeland of the Indo-Europeans

Many scholars hold that the Siberian steppe zone north and east of the Black Sea was, if not the ultimate 'cradle' of the Indo-Europeans, at least a significant staging area for movements to the west into the Balkans and beyond, to Anatolia, and to the south and then east into Iran and India, beginning in the mid-fifth millennium BC. This is what is termed by archaeologists the Kurgan culture, after the Russian word for its characteristic grave monuments or barrows; see Gimbutas (1980); Mallory (1989).

Still other areas have been proposed on sometimes skimpy evidence, ranging from central Europe and the Balkans to northern Europe, and even the circumpolar far North at the end of the last Ice Age. Most recently (Gamkrelidze and Ivanov 1995) an area in eastern Anatolia south of the Caucasus has been proposed, to account for various alleged contact phenomena with neighbouring Semitic, Kartvelian and other language families. This area would have been the starting point for a circular northward movement east of the Caspian Sea, then turning westward into the Kurgan staging area. But the linguistic evidence for the cross-family contact remains controversial. It would appear that the break-up of the Indo-European dialects had already

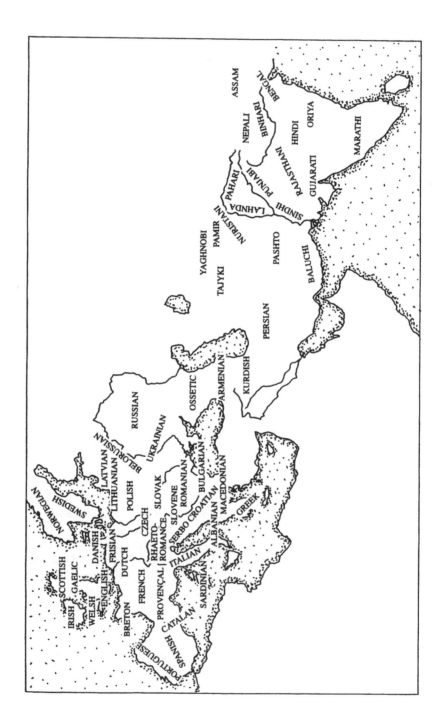

Map 2.2 Indo-European languages in modern times
Used with permission of C. Watkins

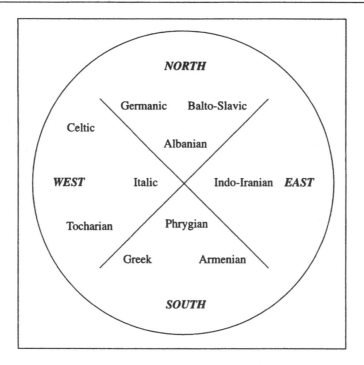

Figure 2.1   Dialectical affinities among ten branches of Proto-Indo-European

taken place in the transpontic Kurgan or a similar staging area. Proto-Indo-European was doubtless spoken over a fairly wide geographical area in Eurasia, and what we reconstruct and term Proto-Indo-European almost certainly refers to a language spoken over a temporal continuum of more than one millennium.

A Grammatical Sketch of Reconstructed Proto-Indo-European

Phonology

In the Indo-European phonological system we distinguish four groups of sounds on the basis of clustering and other morphophonemic rules. These are, in ascending order of syllabicity, *obstruents* (stops and sibilants) (symbol T); *laryngeals* (symbol H); *resonants* (symbol R); and *vowels* (symbol E).

Obstruents

A fairly rich system of stop consonants has been traditionally reconstructed, with five points of articulation (labial, apico-dental, palatal, velar and labiovelar) and three manners of articulation (unvoiced, voiced and voiced aspirated):

I	p	t	$\hat{k}$	k	k^w
II	(b)	d	$\hat{g}$	g	g^w
III	b^h	d^h	$\hat{g}^h$	g^h	g^{wh}

For series III, equivalent notations are ‹bʰ dʰ› etc. For the palatal stops, equivalent notations are ‹k′ g′› etc. For the question of the three tectals ('gutturals') see pp. 38f. below. These are illustrated by the following correspondence charts.

Compare

IE*pet- 'fly, fall' in Hitt. pattar 'wing', Ved. pátati, Avest. pataiti 'falls', Gk pétomai, Lat. petō 'go after', OEng. feðer 'feather', Welsh edn and Ir. én 'bird' (*petno-)

*k̂ekʷ- 'excrement' in Ved. śákr̥t, gen. śaknás, Gk. kópros; *(h₁)ék̂u-o- 'horse' in HLuv. azùwa-, Ved. áśvas, Arm. aspō, Myc. Gk. iqo (Gk hippos), Lat. equos, Goth. aihwa-, OIr. ech (Gaul. epo-, dial. equos), Lith. ašvà 'mare', Toch. B yakwe

*ken- 'fresh, new', Ved. kanisthá- 'youngest', kan(í)yā, Avest. kaine 'maiden', Gk kainós 'new', Lat. recens, Gaul. Cintu-gnātus 'Firstborn', OIr. cét-.

The voiced labial b is disproportionately rare, and correspondence sets are typically limited to few languages, like Hitt. lip- [lib-] 'lick', Luv. lapan- [laban-] 'saltlick', Eng. lip, Lat. labium, IE *leb- (probably imitative); Gk steibō 'trample', Arm. stipem 'press'. Such equations may be posterior to the common period; it is possible, but not demonstrable, that PIE *m reflected an earlier merger of *b and *m. For the others compare:

IE *dek̂m̥ 10: Skt dáśa, Avest. dasa, Gk déka, Lat. decem, Osc. deket-, Goth. taihun, Arm. tasn, OIr. deich n-, OCS desętь, Lith. dēšimts, Toch. B śak

IE *ĝenu-/ĝonu- 'knee': Hitt. genu, Skt jānu, Avest. zānu, Gk gónu, Lat. genu, Goth. kniu, Arm. cunr, OIr, glún, Toch. B keni-, Alb. gju

IE *gʷow- 'bovine': HLuv. waw(a)- (< *gʷ-), Skt gaus, Avest. gaoš, Gk boũs, Lat. bōs (Sabine dialect borrowing); OEng. cū, Arm. kov, Ir. bó, OCS *gov-ędo.

Compare:

IE *bʰerĝʰ- 'high': Hitt. park- [parg-] 'be high', Skt br̥hant- 'lofty', Avest. bərəz- and bərəzant- 'high', OLat. ethnic name Forcti, Gmc ethnic name Burgund-, Arm. barjr 'high', Ir. name Brigit, Toch. B pärk- 'rise' parkare 'long'.

IE *dʰ(e)uh₂- 'smoke': Hitt. tuḫḫ- [tux-] 'smoke', Skt dhūmás, Gk thūmós 'spirit', Lat. fūmus, OCS dymъ, Lith. dúmai.

Table 2.1 Unvoiced stops

Indo-European	Hittite	Sanskrit	Avestan	Greek	Latin	Oscan	Gothic	Armenian	Irish	Old Church Slavic	Lithuanian	Tocharian
*p	p	p	p	p	p	p	f(b)[4]	h(w)[5]	—	p	p	p(p')[8]
*t	t	t	t	t	t	t	þ(d)[4]	t^c	t(th)[6]	t	t	t(c)[8]
*ḱ	k	ś	s	k	c	k	h(g)[4]	s	c(ch)[6]	s	š	k(ś)[8]
*k	k[9]	k(c)[1]	k(c)[1]	k	c	k	h	k^c	c(ch)	k(č, c)	k	k
*kʷ	ku	k(c)[1]	k(c)[1]	p(t)[3]	qu	p	hw	k^c	c(ch)[6, 7]	k(č, c)[2]	k	k

1 c before *e, i, j in Indo-Iran. by the Law of Palatals.
2 č before *e, i, j in Slavic, c before *oi, ai (which became ě, i).
3 t before *e, i in most dialects. Myc. ‹q› = [kʷ].
4 By *Verner's Law*; cf. Chapter 13, pp. 394ff.
5 h-initially, w between vowels.
6 Irish unvoiced t etc. only initially.
7 Ogam Ir. ‹Q› = [kʷ].
8 By inner-Toch. palatalization.
9 Luv. z < *ḱ, k < *k, ku < *kʷ.

Table 2.2 Voiced stops

Indo-European	Hittite[7]	Sanskrit	Avestan	Greek	Latin	Oscan	Gothic	Armenian	Irish[5]	Old Church Slavic	Lithuanian	Tocharian[6]
*b	b	b	b	b	b	b	p	p	b	b	b	p
*d	d	d	d	d	d	d	t	t	d	d	d	t
*g	g	j	z	g	g	g	k	c	g	z	ž	k
*g	g	g(j)[1]	g(j)[1]	g	g	g	k	k	g	g	g	k
*gʷ	gu	g(j)[1]	g(j)[1]	b(d)[3]	u(gu)[4]	b	q	k	b	g(ž, dz)[2]	g	k

1 Skt, Avest. *j* by Law of Palatals.
2 OCS *ž* by Slavic Law of Palatals, *dz* like *c* above; see Chapter 15, p. 429.
3 d before *e* in most dialects. Myc. ‹q› = [gʷ].
4 Lat. *gu* after *n*.
5 Word initially these are stops [b d g], word internally they are voiced continuants [ƀ g đ].
6 With palatalized variants as with unvoiced stops.
7 Probably devoiced word-initially.

Table 2.3 Voiced aspirated stops

Indo-European	Hittite[8]	Sanskrit	Avestan	Greek	Latin[4]	Oscan	Gothic	Armenian	Irish[5]	Old Church Slavic	Lithuanian	Tocharian[7]
*bʰ	b	bh	b	ph	f(b)	f	b	b	b	b	b	p
*dʰ	d	dh	d	th	f(d)	f	d	d	d	d	d	t
*ǵʰ	g	h	z	kh	h(g)	h	g	j	g	z	ž	k
*gʰ	g	gh(h)[1]	g(j)[1]	kh	h	h	g	g	g	g	g	k
*gʷʰ	gu	gh(h)[1]	g(j)[1]	ph(th)[3]	f(u)	f?	b?(w)[6]	j̃	g	g(ž, dz)[2]	g	k

1 Skt *h*, Avest. *j* by the Law of Palatals.
2 *ć* by the Slavic Law of Palatals, *dz* like *c*.
3 *th* before *e*, *i* in most dialects. Myc. ‹φ› = [kʷʰ].
4 Sounds in parentheses are word-internal.
5 As for voiced stops.
6 *b*- is controversial.
7 As for unvoiced stops.
8 Probably devoiced word-initially.

IE *$g^{wh}en$- 'slay, smite': Hitt. *kuen*- [k^wen-], Skt *han*-, Avest. *jan*-, Gk *phónos* 'murder'/ *theínō* 'beat', Lat. (*of-*)*fen*(-*dō*), Gmc *banō* 'murderer', Ir. *gonu* 'kill', OCS *ženǫ* 'drive'.

The Glottalic Theory

The typological rarity ('unnaturalness') of the three series (I) unvoiced: (II) voiced: (III) voiced aspirated (murmured, breathy voiced), together with the rarity of *b*, has led a number of scholars recently to reinterpret the traditional voiced series (II) as an unvoiced ejective (glottalized) one, and the unvoiced (I) as aspirated (with unaspirated allopophones):

I	$p^{(h)}$	$t^{(h)}$	$\hat{k}^{(h)}$	$k^{(h)}$	$k^{w(h)}$
II	p'	t'	$\hat{k}$'	k'	k^w'
III	$b^{(h)}$	$d^{(h)}$	$\hat{g}^{(h)}$	$g^{(h)}$	$g^{w(h)}$

See Gamkrelidze and Ivanov (1995).

While the new 'typological interpretation' may account for some problematic features, it introduces considerable complexities (and 'unnaturalness') elsewhere in the system, and the question still awaits a generally acceptable solution.

The traditional three series of stops (see I–III of chart on p. 34 above) are nowhere preserved intact, but everywhere in the dialects somehow altered. We find the following developments:

1   development of a new series IV, unvoiced aspirates (Indic, pre-Iranian, perhaps pre-Greek and pre-Armenian);
2   series III is devoiced (Greek, possibly pre-Italic);
3   de-aspiration, merger of series II and III as II (Anatolian, Iranian, Balto-Slavic, Phrygian, Celtic, Albanian, Messapic);
4   merger of series I, II, III as I (Tocharian);
5   spirantization (Iranian I, IV → [+continuant], Italic III → [+continuant]);
6   'mutation' (Germanic I, III → '+continuant, α voiced], II → [–voiced]; Armenian I → [+aspirated], II → [–voiced]).

A 'glottalic' restatement (see I–III of chart above) would simplify item (6) but considerably complicate (1) through (5).

Indo-European forms in this chapter, as in most current handbooks, appear in their traditional shape.

The Tectals

Nearly all the languages show good evidence only for·a front/back contrast in the tectals or dorsals ('gutturals'), $k : k^w$ in the western and $\hat{k}: k$ in the eastern dialects: Lat. *centum* '100': *quattuor* '4', Lith. *šiṁtas* '100': *keturì* '4'. Such dialect variation can be typologically paralleled (e.g. in the Athabascan language Kayukon of Alaska). Some scholars therefore assume only four points of articulation in the PIE stops, *p, t, k, kʷ*, despite the classical threeway contrast of reflexes in identical environments, for example, initially before the liquid *r* in Skt *śrad-*: Lat. *crēd-* (IE *ḱr-*); Skt *krávis*: Gk *kréas* (IE *kr-*); Skt (*á-vi-)krītas*: Gk (*a-)príatos* (IE *kʷr-*). New evidence from Luvian as well as other arguments supports the traditional reconstruction of an original threeway contrast *ḱ : k : kʷ*. Compare Luv. *za-/zi-* 'this' < *ḱo-/ḱi-* (Lith. *šìs*, Arm. *-s*), *zīyar(i)* 'lies' < *ḱej-or* (Ved. *śáye* < *ḱej-oj*); *kiša(i)-* 'comb' < *kes-* (OCS *česǫ*), *karš-* 'cut' (Gk *a-kerse-kómēs* 'with unshorn locks'); *kui-* 'who' < *kʷi-* (Lat. *quis*), *-kuwa* < *kʷe* (Lat. *-que*). See Melchert (1987). Most western dialects merged *ḱ, k > k* (the 'centum' solution); the eastern group merged *k, kʷ > k* (the 'satem' [Avest. *satəm* '100'] solution). In the latter case, the front palatals further developed to affricates, then sibilants (see Chapter 4, p. 105).

Sibilants
Beside the wealth of stops, Proto-Indo-European had only a single continuant, the sibilant *s*, allophonically voiced to [z] when followed by distinctively voiced segments, that is, voiced stops. In several languages (independently) *s* is weakened to *h* before vowel: Old Irish, Greek, Armenian, Brythonic.

IE *sekʷ-* 'follow': Lat. *sequitur*, Skt *sácate*, Avest. *hacaitē*, Gk *hépetai* 'follows'

IE *misdʰó-* 'recompense': Gk *misthós*, Avest. *mižda-*, Goth. *mizdō*, OCS *mьizda*;

IE *h₂ster-* 'star': Hitt. *hašter-*, Gk *astér*, Arm. *astł*, Avest. *star-*, OIr. *ser*

Cluster Phenomena
Certain phonological effects are caused by the contact of obstruents in a string. These are context-sensitive rules of IE date. A selection is given below.

Voicing Assimilation
Non-aspirated obstruents assimilate in voicing to a following stop. With the loss of the vowel of IE *ped-* 'foot', the resultant *pd-* appears as *bd-*: Avest. *fra-bd-a-* 'forefoot', Gk *epí-bd-ai* 'day after ['at the foot of'] a festival'. (The voicing of *s* above is simply an instance of this rule.) IE *nigʷ-* 'wash' + *-to-* > *nikʷtó-* 'washed': Skt *niktá-*, Gk *á-niptos* 'unwashed'.

Bartholomae's Law
If the first member of an obstruent cluster is (voiced) aspirated, the assimilation is progressive: $D^h + T \rightarrow DD^h$. This rule is most clearly seen in early Indo-Iranian: Skt *budh-* 'awaken' + *-tá-* > *buddhá*; Indo-Iranian *augh-* 'speak solemnly, aver' +3 sg. mid. *-ta* → Gathic Avest. *aogədā* 'he spoke'. The rule also applied to *s*: *awgʰ-* + 2 sg. mid. *-sa* → Indo-Iran. *augzʰa*, Gathic Avest. *aogəžā*. Outside of Indic the effects of *Bartholomae's Law* have been largely undone by paradigmatic analogy: Young Avest. *aoxta* 'spoke' like Gk *eúkto*, leaving only isolated relics. But that it was an IE rule

is shown by the suffix doublets like *-tro-/ *-d^{h}ro-, *tlo-/ *-d^{h}lo- (Lat. -trum, -brum, -culum, -bulum), whose existence is scarcely to be explained otherwise.

Dental plus Dental
In IE clusters of root-final dental stop followed by morpheme-initial dental stop (like the common third-person singular ending *-ti, -t, the verbal adjective *-to-, agent suffix *-ter-), an s was inserted between the two dentals. From the root *h$_1$ed- 'eat' + 2 pl. ending * -te(-), Hittite e-ez-te-en 'eat!' [etnten] < *ednten (voicing assimilation). Common Indo-Iranian had also *tst- (and *-dzd(^{h})- where the second dental was voiced), whence Indic -tt- (and -dd-), but Avest. -st- (and zd-): Ved. attana 'eat!'. In other branches the result is either -st- (Gk, Balto-Slavic) or -ss- (Italic, Celtic, Germanic); IE *n̥-g^{wh}ed^h-to- 'in-exōrābilis' (*g^{wh}ed^h- 'entreat, pray') in Lat. īnfestus, YAV ajasta- (remade from *ajazda-), with *-dh-t- > *zd^h- in both forms according to Bartholomae's Law (see p. 39).

Dental plus Tectal ('Thorn Clusters')
In a small but important group of words we observe the correspondences Skt kṣ : Gk kt (r̥kṣa- 'bear': árktos). Skt kṣ : Gk khth (kṣám- 'earth': khthṓn); Skt ks : Gk phth (á-kṣi-ta- 'imperishable' á-phthitos). The evidence of Hitt. tekan ['teːgan], gen. taknaš 'earth', hart(a)kkaš 'bear(?)', as well as Toch. A tkaṃ, Toch. B kem made it clear that the correspondences result from metathesized tautosyllabic clusters of dental plus tectal: *tk̂, *d(^{h})ĝ^h, *d^{h}g^{wh}, with differing reflexes dependent on phonetic context.

Geminates
The sequence s+s at morpheme boundary was simplified to single s: root *h$_1$es- 'be' + 2 sg. *-si yielded *h$_1$esi, whence Skt ási, Gathic Avest. ahī, Gk eī(s), Lith. esi. Compare the dental plus dental rule above, which also eliminated geminates. Geminated or long consonants in general were avoided in IE 'ordinary' language, while they played an important role in the onomastic system of hypocoristics (cf. Ger. Fried-rich [friːd–] but Fritz [*fritt-]), appellatives like Gk átta, Goth. atta, Hitt. attaš, 'poppa', and expressive or iconic deformations in poetic language like Gk ópphin 'snake!', synnékhes 'continuously'.

Laryngeals
The term laryngeal is applied (loosely) to a set of h-like sounds in the proto-language, of not entirely specifiable phonetic value. It is probable that they belonged to the natural class of 'gutturals' now recognized by phonologists working with Semitic languages. The PIE laryngeals are here noted h$_1$ h$_2$ h$_3$; equivalent notations are ə$_1$ ə$_2$ ə$_3$, E A O, x̂ x x^W, and other symbols as well. (Some scholars assume only one laryngeal, others four or more. See Kuryłowicz and Mayrhofer 1.121 ff. and Eichner 1988.)

The system of the IE laryngeals was in large part worked out by F. de Saussure in his brilliant *Mémoire* of 1878, from internal structural evidence, corrected by the work of H. Møller (1879), A. Cuny (1912) and J. Kuryłowicz (1927), also on structural grounds. The last further identified Saussure's A = ə, by then recognized as a consonantal element, with Hittite $\underset{\cdot}{h}$. While this material confirmation of the theory was as welcome as it was dramatic, evidence for the laryngeals comes from a variety of sources in many languages, and, for example, despite the absence of a single phonetic continuator, the laryngeals were probably better preserved in Greek than in Hittite.

The basic rules affecting the laryngeals are two: (1) H-coloration, and (2) H-loss.

(1) H-coloration. Laryngeals h_2 and h_3 had the property of colouring (lowering, backing or rounding) an adajacent vowel *e* (and only that vowel) to *a* and *o* respectively; h_1 had no colouring effect. The results were

$$h_1e > h_1e \qquad eh_1 > eh_1$$
$$h_2e > h_2a \qquad eh_2 > ah_2$$
$$h_3e > h_3o \qquad eh_3 > oh_3$$

The new vowels *a* and *o* merged with the previous /a/ and /o/, and increased their frequency and distribution. This change took place already in the proto-language.

(2) H-loss. At a later period, beginning in the proto-language and continuing into the dialects, the laryngeals tended to become lost, with different phonological consequences in different environments and according to dialect. Only a selection of these can be illustrated. When preceded by a short vowel (*e*, *a*, *o* and the high vowels *i* and *u*) and followed by a non-syllabic, the loss of the laryngeal resulted in the corresponding long vowel, by compensatory lengthening. Using the cover symbol H for laryngeal and C for consonant,

$$He > e \qquad eHC > \bar{e}C$$
$$Ha > a \qquad aHC > \bar{a}C$$
$$Ho > o \qquad oHC > \bar{o}C$$
$$Hi > i \qquad iHC > \bar{i}C$$
$$Hu > u \qquad uHC > \bar{u}C$$

Compare IE *peh_2- 'protect', extended form *peh_2-s- *pah_2-s- in Lat. *pās-tor* 'herdsman', Hitt. *paḫš-*. The *o*-grade of the same root is not coloured, but can be lengthened: *$póh_2ju$- in Gk *põu* 'flock (of sheep)' (< *'protected'), *$poh_2yú$- in Ved. Skt *pāyú* 'protector'. When H is lost before a syllabic, compensatory lengthening does not take place: *poh_2i-mén- in Gk *poimén* 'herdsman', Lith. *piemuõ*, gen. *piemeñs* 'shepherd boy'.

H-loss in the dialects as stated above applied only in cases where H was adjacent to a vowel. Where H was not adjacent to a vowel and not in word-initial position, it became syllabic, with different vowel reflexes in the dialects: Skt *i*, most others *a*, but Greek keeps the three distinct as *e, a, o*. These are the reflexes of the older reconstructed 'schwa' *ə* of traditional pre-laryngealist handbooks. Thus:

$ph_2tér$- 'father' in Skt *pitár-*, Gk *patér*, Lat. *pater*, Goth. *fadar*, OIr. *athair*, Arm. *hayr*

dh_3-nó-/-tó- 'given' in Skt *diná-*, Gk *dotós*, Lat. *datus*

d^hh_1s- in Lat. *fānum* 'piece of consecrated ground, temple' < *fas-nom*, Gk *thés-phatos* 'destined by a god, bounded, fatal', *the-ós* 'god', beside e-grade of the following

d^heh_1s- in Osc. *fíísnú* 'piece of consecrated ground, temple' < *$fēs-nā$*, Lat. *fēs-tus (dies)* '(religious) holiday', Arm. *di-k^c* '(pagan) gods'.

/h_1/ for which a phonetic value [h] or [ʕ] has been suggested, has no colouring effect on an adjacent vowel. Its former presence can be inferred, however, from ablaut and vocalization phenomena (pp. 51f) and lengthening effects. Thus:

$h_1és$-ti 'is' in Hitt. *e-es-zi* /ˈest͡si/. Gk *ésti* 'there is', Skt *ásti*, Lat. *est*

h_1s-énti 'are' in Myc. Gk *e-e-si* /ehensi/, Skt *sánti*, Lat. *sunt*, Goth. *sind* negated participle *$n̥$-h_1s-ont-* in Skt *ásat-* 'false'.

/h_2/, for which a velar [x] or pharyngeal [ħ] have been suggested, colours *e* to *a*, but has no colouring effect on *o* or long vowels. It is directly attested in Hitt. and Luv. *ḫ-*, *-ḫ(ḫ)-* and Lyc. *x-*. Compare uncoloured *h_2ow-i-* 'sheep' in Luv. *ḫāwīš*, Lyc. *xawā-* (acc.), Lat. *ovis*, Gk *ó(w)is*, beside coloured *h_2ent-* > *h_2ant-* 'front, forehead' in Hitt. *ḫanza* 'forehead', *ḫantezzi(ya)s* 'first', Lyc. *xñtawati-* 'ruler, king', Gk *antí* 'before', Lat *ante*. Initially before consonant, *$h_2nér$-* 'man, hero' with initial vowel in Gk *anér*, Arm. *ayr* and Phrygian *anar*, lengthening in Skt *sūnára-* 'handsome' < *su-h_2ner-o-*, and loss in Osc. *niir* 'magistrate', Lat. *Ner-ō*, Skt *náram* (acc.), Avest. *nā*, OIr. *nert* 'strength'.

/h_3/, for which a labialized velar [x^w], [$ɣ^w$] or (labialized?) voiced pharyngeal [G], [G^w] has been suggested, colours *e* to *o*, but has no colouring effect on *a* or long vowels. It is directly attested in Hitt. *ḫ-* corresponding to Lyc. zero: IE *h_3ep-* > *h_3op-* in Hitt. *ḫāppar* 'transaction, deal', *ḫappīnant-* 'wealthy', Lyc. *epirije-* 'sell', Lat. *ops* 'power, wealth', *op-ulent-* 'wealthy'. IE *$ĝneh_2$-* > *$ĝnoh_3$-* 'know' in Lat. *(g)nō-scō*, but uncoloured long vowel (lengthened grade, pp. 52f.) in *$ĝnēh_3$-s-* Hitt. *ganeš-zi* 'recognizes', Toch. A *kñās-äṣt* 'du kennst dich aus'.

Under the heading of CLUSTER PHENOMENA we may note some important laryngeal reflexes; only a selection is possible.

RH. Clusters of syllabic liquid or nasal plus laryngeal when followed by a non-syllabic have special reflexes. These are the traditional 'long sonants' $\bar{r}$ etc. as reconstructed in pre-laryngealist handbooks. The basic correspondences in the branches that preserve these distinct are

Indo-European	Sanskrit	Italic, Celtic	Lithuanian (under the accent)
r̥H(C)	īr/ūr	rā	ìr
l̥H(C)	ī/ūr	lā	ìl
m̥H(C)	ān	mā(?)	ìm
n̥H(C)	ā	nā	ìn

[Here as on page 42 Greek has a threefold reflex, with further complications (type -nē- / -ene-, -nā- / -ana-).] The essence of the system is the preservation of a bimoric reflex of the bimoric sequence R̥H, typically by transfer of one mora to the vowel. Lith. ìr etc. with 'acute' (falling) intonation reflects an earlier *īr < *irə < *r̥H(C); contrast ir̃ with 'circumflex' (rising) intonation < *ìr < *r̥(C), consisting of one mora (pp. 44f. below).

IE *pl̥h₁-nó- 'full': in Skt pūrnás, OIr. lán, Lith. pìlnas
IE *ǵn̥h₁-tó- 'born': in Skt jātás, Avest. zātō, Lat. (g)nātus, Gaul. personal name Cintu-gnātus 'First-born'.

Germanic shows no distinction between R̥ and R̥H: Goth. fulls < *fulnaz and -kunds < *-kunðaz.

METATHESIS. The sequences CHi, CHu as zero grades (p. 52) of CeHi, CeHu tend to undergo metathesis:

IE *peh₂wr̥ 'fire': in Hitt. pahhur, zero grade *ph₂ur → *puh₂r in Gk pȳr, Umbr. pir, beside unmetathesized *ph₂ur- before vowel in Gk gen. pyrós, Umbr. abl. pure
IE *seh₂wel > *sah₂wel 'sun' in Dor. Gk āélios, Goth. sauil, beside metathesized *suh₂el (*suwel) in Ved. súvar, antevocalic gen. sūrás = Avest. huuarə, hūrō.

Saussure was the first to note regular cases in Greek where in roots of the structure CeRH the laryngeal disappeared in the o-grade: péra-ssa 'I sold' but pór-nē 'prostitute', -bremé-tēs 'thunderer' but bron-tḗ 'thunder'; tór-nos 'carpenter's tool for drawing a circle' and tór-mos 'hole, mortice, tenon' but tére-tron 'drill'. The rule appears to operate in Hittite as well (tar-mas 'peg, nail' beside Gk tór-mos), and appears regular in its mirror-image as well: HReC- but RoC-.

In WORD-FINAL position the treatment of the laryngeals was probably a function of sentence sandhi (Chapter 4, p. 107) rules: before a word beginning with a non-syllabic we expect lengthening (-EH#C- → -Ē#C-), before a word beginning with a syllabic we expect just loss (-EH#E- → -E#E-) after colouring. The result would be doublets of final -Ē/-E, or -EH/-E, of which we find different reflexes in the dialects. Compare the Luvian abstract suffix -aḫ-(id-) with the feminine abstract suffix *-ā- or its reflex in most of the dialects (nom. sg. CGk -ā, Osc. -ú, Umbr. -u, -a, -o, Slav. -a) from *-ah₂ beside the vocatives (Gk nýmph-a, toxóta, Umbr. -a, Slav. -o) from *-a.

Resonants

Under the term 'resonants' or 'sonants' (cover symbol R) are grouped the two IE nasals m and n, the two liquids r and l, and the semi-vowels (glides) y (equivalent notation i̯, j) and w (equivalent notation u̯).

Syllabicity

These phones in Proto-Indo-European could function either as non-syllabics ('consonantal' R), as above, or as syllabics ('vocalic' R̥), noted m̥, n̥, r̥, l̥, and the high vowels i, u, according to context. The basic rule is that the resonant is non-syllabic when adjacent to a vowel proper (E, see p. 46), and otherwise becomes syllabic before a non-syllabic, iteratively from right to left. Thus in the word for 'dog' /k̑/ /w/ /n/ before syllabic, gen. sg. -os appears as *k̑unós (Gk kynós, Ved. śúnas), but before non-syllabic, instrumental plural *-bhis, as *k̑wn̥bhís (Ved. śvábhis). Exceptions are the initial labials w and m in clusters like *wr-, *wy, *wj-, *mr-, *ml-, *mn- (Gk mnā- 'remember', Skt ā-mnā- 'remember and transmit', Luv. manā- [mnɔ:] or [mǝna:]-, 'see'), as well as the zero grade of nasal infix verbs (page 57), for reasons of paradigmatic unity: *h₃r̥-né-g-ti 'destroys', 3 pl. *h₃r̥-n-g-énti (not **h₃r-n̥-g-énti), Hitt. ḫarnikzi ḫarninkanzi, OIr. orgid 'destroys, kills'.

Reflexes

The PIE complementary distribution of non-syllabic and syllabic variants of resonants is broken up in all IE dialects; these show divergent reflexes of R and R̥. The consonantal resonants are largely preserved intact, as are the syllabic vowels u and i (see pp. 45f.), while the syllabic liquids and nasals are sooner or later replaced in all dialects, typically by sequences of vowel and the consonantal liquid or nasal.

Examples of PIE consonantal liquids and nasals are such widely attested roots as *men- 'think', *nem- 'distribute, bestow', *mer- 'die', *mel-it- 'honey'. Indic and Iranian, in common with a widespread areal feature in Asia, tend to merge the two liquids into one: Iran. r, Ved. r but dialectally l. Indo-European distinguished /m/ and /n/ also in absolute final position (n. sg. *sem '1': en 'in', thematic acc. sg. -om : *mon-stem suffixless loc. sg. -mon, etc.), but some of the languages have merged the two to /n/: Anatolian, Greek, Armenian, Celtic (except Celtiberian and Lepontic).

Syllabic Nasals: Correspondences

Indo-European	Hittite	Sanskrit	Avestan	Greek	Latin	Oscan	Gothic	Armenian	Old Irish[2]	Old Church Slavonic	Lithuanian[3]	Tocharian
m̥	am[4]	a	a	a	em	em	um	am	*am	ẹ(u)	iñ/um	äm
n̥	an	a(n)[1]	a(n)[1]	a(n)[1]	en	en	un	an	*an	ẹ(u)	iñ/uñ	än

1 *an* before vowels.
2 The Common Celtic reflexes are given, which undergo complex changes in Irish.
3 With 'circumflex' (rising) intonation when accented.
4 *un* word-finally.

IE *pód-m̥* 'foot (acc. sg.)': in Hitt. *pādan*, Gk *pód-a*, Lat. *ped-em*, Arm. *otn*
IE *g^wm̥ské*: in Ved. *gáccha*, Gathic Avest. *jasa*, Gk *básk(e)* 'go (ipv.)'
IE *n̥-* 'not-': in Ved. *á-mr̥ta-*, Gk *á-mbrotos*, Lat. *im-mortālis* 'immortal'
Hitt. *am-miyant-* 'small, immature'; Toch. A *ā-knats*, Goth. *un-kunþs*, Arm.
   an-canawt^c 'unknown';
Skt *an-ukta-* 'unsayable', MIr. *an-ocht* 'a metrical fault'

Syllabic Liquids: Correspondences

Indo-European	Hittite	Sanskrit	Avestan	Greek	Latin	Oscan	Gothic	Armenian	Old Irish	Old Church Slavonic	Lithuanian	Tocharian
r̥	ar	r̥	ərə	ra, ar	or	or	awr	ar	ri(ar)[1]	ru	ir, ur	är
l̥	al	r̥	ərə	la, al	ul	ol	ul	al	li(al)[1]	li, lu	il, ul	al

1 The basic reflex is Ri; aR is limited to a few contexts (cf. Chapter 12, p. 357).
2 Myc. and Aeolic Ro, oR.

In Indo-Iranian the syllabic liquid is preserved phonetically, but it is no longer
in complementary distribution with the non-syllabic *r*. In Greek and in Hittite
there is some evidence that the syllabic liquids were similarly preserved until
just before the historical period: the Homeric scansion *ăndrŏtētă* 'manhood'
reflects *anr̥tāta* in a poetic formula of pre-Mycenean date.

Non-syllabic Semi-vowels: Correspondences (Word-initial)

Indo-European	Hittite	Sanskrit	Avestan	Greek	Latin	Oscan	Gothic	Armenian	Old Irish	Old Church Slavonic	Lithuanian	Tocharian
j	y	y	y	z[1]	i	i	j	?	0	j	j	y
w	w	v	v	(w)0[2]	u	v	w	g, v	f	v	v	w

1 Gk *h-* reflects an initial cluster *Hi-*.
2 *w* in Mycenean and many dialects ('digamma').

IE *jugóm* 'yoke': Hitt. *yugan*, Skt *yygám*, Gk *zygón*, Lat. *iugum*, Goth. *juk*,
   OCS *igo* (< *jъgo*)

IE *wih-rós 'strong; man(ly)': Avest. vīrō, Gk *(w)īros* (personal name), Lat. *vir*, Goth. *wairs*, OIr. *fer*, Lith. *výras*, Toch. A *wir* 'young, vigorous'.

Sievers' Law

Under the term Sievers' Law are understood various manifestations in various languages, but primarily in Vedic, of a tendency to a distribution -yE-/-wE- after light sequence, -ijE-/-uwE- after heavy sequence: Ved. *sū́rya-* 'sun', *kā́vya* 'of the poet-seer' to be read and metrically scanned *sū́riya-*, *kā́viya-*. Even in Vedic the longer sequence is regular after heavy, but not infrequent after light sequence as well, and in some branches has been generalized: Lat. *medius*, Osc. *mefiio-*, OIr. *mide* < *medʰjo- beside Ved. *mádhya-* (never *mádhiya-*), Gk *méso-* < *medʰjo-. Related to Sievers' Law is Lindeman's Law, which provides for the optional realization of monosyllables of the structure CRE- as CR̥RE-: *djēws in Gk *Zeús*, Hitt. ᴰ*Šiuš*, *dijēws in Ved. *diyaus*.

Vowels Proper

The vowels of Proto-Indo-European were *e, a, o* plus the high vowels *i* and *u* which were in complementary distribution with the glides *y* and *w*. All five vowels occurred both long and short. These vowels were morphophonemically and distributionally not on a par. Primary short *a* and long *ā* can be reconstructed only for a few roots, albeit some of high frequency; most cases of *a* or *ā* in the dialects resulted from laryngeal colouring. Primary *ī* and *ū* were likewise rare; only after H-loss and compensatory lengthening of preceding vowel (including *i* and *u*), which belongs properly to the history of the individual dialects, do we get long vowels with comparable frequency to their short counterparts. The short high vowels *i* and *u* were usually zero grades (p. 52) of diphthongs *ei* and *eu*; the long vowels *ē* and *ō* were usually lengthened grades (p. 52) of a short *e* and *o*. Short *e* and short *o* were in alternation according to morphological function (p. 51); the short *e* was typically the basic vowel, and short *o* derived from it.

The resultant vowel system can be displayed as a traditional triangle subject to the distributional skewing discussed.

The system was in fact not stable; the wave of compensatory lengthening following H-loss further skewed it, and most branches of the family sooner or later lost the old quantity system and went on to develop new ones.

The disparity in frequency of *ō* and *ā* led to developments which distinguish two dialects in the IE languages of Europe. The *southern* languages, Celtic, Italic, Greek and Armenian, plus Tocharian, maintained the five-vowel triangle by increasing the instances of *a*. The *northern* languages, Balto-Slavic,

Germanic, and Albanian, merged *a* and *o*, and with the exception of Baltic, *ā*, and *ō*, thus creating a vowel rectangle (see Chapter 13, p. 389):

i   u

e   'å'

The vowel *å* would be differently realized according to dialect: Gmc *a*, *ō*, Slav. *o*, *a*, Baltic *a*, *ō*.

e, *o*: the basic *e* is usually the full-grade (see p. 52) of roots, like *b^her- 'carry', *nem- 'distribute', *$g^{wh}en$-; 'smite, slay': Gk *phérō*, Lat. *ferō*, Goth. *bairan*, OIr. *berid*, OCS *bero*, Toch. A, Toch. B *pär-*; Gk *némō*, Goth. *niman*, OIr. *nemed* 'privileged person'; Hitt. *kuenzi* [k^{w}entsi], Gk *then-ón* 'smiting', OCS *ženǫ* 'I drive'. The same roots make *o*-grades *b^hor-, *nom-, *$g^{wh}on$-: Gk *phóros* 'tribute', *nomós* 'pasturage', *phónos* 'murder'. Without attested *e*-grade and possibly non-apophonic: *$b^hosó$- 'naked' in OEng. *bær*, OCS *bosъ*, Arm. *bok*.

a: clear cases of fundamental *a* in common words are the roots:

*dap- in Lat. *daps* 'sacrificial meal', *damnum* 'damage entailing liability', Gk *dapánē* 'expenditure', Arm. *tawn* 'festival'
*g^hans- 'goose' in Gk *khḗn*, Lat. *anser*, OHG *gans*, OCS *gǫsь*, Lith. *žąsìs*;
*sal- 'salt' in Skt *salila-* 'sea', Gk *háls* 'sea', Lat. *sal-*, Goth. *salt*
*alb^ho- 'white' in Hitt. *alpaš* 'cloud', Lat. *albus*, Gk *alphós* 'leprosy'.

i, *u*: examples are the instrumental singular ending *-b^hi(-) in Ved. *paḍbhis*, Myc. Gk *po-pi/popphi* 'with the feet', Gaul. *gobedbi* 'by the smiths'; *$nisdo$- 'nest' in Skt *nīḍas*, *nīdus*, OIr. *net*, OEng., OHG *nest*; *$putlo$- 'son, boy' in Ved. *putrás*, Avest. *puθrō*, Osc. *puklum* (acc. sg.). Underlying short *u* in the particles Hitt. *nu*, Ved. *nú*, Gk *ny*, Lat. *nu-dius* (*tertius*), Lith. *nù* (related to *$néwo$- 'new'), but lengthened in Ved. *nū́*, *nūnám*, Avest. *nū*, *nūrəm*, Palaic *nu-u*, Gk *nȳn*, OCS *nyně* 'now'.

ē, *ō*: these appear typically in lengthened grade categories (see p. 52), like the nominative singular of stems in -R: Gk *patḗr* 'father', ablauting *apátōr* 'fatherless', Skt *pitā́*; IE *$uk^wsó(n)$, stem *uk^wsen- 'ox' in Ved. *ukṣá*, Avest. *uxšan-*, OEng. *oxa*, nom. pl. *oxan*, MWelsh *ych* < *$uchü$ < *$uxsū$, pl. *ychen* < *$uchen$ < *$uxsenes$, Toch. B. *okso*; *$dōm$- 'house' in Hom. Gk *dȭ*, Arm. *tun*, OIr. *dām* 'retinue' < *$dōm-ā$ abstract of *$dōm-ó$- 'belonging to the house'. Long *ō* is also the PIE product of contraction *o* + *e*. Compare the thematic (p. 66) nominative plural *-*ōs* < *-*o-es*, dative singular *-*ōi*, < *-*o-ei*: Ved. *vīrās*, *vīrāy-a* (Avest. *ahurāi*), Osc. *bivus*, *hurtúi*, OIr. voc. pl. *á firu* < *-*ūs* < *-*ōs*, Gaul. (Gk alphabet) *-oui*.

ā: Rare, but compare the words for 'mother', Ved. *mātár-*, Dor. Gk acc. *mātéra*, Gaul. *matir*/[mātīr], Toch. *mācer*, and OIr. *sál* 'ocean, sea' < *$sāl-ó$- 'salty'.

Table 2.4 Vowels proper: correspondences

Indo-European	Hittite	Sanskrit	Avestan	Greek	Latin	Oscan	Gothic	Armenian	Old Irish	Old Church Slavonic	Lithuanian	Tocharian[1]
e	e	a	a	e	e	e	e/i	e	e	e	e	ä[2]
o	a	ā, a[3]	ā, a[3]	o	o	ú, o[4]	a	o	o	o	a	e
a	a	a	a	a	a	a	a	a	a	o	a	ā
i	i	i	i	i	i	i	i	i	i	ь	i	i
u	u	u	u	u	u	u	u	u	u	ъ	u	ä

1 The reflexes are those of Toch. B.
2 With preceding palatalization.
3 ā in open syllables by Brugmann's Law.
4 In the Latin alphabet.

Table 2.5 Long vowels: correspondence charts

Indo-European	Hittite	Sanskrit	Avestan	Greek	Latin	Oscan	Gothic	Armenian	Old Irish	Old Church Slavonic	Lithuanian	Tocharian B
ē	e, i	ā	ā	ē	ē	íí	ē	i	ī	ě	ė	e
ō	a	ā	ā	ō	ō	uu	ō	u	ā, ū[1]	a	ō, uo[2]	a, o[3]
ā	a?	ā	ā	ā	ā	aa	ō	a	ā	a	ō	ā, o[3]
ī	i	ī	ī	ī	ī	íí	ī	i	ī	i	y	i
ū	u	ū	ū	ū	ū	ū, ī?	ū	u	ū	y	ū	ū

1 ū in original final syllables.
2 uo from *oh₂, *oh₃.
3 o in some final syllables.

ī ū: Likewise rare; compare **wīs-ó-* in Gk *īós*, Lat. *vīrus* but **wis-ó-* in Skt *viṣás* 'poison'. The word for 'mouse' (and 'muscle', in accord with a semantic quasi-universal, widespread in the languages of the world), Ved. *mū́s-*, Lat. *mūs*, Gk *mūs*, OHG, ON, OEng. *mūs* is a probable example, in view of Ved. *muṣṇā́ti* 'steals', though some have seen a laryngeal origin in the tectal of Arm. *mukn*.

Diphthongs

The three vowels *e, o, a* combined with the consonantal variants of the high vowels *j, w* to form six diphthongs: *ej, oj, aj, ew, ow, aw*. It is customary to treat the other ER cases (*er, ol, en*, etc.) as sequences, though in Lithuanian they are intonable in the same way as the diphthongs with semi-vowel (*añ, ar̃, án, ár*, like *aĩ, aũ, ái, áu*), and are therefore equally legitimately diphthongs (see Chapter 15, p. 460). The diphthongs with glides are best preserved in Greek and early Italic; in most other dialects their number has been reduced by merger and monophthongization.

IE **dejwós* 'god': in OLat. *deiuos*, Osc. *deívaí*, Gaul. *dēvo-*, Avest. *daēuua-* 'demon';

IE **moj-no-* 'to be exchanged', in OLat. *comoine*, Lat. *commūnis*, Osc. *múíníkú*, Goth. *gamains*, OIr. *moin* 'treasure', *commuin* 'mutual obligation', Skt *menāmenam* 'in exchange', Sicilian Gk (Sophron) *moîton anti moítou* 'like for like'

*kajko- 'one-eyed': in Goth. *haihs*, OIr. *cáech*, Lat. *caecus* 'blind', with the infrequent and therefore expressive *a*-vocalism frequent in words for infirmities and other semantically marked notions.

The diphthong falls together with laryngeal coloured $*h_1aj < *h_2ej$-, as in $*h_2aj$-d^h- 'burn' in Gk *aíth-omai*, Lat. *aed-ēs* 'building' < '*hearth', perhaps Pal. *ḫa-a-ri* < **ḫaj-ari* 'is hot'. We have **ew* in **lewk-ó-*, Gk *leukós* 'white, bright', beside *o*-grade **lowk-éjeti* 'lights' in Ved. *rocáyati*, Avest. *rao-caiieiti*, Hitt. *lukkizzi*; **aw* in *sausó-* 'dry', Gk *aũos*, Lith. *saũsas*, Russ. mobile *súx*, n. *súxo*, f. *suxá*, OEng. *sēar* < Gmc **sauzáz*.

Morphophonemics

Indo-European morphophonemics includes accent, apophony (or 'ablaut'), and root structure.

Accents

A single Indo-European word *accent* can be reconstructed, represented in Vedic by the *udātta* and in Greek by the acute, both noting high pitch: *pitáram* = *patéra*. Accent is reconstructed from other more complicated, innovated and sporadic reflexes in Vedic and Greek, from the accent and intonation systems of Balto-Slavic, from Anatolian, and from the effects of *Verner's Law* in Germanic (see Chapter 13, pp. 394f.).

Aside from atonic or enclitic forms every IE word had a single accent, whose position was governed by rule of word formation and inflection, and whose presence or absence in certain grammatical categories was a function of syntactic rules. Thus in inflection some paradigms had fixed accent on the root or ending, while others had movable accent. In word formation, certain suffix morphemes were inherently accented, others were unaccented and implied root accent. In syntax the verb was unaccented or weakly accented in main clauses but accented in subordinate clauses; but when the verb in a main clause was fronted to sentence-initial position it was accented.

The inherited system underwent profound changes even in those dialects which retained it, like the restriction to the last three syllables in Greek. The remaining dialects have replaced it by newer, independent accent systems, typically linked to the word boundary: accent (stress) on the initial syllable was widespread as a sort of 'default setting', as in early Italic, Goidelic Celtic, and Germanic. This may represent the generalization of an accentual feature already present in the proto-language, as in the usually unstressed Vedic vocative in sentence-initial position, when it is accented on the first syllable.

Apophony ('Ablaut')

Indo-European is profoundly marked by the system of vocalic alternations, expressing morphological functions, which is termed 'ablaut' or apophony. The fundamental form was the vowel *e*, which under certain conditions could appear as *o*, while under certain other conditions the vowel could disappear entirely. We speak of the forms as exhibiting *e-grade*, *o-grade* and *zero grade*. Thus the Indo-European word for 'knee' appears as **ĝenu-* (Hitt. *genu*, Lat. *genu*), **ĝonu-* (Skt *jắnu*, Gk *gónu*), and **ĝnu-* (Hitt. instr. *ganut* 'with the knees', Ved. *jñu-bắdh-* 'kneeling', Gk dat. pl. *perì gnusi* 'about the knees'). In certain cases, termed 'Schwebeablaut', the full grade may appear for example not as **ĝenu-* but as **ĝneu-* (Goth. *kniu*). More limited in extent but still reconstructible for the proto-language are the ablaut vowels *ē* and *ō*, termed 'lengthened grade'. Compare Gk nom. sg. *patér* 'father' (acc. sg. *patéra*) and *apátōr* 'fatherless' (acc. sg. *apátora*), or the cognate of 'knee' in Gk *gōnía* 'angle' < **ĝōnw-ih$_2$*.

When one of the consonants is a resonant R, the latter appears in zero grade as either R̥ or R, depending on the non-syllabic or syllabic nature of the following sound respectively:

TeR-   ToR-   TR̥-T-
                TR̄-E-

as in *e*-grade Gk *tén-ōn* 'tendon', *o*-grade *tón-os* 'stretching', and zero grade *ta-tós*, Skt *ta-tás* < **tn̥-tós* 'stretched' but Skt *ta-tn-e* 'it was stretched'.

When the sonant precedes the fundamental vowel we speak of 'samprasārana ablaut':

ReT-   RoT-   R̥T-

as in *e*-grade *wekʷ*- in Gk (*w*)*épos*, Ved. *vácas*- 'word', *o*-grade *wokʷ*- in Hom. Gk (*w*)*op*- 'voice', zero grade *ukʷ-tó* - in Ved. *uktá*- 'spoken'.

In the fairly common situation where the root contains both a resonant R and a laryngeal H, and Schwebeablaut is in play, we find a full panoply of ablaut variants, as from IE *pelh₁*- 'fill, full':

pelh₁-nes-	Ved. *párīṇas*- 'plethora'
pelh₁-u-	Goth. *filu*, OIr. *il* 'much, many'
polh₁-u-	Gk *polús*, *polloí*, 'many'
pl̥h₁-u-	Ved. *purú*-, Avest. *paoru*- 'id.'
pleh₁-C-	Gk *plḗto* 'filled', Lat. *plēnus*, Arm. *li* 'full'
pleh₁-isto-	Gk *pleîstos*, Avest. *fraēšta*- 'most'
ploh₁-	Ved. perf. *paprātha* 'you filled'
pl̥h₁-no-	Ved. *pūrṇá*- 'full', Lith. *pìlnas*, Goth. *fulls* < *fulnaz*
plh₁-e-	Ved. reduplicated thematic *ápiprata*.

Apophony in the Root

Apophony is found in the root, in suffixes, and in endings. Here we consider only the root.

Typical derivational categories showing *e*-grade are the singular of root athematic presents (*h₁és-ti*, 'is'; *gʷʰen-ti* 'slays'), and aorists (*e-dʰeh₁-t* 'placed', *e-stah₂-t* 'stood'), as well as thematic presents (*sékʷ-or* 'follows', *térh₂-or* 'is able, overcomes'), whence the custom of citing roots in the *e*-grade, since most roots are verbal. In the noun, note the simple thematic adjectives (*néwo*- 'new', *séno*- 'old'), thematic neuter nouns (*wérĝom* 'work', *pédom* 'place'), and the numerous secondary suffixes (p. 64) added to *e*-grade roots like *-tor-*, *-men*, *-es-*.

The *o*-grade is characteristic of the (late?) IE stative perfect in the singular (*wójd-e* 'knows', *(dʰe-)dʰórs-e* 'dares'), the causative-iterative (*lowk-éje-ti* 'lights', *wos-éje-ti* 'dresses'), certain intensive reduplicated presents in the singular (Ved *jaṅghanti* 'slaughters' < *gʷʰen-gʷʰon-ti*), numerous simple deverbal thematic nouns and adjectives (type *gʷʰónos* 'slaying', *gʷʰonós* 'slayer'), and numerous secondary formations.

The zero grade is found outside the singular in the apophonic paradigms of p. 60: (*h₁s-énti* 'they are', *wid-mé* 'we know', *dʰé-dʰh₁-n̥ti* 'they place'), before accented ending in some apophonic noun paradigms, and before accented secondary nominal suffix like *-tó-*, *-nó-* (*ukʷ-tó-* 'spoken') or verbal suffixes like *-ské-* (*gʷm̥-ské-ti* 'is going').

The lengthened grade is found in the singular of some apophonic athematic verb paradigms, alternating with e-grade outside the singular (*$t\acute{e}\hat{k}s$-ti *$t\acute{e}\hat{k}s$-$\d{n}ti$ 'fashion'), before secondary thematic adjective suffix -$\acute{o}$- in the derivational process known as $v\acute{\d{r}}ddhi$ (*dom/*dem- 'household' $\rightarrow$ *$d\bar{o}m$-$\acute{o}$ 'belonging to the household', OIr. $d\acute{a}m$ 'retinue'; *wod-/wed- 'water' $\rightarrow$ *$w\bar{e}d$-o- 'watery, wet', OEng. $wæt$ Luv. Ú.SAL$^{\text{HI.A}}$ -$anza\ witanza$ 'in the watery meadows'.

Morpheme Structure Rules

Under the heading of MORPHEME STRUCTURE RULES we may include the rules for well-formed roots, and certain constraints on the phonological structure of roots.

With a small number of exceptions, chiefly in the pronouns, the canonical shapes for IE roots are the following (Benveniste 1935):

C_1EC_2-

where C_1 and C_2 are different consonants, and E is usually the fundamental vowel $e/o/0$, rarely $a(/0)$;

C_1EC_2-C_3-	(state I)
C_1C_2-EC_3-	(state II)

where the C_3 is different from C_2, and C_1 is equal or lower than C_2 in sonority;

C_1C_2-EC_3-C_4-

where C_4 is different from C_3, and equal to or lower than C_3 in sonority. The sonority hierarchy is T/H < R < E; we find root initial HT- and TH-, root-final -TH and -HT. Well-formed roots are thus *tek-, *ter-, *ret-, but not **tet-; *$terp$-, *$trep$-, but not **$rtep$-, **$petr$-; *$prekt$-, *h_2weks-, but not **$prekl$-, etc. In all cases C_1 may be preceded by an s, with no discernible semantic content ('s-mobile'). Exceptionally, a root may lack an initial C_1 and begin with a vowel (*alb^h-o- 'white'; *$att(a)$ 'father!'). Apparent violations of the identical consonant constraint like *ses- 'sleep' (Hitt. $\check{s}e\check{s}$-zi, Ved. $s\acute{a}sti$), *$m\bar{e}ms$-$\acute{o}$- 'meat' (Ved. $m\bar{a}\dot{m}s\acute{a}$-, Arm. mis, Goth. $mimz$) are doubtless grammaticalized from reduplicated child-language forms.

Further root-structure constraints are that no root may begin and end with a plain-voiced stop (**deg-, **$derg$-, **g^wed-), and that no root may begin with a voiced aspirate and end with an unvoiced stop, or vice versa **b^het-, **b^hejk-, **teb^h-). But the combination of initial s plus unvoiced stop with final voiced aspirate is allowed: *$stejg^h$- 'rise', perhaps *$steb^h$- 'crown, wreathe'.

Morphology

Indo-European languages, particularly in their earlier stages, share a rich and complex morphology of the synthetic type. The independence and autonomy of the word, reinforced by the accent, was such that a variety of morphological elements and processes served as the primary exponents of the syntactic functions. A large part of the success of the comparative method in this family is due to the number and the precision of the agreements among languages in the particulars of morphology. Consider the partial paradigms of the words for 'dog' and 'slay' in various dialects and as reconstructed:

	Hittite	Greek	Vedic	Lithuanian	Old Irish	Proto-Indo-European
Nom.	kuwaš	kúōn	ś(u)vá	šuõ	cú	*ḱ(u)wṓ
Acc.	kuwanan	kúna	śvā́nam	šùnį	coin	*ḱwón-m̥
Gen.	kūnaš	kúnós	śúnas	šuñs	con	*ḱun-és

	Hittite	Vedic	Proto-Indo-European
3 sg. pres. ind.	kuenzi	hánti	*g^{wh}én-ti
3 pl. pres. ind.	kunanzi	ghnánti	*g^{wh}n-énti

The reconstructed forms with their complex interplay of ablaut and accent serve at the same time as a shorthand for the successive morphological as well as phonological changes leading to each of the attested dialect forms.

In early IE languages the fundamental DOMAINS OF MORPHOLOGY are inflection, derivation and composition; combining the latter two we have inflection and word formation

INFLECTION deals with the 'paradigm', the varying forms under which a given inflectible *stem* or lexical entry ('word') may appear in a sentence, as a reflex of its syntactic function.

DERIVATION deals with the formation of inflectible stems, the formation of 'words' minus their inflection. We distinguish *primary* derivation and *secondary* derivation. Primary derivatives are formed at the level of the abstraction we term the *root*; secondary derivatives are inflectible stems formed from other inflectible stems which coexist in the language at the same time, that is, in the same synchronic system.

COMPOSITION deals with the formation of inflectible stems from the combination of an inflectible stem with one or more other meaningful elements.

With a limited class of exceptions, including sentential particles, conjunctions and quasi-adverbial forms (preverbs, postpositions, prepositions, negations), all IE words were inflected. The STRUCTURE OF THE INFLECTED word was *Root* plus *Suffix* plus *Ending*:

R + S + E

(R + S) together constituted the inflectible *stem*. The suffix S is recursive:

(((R + S) + S) + S), etc.

The root contained the basic lexical semantic kernel, with further grammatical meaning supplied by the suffix(es); these typically determined the part of speech ('pars orationis') of the word. Root plus Suffix constituted the stem, which was the domain of derivation (word formation). The open set of stems were the basic lexical stock of the language. Each stem received a single ending, the domain of inflection, which specified its syntactic function in the sentence and assigned the grammatical meaning of the inflectional categories: case and number in the substantive, gender in the adjective; person, number, voice, tense/aspect, mood in the finite verb.

Consider the sentence-initial verb in the Homeric Greek phrase *líssōm' anéra toûton* 'I will entreat that man' (*Iliad* 22.418). Restoration of the elided final (which implies undoing Greek sentence phonetic rules), and segmentation (which implies undoing Greek morphophonemic rules), yields the string

lit-jo-o-mai

containing:

1   a lexical morpheme *lit-* together with a portmanteau meaning. There is in Greek no 'word' *lit-*, an abstraction we may call a 'root' R. There is only (in Homer) a verb *líssomai*, with *litésthai, ellisámēn*; a verb of similar meaning *litaneúō*, a verbal adjective *-llistos* occurring only in composition (p. 56), and a noun occurring only in the plural, *litaí*. The morpheme *lit-* in *líssomai* is followed by three further Greek morphemes of widely different function;

2   a derivational suffix *-jo-* which makes a verb stem, present tense. The suffix establishes the real lexical entry and the part of speech: a verb stem *lit-jo/e-* (R + S) 'pray, entreat'. Only at this point can we talk about translatable meaning;

3   an inflectional suffix *-o/e-*, the sign of the subjunctive mood, with its semantics (grammatical meaning): the narrated event filtered through the attitude of the speaker. The subjunctive stem *lit-jo-o-* ((R + S) + S) is part of the paradigm of the lexical verb stem *lit-jo-* (R + S);

4   finally, an ending *-mai*, a single morpheme but polyfunctional, expressing at once the grammatical categories of *person* (first), *number* (singular), *voice* (middle), which are semantic categories, as well as a purely formal category, *'primary'*, a distributional variant conditioned by the mood-sign subjunctive. Primary endings are associated with non-past-tense,

secondary endings with past tense. The opposition goes back to Proto-Indo-European, though Greek has partly innovated in their distribution.

Each of the morphemes, and their order, faithfully continue the IE situation, even if the *-m-* of the first-person singular ending *-mai* is a Greek innovation. The thematic present suffix *-jo/e-* recurs in most of the family, for example IIr. *- ja-*. The subjunctive sign *-o/e-* combines with the thematic suffix to form a long vowel in IIr. *-ā-* just as in Gk *-ō/ē-*. The root (*-l*)*lit-* has no known cognates outside Greek, but its root structure is perfectly canonical Indo-European, and its apparent zero grade **slit-* (to a putative full grade **sleit-*) is expected before the accented present forming secondary verbal suffix *-jó/é-*, the thematic aorist suffix *-ó/é-* of *litésthai*, and the nominal suffix *-ā́* (< **áh₂-*) of *litaí*.

COMPOSITION involved the combination of two lexical items or notions into a single word: Gk *trí-llistos* 'thrice prayed for', *polú-llistos* 'much prayed for'; IE **n̥-udros* 'waterless' in Ved. *anudrás*, Gk *ánudros*. The possessive (*bahuvrīhi*) type, like Eng. *barefoot*, and the additive (*dvandva*), like Ved. *dvā́daśa* '12' ('2 [and] 10') were well represented in the proto-language; the former type was particularly frequent in personal names as well (cf. Chapter 4, p. 121). Some IE languages have extended and developed composition down to the present day; others have drastically restricted or eliminated it.

In a treatment of this size it is impossible to give a full account of the wealth of reconstructed IE morphology. Nor can we do justice here to the lively and informed controversy that surrounds some areas of PIE morphology and its ancestry. Only salient features of verbal and nominal derivation and inflexion will be given.

While Indo-European shows a clear distinction between verbal and nominal stems, certain features are common to both, like the opposition *athematic* : *thematic* stems. The minimal athematic suffix is zero (-0-); the minimal thematic suffix is the thematic vowel *-o/e-*. A root athematic stem has the structure root + zero suffix before the ending, (R + 0) + E: nom. sg. **pṓd-0-s* 'foot', 3 sg. pres. **gʷʰén-0-ti* 'slays', more simply just **pṓd-s*, **gʷʰén-ti*, beside thematic **éḱw-o-s* 'horse', subjunctive **gʷʰén-e-t(i)* 'may slay'. More complex athematic suffixes end in consonant (**-t-*, **-men-*), while their thematic counterparts end in the thematic vowel (**-to-*, **-mno-*).

The IE verb typically expressed action (the active voice, unmarked), process (the middle voice, subject internal to the action), or state (the perfect). Compare respectively English *murder*, *learn*, *know* with object *French*. The three stood originally in a derivational rather than inflectional ('paradigmatic') relation; many verbs expressed only one of these functions, and where two or more were expressed it was by different stems. This situation is seen most clearly in Vedic, Homeric Greek, and Anatolian. Process and state were related, as shown by the common origin of their endings.

PRIMARY VERBAL STEMS. The ROOT ATHEMATIC ACTIVE formation makes present and aorist stems. One type shows ablaut *e* : 0 with accent shift, as in Gk *eĭ-mi ĭ-men*, Ved. *é-mi i-mási* 'I, we go', Ved. *kṣé-ti kṣiy-ánti* 'he, they dwell', Myc. Gk *kitijesi/ktijensi/*, pple. mid. Gk *-ktĭ-menos*; aor. ipv. 2 pl. Ved. *śrotā*, Avest. *sroatā*, 2 dual. *śrutám/2* sg. *śrudhĭ*, Gk *klȳthi* (with metrical or expressive lengthening). Another type has ablaut *ē* : *e* and columnar accent on the root (see Chapter 9, p. 239) Lat. *ēst, ed-unt* 'he, they eat', Ved. *tắṣṭi tákṣati* 'he, they fashion'.

Several types of REDUPLICATED ATHEMATIC PRESENTS are found. With *i* in the reduplicator and *e* : 0 ablaut Gk *tĭ-thē-mi/tĭ-the-men* 'place', *di-dē-/di-de-* 'bind', Gk pple. *bi-bás (bi-bánt-)* 'striding' = Ved. *jĭ-gat-* (3 sg. *jĭ-gā-ti*). With *e* in the reduplicator and *o* : 0 ablaut Ved. *jaṅghanti* 'slaughters', pple. *jáṅghanat*, gen. *jáṅghnatas*.

NASAL-INFIX PRESENTS: the only morpheme to be infixed in Indo-European is *-n-*, typically forming active transitives. The element *-n-* is infixed between C_2 and C_3 of the root, with *e* : 0 apophony and mobile accent. Thus

*lejkʷ-	'leave'	pres.	**linékʷ-ti/*linkʷ-énti*
*ḱlew-	'hear'		**ḱḷnéw-ti/*ḱḷnw-énti*
*pewh₂-	'purify'		**punéh₂-ti/*punh₂-énti*

Compare Vedic: *riṇák-ti riñc-ánti, śṛṇóti śṛṇvánti, punáti punánti*. The type is preserved most faithfully in Indo-Iranian; other branches have altered the original system. Reduplicated and nasal-infix presents typically formed active root aorists.

The ROOT ATHEMATIC MIDDLE PRESENT makes at least two types of present stems. One has zero-grade root and accent on the endings, IE **dʰugʰ-ó(r)* in Ved. *duhé, áduha[t]* 'gives, gave milk', Hitt. *ištuāri* 'becomes known'. The other has *e*-grade and root accent: IE **ḱéj-o(r)* in Ved. *śáye*, Luv. *zīyar(i)* 'lies', pple. Gk *keí-menos*. IE 3 sg. pres. mid **wés-to(r)*, 3 pl. **wés-n̥to(r)*, underlie Hitt. pres. mid. *weš-ta, wešš-anta*, Ved. impf. mid. *vas-ta, vas-ata*, Gk *hés-to, heí-ato* (with metrical lengthening). A third type with accented *ē*-grade may be attested, IE **h₁és-o(r)* in Hitt. *ēša(ri)* 'sits', Ved. *ắs-te*, Gk *hēs-tai*, Hier. Luv. (SOLIUM) *i-sa- tara/i* -[istra-] 'seat'.

The ROOT ATHEMATIC MIDDLE AORIST appears to show ablaut *o* : 0 and shifting accent, in the aor. 'passives' like *ábodhi abudhran* 'awoke'. An *e*-grade may appear also, as an Avest. *jaini* 'was slain'. Comparable ablaut relations *o* : *e* : 0 have been suggested for the ancestor of Indo-European presents showing both *o* and *e* grade, like Goth. *maliþ*, Hitt. *malli* 'grinds', Luv. *malḫu-* 'crushes' but OIr. *melid* 'grinds', IE **molh₂-/melh₂-*, perhaps with perfect endings.

The PERFECT. Until the discovery of Hittite and Tocharian the perfect was one of the most secure reconstructions in the whole IE verb: it was characterized by a special set of endings: original presential stative value, from which developed resultative, and ultimately just preterite value; a special active participle in

-wos-/-us-*; in most early languages reduplication with *e* except in the verb 'know'; root vocalism *o* : 0 with shifting accent. Homeric Greek shows the vocalism and value clearest: *peíthomai* 'I am persuaded, obey', perf. *pépoitha* *pépithmen* 'I, we trust', *óllumi* 'I destroy' perf. *ólōla* 'I am lost, it's all up with me'. The ablaut and accent are both clear from the effects of Verner's Law in Germanic: OEng. *cēosan* 'choose' (*ĝéws-*) pret. *ic, hē cēas*, (*ĝóws-*) pl. *curon* 'chose' (*ĝus-*). The picture is now more complicated, since Tocharian shows a reflex of the reduplicated perfect participle (Toch. B obl. *peparkos* 'asked') but no reflex of the finite perfect, while Hittite and most other Anatolian languages have a special *ḫi-* conjugation parallel to the obviously inherited *mi-*conjugation, which despite many efforts resists straightforward derivation from the IE perfect as reconstructed. The case is one of the most intensely debated in IE studies today.

Primary THEMATIC formations, present and aorist, place a large and expanding role in the dialects. Their distribution is a mark of recentness; their creation would appear to be one of the latest innovations of Common Indo-European. Their origin appears to be in the middle voice, as in p. 56, where the thematic vowel *o/e* was originally a third-person singular ending. In Hittite, primary thematic presents are found only in the middle voice: 3 sg. *neya(ri)* 'leads' from *neih-o(r)* like Ved. *úpo naya-sva* 'lead hither!' The active (the common type) 3 sg. Ved. *náyati* (from *-e-ti*) was created later by opposition. By Hittite times this had taken place only in secondary, derived verb stems: 3 sg. *-škēzzi* < *-sk-é-ti, -izzi* < *-jé-ti, *-é-je-ti*.

SECONDARY VERBAL STEMS served to form new verbs from existing stems. The most widespread were denominatives, to make verbs from nouns and adjectives, by the suffix *-jé/o-*: Ved. *vasnám* 'sale price', *vasna-yá-* 'fetch a price', Gk *ōnos* 'price', *ōnéomai* 'I offer to buy, make a bid on', Hitt. *ušne-škatta* 'makes a bid on'. The thematic denominative type *-e-jé/ó-* is most clearly attested in Indo-Iranian, Greek, Armenian (*sēr*, gen. *siroy* 'love' → *sirem* 'I love' < *ḱejre-jé-*); other languages have innovated the form in part, like Latin *largus* → *largīrī* (suff. *-ī-je/o-*). The suffix *-je/o-* is added directly to the consonant stems: Ved. *ápas-* 'work' *apas-yáti*, Gk *télos, teles-* 'goal' → *teleíō* 'achieve', Goth. *riqis* 'darkness' → *riqiz-jan*. Stems in R may show zero grade: Gk *ónoma* 'name' → *onomn̥-je/o-*, *onomaínō*, Goth. *namo*, *namin-* 'name' → *namnjan*. An old example is the zero grade of *mélit-* 'honey' in *mlit-jé/ó-* 'take out the honey from the comb', Gk *blíttō*.

For the denominatives to feminine abstracts in *-eh$_2$-* (*-ah$_2$*, later *-ā*, see p. 63) we expect *-ah$_2$-jeló-*, whence *-āje/o-*, as in Lat. *fuga* → *fugāre*. In some languages the *h$_2$* seems after colouring to have been lost before *yod* very early: Hitt. *-aizzi/-ānzi*, Gk *-ăō*.

An old secondary CAUSATIVE-ITERATIVE formation with *o-*grade root and suffix *-éje/o-* is well attested throughout the family. From the root *wes-* 'wear, dress' an active *wos-éje-ti* is attested in Hitt. *waššizzi* 'put clothes on someone', Ved. *vāsáyati*, Gmc. *wazjan*, Alb. *vesh* < *wasje-*. From *lewk-*

'light, shine' we have active *lowk-éje-ti in Hitt. lukkizzi, Ved. rocáyati, Avest. raocaiieiti, OLat. lūmina lūcent 'they light the lamps'.

The suffix *-skéló- forms characterized presents, typically iterative, to zero-grade roots. An old example to the root *preḱ- is *pr̥ḱ-skéló- 'ask, demand' in Ved. pr̥ccháti, Avest. pərəsaiti, Lat. poscō from *por(c)scō, OIr. arcu, Arm. harc'-anem, OHG forscōn 'inquire'. Three languages attest the formation to the verb 'to be' in an existential sense: OLat. escit 'there is', Gk ẽske 'there was' (Alcman), éske (Odyssey, 9.508), Pal. ipv. mid. iška < *h₁s-sḱó 'be (ipv.)'.

Two secondary suffixes are added to adjective stems: a FACTITIVE in *-ah₂- (*-eh₂-), meaning to make something what the adjective denotes, and a STATIVE in *-eh₁- meaning to be what the adjective denotes. Compare Hittite nēwaš (*néwo-) 'new' → newāḫ(ḫ)- (*newéh₂-, newáh₂-) 'make new', maršaš 'false' → maršāḫ- 'falsify', and → marše- 'be false'; Lat. albus → (dē-)albāre 'whiten', albēre 'be white'. In some cases this suffix is part of a so-called 'Caland-system': adj. *gʷr̥h₂-ú- 'heavy' in Gk barús, Ved. gurú-, abstract *gʷr̥h₂-os- in Gk báros, stative *gʷr̥h₂-eh₁- in Aeol. Gk bórētai 'is heavy', Hom. Gk pf. pple. bebareṓs; adj. *h₁rudʰ-ro- 'red' in Lat. ruber, Gk eruthrós, stative *h₁rudʰ-eh₂- 'be red' in Lat. rubēre, OIr. -ruidi, OHG rotēn. A Caland-system in secondary derivation typically exhibits commutation of adjectival suffixes *-u-, *-ro-, *-ent- or substantival *-es- with *-i- as first member of a compound: Ved. r̥j-rás, Gk arg-ós (from *arg-rós) 'swift, bright', in composition Ved. r̥ji-, Gk argi-; note the Greek phrase kúnes argoí 'swift dogs' beside the Vedic possessive compound r̥jí-śvan-, personal name, 'having swift dogs', and Odysseus' dog Árgos.

In VERB INFLECTION, the endings of the finite IE verb marked person (1, 2, 3), number (singular, plural, dual), as well as the 'voices' (genera verbi) active, middle, stative perfect, the modal opposition indicative : imperative, and the opposition primary (marked by a particle -i emphasizing the hic et nunc) : secondary (unmarked, lacking the particle). Certain of these oppositions are neutralized outside of the singular. As noted on p 58, the thematic conjugations are apparently a late IE development out of the athematic middle, but they were fully constituted for secondary verbs before the separation of the Anatolian branch.

In ATHEMATIC ACTIVE paradigm, forms followed by a hyphen are completely specified. The vowel e may ablaut (o, ē, ō). See Table 2.6.

In the THEMATIC ACTIVE paradigm (selections), the thematic vowel is o before R, H, e before T. See Table 2.7.

In the ATHEMATIC MIDDLE paradigm (selections), the details must be tentative; this is another of the controversial areas in current Indo-European studies. See Table 2.8.

Under some circumstances (accent?) the vowel -o- may appear as -e-. The third persons in -t-, -nt- belong to a later chronological layer. Several dialects replaced primary -r by -i, from the active conjugation, whence

Table 2.6 Indo-European athematic active verbal endings

	Indo-European	Hittite	Vedic	Greek
Primary				
1 sg.	*-mi	-mi	-mi	-mi
2 sg.	*-si	-ši	-si	-(s)i
3 sg.	*-ti	-zi	-ti	-ti (Dor.)
1 pl.	*-me	-weni	-mas(i)	-men
		-wani		
2 pl.	*-t(h₂)e-	-teni	-tha	-te
		-tani		
3 pl.	*-(e)nti	-anzi	-a(n)ti	-ensi (Myc.)
1 Dual	*-we-		-vas	
2 Dual	*-t(h₂)o-		-thas	-ton
3 pl.	*-to-		-tas	-ton
Secondary				
1 sg.	*-m	-(n)un	-(a)m	-n
2 sg.	*-s		-s	-s
3 sg.	*-t	-ta	-t	-t
1 pl.	*-me-	-wen	-mā	-men
2 pl.	*-te-		-ta	-te
	(also			
	imperative) -ten			
3 pl.	-(e)nt	-ēr, ir	-(a)n	-n
1 Dual	*-we-		-va	
2 Dual	*-to-		-tam	-ton
3 Dual	*-tah₂-		-tām	-tān (Dor.)
Imperative				
2 sg.	*0, *-dʰi	0, -t	-dhi	-thi
3 sg.	*-tu	-tu	-tu	-tō
3 pl.	*-(e)ntu	-antu	-antu	-ntō

-oj/-toj, *roj/*-ntoj, as in Indo-Iranian and Greek.

The PERFECT endings are clearly related to those of the middle.

From the above paradigms or something like them, the historical paradigms of the different dialects evolved, through a series of divergent innovations, analogical remodelings, and categorial reassignments. Crucial was the role of the athematic third-person singular middle ending -o/e, which was evidently revalued to a suffix -o/e- followed by zero ending, opening the way to the constitution of a full thematic conjugation.

The MORPHOLOGY OF THE NOMINAL SYSTEM subsumes three basic form classes: (1) nouns and adjectives; (2) demonstrative and interrogative pronouns; and (3) personal pronouns. The numerals 1–4 were adjectives, while 5 and up were indeclinable. Adjectives and demonstrative pronouns were inflected for gender, typically with a masculine-neuter stem beside which the feminine stem was a derivative: m.–n. *pih-won- 'fat' in Ved. pívan-, Gk píon- beside f. *pih-wer-ih₂- in Ved. pívarī, Gk píeira, MWelsh

Table 2.7   Indo-European thematic active verbal endings

	Indo-European	Hittite	Vedic	Greek
Primary			(-ā-mi), Gathic	
1 sg.	*-o-h$_2$	-emi	Avest. -ā	-ō
2 sg.	*-e-si	-eši, -iši	-asi	-eis
3 sg.	*-e-ti	-ezzi, -izzi	-ati	-ei
1 pl.	*-o-me-	-aweni	-āmasi	-omen
2 pl.	*-e-te-	-atteni, -itteni	-athas	-ete
3 pl.	*-o-nti	-anzi	-anti	-onti (Dor.)
Secondary				
1 sg.	*-o-m	-anun	-am	-on
2 sg.	*-e-s	-eš, -iš	-as	-es
3 sg.	*-e-t	-et, -it	-at	-et
Imperative				
2 sg.	*-e	-i	-a	-e
3 sg.	*-e-tu	-ittu	-atu	-etō
3 pl.	*-o-ntu	-antu	-antu	-ontō

Iwerydd, stem *Iwerddon* 'Ireland'; thematic m.–n. **new-o-* 'new' beside f.
*new-e-h$_2$-.

ACCENT AND ABLAUT: many scholars now assume a complex set of interdependent ablaut alternations and fixed or mobile accents occurring with each (or many) of the suffix type stem classes (e.g. root nouns, *men*-stems,

Table 2.8   Indo-European athematic middle verbal endings

	Indo-European	Hittite	Vedic	Greek
Primary				
1 sg.	*-h$_2$ar (*h$_2$er)	-ha(ri)	-e	-mai
				-(s)oi (Arc. Cypr.)
2 sg.	*-th$_2$ar (*th$_2$er)	-ta(ri)	-se	
3 sg.	*-or (*-tor)	-a(ri)	-e	
		-ta(ri) (Pal. -tar)	-te	-toi (Arc. Cypr.)
3 pl.	*-ro(r ??)		-re	
				-ntoi (Arc. Cypr.)
	*-ntor	-anta	-ate	
Secondary				
1 sg.	*-h$_2$(a)	-ḫaḫat	-i, -a (opt.)	-mān
2 sg.	*-th$_2$a	-tat	-thās	-so
3 sg.	*-o	-at	-at	
3 pl.	*-ro		-ran	
	(*-nto)	-antat	-ata	-nto
Imperative				
2 sg.	-Ø-			
3 sg.	-ow?			

Table 2.9 Indo-European perfect endings

	Indo-European	Vedic	Greek	Latin
1 sg.	*-h₂a (*-h₂e)	-a	-a	-ī (Faliscan -ai)
2 sg.	*-th₂a (-th₂e)	-tha	-tha	-(is)tī
3 sg.	*-e	-a	-e	-ī[t]
2 pl.	*-e	-a		(Paelign. lexe)
3 pl.	*-ēr, *-ĕr	(Hitt. -ēr, -ir)		(-ēre, -erai
	*-r̥s	-uḥ (Avest. -ərəš)		(Venetic -ers))

etc.). The system of the German and Austrian school (Schindler 1975) recognizes four basic types: 'acrostatic' Ŕ-S-E, nom. *wód-r̥ gen. *wéd-n̥-s 'water'; 'proterokinetic' Ŕ-Ś-E, nom. *h₁órǵʰ-i-s gen. h₁r̥ǵʰ-éi-s 'testicle'; 'hysterokinetic' R-Ś-É, nom. *ph₂-tér gen. ph₂-tr-és; 'holokinetic' or 'amphikinetic' Ŕ-S-É, nom. h₂áws-ōs (h₂éws-ōs) gen. *h₂us-s-és 'dawn'. The system has been criticized as unnatural on grounds of accent typology, and as overly rigid. The prescribed forms do not appear to belong to the same chronological layer (gen. *wéd-n̥-s is attested nowhere, but gen. *bʰrá-tr-s is in Ved. bhrā́tuḥ, ON bróthor). To the degree that for the theory the ablaut is required to be conditioned by the accent, the formations would have belonged to the remote prehistory of the proto-language; ablaut variants and accent are independent variables already in reconstructed Proto-Indo-European, cf. accented zero grade *wĺkʷos in Ved. vŕ̥kas, Gk lúkos, Lith. vil̃kas. Competing systems have been offered, notably by the Dutch school, but comparable objections can be raised to these, and the matter is still very much *sub indice*.

Of obvious and immediate utility is the notion of *internal derivation* in the German and Austrian framework, of the type (R + S)ᵢ → (R + S)ⱼ beside the more usual *external derivation*, of the type (R + S)ᵢ → ((R + S) + S)ⱼ. Compare Ved. bráhman- 'formulation' → brahmán- 'formulator, brahmin', Gk mnẽma 'remembrance' → mnẽmōn 'mindful', *(Ŕ-mn̥) → *(R-món-).

ATHEMATIC NOMINAL SUFFIXES: the simplest is -0-, the root nouns like *pód-s, gen. *péd-s (whence *ped-és) 'foot'; *dóm, gen. *dém-s 'house' in Gk des-pótēs, Gathic Avest. də̄ng patōiš 'master of the house'. Others have a single consonant: acrostatic *nókʷ-t-s 'night', gen. *nekʷ-t-s in Hitt. nekuz mehur 'nighttime'; -s- in nom.-acc. neut. *men-s 'mind' in Gathic Avest. maz-dā- 'place, direct mind', Avest. maṣ ... -dā-, Gathic Avest. mə̄ncā ... (dā-). With ablaut, -r- in nom. *ǵʰés-ōr 'hand' (OHitt. possessed kiššar=šiš), acc. ǵʰes-ér-m̥ (kiššeran), loc. *gʰés-r-i (kišri=tti), kiššari=šmi, Gk kheirí). An -n-stem (a type which becomes limitlessly productive in certain dialects) appears in nom. *h₃or-ō[n] 'eagle', Hitt. ḫarā[š], stem ḫaran-, OHG aro, Eng. erne, Gk ór-n-[is].

The *r/n-stem*, with -r- in the 'strong' cases (nom.-acc.) and -n- in the oblique cases, is well represented in Anatolian, including productive secondary formations, and residually in the other branches: an old example is the word for 'liver' *$h_x y \breve{e}k^w$-ŗ with long root vowel in Gk hḗpar, Lat. iēcur, Avest. yākarə, but short in Ved. yákŗt, and oblique stem Ved. yakn-ás, Gk hḗpat-os < *hēpņ̥(t)-.

An old type of -u- stem appears in the words for 'knee', 'wood', 'lifespan': nom. sg. n. *ĝón-u *dór-u $h_2$óju, Gathic Avest. zānū dārū āiiū, Ved. jánu dáru áyu, Gk gónu dóru ou(kí) 'not'. An apophonic stem variant *ĝénw- dérw- $h_2$éjw- accounts for Hitt. genu(-), Lat. genu(-), Slav. *dérv-o-, Gk ai(w)-ei; but an alternative stem *ĝn-éw- *dr-ew- *h_2y-éw- as in Goth. kniu (thematized), Gathic Avest. yaoš, gen. of āiiū, perhaps Hitt. ganu-t, instr. of genu (unless zero grade) seems very old and unlikely to be due to independent innovation. Zero grades of these words also occur paradigmatically (Gk. gnysi), in composition (Ved. jñu-bādh- 'kneeling', Gk dry-tómos 'cutting oak'), and in derivation (*$h_2$ju-hén- 'vigorous, young' in Ved. yuván-, Lat. iuuen-is).

A curious athematic suffix -it- marking elemental foodstuffs is found in *mél-it 'honey' (Gk mélit-, Hitt. milit, Luv. mallit-, Gmc. mil-) and *sép-it 'wheat' (sp.) (Hitt. šeppit, Gk álph-it- with transferred epithet as root).

Ablauting secondary suffixes with two consonants (rarely three) are common and continue to be productive in the dialects: abstracts *-men-, *-wer-/-wen-, agent *-ter-, verbal adjective *-ent-, possessive *-went-.

FEMININE AND ABSTRACT (COLLECTIVE): the derivational origin of the feminine gender in Indo-European (Kuryłowicz 1964) is clear from the formal relations (see p. 60); note also the Greek 'two-ending' adjectives, type m./f. athánatos, n. athánaton). A suffix morpheme -(e)h_2 is found both in feminine function (thematic type *senah₂-, 'old (f.)' in Gk hḗnē, Ved. sánā-, Lith. senà, perhaps Lyc. lada 'wife'; *swekrúh₂- 'husband's mother' in OCS svekry, Lat. socrus, OHG swigar) and in abstract collective function (type Gk tomḗ 'cutting', neurá 'cord of sinew' beside neûron 'sinew', Luv. zidāḫ-[iša] 'virility' beside ziti- 'man' [earlier *zida-, cf. PN Zidanza] and notably the nominative-accusative neuter singular of the collective which functions as the nominative-accusative neuter plural (Ved. yugá, Gk zugá, Lat. iuga, Goth. juka 'yokes', Hitt. -a, Pal. -a/-ā), still taking a singular verb in Greek, Old Avestan, and Anatolian (Chapter 7, pp. 174f.). Whether the feminine and the collective morpheme are ultimately the same is uncertain. More widely attested in both feminine and collective function is *-ih₂-, with variant *-yah₂-(-yeh₂-): Ved. devī́ (gen. dévyās) 'goddess', vŗkī́s (gen. vŗkías) 'female wolf'.

THEMATIC NOMINAL SUFFIXES: the simplest is -o-, found in some very old primary and secondary formations: masculines like *w[k^w]-o-s 'wolf', *h_2(é)rtḱ-o-s 'bear', neuters like *jug-ó-m 'yoke', *wérĝ-o-m 'work', adjectives like *sén-o- 'old', *néw-o- 'new'. The line between primary and secondary derivatives is hazy; if the first two animals have no recognizable base, the 'horse' *éḱw-o-s is in all likelihood a derivative from 'swift' in Gk ōkýs, Ved. āśús. Other more clearly secondary simple thematic suffixes are the adjectives in accented -ó- marking possession of the base, and adjectives in -ó- with lengthened grade root (*vṛddhi*) marking belonging or relation to the base: Ved. *jyā́* 'bowstring', *$*g^wyah_2$-* (*$*g^wyeh_2$-*) → *$*g^wih_2$-ó-* (Gk *biós* 'bow' ('having a bowstring')); OHG *swehur* 'father-in-law', *swagur* 'brother-in-law', **sweḱuro-* → **sweḱuró-*, **djew-* → **diw-* → **dejw-ó-* 'god'.

The *o*-grade of the root is found in two very productive thematic types: barytone action nouns (type Gk *tómos* 'slice') and oxytone agent nouns and adjectives (type Gk *tomós* 'cutting, sharp'), both beside the Greek root *tem-* 'cut'. We have zero grade in neuters of the type **jug-óm* 'yoke' (Hitt. *iugan*, Ved. *yugám*, Gk *zygón*, Goth. *juk*, OCS *igo*), and in the second element of compounds like **ni-sd-ós* 'nest' (Ved. *nīdás*, Lat. *nīdus*, OIr. *net*, OEng. *nest*) from **sed-* 'sit'; Gk *neo-gn-ós* 'newborn' from *$*newo-ǵṇh_1$-ó-*, with regular loss of laryngeal in this compound position.

A large number of thematic suffixes form secondary nouns and adjectives occurring widely in the historical languages, and commonly formed independently in each. Adjectival *-jo-* and *-ijo-* (partly continuing *$*-ih_2o$-*) express relational notions. From *$*g^wow$-* 'cow, ox' we have Ved. *gávya-*, *gávia-*, also *gavyá-*, (*gávyam ... śatám* 'consisting of 100 cows', *RV*), Avest. *gaoiia-*, Gk *hekatóm-boios* 'worth 100 cows', Armenian *kogi* (*$*g^wowijo$-*) 'butter, *coming from a cow', OIr. *ambue* (*$*ṇ-g^wowijo$-*) 'cowless man'. The last is semantically and sociologically identical with RV *ágos* (gen., 'cowless man') and Gk (Hesiod) *andròs aboúteō* (gen. 'cowless man'); though the formations differ slightly, we have an IE lexeme.

Verbal adjectives in accented **-tó-* (and sometimes **-nó-* in Indo-Iranian), with zero grade of the verbal root, are common in secondary derivation. An old example is **ḱlu-tó-* 'heard, renowned' in Ved. *śrutá-*, Avest. *sruta-*, Gk *klytós*, Lat. *in-clitus*, OIr. *ro-cloth*, OHG *Hlot-hari* (PN, 'whose army is renowned), Arm. *lu* 'known'. Germanic **hlūdaz* 'loud' < **ḱlūtó-* shows expressive lengthening. The suffix, not yet developed by the time of the separation of Anatolian where its function is expressed by **-ént-*, marks semantically 'the accomplishment of the notion of the object': see Benveniste 1948.

Other common secondary thematic types are adjectives in **-nó-* (often paralleling **-tó-*), **-ro-*, **-mo-*, diminutives in **-ko-*, **-lo-*, often with preceding vowel in the dialects: note **-e/onó-* in the past principle of the Germanic strong verb. The adjective for 'hot', substantived 'heat', from the verbal root *$*g^{wh}er$-* 'heat' is widespread: Ved. *gharmá-* 'heat', Avest. *garəma-* 'hot; heat', Lat. *formus* 'warm, hot' (*$*g^{wh}or-mo$-*), Gk *thermós* 'warm', Toch. A *śärme* 'heat', Phrygian *Germiai* 'Hot Springs' (place name, Hellenized), Arm. *ĵerm* 'hot', Alb. *zjarm* 'heat' (*$*g^{wh}er-mo$-*). The suffix is copied in Gmc **warmaz* 'warm', from the root **wer-*.

A suffix **-tero-/-toro-* marking the opposition of two notions is found in many branches, beginning with Anatolian (Hitt. *nun-taras* adv. gen. '*of now', whence 'soon, right away'). 'Other' (of two) is Goth. *anþar*, Skt *ántaras*, Lat. *alter*, beside 'other' (of more than two) in Skt *anyás*, Lat. *alius*, Gk *állos*, Goth. *aljis*. For the syntactic distribution of the suffix, Gk *deksiós* – *aristerós*, *skaiós* – *deksiterós*, both 'right-left'), see Benveniste 1948.

The suffix *-wo-* is found notably in the words for 'alive; *g^wih_3-wo-* in Ved. *jīvás*, Lat. *vīvos*, OIr. *beo*, Welsh *byw*, Goth. *qius* (with shortened *-ĭ-*), and 'dead', *mr-wo-* in OIr. *marb*, W. *marw*. The *-t-* of Lat. *mortuos* and Slavic *mĭrtvŭ* probably is due to *mr-to-* 'destined to die, mortal'.

For the variants of suffix of instrument *-tro-*, *-tlo-*, *-d^hro-*, *-d^hlo-* (Lat. *-trum*, *-c(u)lum*, *-brum*, *-bulum*) see p. 39. An old example is the word for 'plough' *h_2arh_3-trom* in Gk *árotron*, Lat. *arātrum* (with analogical *-ā-*), OIr. *arathar*, Welsh *aradr*, Arm. *arawr*, Lith. *árklas*.

NOUN INFLECTION: the Indo-European noun was inflected for *number, case*, and in adjectives *gender*. Gender was an inherent property of substantives. The familiar three-gender system of masculine, feminine, neuter probably at an earlier date opposed just masculine (animate?) and neuter (inanimate?), with the feminine an original derivational rather than inflectional category. But already in the proto-language the three-way contrast had been attained. Ved. and Avest. *gav-*, Gk *boũs*, Lat. *bōs* (IE*g^wow-) are both feminine 'cow, she-ox' and masculine 'bull, ox'. Number distinguished *singular, plural*, and *dual*. The singular distinguished at least eight, perhaps nine, cases; syncretisms reduced this number in the plural and still more in the dual. The cases were *nominative, vocative, accusative, genitive, dative, instrumental, locative, ablative*, and probably *allative*. Not all the cases can be reconstructed with any confidence.

For consonant stems the clearly reconstructible endings were as in Table 2.10.

Table 2.10   Indo-European athematic nominal endings

	Masculine/Feminine	Neuter	(Greek)
Singular			
Nom.	-s	-0	ánax 'lord'
Voc.	-0		ána
Acc.	-m̥	-0	ánakta
Gen.	-es/-os/-s		ánaktos
Dat.	-ei		Diwei 'to Zeus'
Loc.	-i, -0		ánakti
Plural			
Nom.-Voc.	-es	(coll. -(e)h₂)	ánaktes
Acc.	-ms̥		ánaktas
Gen.	-ōm		anáktōn
Loc.	-su/-si		ánaxi
Inst.	-bʰi(-)		(w)îphi 'by force'
Dual			
Nom.-Acc.	-h₁e?		póde 'two feet'

Table 2.11   Indo-European thematic nominal endings

	Masculine	*Neuter*	*(Greek)*
Singular			
Nom.	-os	-om	híppos 'horse'
Voc.	-e		híppe
Acc.	-om	-om	híppon
Gen.	-os(y)o		híppoio, híppou
Dat.	-ōi < -o-ei		híppōi
			Avest. zastā 'by the
Inst.	-ō < -o-h_1?		hand'
Loc.	-oj		oíkoi 'at home'
Abl. dialectal	-ōt < -o-$h_2$at		OLat. gnaivōd
Plural			
Nom.	-ōs < -o-es		Ved. vŕkās 'wolves'
Acc.	-ons		híppous
Gen.	-ōm < -o-om		híppōn
Inst.	-ōjs		híppois
Loc.	-ojsu/i		Myc. ‹-o-i› -oihi
Dual			
Nom.–Acc.	-oh_1(u)?		híppō

For thematic stems the reconstructible endings were as in Table 2.11.

The inflection of DEMONSTRATIVE and PERSONAL PRONOUNS differed in certain critical respects from that of nouns, notably in an alternation of stem vowel -*i*- with the thematic vowel -*o*/*e*-. as well as in certain endings.

Indo-European had a number of demonstrative pronoun stems of differing ages, some built on or coexisting with deictic particles. Thus *$\hat{k}i$- (Lith. *šìs*) and *$\hat{k}ó$- (Luv. *zaš*, Hitt. *kāš*) beside the particle *$\hat{k}e$ (OLat. *hon-ce* 'hunc', Hitt. *ki-nun* 'now', Gk *ke-eno*- in *keînos*). Others were *$el̥ono$- *$el̥owo$-, and simply *$el̥i$-. In one stage of the proto-language, after the separation of Anatolian, and perhaps Italic and Celtic, the two stems *$so(-)$ and *to- were fused into a suppletive paradigm, later IE *so *sah_2 *tod (Ved. *sá sā́ tád*, Gk *ho hē tó*, Goth. *sa so þata*, Toch. B *se sā te*).

The RELATIVE PRONOUN stem *jo- (perhaps earlier *h_1jo-) is found in Vedic *yá*- and Avestan *ya*, Greek *hós*, Phrygian *ios* (*ni*), Celtiber. *io*(*mui* dat.). In Balto-Slavic this pronoun is suffixed to adjectives to form a definite.

The INTERROGATIVE and indefinite pronoun stem *k^wo-/*k^wi- (*k^wu- in adverbs) is found in all branches of the family; in Anatolian, Italic, Germanic and Balto-Slavic it forms the relative pronoun as well, perhaps via the indefinite function: IE *yós k^wis, *yód k^wid 'who-/whatsoever', Gk *hóstis hótti*, Ved. *yáś cit, yác cit*. Another interrogative stem *mo- is found residually in Anatolian and Tocharian.

PRONOUN INFLECTION differs from the nouns in the final dental for nominative-accusative singular neuter, the optional absence of -*s* in the nominative singular masculine, and in characteristic special forms with inserted -sm- (f. -sj-) in the oblique cases. A partial paradigm of the interrogative indefinite pronoun is:

Nom. *k^wís *k^wíd and *k^wo(s) *k^wod: Lat. quis quid, quod, OLat. quo-i 'quī'; Avest. ciš, cit, kə, kas-, kat; OCS kъ-to čь-to.

Gen. *k^welos(j)o: Avest. kahiiā cahiiā, Gk teo, OCS česo.

Dat. *k^welosmōi

Loc. *k^wesmi: Avest. kahmāi cahmāi, Celtiber. iomui, somui, OCS komu čemu, Umbr. esmei; Avest. kahmi cahmi, Umbr. esme, S. Pic. esme-n, esmí-n.

The cardinal NUMBERS one to four were inflected adjectives, and five to ten were uninflected. (one): *sem- (Gk heís); *oj-no-, *oj-wo-, *oj-ko- (Lat. ūnus, OIr. óen, Goth. ains; Avest. aēuua-; Skt éka-); (two): *d(u)wo-; (three): *trej-es tri-h_2; (four): k^wetwor-es. Three and four had special feminine forms attested only in Indo-Iranian and Celtic, compounded with an old word for 'woman': Ved. tísras, catásras, Avest. tišrō cataŋrō, OIr. teoir, cetheoir, Welsh teir, pedeir. The dissimilation *tri-sr- to *ti-sr- is already Proto-Indo-European. (Five): pénk^{w}e. (six) (k)sweḱs (seven) *septṃ (eight) *(h_3)oḱtō(w) (nine) $h_1$néwṇ. (ten): *déḱṃ. One hundred is a derivative *(d)ḱṃ-tóm 'that which makes 10 (decads)'. The ordinal numerals were suffixed by adjectival *-o- or -to-: for example, *tri-tó-, *septm-ó-.

The PERSONAL PRONOUNS show extensive and irregular allomorphy between the nominative (always stressed, syntactically emphatic) and oblique cases (with both tonic and enclitic forms). Their reconstruction poses particular problems, which cannot be addressed in a treatment of this scope. I give only the first and second singular forms in representative languages:

	Nominative	Accusative	(tonic)	(encl.)	Nominative	Accusative	(tonic)	(encl.)
Greek (Hom.)	egó(n)	emé		me	sú, tū́nē	sé		se
Vedic	ahám	mā́m		mā	t(u)vám	t(u)vā́		t(u)vā
Hittite	uk	ammuk		-mu	zik	tuk		-ta
Gothic	ik		mik		þu		þuk	-ta

A reflexive stem *se(-), *swe(-) marked reference to the subject or the topic of the sentence; it originally referred to all three persons, but was in most branches restricted to third-person function. Non-reflexive pronominal third-person reference was normally by tonic or enclitic demonstrative pronoun.

Syntax

A syntactic description of Indo-European by the traditional method of describing the use of the different parts of speech, for example the different cases of the noun or the moods of the verb, has been done very well in the classical manuals of Delbrück and Wackernagel, to which global reference is made. Here we confine our observations to certain syntactic rules for the simple sentence in Indo-European, relating to the order of constituents of the sentence.

PHRASE STRUCTURE: early Indo-European languages and presumably the protolanguage distinguished verbal sentences where the predicate is a verb (phrase), type NP + VP, Hitt. *zik=wa* URBARRA-*aš kištat* 'you have become a wolf', and nominal sentences, where the predicate is a noun phrase, type NP + NP, Ved. *vŕko hí ṣás* 'for he is a wolf', Gk. *kreíssōn gàr basileús* 'for the king is stronger', or other non-verbal constituent, like the adverb in Gk *metà dè glaukõpis Athénē* 'and grey-eyed Athena (was) with (them)', Hitt. ᵐ*Šippa-LÚ-iš=wa=kan ÚL anda* 'Sippazitis (is) not in (it)'. It is not clear that the latter simply show gapped copula, since they may contrast with an overt copula sentence either stylistically or semantically: Hitt. LÚ.ULÙ.LU=*ku* GUD=*ku* UDU=*ku ēšzi* 'whether it is man or ox or sheep'.

Indo-European was basically an SOV language, and verb-final was the 'default' position in most of the earlier languages and the earlier stages of the later languages; but the operation of a variety of movement rules served to complicate and obscure the word order picture in many of these same languages. The basic rule for the verb phrase was VP → NP + V. The noun phrase was looser: we find NP → Adj. + N or gen. + N in Hittite, where the reverse order may signal a nominal sentence (*ištappulli=šet=a šulīaš* 'but its stopper (is) of lead'), but we find regularly either order in Indo-Iranian and the classical languages.

To the prepositional phrases of the latter correspond in Hittite postpositional phrases (*nēpišaš kattan* 'under heaven'), whose antiquity is to some extent confirmed by the accent of Greek 'prepositions' by 'anastrophe' (*ommátōn ápo* 'from the eyes') agreeing with that of cognates (Ved. *ápa*). When the object of the postposition was a pronoun, Old Hittite formed a possessive syntagma, with the object expressed by enclitic possessive adjective (*katti=šši* 'with him'). This indicates a nominal origin for the pre-/postpositions.

The commonest MOVEMENT RULES in Indo-European are (1) movements of the type 'move-WH', typically interrogatives and relatives, to the 'complementizer' site at the head of the sentence to the left, and (2) 'topicalization' movement, to a site to the left of the complementizer site (Hale 1987). (See Figures 2.2 and 2.3.)

Ved. *kásya bráhmāni jujuṣur yúvānaḥ*
      'whose formulas do the youths enjoy?'
Ved. *yó no dvéṣṭi, ádharaḥ sás padīṣṭa*
      'who hates us, he shall fall low'

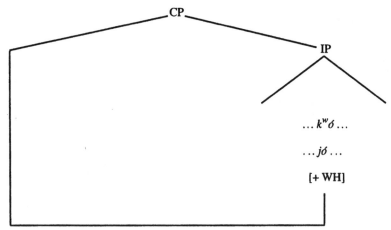

Figure 2.2 'Move-WH' rule in Indo-European

Ved. *brahmā́ kó vaḥ saparyati*
  'which priest honours you?'
Ved. *púro yád asya sampinák*
  'when you smashed his citadels'

Normally only a single constituent or subconstituent appears to the left of the WH-word, but it can be complex:

Ved. *áher yātā́ram kám apaśya indra*
  'What avenger of the serpent did you see, o Indra?'

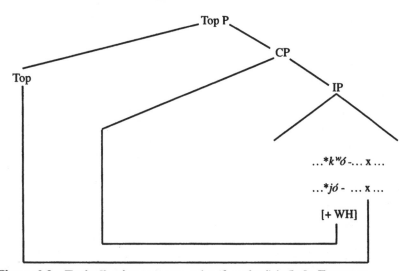

Figure 2.3 Topicalization movement (or 'fronting') in Indo-European

Ved. *ádevena mánasā yó riṣaṇyáti*
'who does harm with ungodly intent'.

Movement to the topicalization site or 'fronting' was a form of emphasis or focusing. The normally atonic finite verb itself was commonly so emphasized (Ved. *áhann áhim* 'he/you slew the serpent'), and received its accent in this position. Sentence-initial was thus the marked position for the verb, beside unmarked sentence-final. When the verb was semantically closely linked or 'compounded' with an adverb ('preverb'), the unmarked position of the (accented) preverb was before the final verb: ... P(...)V # #, optionally separated from it by a single constituent. The preverb could in such structures itself be fronted by movement to the topicalization site, yielding the marked order # # P ... V # # : Hitt. *āppa=wa=mu parna tarna* 'let me go back home'. Fronted verb in topic was characteristic for certain discourse situations like text-initial cataphora and imperatives; compare the widespread tale beginning Skt *āsīd rājā* 'there was a king', Gk *ẽske tis ... wanássōn*, Lith. *bùvo karãlius*, OIr. *boí ri*, Russ. *žyl byl korol'*.

EXTRAPOSITION of constituents to the right of the verb is another common feature. In Greek *Oûtin egṑ pýmaton édomai metà hoîs hetároisin* 'Noman I will eat last among his comrades', the prepositional phrase is extraposed to the right of the verb. The object has been moved to topic; the possessive reflexive pronoun *hoîs* 'his own' refers back to the topic *Oûtin* rather than to the grammatical subject *egó*, as normally.

ENCLITICS tend in IE (and many non-IE) languages to occupy what is loosely termed 'second position' in the sentence: the phenomenon known as *Wackernagel's Law* after its famous codifier (1892). Recent work (Hale 1987) has shown that at least three distinct classes of Wackernagel's Law clitics must be distinguished for Vedic, and that they end up in 'second position' for independent reasons. Thus in the phrase *utá vā yó no marcáyād ánāgasaḥ* 'or also who would harm innocent us', pronominal clitic *nas* (*no*) occupies second position before topicalization, and disjunctive clitic *vā* (and *ca*) second position defined after topicalization. A third type of clitics (*smā* and *cit*) is enclitic to the constituent they modify, and if that constituent is topicalized, it takes the clitic along to the head of the sentence: *áśmānam cid yé bibhidúr vácobhiḥ* 'who split even rock with words'. Such different syntactic history for the position of the different Wackernagel's Law clitics will account, for example, for the consistent precedence of Gk *de* or *te* (and their Old Irish cognates -*d*- and -*ch*-, Watkins 1963) over pronominal clitics.

RELATIVE CLAUSE FORMATION: the testimony of Hittite, Vedic and Greek is unequivocal in pointing to IE correlative relative clauses, usually in the order Relative Clause + Main (Matrix) Clause, with relative pronoun fronted to the complementizer site by WH-movement. Either or both clauses may begin with the sentence introductory particles e.g. Hitt. *nu*, which precede both the fronted WH-word, and any topicalized constituent before it, and thus do not 'count' for fronting. The same holds for Vedic introductory particles (adverbs) e.g. *atha* and the pronoun *sá*, and Greek introductory particles (adverbs), e.g. *éntha*.

In Hittite such sentences are semantically indefinite relatives: *kuiš paprizzi nu apāš-pat* 3 GIN KÙ.BABBAR *pāi* 'Whoever commits a nuisance pays 3 shekels of silver'. In the case of semantically definite relatives some constituent must be topicalized, that is moved into the site preceding the WH-word in the complementizer site. The finite verb is so moved in Hittite *paprizzi kuiš* 3 GIN KÙ.BABBAR *pāi* 'He who commits a nuisance pays 3 shekels of silver'.

There follow thematically similar correlative relative sentences in Hittite, Vedic and Greek, to point up the similarity: they may function as syntactic equations.

Hittite
nu tarḫzi kuiš nu   apāš   KIR₄.TAB.ANŠE   epzi
ptc wins   WH ptc   he   bridle   takes
'And he who wins, (he) takes the bridle'
ᴸᵁKAŠ₄E *tarḫzi kuiš* 1 MANA KU.BABBAR *pianzi*
(prob. *tarḫzi kuiš ḫuyatallaš*)
'the runner who wins, (to him) 1 mina of silver they give',

Vedic
sa yo na ujjeṣyati sa pratamaḥ somasya pāsyati
'(ptc) he who will win, he first will drink of the soma'
sa yo na ujjeṣyati tasya idam bhaviṣyati
'(ptc) he who will win, his this will be'

Greek
hos nyn orkheston . . . atalotata paizei to tode k[ ] . . .
'he now of the dancers who most sportively plays, his (is) this *k*.'
hoppóteros dé ke nikḗsēi . . . gynaîka te oîkad' agésthō
'whichever should win . . . let him take the woman home'

See Watkins 1976.

Early IE languages are notable for the supple SYNTAX OF THE PARTICIPLE, which may 'transform' finite verbs into noun phrases. With the last Greek relative clause above compare *tôi dé ke nikḗsanti phílē keklḗsēi ákoitis* 'to the one having-won (= who should win) you will be called dear wife'. Note the presence of the enclitic particle *ke* (Hitt. *-kan*) in both. The performative statement, speech act of pledge and self-engagement expressed by the syntactic minor rule of the demonstrative in Vedic *ayám te asmi* 'I here(by) am yours', is transformed to a participle phrase in the complex *mā mā́m imā́m táva sā́ntam . . . nī́ gā́rit* 'Let him not swallow . . . me, being here(by) yours'. The participle reinforces a performative statement: 'I hereby pledge myself to you, Atri. Don't let Svarbhānu destroy me.' Just so the finite verb of existence in another speech act, that of the confessional formula in Hitt. *ēšziy=at iyawen=at* 'It is. We did it' is transformed to the participle in the personal confession *ašān=at iyanun=at* (lit.) 'It (is) being. I did it'. In the syntactic use of Hitt. *ašant-* here we can glimpse the background of Latin *sōns, sontis* 'guilty', the old present participle of *esse* 'be'.

Note
For invaluable criticism, comments, and suggestions I am deeply indebted to the editors, and to Bernard Comrie, Benjamin Fortson, Andrew Garrett, Mark Hale, Eric Hamp, Ioannis Ikonomou, Stephanie Jamison, Jay Jasanoff, Joshua Katz, Craig Melchert, Steve Peter, Charles Reiss and Bert Vaux.

References
Benveniste, Emile (1935) *Origines de la formation des noms en indo-européen*, Paris: Maisonneuve.
────── (1948) *Noms d'agent et noms d'action en indo-européen*, Paris: Maisonneuve.
────── (1969) Le vocabulaire des institutions indo-européennes, Paris: Minuit.
Brugmann, Karl and Delbrück, Berthold (1897–1916) *Grundriss der vergleichenden Grammatik der indogermanischen Sprachen*, 2nd edn, Strasburg: Trübner.
Eichner, Heiner (1988) 'Anatolisch und Trilaryngalismus', in Alfred Bammesberger (ed.), *Die Laryngaltheorie*, Heidelberg: Winter, pp. 123–51.
Gamkrelidze, Thomas V. and Ivanov, Vjačeslav V. (1995) *Indo-European and the Indo-Europeans*, Berlin: Mouton de Gruyter.
Gimbutas, Marija (1980) 'The three waves of the Steppe People into East Central Europe', *Actes Suisses d'Anthropologie* 43.2.
Hale, Mark (1987) 'Notes on Wackernagel's law in the language of the Rigveda', in Calvert Watkins (ed.), *Studies in Memory of Warren Cowgill (1929–1985)*, Berlin: de Gruyter, pp. 38–50.
Kuryłowicz, Jerzy (1927) 'ə indo-européen et h hittite, *Symbolae in honorem Ioannis Rozwadowski*, Cracow: University of Jagiellonski, pp. 95–104.
────── (1964) *The Inflectional Categories of Indo-European*. Heidelberg: Winter.
Kuryłowicz, Jerzy and Mayrhofer, Manfred (eds) (1969–86) *Indogermanische Grammatik*, Heidelberg: Winter.
Mallory, J. P. (1989) *In Search of the Indo-Europeans: Language, Archeology and Myth*, London: Thames & Hudson.
Meillet, Antoine (1937) *Introduction à l'étude comparative des langues indo-européennes*, Paris: Hachette.
Melchert, H. Craig (1987) 'Proto-Indo-European velars in Luvian', in Calvert Watkins (ed.), *Studies in Memory of Warren Cowgill (1929–1985)*, Berlin: de Gruyter, pp. 182–204.
Pokorny, Julius (1948–69) *Indogermanisches etymologisches Wörterbuch*, Bern: Francke.
Schindler, Jochem (1975) 'Zum Ablaut der neutralen s-Stämme des indogerman-

ischen', in Helmut Rix (ed.), *Flexion und Wortbildung*, Wiesbaden: Reichert.

Wackernagel, Jakob, (1926–8) *Vorlesungen über Syntax*, 2nd edn, Basel: Birkhäuser.

Watkins, Calvert (1963) 'Preliminaries to a historical and comparative analysis of the syntax of the Old Irish verb', *Celtica* 6: 1–49.

—— (1976) 'Towards Proto-Indo-European syntax: problems and pseudo-problems', in S. Steever (ed.), *Papers from the Parasession on Diachronic Syntax*, Chicago: Chicago Linguistic Society, pp. 305–26.

3 The Indo-European Linguistic Family: Genetic and Typological Perspectives

Bernard Comrie

Introduction: Genetic and Areal Affiliations

The other chapters in this book are essentially inward-looking in terms of their Indo-European perspective, examining reasons for positing the genetic unity of the Indo-European languages and ways of accounting for their differentiation from a single ancestor language. This chapter, by contrast, is outward-looking, seeking to identify some salient features of Indo-European against a background of the range of structural diversity found across the languages of the world – in other words, to typologize Indo-European. The emphasis in this typological chapter will be on Proto-Indo-European and the early attested IE languages.

In order to put the typology of early Indo-European into historical perspective, it is important to consider with what other languages Proto-Indo-European might have genetic affiliations and with what other languages Proto-Indo-European might have been in areal contact; in some cases, the answers to the two questions might be the same, since if Proto-Indo-European does have genetic relatives, then at some point it must also have been in areal contact with them. Where early Indo-European shares typological characteristics with other languages and language families, distant genetic affiliations or areal contact are a plausible reason for these similarities.

The question of possible more distant genetic affiliations of the IE language family is one fraught with controversy, often even with emotional polemic, and no attempt will be made here to impose a particular viewpoint. One thing that is clear is that Indo-European itself is a well-defined genetic unit, that is, any two arbitrarily selected IE languages are genetically closer to one another than they are to any non-IE language. Thus what is at issue is not so much the nature of Indo-European but whether or not Indo-European forms part of a larger genetic unit (in much the same way as the Germanic languages form a genetic unit within the larger IE family). The various suggestions that have been made for more distant genetic affiliations are far from as tightly argued as are those for the internal genetic unity of Indo-European itself, but none the less there are some tantalizing hints of broader genetic links that deserve further consideration. For instance, in Proto-Indo-European the first and second person pronouns are characterized, at least in some morphological forms, by stems containing *m- and *t- respectively. Essentially this same pattern, with m- (or sometimes another labial) for first person and t- for second person, is found across a number of other language families of northern Eurasia: Uralic, Yukaghir (which many scholars consider to form, with Uralic, a Uralic-Yukaghir genetic unit), Turkic, Mongolian, Tungusic (which three, many scholars consider to form a single, Altaic family, perhaps also including Japanese and Korean), Chukotko-Kamchatkan (in north-eastern Siberia), and Eskimo-Aleut (in northern North America). Since the probability of this same pattern being replicated independently by chance in so many instances is low, and since personal pronouns are relatively immune to borrowing, this suggests that there may be a distant genetic relation among these languages, which Greenberg (forthcoming) has subsumed, along with some others, in a putative Eurasiatic family. Other scholars have placed equal or more emphasis on possible genetic relations to languages to the south and east, in particular Afroasiatic (the family which includes Semitic as one of its branches, with such languages as Arabic and Hebrew), Kartvelian or South Caucasian (spoken to the south of the main range of the Caucasus and including Georgian as its major representative), and Dravidian (whose member languages are spoken primarily in southern India); they prefer Nostratic as the name of the larger genetic unit to which they would assign Indo-European (e.g. Illič-Svityč 1971–84).

In dealing with areal contacts between Indo-European and other language families, and the possibility of similarities that may have arisen through areal influence, it is important to restrict our attention to languages with which Proto-Indo-European was in contact, since later contacts between individual IE languages and non-IE languages belong properly to the history of those individual languages. The precise range of areal contacts entered into by Proto-Indo-European will of course depend on the solution to such controversial questions as the location of the PIE homeland and the geographic location of the other languages at the time in question. Suffice it to say that plausible candidates for substantial areal contact with Proto-Indo-European include the proto-language or some individual languages of the following families: Uralic, Afroasiatic (more specifically: Semitic), Kartvelian, possibly also North Caucasian (i.e. the indigenous languages of the northern Caucasus, including North-west Caucasian and Nakh-Daghestanian or North-east Caucasian).

Phonological Typology

From a typological perspective, the vowel system of late Proto-Indo-European, that is, the stage immediately preceding the break-up of the parent language, would hardly elicit surprise, containing as it does the most common five-vowel system in the world (i–e–a–o–u), superimposed on which is a two-way opposition of vowel length, plus the 'schwa'-vowel standing outside the length opposition. By contrast, the consonant system, more specifically the obstruent system, is highly skewed, with a preponderance of stops distinguished by a rich set of places of articulation (perhaps as many as five: labial, dental, palatal, velar, labiovelar) and of phonation types (perhaps as many as four: voiceless unaspirated, voiceless aspirated, voiced unaspirated, 'voiced aspirated'), but only a single fricative phoneme (s). While obstruent systems with so many stops and so few fricatives are not unknown, being found for instance quite typically in the indigenous languages of Australia, they are certainly unusual across languages of the world as a whole. And indeed, a substantial part of the further reconstruction back to early Proto-Indo-European has been concerned with providing a typologically more plausible account of the consonant system – but with the result that in turn a new vowel system has been proposed that stands at the boundaries of typological plausibility.

Perhaps the most important step in this shift of typological perspective came with the Laryngeal Theory, which gradually stripped away the oppositions of quantity and quality in the vowel system: i and u can be treated as allophones of y and w respectively; o is to a large extent a morphophonemic alternant of e under ablaut; a neater overall account can be given of ablaut if it is assumed that the long vowels reflect an earlier sequence of short vowel plus laryngeal, and schwa can then in turn be considered a syllabic laryngeal; many remaining instances of the vowels a and o can plausibly be considered reflexes of laryngeal–vowel or vowel–laryngeal sequences if one assumes that there were three laryngeals, the late PIE differentiation of vowel qualities (e–a–o) reflecting an early differentiation of laryngeals (h_1–h_2–h_3), perhaps mirroring the palatal–velar–labiovelar opposition (see also Chapter 2, pp. 40–4). Thus early Proto-Indo-European, or at least this widely accepted version of early Proto-Indo-European, ends up with a more balanced obstruent system through the introduction of the three 'laryngeals' (at least some of which are probably fricatives), but by the same token ends up with a typologically highly unusual vowel system: perhaps just a single vowel, symbolized *e. While it is probably true that no absolutely convincing case has been made for any attested and well-described language of the world that it is monovocalic, there are some languages that certainly come close, including, interestingly, the North-west Caucasian languages (Abkhaz–Abaza, Circassian, Ubykh), which have very restricted vowel inventories and very rich consonant inventories (Hewitt 1981: 205–7). In terms of areal typology, and perhaps more distant genetic comparison, it is also worth noting that the Semitic languages, especially phonologically more conservative Semitic languages like Arabic, have relatively small vowel inventories (Classical Arabic has *i–a–u*, long and short) but rather rich consonant inventories. Both North-west Caucasian and Semitic languages are particularly rich in 'laryngeal' consonants, that is, consonants produced at the back of the upper vocal tract.

The late PIE obstruent system provides another apparent typological anomaly in the range of phonation types. Since the evidence for the voiceless aspirated series is rather marginal, perhaps reflecting an innovation of Indo-Iranian rather than a feature of the proto-language, the phonation types can plausibly be reduced to three: voiceless unaspirated, voiced unaspirated, and voiced aspirated. But it was then argued that, typologically, the presence of a voiced aspirated series necessarily presupposes the existence of a voiceless aspirated series. Either one goes back to the fourway opposition of phonation types, or one reanalyses the phonetic nature of one or other of three other phonation types. Actually, the term 'voiced aspirate' is something of a misnomer, since in strict phonetic terms voicing and aspiration are incompatible; rather, what is meant is 'breathy (or murmured) voice', and the question therefore boils down to whether a breathy voiced series is possible in the absence of voiceless aspirates. If one assumes that it is not, then phonetic reanalysis is required, as in the Glottalic Theory (Gamkrelidze and Ivanov 1984; ch. 1), which holds that the so-called voiced unaspirated stops were in fact glottalized stops, with the voiceless unaspirated stops being phonologically classifiable rather as voiced unglottalized, while the so-called voiced aspirated stops can be classified phonologically simply as voiced stops (see Chapter 2, p. 38). The typological debate has, however, been reopened by the discovery of languages in West Africa that have essentially the threeway opposition of phonation types proposed for Proto-Indo-European (Stewart 1989: 231–9). It should be noted that the typological argument just outlined is not the only evidence in favor of the Glottalic Theory, and if the Glottalic Theory is accepted then Proto-Indo-European would share a striking typological feature with North Caucasian, Kartvelian and possibly Semitic (the so-called 'emphatics' show up in some Semitic languages, e.g. Amharic, as glottalized consonants; their value in Proto-Semitic is unclear). (For a more detailed consideration of these phonological problems, reference may be made to Comrie 1993.)

We have already alluded to the most striking morphophonemic alternation of Proto-Indo-European, namely ablaut, whereby the basic vowel *e* appears, under appropriate circumstances, as *o* or is even deleted altogether. Somewhat similar patterns of changes in vowel quality and loss of vowels have been investigated from the viewpoint of areal typological similarities to Indo-European in the Kartvelian languages (Gamqreli3e and Mačavariani 1965).

Morphological Typology

In speaking of the morphological typology of Proto-Indo-European, there are three main topics that deserve attention: (a) the general morphological type, in terms of the classification into isolating, agglutinating and fusional languages; (b) the distinction of words into word classes or parts of speech; (c) the most salient categories that are expressed morphologically. Kuryłowicz (1964) is a masterly discussion of this area of Indo-European linguistics.

Morphological Type

In terms of the classification of morphological types, early Indo-European is fusional. It is distinct from an isolating language, in which each word consists of one and only one morpheme, in that it has many words consisting of more than one morpheme, for example, Lat. *virī* 'man (gen. sg.)', where the one word includes expression of the lexical item ('man'), of singular number, and of genitive case, that it, three morphemes. It is distinct from an agglutinating language in that it is frequently impossible to segment a word into morphs (formatives, sequences of phonemes) corresponding to its constituent morphemes. In Lat. *virī*, for example, there is no segmentable morph expressing singular number (cf. acc. sg. *virum*), nor is there a segmentable morph expressing genitive case (cf. gen. pl. *virōrum*). Indeed, the fusional nature of early Indo-European morphology is exacerbated by the fact that the major parts of speech fall into inflectional classes, such that the same combination of morphemes often finds different expression in different inflectional classes: thus, genitive singular can also be realized in Latin as *-ae* (e.g. *mensae* 'table (gen. sg.)'), *-is* (e.g. *rēgis* 'king (gen. sg.)'), and so on. In the classification of morphological types, a fourth type is sometimes introduced, namely polysynthetic, referring to a language where typically a large number of morphemes are combined into a single word. Although early Indo-European is fusional, it is not polysynthetic. In nouns, for instance, only two categories are expressed inflectionally (case, number), while in verbs the range of categories expressed is of the order of person–number (of the subject), tense–aspect, mood, voice, finiteness, in sharp contrast to typical polysynthetic languages which readily include a dozen morphemes in a single word, such a word often functioning as a complete sentence. Indeed, it is remarkable that despite the complexity of the morphology of the early IE languages, easily testified to by anyone who has had to master the morphology of an early IE language, this complexity is due not to any large number of morphological categories expressed, but rather to the fusional expression of the few categories that are expressed.

While fusional morphology characterizes the earliest attested IE languages and is indeed still characteristic of many modern languages (e.g. Icelandic and the Baltic and Slavic languages), and forms part of the reconstruction of late Proto-Indo-European, the application of internal reconstruction to the product of comparative reconstruction has been able to strip away some, but by no means all, of the fusional nature of early Indo-European and point to an earlier stage of Proto-Indo-European which was more agglutinative; for rather strikingly different reconstructions of this type, reference may be made to Szemerényi (1989) and Beekes (1990). The fusional nature of Late Proto-Indo-European stems in part from intervening phonological changes that obscured similarities and to the influence of analogy, which further obscured the original pattern. A simple example is provided by the accusative singular in Ancient Greek, whose two major exponents, *-n* and *-a*, though quite different synchronically, both derive from PIE *-m*, non-syllabic and syllabic respectively. Historically, Ancient Gk *-n* is the reflex of PIE non-syllabic *m* and is thus expected after a syllabic segment, as in *lógon* 'word (acc. sg.)', while *-a* is the reflex of syllabic *m* and is thus expected after a non-syllabic segment, as in *phýlaka* 'guard (acc. sg.)'. But dental stems with unaccented final syllable take the *-n* allomorph, with deletion of the stem-final dental, as in *érin*, accusative singular of *éris* (stem *erid-*) 'strife' (cf. *elpída*, accusative singular of *elpís* 'hope', with an accented final syllable). Even this distribution is disturbed by exceptions like *kleís* (stem *kleid-*) 'key', whose accusative singular is usually *kleîn*, rarely *kleîda*. Such subsequent phonological and analogical changes even lead to difficulty in separating stem from inflection, so that in declining a Latin noun like *hortus* 'garden' synchronically, it is usual to segment along the lines nom. sg. *hort-us*, voc. sg. *hort-e*, gen. sg. *hort-ī*, dat.–abl. sg. *hort-ō*, thus losing sight of the etymological stem *horto-* (of which *horte* is an ablaut variant).

Of the languages with which early Indo-European was in areal contact, fusional morphology is particularly characteristic of the Semitic and Kartvelian languages.

Word Classes (Parts of Speech)
The most readily distinguishable word class in Proto-Indo-European is the verb, which has a number of categories not shown by any other word class, e.g. person–number, tense–aspect, and mood. Within the remainder, the core class is composed of substantives (nouns, in the narrow sense of this term), which are characterized by the categories of case and number. These same categories characterize a number of other word classes that are distinguishable, to different degrees, from substantives. Thus, pronouns show the same categories as substantives, but follow a different inflection in some respects, for example, with nominative singular neuter in *-d* rather than *-m*, e.g. Lat. *illud* 'that (nom. sg. n.)' versus *bonum* 'good (nom. sg.)'; the personal pronouns, originally restricted to the first and second persons (demonstratives being used in place of third person pronouns) have an even more idiosyncratic

declension, with some suppletion between the nominative and oblique cases, a phenomenon to which we return in **Morphological Categories**, pp. 81ff. The distinguishability of a separate class of adjectives is even more questionable for Proto-Indo-European, and in the early IE languages adjectives differ little from substantives, the most important difference being that adjectives show a fully productive inflectional category of gender (e.g. Lat. m. *bonus*, f. *bona*, n. *bonum*), whereas with nouns gender is at best a derivational category, for example, *victor* 'conqueror (male)', *victrix* 'conqueror (female)'. In individual early IE languages, however, further distinctions arise between substantives and adjectives. In Ancient Greek, for instance, they may have different accentual patterns, as when the genitive plural of first-declension nouns is always accented -*ōn* (e.g. *khōrōn*, genitive plural of *khôrā* 'land') while that of first-declension adjectives is not so accented if the nominative singular does not have final accent (e.g. *aksíōn*, genitive plural of *aksíā* 'worthy (f.)'). The treatment of adjectives, that is, of items expressing prototypically qualities rather than entities (substantives) or activities (verbs), as similar or identical to substantives seems to be particularly characteristic of languages of Europe, northern Asia and northern Africa, that is, those languages with which Indo-European has been in areal contact and with which it may have distant genetic affiliations. According to ongoing typological investigations by R.M.W. Dixon, outside this area this treatment of quality-words is widespread only in Australia, parts of Mexico and California, and the Philippines; over most of the world quality-words are either treated like verbs or form a small, closed class of adjectives (with other quality-words treated either as verbs or as substantives). Participles, incidentally, are not strictly a separate word class: they are rather adjectives derived from verbs and thus showing some verbal categories in addition to the categories expressed in an adjective.

Many adverbs are etymologically, and sometimes even synchronically, case forms of nominals, for example, Lat. *partim* (< acc. sg.) 'partly', Skt *divā* (< instr. sg.) 'by day', or nominals with case-like suffixes, e.g. Ancient Gk *póthen* 'whence?' However, there is also a set of primarily short adverbs for which at least no such substantival origin is clear, for example, *$h_1$en* 'up' (cf. Ancient Gk *aná*), *upér(i)* 'above' (cf. Skt *upári*), *pro* 'forwards' (cf. Skt *prá*). Many of the last-named items also show up as prepositions (or postpositions, which we may together call adpositions) and also as verbal prefixes in some early and most contemporary IE languages, but one of the striking typological characteristics of Proto-Indo-European seems to have been the lack of adpositions. The items in question were earlier adverbs, and their use as adpositions or prefixes is secondary. In Proto-Indo-European the grammatical and semantic roles of noun phrases were expressed primarily by means of case, with those adverbs that were later to become adpositions at best further specifying the semantics of the case in question; the reinterpretation in favour of an adposition governing a particular case came later. Clear traces of the earlier system are visible in Homeric Greek, in comparison with the later use of the items in question as strict prepositions in classical Attic prose. Thus, the adverbial use of *perí* 'about' is clear in *gélasse dè pāsa perì khthón* (*Iliad* 19.362) 'and all the earth laughed around'. While *katá* 'down' appears as a verbal prefix in *kat-édomai* 'eat up', it is still possible for it to be separated from its verb, as in *hoì katà boûs Hyperíonos Ēelíoio ésthion* (*Odyssey* 1.8–9) 'they ate up the cattle of Hyperion the Sun-god'. And even in adpositional usage, while preposition is the norm, postposition is also found, as in *theōn ek thésphata éidē* (*Iliad* 5.64) 'he knew the decrees from the gods' (cf. Chapter 9, p. 258). This wide range of usages is still found with some items in English, for example, *up*, which is a preposition in *up the Nile River*, a prefix in the verb *to uplift* (used primarily in metaphorical senses), and an adverb in *to lift up* (used primarily in the literal sense; see Chapter 14, p. 448). And while across most of Indo-European such items, in becoming adpositions, became prepositions, there are also languages, such as Hittite, where postpositions are the norm, and individual items that are postpositional even in languages that normally have prepositions, for example, Lat. *mēcum* 'with me'. Weakly developed adpositions, or adpositions that are for the most part clearly of secondary origin, alongside a well-developed case system are also characteristic of Uralic and Kartvelian languages, in this respect contrasting sharply with Semitic, with its limited case system (e.g. Classical Arabic has only nominative, accusative and genitive) and prepositions of no clear non-prepositional origin (e.g. Classical Arabic *fī* 'in', *min* 'from').

Although the numerals form a clearly defined semantic class, they are not to be treated as a single word class in morphological terms, combining items that are adjectival (or, in some instances in some languages, pronominal), invariable and substantival. Whether Proto-Indo-European had clause-combining conjunctions is questionable, since clause-combining probably originally involved the use of non-finite verbal forms (see **Clause Combining**, pp. 94–5); the most plausible candidate is the word for 'if', Ancient Gk *ei*, Goth. *ei* suggesting originally a locative of the anaphoric pronoun $*h_1e$ 'that, the aforementioned'. The enclitic coordinating conjunctions $*-k^we$ 'and' and $*-ue$ 'or' have widespread reflexes. Finally, Proto-Indo-European had a number of invariable particles and, of course, interjections.

Morphological Categories
As noted in **Morphological Type**, pp. 78f., despite the complexity of early IE morphology the actual number of categories expressed morphologically is rather small. While the reconstruction of the PIE forms for most of these categories is relatively straightforward, the reconstruction of their precise meaning, or more generally function, is typically fraught with greater difficulty, given the extent to which etymologically identical forms have diverged in use in different languages.

The only morphological categories expressed in nominals (nouns, adjectives, pronouns) are gender, number and case, and of these gender is inflectional only in adjectives and some pronouns, perhaps reflecting an earlier stage where gender was always derivational rather than inflectional and where adjectives were indistinct from nouns. The absence of a category of possession (i.e. affixes for 'my', etc.) is in striking contrast to Uralic and Semitic, although in Uralic, at least, the development of this category is probably quite recent (as seen, for instance, in the number of languages attaching possessive suffixes after case suffixes).

Speculations on the areal typological affinities of the gender system are hampered by uncertainty over whether the PIE system was basically masculine–feminine–neuter (as in Sanskrit, Ancient Greek, Latin, etc.) or animate–inanimate (as in Hittite: see Chapter 7, p. 177). While the formally distinct feminines in *-h_2 (e.g. *-$\bar{a}$ < *-e-h_2, *-$\bar{i}$ < *-i-h_2) are clearly a relatively late grammaticalization of a derivational pattern, it is not clear how late this process is. Of the areally related languages, gender is completely absent from Uralic and Kartvelian, while Semitic has a masculine–feminine opposition, including apparently idiosyncratic gender assignments reminiscent in type of the early (and many modern) IE languages; North-west Caucasian has a masculine–feminine–neuter system, but with the gender assignment of nouns predictable directly from their semantic humanness and their biological sex. The number system, singular–dual–plural, of Proto-Indo-European is widespread among the languages of the world, being found for instance in some Uralic and Semitic (though not Kartvelian) languages; simplification of such a system to a singular–plural opposition, as has happened over most of Indo-European, is again widespread crosslinguistically, again with parallels in Uralic and Semitic.

The case system of early Indo-European represents a moderate-sized inventory (seven plus the vocative, on the standard reconstruction), certainly richer than that of Semitic, but not nearly so rich as that of Hungarian or some Daghestanian languages. As one might expect typologically from an inventory no larger than this, other means were used to encode finer distinctions, recourse being had in particular to those adverbs that later became adpositions (**Word Classes**, pp. 79f.). Indeed, even looking at the early IE languages one can discern a continuing development away from reliance on case towards reduction in the number of cases or at least in their functional range and towards greater reliance on adpositions; witness, for instance, the demise of the accusative as a means of indicating motion towards (e.g. Lat. *Rōmam* 'to Rome'), its replacement in this function by prepositional phrases (e.g. Vulgar Lat. *ad Roma*(*m*)), and the restriction of its functions to the syntactic one of indicating direct objects. Extrapolating backwards, one might hypothesize that at an earlier stage the cases had even more semantic and less syntactic content. This would fit in with some other claims made on the basis of internal reconstruction with respect to early Indo-European.

For instance, the distribution of the PIE nominative singular suffix *-s is rather strange, being absent in particular from neuter nouns. There are three main kinds of case-marking systems for subjects and objects found across the languages of the world. In the 'nominative–accusative system', one case (nominative) is used for both intransitive subjects and transitive subjects (or agents), while another case (accusative) is used for the direct object (patient) of transitive clauses. In the 'ergative–absolutive system', one case (absolutive) is used for both intransitive subjects and the direct objects (patients) of transitive clauses, while another case (ergative) is used for the subject (agent) of a transitive clause. In the 'active–inactive system', one case (active) is used for both subjects (agents) of transitive verbs and for semantically more agent-like (whence: active) subjects of intransitive verbs, while another case is used for both direct objects (patients) of transitive verbs and for semantically more patient-like (whence: inactive) subjects of intransitive verbs. (See, for instance, Harris 1990 and references cited there.) The early IE languages are traditionally described in terms of the nominative–accusative system, although this loses sight of the fact that neuter nouns in fact never show a distinction between nominative and accusative and indeed in o-stems have a nominative–accusative inflection *-m which is identical to the accusative of masculine nouns of this declension. In Proto-Indo-European, the most clear-cut nominative–accusative system is found with the personal pronouns, which in the first person typically go as far as to have suppletion between the stem used in the nominative and that used in the accusative and other oblique cases, for example, Lat. nom. *ego* 'I', acc. *mē*, Skt nom. *vayám* 'we', acc. *asmán*. If those paradigms where the so-called nominative singular is in *-s are not analysed, at least for early Proto-Indo-European, as nominative–accusative, the question arises whether they formed part of an ergative–absolutive or of an active–inactive case-marking system. Here, cross-linguistic studies of languages with split case-marking systems, that is, which combine two or more of the three case-marking systems in various ways, can throw light on the problem (Silverstein 1976). Crucial to this area of study is the so-called 'Animacy Hierarchy', which arranges noun phrases in terms of their inherent animacy, as follows (though individual languages may make more or fewer distinctions): first/second-person pronouns > human noun phrases > other animate noun phrases > inanimate noun phrases. In languages which have a split in their case-marking system conditioned by the Animacy Hierarchy and which combine nominative–accusative case marking with one or more other case-marking systems, it is always the case that the nominative–accusative system is used for noun phrases highest in animacy. This fits in perfectly with our observation that PIE personal pronouns, restricted to first and second persons, show the most clear-cut nominative–accusative case-marking system. In languages where the ergative–absolutive system is combined with other case-marking systems, it is always the case that the ergative–absolutive system is found with noun phrases lowest in animacy. This is not consistent with the observation that PIE *-s is most characteristic of masculine nouns and least characteristic of neuter nouns, the latter being typically lowest in animacy in Proto-Indo-European. The only way in which the IE evidence can be reconciled with the cross-linguistic distribution of ergative–absolutive case marking would be to claim that *-s was originally an ergative case marker, that neuter nouns rarely or never appeared as agents of transitive verbs, and that neuter nouns thus rarely or never showed up in the form in *-s. Subsequently, the use of *-s spread from transitive to intransitive verbs, thus beoming a gender-restricted nominative. If, however, we assume that the *-s was originally a marker of the active case, then the need to adopt this kind of argumentation evaporates: the inflection was simply used to mark those noun phrases that are more 'active', whether subjects of transitive or intransitive verbs, thus including masculine nouns in preference to neuter nouns; this has the effect of assigning greater semantic content to this suffix. The problem of the original function of *-s still cannot, however, be regarded as definitively solved: in languages with active–inactive case marking, for instance, the nature of the verb (dynamic or stative) is usually the crucial factor in determining the case of the intransitive subject, whereas on the active–inactive analysis of the PIE case-marking system the verb plays no role, only the inherent animacy of the subject noun phrase. In sum, while the PIE case system has anomalies in terms of the nominative–accusative case marking, the assumption of an ergative–absolutive or active–inactive case-marking system serves only to eliminate these anomalies at the expense of introducing others (see further Comrie 1994).

The major verbal categories are person–number, tense–aspect, mood, voice and finiteness, though with the exception of person–number the semantic characterization of categories is even more elusive with verbs than it is with nouns. The person–number inflections quite straightforwardly encode the person–number of the subject, irrespective of whether or not the subject is agentive, that is, following a strict nominative–accusative system; there is no inflection on the verb for any other argument, in contrast to the object agreement found in Semitic and some Uralic languages and the polypersonal agreement found in Kartvelian languages (subject, direct object, indirect object) and especially in North-west Caucasian languages (where verbs may in addition agree with adpositional objects).

On the basis primarily of Ancient Greek and Indo-Aryan, the conventional reconstruction of the PIE tense–aspect system comprises the following categories: present, imperfect, aorist, perfect. This system rests on three oppositions: that between non-past and past tense, seen clearly in the opposition between present and imperfect; that between imperfective and perfective aspect, seen in the opposition between present and imperfect on the one hand, and aorist on the other, and that between perfect and non-perfect, corresponding to the distinction between the perfect and the rest (for these terms, see Comrie 1976). Of these, the imperfect is clearly a more recent development, essentially a past tense based on the present stem, so a more accurate picture might be the following: present, aorist, perfect. Since, in this system, there is no opposition of tense, it can be reformulated as imperfective, aorist (perfective), perfect. It is noteworthy that in this reconstruction, aspect is more important than tense, although by the time of the early IE languages tense, in particular the past–non-past opposition, has become crucial. Many branches of Indo-European have simpler systems, though often with traces of the earlier richness. Latin and Germanic, for instance, have no synchronically distinct tense–aspect as a reflex of the PIE perfect, although etymologically perfect formations lie behind the Latin preterite *pepercī* 'I have spared' and the present *nōvī* 'I know', behind the Gothic preterite *gaígrôt* 'I have wept' and present *wait* 'I know'. Hittite is unusual, for so ancient an IE language, in having not even traces of the earlier richness, since its verbal system operates in terms of a past–non-past opposition with no distinctions of aspect; whether this represents innovatory loss or the retention of an archaic system predating that of the IE languages remains unclear.

Two developments in Proto-Indo-European served to develop the past–non-past opposition in the system. One is the opposition between primary and secondary inflections. Despite the terminology, the secondary inflections are original, the primary inflections being formed from them with a final -*i*. The function of the final -*i* was to indicate present time reference, as in the Ancient Greek present *títhēmi* 'I put (pres.)' in contrast to the imperfect *etíthēn* 'I was putting, used to put', with -*n* from *-*m*. The development of the primary inflections gives a form with clearly present tense, in principle sufficient to distinguish this from other time references. The second is the development of the augment, *e*-, perhaps originally a temporal adverb, to indicate past time reference, as in the Ancient Greek imperfect form just cited and in the aorist *élyse* 'he loosed'. The augment is attested only in Indo-Iranian, Greek, Armenian and Phrygian, and may have been a local innovation. Thus, at least for those branches of Indo-European with the augment, there is a distinct present tense with -*i* and a distinct past tense with *e*-. If some branches never had the augment, then they are characterized throughout by a distinct present tense with -*i*.

In this general schema of tense in late Proto-Indo-European, the only incompatibility for the secondary inflections is with present time reference, thus leaving them in principle free to express either past or future time reference, or indeed absence of time reference. Traces of this situation can be seen in the use of secondary inflections with the optative (since wished-for states of affairs can be seen as standing outside real time) and in the Vedic injunctive, morphologically an augmentless past, which often has future time reference, for example, *índrasya nú vīryāni prá vocam* (*RigVeda* I.32.1) 'I will now proclaim the heroic deeds of Indra', *kó no mahyâ áditaye púnar dāt* (*RigVeda* I.24.1) 'who will give us back to great Aditi?' (see Chapter 4, p. 116). Subsequently, however, the secondary inflections came to be more specifically tied to past time reference, at least in the indicative, so that in most early IE languages that retain the imperfective–perfective aspectual opposition we find the past–non-past opposition reflected in that between present on the one hand and imperfect and aorist on the other, and the imperfective–perfective opposition reflected in that between present and imperfect on the one hand and aorist on the other (Comrie 1990).

It will be noted that there is no future tense reconstructible for Proto-Indo-European. All of the forms that can be referred to as future tenses in IE languages are later formations, paralleling ways of forming future tenses that are found in many languages of the world (Ultan 1976), for instance modal formations (e.g. Lat. *erō* 'I shall be' from the subjunctive, Eng. *I will go* with an auxiliary originally meaning 'want' and *I shall go* with an auxiliary originally meaning 'must'), inchoative formations (e.g. Ger. *ich werde gehen* 'I will go' with an auxiliary originally meaning 'become', OCS *mĭněti načĭnǫtŭ* 'they will think' with an auxiliary originally meaning 'begin'), or simply the present tense with future time reference (e.g. Ger. *ich gehe morgen* 'I (will) go tomorrow'). As in some other languages that lack a distinct future tense (e.g. Finnish, Hungarian, Georgian), the use of a present-tense form with telic or perfective meaning often gives future-tense reference, most clearly in the West and East Slavic languages, where the perfective of the present has basically future time reference, e.g. Russ. *ja brošu* (pfv.) 'I will throw', cf. *ja brosaju* (ipfv.) 'I throw'. It will be noted that this presupposes the development of the PIE present tense, with its primary endings, into a more general non-past tense.

This leaves the perfect. Although in some early IE languages the perfect seems to have been well integrated into the verbal paradigm, for instance in Sanskrit and to a large extent in classical Attic Greek, there are clear signs that its relation to the rest of the paradigm was once much looser, the perfect being in origin a stative derivative of the verb stem, as seen for instance in the diathesis changes that characterize many perfects in relation to the rest of the paradigm, for example, in Ancient Greek *peíthō* 'persuade' has as one of its perfects *pépoitha*, with the meaning not 'I have persuaded' but rather 'I trust', that is, as a result of having been persuaded. Where we find such diathesis changes, the phenomenon always involves expression of a state of affairs where the subject is affected. The inflections of the perfect in Proto-Indo-European are also close to those of the middle voice (see below). From this one can conclude that the IE perfect was originally a voice-neutral derived form and that its original value was to express a state, this state being attributed naturally to that entity most affected. Since the perfect was derived typically from dynamic verbs, its value was more specifically expression of a state resulting from a previous action, as 'to trust' is the state resulting from a previous action of persuasion. The changes in diathesis, while perhaps appearing idiosyncratic in the synchronic description of early IE languages, find a natural explanation on the basis of this assumption about the original value of the perfect and general typological observations on the nature of resultative constructions (for which see Nedjalkov 1988). In many languages, the perfect subsequently shifted value semantically, de-emphasizing the resultant state and emphasizing more the earlier action, with the result that such forms often became general perfective pasts, supplanting or merging with the aorist, as in Sanskrit and Latin, or even general past tenses, as in Germanic. This is a diachronic shift that has taken place cyclically in a number of IE languages: for instance, Latin developed a new periphrastic formation with resultative meaning, for example, *habeō litterās scrīptās* 'I have the letters written', which has eventually given the perfective past *ho scritto* 'I wrote' of spoken Italian.

We may now compare the reconstructed PIE tense–aspect system with that of other languages plausibly in areal contact or possibly genetically related to Indo-European. The closest parallel to the core present–imperfect–aorist systems of many early IE languages is perhaps found in the Kartvelian languages, with its core present–imperfect–aorist system. The basic distinction between past and non-past is found in nearly all languages of Europe, including Basque and the Finno-Ugric languages. The system is radically different from that found in the Semitic languages. However, it should be recalled that even within Indo-European we can plausibly reconstruct back from the system of such early IE languages as Ancient Greek to a rather different earlier system with much heavier emphasis on aspect than on tense, so the similarities between Indo-European and many of its neighbours may well be more representative of areal contact than of any deeper genetic relations that may exist. (For further discussion of the typology of tense–aspect systems in languages of Europe, see Comrie 1990.)

The distinct moods in Proto-Indo-European were the indicative, subjunctive, optative and imperative, perhaps also injunctive, although as a morphologically clearly distinct form the injunctive is limited to Sanskrit. Given the rather undeveloped state of cross-linguistic studies on the typology of mood systems, it is difficult to say much of typological relevance with respect to moods. The role of the subjunctive in the development of future tense forms has already been alluded to. One interesting observation with respect to the imperative is that both Sanskrit and Latin, and therefore probably Proto-Indo-European, distinguish between an imperative with more proximate time reference (e.g. Skt *ihí*, Lat. *ī* 'go') and an imperative with more distant time reference (Skt *itất*, Latin *ītō*).

In most general linguistic studies of voice, the paradigm case of voice has usually been taken to be the opposition between active and passive, that is, the relation as illustrated in English *The dog bit the cat* versus *The cat was bitten by the dog*. Following the terminology of Klaiman (1991), we may refer to this as 'derived voice', since the passive can be viewed as derived from the active (with preservation of at least the basic meaning). In Proto-Indo-European, however, there is no evidence for an active–passive distinction, and the forms (synthetic or, more usually, analytic) that are specifically passive in individual IE languages are all clearly later developments. The only voice distinction characteristic of Proto-Indo-European is rather that between active and middle, a voice distinction of a type that Klaiman refers to as 'basic voice', since the active and the middle do not share the same meaning. The characteristic of the middle voice is that the subject is affected by the action of the verb, a distinction well illustrated by the traditionally cited opposition between Ancient Gk *lýō* (act.) *toùs aikhmalô- tous* 'I free the prisoners' and *lýomai* (mid.) *toùs aikhmalôtous* 'I ransom the prisoners', where in the second example the subject gains benefit from the action. As shown by Klaiman (1991: ch. 2) such basic voice systems are by no means infrequent across the languages of the world. However, I am not aware of basic voice systems in the languages likely to have been in direct areal contact or possible distant genetic relation with Proto-Indo-European. The closest would perhaps be the systems of verbal derivatives (Hebrew *binyanim*) in the Semitic, and more generally Afroasiatic, languages. In addition, the Dravidian languages have a basic voice system very similar to that of Proto-Indo-European.

Non-finite verbal forms are characteristic of all the early IE languages and in most instances the parallels in formation are so clear that PIE forms can be reconstructed with minimal difficulty. As will be seen in **Clause Combining**, pp. 94–5, non-finite verbal forms played a crucial role in clause combining in Proto-Indo-European. Verbal adjectives (participles) include the present participle active (e.g. Skt *bhárant-*, Goth. *bairands* 'carrying'), the perfect participle active (e.g. Ancient Gk *eidôs* 'knowing', OCS *nesŭ* 'having carried'), the middle participle (e.g. Ancient Gk *hepómenos* 'following'), and the **-to-/*-no-* verbal adjective (e.g. Skt *syūtá*, Lith. *siútas* 'sewn'). Verbal nouns were of various morphological formations, originally part of the derivational rather than the inflectional morphology, though various case forms of such verbal nouns became generalized lexically and specialized syntactically to give infinitives, a category found in most IE languages but not going back to a single PIE ancestor form. There is less clear evidence for forms reconstructible to Proto-Indo-European that are specifically verbal adverbs (gerunds or converbs, in Slavicist and Turkologist terminology, with such meanings as 'while doing . . .'), such forms as the Russian gerund (verbal adverb) *čitaja* '(while) reading', etymologically a frozen nominative case form of a participle, being later language-specific formations. Most of the languages with which Proto-Indo-European may have been in areal contact or genetic affiliation have systems of non-finite forms, reaching particular richness in the Uralic and especially the Altaic languages, which latter in particular have verbal adverbs (usually called gerunds or converbs).

Syntactic Typology

Constituent Order

Much of the discussion of the syntactic typology of Indo-European in recent years has centered on the question of word-order typology, with quite different assessments being given on such questions as the order of subject (S), verb (V) and object (O) in Proto-Indo-European. Thus, Lehmann (1974) argues that Proto-Indo-European was basically an SOV language, with other constituent orders that one would expect, cross-linguistically, to co-occur most frequently with this word order, such as the adjective (A) and genitive (G) before the noun (N), that is, AN, GN, and adpositions (Ad) following the dependent noun phrase (NP), that is, NPAd. In terms of the dependency approach to syntax, in which each constituent typically has a head and one or more dependents (arguments), Proto-Indo-European would thus be a head-final language, with the head (verb of a verb phrase, noun of a noun phrase, adposition of an adpositional phrase) at the end of that phrase. Lehmann's database consisted primarily of citations of examples consistent with these orders from the early IE languages, although he was, of course, aware that deviations from some or all of these constituent orders are frequent in the early IE languages: these deviations were to be treated in terms of departures in the individual early IE languages from the word order of Proto-Indo-European, or as marked constituent orders allowed in Proto-Indo-European. Friedrich (1975) argues, on the basis of a statistical analysis of the early IE languages, that for several of the constituent-order parameters there is at least as much evidence for assuming some other constituent order, with a trichotomization of the early IE languages into SOV (e.g. Indo-Aryan, Anatolian, Tocharian), SVO (e.g. Greek, on Friedrich's assessment), and even VSO (Celtic, also Proto-Slavic on Friedrich's assessment). Watkins (1976) suggests that it is methodologically unsound to rely on statistical analyses of early IE languages (perhaps especially given that some of the earliest attestations of individual branches of Indo-European are separated by thousands of years from the break-up of late Proto-Indo-European); rather, emphasis should be placed on expressions that can otherwise be judged as archaic in the attested texts. In cases where such archaic formulations can be clearly identified, they point rather clearly to Proto-Indo-European as basically an SOV language, and both this conclusion and Watkins' method-ology have been generally accepted in the field. The evidence for whether Proto-Indo-European was AN or NA and whether it was GN or NG is indecisive. As noted above, the proto-language probably lacked adpositions, so the question of postpositional versus prepositional belongs properly to the history of the individual branches.

It should be noted that many individual branches show changes in basic constituent order over their recorded histories. While in some cases this involves a movement from more SOV to more SVO, as with the Romance and

Germanic languages, it is equally likely to involve the opposite movement, as in Indo-Aryan: modern Indo-Aryan languages are much closer to consistent SOV order, and in particular to the requirement of verb-finality, than is Sanskrit. It is thus not possible to take directions of development found in the historically attested languages and project these same directions back indefinitely into the past.

While Proto-Indo-European was probably basically SOV, it also, on the basis of the attested early IE languages, allowed considerable freedom of constituent order, for instance with constituents being proposed for purposes of pragmatic highlighting. This relative freedom of constituent order was facilitated by the rich morphology, in particular the marking of case on noun phrases, permitting recovery of grammatical relations irrespective of constituent order, to a lesser extent by verb agreement with the subject, since this serves as an additional means of identifying the subject. As indicated in **Agreement**, pp. 91f., agreement among the individual words of a noun phrase, for instance, meant that it was even possible to move words out of constituents, so that an adjective might be separated from its head noun; in this sense, Proto-Indo-European can be characterized as having freedom of word order, and not just of constituent order (Chapter 14, p. 449).

One systematic set of exceptions to the general constituent-order principles outlined above is provided by enclitics, that is unstressed items that are necessarily pronounced as a single stress unit with the preceding stressed word (see especially Hittite, Chapter 7, pp. 187f.). Of particular interest are sentence enclitics, whose position is determined relative to the sentence as a whole, since in many early IE languages such enclitics appear as the second word in the sentence. This set of enclitics includes in particular unstressed forms of object pronouns, such as Ancient Gk *mé* 'me (acc.)', *moí* 'to me (dat.)', and a number of sentence particles, such as Ancient Gk *té* 'and'. (In citing Ancient Greek enclitics in isolation, it is usual to mark them as if accented. Despite the use of the accent in all environments, such Ancient Greek particles as *gár* 'for, because' and connective *dé* have all the word-order properties expected of enclitics.) This sentence-second position for enclitics has come to be called, at least in IE studies, *Wackernagel's Law* after an early formulation of the regularity by Jacob Wackernagel (cf. Chapter 2, p. 70). In many instances the notion of sentence-second position is interpreted absolutely literally, so that an enclitic will, if appropriate, separate the constituents of a single phrase, as in Ancient Gk *hē gàr eiōthyĩá moi mantikḗ* ... (Plato, *Apologia* 40A) 'for the divination that is customary to me ...' Recent work on the behaviour of clitics cross-linguistically has established that second-position enclitics, including instances where this is interpreted literally as positioning after the first stressed word of the sentence, is widespread across the languages of the world (see, for instance, Klavans 1982).

Although recent discussions of PIE constituent order have concentrated primarily on the order of constituents, it is also worth commenting briefly on the order of morphemes within the word. The inflectional morphology of Proto-Indo-European, and still of most modern IE languages, is almost exclusively suffixing, that of nominals exclusively so. The only inflectional verbal prefixes are the augment and reduplication; the only infix in Proto-Indo-European is the present stem infix -*n*- of the verb, for example, *vincō* 'I conquer', compare perfect *vīcī* and past participle passive *victus*. This restriction of inflections to suffixes is also found in the Uralic (and Altaic) languages, and is in striking contrast to the frequent use of prefixes in reflectional morphology of the verb in Kartvelian and Semitic languages and to an even greater extent in the inflectional morphology of the North Caucasian languages. The derivational morphology of Proto-Indo-European is likewise primarily suffixing; suffixing derivational morphology is found virtually without exception in Turkic languages and also for the most part in Uralic languages. Prefixing in the early attested IE languages consists primarily of preverbs (i.e. adverbs that have been fused to the verb as prefixes, see **Word Classes**, pp. 79f.), in which case one is dealing etymologically more with compounding than with prefixing, and it is significant that in those Uralic languages that have widespread prefixing, such as Hungarian, the prefixing is likewise primarily of this kind, for example, *el-megy* 'go away', where *el-* is in origin an adverb meaning 'away'.

Agreement

One of the characteristics of the syntactic structure of the early IE languages is the extent to which the constituents of a multi-word phrase must agree. Within a noun phrase, adjectives (including attributive pronouns, such as demonstratives used attributively) must agree in gender, number and case with their head noun. (There is no agreement of a genitive with its head noun, a possibility found in a limited way in Kartvelian languages.) Agreement of adjectives with their head nouns is found in the Kartvelian and Semitic languages, though not in Turkic or, for the most part, Uralic languages, and indeed the Balto-Finnic branch of Uralic, which does have adjective agreement in noun phrases, is the branch of Uralic most subject to IE influence.

Within the clause, the finite verb must agree in person–number with its subject, while predicative adjectives must agree in gender, number and case with their subject. The major exception to this generalization is that finite verbs normally stand in the third-person singular (arguably the default form) when the subject is neuter plural in a number of early IE languages; however, this may simply reflect the fact that the neuter plural was originally a collective formation (analogous to the singular of *ā*-stems, i.e. *h_2-stems), rather than a true plural. (Agreement of predicative adjectives in case is most clearly visible when the subject is in some case other than the nominative, for example, with the accusative subject of an infinitive in Latin, as in *lēgem brevem esse oportet* 'it is fitting for a law to be brief' (Seneca,

Epistulae morales, 94.38)). As already noted in **Morphological Categories**, pp. 81f., agreement of the predicate with the subject is found in most other languages of the area, including Uralic, Turkic, Kartvelian, North Caucasian and Semitic, although some of these, in particular Kartvelian, North Caucasian and Semitic, also allow indexing in the verb of arguments other than the subject, a possibility not found in the early IE languages and not reconstructible for Proto-Indo-European.

In terms of the typological distinction between head marking and dependent marking introduced by Nichols (1986), Proto-Indo-European is overwhelmingly dependent marking: within the clause, the relation between predicate (head) and arguments (dependents) is shown primarily by case marking the arguments; within the noun phrase the relation between the head noun and its attributes (dependents) is shown primarily by having the dependents marked to show agreement with the head noun. Subject–predicate agreement is the only instance of head marking, since here the predicate (head) is marked to show agreement with one of its arguments (dependents). As noted by Nichols (1986: 75–6), cross-linguistically head marking at the clausal level is not unusual in languages that are otherwise basically dependent marking, and patterns similar to that found in Proto-Indo-European are also found in most Uralic, in Semitic and in Kartvelian languages.

In a sense, it is perhaps misleading to refer to this phenomenon as agreement in Proto-Indo-European and many IE languages, since it is typically possible to omit the subject whose person–number is indexed in the verb and the head noun whose gender, number and case are indexed in the attribute, if the omitted items are recoverable from the broader context, as when Latin first-person singular *amō* means 'I love', third-person singular *amat* means '(s)he loves', or masculine singular *bonus* means 'good man'. Furthermore, it is possible for the constituents of a noun phrase to be separated from one another, for instance for the attributive adjective to be separated from its head noun, as in Lat. *Catōnem vīdī in bibliothēcā sedentem multīs circumfūsum Stōicōrum librīs* (Cicero, *De finibus bonorum et malorum*, III.2, 7 (536)) 'I saw Cato sitting in a library, surrounded by many books of the Stoics', where *Catōnem, sedentem* and *circumfūsum* are all separated from one another and *multīs* is separated from *librīs*. On this basis, one might argue, following Hale's (1982) characterization of non-configurational languages, that in Proto-Indo-European and at least residually in some early IE languages, items in agreement do not really form a single constituent, but are rather distinct constituents in apposition, that is, *puer amat* is 'he, the boy, loves' rather than 'the boy loves', and *bonus puer* is 'the good one, the boy' rather than 'the good boy'. Over the recorded history of the IE languages, however, these possibilities for breaking up phrases in this way have decreased sharply, and the configurationality of most attested IE languages is hardly to be doubted.

Clause-structure Typology

At their earliest attestations, the various branches of the IE family show rather consistently nominative–accusative clause structure, with the same case (nominative) being used for both intransitive and transitive subjects, and a different case (accusative) being used for direct objects; verb agreement is consistently with the subject, whether transitive or intransitive. Attested deviations from nominate–accusative structure are of two kinds. First, some (originally) derivational forms have ergative–absolutive syntax in PIE languages, as in many other languages of the world, for example, the resultative participle in *-to-/*-no-, as in Skt gatá- 'having come' vs syūtá- (having been) sewn' (see Nedjalkov 1988 for the typological background). Second, forms based on such elements are quite likely to have ergative–absolutive syntax, such as the periphrastic perfect in Sanskrit.

There are, however, certain features of Proto-Indo-European that appear somewhat anomalous against the background of the nominative–accusative system, and these have led a number of investigators to propose recently that Proto-Indo-European at some stage had either ergative–absolutive or active–inactive clause structure (Gamkrelidze and Ivanov 1984: ch. 5). Perhaps the most striking piece of evidence is the existence of the nominative singular in *-s, occurring in many declensional classes but noticeably absent from neuter nouns (see **Morphological Categories**, pp. 83f.). However, even if it is accepted that the case-marking system of Proto-Indo-European was ergative–absolutive or active–inactive, it is important to note one phenomenon that has been noted repeatedly in the cross-linguistic study of case-marking systems in relation to clause structure: the case-marking system of a language does not necessarily mirror its clause-structure type (e.g. Anderson 1976). It is thus misleading to regard such terms as nominative–accusative, ergative–absolutive or active–inactive as providing uniform characterizations of the whole of a language's structure.

In the early IE languages, there is no direct evidence for inherited non-nominative–accusative clause structure. With respect to ergative–absolutive structure, as noted in **Morphological Categories**, pp. 83f. there are problems even in assuming an ergative–absolutive case-marking system for Proto-Indo-European. In languages with active–inactive case marking, nouns appear in the active when they denote the active participant in an event (e.g. *the man* in *the man hit the dog*, or *the man ran away*), in the inactive when they denote the inactive participant in an event (e.g. *the man* in *the dog bit the man*, *the man died*, or *the man is good*). Crucially, a given noun phrase as single argument of an intransitive predicate can appear in either the active or the inactive. This is not, however, found in the early IE languages; even though there are a few impersonal verbs that take a single non-nominative argument (e.g. Lat. *mē pudet* 'I am ashamed'), adjectives, which are the prime instances of inactive predicates, take nominative subjects. The direct evidence shows only that Proto-Indo-European had an opposition between more animate nouns (with nominative singular in *-s) and less animate nouns, but distinctions of this kind are widespread in languages with nominative–accusative clause structure (e.g. the Bantu languages) and languages with ergative–absolutive clause structure (e.g. the Australian language Dyirbal), having no necessary correlation with active–inactive clause structure. The evidence of the early IE languages points to nominative–accusative clause structure, and the reconstruction of active–inactive or ergative–absolutive clause structure or even case marking for Proto-Indo-European involves a high degree of speculation. In areal terms, nominative–accusative case marking and clause structure is shared with the Uralic and Semitic languages, and more distantly with the Altaic languages, while Caucasian languages typically have a high degee of ergative–absolutive or active–inactive structure in at least case marking or verb agreement.

Clause Combining

Although subordinate clauses, introduced by subordinating conjunctions, are the prime means of combining clauses into longer sentences in most of the modern IE languages, very few of these conjunctions can be reconstructed back to Proto-Indo-European (cf. **Word Classes**, p. 81). One recent study (Beekes 1990: 266–7) lists only a handful of derivatives of the relative pronoun (*jo- or *k^{w}o- according to dialect) plus the conditional *h$_1$ei 'if' (apparently the locative of an anaphoric pronoun), and it should be noted that no single reconstructed form is given for the relative pronoun (but see below on correlative relative clauses). It is thus highly plausible that Proto-Indo-European made relatively little use of finite subordinate clauses, preferring instead various non-finite constructions, which are richly reflected in the early IE languages.

Participial constructions serve readily as substitutes for many relative clauses, for instance substituting 'the man having fed the dog' for 'the man that fed the dog' and 'the man having been bitten by the dog' for 'the man that the dog bit'. The forms of the participles are clearly reconstructible back to the parent language (see **Morphological Categories**, p. 88). They can also serve in adverbial function, most obviously in cases where the subject of the adverbial construction is the same as that of the main clause, for example, substituting 'having fed the dog, the man went home' for 'when the man (had) fed the dog, he went home'; the appearance of special verbal adverb forms, such as the absolute participle in Sanskrit or the gerund in many Slavic languages, is a later development. However, a participle in the appropriate case can also be assigned to a noun in a case other than the nominative, thus substituting 'the dog bit the having-fed-it man' for 'the dog bit the man when he (had) fed it'. Finally, the existence of so-called absolute constructions permits the expression of such adverbial notions even where there are no coreferential noun phrases in the two clauses, as when 'the man having fed the dog (or: the dog having been fed by the man), the cat ran away' is substituted for 'when the man (had) fed the dog, the cat ran away'. Although different early IE languages differ in the case used in the absolute construction (locative in Sanskrit, genitive in Greek, ablative in Latin, dative in Gothic, Baltic and Slavic), the basic syntactic pattern is shared by all these languages and seems therefore reconstructible back to the parent language.

While no infinitive as such is reconstructible for Proto-Indo-European, the infinitives of individual languages represent specializations of case forms of action nominals that are reconstructible back to the proto-language (see **Morphological Categories**, p. 88). Occasionally more than one case form survives, as in the contrast in Old Church Slavic between the infinitive (e.g. *dělati* 'to do', deriving from a dative) and the supine (e.g. *dělat*, deriving from an accusative). Thus Proto-Indo-European had verbal nouns rather than an infinitive, the infinitives of the individual branches representing dialect-specific integrations of verbal nouns into the inflectional system (Disterheft 1980).

The widespread use of non-finite devices for combining clauses links Indo-European particularly closely typologically to the Uralic and Altaic languages. Nearly all attested Altaic languages make almost exclusive use of non-finite means for combining clauses (the few exceptions being under clear IE influence, for example, the use of the finite subordinating conjunction *ki* borrowed from Persian in Turkish and, especially, Azerbaijani). In Uralic, finite subordinating clauses occur primarily in those languages that have been under the longest influence from Indo-European, for instance Balto-Finnic (including Finnish), where they are none the less paralleled by a rich set of non-finite constructions that are used especially in more literary and archaic styles. There is, however, one difference between Indo-European on the one hand and Uralic and Altaic on the other. In comparison with the rich syntactic and semantic range of non-finite forms found in the Uralic and, especially, the Altaic languages, the early IE languages have a much more restricted set of oppositions among non-finite verb forms, and there is no reason to suppose the Proto-Indo-European had a system that was much richer than this (given that the early attested languages have non-finite verb systems very close to one another).

One kind of finite subordinate-like construction that Proto-Indo-European, on the evidence of the early IE languages, may well have had is the correlative construction, in particular as a way of expressing relative clauses, as in constructions of the type 'who/which man feeds the dog, he/the man is good' for 'he/the man who feeds the dog is good'. The richer set of subordinating conjunctions and subordinate clauses found in even the early IE languages plausibly reflects a further development of this kind of construction, whence the close formal links between many subordinating constructions and the relative pronoun (see further Haudry 1973).

References

Anderson, Stephen R. (1976) 'On the notion of subject in ergative languages', in Charles N. Li (ed.), *Subject and Topic*, New York: Academic Press, pp. 1–23.

Beekes, R. S. P. (1990) *Vergelijkende taalwetenschap: een inleiding in de vergelijkende Indo-europese taalwetenschap* (Aula Paperback 176), Utrecht: Het Spectrum. (English translation: Robert S. P. Beekes, *Comparative Indo-European Linguistics: An Introduction*, Amsterdam: John Benjamins, 1995.)

Comrie, Bernard (1976) *Aspect* (Cambridge Textbooks in Linguistics), Cambridge: Cambridge University Press.

—— (1990) 'The typology of tense–aspect systems in European languages', *Lingua e stile* 25: 209–18.

—— (1993) 'Typology and reconstruction', in Charles Jones (ed.), *Historical Linguistics: Problems and Perspectives*, London: Longman, pp. 74–97.

—— (1994) 'Was Proto-Indo-European ergative?', *Bulletin of the Language Institute of Gakushuin University* 17: 3–14.

Disterheft, Dorothy (1980) *The Syntactic Development of the Infinitive in Indo-European*, Columbus, Oh.: Slavica.

Friedrich, Paul (1975) *Proto-Indo-European Syntax* (Journal of Indo-European Studies, Monograph 1), Butte, Mont.: Journal of Indo-European Studies.

Gamkrelidze, Tamaz V. and Ivanov, Vjačeslav V. (1984) *Indoevropejskij jazyk i Indoevropejcy*, 2 vols, Tbilisi: Izd-vo Tbilisskogo Universiteta. (English translation: Thomas V. Gamkrelidze and Vjačeslav V. Ivanov, *Indo-European and the Indo-Europeans*, 2 vols, Berlin: Mouton de Gruyter, 1994–5.)

Gamqreliʒe, Tamaz (= Gamkrelidze, T. V.) and Mačavariani, Givi (= Mačavariani, G. I.) (1965) *Sonantta sistema da ablauti kartvelur enebši*, Tbilisi: 'Mecniereba'; (includes Russian résumé; German translation, primarily of the résumé: T. V. Gamkrelidze and G. I. Mačavariani, *Sonantensystem und Ablaut in den Kartwelsprachen*, Tübingen: Gunter Narr, 1982.)

Greenberg, Joseph H. (1966) 'Some universals of grammar with particular reference to the order of meaningful elements', in Joseph H. Greenberg (ed.), *Universals of Language*, 2nd edn, Cambridge, Mass.: MIT Press, pp. 73–113.

—— (forthcoming) *Indo-European and its Closest Relatives: The Eurasiatic Language Family*, Stanford, Calif.: Stanford University Press.

Hale, Kenneth (1982) 'Preliminary remarks on configurationality', *North-Eastern Linguistic Society* 12: 86–96.

Harris, Alice C. (1990) 'Alignment typology and diachronic change', in Winfred P. Lehmann (ed.), *Language Typology 1987: Systematic Balance in Language*, Amsterdam: John Benjamins, pp. 67–90.

Haudry, Jean (1973) 'Parataxe, hypotaxe et corrélation dans la phrase latine', *Bulletin de la Société de Linguistique de Paris* 68(1): 147–86.

Hewitt, B. G. (1981) 'Caucasian languages', in Bernard Comrie (ed.), *The Languages of the Soviet Union*, Cambridge: Cambridge University Press, pp. 196–237.

Illič-Svityč, V. M. (1971–84) *Opyt sravnenija nostratičeskix jazykov*, 3 vols, Moscow: Nauka.

Klaiman, M. H. (1991) *Grammatical Voice*, Cambridge: Cambridge University Press.

Klavans, Judith L. (1982) *Some Problems in a Theory of Clitics*, Bloomington, Ind.: Indiana University Linguistics Club.

Kuryłowicz, Jerzy (1964) *The Inflectional Categories of Indo-European*, Heidelberg: Carl Winter.

Lehmann, Winfred P. (1974) *Proto-Indo-European Syntax*. Austin, Tex.: University of Texas Press.

Nedjalkov, V. P. (ed.) (1988) *Typology of Resultative Constructions* (Typological Studies in Language 12), Amsterdam: John Benjamins. (Translation and revision of V. P. Nedjalkov (ed.), *Tipologija rezul'tativnyx konstrukcij*, Leningrad: 'Nauka' 1983.)

Nichols, Johanna (1986) 'Head-marking and dependent-marking grammar', *Language* 62: 56–119.

Silverstein, Michael (1976) 'Hierarchies of features and ergativity', in R. M. W. Dixon (ed.), *Grammatical Categories in Australian Languages*, Canberra: Australian Institute of Aboriginal Studies, pp. 112–71.

Stewart, John M. (1989) 'Kwa', in John Bendor-Samuel (ed.), *The Niger-Congo Languages*, Lanham, Md.: University Press of America, pp. 217–45.

Szemerényi, Oswald (1989) *Einführung in die vergleichende Sprachwissenschaft*, 3rd edn, Darmstadt: Wissenschaftliche Buchgesellschaft. (English translation: Szemérenyi, Oswald, *Introduction to Indo-European Linguistics*, Oxford: Clarendon Press, 1996.)

Ultan, Russell (1978) 'The nature of future tenses', in Joseph H. Greenberg, Charles A. Ferguson and Edith A. Moravcsik (eds), *Universals of Human Language*, vol. 3, *Word Structure*, Stanford, Calif.: Stanford University Press, pp. 83–123.

Watkins, Calvert (1976) 'Towards Proto-Indo-European syntax: problems and pseudo-problems', in Sanford B. Steever, Carol A. Walker and Salikoko S. Mufwene (eds), *Papers from the Parasession on Diachronic Syntax*, Chicago: Chicago Linguistic Society, pp. 305–26.

4 Sanskrit

Romano Lazzeroni

The *Aryan* group of IE languages consists of Sanskrit and the other IE dialects of India, Iranian and the Kafir languages of North-west India. The original homeland of the Indians, or rather of the IE tribes who had penetrated into India, can be traced to a region outside India, north-west of India itself. From here, probably around the middle of the second millennium BC, the forebears of the Indians moved into India, conquering the non-IE native peoples. These peoples had a flourishing civilization, the so-called 'Indus Valley civilization', whose most important archaeological remains have been recovered by the excavation of Mohenjo-daro and Harappa (Thumb and Hauschild 1958).

The *Aryans* are the only IE peoples of whom linguistic traces remain outside their historical homelands, in Asia Minor and Mesopotamia. The Hurrian kingdom of the Mitanni was dominated by an Aryan aristocracy which reached the greatest extent of its power in the first half of the second millennium BC. The rulers of the Mitanni had names with a clear Aryan stamp; moreover, in a treaty, written in Akkadian, between the Hittite king Suppiluliuma and the Mitanni king Mattiwaza, the guarantors of the oath are named as Mitra, Varuṇa, Indra and Nāsatya. The first three deities are part of the Indian pantheon; in the Vedic hymns, the name of the fourth is an epithet of the twin deities, the Aśvins. Finally, in a text about horse rearing written in Hittite by the Mitanni Kikkuli, a handful of numerals and horsemanship terms are of Indian derivation: *aika* 'one' (Skt *eka-*), *panza* 'five' (Skt *pañca*), and so on. These numerals appear in compounds with the noun *wartanna* (Skt *vartana-*) 'circle, ring' (Mayrhofer 1974).

Figure 4.1, taken from *Les Langues du monde* by A. Meillet and M. Cohen, shows the extent of the kingdom of the Mitanni.

The Aryan linguistic remains outside India resemble Sanskrit more than Iranian, compare *aika* 'one' beside Skt *eka-* but Iran. **aiwa-* (Avest. *aēwa-*, OPers. *aiva-*). Nor are there traces of Iranian phonetic features: *-s-* is preserved as in Sanskrit, while in Iranian it becomes an aspirate; the cluster *-sw-* becomes *-sv-* as in Sanskrit, while in Iranian it becomes *-sp-*.

Sanskrit and Iranian share a large number of common features, both linguistic and cultural. On the basis of these features it is usual to speak of an 'Indo-Iranian unity'. The vocabulary is largely shared (even the ethnic name *Aryan*); the nominal declension and verbal flexion are structured almost identically;

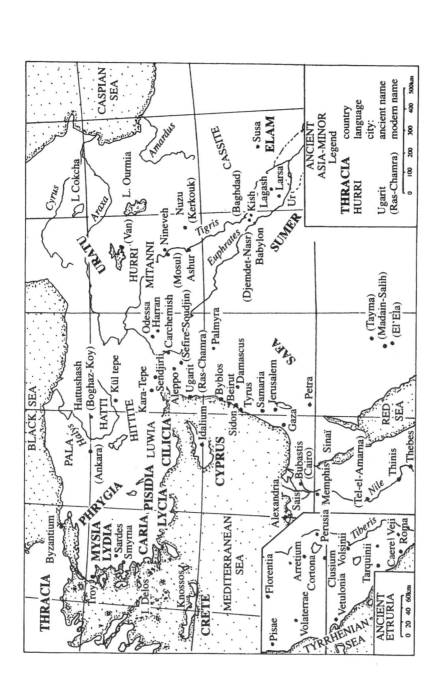

Map 4.1 Ancient Asia-Minor
Source: A. Meillet and M. Cohen, *Les Langues du monde*, 1959

as regards sound changes, $*\breve{e}$, $*\breve{o}$, $*\breve{a} > *\breve{a}$; $*m$, $*n > a$; $*s > \acute{s}$ when preceded by i, r, u, k (in Sanskrit we have s, where the retroflexion is due to a subsequent development); $*\partial > i$; the IE pure velars and labiovelars develop in one way before i and before $a < *e$ and in a different way elsewhere (see p. 105); $*l > r$. Common to Sanskrit and Iranian is Bartholomae's Law, according to which a voiced aspirate stop followed by a voiceless stop is replaced by a cluster consisting of a voiced stop followed by a voiced aspirate: $*bud^h\text{-}tas$ 'enlighted, awakened' $> buddhas$, whence the name *Buddha*.

Nevertheless, there are important differences between Sanskrit and Iranian: in Iranian $*(\text{-})s\text{-}$ becomes $(\text{-})h\text{-}$ as in Greek and Armenian, while in Sanskrit it is preserved; in Sanskrit the voiced aspirates $*b^h$, $*d^h$, $*g^h$ remain as such, while in Iranian they lose their aspiration as in Slavic and several other IE languages; in Sanskrit – probably through the influence of a non-Aryan substratum – there appears a series of retroflex phonemes (t, th, d, dh, n, s) which do not exist in Iranian (see Chapter 5, pp. 125f.).

Some of these unitarian features are not in fact such, or are only partially so when their geographical distribution is taken into account: $l > r$ is common to Iranian and the ancient dialects of western India (those from which Vedic developed) but is less pronounced in central India, and in eastern India precisely the opposite development ($r > l$) takes place.

An examination of the relative chronology of shared and divergent features shows that the former are older than the latter. In addition, as we have seen, some of the features specific to Iranian also occur in the languages of the central IE group, for example in the Slavic languages, and in Greek and Armenian.

This shows that the so-called Indo-Iranian unity is the result of a complex process of development which may be summarized as follows:

1   Sanskrit and Iranian derive from a substantially uniform IE tradition. There was a period of extensive contact between the two languages during which the common features developed, probably spreading out from an epicentre situated to the west of India. This is indicated, for example, by the geographical distribution of $l > r$.

2   There subsequently occurred a process of fragmentation, as a result of which Sanskrit split off and developed a set of features of its own, while Iranian began moving (or continued moving) towards central Indo-European areas and underwent a series of shared innovations with them.

The model is one of a linguistic and cultural community (rather than a complete unity as such) which at a certain point broke up.

One confirmation of this comes from the vocabulary: the Indian word for 'god' (*deva-*) corresponds to the Iranian word for 'demon' (*daēva-*); Indra is a god in the Indian world and a demon in the Iranian world; on the other hand, the Iranian word for the deity (Avest. *baγa-*) is also shared by the Slavic languages (OCS *bogŭ*, Russ. *bog*).

The transposition of the names of deities into names of demons is typical of a change of religion. In the same way the pagan gods became demons in popular Christian tradition: the gods of the old religion came to be the demons of the new. It was no doubt the rise of Zoroastrianism in the Iranian world that occasioned the linguistic and cultural split between the Iranian and Indian areas (Lazzeroni 1968).

The Aryan dialects of India in the historical territories (i.e. leaving aside the Indian linguistic remains in Asia Minor) may be divided up as follows:

Vedic

This is the literary language of the Vedic tradition (the oldest document, the RigVeda 'Veda of the Chants', goes back to around 1000 BC) and may be divided into Early and Later Vedic. The difference is not so much diachronic as diatropic and diastratic. Early Vedic (essentially the language of the oldest parts of the RigVeda) was based on a western dialect; in Later Vedic (recorded in the less ancient parts of the RigVeda, in the Atharva Veda and the rest of Vedic literature) there were more features deriving from central dialects. These features were also present in Early Vedic, but occurred less frequently.

According to the popular interpretation, the ancient RigVeda is a collection of hymns composed in the western regions of India – and some outside India itself – before the Indians moved eastwards; the works regarded as Later Vedic, on the other hand, are believed to have been composed after the Indian expansion towards the centre of the peninsula. This theory fails to take account of the following information:

1   Some texts classed as 'Later Vedic', for example, some of the hymns in the Atharva Veda, are in fact very ancient, probably of IE ancestry.
2   Central dialect features are also present in the oldest parts of the Rig-Veda.
3   The same central features are, from the IE point of view, conservative features and some show popular characteristics.
4   As well as the linguistic difference between Early and Later Vedic there is a difference in content: the eulogistic hymns are ancient in character, while the exorcising, magic, speculative and philosophical hymns have a more recent stamp. The diatopic difference is thus reduced to a diastratic one: the eulogistic hymns belong to a 'high' variety of the language, permeated by (innovative) features originating in those western dialects where the genre developed; the other compositions – less tied to the eulogistic tradition – are more open to the non-western (conservative) elements of the spoken language (Renou 1957; Lazzeroni 1985).

Sanskrit

This is the language of the classical literature of India, heavily formalized and standardized (*saṃskṛta-* 'perfected'). What we call Classical Sanskrit is the language codified by Pāṇini, the most famous of the Indian grammarians (fifth to fourth centuries BC). The basis of Sanskrit is a dialect of the central region of India (*Madhyadeśa*) and Sanskrit thus shares many features with Later Vedic.

The differences between Vedic and Sanskrit are of two sorts:

1   on the one hand, Vedic preserves very ancient IE features which are absent in Sanskrit, for example, the injunctive and subjunctive, some of the verb endings, the infinitive expressed with a noun of action declined according to its syntactic function;
2   on the other hand, Vedic exhibits a series of innovations where Sanskrit has contrasting conservative forms:

> the *-a-* stem nominative plural *-āsas* (Sanskrit has *-ās* < *-ōs*);
> the *-a-* stem instrumental plural *-ebhis* (Sanskrit has *-ais* < *-ōjs*);
> the first-person plural active ending *-masi* (Sanskrit has *-mas* < *-me/os*, cf. Dor. Gk *-mes*, Lat. *-mus*).

These innovations, also shared by Iranian, go back to a period of Indo-Iranian linguistic and cultural contact. The 'Indo-Iranian unity', then, increasingly appears to be the product of a Vedic and Iranian cultural community.

The Prākrits

These belong to the Middle Indian tradition (300 BC to AD 200); they do not derive from Sanskrit in the same way that the Romance languages derive from Latin, but rather from a parallel tradition going back to the Vedic period. Indeed, some innovative features are shared by Vedic and the Prākrits but not by Sanskrit, for example, the *-a-* stem nominative plural *-āsas* and dative plural *-ebhis*. However, the Prākrits do not go back directly to the dialect which formed the basis of Vedic, but rather to a parallel tradition (the so-called Vedic Prākrits): indeed, some features of the Prākrits are shared by other IE languages but not by Vedic, for example, Prākrit *tārisa-* 'such a', Gk *tēlíkos*, Lat. *tālis*. The most important of the ancient Prākrits is Pāli ('rule, canon'), the language of the canon of the Buddhist faith.

The inscriptions of Aśoka (272–231 BC) are written in a language similar to Pāli. The Prākrits are literary languages, handed down through poetry and drama. The modern Aryan dialects of India go back to the spoken dialects on which the Prākrits were based (Pischel 1965; Grierson 1967).

Figure 4.2 shows the linguistic situation in India today (the white areas represent those parts occupied by non-IE (Dravidian or Muṇḍa languages).

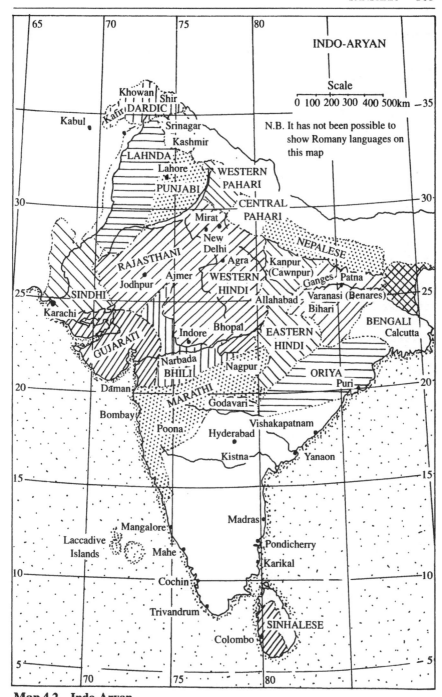

Map 4.2   Indo-Aryan
Source: A. Meillet and M. Cohen, *Les Langues du monde*, 1959

Sanskrit Phonology

The principal change in the Sanskrit vowel system with respect to that of Indo-European is the reduction of the three IE vowels ĕ, ŏ, ă to the single quality ă:

Skt *asti* > **esti*, Lat. *est*
Skt *rājan-* 'king' < **rēĝ-*, Lat. *rēx*
Skt *pati-* 'lord, master' < **poti-*, Lat. *potis*
Skt. *vāk* 'word' < **wōkʷs*, Lat. *vōx*
Skt *akṣa* 'axle' < **akso-*, Lat. *axis*
Skt *bhrātar-* 'brother' < **bʰrátēr-*, Lat. *frāter.*

The qualities of the first elements of the diphthongs merged (**ej, *oj, *aj* > **aj; *ew, *ow, *aw* > **aw*) and these then monophthongized (**aj* > *e*; **aw* > *o*):

Skt *eti* 'goes' < **ejti*, Gk *eîsi*
Skt *veda* 'I know' < **wojda*, Gk *(w)oîda*
Skt *edhas-* 'firewood' < **ajdʰos-*, Gk *aíthos*, Lat. *aedes*
Skt *bodhati* 'he is awake' < **bʰewdʰeti*, Gk *peýthomai*
Skt *loka-* 'free space' < **lowko-*, OLat. *loukom* (acc.)
Skt *ojas-* 'strength' < **awĝos-*, Lat. *augeo.*

The long diphthongs shortened their first elements and became *ai, au*:

Skt *vṛkais* (inst. pl. of *vṛka-* 'wolf') < **wḷkʷōjs*, Gk *lýkois* (dat. pl.)
Skt *dyaus* 'heaven' < **djews*, Gk *Zeús*
Skt *naus* 'ship' < **nāws*, Gk *naús*, Lat. *nāvis.*

Indo-European schwa (*ə*) became *i* in all positions:

Skt *pitar-* 'father' < **pəter-*, Lat. *pater*
Skt *sthiti* 'standing' < **stəti-*, Lat. *statio.*

For a discussion of the so-called 'laryngeals', see Chapter 2, pp. 40f.
    The final outcome was that the IE vowel triangle

/i(ː)/   /(uː)/
        /e(ː)/   /o(ː)/
                /a(ː)/

in which the long vowel and short vowel systems were symmetrical, split up into two asymmetrical triangles:

			/iː/			/uː/		/i/	/u/

/eː/   /oː/

/aː/   /a/

The long vowel system contained /eː/ and /oː/, but for these vowels length was not phonologically relevant, because they did not contrast with the corresponding short vowels. They can also be represented as morphophonological variants of the bi-phonemic clusters *ai* and *au*.

Sanskrit preserves the IE liquid sonant *r̥*, with which *l̥* also merges:

Skt *mr̥tyu-* 'death' < **mr̥t-*, Lat. *mors*
Skt *pitr̥su* (loc. pl. of *pitar-* 'father') < **pətr̥su*, Gk *patrási* (dat. pl.)
Skt *pr̥thu-* 'broad' < **pl̥tu-*, Gk *platýs*
Skt *vr̥ka-* 'wolf' < *wl̥kʷo-*, Goth. *wulfs*.

The IE nasal sonants *m̥* and *n̥* become *a*:

Skt *sapta* 'seven' < **septm̥*, Lat. *septem*
Skt *mati-* 'thought' < **mn̥ti-*, Lat. *mens*.

In the consonant system the most important changes involve the system of the velars. The reflexes of the IE pure velars and the labiovelars are identical. These are represented below.

Table 4.1   Reflexes of Indo-European velars and labiovelars

			A	B
*k,	**kʷ*	>	c	k
*g,	**gʷ*	>	j	g
*gʰ,	**gʷʰ*	>	h	gh

Column A in Table 4.1 represents the development before **i* and before *a* < **e*; column B the development in all other positions. The IE palatals *k̂*, *ĝ*, *ĝʰ* became *ś*, *j*, *h* respectively. Thus the non-conditioned reflexes of the voiced and voiced aspirated palatals fell together with the conditioned (A) reflexes of the corresponding labiovelars and the voiced and voiced aspirated pure velars (cf. the Iranian developments, Chapter 5, pp. 132f.).

k̂: Skt *daśa* < **dek̂m̥*, Lat. *decem*
k̂ʷ: Skt *cit* < **kʷid*, Lat. *quid*: Skt *ca* < **kʷe*, Lat. *-que*, but Skt *kas* < **kʷos*, Lat. *quo-d*
ĝ: Skt *juṣṭa-* 'pleasing' < **ĝusto-*, Lat. *gustus*
g/gʷ: Skt *yuga-* < **jugo-*, Lat. *iugum*, but *jīva* 'alive' < **gʷīwo-*, Lat. *vīvus*

ĝʰ: Skt *lehmi* 'I lick' < **lejĝʰmi*, Gk *leíkhō*

gʷʰ: Skt *hanti* 'he kills' < **gʷʰenti*, Gk *theínō*, but *ghnanti* 'they kill' < **gʷʰnonti*, Gk *é-pe-phn-o-n*

In a prehistoric stage of Sanskrit, the IE velars and labiovelars thus had two combinatory variants. For example, before **e* became *a*, the alternation between *k* and *c* was governed by the phonetic environment. When **e* became *a*, one of the conditions for the automatic selection of *c* was lost and so the two allophones became phonologized.

The discovery of the rule governing the development of the velars (the Law of Palatals) was of great importance in the history of comparative linguistics because it made it possible to take the vowel *e* back to a prehistoric stage of Sanskrit and therefore to the IE vowel system. Thus there was proof that the IE vowel system was better preserved in the western languages (e.g. Greek and Latin) than in Sanskrit. Until the discovery of the Law of Palatals the IE vowel system had been reconstructed on the basis of that of Sanskrit, with the postulation of an original vowel *a* which had 'split' into *e, a, o* in the western languages.

Also characteristic of the Sanskrit consonant system are the retroflex consonants *ṭ, ṭh, ḍ, ḍh, ṇ, ṣ*. These are sometimes combinatory variants: for example, *n > ṇ* if preceded, even at some distance, by *r* or *ṣ*: *nagarāṇi*, nominative plural of *nagara-* 'city' (but *phalāni*, nom. pl. of *phala-* 'fruit'). Thus *r*, which has the same effect as *ṣ*, must also have had a retroflex articulation. Frequently, however, these retroflex consonants are not conditioned by the phonetic environment and have phonemic status. It is probable that they were, at least in part, due to borrowings from the Prākrits (where *r* can be lost, causing the retroflection of a following dental), or to the influence of the pre-IE substrata in India (Gonda 1971).

The consonant system of Sanskrit is given in Table 4.2. The forms in square brackets have a limited distribution: *ṅ* occurs as a phoneme only in final

Table 4.2 The consonant system of Sanskrit

	Occlusive Voiceless	Voiced	Nasal	Semi-vowel	Liquid/vibrant	Fricative Voiceless	Voiced
Pharyngeal						[ḥ]	h
Velar	k kh	g gh	[ṅ]				
Palatal	c ch	j jh	[ñ]	y		ś	
Retroflex	ṭ ṭh	ḍ ḍh	ṇ		r	ṣ	
Dental	t th	d dh	n		l	s	
Labiodental				v			
Labial	p ph	b bh	m [ṃ]				

position and is otherwise a combinatory variant of the nasal before velar phonemes; *h* is a combinatory variant of *s* in absolute final position or when followed by a word with initial voiceless dental, labial, velar, and so on.

We have reliable information on accentuation only in the case of Vedic: in the Vedic texts the accent is represented by a special system of diacritics. At this period the accent was predominantly musical; it was not restricted to a particular position and essentially corresponded to that of the IE accent, as shown by comparison with Greek, and with Germanic in cases where Verner's Law operates: Ved. *dhūmás*, Gk *thȳmós*: Ved. *pádam* (acc.), Gk *póda* (acc.); Ved. *padás* (gen.), Gk *podós* (gen.); Ved. *pitá̄*, Gk *patḗr*, Goth. *fadar*; Ved. *bhrá̄tā*, Gk *phrá̄tēr*, Goth. *brōþar* (cf. Chapter 13, pp. 394f.). The present-day pronunciation of Sanskrit specifies an expiratory accent governed by a sort of 'law of penultimates' as in Latin. It is probable that this type of accentuation goes back to the classical age (Wackernagel 1896).

A prominent characteristic of Sanskrit phonetics is *sandhi* ('composition'), that is, the set of rules governing the modification of word endings in relation to the following word. For example, *-as* > *-o* when the following word begins with a voiced consonant: *Caṇḍaravo nāma* 'Caṇḍaravas by name' = *Caṇḍaravas nāma*; *-e*, *-o* > *-a* if the following word begins with a vowel other than *a*: *nagara iha* 'here, in the city' = *nagare* (loc.) *iha*, and so on (Allen 1962).

Morphology

The nominal morphology exhibits many archaic features. For example, the three numbers (singular, dual and plural) and eight cases (nominative, vocative, accusative, genitive, dative, ablative, locative, instrumental) are preserved. The system of three grammatical genders is the result of an innovation, the creation of the feminine, which had taken place in late Indo-European: previously the basic opposition had been between the animate gender (without a distinction between masculine and feminine) and the neuter gender (cf. the discussion in Chapter 7, p. 177). In the development of this innovation Sanskrit has gone further than other IE languages such as Greek and Latin. In Latin and Greek, nouns in *-o* and *-ā* may be either masculine or feminine; this represents a relic of the system which preceded the introduction of the feminine. In Sanskrit, however, the contrast between masculine and feminine has been fully generalized: all nouns in *-a-* (< *-o-*) are masculine and all nouns in *-ā-* (< *-ā-*) feminine. Because of the merger of the vowel qualities, the quantitative opposition has thus become a distinctive character-istic of the gender contrast. Consequently, the whole vowel-stem declension has been reorganized around this contrast. It is because of this that feminine nouns in *-i-* have, alongside the inherited forms (which are the same as those of the masculine), forms taken from the feminines in *-ī*: feminine *matis* 'thought', genitive *mates* (like masculine *agnis* 'fire', genitive *agnes*) but also *matyās* (like *devyās*, genitive of feminine *devī* 'goddess').

Table 4.3   Nominal stems in -a-

	Singular	Dual	Plural
Nom.	devaḥ	devau	devāḥ
Voc.	deva	devau	devāḥ
Acc.	devam	devau	devān
Gen.	devasya	devayoḥ	devānām
Dat.	devāya	devābhyām	devebhyaḥ
Abl.	devāt	devābhyām	devebhyaḥ
Loc.	deve	devayoḥ	deveṣu
Instr.	devena	devābhyām	devaiḥ

Indo-European nominal derivation is well preserved in Sanskrit: still productive are the agent nouns in *-tar* (Gk *-tēr/-tōr*), verbal abstracts in *-es-/-os-* (Skt *janas* 'race, descent', Gk *génos*, Lat. *genus*), nouns of action in *-ti-* (Skt *matis* 'thought' < **mṇtis*, Lat. *mens*), heteroclitic nouns in *-r-/-n-*; adjectives in *-ro-* (> Skt *-ra-*), and so on. Table 4.3 shows the paradigm of a noun in *-a-* (< **-o-*): *devas* 'god'.
Note the following:

Singular
nom. *devas* < **dejwos* (Gk *híppos*, Lat. *lupus*)
acc. *devam* < **dejwom* (Gk *híppon*, Lat. *lupum*)
gen. *devasya* < **dejwosjo* (Gk *híppoio*, OLat. *Valesiosio*)
dat. *devāya* < **dejwoj* (Gk *híppōi*, Lat. *lupō* < *lupōi*; Skt *-a* is due to an unexplained Indo-Iranian innovation)
abl. *devāt* < **dejwōd* (OLat. *meritod*)
loc. *deve* < **dejwoi* (Gk. *oíkoi* 'at home', Lat. *domi* < **domoi*)

Plural
nom. *devās* < **dejwōs* (Goth. *wulfos* 'wolves', Osc. *Núvlanús* 'the Nolāni, inhabitants of Nola' with ‹ú› = /0/)
acc. *devān* < **dejwons* (Gk *híppous*, Lat. *lupos* < *-ons*; the Skt long vowel is the result of an innovation)
gen. *devānām* < **dejwōnōm* (the IE reconstructed form is **dejwōm*: OLat. *Romanom*, Gk. *híppōn*, Ved. *devām*; *-ānām* is an Indo-Iranian innovation)
dat./abl. *devebhyas* < **dejwobʰjos* (the IE form can be reconstructed as **dejwobʰos*: Skt *-oi-* is of pronominal origin; the **-bʰjos* form of the morpheme – for **bʰos* (Lat. *-bus*) – is obscure)
loc. *deveṣu* < **dejwojsu* (Gk. *híppoisi* (dat.), with different final vowel)
instr. *devais* < **dejwōjs* (Gk. *híppois* (dat.) Lat. *lupis* < *-ōis*)

Dual
nom./acc./voc. *devau* < **dejwōu* (in Vedic we also have *devā* < **dejwō*, Gk

Table 4.4   Nominal stems in -*n*-

	Singular	*Dual*	*Plural*
Nom.	rājā	rājānau	rājānaḥ
Voc.	rājan	rājānau	rājānaḥ
Acc.	rājānam	rājānau	rājñaḥ
Gen.	rājñaḥ	rājñoḥ	rājñām
Dat.	rājñe	rājabhyām	rājabhyaḥ
Abl.	rājñaḥ	rājabhyām	rājabhyaḥ
Loc.	rājani, rājñi	rājñoḥ	rājasu
Instr.	rājñā	rājabhyām	rajabhiḥ

híppō; the polymorphism -*ō*/-*ōu* probably originated in IE phonotactic variants)

Table 4.4 shows the paradigm of a masculine -*n*- stem: *rājan*- 'king'. The stem shows alternation between the full grade *rājan*- (< *rêĝen-*)/*rājān*- (< *rêĝon-*) and a reduced grade which, depending on phonotactic conditions, appears as *rājñ*- (< *rêĝn-*) or *rāja*- (< *rêĝn̥-*). As regards the endings, we note the following:

Singular
gen. -*as* < *-*es*/-*os* (Lat. *rēgis* < *rēg-es*; Gk *pod-ós*); dat. -*e* < *-*ei* (OLat. *virtutei*, Cypriot Gk *Diweí-philos*)

Plural
nom. -*as* < *-*es* (Gk. *pódes*); acc. -*as* < *-*n̥s* (Lat. *pedes* < *pedens* < *pedn̥s*); instr. -*bhis* < *bʰis* (Hom., Myc. Gk -*phi*)

The adjectives follow the noun flection, as in Indo-European. Adjectives with two endings have an opposition between the animate and neuter genders; these are the vestiges of a period when the opposition between masculine and feminine was not expressed at the grammatical level. Adjectives with three endings distinguish masculine, feminine and neuter; when the masculine is in -*a*- (< *-*o*-) the feminine regularly shows -*ā*- (Lat. *bonus*/*bona*; Gk *mikrós*/ *mikrá*; Skt *pāpas*/*pāpā* 'bad' (m./f.). Otherwise the feminine is formed with the suffix -*ī*: *uru*-/*urvī* 'broad'.

Extremely archaic are the several instances of suffixal suppletion where the masculine in -*van* contrasts with the feminine in -*varī*: *pīvan*-/*pīvarī* 'fat', Gk *pī̆(w)ōn*/*pí(w)eira*.

The comparative is the synthetic type, formed with the suffix -*iyas*- (Lat. -*ios*- in accusative singular *mel-ior-em* 'better', Gk nominative plural *beltíous* 'better' < *belt-jos-es*) added to the full grade root: *ugras* 'mighty', comp. *ojīyas*-; *dūras* 'far', comp. *davīyas*-. Another comparative suffix is -*tara*- (Gk

-tero-) added to the adjectival stem: *dūra-taras* 'further'. The corresponding superlative suffixes are *-istha* (Gk. *-isto-*) and *-tama* (< *-tomo*, Lat. *optimus* < *op-tomos*).

In Indo-European the two types were functionally distinct, and in some cases this is still perceptible in Sanskrit and Greek: *-tero-* and *-tomo-* indicate a separative-spatial value, *-jos-* and *-istos* a qualitative-dimensional value (Benveniste 1948).

With respect to the noun system, the pronouns exhibit the following IE characteristics:

1. frequent suppletion of the stem (*aham* 'I', acc. *mām*, Gk *egó(n)*, gen. *emoû*; Lat. *ego*, gen. *mei*)
2. in some cases, a special set of endings, different from those of the nouns (n. nom. sing. *ta-t* 'that', Lat. *istu-d*, Gk *tó* < *to-d* beside Skt *yuga-m*, Gk *zygó-n*, Lat. *iugu-m*)
3. infixed elements (Skt acc. *ta-m* 'that', abl. *ta-sm-āt* beside *deva-m*, *devā-t*
4. scope for expansion by using particles (Gk *hoûtos* and *houtos-í* 'this'); some of these are reanalysed as inseparable parts of the pronoun: Lat. *id-em*, gen. *eius-dem*, Skt *id-am* (n. nom.-acc. sg.)

The most common demonstrative pronouns are: m. *ayam*, f. *iyam*, n. *idam* 'this'; m. *asau*, f. *asau*, n. *adam* 'that'; *sa*, *sā*, *tat*, corresponding to the Greek article (and pronoun) *ho*, *hē*, *tó*, is the anaphoric pronoun, also used as a personal pronoun, usually in the third person, but also in the second person:

sá no mṛla mahấṅ asi
you to-us propitious great are
'you are propitious to us, you are great'

(RigVeda, I, 36, 12)

As a noun determiner in the noun phrase, the anaphoric pronoun also came to develop the meaning of an article (Renou 1961).

It is not possible here to take account of all the pronominal forms. We mention only some of the forms of *sa*, *sā*, *tat*: nominative = Gk *ho*, *hē*, *tó*; masculine accusative *tam*, feminine accusative *tām*, Gk *tón*, *tén*; masculine genitive *tasya*, Gk *toîo*; plural: masculine nominative *te*, Hom. Dor. Gk *toí*; masculine instrumental *tais*, Gk (dat.) *toîs*; feminine genitive *tāsām*, Gk *tôn* < *tāōn*: masculine locative *teṣu*, Hom. Ion. Gk *toî si* (dat.). In the masculine singular dative, ablative and locative there appears an infix *-sm-* which recurs in various other languages, for example, Gothic dative *þamma*, and so on.

The interrogative pronoun is formed from the IE interrogative-indefinite stem *k^wo-/k^we-*, *k^wi-*: masculine *kas*, feminine *kā*, neuter *kim* (and *kat*). The flection is as for *sa*. The form *ka-* continues the strong grade of the stem,

*k^wo-. According to p. 105, *k^we- and *k^wi- ought to give *ca*- and *ci*-. These forms have been lost from the paradigm but survive in the particles *cana*- and *cit*. These, when added to the interrogative, form the indefinite: *kas* 'who', but *kas cit* 'someone'. The form *cit* corresponds etymologically to Lat. *quid* and Gk *tí* < *k^wid and is thus the old nominative case of the neuter singular of the interrogative pronoun. The Sanskrit indefinite pronoun is formed, then, by repeating the stem of the interrogative. This is an IE principle of formation: the Latin indefinite *quisquis* 'whoever, anyone' is formed by means of repetition of the interrogative *quis* 'who'.

The relative pronoun is *yas* (f. *yā*, n. *yat*), cf. Gk *hós*, *hḗ*, *hó* (< *yos, *$yā$, *yod).

The cardinal numerals from one to four are declined for all three genders: masculine *trayas*, feminine *tisras* neuter *trīṇi* 'three'. Those from five to ten are also declinable, but without distinction of gender: *pañca* 'five', instrumental *pañca-bhis*, and so on. Whereas the inflexion of the first four cardinal numerals is Indo-European, that of the other six is an innovative feature: Vedic still had the indeclinable forms. The numerals from eleven to nineteen take the form of copulative compounds: *ekadaśa* 'eleven' (lit. 'one-ten'); *caturdaśa* 'fourteen' (lit. 'four-ten'), etc.

Most of the ordinal numerals are formed with the suffix -*ma* (*saptama*, *daśama*, Lat. *septimus*, *decimus*) or with the suffix -*tama* (*pañcaśat* 'fifty', *pañcaśattamas* 'fiftieth'). Both of these suffixes are also superlative morphemes (on -*ma* < *-*mo* cf. Lat. *summus* < *-*sub-mos*). The use of the same suffix to form the ordinals and the superlative goes back to Indo-European and derives from the spatial meaning of the suffix: the ordinal points to the final term in a series indicating the completion of a whole (Benveniste 1948).

The first- and second-person personal pronouns are declinable, do not distinguish grammatical gender, exhibit instances of suppletion and form their plurals using a different stem from that of the singular: *aham* 'I' (acc. *mam*. instr. *mayā*, etc.); *tvam* 'you (sg.)' (acc. *tvām*. instr. *tvayā*, etc.)/*vayam* 'we' (acc. *asmān*, instr. *asmabhis*, etc.; nom. acc. dual *āvām*); *yuyam* 'you (pl.)' (acc. *yuṣmān*. instr. *yuṣmabhis*; nom. acc. dual *yuvām*).

It is not possible to take account here of all of the forms. We note the main ones: *aham* < *$eĝ(^h)om$, Lat. *egō*, Gk *egó(n)*; *tvam* < *tw-om (ending by analogy with the first person), Dor. Gk *tý*, Lat. *tū*; *vayam* has the same stem as Goth. *weis*, Ger. *wir* and *yuyam* has the same stem as Goth. *jus* 'you (pl.)'; in their first syllables, *asmān* and *yuṣmān* have *ns and *us respectively (*y*- in *yuṣmān* is by analogy with nom. *yuyam*); these represent the reduced grade of the stem attested in Lat. *nos*, *vos*.

For the third person pronoun, *sa* is used; see p. 110.

Verb Conjugation

The Sanskrit verb system is organized around a fundamental distinction between *processes* and *states arising from processes*. Within each of these notions there is a present/past tense distinction.

In the representation of actions, the present is expressed using the present flection, and the past is expressed using the imperfect flection (formed from the present stem) and the aorist flection (formed from an independent stem). In the representation of states, the present is expressed by the perfect flection (cf. Skt *veda* 'I know' as the result of 'having seen, having discovered') and the past by the pluperfect flection.

This formal organization of the grammatical *signifiés* reflects both features of common Indo-European and others which have developed in a more restricted area than that covered by Indo-European. They form part of a number of features linking the Sanskrit verbal system to those of Iranian and Greek (cf. Chapter 5, pp. 144f.; Chapter 9, pp. 249–56).

At the functional level, it should be noted that the Sanskrit imperfect and the aorist do not have the same value as the corresponding 'tenses' in Greek. In Greek these mainly express aspectual distinctions; in Sanskrit, although the notion of aspect is not absent, the distinction is predominantly one of tense: the imperfect indicates the distant past, the aorist the recent and immediate past (Gonda 1962). Moreover, the future tense is expressed grammatically in Sanskrit, which also occurs, though rarely, in Vedic (see p. 115).

The moods are the indicative, subjunctive, optative, injunctive and imperative. The basic distinction is between the representation of an action as unmarked for mood (indicative) and as visualized (i.e. imagined, not perceived as real). Within the representation of visualized actions, the subjunctive is contrasted with the optative by the feature 'likelihood of realization': the subjunctive expresses an action whose realization is considered certain, the optative an action whose realization is regarded as possible (Gonda 1956).

The injunctive as a mood stands outside the rest of the system. It has the value of an indicative signifying both the 'general' present (i.e. the non-time-specific present of timeless assertions such as 'the gods live in heaven') and the preterite, and a set of modal values which from time to time are superimposed on those of the subjunctive, optative and imperative (see p. 116).

There are three numbers, singular, dual and plural, each inflected for all three persons. There are also three voices, active, middle and passive. While the first two are of IE origin, the formal expression of the passive is the result of an innovation. An IE passive cannot be reconstructed. Each language has come to express the passive – if it does so at all – in its own way (see p. 115).

The present stem (from which the imperfect is also formed) is characterized by a high degree of polymorphism. The Indian grammarians distinguished ten stem classes:

1   full grade with accent on the root: *bhárati* 'he bears', Gk *phérō*
2   radical: *asti* 'he is', Gk *estí*

3   reduplicated: *bi-bhar-ti* 'he bears', Gk *mímno* 'I wait', Lat. *sisto*

4   with suffix *-ya*: *pacyate* 'he cooks', Gk *péssō* 'id' < **pekʷjō*

6   reduced grade with unaccented root: *tudáti* 'he strikes', Gk *gráphō* 'I write' < **gr̥bʰō*

10   with suffix *-aya* (properly *-ay-a*): *tarṣayati* 'he burns' < **tors-ej-e-ti*, Lat. *torreo* < **torsejō*.

Classes (5), (7), (8) and (9) comprise various types of stem with the addition of a nasal: *yunakti* 'he joins' < *ju-n-eg-ti*, Lat. *iungo*; *tanoti* 'he pulls' < **tn̥-n-ew-ti*, and so on.

Virtually any verbal root can form more than one present stem: *bharati* (Class (1)), *bharti* (Class (2)), *bibharti* (Class (3)). Similarly, in Greek we have *leípō* and *limpánō* 'I leave', *ménō* and *mímnō* 'I wait', *ékhō* (< **segʰō*) and *ískhō* (< **si-sgʰ-ō*) 'I have'. Only rarely is any functional distinction between the stems perceptible: for example, *-aya* usually (but not exclusively) forms causatives (*bhārayati* 'he causes to bring', Gk *phoréō*); the infix *-n-* seems sometimes to have transitivizing value (Joachim 1978). But on the whole, unequivocal functional distinctions cannot be recognized; and above all there is no certainty, even when they do exist, that they go back to Indo-European. In short, we have the impression that the present-stem polymorphism is the residue of a collapsing system which has almost completely ceased to be functional.

The flection can be thematic or athematic. Classes (1), (4), (6) and (10) follow the thematic flection, the others the athematic flection.

In the thematic flection the thematic vowel *a/ā* (< **e/o*) is introduced between the stem and the ending: *bhar-a-ti*, *bhar-ā-mas* 'he bears, we bear', Gk. *phér-o-men*, *phér-e-te* 'we bear, you (pl.) bear'. In the athematic flection the endings are added directly to the stem: *bharti* 'he bears'. Lat. *fert* < **bʰer-ti*; *asti* 'is', Lat. *est*, Gk *estí* (< **es-ti*).

The athematic flection is also characterized by ablaut alternation in the stem: in the singular active indicative the full grade appears (*a* < **e*; *e* < **ej*; *o* < **ew*, etc.) and in the other forms the reduced grade (0, *i*, *u*) appears: *asti* < **es-ti*, but *smas* < **s-me/os*; *eti* 'he goes' < **ej-ti*, but *imas* 'we go' < **i-me/os*; *tanoti* 'he pulls' < **tn̥-n-ew-ti*, but *tanumas* 'we pull' < **tn̥-n-u-me/os*.

With respect to the present, the forms of the past are characterized by the augment and by a special set of endings. The augment, which also appears in Iranian, Greek and Armenian, is a particle *a-* (< **e-*) prefixed to the verbal stem: Skt *abharam* (< **e-bʰer-o-m* (1 sg. impf.)), Gk *é-pher-o-n*.

The endings are traditionally classified into two series, the 'primary' and the 'secondary' endings.

The primary endings are characteristic of the present indicative, the secondary endings of the past indicative and of the other moods. Like the other moods, the IE subjunctive had the secondary endings. The Sanskrit subjunctive, as the result of an innovation shared also by Iranian and Greek,

Table 4.5 Pimary and secondary verbal endings

	Singular Active	Middle	Dual Active	Middle	Plural Active	Middle
Present indicative (primary) endings						
1	-mi	-e	-vaḥ	-vahe	-maḥ	-mahe
2	-si	-se	-thaḥ	-the	-tha	-dhve
3	-ti	-te	-taḥ	-te	-nti	-nte
Imperfect (secondary) endings						
1	-m	-i	-va	-vahi	-ma	-mahi
2	-s	-thāḥ	-tam	-thām	-ta	-dhvam
3	-t	-ta	-tām	-tām	-n	-nta

has the primary endings. The imperative has, in part, its own special endings. The two series of endings are shown in Table 4.5.

It is not possible here to comment on the endings individually. It will suffice to note that one group of primary endings is distinguished from the corresponding secondary endings by the presence of *-i*:

Active: *-mi, -si, -ti, -nti/-m, -s, -t, -nt* (> *n*)
Middle: *-te* (< **-taj*), *-nte* (< **-ntaj*)/*-ta, -nta*

This system must be of IE origin since it appears in an almost identical form in Greek and many other languages.

The imperfect is formed from the present stem. The aorist is formed either directly from the root (root aorist) or by adding a formant *-s-* to the root (sigmatic aorist). There is also a thematic aorist formed by adding the thematic vowel to the root, usually in the reduced grade. All of these formations are of IE origin: in Greek the root aorist is represented, for example, by *ébēn* 'I went' (pres. *baínō*), the thematic aorist by *élipon* 'I left' (pres. *leípō*) and the sigmatic aorist by *élysa* 'I loosed' (< **e-lu-sm̥*, pres. *luō*). The root aorist is formally identical to an imperfect of Class (2) and the thematic aorist to an imperfect of Class (6). The non-sigmatic imperfect and aorist are thus distinguished only by their relation to the present: *adadhām* 'I put' is recognized as the imperfect and *adhām* 'I have put' as the aorist of *dadhāti* 'I put' because the former is formed from the same reduplicated stem *dadhā-* as the present *dadhāti*, while the latter is formed from the non-reduplicated root *dhā-* which does not appear in the present. But *apāt* 'he protected', although a root formation like *adhāt*, is recognized as imperfect because the present is also formed from that root: *pāti*.

The same occurs in Greek: *ébēn* 'I went' and *édrakon* 'I saw' are symmetrical with *éphēn* 'I said' and *égraphon* 'I wrote' respectively. But the first two are recognized as aorist in relation to the present *baínō* and *dérkomai*, the others as imperfect in relation to the present *phēmí* and *gráphō*.

The perfect, characterized by reduplication and a special set of endings, continues IE features. The root is in the full grade (Skt $a/\bar{a}$, o, $e < *o$, $*ow$, $*oj$) in the singular active indicative: otherwise it is in the reduced grade.

The same features appear in Greek (perf. *léloipa*/pres. *leípō*) and in the Germanic strong preterite (Goth. *band* 'I tied' $< *b^hond^ha$; 1 pl. *bundum* $< *b^h\underset{\circ}{n}d^h$-). The reduplication vowel is a ($< *e$) and so if the verbal base begins with a velar consonant the reduplication consonant is the corresponding palatal (see p. 105 above): $k\underset{.}{r}$- 'do', perf. *cakāra*; if the base contains i or u the reduplication vowel is i or u.

The perfect middle is the result of an innovation, produced through symmetry with the present. Originally the perfect, in its stative meaning, had an intrinsic middle value and thus no need for specific middle forms. In fact, it frequently happens that a perfect active belongs to an otherwise middle paradigm (Renou 1925). The same occurs in Greek: pres. *gígnomai*/perf. *gégona*; pres. *dérkomai*/perf. *dédorka* (see Chapter 3, p. 81).

The endings of the perfect are as in Table 4.6.

The future is formed by adding the suffix *-sya* (or *iṣya*) to the root, usually in the full grade. The conjugation is identical to that of the thematic presents: *dā*- 'give'/*dāsyati* 'will give'; *kṛ*- 'do'/*kariṣyati* 'will do'. The morpheme *-sya* ($< *sjo/e$) probably continues an old desiderative suffix. This formation occurs in Lithuanian as well as in Sanskrit and Iranian and can also be assumed for a prehistoric phase of the Slavic languages. It is thus an inherited formation, albeit limited to one dialect region of the IE area. No future formation can be attributed to common Indo-European.

The passive is formed with the suffix *-ya-* (stressed *-yá-* in Vedic) which is added to the verbal base in the reduced grade. The endings are those of the middle: *bandh-* 'tie'/*badhyate* ($< *b^h\underset{\circ}{n}d^h$-) 'is tied'. The flection is as for a present of the fourth class.

Common Indo-European had no passive. Sanskrit has developed one apparently by modifying Class (4) presents with intransitive value: *jāyate* ($< *\hat{g}\underset{\circ}{n}\partial\text{-}j\text{-}e\text{-}toj$) 'comes forth' > 'is born'. Outside the present system, the passive is expressed by the middle. An aorist passive in *-i*, limited to the third-person singular (*kṛ*- 'do'/*akāri* 'has been done'), is obscure.

Table 4.6   Perfect endings

	Singular		Dual		Plural	
	Active	Middle	Active	Middle	Active	Middle
1	-a	-e	-va	-vahe	-ma	-mahe
2	-tha	-se	-athuḥ	-āthe	-a	-dhve
3	-a	-e	-atuḥ	-āte	-uḥ	-ire

Note: 1 sg. *-a* < *-a* (Skt *dadarśa*, Gk *dédorka* 'I have seen'); 2 sg. *-tha* < *-tha* (Skt *vettha* 'you know', Gk *oîstha*); 3 sg. *-a* < *-e* (Skt *veda*, Gk *oîde*).

The subjunctive continues an IE formation. In the athematic verbs this is formed by adding the thematic vowel to the full-grade root (*asti* 'is'/subj. *asat*(*i*); Lat. *est*/subj. (> fut.) *erit* (< **es-e-t*)) and in the thematic verbs by lengthening the thematic vowel (*bharati* 'he bears'/subj. *bharāt*(*i*); Gk *phérei* 'he bears'/subj. *phérēi*).

In the first-person singular the ending is *-āni* (also *-ā* < **-ō* in some Vedic remains, see Chapter 5, pp. 144f.).

The optative also continues an IE formation. In the athematic flection it is formed by adding the morpheme *-yā/-ī* (< **-jē/-ī*) to the reduced-grade verbal stem: *as-* 'to be': opt. 3 sg. *syāt*, 3 pl. *syuḥ*, cf. the Latin subjunctive (< opt.) 3 sg. (OLat.) *siet*, 3 pl. *sīnt*.

The thematic optative is formed by adding the suffix *-e-* (< **-oj-*, to be analysed as thematic vowel *o* + optative suffix *ī*) to the stem: *bharati* 'he bears'/opt. *bharet* < **bherojt*, Gk *phéroi*.

The imperative continues forms which are in part those of the subjunctive, in part those of the injunctive (see paragraph below) and in part specific. In the second person of the thematic flection the pure stem appears: *bhara* 'bear!', Gk *phére*, Lat. *lege*; in the athematic flection the morpheme *-dʰi* is used: *śrudhi* 'listen!', Gk *klŷthi*.

Formally, the injunctive looks like an imperfect or an aorist (less frequently, like a pluperfect) without the augment. This is a vestige of a (palaeo-) IE system in which the grammatical expression of tense did not exist. A form such as **bheret*, from which the Sanskrit injunctive *bharat* derives, expressed the relation of the verbal lexeme to person, mood and voice, but not to tense. Tense was indicated by lexical elements (e.g. adverbs) or by deictic particles. Indeed, in late Indo-European, the grammatical expression of tense arose as a result of the grammaticalization of deictic particles. The present was indicated by adding **-i* (originally a sign of the *hic et nunc*) to the endings **-m*, **-s*, **-t*, **-nt*; the past was formed by prefixing **e-* (the so-called 'augment', Skt *a-*, Gk *e-*, Arm. *e-*, originally a sign of the *illic et tunc*) to the verbal stem. The injunctive **bheret* > Skt *bharat* 'he bears' (as a non-time-specific action) is the basis of **bhereti* > Skt *bharati* 'he is bearing' (as a current, present action) and of **ebheret* > Skt *abharat* 'he bore'. The injunctive was, then, originally a non-time-specific present, and the endings usually termed 'secondary' are in fact the original endings (see Chapter 3, pp. 81f.).

The functional values of the Sanskrit injunctive are specified by the formation of the new indicative *bharati* with the value of an immediate present. In contrast with *bharati*, *bharat* took on the values 'non-immediate', 'non-present' and non-indicative', thus becoming the mark for the general (non-immediate) present, the past (non-present) and a number of the non-indicative moods.

Within this new system, tense was expressed only in the indicative mood, as in *bharati*; indeed, the other moods show no sign of the grammatical expression of tense: those of the past (e.g. the aorist moods) do not take the augment, and those of the present do not modify the original endings with -*i* (using the traditional formulation, these moods have the 'secondary' endings).

The Vedic injunctive is a residual form. In Classical Sanskrit it disappears, surviving only in the expression of the negative imperative (Hoffmann 1967; Lazzeroni 1977, 1984).

The nominal forms of the verb: the active participle is formed with the suffix -*nt*- and preserves the alternating IE flection as mentioned on pp. 107f.: nom. sg. *bharan* 'bearing', acc. *bharantam*, nom. pl. *bharantas*, acc. *bharatas* (< **bherṇt-*).

The middle participle ends in -*māna* in the thematic verbs (*bharamānas*) and in -*āna* in the athematic verbs (*dviṣānas/dveṣṭi* 'hate'). The form -*māna* is certainly related to the suffix -*meno* of the Greek middle participle (*pherómenos*) and to the suffix -*mno* in Latin formations such as *alumnus* (from *alere*). The etymology of -*āna* (which also appears in the perfect middle participle) is unclear.

The perfect active participle is formed with the suffix -*vas/-uṣ/-vat* (alternating as on pp. 107f.: -*uṣ* appears before vocalic endings). This is an IE formation: Gk *eidós* 'knowing' (< **wejd-wōs*), f. *eidyîa* (< **wejd-us-ja*), gen. *eidótos* (< **wejd-wot-os*), n. nom./acc. *eidós* (< **wejd-wos*).

The perfect passive participle is formed by means of the addition of the suffixes -*ta* or -*na* (< **-to*, **-no*) to the reduced-grade root: *kṛ*- 'do'/*kṛtas*; *kṣi*- 'destroy'/*kṣitas*, *kṣiṇas*.

These formations are also inherited. In Greek we have *teínō* 'pull'/*tatós* 'pulled' (< **tṇ-tos*), *házomai* 'worship' (< **jagjomai*)/*hagnós*; in Latin, (*re*)*pleo* 'fill'/*repletus*, *plenus*.

The suffix which forms the *participle of necessity* (gerundive) is -*ya*. Its value follows a special Sanskrit use of the derived adjectival suffix **-jo* (cf. Gk *házomai* 'I worship, venerate'/*hágios* 'holy' (= 'venerable'). In late Vedic tradition and in Classical Sanskrit there also appear other suffixes which it is not possible to mention here.

The infinitive morphemes in the various IE languages are fossilized case forms of verbal nouns. This leads us to suppose that the IE infinitive was a regularly declined verbal noun, whose case was determined by its syntactic function (dative of purpose, accusative of object or of movement, etc.). Vedic preserves this primitive situation virtually intact: a series of verbal nouns (in -*ti*-, -*tu*-, -*as*-, etc.), declined for all cases, function as infinitives. In Classical Sanskrit (and already in the late Vedic tradition) the accusative -*tum* of the verbal nouns in -*tu*- became fossilized in the function of an infinitive: *kartum* (< *kṛ*-) 'to do'.

This suffix corresponds to the Latin supine suffix (*factum*, *dictum*, etc.). It should be noted that in Latin a trace of the directional value which caused the accusative to be chosen is preserved in the fact that the declension of the supine pertains to verbs of motion: ***venerunt** legati pacem **postulatum*** 'the envoys **came to sue for** peace'.

Finally, there exist various absolute formations which are more or less equivalent in meaning to the English present participle. The most common suffixes are *-tvā-* and *-va-*. The former is the instrumental of a noun of action in *-tu-*: *kṛtvā* 'doing, having done' (lit. 'with the doing'). The etymology of *-ya-* is obscure.

The system outlined here was alive in Vedic (where there were also other formations, such as the precative, which it is not possible to discuss here), but already in the late Vedic literature, and above all in Classical Sanskrit, it underwent important modifications. The injunctive and the subjunctive disappeared (both surviving only in some imperative forms); the aorist became increasingly rare and was replaced by the imperfect or the perfect; the root aorist came to be limited to the vocalic stems only; a periphrastic perfect and future made headway. The former was formed by the addition of *-am* (probably the accusative of a verbal noun) to the verbal root, and the perfect of *kṛ-* 'do' or *as-* or *bhū-* 'be': *und-* 'bathe', perf. *undam cakara* 'I have bathed' (lit. 'I have done the bathing'?). The periphrastic future was formed with the nominative *-tā* of an agent noun in *-tar* derived from the verbal base, and the present of *as-* 'be': *dātāsmi* 'I shall give' (= *dātā asmi* 'I am the giver'). But the most important change was the extensive development of the passive participial phrase at the expense of finite forms:

adarśanam   *gatas*
into-the-invisibility   gone (sc. 'he was')
'he disappeared'

Tables 4.7 to 4.10 show some verbal paradigms.

Word Classes

The invariable word classes are the conjunctions, adverbs and prepositions.

In Sanskrit, subordinating syntax is not highly developed. The following list contains the main coordinating conjunctions, both in sentences and noun phrases:

copulative: *ca* (< *$*k^we$*, Gk. *te*. Lat. *-que*), *api, tathas, atha*
disjunctive: *va* (Lat. *-ve*)
adversative: *tu*
causal: *hi, tat, tasmāt, athas*

Note that some of these conjunctions (*tatas, tasmāt, tat*) are case forms and adverbial forms of the anaphoric pronoun (p. 110). The subordinating conjunctions, on the other hand, are case forms and adverbial forms of the relative pronoun: *yad* (declarative, causal and final); *yena* (causal and final);

Table 4.7   Thematic conjugation: *bhṛ* 'bear', Class 1

ACTIVE			MIDDLE		
Singular	**Dual**	**Plural**	**Singular**	**Dual**	**Plural**
Present Indicative			Present Indicative		
bharāmi	bharāvaḥ	bharāmaḥ	bhare	bharāvahe	bharāmahe
bharasi	bharathaḥ	bharatha	bharase	bharethe	bharadhve
bharati	bharataḥ	bharanti	bharate	bharete	bharante
Present Optative			Present Optative		
bhareyam	bhareva	bharema	bhareya	bharevahi	bharemahi
bhareḥ	bharetam	bhareta	bharethāḥ	bhareyāthām	bharedhvam
bharet	bharetām	bhareyuḥ	bhareta	bhareyātām	bhareran
Present Imperative			Present Imperative		
bharāṇi	bharāva	bharāma	bharai	bharāvahai	bharāmahai
bhara	bharatam	bharata	bharasva	bharetām	bharadhvam
bharatu	bharatām	bharantu	bharatām	bharetām	bharantām
Imperfect Indicative			Imperfect Indicative		
abharam	abharāva	abharāma	abhare	abharāvahi	abharāmahi
abharaḥ	abharatam	abharata	abharathāḥ	abharethām	abharadhvam
abharat	abharatām	abharan	abharata	abharetām	abharanta

Table 4.8   Athematic conjugation: *dviṣ-* 'hate', Class 2

ACTIVE			MIDDLE		
Singular	**Dual**	**Plural**	**Singular**	**Dual**	**Plural**
Present Indicative			Present Indicative		
dveṣmi	dviṣvaḥ	dviṣmaḥ	dviṣe	dviṣvahe	dviṣmahe
dvekṣi	dviṣṭhaḥ	dviṣṭha	dvikṣe	dviṣāthe	dviḍḍhve
dveṣṭi	dviṣṭaḥ	dviṣanti	dviṣṭe	dviṣāte	dviṣate
Present Optative			Present Optative		
dviṣyām	dviṣyāva	dviṣyāma	dviṣīya	dviṣīvahi	dviṣīmahi
dviṣyaḥ	dviṣyātam	dviṣyāta	dviṣīthāḥ	dviṣīyāthām	dviṣīdhvam
dviṣyāt	dviṣyātām	dviṣyuḥ	dviṣīta	dviṣīyātām	dviṣīran
Present Imperative			Present Imperative		
dveṣāṇi	dveṣāva	dveṣāma	dveṣai	dveṣāvahai	dveṣāmahai
dviḍḍhi	dviṣṭam	dviṣṭa	dvikṣva	dviṣāthām	dviḍḍhvam
dveṣṭu	dviṣṭām	dviṣantu	dviṣṭām	dviṣātām	dviṣatām
Imperfect Indicative			Imperfect Indicative		
adveṣam	adviṣva	adviṣma	adviṣi	advisyahi	adviṣmahi
advet	adviṣṭam	adviṣṭa	adviṣṭhāḥ	adviṣāthām	adviḍḍhvam
advet	adviṣṭām	adviṣan	adviṣṭa	adviṣātām	adviṣata

Table 4.9 Aorist conjugation: *dā-* 'give', root aorist

ACTIVE

Singular	Dual	Plural
adām	adāva	adāma
adāḥ	adātam	adāta
adāt	adātām	aduḥ

ni- 'lead', sigmatic aorist

ACTIVE

Singular	*Dual*	*Plural*
anaiṣam	anaiṣva	anaiṣma
anaiṣīḥ	anaiṣṭam	anaiṣṭa
anaiṣīt	anaiṣṭām	anaiṣuḥ

Notes: Athematic conjugation. 3 pl. pres. ind. act. *dviṣanti*, impf. *adviṣan* from **-e/onti* and **-e/ont* respectively. This is the full grade of the ending **-nti*, **-nt* (> Skt *-n*) of the thematic forms. 3 pl. pres. ind. mid *dviṣate*, impf. *adviṣata < -ṇtai* (< **-ntoj*), *-ṇta* (< **-nto*): *dviṣate* **dviṣṇte*, l sg. impf. act. *adviṣam < *adviṣṃ* (> *adviṣa* as in the Gk aor. *élysa < *elusṃ*) remodelled with *-m* from the thematic conjugation. The same is true of the aor. *anaiṣam*.

Table 4.10 Perfect conjugation: *kṛ-* 'do'

ACTIVE			MIDDLE		
Singular	Dual	Plural	Singular	Dual	Plural
cakắr	cakṛva	cakṛma	cakre	cakṛvahe	cakṛmahe
cakartha	cakrathuḥ	cakra	cakṛṣe	cakrāthe	cakṛdhve
cakāra	cakratuḥ	cakruḥ	cakre	cakrāte	cakrire

yatas (causal); *yathā* (comparative); *yadi* (conditional and concessive); *yāvat* (temporal).

In the IE languages the adverbs are often fossilized case forms: for example, Greek *aién* 'always' continues an old form of the locative of *aiṓn* 'time' (properly 'in the time'); Latin *saepe* 'often' may be the nominative case of an old neuter noun. The same can be perceived in Sanskrit, but with the qualification that since the IE paradigm is essentially preserved in all its cases, it is sometimes difficult to distinguish the adverbial forms from those of the nominal declension: *dūreṇa* (instr.) 'far'; *balāt* (abl.) 'strongly'; *ciram* (acc.) 'for (since) a long time', etc.

There is also a series of adverbial suffixes: *-vat* (modal: *ṛṣi-vat* 'like a seer (*ṛṣi-*)'); *putravat* 'like a son (*putra-*)'; *-tas* (separative, 'originating in': Gk *-tos* in *ektós* 'outside', Lat. *intus, radicitus*): *dūratas* 'from afar'; *sarvatas* 'from all parts'; *-tra* (local): *sarvatra* 'wherever', etc.

A series of particles – mainly of IE origin – has adverbial value when used absolutely, prepositional value when linked with a noun, and preverbal value when linked with a verb: *antar* 'between'; *pari* 'around'; *upa* 'near'; *prati* 'against', etc. Thus we have *pari tvā* 'around you (*tvā*)'; *pari dhā-* 'put around, surround' (*dhā-* 'put'), etc. Semantically, these particles are broadly autonomous: as preverbs they are (for the most part) separable from the verb, and as prepositions they can follow the noun, effectively functioning as postpositions: *madhyaṁdinaṁ pari* 'around midday'.

Word Formation

Derivation occupies an important place. It is manifested in an extremely extensive series of suffixes which it is not possible to list here. For example, *-tar-* (Gk *-tēr-/-tōr-*, Lat. *-tor*) forms agent nouns (*dātar-* 'one who gives, giver'); *-ti-* (Gk *-si-*, Lat. *-ti-* in *na-tio*) forms verbal abstracts (*dṛś-* 'see'/*dṛṣti-* 'vision'); *-tra* (< **tro*) forms instrument nouns (*vas-* 'to dress'/*vastra-* 'clothing'; *śru-* 'listen'/*śrotra-* 'ear', etc.

As is clear even from the few examples cited, Sanskrit words have a high degree of (semantic) transparency, their constituents usually being easily recognizable in a clear diagrammatic relationship. This has been recognized as a characteristic inherited from Indo-European (Belardi 1985).

Another process of derivation extensively employed is the so-called '*vṛddhi* grade derivation'. This consists of the lengthened grade of the derived word, according to the following relationship (cf. Chapter 2, pp. 52f.):

Base form	Derived form
a	*ā*
i, e	*ai*
u, o	*au*
ṛ	*ār*

deva- 'god': *daiva-* 'godly, divine'; *Varuṇa*: *Vāruṇa-* 'belonging to Vāruṇa', etc. This type of derivation is of IE origin, cf. Gk *énos* 'year': *ēnis* 'of one year'; *oîs* 'ram': *óia* 'sheepskin', etc. However, in no IE language is the type as widespread as in Sanskrit, where its development may have been aided by the merger of vowel qualities (p. 104) which rendered impracticable derivation based on quantitative ablaut (Lat. *tego*: *toga*, etc.).

Nominal compounding is an IE feature. Present to a moderate degree in Vedic, it underwent an unusual development in the passage to Classical Sanskrit, where compounds of up to ten members can appear.

In the compound – which in its oldest form consisted of two elements – only the last element is declined. The others correspond to the pure stem. The three basic types (within which there are various subclasses which cannot be listed here) are:

1   Copulative (or *dvandva* 'pair'): a relationship of correlation exists
     between the elements: *hastyaśvās* (nom. pl.) 'elephants (*hasti-*) and
     horses (*aśva-*)'; *śuklakṛṣṇa-* 'light' (*śukla-*) and dark (*kṛṣṇa-*)'; cf. Gk
     dṓdeka, Lat. *duodecim* '12' (lit. '2 and 10'), Gk *nykhthḗmeron* 'night and
     day', etc.
2   Determinative (or *tatpuruṣa-* 'his servant'): the first element (a noun or
     adjective) determines the second: *mahādeva-* 'the great (*maha-*) god
     (*deva-*)'; *devadatta-* 'given (*datta-*) by god (*deva-*)'; cf. Gk *akrópolis*
     'high city', *theoeíkelos* 'godlike', Lat. *agricola* 'farmer' (= 'he who
     cultivates the fields')
3   Possessive (or *bahuvrīhi* 'having much rice'): these are the so-called
     exocentric compounds, those with adjectival value, which refer to an
     entity external to the compound itself: *dvipad-* 'biped' (= 'having two
     feet'); *divyarūpa-* 'having divine form' (*rūpa-* 'form'), etc.; cf. Gk
     rhododáktylos 'rosy-fingered', in Vedic, where the accent is free, the
     possessive compound is distinguished from the determinative by the
     position of the accent: *rājaputrá-* 'son (*putra-*) of the king'/*rā́japutra-*
     'having kings as sons'.

Syntax

Here we cannot give an account of even the main features of Sanskrit syntax.
Moreover, many elements still require a more detailed analysis after the
fundamental work by Delbrück (1888). Some syntactic features (the development of nominal and participial phrases, compounding, coordination and
subordination) have already been discussed in the section on morphology. Here
word order alone will be discussed. In Sanskrit, the syntactic function of a word
is indicated in its case-bearing morphemes: the order of constituents within the
sentence does not have grammatical function and is thus largely free.

     This is clearest in the Vedic poetry: rhythmical, metrical, phono-symbolic
and stylistic requirements take precedence over those of word order (Gonda
1952). In prose, however, the basic order is the sequence SOV. This
corresponds to the IE order.

viśah   kṣatriyāya   baliṁ haranti
farmers   to-the-master   tax   they-pay
'The farmers pay the tax to the master.'

If, as in the example cited, the sentence contains an indirect object, this
precedes the direct object:

chandāṁsi yuktāni   devebhyo   ajñam   vahanti
verses   ornate   to-the-gods   sascrifice they-bear
'The ornate verses bring the sacrifice to the gods.'

The determiner precedes the object determined and thus the adjective and genitive precede their governing noun:

Manor   jāyā
of-Manu   the-wife
'Manu's wife'

but the noun in apposition and the participle follow it: *chandāṁsi yuktāni*. The infinitive precedes the predicate; the absolutive follows the subject, but precedes the direct and indirect objects of the predicate. The position of the enclitics is significant. The sentence enclitics occupy second position in the order of constituents. The same is true of a set of auxiliary words (particles, pronouns, etc.) which, although stressed, behave like the enclitics. This phenomenon goes by the name of 'Wackernagel's Law' and goes back to Indo-European (see Chapter 2, p. 70 and Chapter 7, pp. 187f.).

References

Allen, Sidney (1962) *Sandhi*, The Hague: Mouton.

Belardi, Walter (1985) 'Considerazioni sulla ricostruzione dell'indoeuropeo', in *Tra linguistica storica e linguistica generale*. Written in honour of Tristano Bolelli (edited by R. Ambrosini), Pisa: Pacini, pp. 39–66.

Benveniste, Émile (1948) *Noms d'agent et noms d'action en indo-européen*, Paris: Maisonneuve.

Burrow, T. (n.d.) *The Sanskrit Language*, London: Faber & Faber.

Delbrück, Berthold (1888) *Altindische Syntax*, Halle a.S.: Verlag der Buchhandlung des Weisenhauses.

Di Giovine, Paolo (1990–6) *Studio sul perfetto indoeuropeo*, I, II, III, Rome: Dipartimento di studi glottoantropologici.

Gonda, Jan (1951) *Remarks on the Sanskrit Passive*, Leiden: Brill.

——— (1952) *Remarques sur la place du verbe dans la phrase active et moyenne en langue sanscrite*, Utrecht: Oosthoek.

——— (1956) *The Character of the Indo-European Moods*, Wiesbaden: Harrassowitz.

——— (1962) *The Aspectual Function of the Rgvedic Present and Aorist*, Den Haag: Mouton.

——— 'Old Indian' in *Handbuch der Orientalistik*, II, 1, 1), Leiden and Cologne: E. J. Brill.

——— (1979) *The Medium in the Rgveda*, Leiden: Brill.

Grierson, George A. (1967) *Linguistic Survey of India*, 11 vols repr. New Delhi: Motilal Banarsidass.

Hoffmann, Karl (1967) *Der Injunktiv im Veda*, Heidelberg: Winter.

Joachim, Ulrike (1978) *Mehrfachpräsentien im Rgveda*, Frankfurt am Main: Lang.

Lazzeroni, Romano (1968) 'Per una definizione dell'unità indo-iranica', *Studi e saggi linguistici*. Supplement to *L'italia dialettale* 8: 131–59.

——— (1977) 'Fra glottogonia e storia: ingiuntivo, aumento e lingua poetica indoeuropea', *Studi e saggi dialettale*. Supplement to *L'italia dialettale* 17: 1–30.

——— (1984) 'La formazione del sistema dei tempi e degli aspetti nel verbo sanscrito', *Atti del Sodalizio Glottologico Milanese*, 24: 55–63.

—— (1985) 'Il vedico come lingua letteraria', in *La formazione delle lingue letterarie*, in *Atti del convegno della Società Italiana di Glottologia* (Siena, 16–18 April 1984), Pisa: Giardini, pp. 81–91.

Mayrhofer, Manfred (1956–80) *Kurzgefasstes Etymologisches Wörterbuch des Altindischen*, Heidelberg: Winter.

—— (1974) *Die Arier im Vorderen Orient – Ein Mythos?* Vienna: Verlag der Österreichischen Akademie der Wissenschaften.

—— (1986) *Etymologisches Wörterbuch des Altindoarischen*, Heidelberg: Winter.

Pischel, R. (1965) *Comparative Grammar of the Pracrit Languages*, New Delhi: Motilal Banarsidass (transl. of *Grammatik der Prakrit Sprachen*, Strasburg: Trübner, 1900).

Renou, Louis (1925) *La valeur du parfait dans les Hymnes Védiques*, Paris: Champion.

—— (1952) *Grammaire de la langue védique*, Paris and Lyons, IAC.

—— (1957) 'Introduction générale' to the new edition (1957) by Wackernagel (1896–1954).

—— (1961) *Grammaire sanskrite*, Paris: Maisonneuve.

Sani, Saverio (1991) *Grammatica sanscrita*, Pisa: Giardini.

Thumb, Albert and Hauschild, Richard (1958–9) *Handbuch des Sanskrit*, 3rd edition revised by R. Hauschild, I, 1 and I, 2, Heidelberg: Winter.

Wackernagel, Jakob (1896–1954) *Altindische Grammatik*, vols I, II.1 (anastatic reprint of *Nachträge* by A. Debrunner, 1957); II.2; III, Göttingen: Vandenhoeck & Ruprecht.

5 The Iranian Languages

Nicholas Sims-Williams

At the present day, IE languages of the Iranian group are spoken over a wide area including virtually the whole of Iran, Afghanistan and Tajikistan, together with the neighbouring parts of Turkey, Syria, Iraq, Pakistan and Uzbekistan and larger or smaller enclaves in Oman, Armenia, Georgia, Azerbaijan, Turkmenistan and western China (see the map at the end of Schmitt (ed.)'1989). In medieval times Iranian languages such as Sogdian and Khotanese were well established even further east, in the area which later became Chinese Turkestan (Xinjiang); at a still earlier period, the original homeland of the Iranian-speaking peoples seems to have lain to the north-east of the present state of Iran.

Iranian and Indian

This chapter concentrates on the earliest attested Iranian languages, Avestan and Old Persian, which are naturally the most important for IE studies. These two Old Iranian languages are described to a large extent in terms of their similarities to and differences from the closely related Old Indian, a procedure justified in the first place by pragmatic considerations. Old Indian (Vedic and Sanskrit) is attested by a huge and varied corpus of literature, written in a clear, almost phonemic script which allows the phonological and morphological structure of the language to be clearly perceived. On the other hand, each of the attested Old Iranian languages is known from a limited corpus – in the case of Old Persian, a tiny corpus – of rather repetitive and monotonous texts, one written in an ambiguous cuneiform writing system, the other by means of an over-elaborate, almost phonetic alphabet, whose intricacies obscure rather than illuminate its grammatical structure. Although some of these deficiencies are made good by the more abundant Middle and Modern Iranian material, it cannot be denied that Iranian evidence is usually more difficult than Indian for a student of Indo-European to evaluate.

From a theoretical point of view, too, it is proper to treat the Iranian languages in constant comparison with Indian, since the two groups are not merely closely related but jointly constitute a single Indo-Iranian branch of the IE family, as is indicated by the innumerable phonological, morphological and lexical isoglosses which they share to the exclusion of all other branches of Indo-European. One such isogloss is the use of OInd. *árya-*, Avest. *aⁱriia-*, OPers. *ariya-* (from which the name of the country 'Iran' derives) as a self-designation for the speakers of Indo-Iranian, whence the alternative term 'Aryan'. The closeness of the relationship between Indian and Iranian is most clearly demonstrated by the fact that it is possible to find not just words but whole sentences in Vedic or Avestan which may be transposed from the one language into the other merely by observing the appropriate phonological rules; for example, Avest. *təm amauuantəm yazatəm sūrəm dāmōhu səuuištəm miθrəm yazāi* 'this powerful, strong (being) worthy of worship, Mithra, the strongest amongst creatures, I shall worship' (Yasht 10.6) = Ved. **tám ámavantam yajatám śúran dhámasu śáviṣṭham mitrám yajai* (cf. Jackson 1892: xxxi–xxxii; also Chapter 4, pp. 98f.).

Despite the overwhelming similarity of Indian and Iranian, each is distinguished from the other by a number of characteristic innovations. Phonological innovations on the Indian side include the loss of the Indo-Iranian (II) diphthongs **aj*, **aw* (> *e, o*) and voiced sibilants (**z, *ź*, etc.) and the development of a series of retroflex consonants (*ṭ, ṇ, ṣ*, etc.), whilst Iranian languages typically show the loss of the voiced aspirates **bʰ, *dʰ, *gʰ*, etc. (> *b, d, g*), the development of the voiceless fricatives *f, θ, x* (from II **p, *t, *k* before consonants, and from **pʰ, *tʰ, *kʰ*), the depalatalization of II **ć, *ȷ(ʰ)* (> **ts, *dz*; OPers. *θ, d*, Avest. *s, z*), and the change of **s* (in most positions) to *h*. Some apparent exceptions to these isoglosses may be due to the reversal of a sound change: for instance, Avestan *pt* (as in *hapta* 'seven') may derive from the expected **ft* (as attested, directly or indirectly, in all other Iranian languages, e.g. Pers. *haft*) rather than preserving II **pt* (cf. OInd. *saptá*). In other cases, however, it is clear that a development characteristic of Iranian cannot in fact have been fully carried through at the Common Iranian stage: cf. for instance, p. 136 on evidence for the survival of the palatal **ć* in certain clusters. Similarly, the development of **s* to *h*, though common to Avestan, Old Persian and all later Iranian languages, is demonstrably later than the earliest attestations of Iranian in Ancient Near Eastern sources (cf. p. 127 below on the divine name *Assara mazaš*). Thus, at least in phonology, the innovations attributable to Common Iranian are comparatively few in number (though significant in kind).

It is in part as a result of the fact that Common Iranian cannot have differed greatly from Common Indo-Iranian (or 'Aryan') that it is difficult to determine the precise status of the so-called 'Nuristani' languages (formerly known as 'Kafiri'). This group of languages, recorded in modern times in the north-east of Afghanistan and neighbouring parts of Pakistan, undoubtedly belongs to the Indo-Iranian family, but it is not yet clear whether it is to be regarded as a third, independent subgroup beside Indian and Iranian (Morgenstierne 1973a: 327–43) or as an archaic form of Iranian, much influenced by several millennia of proximity to languages of the Indian group (cf. Mayrhofer 1983).

Origins

The original homeland of the Aryans, the speakers of Common Indo-Iranian, cannot be precisely identified, but is thought to have been in western Central Asia, to the east and north-east of the Caspian Sea. At a time when 'proto-Indian' and 'proto-Iranian' (i.e. the ancestral dialects from which the Indian and Iranian languages respectively derive) had already become differentiated to some extent, perhaps about the beginning of the second millennium BC, two groups of 'proto-Indian' or 'Indo-Aryan' speakers began to migrate from this homeland, one towards the west (cf. Chapter 4, p. 98, on traces of the Indo-Aryans in the Hurrian empire of Mitanni in northern Mesopotamia) and the other towards India. At a later date, Iranian tribes too began to migrate westwards, reaching central and western Iran by the middle of the ninth century BC, at which period they are referred to for the first time in Assyrian sources; whether they had come from the north-east by the most direct route, to the south of the Caspian, or more circuitously through the Caucasus is still a matter of debate. (For a more detailed summary and references to the literature on the prehistory of the Aryans see Schmitt 1987.) From the ninth century BC onwards, a scattering of Iranian linguistic material is to be found in Mesopotamian sources, beginning with the names of the Medes (*Matai*) and Persians (*Parsuaš*) and most notably including the name of the principal deity of the Iranians in the form *Assara mazaš* (= Common Iranian **Asura-mazdās*, later **Ahura-mazdāh*, cf. OPers. *Auramazdā*, Avest. *Ahurō Mazdā̊*).

The Iranian Languages

Only two Old Iranian languages are attested by texts, namely Avestan and Old Persian. Others, such as Median and Scythian, are only known to us through occasional words and names transmitted in texts in other languages.

Avestan is the language of the Zoroastrian scriptures, the Avesta, the earliest parts of which are the Gāthās ('Songs') of Zoroaster or Zarathushtra – whom tradition places in the sixth century BC, though many scholars argue, partly on linguistic grounds, for a date five centuries or more earlier – and the *Yasna Haptaŋhā'ti* 'Service consisting of seven chapters'. These texts, together with a few short prayers, are preserved in 'Gathic' or Old Avestan, a highly archaic dialect comparable to Vedic in its stage of development. Later Avestan, also known as Younger Avestan, is attested by a much larger corpus of texts, including the *Yashts* (hymns in honour of individual divinities) and the *Vīdēvdād* ('Law against the demons'). The manuscript tradition of the Avesta derives from an archetype created at some time during the Sasanian

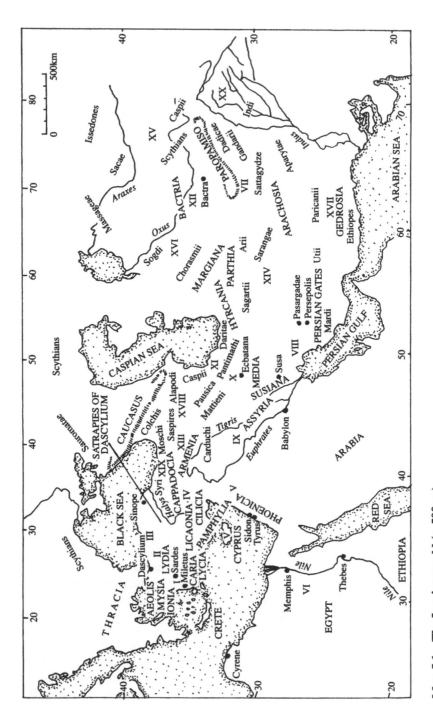

Map 5.1 The Iranian world (c. 500 BC)
Source: R. Ghirshman, *Iran*, Penguin Books, 1954: 143

period (224–651 AD), when these orally transmitted texts were written down, probably for the first time, in a specially invented and extremely elaborate alphabetic script (see Hoffmann and Narten 1989).

The Avestan orthography was designed to preserve the traditional pronunciation with great accuracy and contains much phonetic detail which is irrelevant for the comparativist. For example, the word for 'land' appears in such different forms as *da^iŋhu-* and *dax̌iiu-*, both representing what is etymologically and probably phonemically **dahyu-*. A particularly confusing feature of the Avestan writing system is the frequent notation of anaptyctic and epenthetic vowels. In this chapter such unetymological vowels will be written superscript, as in *daδā^iti* 'he gives' (= OInd. *dádāti*) – as opposed to the diphthong *āi* in *āiδi* 'come!' – or OAvest. *d^aibitiia-* 'second' (= OInd. *dvitī́ya-*). Note too that the semi-vowels *j* and *w* are regularly represented by *ii* and *uu* (which can equally represent the sequences *iy* and *uw*) and that *ī*, *ū* are not consistently distinguished from *i, u*.

Old Persian, which is known from inscriptions of the Achaemenian period (sixth to fourth centuries BC), represents a later stage of linguistic development as well as a different dialect from the language of the Avesta. Like Avestan, it is written in a specially invented script, in this case a form of the cuneiform writing commonly used in the ancient Near East. The Old Persian script combines syllabic and alphabetic principles. For example, there are two *t*-signs, of which *t^u* is syllabic (representing [tu(:)], since *ī* and *ū* are not distinguished from *i* and *u*) whilst *t* can represent either a syllable [ta, tə] or the simple consonant [t]. Since there is no sign for **t^i* (though comparable signs such as *d^i* do exist), [ti] or [ti:] has to be written by means of two signs (*t-i*), a combination which can also denote [tai]. The fact that a sign such as *t* has both syllabic and consonantal values is the source of much ambiguity, as is the fact that in most cases a nasal is not written before another consonant. As a result of these two deficiencies, for instance, the third-person singular present indicative active and middle (-*ti* and -*tai*) and the equivalent plural endings (-*nti* and **-ntai*) are all indistinguishable in writing. In this chapter, for the sake of clarity, Old Persian forms will generally be cited in phonemic transcription rather than in transliteration. (On the Old Persian writing system see further Hoffmann 1976: 620–45.)

Only a brief survey can be given here of the great variety of languages attested at the Middle Iranian stage. Western Middle Iranian is represented by Middle Persian, which is essentially, though not in every detail, a later form of the same dialect as Old Persian, and by Parthian. The Eastern Middle Iranian languages include Khotanese and the closely related Tumshuqese, which are the most conservative of the Middle Iranian languages in their morphology, Sogdian, Bactrian and Choresmian. Amongst the even more numerous Modern Iranian languages we shall occasionally have reason to refer to Persian (or New Persian), Pashto, Ossetic and the Shughni group. Further information on these and other Iranian languages may be found in the relevant chapters of the *Compendium Linguarum Iranicarum* (Schmitt 1989).

Phonology

The vocalic system of Common Iranian is almost identical to that of Old Indian. The main difference is the lack of $\breve{e}$ and $\breve{o}$, the diphthongs from which Old Indian *e* and *o* derive being preserved in Old Iranian as *ai* (Avest. *aē* or *ōi*) and *au* (Avest. *ao* or *əu*). Compare OPers. *daiva-*, Avest. *daēuua-* '(evil) god, devil' = OInd. *devá-* 'god'; OPers. *rautah-* 'river' = OInd. *srótas-* 'stream'. The comparatively rare long diphthongs *āi* and *āu*, which are shortened in Indian, also survive in Old Iranian, compare Avest. instr. pl. *yasnāiš* 'by sacrifices' = OInd. *yajñáiṣ*; Avest. nom. sg. *gāuš* 'ox, cow' = OInd. *gáus*.

The etymological origins of the Iranian vowels *a*, *i*, *u*, *ṛ* (= [əʳ]), *ā*, *ī*, *ū* are in general the same as those of the equivalent Old Indian vowels. In particular, as in Indian, IE **a*, *e*, *o*, *ṇ*, *ṃ* fall together as *a* and the corresponding long vowels (including those which ultimately derive from short vowel + laryngeal) as *ā*. Brugmann's Law, according to which IE **o* gives *ā* in open syllables, seems to apply in the same circumstances in both branches of Indo-Iranian, for example, Avest. nom./acc. sg. *dā̆ru*, OInd. *dā́ru* 'wood' = Gk δόρυ. However, the contexts in which the IE laryngeals are vocalized (to Iran. *i*, OInd. *ĭ*, e.g. OPers./Avest. *pitar-*, OInd. *pitár-* 'father' < IE **ph₂ter-*) are more restricted in Iranian, resulting in many cases of the correspondence Iranian 0 : OInd. *ĭ*, e.g. OAvest. *dugᵊdar-*, Later Avest. *duɣðar-* = OInd. *duhitár-* 'daughter' < IE **dʰugh₂ter-*; OAvest. *varᵊntē* = OInd. *vṛṇītē* 'chooses' < **wḷ-nH-toi*. Where Old Indian has *ir*, *ur* (before vowels) or *īr*, *ūr* (before consonants) from IE **ṛH* or **ḷH*, Iranian has uniformly *ar*:

Avest. *sarah-* = OInd. *śíras-* 'head' < **ḱṛh₂os-*
OPers. *paru-* = OInd. *purú-* 'much' < **pḷh₁u-*
OPers. *darga-*, Avest. *darᵊga-* = OInd. *dīrghá-* 'long' < **dḷh₁gʰo-*
Avest. *varᵊnā-* = OInd. *ū́rṇā-* 'wool' < **h₂wḷh₁neh₂-*

Since short *a* and long *ā* probably differed markedly in quality as well as in quantity (as they do both in Sanskrit and in many modern Iranian languages), the system of simple vowels in Common Iranian may be represented diagrammatically in Figure 5.1.

This simple system seems to survive almost unchanged in Old Persian (in so far as the inadequate cuneiform orthography allows one to tell), though the unitary sound *ṛ* had probably developed to a sequence of vowel + consonant, most likely [ər] (written *a-r-* in initial position, but distinct from the sequence [ar], as is proved by its different fate in Middle and New Persian). A similar development is found in Avestan, where *ṛ* usually gives *ərə* (i.e. *ər*ᵊ) as in

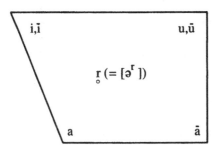

Figure 5.1   Simple vowels

kərᵊnao'ti 'makes' = OInd. *kṛnóti*. But many other outcomes of *ṛ* are found in Avestan, e.g. *ar* before *š* (*aršti-* 'spear' = OPers. *a-r-š-t-i-* [ərsti-], OInd. *ṛstí-*), *əhr* before *k, p* (*vəhrka-* 'wolf' = Pers. *gurg* < OPers. **vərka-*, OInd. *vṛ́ka-*, see p. 138), *ir* before *y* (pres. stem *kiriia-* 'to be done' = OPers. *kəriya-* < **kṛya-*, OInd. *kriyá-*), *rə* after *t* (pres. stem *trəfiia-* 'to steal' = Sogd. *čəf-* < **tṛfya-*, cf. OInd. °*tṛp-* 'stealing').

The example of *ṛ* may serve to illustrate the complexity of Avestan vocalism. It is not possible here to detail the development of all the vowels, but The most important contextual changes must be noted. These include the (re)appearance of mid-high vowels *ĕ* and *ŏ*. In final position **-ai* and **-au* give *-ĕ* and *-ō* (or *-uuō*) respectively (e.g. 3 sg. pres. mid. ending *-tĕ* = OPers. *-tai*, OInd. *-te* < **-taj*, IE **-toj*) while **-yă* gives Later Avest. *-e* (e.g. *a-* stem gen. sg. ending Later Avest. *-ahe* = OAvest. *-ahiiā*, OPers. *-ahəyā*, OInd. *-asya*, IE **-osjo*). Internally, *a* often becomes *e* between two palatal sounds, as in OAvest. *yehiiā*, Later Avest. *yeṅhe* 'of whom' (= OInd. *yásya*), and *o* between *p/g/m/v* and *u*, as in *po"ru-* 'much' (= OPers. *paru-*, see p. 130). Final *-ō* (OAvest. *-ō* or *-ə̄*) and *-ā̊* most often derive, via **-ah* and **-āh*, from **-as* (IE **-os, *-es*) and **-ās* respectively, e.g. *yō* (OAvest. *yə̄*) 'who' (nom. sg. m.), *yā̊* 'who' (nom. pl. f.). Before nasals, especially in final syllables, *a* and *ā* normally develop into *ə* and *ą* (= [aã]) respectively, so that *-əm* and *-ąm* are the regular accusative singular endings of *a-* stems and *ā-* stems. The *ə* which arises thus is subject to further changes, for instance, to *i* after a palatal, as in °*činah-* 'desire' < **čənah-* (beside OPers./Avest. °*čanah-*, OInd. *cánas-*). The sequences **(i)yə, *(u)wə* frequently contract to *ī, ū* (or *i, u*, since the length of these vowels is not consistently noted in Avestan), **aya, *awə* to *aē, ao*. Compare *īm* 'this' (= OPers. *iyam*, OInd. *iyám*, nom. sg. f.); Later Avest. *tūm* 'thou' (= OAvest. *tuuə̄m*, OPers. *tuvam*, OInd. *tuvám*, nom.); *aēm* 'this' (beside OAvest. *aiiə̄m*, OInd. *ayám*, nom. sg. m.); *baon* 'they became' (= OInd. *(á)bhavan*).

The consonantism of the Iranian languages diverges much more fundamentally from that of Old Indian. Two major innovations in Iranian are the loss of all aspirates and the appearance of a series of fricatives (f, θ, x) unknown to Old Indian. In most cases these fricatives derive from p, t, k in pre-consonantal position, but they also correspond to the Old Indian voiceless aspirates ph, th, kh (in all positions). The voiced aspirates (IE $*b^h$, $*d^h$, $*g^h/g^{wh}$, OInd. bh, dh, gh) merely lose their aspiration, thus merging with the original non-aspirate series:

Iran. p = OInd. p: OPers./Avest. *pitar*, OInd. *pitár-* 'father'
Iran. f = OInd. p: Avest. *friia-*, OInd. *priyá-* 'dear'
    = OInd. ph: Avest. *kafa-* 'foam', OInd. *kapha-* 'slime'
Iran. t = OInd. t: OPers. *tuvam*, OAvest. *tuuəm*, Later Avest. *tūm* (see
        p. 131), OInd. *tuvám* (nom.) 'thou'
Iran. θ = OInd. t: OPers. *θuvām*, Avest. *θβąm*, OInd. *tvā̆m* (acc.) 'thee'
    = OInd. th: Avest. *paθō*, OInd. *pathás* (gen. sg.) 'way'
Iran. k = OInd. k: Avest *kuθra*, OInd. *kútra* 'whither?'
Iran. x = OInd. k: OPers/Avest. *xšap-*, OInd. *kṣap-* 'night'
    = OInd. kh: Avest. *xā-*, OInd. *khā̆-* 'spring, well'
Iran. b = OInd. b: Oss. *bal* 'group', OInd. *bála-* 'power' (?)
    = OInd. bh: OPers./Avest. *brātar-*, OInd. *bhrātar-* 'brother'
Iran. d = OInd. d: Avest. *dantan-*, OInd. *dant-* 'tooth'
    = OInd. dh: Avest. *daēnu-* 'female', OInd. *dhenú-* 'cow'
Iran. g = OInd. g: Avest. *ga^{i}ri-*, OInd. *girí-* 'mountain'
    = OInd. gh: Avest. *garəma-*, OIns. *gharmá-* 'heat'

Despite their loss of aspiration in Iranian, the IE voiced aspirates are still occasionally distinguishable from the equivalent non-aspirates by the effects of Bartholomae's Law, according to which a combination such as $*g^h+t$ was assimilated to $*gd^h$ in Indo-Iranian (and perhaps already in Indo-European, cf. Chapter 2, p. 39), whereas $*g+t$ gave $*kt$. By this rule, which applied to all combinations of voiced aspirate + voiceless stop or sibilant, one may deduce from a form such as OAvest. *aogədā* 'he said' (= *aog* + morpheme *-tā*) that the root *aog* originally ended in an aspirate $*g^h$ or $*g^{wh}$; in this case $*g^h$ is confirmed by Gk εὔχεσθαι and so on. Unfortunately the contrary deduction cannot usually be made from the presence of a voiceless cluster, since the effects of Bartholomae's Law tended to be cancelled out by the restoration of the normal form of the morpheme, as in Later Avest. *aoxta* for OAvest. *aogədā*, OPers./Later Avest. *basta-* 'bound' for expected *$*bazda-$* (= OInd. *baddhá-*).

    Common Iranian was rich in both sibilants (s, z, $š$, $ž$) and affricates ($č$, $ǰ$, i.e. $t\!š$, $d\!ž$ – differing from the Indian c, j, which, at least in the earliest period, were palatal stops – and possibly c, j, i.e. ts, dz). These stem in part from IE $*s$ and in part from the 'two series of palatals', that is (a) IE $*\acute{k}$, $*\acute{g}$, $*\acute{g}^h$ (> OInd. $\acute{s}$, j, h); and (b) IE $*k/k^w$, $*g/g^w$, $*g^h/g^{wh}$ when secondarily palatalized before IE $*e$, $*i$, $*j$, and so on (> OInd. c, j, h). The history of these sounds is rather complicated, but is worth examining in some detail in view of the fact that Iranian here retains evidence of distinctions which are lost in Old Indian.

For Indo-European only one sibilant is to be assumed, namely $*s$ (with the allophone $*z$ in clusters such as $*zd$). In addition to its role as an independent phoneme, IE $*s$ has a secondary origin as an automatic feature of the juncture of two dental stops (see Chapter 2, p. 40): $*t+t/*d+t = *tst$, $*d^h+t = *dzd^h$, e.g. IE $*sed+to- = *setsto-$ 'seated' > OInd. *sattá-*, Middle Pers. [*ni*]*šast* (< OPers. *[ni]šasta-*), Lat. *sessus*, cf. also OIr. *sess* 'seat', etc.; $*w\underset{\circ}{r}d^h+to- = *w\underset{\circ}{r}dzd^ho-$ 'increased' > OInd. *v\underset{\circ}{r}ddhá-*, Avest. *vərəzda-* (the development of a voiced group in the latter case being a further instance of Bartholomae's Law, on which see above). As these examples indicate, the resulting clusters were simplified in different ways in Indian, where the sibilant disappeared, and in Iranian, where the first of the two dental stops was lost, giving the regular correspondences Indian *tt* : Iranian *st* and Indian *ddh* : Iranian *zd*.

In Indo-Iranian, much as in Slavic (see Chapter 14, pp. 423f.), IE $*s$ and $*z$ underwent a split, becoming Ind. *ṣ̌*, *ẓ̌*, Iran. *š*, *ž*, after the sounds collectively known as RUKI (i.e. *r*, *\underset{\circ}{r}*; *ŭ*, *ău*; *k* and other velars and palatals; *ĭ*, *ăi*) but remaining, at least in the first instance, unchanged in other contexts. For example: loc. pl. ending Avest. *-šu* (OInd. *-ṣu*) after stems in *u* (etc.) but *-su* after stems in *ant*; Avest. *mižda-* 'reward', OInd. *mīḍhá-* < $*mizdhá-$, IE $*miz-d^h(h_1)o-$ (Gk μισθός) but OPers./Avest. *Mazdā-* (divine name), OInd. *medhā́-* 'wisdom' < $*mazdhā́-$, IE $*m\underset{\circ}{n}z-d^heh_1-$. (Note that the Iranian forms with *z* and *ž* here clarify their Indian counterparts, which have become opaque as a result of the loss of voiced sibilants in Old Indian.) This change does not affect Iran. *st*, *zd* < $*tst$, $*dzd^h$, showing that the sibilant was still protected by the preceding stop when the RUKI rule operated: Avest. *vista-* 'known' < $*witsto- = *wid+to-$ (Gk Ϝιστός, OIr. *fess*). In Iranian (but not Indian) the change to *š*, *ž* also takes place after a labial: Avest. *diβža-*, OInd. *dípsa-* < $*di(d)bz^ha-$, desiderative of Avest. *dab*, OInd. *dabh* 'to injure, deceive'.

Finally, those instances of IE $*s$ which had so far survived unchanged in Iranian underwent a further split, *s* remaining in groups such as *sn*, *sp*, *st*, $*ts$ (> *s*) but becoming *h* in all other contexts, e.g. OPers. *a(h)mi*, Avest. *ahmi*, Khot. *īmä* 'I am', OPers. *hanti*, Avest. *hənti*, Khot. *īndä* 'they are' (= OInd. *ásmi*, *sánti* < IE $*h_1esmi$, $*h_1senti$), but OPers. *asti*, Avest. *asti*, Khot. *aštä* 'he is' (= OInd. *ásti* < IE $*h_1esti$); *ā*-stem loc. pl. Avest. *-ā-hu* (= OInd. *-ā-su*). Although this development is found in all Iranian languages it must be comparatively late, since proto-Iranian forms with *s* (for later *h*) are preserved in ancient Near Eastern sources (see p. 127).

An important implication of this fact is that the development of the IE 'first palatal series' ($*\hat{k}$, $*\hat{g}$, $*\hat{g}^h$) to sibilants (*s*, *z*), which occurs in Avestan and all branches of Iranian other than Old Persian (and later dialects of south-west Iran), must also be later than the Common Iranian period, since the *s* arising from IE $*\hat{k}$ does not participate in the change of IE $*s$ to *h*. As a plausible intermediate stage between the attested Iranian series (Avest. *s*, *z*, *ẓ*; OPers. *θ*, *d*, *δ*) and the presumed Indo-Iranian palatal affricates *$*ć$, *$*ǰ$, *$*ǰ^h$ (< IE *$*ḱ$, *$*ǵ$, *$*ǵ^h$) the dental affricates *$*\underline{ts}$ and *$*\underline{dz}$ may be reconstructed for Common Iranian. In Figure 5.2 the postulated development of this 'first series' of palatals is set beside that of the 'second series' (i.e. the Indo-Iranian palatal stops arising from the secondary palatalization of IE velars or labiovelars, which eventually gave palatal affricates in Iranian) in order to show how the resulting Iranian and Indian forms disambiguate one another.

As Figure 5.2 shows, only the voiceless sounds (Ind. *ś*, Iran. *$*\underline{ts}$ < IE *$*ḱ$; Ind. *c*, Iran. *č* < IE *$*k/k^w$ before a palatal) are etymologically unambiguous. Each of the voiced sounds, OInd. *j* and *h*, Iran. *$*\underline{dz}$ and *ǰ*, has a double origin, since Old Indian confuses the two palatal series while Iranian (as always) confuses aspirates and non-aspirates. However, the ambiguity is resolved in the case of words preserved in both branches of Indo-Iranian, each of which preserves the distinction lost in the other.

Iran. *$*\underline{ts}$ = OInd. *ś*: OPers. *θard-*, Avest. *sarᵊd-*, cf. OInd. *śarád-* 'year' (IE *$*ḱ$)

Iran. *$*\underline{dz}$ = OInd. *j*: OPers. *yad*, Avest. *yaz*, OInd. *yaj* 'to worship' (IE *$*ǵ$)
= OInd. *h*: OPers. *adam*, Avest. *azᵊm*, OInd. *ahám* 'I' (IE *$*ǵ^h$)

Iran. *$*č$ = OInd. *c*: OPers. *či*, Avest. *čiṯ*, OInd. *cit* (enclitic) 'also, even' (IE *$*k^w$)

Iran. *$*ǰ$ = OInd. *j*: Avest. *ǰaⁱni-*, OInd. *jáni-* 'woman' (IE *$*g^w$)
= OInd. *h*: OPers./Avest. *ǰan*, OInd. *han* 'to strike, kill' (IE *$*g^{wh}$)

The depalatalization seen in the unconditioned reflexes of the IE palatals

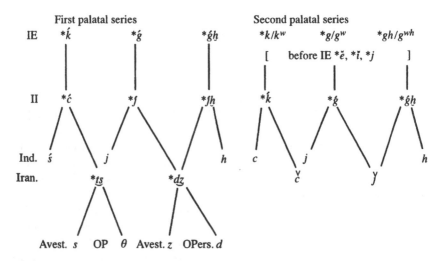

Figure 5.2   Reflexes of the IE palatals

(Avest. *s*, *z*; OPers. *θ*, *d*) failed to take place in most combinations with consonants, where the usual outcome in all Iranian languages is palatal *š*, *ž*, as in Avest. *fšu-* beside *pasu-* 'sheep' (OInd. *paśú-*, IE *p(e)k̑u-*). In most cases the Old Indian equivalent is retroflex *ṣ*, *ẓ*, cf. Avest. *ašta* 'eight' = OInd. *aṣṭá* (IE *ok̑tō*); Avest. *mǝrǝždika-* 'mercy' = OInd. *mr̥ḍīká-* (< *mr̥ẓdīká-*, IE *-ĝd-*). An important special case is that of IE *sk̑*, which gives OInd. *(c)ch*, Iran. *s*, as in the inchoative present stem OInd. *gáccha-* 'to come', Choresmian [*n*]*γs-* < *[*ni*]*gasa-* 'to arrive' (a more archaic form than Avest. *jasa-*), all < IE *g̑ʷm̥-sk̑o-* (Gk βάσκε). Regarding IE *k̑w* (> OPers. *s*, Khot. *śś* [š], elsewhere *sp*), *g̑(ʰ)w* (> OPers. *z*, Khot. *ś* [ž], elsewhere *zb*), and *k̑r* see p. 136.

Finally, we should note the outcome of IE clusters of velar, labiovelar, or palatal + *s*. All such groups give OInd. *kṣ*, whilst Iranian distinguishes four possibilities: (a) *xš* < *k(ʷ)s*, e.g. Avest. *vaxšiia-*, OInd. *vakṣyá-*, fut. of *vak* 'to speak'; (b) *gž* < *g(ʷ)zʰ* (for *g(ʷ)ʰ+s* by Bartholomae's Law), e.g. OAvest. *aogǝžā* 'saidst'; (c) *š* < *k̑s*, e.g. Avest. *mošu*, OInd. *makṣú* 'quickly'; (d) *ž* < *g̑zʰ* (for *g̑ʰ+s*), e.g. OAvest. *dīdǝrǝža-*, desiderative of *darǝz* 'to make firm' (OInd. *dr̥m̥hati*).

The following schema shows the minimum complement of consonantal phonemes to be assumed for Common Iranian. An asterisk (*) indicates those which do not survive as such in any attested language.

p		f	b			m		w	
t		θ	d			n	l		
	*ts	s		*dz	z		r		
	č	š		ǰ	ž			y	
k		x	g						*H

Regarding the reappearance of IE *l* (> OPers./Avest. *r*) as *l* in later Iranian see next paragraph. On the reconstructions *ts* and *dz* see pp. 133–4. The symbol *H* represents a consonant deriving from the IE laryngeals, whose survival, at least in certain positions, is indicated by metrical and other considerations; for example, OAvest. *mazdā̊*, a form which is disyllabic as nominative singular but trisyllabic as genitive singular, indicating nom. *mazdaH-s* (> *mazdās*) ~ gen. *mazdaH-as*.

Not all of the phonological developments shared by Avestan and Old Persian can be ascribed to Common Iranian. The change of *s* to *h* (except in certain groups), which occurs in all attested Iranian languages, cannot have been completed until after the arrival of Iranian speakers in western Iran, as has already been pointed out. The replacement of *l* (and *l̥*) by *r* (and *r̥*), which Avestan and Old Persian have in common with Vedic, was nevertheless not universal in Iranian, as is shown by the later reappearance of dialectal forms with *l* < IE *l*, for example, Pers. *lištan* 'to lick' beside Avest. *raēz* (IE *lejg̑ʰ*, Gk λείχω). Similarly, the two Old Iranian languages share a development of IE *$k(^w)j$ to *šy*, as in OPers. *šiyav*, Avest. *š(ii)auu* 'to go' (IE *$kjew$-, OInd. *cyav*, Gk σεύομαι and κῑνέω), but the preservation of an affricate in Khot. *tsū*- [tsʰuː-], Tumshuqese *cch*- 'id.' indicates that only the intermediate stage *čy* is to be attributed to Common Iranian.

The most important isogloss separating Old Persian from Avestan is to be seen in the treatment of the 'first palatal series', IE *$\acute{k}$, *$\acute{g}$, *$\acute{g}^h$, which are thought to have developed via palatal affricates (II *$\acute{c}$, *$\acute{j}$, *$\acute{j}^h$) and dental affricates (Common Iranian *$t\underline{s}$, *$d\underline{z}$) and which give θ and *d* in Old Persian (and later dialects of south-west Iran) but *s* and *z* in Avestan and all other Iranian languages (see pp. 131f.). The treatment of the IE combinations *$\acute{k}w$ and *$\acute{g}(^h)w$ provides a threeway isogloss, giving *sp*, *zb* in most Iranian languages (including Avestan), *s*, *z* in Old Persian and *š*, *ž* in the group of north-eastern Iranian Saka (Scythian) languages represented by Khotanese. Examples: Avest. *aspa*-, OPers. *asa*-, Khot. *aśśa*- [aʃa-] 'horse' (= OInd. *áśva*-, IE *-$\acute{k}w$-); Parthian *əzbān*, OPers. *həzan*-, Khot. *biśāa*- [βiʒaːa-] 'tongue' (cf. OInd. *jihvā́*-, IE *-$\acute{g}^hw$-). Since the palatals *š*, *ž* can hardly be derived from *$t\underline{s}w$ and *$d\underline{z}w$, it is simplest to assume Common Iranian *ćw and *ȷw. The palatal nature of II *$\acute{c}$ < IE *$\acute{k}$ seems also to have been preserved up to the Common Iranian stage in the case of the cluster *ćr, cf. Khot. *śśāra*- [seṛa-] 'good' (= Avest. *srīra*-, OInd. *śrīla*- 'beautiful', cf. Gk κρείων). In Old Persian *ćr gives *ç* (a sibilant of unclear phonetic character), a development which may have proceeded via *$t\underline{s}r$ and *θr, since *ç* is also the outcome of Iran. *θr < IE *tr or *tl, as in *puça*- 'son' (= Avest. *puθra*-, OInd. *putrá*-).

It is not surprising to find that it is the languages spoken at the fringes of the Iranian world – Old Persian in the extreme south-west and the languages of the nomadic Saka peoples of the Eurasian steppes – which stand out as aberrant in respect of the old isoglosses mentioned above. In each case, Avestan represents the Iranian mainstream. Avestan is often regarded as an Eastern Iranian language, which is no doubt correct from a purely geographical point of view, but it shows none of the phonological developments which are characteristic of Eastern Iranian in later periods, such as the voicing of the fricative in the groups *xt and *ft or the depalatalization of *č. Avestan does indeed have its peculiarities, such as the reversion of *ft to *pt*, the development of *rt to *š*, or the frequent insertion of a nasal *ŋ* before *h* (e.g. *aŋhat̰*, 3 sg. subj. of *ah*- 'to be', OInd. *ásat*), but they do not seem likely to be very ancient, nor do they provide evidence of a particularly close relationship with any other Iranian language.

Morphophonology

At the end of the word certain special phonological changes take place. In the attested Old Iranian languages the original distinctions between long and short final vowels are lost. In general, Old Persian and Old Avestan tend to lengthen short final vowels, while Later Avestan shortens many that were originally long. In the *a*-declension, for instance, both the vocative singular (originally *-*a*) and the instrumental singular (originally *-*ā*) appear as OPers./OAvest. -*ā*, Later Avest. -*a*, so that the length of the final vowel no longer has any phonemic (or etymological) significance. The merging of long and short final vowels was not universal, however; cf. Morgenstierne (1973a: 108–9) on remnants of a distinction between *-*a* and *-*ā* in Shughni and other modern Iranian languages of the Pamir mountains.

A feature common to all the Iranian languages is the loss of final *-*h* (< IE *-*s*). In some languages the loss of *-*h* is accompanied by a change in the quality of the preceding vowel, whereby *-*ah* > Avest. -*ō* (OAvest. also -*ə*), Khot. -*ä* [-e], Sogd. -*i*, and *-*āh* > Avest. -*å*, Khot. -*e* [-ɛ:] (but Sogd. [-*a*; cf. the similar changes accompanying the loss of final *-*m* in Middle Iranian: *-*am* > Khot./Sogd. -*u*; *-*ām* > Khot. -*o* but Sogd. -*a*). In Old Persian, on the other hand, *-*h* is lost without trace, as are *-*d*/-*t* and perhaps some other final consonants, so that *-*ah*/-*ad* and *-*āh*/-*ād* give -*a* and -*ā* respectively (thus re-establishing the recently lost phonemic distinction between long and short final vowels). Such developments had a significant impact on the morphology of the Iranian languages, as may be seen from the paradigm of the *a*-stems in Table 5.1.

The changes typical of absolute word-final position are sometimes found also internally, in compounds and before particular morphemes: compare Avest. *vačō.marᵊta*- 'recited aloud' and instr. pl. *vačəbiš*, both from *vačah*- 'speech, word' with the same treatment of *-*ah* < *-*as* as occurs in final position in the nom./acc. sg. *vačō*/*vačə* (= OInd. *vácas*, Gk (*F*)ἔπος). In other cases, however, compound-juncture is treated as internal position, as in Avest. *vačas.tašti*- 'strophe', where the original *s 'reappears' in accordance with the regular treatment of the IE cluster *st. Such combinatory variants as *vačas*° are referred to as sandhi forms, 'sandhi' being the Sanskrit term for the 'combination' both of elements within a word and of words within a sentence (see Chapter 4, p. 107); in Old Iranian, however, the occurrence of sandhi is almost entirely restricted to the juncture of elements within a single accentual unit, that is, of morphemes in a word, of words in a compound or of a clitic with its host as in Avest. *fraδātaē-ča* 'and (it) will prosper' (= *frāδáⁱte, 3 sg. subj. mid. of *frād* + encl. -*ča* 'and', see Hoffmann 1975: 262ff.), *kas-čiṱ* 'someone' (= nom. sg. m. *kō* 'who?' + encl. indefinite particle -*čiṱ*), OPers. *kaš-či*. As these examples show, the forms occurring in sandhi before enclitics often preserve older phonological forms of the inflections: -*taē*° < IE *-*toj* (see pp. 130f.), *kas*° < IE *kʷos. The shortening of the vowel in the first syllable of *fraδātaē-ča* is probably due to a shift of accent to the syllable preceding the particle -*ča* (= Gk τε, Lat. -*que*, etc.).

Since the accent is not noted in writing in any Old or Middle Iranian language, its position and nature can only be deduced – as in Germanic – from its observable effects. In Avestan the most important phonological change connected with the accent is the devoicing of *r* (and *ər* < **r̥*) before *k*, *p*, *t*, which is restricted to forms in which the accent falls on the syllable containing *r*. The working of this rule, which results in written *hrk*, *hrp* and (**hrt* >) *š*, indicates the existence of a free accent, which is often though not always on the same syllable as in the equivalent Vedic form, e.g. *vəhrka-* 'wolf', *aməša-* 'immortal' = Ved. *vŕ̥ka-*, *amŕ̥ta-*, but *mahrka-* 'destruction' = **márka-* (as against Ved. *marká-*). The formation of a compound or the addition of a suffix or enclitic (see p. 137) can result in a shift of accent, as in *amərᵊta-tāt-* 'immortality' (cf. Ved. *sarvá-tāt(i)-* beside *sárva-*). See Mayrhofer in Schmitt 1989: 12–13; Beekes 1988: 55–69.

Whether the Avestan accent was still a musical (pitch) accent like that of Greek and Vedic or a dynamic (stress) accent is controversial, but there is no doubt that most middle and modern Iranian languages have developed a strong stress accent, which often causes syncope in unstressed syllables. In many Iranian languages the position of the stress has come to be wholly determined by the quantitative shape of the word, but a free stress, possibly reflecting the IE accent, is still found in some modern Eastern Iranian languages; cf. Morgenstierne 1973b on the difference in stress in such pairs as Pashto *wúča* (f.) 'dry' (= Ved. *śúṣkā-*) and *ričá* 'nit' (= Ved. *likṣā́-*).

The original close relationship between accent and ablaut (see Chapter 2, pp. 50–2) has become effaced in Iranian, as in other branches of IE, to the extent that the accent can fall on any syllable, regardless of its vocalism. As a result of the merger of **ĕ̆* and **ŏ̆* in Indo-Iranian *ă̆*, the IE qualitative ablaut has disappeared, although the palatalization of the IE (labio)velars before **ĕ̆* occasionally allows its former presence to be discerned, as in the inflection of OAvest. *aogah-* (n.) 'strength', acc. sg. *aogō*, instr. sg. *aoǰaŋhā* < **h₂ewg-os*, **h₂ewg-es-eh₁*, cf. Gk μένος, μένεος (Hoffmann 1958: 14–15) or the interrogative pronoun Avest. *ka-*, *ča-* < **kʷo-*, **kʷe-* (see p. 143). Some such contrasts between forms with and without palatalization survive into Middle Iranian, as in Parthian *paryōž* beside *paryōγ* 'victory' or Khot. *tcamäna*, instr. sg. of *kye* 'who'. On the other hand, the quantitative ablaut (the IE alternation $0 \sim e/o \sim \bar{e}/\bar{o}$) is well preserved and productive in Indo-Iranian, where it appears as $0 \sim a \sim \bar{a}$, or, in combination with a following semi-vowel or consonant, $i/y \sim ai/ay \sim \bar{a}i/\bar{a}y$, *r̥/r* ~ *ar* ~ *ār*, *a/n* (< **n̥/n*) ~ *an* ~ *ān*, etc. It is to be noted that the Indo-Iranian long grade (*ā* etc.) does not always derive from an IE long grade but can also represent the *o*-grade by Brugmann's Law (see p. 130).

These alternations, which can occur in any part of a word (root, suffix or ending), are of great importance for the historical morphology of Iranian (see also pp. 149–50 on the function of 'vr̥ddhi' in word formation). Ablaut occurs both within a single paradigm, a particular grade of the root and/or suffix being associated with each individual ending, and between contrasting paradigms. Ablaut of the root is most often attested in formations without suffix, particularly in root-presents such as *ah-/h-* 'to be' and reduplicated presents such as *dadā-/dad-* 'to give' (< **de-deh₃-/*de-dh₃-*). In formations containing a suffix (or infix) it is usually this element which shows alternation, for example nouns in *-tār-/-tar-/-tr̥-* (*-θr-*), athematic optatives in *-yā-/-ī-* or present stems with infixed *-na-/-n-*. The preservation of an alternation in both root and suffix, as in Avest. nom. sg. *paṇtā̊*, gen. sg. *paθō* 'path' (< IE **pent-oh₂-s/*pn̥t-h₂-es*) is exceptional.

Each individual form in such an alternating paradigm is characterized by a particular ablaut grade of the stem as well as by a specific ending. In the root-present, for instance, the first-, second- and third-person singular present indicative active generally require the full grade of the stem (as in OAvest. *mrao-mī* etc. from *mrauu-* 'to say'), while the equivalent middle forms require the zero grade (°*mru-yē* etc.). Similarly, a *u*-stem such as OPers. *Kuru-* 'Cyrus' has the zero grade of the stem in the nominative singular (*Kur-u-š*) but the full grade in the genitive singular (*Kur-au-š*). Occasionally the occurrence of an abnormal ablaut grade (e.g. the long grade of the root in OAvest. *stāumī*, 1 sg. pres. indic. act. of *stauu* 'to praise', or the long grade of the suffix in OPers. *dahəyāuš*, nom. sg. of the *u*-stem *dahəyu-* 'country') indicates that a category such as 'root-present' or '*u*-stem' is not unitary but is made up of stems which originally belonged to various classes characterized by different configurations of accent and ablaut.

The endings do not normally display ablaut variation within a single paradigm, but only between contrasting paradigms (but see pp. 141–2 on the inflection of Avest. *xratu-*). Thus the genitive singular ending is attested as **-as* (IE **-es/-os*) in Avest. *rāiiō, uxšnō,* and OPers. *piça* (< **piθras*, cf. Gk πατρός, Lat. *patris*) from the stems *raiii-* 'wealth', *uxšan-* 'bull' and *pitar-* 'father' but as **-s* in Avest. *garōiš*, OAvest. *čašmə̄ṇg* (with *-ṇg < *-nh < *-ns*) and *nər°š* from the stems *gaʼri-* 'mountain', *čašman-* 'eye' and *nar-* 'man'. Not all of the individual forms attested are ancient: *nər°š*, for instance, with its remarkable combination of zero grade in both stem and ending, is probably an innovation for expected **narō* (cf. OInd. *nárah̥*, Gk ἀνδρός). Nevertheless, since the innovation must have been based on an already existing form – in this case perhaps **brá-tr̥-š* (= OInd. *bhrátur*, ON *bróðor*), gen. sg. of *brātar-* 'brother' (see Hoffmann 1976: 598) – such a form can justifiably be used as evidence that Iranian inherited *r*-stems with 'acrostatic' accent and the associated type of ablaut (see Chapter 2, pp. 51f.).

Morphology

Nouns

In Avestan, as in Old Indian, the system of three genders, three numbers and eight cases is well established (though it is only in the singular of a few declensions that all eight cases are formally distinct). During the later history of Iranian this system was gradually simplified. Old Persian has already reduced the cases to six by conflating the dative with the genitive and the instrumental with the ablative; Khotanese has gone further, retaining only remnants of the neuter gender and the dual number, while Sogdian has replaced most of the old plural inflections by forms derived from a collective noun in *-tā-. Many modern Iranian languages have dispensed both with the case system and with grammatical gender, so that in New Persian, for instance, the only morpheme surviving from the Old Iranian system of nominal inflection is the plural in -ān (< OPers. gen. pl. -ānām).

In Old Iranian the various declensions are principally distinguished by the final sound of the stem: stems in a, ā, i, r, etc. They are further divided into subclasses by gender (e.g. stems in a into masculines and neuters) and, to a limited extent, by the different accent and ablaut patterns referred to on p. 139. The number of distinct declensions is very much reduced in Middle Iranian, where there is a marked tendency to transfer masculine and neuter nouns to the a-declension and feminines to the ā-declension.

The most common declension in all Iranian languages is that of the masculine a-stems (IE *o-stems), whose inflection in Avestan (exemplified by yasna- 'sacrifice, worship' = Ved. yajñá-), Old Persian, Khotanese and Sogdian is shown in Table 5.1, together with the corresponding Vedic forms. (Only a selection of the numerous variant forms attested, especially in Avestan and Khotanese, is included in the table.)

This type of stem seems always to have had a fixed accent (with the exception of the vocative forms, which in Vedic are either unaccented – cf. Sogd. encl. voc. sg. βaγ 'sir!' beside stressed βaγá – or accented on the first syllable regardless of the position of the accent in the rest of the paradigm – a rule for which there is some evidence also in Avestan, see Hoffmann 1975: 266 and cf. Gk ἄδελφε ~ ἀδελφός, etc.). As for the individual endings, the majority of the Iranian forms are directly comparable with their Old Indian equivalents, on the etymologies of which see Chapter 4, pp. 107f.. The Avestan/Old Persian instrumental singular in -ă̄ corresponds to the rarer Vedic instrumental in -ā rather than to that in -ena (which is of pronominal origin, as is Khot. -na < OIran. *-anā). The usual Avestan dative singular -āi, which may be compared directly with Greek -ῳ, is more archaic than OAvest. -āi.ā, OInd. -āya; the final -ă̄ of the latter form seems to be a fossilized postposition, which may be found also in some Iranian ablative singular, locative singular and locative plural forms. In the nom.-acc.-voc. dual the Iranian forms agree with Vedic -ā (= Gk -ω, cf. also Lat. ambo) rather than -au; the two forms are thought to be old sandhi variants. In the remaining cases of the dual the Iranian and Indian forms are not precisely comparable, the most important difference being the preservation of a distinction between genitive and locative dual in Avestan. In the nominative/vocative plural the regular equivalents of Old Indian -ās and -āsas are the rare endings Avestan -ă̄ and -ă̄ŋhō, Old Persian -āha, which seem to be particularly favoured for words pertaining to the sacral sphere (Avest. aməšă̄ 'the immortal ones', yazată̄ŋhō '(beings) worthy of worship', OPers. bagāha 'gods'). The usual form in both

Table 5.1 Declension of masculine *a*-stems (IE stems in *o)

	Vedic	Avestan	Old Persian	Khotanese	Sogdian
Singular Nom.	yajñ-ás	yasn-ō	-a	-ä	-i
Acc.	yajñ-ám	yasn-əm	-am	-u	-u
Instr.	yajñ-ā́	yasn-a	-ā	-na	(= abl.)
Dat.	yajñ-ā́ya	yasn-āi, OAvest. also -āi.ā	(= gen.)	(= gen.)	(= gen.)
Abl.	yajñ-ā́t	yasn-āt, Later Avest. also -āδa	-ā	(= instr.)	-a
Gen.	yajñ-ásya	yasn-ahe, OAvest. -ahiiā	-ahəyā	-i	-e
Loc.	yajñ-é	yesn-e, yasn-aiia	-ai, -ayā	-ⁱa	-ya
Voc.	yájñ-a	yasn-a	-ā	-a	-a
Dual Nom.-Acc. Instr.-Dat.	yajñ-ā́, -áu	yasn-a	-ā	-a	
-Abl.	yajñ-ábhyām	yasn-aēⁱbiia	-aibiyā		
Gen.	yajñ-áyos	yasn-aiiå̄			
Loc.	(= gen.)	yasn-aiiō			
Voc.	yájñ-ā, -au	yasn-a			
Plural Nom.	yajñ-ā́s, -ā́sas	yasn-a	-ā	-a	-a
Acc.	yajñ-ā́n	yasn-ą, OAvest. -ə̄ng	(= nom.)	(= nom.)	
Instr.	yajñ-áis, -ébhis	yasn-āiš	-aibiš	-yau	
Dat.	yajñ-ébhyas	yasn-aēⁱbiiō	(= gen.)	(= gen.)	
Abl.	(= dat.)	(= dat.)		(= instr.)	
Gen.	yajñ-ā́nām	yasn-anąm	-ānām	-ānu	-ān
Loc.	yajñ-éṣu	yasn-aēšu, -aēšuua	-aišuvā	-uvo'	
Voc.	yájñ-ās, -āsas	yasn-a		(= instr.)	

Avestan and Khotanese is -*a*, which has been explained as an IE collective in
*-*ā* (< *-*eh₂*), compare Lat. *loca* ~ *locus* (Hoffmann 1958: 13); OPers. -*ā* and
Sogdian -*a* are ambiguous and may equally well derive from *-*ā* or *-*ās* (or
both).

Although Iranian inherited many varieties of stem showing ablaut variation
(originally associated with a mobile accent), these seldom survive as
independent types. As a result of a tendency to harmonize the inflection of all
stems ending in the same sound (e.g. all stems in *u*), forms deriving from
different ablaut types may be combined in the inflection of a single word,
often making it difficult to discern its original ablaut pattern. This point may
be illustrated by the *u*-stem Avest. *xratu*- (m.) 'mental power, intention, etc.'
(= OInd. *krátu*- 'power'), of which all the attested forms are shown in Table
5.2. (The only forms which occur in Old Persian are the two acc. sg. forms

Table 5.2   Declension of Avestan *xratu-*

	Singular		Plural
	Old Avestan	*Later Avestan*	*Old Avestan*
Nom.	xratuš	xratuš	xratauuō
Acc.	xratūm	xratūm, xraθβəm	xratūš
Instr.	xratū, xraθβā	xraθβa	*xratubīš
Dat.		xraθβe	*xratubiiō
Abl.	(= gen.)	xrataot̰	(= dat.)
Gen.	xratə̄uš	xratə̄uš, xraθβō	*xratunąm
Loc.	xratå		*xratušū
Voc.		[hu]xratuuō	(= nom.)

xratum and *xraθum*, the latter showing generalization of *θ* from a form such as instrumental singular **xraθuvā* = Avest. *xraθβå̆*.)

In the paradigm in Table 5.2 the suffix appears in the zero grade as **u* (Avest. *ŭ*) or **w* (> Avest. *β* after *θ*), in the full grade as **au* (Avest. *ə̄u/ao*, in final position *ō/uuō*) or **aw* (Avest. *auu*), and in the long grade as **āu* (> Avest. *å̆* in final position). Note also the occurrence of two ablaut variants of the ending itself in the instrumental singular (*-ū < *-u-h₁*; *-βā < *-w-eh₁* or **-w-oh₁*) and genitive singular (*-ə̄uš < *-ew-s*; *-βō < *-w-es* or **-w-os*). The etymologies of the remaining endings are as follows. Singular: nom. *-š < *-s*; acc. *-m < *-m* (Later Avest. variant *-əm* borrowed from the *a*-stems); dat. *-ē̆ < *-ei*. Originally the ablative singular was formally distinct from the genitive only in the *a*-declension; Later Avest. *xrataot̰* exemplifies a tendency to create special ablative forms by borrowing the final *-t̰* of the *a*-stems. The locative and vocative singular are both endingless but differ in the grade of the suffix. Plural: nom./voc. *-ō < *-es*; acc. *-(ū)š < *-(u-)ns*; instr. *-bīš < *-bʰis*; dat./abl. *-biiō < *-bʰjos*; loc. *-šū̆ < *-su*. The genitive plural (like that of the *a*-stems and most other declensions) was remodelled in Indo-Iranian after that of the *n*-stems, but the older ending *-ąm* (< **-ōm*, Gk *-ων*) is occasionally attested, as in Later Avest. *yāθβąm* (beside *yātunąm*), genitive plural of *yātu-* 'sorcerer'.

In general adjectives are inflected exactly like nouns, though a few common adjectives, such as Avest. *vīspa-* 'all' and its cognates, display some of the peculiarities of pronominal declension (see p. 143), e.g. Sogd. abl. (originally instr.) sg. m. *wispna*, Later Avest. nom. pl. m. *vīspe* (= Khot. *biśśä*, contrast OAvest. *vīspå̄ŋhō*), gen. pl. m. *vīspaēšąm* (beside *vīspąnąm*). The feminine forms of adjectives are usually derived from a separate stem in *-ā* or *-ī* (even where the masculine/neuter stem belongs to a class, such as the *u*-declension, which includes feminine nouns). Examples from Avestan: *sūra-*, f. *sūrā-* 'strong'; *poʰru-*, f. *paoˢrī-* 'much'; *bərˢzaṇt-*, f. *bərˢzaˢtī-* 'high'.

As in Old Indian, comparatives and superlatives can be formed in two ways: with the suffixes *-tara-* and *-tama-* added to the stem of the positive (e.g. Avest. *aš.aoǰah-*, *aš.aoǰas-tara-*, *aš.aoǰas-təma-* 'possessing much, more, most power') or with the suffixes *-yah-* and *-išta-* added directly to the underlying root in the full grade (e.g. Avest. *uγ-ra-*, *aoǰ-iiah-*, *aoǰ-išta-* 'strong/er/est'). Also formed directly from the root is the compound form in *-i-*, as in Avest. *tiži.asūra-* 'sharp-tusked' (< **tiǰ-i-* beside *tiγ-ra-* 'sharp'), *bər°zi.čaxra-* 'high-wheeled' (beside *bər°z-aṇt-*), cf. OInd. *r̥j-i-*, Gk ἀργ-ι- as compound form of *r̥j-rá-*, ἀργός (< **ἀργ-ρό-ς* 'swift; bright', etc. (cf. Chapter 2, p. 59).

Pronouns

The principal Avestan demonstrative pronouns are *hō* (nom. sg. m.), *hā* (nom. sg. f.), *tat̰* (nom. sg. n.) 'this; he, she, it', and its compound *aēšō, aēša, aētat̰*; *aēm, īm, imat̰* 'this'; and *hāu, hāu, auuat̰* 'that'. In their inflection these show the same kinds of peculiarities as the equivalent Old Indian forms (see Chapter 4, p. 110), including the employment of suppletive stems, often opposing the nominative singular masculine and feminine (e.g. *hō, hā*) to the rest of the declension (stem *ta-*), and the prefixation or suffixation of deictic particles (e.g. *aē-* in *aē-ša-* etc., *-am in *aēm, īm* = OInd. *ay-ám, iy-ám*). The use of certain endings different from those of nouns (e.g. nom./acc. sg. n. in *-t̰*, instr. sg. m./n. in *-na*, nom. pl. m. in *-e*) and the infixation of additional elements between the stem and ending (e.g. *-hm-* and *-hy-* respectively in several cases of the m. and f. sg., *-h-/-š-* in the gen. pl.) may be exemplified by the following forms of the demonstrative Avest. *aēm* 'this' (stems *ay-/i-*, *a-* and *ima-*): nom. sg. n. *ima-t̰*, instr. sg. m. *a-na*, dat. sg. m. *a-hm-āi*, dat. sg. f. *a-ⁱŋh-āi* (< *a-hy-āi), nom. pl. m. *im-e*, gen. pl. m. *aē-š-ạm*, gen. pl. f. *ā̊-ŋh-ạm*. The Old Persian forms follow the same principles.

Similar irregularities occur in the inflection of the relative pronoun, Avest. *yō* (OAvest. *yə̄*), *yā, yat̰*, OPers. *haya, hayā, taya* (where the relative has been compounded with the demonstrative **hā̊-*, **ta-*), and of the interrogative pronouns. In Old Iranian, unlike Old Indian (see Chapter 4, p. 110), all of the four interrogative stems, *ka-, kā, ča-* and *či-*, still function as pronouns and tend to combine into a suppletive system like that of the demonstratives: Avest. *kō, kā, čit̰* (nom. sg. m., f., n.), cf. OPers. *kaš-či* 'someone', *čiš-či* 'something'.

The inflection of the personal pronouns differs even more markedly from that of nouns, as may be illustrated by the following selection of first person forms:

nom. sg. Avest. *azə̄m*, OPers. *adam*
acc. sg. Later Avest. *mạm*, OPers. *mām*
dat. sg. OAvest. *maⁱbiiā, maⁱbiiō*, Later Avest. *māuu°iia*
gen. sg. Later Avest. *mana*, OPers. *manā*
nom. pl. Avest. *vaēm*, OPers. *vayam*
dat. pl. OAvest. *ahmaⁱbiiā*

gen. pl. Later Avest. *ahmākəm*, OPers. *amāxam*
(cf. OInd. *ahám, mằm, máhya(m), máma, vayám, asmábhya(m), asmākam*).

It will be noted that, as in Old Indian, these forms show no distinction of gender, and that the singular and plural forms are derived from apparently unrelated stems. A further peculiarity of the personal pronouns is the existence of alternative unaccented (enclitic) forms in certain cases, e.g. 1 sg. Avest. *mā*, OPers. *-mā* (acc.), OAvest. *mōi*, Later Avest. *mē*, OPers. *-mai* (gen./dat.). In the plural, Old Avestan preserves a distinction between the enclitic accusative *nā̊* 'us', *vā̊* 'you' (cf. Latin *nōs, vōs*) and the enclitic genitive/dative *nə̄, və̄*, while Later Avest. *nō* and *vō*, like OInd. *nas* and *vas*, are used for all three cases. Finally, we may note the Old Avestan nominative singular feminine forms *θβōi* and *xᵛaē[čā]* (from the possessive adjectives *θβā̊-* 'thy', *xᵛă̆-* '(one's) own'), whose ending may be compared with that of Latin *quae* etc. (Hoffmann 1958: 16).

Verbs

In Old Iranian, and especially in Avestan, the inflection of the verb is extremely rich as a result of the numerous intersecting categories into which its forms are classified: person (first, second or third), number (singular, dual, plural), mood (indicative, injunctive, subjunctive, optative, imperative, participle, infinitive), tense (present, aorist, perfect, etc.) and voice (active, middle or passive). In general, the category of tense is indicated by the stem of the verb; that of mood by the presence or absence of a modal suffix following the tense-stem, the presence or absence of the augment *a-* before the tense-stem and the choice of ending; those of person, number and voice by the verbal endings alone (except in the case of the passive present stem in *-ya-*). The following survey (based on the comprehensive description of Kellens 1984) is primarily concerned with Avestan; Old Persian provides examples of most of the corresponding types and categories but no complete paradigms.

Present stems can be formed in many ways, of which only the principal types can be mentioned here. The most important division is that between 'thematic' and 'athematic' presents. The thematic presents are formed by adding to the root (in a particular, invariable ablaut grade) a suffix consisting of or ending in *-a-* < IE *-e/o-*:

Avestan *θβərᵊs-a-* 'to fashion' (zero grade of root + suffix *-a-*)
bauu-a- 'to become' (full grade + *-a-*)
bū̆ⁱδ-iia- 'to notice' (zero grade + *-ya-*)
zb-aiia- 'to invoke' (zero grade + *-aya-*)
baṇd-aiia- 'to bind' (full grade + *-aya-*)
xšnāuu-aiia- 'to satisfy' (long grade + *-aya-*)
ja-sa- 'to come, go' (zero grade + *-sa-* < IE 'inchoative' *-sko-*).

The various types of athematic present have in common certain endings different from those of thematic stems (see below on the indicative and imperative) and the occurrence of ablaut alternation in the stem:

jan-/γn- 'to strike' (root-present)
da-dā-/da-d- 'to give' (reduplicated present)
vi-na-d-/vi-n-d- 'to find' (infixed nasal)
dᵊbᵊ-nao-/*dᵊbᵊ-nu- 'to deceive' (zero grade + *-nao-/-nu-*)
stərᵊ-nā-/stərᵊ-n- 'to spread' (zero grade + *-nā-/-n-*)

In origin the last two classes are special cases of the preceding type, the nasal infix having been inserted into a root with final *-w-* or *-H-*, cf. *ā.dᵊbao-man-* 'deception' (which demonstrates the existence of a root *dbav* beside *dab*), *starᵊta-* 'spread' (< **st_r̥h₃-to-*, Gk στρωτός), etc.

Certain types of present stem, notably the passives in *-ya-*, causatives in *-aya-* and future stems in **-sya-* (> *-hya-*, *-šya-*), express a special or modified sense of the verb:

jan-iia- 'to be struck' (beside *jan-/γn-* 'to strike')
jām-aiia- 'to cause to go' (beside *ja-sa-* 'to come, go')
bū-šiia-nt- (fut. part. act.) 'about to be' (beside *bauu-a-nt-* (pres. part. act.) 'being').

The future stem is most often attested by its participles, the sense of the future indicative being more commonly expressed by the present subjunctive. The passive stem in *-ya-* (which in Iranian, unlike Old Indian, takes middle or active endings indifferently) is also comparatively rare, in part as a result of the fact that a passive sense can alternatively be expressed by the use of the normal (non-passive) present stem with middle instead of active endings, for example, *vaēna'te* (mid.) 'is seen, seems' as opposed to *vaēna'ti* (act.) 'sees'.

The principal types of aorist stem are the sigmatic aorist, for example, *xšnāu-š-/xšnao-š-* 'to satisfy', in which the suffix **-s-* (> *-s-*, *-h-*, *-š-*) is combined with alternation between the long grade and full grade of the root, and the root-aorist, for example, *jam-/γm-* 'to come, go', which displays alternation between the full grade and zero grade as in the most common type of root-present (though the distribution of the two alternants is slightly different in the aorist). The perfect stem is usually formed by reduplication, for example, *va-uuac-/va-oc-* 'to say'. As in other IE languages, the verb 'to know' irregularly forms an unreduplicated perfect stem *vaēd-/vid-*, cf. OInd. *véda*, *vidmá*, Gk (F)οἶδα, (F)ἴδμεν (see Chapter 9, p. 251), etc. The role of the aorist and perfect stems is very much restricted in Later Avestan – even more so in Old Persian – a development marking the first stage in the creation of the Middle Iranian verbal system (based on the present stem and a new 'past stem' derived from the past participle in *-ta-*).

Table 5.3   Secondary endings

	Active	Middle
Singular		
1	-m/-əm	-i
2	*-s (> -h, -š, etc.)	*-sa (> -ha, -ša, etc.)
3	-t̰	-ta
Plural		
1	-ma	-ma͜idi
2	-ta	-dūm/-δβəm
3	{ -ən (< *-ent/*-ont) -n (< *-nt) -at̰ (< *-ṇt)	{ -nta -ata (< *-ṇto)

It is convenient to begin a survey of the formation of the moods with the injunctive, which is formed by the addition of the so-called 'secondary' endings – which actually represent the verbal endings in their most basic forms, see Chapter 4, p. 113 – directly to the present or aorist stem. The 'secondary' endings (omitting those of the dual, since they are poorly attested and often etymologically obscure) are as in Table 5.3. With the exception of second-person singular middle *-sa (cf. Gk ἔθου, Hom. Gk ἔθεο < *e-dʰh₁-so, etc. as against OInd. -thās) and third-person plural active -at̰ (< *-ṇt), an archaic ablaut variant lost in Old Indian, these endings correspond precisely to the equivalent Old Indian forms.

The imperfect is formed, as in Old Indian, by prefixing the augment a- (= OInd. a-, Gk ε-, Arm. e-) to the present injunctive. The imperfect is well attested in Old Persian, and in some later Iranian languages such as Sogdian, but comparatively rare in Avestan, where the present injunctive has largely taken over its function as a past tense. The even rarer aorist indicative, of which a few forms are attested in Old Avestan and Old Persian, is similarly formed by the prefixation of the augment to the aorist injunctive. The present and perfect indicatives, however, are characterized in a different way, by the use of endings distinct from those of the injunctive.

The so-called 'primary' endings of the present indicative (again omitting the dual forms), as attached to athematic pres. stems, are as in Table 5.4. All of these endings have exact cognates in Old Indian. The inflection of thematic stems differs only in the first-person singular active, where Old Avestan attests the ending -ā (= Gk -ω, Lat. -ō, etc.) as against OPers./Later Avest./ OInd. -ā-mi. The thematic vowel, in general a, appears as ā (< *o by Brugmann's Law, see p. 130) in first-person plural active -ā-mahi and middle -ā-ma͜ide; on the other hand, the thematic first-person singular middle has merely -e < *-ai where *-āj < -*a-ai might have been expected. Since the thematic present indicative is well attested in most Iranian languages, it is possible to give some complete paradigms, at least of the singular and plural

Table 5.4   Primary endings

	Active	Middle
Singular		
1	-mi	-e
2	*-si (> -hi, -ši, etc.)	*-sai (> -he, -še, etc.)
3	-ti	-te
Plural		
1	-mahi	-ma^{i}de
2	*-θa	-duiiē
3	{ -ənti	{ -nte
	-nti	-a^{i}te (< *-ņtoi)
	-at^{h}ī (< *-ņti)	

Table 5.5   Conjugation of the thematic present indicative active

	Avestan	Old Persian	Khotanese	Sogdian
1 sg.	bar-ā-mi	bar-ā-mi	barīmä	βarām
2 sg.	bar-a-hi		bīri	βare
3 sg.	bar-a-^{i}te	bar-a-ti	bīdä	βarti/βart
1 pl.	bar-ā-mahi	bar-ā-mahi	barāmä	βarēm
2 pl.	bar-a-θa		baḍa	βarθa/βarta
3 pl.	bar-ə-nti	bar-a-nti	barīndä	βarand

Table 5.6   Conjugation of the thematic present indicative middle

	Avestan	Old Persian	Khotanese
1 sg.	ba^{i}r-e	bar-ai	bare
2 sg.	bar-a-he		bara
3 sg.	bar-a-^{i}ti	bar-a-tai	baḍe
1 pl.	bar-ā-ma^{i}de		barāmane
2 pl.	(OAv.) bar-a-duiiē		barīru
3 pl.	bar-ə-nte		barāre

forms, based on the present indicative of *bar*, present stem *bar-a-* (act.) 'to carry', (mid.) 'to ride', see Tables 5.5 and 5.6.

The second-person plural active ending *-ta* in Khot. *baḍa*, Sogd. *βarta* (beside *βarθa*) is a secondary ending borrowed from the injunctive etc., as is the second-person singular middle *-ha* in Khot. *bara*; the Khotanese second-person plural middle ending *-īru* is borrowed from the optative. The ending of Khotanese first-person plural active *barāmä* seems to correspond more closely with Classical Sanskrit -mas than with its Vedic variant -masi (= OPers./Avest. -mahi). A more significant division amongst the various Iranian languages is found in the third-person plural middle, where Khotanese and some other languages attest an ending *-ārai (= Avest. -āⁱre) or *-rai (= OInd./Avest. -re). In Avestan, as in Old Indian, this ending is restricted to a small group of root-presents, some of which also have a third-person singular middle in -e rather than -te. These special endings, which are also found in the pf. indicative middle, seem originally to have characterized a particular subclass of root-presents (with a fixed accent on the root and ablaut alternation between long grade and full grade instead of between full grade and zero grade, see Narten 1968).

The endings of the pf. indicative active (singular and plural) are as follows: Sg. 1 -a, 2 -θa, 3 -a; Pl. 1 -ma, 3 -arᵊ or -ərᵊš. It is not clear which of the two third-person plural endings is to be equated with Old Indian -ur (< *-r̥r = -arᵊ or *-r̥s = -ərᵊš). The endings of the pf. indicative middle, in so far as they are attested, are the same as those of the present indicative middle, with third-person singular -e and probably third-person plural *-re (cf. Khot. byaure 'they exist' < *abi-āf-rai, originally third-person plural pf. middle of abi-āp 'to find, obtain'), see above.

The subjunctive is characterized by a suffix -a-, which is inserted between the stem (whether present, aorist or perfect) and the endings. In the case of thematic stems, the subjunctive suffix combines with the final vowel of the stem to a long ā. The endings are a mixture of primary and secondary – the choice being fixed in some cases and free in others – except in the first-person singular, where Old Avestan active -ā and middle -āi are later replaced by the special endings -āni (= OInd. -āni beside -ā, see Chapter 4, p. 116) and -āne respectively.

The optative is similarly characterized by the insertion of a suffix between the present, aorist or perfect stem and the endings, which in this case are always the secondary endings, apart from the special endings third-person plural active -ārᵊ or -ārᵊš (beside secondary -n) and first-person singular middle -a. In the case of most athematic stems, the optative suffix shows ablaut alternation between -yā- and -ī- (from *-jeh₁-/*-ih₁-). In all other cases the suffix is a non-alternating -ī-, which combines with the final vowel of thematic stems to form the diphthong *ai (< Avest. aē or ōi). A special feature of Iranian (attested in Avestan, Old Persian and Sogdian) is the employment of the augment with certain optative forms which express a repeated or habitual action in the past (cf. p. 150).

The endings of the imperative are added directly to the present or aorist stem. (No perfect imperative is attested.) Active: 2 sg. (thematic) -∅, (athematic) -di, 3 sg. -tu; 2 pl. -ta, 3 pl. -əntu or -ntu. Middle: 2 sg. *-swa (> -suua, -huua, -šuua), 3 sg. -tąm or -ąm; 2 pl. -dūm or -δβəm, 3 pl. -ntąm. These endings, all of which have exact cognates in Old Indian, are peculiar to the imperative (except for those of the second-person plural, which are identical with the secondary endings). There is no first-person imperative in Iranian.

Present and aorist stems form their active participles by means of the suffix -*aṇt-*/-*at-* (athematic) or -*ṇt-* (thematic), while perfect stems employ the suffix -*uuah-*/-*uš-*. All three types of stem form their middle participles in the same way, with the suffix -*āna-* (athematic) or -*mna-* (thematic). The latter form may be directly equated with Greek -μενος (< *-*mh₁no-*), while its Old Indian equivalent -*māna-* shows the influence of the athematic suffix -*āna-* (< *-*m̥h₁no-*). Certain other verbal adjectives or participles are not formed from a tense-stem but directly from the root, the most important being the 'past participle' in -*ta-*, which has a passive sense in the case of transitive verbs, and which comes to provide the basis for all the past-tense formations in most Middle and Modern Iranian languages. Various types of infinitive are attested in Avestan, although none of them is common. As in the case of the participles, some are derived from a tense-stem, others directly from the root. The Old Persian infinitives, on the other hand, are all of a single type (not found in Avestan or Old Indian), the suffix -*tanai* being added to the full grade (IE *e*-grade) of the root, for example, *čartanai* 'to do' from the root *kar*.

Word Formation

As in Old Indian, the principal means of creating new words in Iranian are suffixation and the formation of compounds. The individual suffixes and types of compound are also largely identical with those found in Indian, see Chapter 4, pp. 121f., and need not be described again here. A peculiarity of Avestan, of which traces survive in some Middle Iranian languages, is the tendency to replace the bare stem by the nominative singular form, both in compounds and before certrain suffixes, e.g. *bāzuš.aoǰah-* 'strong-armed', *daēuuō.dāta-* 'devil-created', *daēuuō.təma-* 'arch-devil' (beside *bāzu.-stauuah-* 'as thick as an arm', *daēuua-iiasna-* 'devil-worshipper', etc.). A further Avestan development is the employment of the compound form in -*ō*°, originally the nominative singular masculine of the *a*-declension (cf. *daēuuō.dāta-* etc.), without regard to the gender or declension of the stem, as in *daēnō.sāč-* 'well versed in the religion' (from the feminine noun *daēnā-*) or *karhr ͣpō.tāt-* (a collective noun derived from *karhr ͣpan-*, the designation of a class of priests). Similarly in Sogdian, a feminine *ā*-stem such as *xānā* < *xānākā-* 'house' appears before certain suffixes as *xānē-* < *xānāki-* (-*i* being the nominative singular masculine ending of the Sogdian *a*-declension, cf. Table 5.1, p. 141), e.g. plural *xānē-t* 'houses', in origin a collective noun with suffix *-tā-*.

The use of 'vṛddhi' of the first syllable as a derivational device (see Chapter 4, p. 121) is well established in Iranian, although it never became common as it did in Classical Sanskrit. As parallels to the Old Indian forms with $\bar{a}$ and $\bar{a}r$ as vṛddhi of a and $r̥/ar$ respectively one may cite such forms as Avest. *hāuuani-* '(time) appropriate for pressing' from **hauuana-* 'act of pressing' (OInd. *sávana-*); *vārᵊθrayni-* 'victorious' from *vərᵊθrayna-* 'victory'; OPers. *Mārgava-* 'inhabitant of *Margu-*'. Some Iranian languages seem to have agreed with Old Indian also in using the long diphthongs *āi, āu* (= OInd. *ai, au*) as vṛddhi of *i* and *u*, compare the Old Persian month name *Θāigrači-*, probably from **θigra-ka-* 'garlic' (cf. Persian *sīr* 'id.' < **θigra-*), MPers. *wāspuhr* (< **wāispuhr*) 'principal' from *wispuhr* 'prince', etc. In such cases, however, Avestan consistently follows an older derivational pattern in employing the short diphthongs **aj, *aw* (> *aē, ao*, etc.), as in *duuaēpa-* 'island' from **dwi-āp-* 'two waters' (contrast OInd. *dvīpá-* 'island' < **dwi-h₂p-o-*, without vṛddhi), *daožaŋᵛha-* 'hell' from *duž-ahu-* 'id.' (literally 'evil existence').

Syntax

Much less study has been devoted to the syntax of the Iranian languages than to their phonology and morphology. Here it must suffice to mention some of the more important points in which they differ from Old Indian.

One of the most remarkable features of Old Iranian nominal syntax is the ability of the instrumental plural form to substitute for other cases of the plural, as in Avest. *vīspāiš aoi karšuuąn yāiš hapta* 'to all the seven continents' (instr. *vīspāiš, yāiš* for acc.), OPers. *XIV raučabiš θakatā āha* '14 days had passed' (instr. *raučabiš* for nom.). Compare also the use of the instrumental plural for the vocative plural in Khotanese (Table 5.1, p. 139) and as a generalized oblique case of the plural in some of the modern Iranian languages of the Pamir mountains (Wakhi *-əv* < **-aibiš*, etc.). Equally noteworthy is the use of the relative pronoun (Avest. *yā̆-*, OPers. *hayā-/taya-*, see p. 143) in attributive constructions such as Avest. *daēum yim apaošəm* 'the demon Apaosha' (acc.) or OPers. *dahəyūnām tayaišām parūnām* 'of many lands', a usage which results from the reinterpretation of a nominal relative clause such as Avest. *daēuuō yō apaošō*, originally 'the demon who (is) Apaosha', and the attraction of the relative pronoun (and predicate) into the case of the antecedent, giving *daēum yim apaošəm* for **daēum yō apaošō* (see Reichelt 1909: 370–1).

Several characteristic features of the syntax of the verb in Old Iranian have already been referred to on p. 148, including the use of the injunctive in place of the imperfect as the normal narrative past tense, which is peculiar to Avestan, and the use of the optative (sometimes with augment) to express a repeated or habitual action in the past, for example, Avest. *tūm zəmargūzō ākərᵊnuuō vīspe daēuua, zaraθuštra, yōi para ahmāt̰ vīrō.raoδa apataiiən paˁti āiia zᵊmā* 'you, Zarathushtra, drove underground all the demons who previously *used to go about* on this earth in human form'; OPers. *yaθā-šām hacā-ma aθahəya, avaθā akunavayantā* 'as was said to them by me, so *they used to do'*; Sogd. *čāf awya nāra awī δasta nīyāse, əhr 'ti-šī xa nāra čan δasta wāpate* 'however many pomegranates *she took* in (her) hands, the pomegranates *fell* from her hands'.

The loss of the IE perfect system, which is incipient in Later Avestan and almost complete in Old Persian, is made good by the creation of a new type of perfect based on the past participle (with an obligatory passive construction, the agent being originally in the dative, replaced in Old Persian by the genitive): Avest. *yezi-ča hē aniia aya šiiaoθna frauuaršta* 'and if he has committed other evil deeds'; OPers. *ima taya manā kərtam* 'this (is) what I have done' (lit. 'what (has been) done by me'). In many later Iranian languages this construction comes to express a simple past tense, as in MPers. *man kard* 'I did (it)'. Another verbal periphrasis which later becomes widespread, especially in Eastern Middle Iranian, is the so-called 'potential construction'. This is first attested in Old Persian, where the past participle of a transitive verb is used with the auxiliary *kar* 'to make' (in the active) or *bav* 'to become' (in the passive) to express either a potentiality or the consummation of an action: *nai āha martiya ... haya avam Gaumātam tayam magum xšaçam dītam čaxriyā* 'there was no one ... who *could have deprived* that Gaumāta the magus of the kingship'; *yaθā kantam abava, pasāva θikā avaniya* 'when *it had been dug*, then it was filled with gravel'. In Middle Iranian the potential construction also occurs with intransitive verbs (aux. 'to become', Sogd. *βw-*, Khot. *häm-*), for example, Sogd. *ne nipasta βōt* 'he cannot lie down'; Khot. *ku vā drai māśtä parräte hämäte, balysä rrundu kṣamotte* 'when three months *had passed*, the Buddha took leave of the king'.

References

In addition to bibliographic details of works cited in this chapter the following list includes a selection of basic literature on the Iranian languages, especially Avestan and Old Persian.

The most up-to-date survey of the whole field is to be found in the *Compendium Linguarum Iranicarum* (Schmitt (ed.) 1989), which includes chapters on the prehistory of the Iranian languages (pp. 4–24, by M. Mayrhofer), on Old Persian (pp. 56–85, by R. Schmitt), both in German, and on Avestan (pp. 32–55, in French, by J. Kellens). For Avestan see also K. Hoffmann 1987. An earlier article by the same author (Hoffmann 1958) gives an incisive characterization of the special features of Old Iranian, as compared with Old Indian, and is still well worth consulting, as is its companion chapter on Middle Iranian (Henning 1958). These surveys supplement but do not replace Geiger and Kuhn 1895–1903, whose chapters on the Old Iranian languages (pp. 1–248, by Chr. Bartholomae), though in many respects dated, remain unsurpassed in comprehensiveness.

The standard edition of the Avesta is that of K. F. Geldner (1886–96, in the original script). The dictionary of Bartholomae (1904) has likewise not been superseded. Most beginners will find that a reader such as Reichelt 1911, which includes selected texts in transliteration together with notes and glossary, provides a convenient introduction to Avestan. The most accessible systematic grammar is that of A. V. W. Jackson (1892), whilst that of H. Reichelt (1909) is especially valuable for the long section on syntax (pp. 218–387). A modern treatment of Avestan phonology and morphology is provided by Hoffman and Forssman 1996; see also Kellens 1984 and 1995 on the morphology and syntax of the Avestan verb.

All the works mentioned above cover both Old and Later Avestan, though their treatment of the former tends to be less complete as a result of the frequent obscurity of the Gāthās. Modern editions of the Old Avestan texts, with translation and commentary, include Insler 1975 (Gāthās only), Narten 1986 (Yasna Haptaŋhā'ti only), Kellens and Pirart 1988–91, and Humbach 1991. The phonology and morphology of Old Avestan are treated in Beekes 1988 (cf. also Kellens and Pirart 1988: 42–88 on 'phonétique et graphie'), aspects of its syntax in Kellens and Pirart 1990, which also contains a complete lexicon to the Old Avestan texts.

The most comprehensive edition of the Old Persian inscriptions is that of R. G. Kent (1953; supplemented by Mayrhofer 1978). The longest and most important inscription, that of Darius at Bisitun, has recently been re-edited by R. Schmitt (1991). Kent's book also contains a historical grammar (more detailed but less reliable than Schmitt 1989: 56–85) and a lexicon.

Bartholomae, Christian (1904) *Altiranisches Wörterbuch*, Strassburg: Trübner.

Beekes, Robert S. P. (1988) *A Grammar of Gatha-Avestan*, Leiden: Brill.

Geiger, Wilhelm and Kuhn, Ernst (eds.) (1895–1903) *Grundriss der iranischen Philologie*, vol. I, Strassburg: Trübner.

Geldner, Karl F. (1886–96) *Avesta: The Sacred Books of the Parsis*, 3 vols, Stuttgart: Kohlhammer.

Henning, W. B. (1958) 'Mitteliranisch', in Spuler 1958: 20–130.

Hoffmann, Karl, (1958) 'Altiranisch', in Spuler 1958: 1–19; repr. Hoffmann 1975: 58–76.

—— (1975), (1976), (1992) *Aufsätze zur Indoiranistik*, 3 vols, Wiesbaden: Reichert.

—— (1987) 'Avestan language', in Yarshater 1982–: vol. III/1, 47–62; repr. Hoffmann 1992: 864–79.

Hoffmann, Karl and Forssman, Bernhard (1996) *Avestische Laut- und Flexionslehre*, Innsbruck: Institut für Sprachwissenschaft der Universität.

Hoffmann, Karl and Narten, Johanna (1989) *Der Sasanidische Archetypus: Untersuchungen zu Schreibung und Lautgestalt des Avestischen*, Wiesbaden: Reichert.

Humbach, Helmut (1991) *The Gāthās of Zarathushtra and the Other Old Avestan Texts*, 2 vols, Heidelberg: Winter; revised and expanded English version of *Die Gathas des Zarathustra*, Heidelberg: Winter, 1959.

Insler, Stanley (1975) *The Gāthās of Zarathustra* (Acta Iranica 8), Tehran and Liège: Bibliothèque Pahlavi (distributed by E. J. Brill, Leiden).

Jackson, A. V. Williams (1892) *An Avesta grammar in comparison with Old Indian*, Part I, *Phonology, Inflection, Word-formation, with an Introduction on the Avesta*, Stuttgart: Kohlhammer.

Kellens, Jean (1984) *Le Verbe avestique*, Wiesbaden: Reichert.

—— (1995) *Liste du verbe avestique*, Wiesbaden: Reichert.

Kellens, Jean and Pirart, Eric (1988), (1990), (1991) *Les textes vieil-avestiques*, vol. I, *Introduction, texte et traduction*, vol. II, *Répertoires grammaticaux et lexique*, vol. III, *Commentaire*, Wiesbaden: Reichert.

Kent, Roland G. (1953) *Old Persian: Grammar, Texts, Lexicon*, 2nd edn, New Haven: American Oriental Society.

Mayrhofer, Manfred (1978) *Supplement zur Sammlung der altpersischen Inschriften*, Vienna: Verlag der Österreichischen Akademie der Wissenschaften.

—— (1983) 'Lassen sich Vorstufen des Uriranischen nachweisen?', *Anzeiger der phil.-hist. Klasse der Österreichischen Akademie der Wissenschaften* 120: 249–55.

Morgenstierne, Georg (1973a) *Irano-Dardica*, Wiesbaden: Reichert.
—— (1973b) 'Traces of Indo-European accentuation in Pashto?', *Norsk tidsskrift for sprogvidenskap* 27: 61–5.
Narten, Johanna (1968) 'Zum "proterodynamischen" Wurzelpräsens', in: *Pratidā-nam: Indian, Iranian and Indo-European Studies Presented to F. B. J. Kuiper*, The Hague: Mouton, pp. 9–19.
—— (1986) *Der Yasna Haptaŋhāiti*, Wiesbaden: Reichert.
Reichelt, Hans (1909) *Awestisches Elementarbuch*, Heidelberg: Winter.
—— (1911) *Avesta Reader*, Strassburg: Trübner.
Schmitt, Rüdiger (1987) 'Aryans', in Yarshater 1982–, II/7: 684–7.
—— (ed.) (1989) *Compendium Linguarum Iranicarum*, Wiesbaden: Reichert.
—— (1991) *The Bisitun Inscriptions of Darius the Great: Old Persian Text*, London: School of Oriental and African Studies.
Spuler, Bertold (ed.) (1958) *Handbuch der Orientalistik*, part 1, vol. IV, *Iranistik*, section 1: *Linguistik*, Leiden and Cologne: Brill.
Yarshater, Ehsan (ed.) (1982–) *Encyclopaedia Iranica*, vols. I–IV, London: Routledge & Kegan Paul; vols V–VII: Costa Mesa: Mazda Publishers.

6 Tocharian

Werner Winter

'Tocharian' is the term commonly used to designate two closely related languages documented in texts from the middle and end of the first millennium AD discovered around the turn of the twentieth century and later in what is now Xinjiaáng. Native names of the languages have not survived, and the identification of the speakers of 'Tocharian' with the *Tochari* and *Tókharoi* of Latin and Greek is far from certain.

There is indirect evidence that speakers of the two languages were present in the general area at least as early as the last pre-Christian centuries. There are clear indications that one of the languages, Tocharian B (Toch. B), also frequently called 'West Tocharian', was in actual use in the region of Turfan, Qarašahr, Šorčuq and Kuča. Tocharian A (Toch. A) texts have come to light only in the easternmost of these settlements; there is, though, no evidence that Tocharian A was more than a literary language even here.

Our sources are, often extremely fragmentary, texts of religious and learned content (for Tocharian A and Tocharian B) and monastery records, secular administrative documents, an occasional letter, and a fair number of graffiti (all Tocharian B only); texts of the first type are as a rule Tocharian adaptations of Indic originals, sometimes in the form of straightforward bilingual documents, more commonly translations and reformulations of Sanskrit texts which often are known directly or through translations into other languages of Buddhism.

The fact that so many of the texts had parallels elsewhere made it fairly easy to analyse texts of the first category and to reach insights into aspects of lexicon, grammar and semantics of Tocharian B and Tocharian A; the non-Tocharian subject matter of these texts made it, however, next to impossible to use them as a source of information about the Tocharians. Texts of the second type can contribute more in this respect; however, time and again details of the proper interpretation will still elude us.

It is reasonable to assume that the ancestors of the Tocharians migrated to their historical homelands at a fairly recent date.[1] While it has of late become a popular notion to think that the Tocharians separated early from the main body of Indo-Europeans, there is no direct evidence to support such a conclusion (the arguments for an identification with archaeologically determinable cultures are almost necessarily largely circular). The earlier view that the forebears of the Tocharians were part of the Indo-Europeans of Europe, a view based on linguistic criteria, derives additional support from the fact that the evidence of wall paintings proves that at least part of the upper strata of Tocharian society were of a European phenotype.

The two Tocharian languages differ too much from each other to be considered dialects of a single language. Such differences include: in Tocharian B, pre-final vowels other than *i were preserved; Common Tocharian (Toch.) diphthongs were retained; some Common Tocharian consonant developments were preserved better in Tocharian A. Nominal inflection was less thoroughly reshaped in Tocharian B than in Tocharian A; parts of the verbal system of Tocharian A, on the other hand, are more archaic in Tocharian A. While the lexicon shows much overlap between Tocharian B and Tocharian A, there are again major areas of disagreement – the fact that such divergence is found in particular in the area of central Buddhist terminology may reflect different Buddhist traditions that came to affect the two languages.

In spite of the disagreements just mentioned, the comparison of Tocharian B and Tocharian A, together with procedures of internal reconstruction applied to the data, makes it possible to arrive at a reasonably clear picture of an immediate antecedent of Tocharian B and Tocharian A, 'Common Tocharian'. Common Tocharian may be said to have been characterized, inter alia, by the properties to be discussed in the following.

Phonology
Consonants belonged to two almost all-pervasive sets, a plain and a palatalized one. The system of short vowels resembled that of such languages as Greek or Latin (with a high central vowel *i added that reflected earlier *e i u). Vowel length apparently was phonemic in Common Tocharian; a thorough reshaping of the pattern occurred after the development of Tocharian B and Tocharian A. Only some of the old word-final consonants survived unchanged; clusters of initial and internal consonants were disrupted by inserted vowels more often than in other IE languages. The pattern of word accent as found underlyingly in Tocharian B can be taken to reflect that of Common Tocharian, which means that the PIE system of accent distribution did not survive into Common Tocharian.

Morphology
Nouns: number included singular, dual and plural. The declension was characterized by a two-tiered system: nominative, accusative and genitive (partly based on PIE dative forms) contrasted with 'secondary cases' consisting of combinations of accusative and postpositions. Nominal paradigm formation was often based on a two-stem principle, with stem one for the nominative singular and stem two for all other case forms. The three-gender system of PIE had been replaced by a new one consisting of masculine, feminine and alternating nouns.

Adjectives: number included again singular, dual and plural. The case system had been reduced to the 'primary' cases, with accusative often selected instead of the genitive in complex nominal phrases. The forms showed traces of older adjectival inflection alongside the patterns transferred from the deictics. Feminine plural forms had in part been replaced by collective formations. Stem gradation prevailed, though in a form somewhat different from that found in other IE languages.

Deictics: these matched adjectives in having contrasting stems for masculines and non-masculines; likewise, the case system contained only primary cases. The neuter survived as a nominal form referring to entire clauses; as such, it could be used in both primary and secondary cases.

Personal pronouns: forms for singular, dual, and plural can be reconstructed, with separate stems for the singular. Both primary and secondary cases were formed.

Verbs: the parameters of person (first, second, third), number (singular, dual, plural), tense (non-past, past), aspect (durational, non-durational), mood (indicative/subjunctive, optative, imperative), diathesis (active, mediopassive) can safely be assumed to have been reflected in finite verb forms; of non-finite forms, participles, gerunds, infinitives, privatives can be ascribed to Common Tocharian in spite of some divergence between Tocharian B and Tocharian A in details of form.

Syntax

All statements about Tocharian syntax suffer from the fact that most of the Tocharian B and Tocharian A texts are translations. Nevertheless, some points are reasonably clear: the so-called 'group inflection' was a natural consequence of the fact that only accusative forms could be combined with postpositions. The evidence of prose texts suggests that a basic 'word order' SOV can be posited for Tocharian A and Tocharian B, which makes it possible to assume the same for Common Tocharian. As this basic order can be said to have been complemented by A + N, G + N, N + Postpos, a pervasive pattern Modifier + Head can be posited for Common Tocharian.

In the following, the general comments just made will be discussed in greater detail.

Phonology

Consonant Systems
The inventories of Tocharian B and Tocharian A can be said to have been:

Plain	*Palatalized*
p	
t	č ‹c› [tʃ]
c ‹ts› [ts]	
k	ś
m	

n	ń ‹ñ› [ɲ]
s	š ‹ṣ› [ʃ]?
r	
l	l′ ‹ly› [ʎ]
w	y

Toch. B /y/ is both the palatalized counterpart of Toch B. /w/ and a plain consonant; in Tocharian A, there are no more than hints as to the existence of an earlier /w̌/. In Tocharian A, /ś/ is the palatalized counterpart of both /c/ and /k/; in Tocharian B, only the latter pairing remained productive.

For Common Tocharian, the following system may be reconstructed:

Plain	Palatalized
p	ṕ
t	č
c	ć
k	ś
kʷ	
m	ḿ
n	ń
s	š
r	
l	l′
w	w̌ [y]
y	

PIE *p b bʰ yielded CToch. *p/ṕ; PIE *t dʰ resulted in CToch. *t/c; PIE *d became CToch. *c/ć, except that it was lost before continuant; PIE *ḱ ĝ ĝʰ and *k g gʰ developed to CToch. *k/ś; PIE labiovelars yielded CToch. *kʷ (in some environments *k) beside *ś. PIE *m was reflected by CToch. *m/ḿ, PIE *n by CToch. n/ń, PIE *r by CToch. *r, PIE *l by CToch. *l/ĺ, PIE *w by CToch. *w/w̌, and PIE *y by CToch. *y. Reflexes of PIE aspirates apparently lost their aspiration preceding other aspirates.

Vowel Systems
The vowel systems of Tocharian B and Tocharian A differ:

Tocharian B	i		ɨ		u
		e		o	
			a		

Tocharian A	i		ɨ		u
		e		o	
			a		
		ē		ō	
			ā		

Toch. A *e, o, ē, ō* resulted from monophthongization of earlier *ai *au, *āi, *āu; it is hence possible to reconstruct a pre-Toch. A system as follows:

i   ɨ   u
           'a'
           'ā'

The difference between pre-Toch. A *'*a*' and pre-Toch. A *'*ā*' probably was one of tongue height. Toch. A *a* corresponds very frequently to both Toch. B *e* and Toch. B *o*; it thus seems appropriate to reconstruct a short-vowel system of Common Tocharian identical with that of Tocharian B. For a partly parallel long-vowel system, the evidence is strongest for CToch. *ē deriving from both PIE *ē and PIE *ō; it seems probable that at least some instances of Toch. B ‹o› reflect a CToch. *ō.

While there was a great deal of interference with regular development through, for example, umlaut phenomena and pre-pausal changes, clear patterns nevertheless can be noted.

PIE *e yielded CToch. *i preceded by a palatalized consonant (in word-initial position, CToch. *y- developed). PIE *o is reflected by CToch. *e following a plain consonant. PIE *ē became CToch. *ē after palatalized consonant, while CToch. *ē after plain consonant was the reflex of PIE *ō. PIE *ā resulted in CToch. *ō, while PIE *a was retained as CToch. *a. Both PIE *i and PIE *u became CToch. *i. What are taken to be reflexes of PIE *ī and PIE *ū in other IE languages are to be reconstructed for CToch. as sequences of semivowels followed by *a or *i, depending on the nature of the PIE laryngeal that caused the lengthening of *ī and *ū. PIE *n m r l in syllable-peak position were reflected by CToch. *-*iR*- in non-initial position and by *ēR- initially.

Laryngeals
Questions remain as to the reflexes of laryngeals. PIE *h$_1$ definitely yielded CToch. *a in peak position (cf. Toch. B *pācer* 'father'); the same seems to have been the case for PIE *h$_3$ (cf. Toch. A *knānmāṃ* 'knowing'). For PIE *h$_2$ the only strong case for a development to CToch. *a is the marker of the mediopassive present participle; but the neuter dual and the optative marker (both CToch. *yi < *-*yE*) provide powerful counterarguments.

Suprasegmentals
The place of the word accent can be determined in 'Central' and 'Eastern' Tocharian B texts on the basis of vowel alternations. On the phonemic level, no single general rule of accent distribution can be given; in terms of morphophonemics, however, a simple statement is possible: in all accented forms, the place of the accent was on the second syllable of a word. In the case of morphophonemically disyllabic forms, the accent was retracted to the first syllable. It can be assumed that the underlying

Tocharian B pattern can be projected back into Common Tocharian, which means that Common Tocharian accent deviated radically from that of late Proto-Indo-European.

The word accent of Tocharian A is as yet poorly understood; it seems that a leftward retraction occurred when this syllable contained a non-high vowel.

Even less is known about phrasal and clausal accentuation patterns. There is evidence indicating that monosyllabic verb forms, like various particles, lacked accent; whether this applied to polysyllabic finite verb forms too, cannot be said at this point.

Paradigmatic Morphology

Like other IE languages, Tocharian B and Tocharian A preserved, apart from relatively few synchronically unchangeable items, two major form classes, one with forms subject to case marking, the other, with person marking. Shifts in class membership were easily exacted; some of these shifts appear to have had unlimited productivity (e.g. participle or infinitive formation).

Nouns

Nouns are morphologically modified for number (singular, dual, plural) and case. Three genders (masculine, feminine, alternating) are found. Two major declension-based types can be distinguished, characterized by (a) nominative plural ≠ accusative plural; (b) nominative plural = accusative plural. In the singular, plural forms of type (b) are normally matched by forms identical for nominative and accusative; type (a) forms are commonly found beside singular forms differing for nominative and accusative, but in CToch. *-e- stems this is the case only if the noun denotes a human being.

In the singular, nominative and accusative forms of Tocharian B and Tocharian A are characterized by the absence of an overt ending (except where [+human] is signalled); in Tocharian A, this has led to an almost complete convergence of the two case forms, while in Tocharian B preserved stem alternation prevented a formal identity of nominative and accusative except in descendants of PIE *-o- masculines and of PIE neuters.

In the genitive singular, very few direct traces of PIE genitive forms survived; in kinship terms and proper names, the reflex of a PIE dative (Toch. B Toch. A -i) is found. Elsewhere, the case is marked by Toch. B -ntse, Toch. A -ys < CToch. *-nse.

The vocative singular, attested as a live category in Tocharian B, varies too much across declensional classes to permit generalizations. Nominative and accusative dual agree in form both in Tocharian B and Tocharian A.

In plurals of type (a) in Tocharian A, the accusative ending is always Toch. A -s, while in the nominative Toch. A -ñ is found after stem-final vowel, Toch. A -i (with or without preceding palatalization) in consonant stems (except for Toch. A lāñś 'kings', Toch. A pracre 'brother'). In Tocharian B, the accusative ending is Toch. B -m throughout. The nominative has a marker Toch. B -i in

Toch. B *e*- stems, an ending Toch. B *-ñ* in stems ending in other vowels, and an ending Toch. B *-i* (following a palatalized consonant) in consonant stems (an exception is Toch. B *lāñc* 'kings'). In plurals of type (b), the ending is always Toch. B *-a* (normally matched by zero in Toch. A); in addition, plural is marked by a stem change (cf. Toch. B *palsko*, Toch. A *pältsäk* 'thought': Toch. B *pälskonta*, Toch. A *pälskant* 'thoughts').

The genitive plural in Toch. B ends in Toch. B *-ts* or Toch. B *-m̥ts*, the latter probably originally limited to nouns of type (a). In Tocharian A, the ending is Toch. A *-śśi*; in nouns of type (b), the ending of the genitive singular is found beside that of the plural (cf. Toch. A *lwākis*: Toch. A *lwāśśi* 'of animals'). A Common Tocharian form can only be reconstructed if one assumes that Toch. B /c/ ‹ts› and Toch. A *-(ś)ś(i)* both derived from underlying CToch. *-ć-*.

The secondary cases in both Tocharian B and Tocharian A are based on forms of the accusative followed by postpositions (which in Tocharian A were fused with the noun to yield single word forms, while in Tocharian B univerbalization affected only the ablative and the rare causal). With the exception of the locative, there is no equivalence in the forms of Tocharian B and Tocharian A, as clearly shown by a listing:

	Tocharian B	Tocharian A
Abl.	-mem̥	-ṣ
Dat. ('allative')	+śc	-ac
Instr. ('perlative')	+sa	-ā̲
Loc.	+ne	-am̥
Com.	+mpa	-aśśäl
Causal	=ñ	———
Proximative	+spe	———

The discrepancies between Tocharian B and Tocharian A are to be explained by differing results of decomposition processes affecting sequences of Common Tocharian accusative forms of the singular or the plural followed by postpositions which were only in part identical in the two languages.

Adjectives
Plural forms of the adjective in Tocharian B are of type (a) (see p. 159) in the masculine, of type (b) in the feminine; in Tocharian A, the masculine has type (a) throughout, while in the feminine, depending on form class, both (a) and (b) occur. In the singular, again depending on class, formal identity or non-identity between nominative and accusative is found in both Tocharian B and Tocharian A. In the dual, these case forms never differ. A neuter form, identical for both cases, occurs only in the singular.

In all genders, the nominative singular is markerless in Tocharian B and Tocharian A. The accusative singular is characterized either by stem change or the addition of a final nasal to the overt or underlying form of the nominative; in Toch. B, *-aN is reflected by Toch. B -ai. The genitive singular feminine ends in Toch. B -ai, Toch. A -e; that of the masculine in Toch. B -epi (-pi after vowel), Toch. A -yāp/-āp, added to the stem of the accusative (without the nasal ending). A few genitive masculine forms ending in Toch. B -e (< PIE *-os) survived.

The nominative plural masculine shows a variation identical with that incurred in nouns: Toch. B -i is found in -e- stems, Toch. B -ñ in stems ending in other vowels, palatalization in consonant stems; an accusative is formed by the addition of a nasal to the stem. Corresponding endings of the nominative are Toch. A -e, Toch. A -ñ, palatalization, or Toch. A -i preceded by palatalization. For the accusative plural masculine, the basic ending is Toch. A -s which is often added not to the stem but to the form of the nominative; merging of paradigms has led to further irregularity.

The feminine singular is characterized by a gender-shifting suffix Toch. B -ya-, Toch. A -yā- common to all case forms. In the feminine plural, two conflicting patterns can be observed: either the stem of the singular is retained in the plural – as in all type (a) forms of Tocharian A and in some Tocharian B paradigms – or a masculine singular form (nominative or accusative) is used as a basis for a type (b) form. Dual forms are derived from either masculine (= neuter) or feminine stems; the assignment of specific forms to genders is, however, beset with difficulties.

Adjectival patterns of Tocharian B and Tocharian A have enough in common to permit the reconstruction of their Common Tocharian antecedents. Two types of declension have to be recognized – one in which the accusative singular masculine is characterized by the addition of a nasal ending, the other, by a change of stem over against the nominative. The second type shows a stronger influence of the inflection of deictics than the first one; the relative recency of this development is shown by the contrast of the accusative forms of 'other' found in Toch. A ālamwäc: Toch. B ālyauce 'each other'.

Deictics

The morphologically simplest type of deictic is found in Tocharian B; the nominative singular forms masculine Toch. B se, feminine Toch. B sā, neuter Toch. B te are close parallels to, for example, Gk ho hē tó. The second stem of the feminine (acc. Toch. B tā, pl. Toch. B toy) is likewise simple and highly archaic, except that the accusative singular form shows no trace of an underlying final nasal (neither does the accusative masculine singular, Toch. B ce). Among forms to be related to the simple stem of the neuter are Toch. B tane /tï+ne/ 'here, there' and possibly Toch. B tsa 'indeed'.

The same vocalism as in Toch. B tane is found in the stems of the complex deictics Toch. B su, Toch. A säm (= Skt sas), Toch. B samp (= Skt asau), and

Table 6.1   Deictic pronouns

	Masculine	Feminine	Neuter
Singular			
Nom.	*se / *si-	*sa	*te / *ti-
Acc.	*cē	*ta	*te / *ti-
Gen.	*cipi	*tay	*tense
Plural			
Nom.	*cēy	*tōy	
Acc.	*cēns	*tōns	
Gen.	?	?	

Toch. A *säs* (= Skt *ayam*), while the forms signalling close deixis (Toch. B *sem*, Toch. A *sam*) are derivable from the fuller base form. The modifying elements were added to complete forms of the simplex, not to a stem, and are therefore to be considered particles, not suffixes.

The genitive singular masculine deviates from other forms of the second stem in showing a vocalism Toch. B -*i*- rather than Toch. B -*e*- as in the adjective. The genitive singular neuter has a nominal rather than a pronominal ending.

Based on what seem to be the more archaic components of the Tocharian B system, the Common Tocharian simple deictic paradigm may be reconstructed as in Table 6.1.

In Tocharian B, the forms of the feminine plural seem to have been reassigned to different deictic paradigms once type-(b) inflection had become the rule in the feminine.

There is not enough evidence to reconstruct a subparadigm of the dual.

Palatalization in the second stem of the masculine is to be viewed as reflecting a generalization of *tē* of the accusative singular, in its turn reshaped after the accusative of personal pronouns (cf. Lat. *mē*, *tē*); feminine Toch. B *tā* does not continue PIE *tām*, but a form without a nasal, and thus shows an influence of the accusative singular masculine.

Cardinals

The Tocharian cardinals are characterized for gender (one to four in Toch. A, one, three to four in Toch. B), number ('one' only) and case. Major parts of the Common Tocharian inventory of terms for the lower numbers can be reconstructed (see also Chapter 2, p. 67):

'one'   masculine CToch. *ṣēs (Toch. A *sas*, Toch. B *ṣes-*), feminine CToch. *ṣina (Toch. B *sana*, Toch. A *säm*); second stem masculine CToch. *ṣeme- (Toch. B *ṣeme*, Toch. A *ṣom*), feminine CToch. *ṣōmō- (Toch. B *ṣomo*, Toch. A *ṣom*)

'two'   masculine CToch. *wu (Toch. A wu), feminine CToch. *wey
             (Toch. A we, Toch. B wi)
'three'   masculine CToch. *treyi (Toch. B trai, Toch. A tre), feminine
             CToch. tirya (Toch. B tarya, Toch. A tri)
'four'   masculine CToch. *śitweri (Toch. B śtwer, Toch. A śtwar),
             feminine CToch. *śitwara (Toch. B śtwāra)
'five'   CToch. *pinśi (Toch. B piś, Toch. A päñ)
'six'   CToch. *śiki (Toch. A ṣäk)
'seven'   CToch. *śipti (Toch. A ṣpät)
'eight'   CToch *okti (Toch. B okt, Toch. A okät)
'nine'   CToch *ńiwi (Toch. B Toch. A ñu)
'ten'   CToch. *ćiki (Toch. B śak, Toch. A śäk)

Of higher numerals, CToch. *kinte '100' can safely be reconstructed on the
basis of Toch. B kante, Toch. A känt; Toch. B yaltse, Toch. A wälts can be
derived from CToch. *wilce '1,000'.

While the 'teens' do not permit setting up a Common Tocharian prototype,
the decades thirty to ninety can be fairly well reconstructed:

'thirty'   CT *tiryaka (Toch. B täryāka)
'forty'   CT *śitwaraka (Toch. B śtwārka, Toch. A śtwarāk)
'fifty'   CT *pinśaka (Toch. B piśāka)
'sixty'   CT *śikiska (Toch. B ṣkaska, Toch. A säksäk)
'seventy'   CT *śiptinka (Toch. B ṣuktaṅka, Toch. A ṣäptuk)
'eighty'   CT *oktuka (Toch. A oktuk)
'ninety'   CT *ńiwimka (Toch. B ñumka)

Toch. B ikäṃ, Toch. A wiki 'twenty' yield no clear Common Tocharian
preform.

The ordinals show a term for 'first' independent of that for 'one' (Toch. B
pärweṣṣe, Toch. A maltow-inu); a CToch. *pirwe can be reconstructed from
the Tocharian B word and Toch. A pärwat 'first-born son'. Ordinals from
'2nd' through '6th' contain a suffix CToch. *-te; so does Toch. B ikante
'20th'. '7th' through '9th' have a suffix identifiable as CToch. *-nte. Ordinals
based on decads have a complex suffix -nci in Tocharian A.

Personal Pronouns

These are commonly characterized for case and number in IE languages, with
number distinction signalled by stem alternation. In addition, there tends to
be a contrast not only in endings, but also in stems between nominative and
non-nominative forms. Tocharian proves to be fairly conservative here; there
is, however, a striking innovation to be noted: Tocharian A distinguished a
masculine from a feminine first-person singular.

The following reconstruction can be proposed:

Singular

'I'	CToch. *ńiśi (Toch. B ñäś)		'thou'	CToch. *tiwe (Toch. B tuwe, Toch. A tu)
'me'	CToch. *ńiśi (Toch. B ñäś)		'thee'	CToch. *ciwi (Toch. B ci, Toch. A cu)
'my'	CToch. *ńi (Toch. B Toch. A ñi)		'thy'	CToch. *tińi (Toch. B tañ, Toch. A tñi)

Dual

'we, us'	CToch. *we-ne (Toch. B we-ne)		'you'	CToch. *ye-ne (Toch. B ye-ne)
'our'	?		'your'	?

Plural

'we, us'	CToch. wesi (Toch. B wes, Toch. A was)		'you'	CToch. *yesi (Toch. B yes, Toch. A yas)
'our'	?		'your'	?

The masculine form Toch. A näṣ 'I, me' may reflect an old plural form while its feminine counterpart Toch. A ñuk could derive from the singular. Only the forms of the second-person singular nominative and accusative have clear IE equivalents (cf. Skt tvam, Gk sé).

Verbs

The finite forms of the Tocharian verb signal morphologically the following properties:

number (singular, dual, plural)
person (first, second, third)
tense (non-past, past)
aspect (durational, non-durational; durational aspect was marked by suffixation if a verb stem was inherently non-durational – a primarily durational verb stem could not be shifted by affixation)
mood (indicative, optative, imperative; the so-called subjunctive is the non-past of the non-durational aspect)
voice (active, mediopassive – with special intransitive/passive subparadigms in some form classes)
(in)transitivity (marked in a number of form classes)

Non-finite forms are: participles (present active, present mediopassive, preterite), gerunds (of both aspects), infinitives (neutral as to voice, with special intransitive/passive forms attested for some verbs); abstract nouns are based on gerunds; a number of adjectival and nominal derivatives with limited productivity are to be noted.

In Tocharian B and Tocharian A, there was a highly developed system of causatives derived from non-causatives – partly from basic stems, partly from complex ones (erroneously called *Grundverben*) which frequently were denominative formations. Both causatives and complex non-causatives were notably productive form classes.

Basic stems were either athematic or thematic formations. An athematic first (i.e. 'present') stem was matched by an athematic second ('subjunctive') stem. A thematic first stem had beside it a morphologically identical second stem. A basic athematic second stem (in Tocharian A frequently extended by a suffix -*ñ*-) formed a thematic present stem with a suffix Toch. B Toch. A -*s*- or Toch. B -*sk*- (Toch. A -*s*) depending on the place of the phonological accent; Toch. B Toch. A -*n*- or a change-over to thematic inflection in the first stem were further, less common, shift indicators.

Complex stems were usually characterized by a suffix Toch. B -*a*-, Toch. A -*ā*- (the latter subject to syncope) in the subjunctive stem. In the case of transitive verbs, present stems were derived by an insertion of a suffix -*n*- before Toch. B -*a*-, Toch. A -*ā*-. Intransitive complex verbs, on the other hand, had present-stem forms marked by either a suffix Toch. B -*e*-, Toch. A -*a*- or Toch. B -*o*-, Toch. A -*a*-.

In addition to the formations just enumerated, there were others with a more limited distribution, such as denominative verbs. Suppletion occurred both with a utilization of etymologically unrelated stems and with stems which, though related, disrupted normal paradigmatic patterns.

The affixes used in Tocharian B and Tocharian A paradigms permit in many cases a reconstruction of Common Tocharian antecedents by mere comparison; frequently, however, discrepancies occur which call for the assumption of either innovations in one or both languages, or of the coexistence of competing forms in Common Tocharian; a decision will usually depend on evidence from outside Tocharian. Thus, the forms of the present participle of the mediopassive (Toch. B -*mane*, Toch. A -*mām*) permit the reconstruction of CToch. *-*mane*, and a prefix *-*pi̯*- can safely be posited for the Common Tocharian imperative. Tocharian A and Tocharian B differ in the formation of the present participle of the active (Toch. A -*ant*, Toch. B -*eñca*); here Tocharian B can be identified as the innovating language so that CToch. *-*enta* can be reconstructed. The infinitive in Toch. B Toch. A -*tsi* is derived from the subjunctive stem in Tocharian B, from the present stem in Tocharian A: here no decision as to the state of affairs in Common Tocharian seems possible. On the other hand, if several non-past forms in Tocharian B appear to be based on forms with PIE secondary endings, while Tocharian A shows descendents of primary ones, it becomes possible to assume that reflexes of both primary and secondary endings survived until Common Tocharian times.

The patterns of stem formation throughout the various paradigms may be illustrated by a few examples:

Unextended forms, athematic

Toch. B Toch. A *sälp-* 'glow': pres. Toch. B *sälpamane*, Toch. A *sälpmāṃ*; subj.: Toch. B *sälpalle*, Toch. A *sälpiṣ*; pret. Toch. B *sälpare*; PPP Toch. B *sälpau*, Toch. A *sälpont*

Toch. B Toch. A *lkā-* 'see': pres. Toch. B Toch. A *lkātär*; subj. Toch. B *lkānme*; pret. Toch. B *lyakāwa*; PPP Toch. B *lyelyku*

Unextended forms, thematic

Toch. B *klyaus-*, Toch. A *klyos-* 'hear': pres. Toch. B *klyauṣäṃ*, Toch. A *klyossi*; subj. Toch. B *klyṣäṃ*, Toch. A *klyoṣäṣ*; pret. Toch. B *klyauṣāwa*, Toch. A *klyoṣā*; PPP Toch. B *keklyauṣu*, Toch. A *kaklyuṣu*

Toch. B *lāṃs-*, Toch. A *wles-* 'work': pres. Toch. B *lāṃṣtär*, Toch. A *wleṣtär*; subj. Toch. B *lāṃṣtsi*, Toch. A *wleṣit*; pret. Toch. B *lamṣṣānte*, Toch. A *wleṣāt*; PPP Toch. B *lalāṃṣuwa*, Toch. A *wāwleṣu*

Basically non-durational verbs, with athematic subjunctive

Toch. B *kau-*, Toch. A *ko-* 'kill': pres. Toch. B *kauṣäṃ*, Toch. A *koṣänt-*; subj. Toch. B *kowän*, Toch. A *kolune*; pret. Toch. B *kowsa*, Toch. A *kosām*; PPP Toch. B *kakawu*, Toch. A *kāko*

Toch. B Toch. A *pärk-* 'ask': pres. Toch. B *prekṣalle*, Toch. A *prakṣäl*; subj. Toch. B *preku, parkälle*, Toch. A *pärkñäm*; pret. Toch. B *preksane, parksantene*, Toch. A *prakäs, präksāt*; PPP Toch. B *peparku*, Toch. A *papräku*.

Toch. B Toch. A *āl-* 'keep away': pres. Toch. B *alaṣṣälle*, Toch. A *ālsanträ*; subj. Toch. B *āltsi*, Toch. A *ālñäl*; pret. Toch. A *ālsāt*; PPP Toch. B *ālu*, Toch. A *ālu-*

Toch. B Toch. A *yām-* 'make': pres. Toch. B *yamaskau* (Toch. A *ypam*); subj. Toch. B *yamäṃ*, Toch. A *yāmäṣ*; pret. Toch. B *yamaṣṣa*, Toch. A *yāmäṣ*; PPP Toch. B Toch. A *yāmu*

Extended forms

Toch. B Toch. A *āra-* 'cease': pres. Toch. B *orotär*, Toch. A *aratär*; subj. Toch. B *āraṃ*, Toch. A *āraṣ*; pret. Toch. B *arāre*, Toch. A *ārar*

Toch. B *kauta-*, Toch. A *kota-* 'split': pres. Toch. B *kautanoñc*, Toch. A *kotnatsi*; subj. Toch. B *kautalñe*, Toch. A *kotlune*; pret. Toch. B *kauta*, Toch. A *kot*; PPP Toch. B *kakautau*, Toch. A *kākotu-*

Toch. B Toch. A *muskā-* 'be lost': pres. Toch. B *musketär*; subj. Toch. B *muskälñe*, Toch. A *muskālune*; pret. Toch. B *muska*, Toch. A *muskāt*; PPP Toch. B *muskau*

Toch. B Toch. A *tärkā-* 'let go': pres. Toch. B *tärkanaṃ*, Toch. A *tärnāṣ*; subj. Toch. B *tārkaṃ, tarkalñe*, Toch. A *tarkam, tärkālune*; pret. Toch. B *cärkāwa, tärkānte*, Toch. A *cärk, tarkar*; PPP Toch. B *tärkau*, Toch. A *tärko*

Causatives based on unextended stems

Toch. B *lak-äsk-*, Toch. A *läk-s-* 'show': pres. Toch. B *lakäskemane*, Toch.

A *läksant-*; pret. Toch. B *lakässame*, Toch. A *laläksāwā*; PPP Toch. B *lelakässor*, Toch. A *laläksu*

Toch. B *kātk-äsk-*, Toch. A *kātk-äs-* 'gladden': pres. Toch. B *kātkästärme*, Toch. A *kātkāstär*; subj. Toch. B *kātkässi*; PPP Toch. B *kakātkässu*, Toch. A *kākätksu-*

Causatives based on extended stems

Toch. B *yāt-äsk-*, Toch. A *yāt-äs-* 'control': pres. Toch. B *yātässeñca*, Toch. A *yātässi*; subj. Toch. B *yātässi*; pret. Toch. B *yātässatai*; PPP *yayātässu*

Toch. B *wik-äsk-*, Toch. A *wik-äs-* 'remove': pres. Toch. B *wīkäskau*, Toch. A *wikäst*; subj. Toch. B *wīkässi*, Toch. A *wikāsam*; pret. Toch. B *yaika*, Toch. A *wawik*; PPP Toch. B *yaiku*, Toch. A *wawiku*

Toch. B *śars-äsk-*, Toch. A *śärs-äs-* 'teach': pres. Toch. B *śarsässäme*, Toch. A *śärsäst*; subj. Toch. B *śarsässi*; pret. Toch. B *śārsame*, Toch. A *śaśärs*; PPP Toch. B *śeśśarsos*

In the optative, the singular forms are: 1 Toch. B Toch. A *-m*, 2 Toch. B Toch. A *-t*, 3 Toch. B *-0* Toch. A *-s*; elsewhere, non-past endings are used. In the imperative, there is considerable agreement between Toch. B and Toch. A:active singular 2 Toch. B Toch. A *-0*, plural 2 Toch. B Toch. A *-s*; mediopassive singular 2 Toch. B Toch. A *-r*, plural 2 Toch. B *-t*, Toch. A *-c*, dual 2 Toch. B *-yt*.

At least partial agreement is also found in non-finite forms: the active present participle ended in Toch. B *-eñca*, Toch. A *-ant*; its mediopassive counterpart was Toch. B *-mane*, Toch. A *-mām*; the past participle, Toch. B

Table 6.2 Endings of finite forms

	Active		Mediopassive	
	Tocharian B	Tocharian A	Tocharian B	Tocharian A
Non-past				
1 sg.	-u/-w	-m	-mar	-mār
2 sg.	-t	-t	-tar	-tār
3 sg.	-m	-s	-tär	-tär
1 pl.	-m	-mäs	-mtär	-mtär
2 pl.	-cer	-c	-tär	-cär
3 pl.	-m	-y(ñc)	-ntär	-ntär
3 dual	-tem			
Past				
1 sg.	-wa	-ā/-wā	-mai	-e/-we
2 sg.	-sta	-st	-tai	-te
3 sg.	-sa/-a	-sā-/-ā-	-te	-t
1 pl.	-m	-mäs	-mte	-mät
2 pl.	-s	-s	-t	-c
3 pl.	-r/-re	-r	-nte	-nt
3 dual	-ys	*-ynas		

Toch. A -*u*, with or without reduplication depending on form class. The gerund was formed in Toch. B -*lle*, Toch. A -*l*, both derivable from PIE *-*lyo*-; the gerund-based abstract ended in Toch. B -*lläññe* (-*lñe*), Toch. A -*lune*. The infinitive had the suffix -*tsi* in Toch. B and Toch. A. The privative had a complex suffix -*tte* in Toch. B, while its counterpart Toch. A -*t* may reflect simple PIE -*to*-. A semi-productive adjectival formation based on PIE *-*mōn*- is found in forms with Toch. B -*mo*, Toch. A -*m*. Several classes of deverbative nouns with severely limited productivity can be reconstructed for Common Tocharian from Tocharian B and Tocharian A data.

A brief survey such as that offered here can give no more than a partial picture of Tocharian and of aspects of its prehistory. Still, even the limited information should have made it clear that Tocharian A and Tocharian B, just as other IE languages, present evidence for both innovations and retentions, which means that Tocharian can contribute important insights for a reconstruction of Proto-Indo-European.

Note: This view has been revised in winter 1997.

References

Krause, Wolfgang (1952) *Westtocharische Grammatik*, vol. I, *Das Verbum*, Heidelberg: Winter.

Krause, Wolfgang and Thomas, Werner (1960) *Tocharisches Elementarbuch*, vol. I, *Grammatik*, Heidelberg: Winter.

Pinault, Georges-Jean (1989) 'Introduction au tokharien', *LALIES* 7: 5–224.

Sieg, Emil, Siegling, Wilhelm and Schulze, Wilhelm (1931) *Tocharische Grammatik*, Göttingen: Vandenhoeck & Ruprecht.

Thomas, Werner and Krause, Wolfgang (1964) *Tocharisches Elementarbuch*, vol. II, *Texte und Glossar*, Heidelberg: Winter.

Van Windekens, Albert Joris (1976), (1979), (1982) *Le tokharien confronté avec les autres langues indo-européennes*, vol. I, *La Phonétique et le Vocabulaire*; vol. II.1, *La Morphologie nominale*; vol. II.2, *La Morphologie verbale*, Louvain: CIDG. (To be used with much caution.)

Winter, Werner (1997) 'Lexical archaisms in the Tocharian languages', in Hans Henrich Hock (ed.), *Historical Indo-European and Lexicographical Studies. A Festschrift for Ladislav Zgusta on the Occasion of his 70th Birthday*. Berlin–New York: Mouton de Gruyter, pp. 183–93.

7 *The Anatolian Languages*

Silvia Luraghi

The Anatolian Languages

The Anatolian branch of IE comprises several languages that spread across Anatolia in the course of the second and first millennia BC. On the delimitation of the Anatolian linguistic group, see Carruba (1981a: 47, 1981b). On the geographical spread of the Anatolian languages, see Map 7.1.

There is no continuity in the attestations of any of these languages, so for convenience they may be divided into languages of the second millennium and those of the first:

Second millennium: Hittite, Cuneiform Luwian, Palaic
First millennium: Hieroglyphic Luwian, Lycian, Milyan, Lydian, Carian

The relationships within the Anatolian linguistic group are represented by the 'family tree' in Figure 7.1. The 'family tree' shown in the figure is based

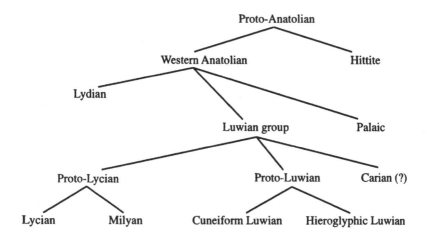

Figure 7.1   Anatolian linguistic group

169

essentially on Oettinger (1978) (although Oettinger posits the existence of an intermediate unit between the Luwian and Palaic groups); on the position of Carian, see Carruba (1981a) and Giannotta *et al.* (1995). We shall discuss specific problems concerning subdivision whenever they occur.

The attestations cover approximately one millennium, beginning around 1650 BC (or 1570 BC, according to the short chronology) and ending around 330 BC, with a gap of almost a century and a half at the end of the second millennium. On all the problems regarding the chronology of the Near East in the second millennium BC, see the *Cambridge Ancient History*.

Problems of the Writing Systems

The Anatolian sources have come down to us in three types of script: cuneiform, from the second millennium; hieroglyphic, attested in both the second and first millennia; and alphabetic, from the first millennium. The type of script employed has very important consequences for our understanding of Anatolian phonetics (see also **Phonology**, pp. 174f.). For example, the cuneiform syllabary does not lend itself to the transcription of complex consonant groups, which therefore have to be rendered with the addition of a written supporting vowel.

The same is true of hieroglyphic, which presents even greater problems. Hieroglyphic is a script which originated in Anatolia (unlike cuneiform, which, as is well known, was introduced there from Mesopotamia; see Pugliese Carratelli and Meriggi (1978) and Hawkins (1986)). It is a syllabary similar to cuneiform in that the signs have sometimes an ideographic and sometimes a syllabic value. Only in the first millennium is Anatolian hieroglyphic clearly associated with a particular language (Luwian); the highly ideographic attestations from the second millennium make it practically impossible to establish which language (Hittite or Luwian) hieroglyphic was used for. Since Anatolian hieroglyphic was not used for any other independently known language, the assignment of a precise value to each sign has been a particularly complex matter and still leaves room for uncertainty.

The alphabetic scripts obviously present fewer problems; they are all derived in some way from Greek alphabets of the red type (Eastern alphabets; see Rosenkranz (1978: 32)).

Hittite

Among the Anatolian languages, by far the best attested is Hittite, which is know to us from a large number of clay tablets written in the cuneiform syllabary, for the most part originating from the archives of the capital of the Hittite kingdom, Hattusas (now Boğazkale) in northern Anatolia, about 100 kilometres east of Ankara. The fundamental works for a knowledge of Hittite are Friedrich (1952) and (1960) and the part so far published of the *Chicago Hittite Dictionary*, the *Materialien zu einem hethitischen Thesaurus* and Puhvel (1984).

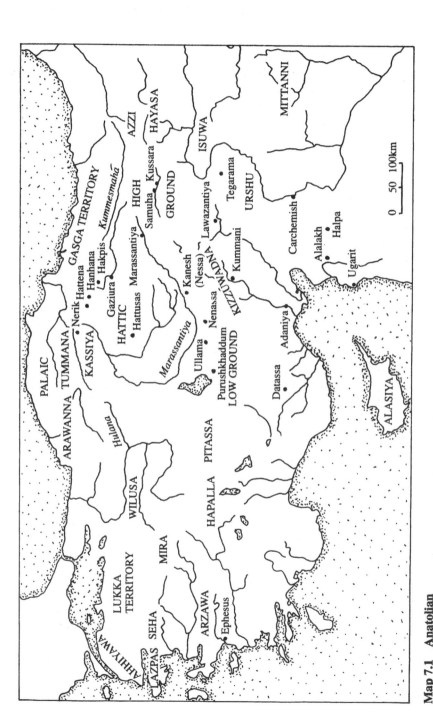

Map 7.1 Anatolian
Source: J. Mellaart, *The Archaeology of Ancient Turkey*, London: Bodley Head, 1978

The tablets were deciphered in 1915–17, by the Czech scholar Hrozný (see Friedrich 1966); this is thus a relatively recent area of study. The Hittite texts in our possession cover a span of around 500 years (or less, according to the 'short chronology') and are of various types; we have historical texts (mainly treaties and annals produced under various kings), legal texts (of which the best known is the collection of Laws), letters, religious and mythological texts and many rituals, oracles and descriptions of religious festivals. Consequently, Hittite does not present substantial problems of interpretation.

Cuneiform Luwian

Luwian of the second millennium is termed 'Cuneiform Luwian', because it is written in the cuneiform syllabary, unlike Luwian of the first millennium, for which hieroglyphic is always used. Cuneiform Luwian is known to us through a certain number of Hittite ritual tablets containing parts which were recited in Luwian, the rituals themselves having originated in Luwian territory. Luwian was spoken in the south of the Anatolian peninsula and the extent of its effective spread throughout the population must have been greater than that of Hittite, as is shown by the fact that languages of the Luwian group survived the population migrations which took place in the Near East at the end of the second millennium. Moreover, Luwian also exercised a certain influence over Hittite during the course of the centuries. Proof of this are the numerous Luwian words found in Hittite texts; these words are often indicated in a conventional way by the scribe. A grammatical sketch of Luwian, based mainly on Cuneiform Luwian, may be found in Laroche (1959); the most up-to-date work on Cuneiform Luwian is Starke (1985).

Palaic

Also attested through Hittite rituals, but to a much lesser extent than Luwian, is Palaic, a language which was spoken in the mountainous region to the north of the Hittite area, towards the Black Sea (see Carruba 1970; Melchert 1984). The Palaic peoples were very quickly overwhelmed by the invasions of the Kaskas, a non-IE people from the East, who swept them away and for centuries kept attacking the Hittite kingdom. Even at the time when the texts containing the Palaic formulae were written, Palaic must already have been a dead language.

Hieroglyphic Luwian

Hieroglyphic Luwian is attested until the middle of the first millennium. It is a very important source not only from the linguistic but also from the cultural point of view, in that it is the only one which gives us any information about the centuries bridging the two millennia, during the break caused by the so-called Peoples of the Sea. The sources consist mainly of long inscriptions, produced at the behest of the lords of small local monarchies, celebrating their deeds (see Meriggi 1966; Hieroglyphic Luwian has also been studied by Hawkins in many studies published over the last twenty years; see also Marazzi 1990).

Lycian and Milyan

Until recently, Lycian and Milyan were considered to be two varieties deriving from a common 'Proto-Lycian'. In conformity with this theory, the two languages were long designated Lycian A (= Lycian) and Lycian B (= Milyan). In the last ten years, however, the traditional view has been called into question. For example, Carruba (1981a: 47) writes that Milyan is 'una lingua diversa, ... che non è escluso sia imparentata più strettamente con il luvio' ('A different language, ... which is not to say that it is not most closely related to Luwian'). Starke (1982), examining the nominal declension in the languages of the Luwian group, notes that Lycian and Milyan do not share any common innovation with respect to Cuneiform Luwian and Hieroglyphic Luwian and thus should not be considered as more closely related to each other. Consequently, the Luwian branch of the family tree in Figure 7.1 would be redrawn as in Figure 7.2. However, it is very difficult to assess the position of Milyan, because it is basically known from a single source, the so-called 'bilingual from Xanthos'. Lycian is better attested. Our knowledge is based on epigraphic texts, funerary and religious in nature, and, especially as far as onomastics is concerned, locally minted coins. Melchert (1994: 125) points out that 'Lycian shares a number of innovative features with Luwian ... However, some of the relevant features are also shared with Lydian, while Luwian agrees with Hittite and Palaic in other respects. It thus seems more prudent at this point to view the Anatolian languages as a continuum of dialects.' Other objections to the present 'family tree', as well as bibliography on the subject, may be found in Gusmani (1990).

Lydian

Lydian is known to us through funerary inscriptions and poetic texts. Both the rather small number of texts and their extremely uniform nature make them difficult to understand, so much so that their IE character long remained in doubt. Within the Anatolian languages, Lydian appears rather isolated; it is

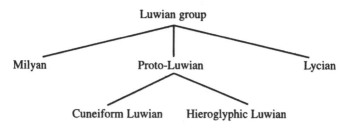

Figure 7.2   Luwian branch

also possible that it should be seen as a separate branch of Anatolian, different from both Hittite and the Luwian/Palaic group. A grammatical outline of Lydian may be found in Gusmani (1964); see also Carruba (1969a) and, for an up-to-date bibliography, Gusmani (1981).

Carian

Carian (see Rosenkranz 1978: 8) is in fact a *Restsprache*. We cannot be completely sure that it belongs to the Anatolian group, or even to the IE linguistic family. Carruba (1981a) places it close to the Luwian subgroup of Anatolian, mainly on the basis of his study of the onomastics; however, this is a hypothesis which cannot easily be proved. Beside Carian, one should still add Pisidian and Sidetic attested through onomastics (see Melchert 1994: 44–5).

Phonology

Since it is the best-attested Anatolian language, Hittite is obviously of central importance for comparison. To some extent, the Hittite writing system limits our understanding of Anatolian phonology, in part because of the very nature of cuneiform as a syllabic script (for example, the inability to transcribe complex consonant clusters); in part because of particular Hittite scribal practices. Amongst these, one peculiarity is the confusion of voiceless and voiced stops, attested particularly in the case of the dentals.[1] Basically, the signs -*d*V- and -*t*V- are employed interchangeably in different occurrences of the same word. Moreover, in the case of syllables of the type VC, only the sign with a voiceless stop is normally used; finally the frequency of signs with voiced labials or velars is rather low, even for syllables of the type CV. However, from an observation of the distribution of spellings with double and single consonants in the oldest texts, it appears that the voiceless stops were spelled as double consonants and voiced ones as single consonants. This regularity is most consistent in the case of dental stops in older texts; in later texts one sometimes finds irregular variation.

Vowels

Anatolian reduces the inventory of vowel phonemes inherited from Indo-European, in that it merges the vowel qualities *a* and *o*. Moreover, the status of the opposition between long and short vowels is unclear, but it does not continue the IE contrast.[2]

The vowels *e* and *i* are frequently interchanged in Hittite cuneiform spelling; however, this does not mean that there were not two distinct phonemes /e/ and /i/ in Hittite; this is shown by the pair *et* 'eat!' vs *it* 'go!', a contrast which may also be encountered in later Hittite. As shown by Melchert (1983), in Hittite we find the two vowels as the reflexes of IE */e/ and */i/ in roots, suffixes and inflectional endings. For example, the word *eshar* 'blood' must contain a phoneme /e/ (cf. Gk *éar*) continuing IE */e/, despite the fact that the spelling *isḫar*, too, is sporadically attested. However, the reconstruction of an Anatolian */i/ remains a problem, given that Hittite /i/ generally corresponds to a vowel of different quality in the other languages (see Meriggi 1981). The **e/o* ablaut is preserved as an alternation *e/a*, for example, Hittite *peda* 'place' and *pata-* 'foot', which both derive from the IE root **ped-/pod-*. The IE diphthongs are not preserved; in Hitt. **ew, ow > u* (*luk-* 'to be light' < **lewk* 'white'), while **ej, oj* gives the varying spelling *e/i* mentioned above.

The development of the semi-vowels, **w* and **j* is examined in Melchert (1983). Indo-European */w/ is normally preserved: Hitt. *watar*, gen. *wetenas* 'water' (Gmc **water*, Gk *hýdor*, gen. *hýdatos* < **hudn̥tos*), CLuw. *hawi-* 'sheep' (Lat. *ovis*); in Hitt. /w/ > /m/ by dissimilation when it follows or precedes the vowel /u/, cf. Hitt. *sumes* < IE **suwes* (secondary form of **swes*, see Melchert 1983: 27).

According to some scholars, a vowel /o/ is attested in Hittite, where it is spelled *u* (/u/ is consistently spelled *ú*), but it is not a reflex of IE /o/ (see Eichner 1980).

Consonants

The stops (see Shevoroshkin 1988; Melchert 1994) are reduced to two series, voiceless and voiced. The IE voiced aspirates lose their aspiration and their reflexes merge with those of the non-aspirated voiced stops. The labiovelars are on the whole preserved as such; only in Lycian they are de-labialized (the attested forms allow this to be established with certainty only for the voiceless series). The development of the labiovelars should show the Anatolian languages to be of the 'centum' type; the development of the palatals, however, is not so clear.

IE */p/ > Anat. */p/, cf. Hitt. *pada-* 'foot', *appa* 'behind' (Gk *apó*); Anat. */p/ > Lyd. /f/

IE */bʰ/ > Anat. /b/, cf. Hitt. *nepis-* 'sky' (Lat. *nebula*, Gk *nephélē*)
(There are no certain examples of IE */b/)

IE */t/ > Anat. */t/, cf. Hitt. *ḫastai* 'bone', *katta* 'down' (Gk *katá*); Anat. */t/ before /i/ > /z/ in Hittite, cf. *eszi* 'he is'

IE */dʰ/ > Anat. */d/, cf. Hitt. *teḫḫi* 'I place' (Gk *tithēmi*, OInd. *dadhāmi*, Lat. *faciō*)

IE */d/ > Anat. */d/, cf. Hitt. *pada-* 'foot'

IE */k/ > Anat. */k/, cf. Hitt. *katta*, HLuw. *katta* 'down', Hitt. *kars-*, CLuw. *kars-* 'to cut';[3] Anat. */k/ before /i/ > Ø in the languages of the Luwian group.

IE */k̂/ does not have a single reflex in Anatolian. In the languages of the Luwian group we have assibilation, while in the other languages the reflexes merge with those of */k/; cf. Hitt. *karawar-* 'horn', HLuw. *zurni* 'id.' (Gk *kéras*, Lat. *cornu*, Goth. *haurn*, Avest. *sruuvā-*), Hitt. *kas* 'this',

CLuw. *za-* 'id.' (Arm. *sa-*); for the Hittite reflex compare also Hitt. *gank-* 'to hang, suspend' (OI *hanga*). The uniformity of the Luwian group as regards the treatment of voiceless palatals appears to be confirmed by other words, attested only in Lycian, such as Lyc. *esbe*, HLuw. *azu(wa)-* 'horse' (Skt *aśva-*), Lyc. *sñta* '100' (or perhaps '10') (Lat. *centum*, Skt *śatam*)[4]

IE *g^h/, */$\hat{g}^h$/ > Anat. */g/, cf. Hitt. *kessera-* 'hand' (Gk *kheír*), Hitt. *mekki-*, HLuw. *maia-* 'very' (Gk *mega-*) (on the loss of the medial velar in Luwian, see below)

IE */g/, */$\hat{g}$/ > Anat. */g/, cf. Hitt. *genu-* 'knee'; Anat. */k/, */g/ – /i/ and in medial position > 0 in the languages of the Luwian group, cf. CLuw. *issari-* 'hand' (Hitt. *kessera-*), CLuw. *maia-*, cited above, CLuw. *tiyammi* 'earth' (Hitt. *tekan*, Gk *khthón*)

IE */k^w/ > Anat. */k^w/, cf. Hitt. *kuis*, CLuw. interrogative and relative pronoun *kuis* (Lat. *quis*); Anat. */k^w/ > Lyc. /t/, cf. the relative pronoun *ti-*

IE */g^{wh}/ > Anat. */k^w/, cf. Hitt. *kuen-* 'kill', Skt *han-*

IE */g^w/ > Anat. */w/, cf. Luw. *uana-* 'woman' (Eng. *queen*).

The velar and palatal voiceless stops have two distinct developments in the languages of the Luwian group, while in the others they share the same development. Consequently, it is difficult to reconstruct a Proto-Anatolian form for the palatals, unless we wish to suppose that IE */$\hat{k}$/ > Anat. */$\hat{k}$/, which subsequently > /s/ (or /z/) in Luwian and /k/ in Hittite. However, this smacks of an *ad hoc* solution. The most balanced conclusion is perhaps that offered by Tischler, who writes on this subject:

> Daß das Luwische Reflexe aller drei Gutturalreihen zeigt, ist also in keiner Weise einzigartig, überraschend ist lediglich, daß das eng verwandte Hethitische sich diesbezüglich so anders verhält. Das wird erst dann verständlich, wenn man sich von der Vorstellung frei macht, daß die indogermanische Grundsprache bis zur Aufspaltung in die verschiedenen Einzelgruppen einheitlich war.[5]

The liquids and the voiceless fricative */s/ are preserved as such, compare Hitt. *melit*, Luw. *mallit-* 'honey', Hitt. *laman* 'name' (initial /l/ is due to nasal dissimilation), HLuw. *atima* 'id.' (with a prothetic vowel and dissimilation of a different sort from that attested in Hittite), Hitt. *kessera-*, Luw. *issari-* 'hand'. As in Greek and Armenian, /r/ is not found in word-initial position. On the voiceless fricative, compare Hitt. *hassa-* 'hearth' (Lat. *ara*) and also the nominative singular of the common gender, -*s*, attested in all the Anatolian languages except Lycian and Milyan, where Anatolian final */s/ > Ø.

As is known, the decipherment of Hittite has provided concrete evidence for the Laryngeal Theory outlined by Saussure in his *Mémoire* of 1878. Besides, the Anatolian data have demonstrated the essentially consonantal character of the laryngeals (see Chapter 2, p. 40).

Indo-European $*/h_1/$ > Anat. 0, cf. Hitt. *eszi* 'he is' < IE $*h_1esti$: this development is found in pre- and post-vocalic initial and medial positions.[6] IE $*/h_2/$, $*/h_3/$ are continued in a sound which is probably a fricative before vowels and sonants, cf. Hitt. *ḫarki* 'white' (Lat. *argentum*); Hitt. *ḫastai*, Luw. *ḫassa* 'bone' (Gk *ostéon*); CLuw. *hawi*, HLuw. *hawa*, Lyc. *χawa-* 'sheep'; Hitt. *ḫulana* 'wool' (Skt *ūrṇa*). IE $*/h_2/$ is also preserved in post-vocalic position, while IE $*/h_3/$ > Ø; cf. Hitt. *newaḫḫ-* 'to renew' < $*neweh_2$- (Lat. *novāre*).

In addition, IE $*/H/$ is vocalized, becoming /a/ in consonantal environments (this is the $*/ə/$ of traditional reconstruction); this happens both medially, as in the other IE languages, and initially, where in the other languages $*/H/$ normally > Ø, cf. Hitt. *asanzi* 'they are' < IE $*h_1sénti$ (Skt *santi*, Lat. *sunt*).

Morphosyntax of the Main Word Classes

Nouns and Adjectives
Anatolian had eight cases (nominative, accusative, genitive, dative-locative, directive, instrumental, ablative and vocative), two numbers (singular and plural) and two genders (common and neuter). There is disagreement over what the common gender represented (possibly an IE common gender where masculine and feminine were not yet distinguished; or syncretism of the IE masculine and feminine); answers to this question are often based not only on the interpretation of data but also on the position assigned to Anatolian within the IE languages. This is discussed further in **The Position of Anatolian** (pp. 190f.).

The nominal endings of the Anatolian languages and those of Common Anatolian may be seen in the overview in Table 7.1.

Nominative and Accusative
The common nominative and accusative do not present problems; the presence of 0 in Lycian and Milyan is due to the regular loss of final -*s*; see Consonants, pp. 175f.. The nominatives in -*s* and -*z* in these two languages are those of the stems in -*ant*-. As regards the nominative-accusative neuter singular, the only noteworthy point is the extension of the pronominal ending -*d* to the nouns in Lydian and, partially, in Palaic. In the plural, the Luwian endings in -*nz*- carry on the Anatolian accusative ending *-ns*. The value of the Luwian plural in -*sa* is doubtful (perhaps collective).

Dative-locative and Directive
The directive is preserved as a case distinct from dative-locative only in Old Hittite, where it is used with nouns denoting inanimate entities to express

Table 7.1 Nominal endings of the Anatolian languages

	Anatolian	Hittite	Palaic	Cuneiform Luwian	Hieroglyphic Luwian	Lycian	Milyan	Lydian
Singular								
Nom.	*-s	-s	-s	-s	-s	Ø, -s	Ø, -z	-s
Acc.	*-n	-n	-n	-n, -an	-n, -an	~, -n	~, -n	-v(a)
Neuter Nom.-Acc.	*-n, Ø	-n, Ø	-n, Ø, -t	-n, Ø	[-n, Ø]	~, Ø	~, Ø	-d
Gen.	*-as	-as	-as					
Dat.-Loc.	*-i	-(a)i -ya	-(a)i	-i, -ya, -a	-i, iya, -a	-i, iye, -a	-i	-λ(b)
Dir.	*-a	-a	-a					
Inst.	*-t	-it	-at?	-ati	-ati, -ari	-edi, -adi	-edi, -adi	-ad
Abl.	*-az	-az						
Voc.	*Ø, -e	Ø, -e						
Plural								
Nom.-Voc.	*-es	-es, -us, -as	-es	-nzi	-nzi	-i	-iz	-is?
Acc.	*-ns	-us	-anza?	-nz	-nzi	-s	-z	-as
Neuter Nom.-Acc.	*Ø, -a	Ø, -a	-a, -sa?	-a, -sa	-a, -sa	-a	-a	-a
Gen.	*-an, -as	-an, -as	?			-ã/ẽ (?)		-an
Dat.-Loc.	*-as	-as	-as	-nz	-nz	-e	-z	
Dir.								
Abl.		(-az)		} -nzati?				
Inst.		(-it)						

Notes: (a) IPA [ŋ] (b) IPA [ʎ]

Source: Based mainly on Meriggi (1981) and, for the languages of the Luwian group, on Starke (1982).

'motion towards', in sentences containing verbs of motion (e.g. ^{URU}Har-aḫsuwa= *as aras* 'he (*-as*) arrived at the city of Harahsu (dir.)', *Keilin-schriften aus Boğazköy* XXII 2 ii 7). Both in later Hittite and in the other Anatolian languages, the directive merges with the dative-locative; this is also the case in Old Hittite with the stems in *-i-*. The IE origin of the *-a* ending of the directive is controversial. In addition, there is also a locative with ending 0 attested in Hittite. This form is subject to lexical restrictions, in that it is mainly used with nouns referring to natural locatives, such as the Hittite form *dagan* 'on the ground', locative of *tekan* 'ground'. In some cases, as in this example, the formation of the 0 locative involves a vowel gradation different from that of the nominative; in other cases, however, the vowel does not undergo any change (see Neu 1980).

Genitive
A characteristic of the Luwian group is that it has lost the genitive, which is replaced by adjectival formations (see Chapter 9, p. 258), with a suffix *-assi-* (CLuw.). This suffix derives adjectives from nominal stems which are then declined.[7] The replacement of the genitive with a denominal adjective also happened in Lydian, where the suffix *-ali-* is used. This suffix has given rise to an ending which has also been extended to the dative.

The genitive in *-an* is attested in Old Hittite: it is possible that it had a collective rather than a plural value. Probably Lycian, too, preserves a genitive plural ending *-ā*, *-ē*, related to the Hittite genitive in *-an*.

Ablative and Instrumental
Only Hittite has two different inflectional endings for the ablative and instrumental. These two cases are functionally distinct only in Old Hittite; in the texts of the later period there appears first a functional syncretism, then a tendency for the instrumental ending to disappear.

Vocative
The origin of the Hittite vocative in *-i* (*-u-* stems) is unknown. The *-nt-* stems preserve final *-t* in the vocative, unlike what happens in the other IE languages.

Absence of the Concrete Cases in the Plural
In Table 7.1 there are no ablative or instrumental plural forms (except for Hittite, where these are given in parentheses, in that they are in fact singular endings, see below); the directive appears to have undergone syncretism with the dative-locative. Basically, the plural has only the grammatical cases and not the concrete cases. In addition, the neuter seems not to have a true plural. This fact has to be seen in the light of another phenomenon which may be clearly observed in Old Hittite: the concrete cases are used only for the neuter. It will be remembered, then, that the ending of the nominative-accusative neuter plural in Indo-European was in fact a collective ending (cf. Chapter 2,

p. 63). This was surely still true in the Anatolian languages, where the nominative neuter regularly agrees with the predicate in the singular (also well attested in Greek, the so-called *skhêma Attikón*). In Hittite, from the oldest texts onwards, the neuter ablative and instrumental are used both in contexts where the singular would be required and where the plural would be required (cf. expressions such as *issaz= smit* 'from their mouths', where *issaz* may be analysed as ablative singular).[8]

Pronouns

The first- and second-person pronouns are well attested in Hittite; in the other Anatolian languages the paradigms are not preserved fully. The IE character of the Hittite personal pronoun inflection is shown above all by the suppletion which contrasts the nominative stem with that of the other cases. The paradigms are as in Table 7.2.

The nominative of the personal pronouns is also attested in the so-called emphatic form, with the addition of an enclitic particle -*a*; consequently, we have forms such as Hittite *uga*, analogous to Latin *egō* and Greek *egó*. The Hittite vocalic alternation between the nominative and the oblique cases in the second singular pronoun is matched by the Palaic forms *ti, tu*. The genitive in -*el* is found only in Hittite, where it has been generalized in the pronominal flection. The ablative forms are more stable; they are formed with a suffix -*ed*- deriving from the demonstrative pronoun flection, and they originated within the case-attraction construction. This construction is used to express inalienable possession. The noun referring to the possessor is 'attracted' into the same case as the noun denoting the object possessed, as in the expression *ammedaz ŠU-az* 'with my hand' literally 'with me with the hand' (see Luraghi 1990b).[9]

In all persons, the Anatolian languages have weak pronominal forms in the oblique cases; alongside the accusative/dative forms of the unaccented first- and second-person pronouns, we also find a third-person singular and plural dative pronoun, which in Hittite derives from the IE reflexive pronoun. The third-person nominative and accusative are rendered with the forms of the enclitic demonstrative -*a*-, attested throughout Anatolian. Only in Hittite do

Table 7.2 Luwian branch

	First-person singular	First-person plural	Second-person singular	Second-person plural
Nom.	uk	wes	zik	sumes
Acc./Dat.	ammuk	anzas	tuk	sumas
Gen.	ammel	anzel	tuel	sumel, sumenzan
Abl.	ammedaz	anzedas	tuedaz	sumedaz

we have the third-person strong forms *sel* (gen.) and *sez* (abl.) from the stem
**se-*.

The paradigms of the enclitic third-person pronoun may be reconstructed
as in Table 7.3.

The reflexive is expressed not only by means of the middle voice of the
verb (see **Verbs**, pp. 182f.) but also by an enclitic particle, attested in Hittite
as *-z(a)*, in Luwian, Palaic, Lycian and Milyan as *-ti* and in Lydian as *-(i)t*,
whose origin is obscure.

Table 7.4 shows the inflection in Hittite of the demonstrative pronoun *apas*
'that', also used as an anaphoric pronoun. The Common Anatolian form of
this pronoun may be reconstructed as **aba-*; this root is also attested in the
other Anatolian languages and functions as an anaphoric pronoun in Luwian
(CLuw. *apa*, HLuw. *(a)pa-* or *(a)pi-*) and in Lydian (*bi-*); Lycian *ebi-*, on the
other hand, appears to function only as a demonstrative (see Meriggi 1981:
324).

Table 7.3   Enclitic third-person pronoun

	Hittite	Palaic	Cuneiform Luwian	Hieroglyphic Luwian	Lycian	Lydian
Singular						
Nom.	-as	-as	-as	-as	-ne?	-is
Acc.	-an	-an	-an	-an	-ene, -e?	-av
Neut.						
Nom.-Acc.	-at	-at	-ata	-ata	-ede	-ad
Dat.	-si	-du, -si	-du	-tu	-ije, -i?	-mλ
Plural						
Nom.	-e, -at	-e, -as	-ata	-ata	-ne?	
Acc.	-as, -us		-ata	-ata	-ne	-as
Neuter						
Nom.-Acc.	-at, -e	-e	-ata	-ata	-ija	-ad
Dat.	-smas	-si?	-mmas	-ma^{n}za	-ije?	-ms

Source: Carruba 1985: 97.

Table 7.4   The demonstrative pronoun *apas*

	Singular	Plural
Nom.	apās/abās	apē
Acc.	apūn	apūs
Neuter Nom.-Acc.	apāt	apē
Gen.	apēl	apēnzan
Dat.-Loc.-Dir.	apēdani	apēdas
Inst.	apēz	
Abl.	apit/apēdanda	

After Old Hittite, all the demonstrative pronouns show a tendency towards syncretism affecting the accusative and the nominative plural of the common gender (the ending *-us* is used for both cases; to a more limited extent, the ending *-e* is extended to the accusative). In addition, the oblique cases, too, tend to merge in the plural (the dative ending is extended to the genitive, the original genitive ending becomes less frequent), where the plural form of the pronouns tends to be structured according to a paradigm which contrasts a form, or rather, two allomorphs, for the direct cases (nominative and accusative) with a form for the oblique cases.

A peculiarity of Hittite is the presence of enclitic possessives in all persons.[10] Although generally called 'possessive pronouns', these are really adjective forms; they exhibit a regular declension and agree in gender, number and case with their nominal head, which hosts them. Consider the following examples: *attas= mas* 'of my father (gen.)'; *ishi= ssi* 'to his master (dat.)'; *parna=ssa* 'to his house (dir.)'; *issaz=smit* 'from their mouths (abl.)'.

Possessives take on the value of pronouns when they are used with local adverbs (see **Adverbs**, p. 186) as in the expressions *ser= samet* 'above them', *katti= ssi* 'with him'.

Interrogative, relative and indefinite pronouns, and adjectives all derive from the IE type with initial labiovelar, cf. Hitt. *kuis, kuit*, CLuw. *kuis, kui*, Pal. *kuis, kuid*, Lyc. *ti-* (see Carruba 1983), Lyd. interrogative and relative pronoun *qi-*; Hitt. indefinite pronoun *kuiski, kuitki*. The pronoun *kuis, kuit* in Hittite has the forms given in Table 7.5.

On the formation of relative clauses, see **Subordinate Clauses**, p. 189.

Verbs

The Anatolian verbal system differs greatly from the system traditionally reconstructed for Indo-European, which is based mainly on Greek and Old Indic. The Anatolian verb only has two finite moods, indicative and imperative, two tenses, present- future and preterite, and two voices, active and mediopassive (we shall see below that the term mediopassive is perhaps not ideal to describe the function of that voice). In the present, in the singular only, and in the first person singular of the preterite the verbs are divided into two conjugations, one in *-mi* and one in *-ḫi*. While the IE origin of the *-mi*

Table 7.5   The pronoun *kuis/kuit*

	Singular	Plural
Nom.	kuis	kues
Acc.	kuin	kueus
Neuter Nom.-Acc.	kuit	kue
Gen.	kuel	
Dat.-Loc.	kuedani	kuedas
Abl.	kuez	

conjugation is unequivocal, the origin of the -*ḫi* conjugation has given rise to greater controversy. On the one hand, there are similarities between the -*ḫi* conjugation and the IE perfect; on the other hand, the -*ḫi* conjugation can also be compared with the IE middle. Note also that this conjugation is attested with certainty only in Hittite; among the other languages, Luwian and Palaic probably have the third-person singular form. The reconstruction of the verb endings for Proto-Anatolian is extremely doubtful; the synopsis in Table 7.6 shows, as far as is possible, the paradigms of the historical languages.

The conjugation of the mediopassive is fully attested only in Hittite; its paradigms are listed in Table 7.7.

Only in the third-person singular present is there a difference between the conjugation in -*mi* (ending -*ta(ri)*) and that in -*ḫi* (ending -*a(ri)*). The forms with the suffix -*ri*, which at first had suggested an exact correspondence

Table 7.6   Verb endings for Anatolian languages: active

	Hittite	Palaic	Cuneiform Luwian	Hieroglyphic Luwian	Lycian	Lydian
Present indicative active						
1 sg.	-mi -ḫi	——	-wi	-w, -wi	——	-u, -v
2 sg.	-si -ti	-si	-si	-s(a)	——	-s
3 sg.	-zi -i	-ti -i	-ti -i	-ti -i(?)	-t/di	-t, -d
1 pl.	-weni	-wani	——	——	——	——
2 pl.	-teni	——	——	——	——	——
3 pl.	-anzi	-anti	-nti	-ti	-ti	-t, -d
Preterite active indicative						
1 sg.	-un -hun	-ha	-ha	-ha	-χa	-id
2 sg.	-s -(s)ta	-is	-s	——	——	——
3 sg.	-t(a) -(s)ta	-t	-ta	-ta	-te	-l
1 pl.	-wen	——	-man	-min	——	——
2 pl.	-ten	——	——	——	——	——
3 pl.	-er	-nta	-nta	-ta	-te	——

Table 7.7   Verb endings for Anatolian languages: mediopassive

	Mediopassive *Present*	*Preterite*
1 sg.	-ḫa, -ḫari, ḫaḫari	-ḫat(i), -ḫaḫat(i)
2 sg.	-ta	-ta, -tat(i)
3 sg.	-ta, -tari -a, -ari	-(t)at(i)
1 pl.	-wasta, -wastari, -wastati	-wastat(i)
2 pl.	-duma, -dumari, -dumati	-dumat
3 pl.	-anta, -antari	-antat(i)

between the Hittite and the Latin middle, are in fact the most recent (cf. Neu 1968). Forms with this suffix are attested also in the present middle of Luwian and Palaic (see Meriggi 1981).

The link between the *-ḫi* conjugation and the IE perfect is unclear, so much so that some scholars believe that the *-ḫi* conjugation may have had a number of different origins. Eichner (1975) elucidated the correspondence between a group of verbs in *-ḫi* and the Germanic preterite-presents (see Chapter 13, pp. 404–5). One example is the root *sag-* 'to know' (cf. Lat. *sagire*, Goth. *sokjan*), which forms a present *saggaḫḫi*, formed with the same ending $*-h_2a$ that we find in the perfect of the other IE languages and the addition of a suffix *-i*, by analogy with the verbs in *-mi*; the forms without addition of *-i* have given rise to a preterite. The *-ḫi* conjugation then came to have a present, continuing the original stative value of the IE perfect, and a preterite, continuing its form. From a formal point of view, this process must have been the origin of all the verbs in *-ḫi*; but from a semantic point of view, the verbs in *-ḫi* which can be derived through the value of preterite-presents are limited in number. Neu (1985), partly based on the conclusions of Eichner, provides an analysis of the origins of voice in Indo-European, which is conditioned by the necessity to explain the facts of Anatolian. In addition, Neu elucidates the links between perfect and middle in Indo-European, which were probably still reflected in the stative value of some old Hittite 'media tantum' (see Neu 1968). The derivation of the *-ḫi* conjugation from the IE perfect is, however, still controversial; for example, Jasanoff (1979) prefers to link the *-ḫi* conjugation to the thematic inflection of the other IE languages.

Semantic and syntectic properties of the Anatolian verb are mostly known from Hittite, to which I shall refer in the remaining part of this section.

Modality

Apart from assertive and imperative modality, expressed by means of the indicative and imperative moods, the Hittite verb can also denote potential and contrary-to-fact modality, by means of the particle *man* and the present indicative (potential) or preterite indicative (contrary-to-fact).

Voice

The original value of the Hittite middle is disputed; however, most likely the opposition active/middle continued an original opposition between active and stative, as is evident above all in Old Hittite (see Neu 1968). Among other things it is to be noted that in the oldest texts each verb exhibits, with few exceptions, only forms belonging to one of the two voices. The processual middle must also have been ancient; in addition, the forms of the middle often have reflexive or (in the case of the third-person singular) impersonal value. Relatively rare, and attested only in documents later than the oldest phase, is the use of the middle as a true personal passive. The function of the passive is otherwise conveyed by lexical passives (e.g. *ak-* 'die' as the passive of *kuen-* 'kill') or by the third-person active plural, which is widely employed as an impersonal form (cf. Luraghi 1990a: 39 and n.75).

Periphrastic Forms

A peculiarity of Hittite with respect to the other IE languages is the existence of a large number of periphrastic verb forms, for the most part already attested in the older period, whose use becomes more frequent in the course of time. Periphrastic constructions are the following:

1   *har(k)-* 'hold', 'have', +n. nom.-acc. of the participle, with the value of a durative perfect (see Boley 1984)
2   *es-* 'be', + participle, initially agreeing with the subject (predicative participle), later in the form of a nom.-acc. n., indicating an advanced degree of grammaticalization of the construction. The sense is that of a pluperfect (see Houwink Ten Cate 1973)
3   *dai-, tiya-* 'take' + (invariable) supine, with inchoative value (see Kammenhuber 1955)
4   *pai-* 'go', or *uwa-* 'come', with the indicative, which give rise to a serial construction; they emphasize the temporal sequence of a certain action with respect to a preceding action (usually translated as 'it happened that', 'and then', see Luraghi (1993)).

Derivative Verbs

Hittite makes extensive use of derivative verbs, both deverbatives and denominatives. Among the most commonly used suffixes also attested in other IE languages we have *-sk-*, for deverbatives with iterative value, and *-nu-*, which forms causatives, mainly deverbative (the denominative causatives, also called 'factitives', are generally formed with the suffix *-ahh-*) (see Friedrich 1960: 73–6 and Luraghi 1992).

Non-finite Forms of the Verb

(see Kammenhuber 1954, 1955) Hittite has only one participle, formed with the suffix *-nt-*, also attested in other IE languages. Unlike elsewhere, however, the Hittite participle in *-nt-* does not have a present, but rather a perfect, value: *akkanza* 'died', participle of *ak-* 'die'; *appanza* 'the prisoner' (i.e. he who has been captured), from *ep-* 'take', *panza* 'gone', from *pai-* 'go'. Unlike Hittite, all the other Anatolian languages instead have a participle in *-mi-*, which also has the value of a past participle. Both of the participles are attested in Luwian and Palaic, but it is difficult to establish whether there is any semantic difference between them.[11]

The infinitive in Hittite is formed with the suffixes *-uwanzi*, as in *uwauwanzi* 'to come' (root *uwa-*) and *-anna*, as in *adanna* 'to eat' (root *ed-*). This second type of infinitive is also attested in the other Anatolian languages, for example, CLuw. *aduna* 'to eat' and Pal. *ahuna* 'to drink'. Finally Hittite has a verbal noun, formed with the suffixes *-war* (gen. *-was*), for verbs with an infinitive in *-uwanzi*, and *-atar* (gen. *-annas*) for verbs with an infinitive in *-anna*.

Adverbs

This section will be limited to providing a simplified treatment of the so-called 'local adverbs' or 'dimensional adverbs' of Hittite, in so far as these are of particular interest for comparison with the other IE languages (see Starke 1977 and Boley 1985). Local adverbs make up a coherent system in old Hittite, where they are divided into two corresponding series of static and dynamic adverbs:

Static adverbs	*Dynamic adverbs*
andan 'within'	*anda* 'into'
appan 'behind'	*appa* 'backwards', 'again'
kattan 'under'	*katta* 'downwards'
piran 'in front of'	*para* 'forwards'
ser 'on'	*sara* 'upwards'

The static adverbs are forms whose nominal origin is still clear; in fact, they can be used with the genitive of a noun, in constructions similar to those attested in other IE languages (cf. Lat. *causā gratiā*), and they can take enclitic possessive pronouns (see **Pronouns**, pp. 180–2). The dynamic adverbs are of more recent origin than the static adverbs, as is clear, among other things, from the greater regularity of their formation (the root has the same vowel in all the dynamic adverbs). They are derived from the corresponding static forms with the addition of the directive ending *-a*.[12] They are used exclusively with verbs of motion, in sentences which can also contain a complement of motion in the directive.

Etymologically, the Hittite spatial adverbs are related to the adverb-preverb-prepositions of the other IE languages (see Chapter 8, **Prepositions**, p. 222 and Chapter 9, pp. 257–8). Their use as postpositions or preverbs, however, is extremely limited in Old Hittite, where this happens only in the case of *piran* + dative-locative and *para* + ablative (postpositions) and for a few verbs, which, with the addition of the adverb-preverb, exhibit a meaning and valency different from the simple verb (see Luraghi 1990a: 33–5).

The contrast of static and dynamic adverbs disappears after Old Hittite, parallel to the disappearance of the opposition between directive and dative-locative. At the same time, the use of the adverbs as postpositions or preverbs undergoes considerable development. (However, in writing the preverbs are usually still separate from the verb.)

Sentence and Phrase Structure

Constituent Order in the Simple Sentence

The order of constituents in the Anatolian languages is free as regards the nominal constituents, as is generally the case in inflected languages, but fixed as regards the position of the verbs and enclitics. The simple sentence is characterized by two pivotal points, the verb, which delimits its rightmost boundary, and the enclitics, often supported by a connective, which delimit its leftmost boundary.

Let us analyse the following example:

(a) *nu= za*   ŠA ^{HUR.SAG} *Tarikarimu* ^{URU} *Kaskan   tarahhun*
    conn. refl.   of   *T.*   *K.* : acc. I-defeated

(b) *n=   an=   kan kuenun*
    conn. pron.3sg.acc.=part. killed

(c) ^{HUR.SAG} *Tarikarimun= ma   dannattahhun*
          T. : acc.   -conn. emptied

(d) KUR ^{URU} *Zihariya ya   human   arha   warnun*
    land   *Z.*   and   all : acc. prev. burnt

'(a) The Kaskas of the Tarikarimu mountains I defeated, (b) I massacred them. (c) I cleared the mountains of Tarikarimu of people (d) and set alight the whole land of Zihariya.'

(Annals of Muršiliš 80)

All the sentences contain one or more enclitics (i.e. *-za, -an, -kan, -ma* and *-ya*), phonologically hosted by the first word of the sentence. In sentences (a) and (b), the first word, which serves as a support for the enclitics, is the connective *nu*.

The regular presence of chains of enclitics is a characteristic of the Anatolian languages. The enclitics are placed in fixed positions; each sentence may contain a maximum of six (see Carruba 1985 and, on Hittite, Luraghi 1990a: 13–15):

1   Connectives or coordinating conjunctions: Hitt. *-ma, -a, -(y)a*; Pal. *- (y)a, -pa*; CLuw. *-ḫa, -kuwa*; HLuw. *-ha*; Lyc. *-me, -be*; Mil. *-me, -be, -ce*; Lyd. *-k, -(u)m*[13]

2   A particle of reported speech, Hitt. and Pal. *-wa(r)-*; Luw. *-wa-*; Lyc. and Mil. *-(u)we- <* IE **wer-*; cf. Lat. *verbum*, Hitt. *weriya-* 'call'[14]

3   (In Hittite), nominative or accusative forms of the enclitic third-person pronoun

4   (In Hittite), oblique forms of the first- or second-person pronouns, or dative forms of the third-person pronoun

5   (In Hittite), reflexive particle

6   Particles of spatial reference: Hitt. *-(a)n, -(a)pa, -(a)sta, -kan, -san*; Pal. *-(n)tta, -pi*; CLuw. *-tta, -tar*; HLuw. *-ta, -pa*; Lyc. *-te, -pi, -de*; Mil. *-te*, Lyd. *-(i)t* (Carruba 1985: 95).

The order of the enclitics attested in Hittite for the positions (3)–(5) is different from the order attested in all the other languages, in which we find:

3   reflexive particle
4   oblique forms of the pronouns
5   nominative or accusative of the third-person pronoun.

In Hittite, too, the dative plural forms of the third-person pronoun precede the possible nominative or accusative forms.

The position of the enclitics near the leftmost margin of the sentence in Anatolian has correspondences in the other IE languages, in which, as observed by Wackernagel several decades before the decipherment of Hittite, unaccented particles and pronouns tend to be situated in this position, after the first accented word (see Luraghi 1990c). 'Wackernagel's Law' is attested in Anatolian with much greater regularity than is encountered in the other IE languages (cf. Chapter 2, p. 70).

Using the terminology employed by Rosenkranz (1979: 223), we may call the enclitic chain an *Informationskette* or 'chain of information', in that it contains forms which specify the relationship of the sentence to the preceding context, or relationships within the sentence itself. Connectives, which link the sentence to its context, precede pronouns and particles, whose function is specified within the sentence (i.e. a division into *textrelevante* (text-relevant) and *kernrelevante* (core-relevant) enclitics is made, again using Rosenkranz's terminology).

Connectives and Particles
Among the enclitics listed above, the spatial particles are of particular interest, since they do not correspond to anything in the other IE languages. These particles, whose etymology is difficult, occur on the whole in sentences which also contain complements of place or adverbs and have the function of specifying a particular spatial relationship within the sentence. In later Hittite, the number of particles used is greatly reduced; in practice, the use of the particle *-kan* becomes generalized with some verbs, even without spatial reference. The function of *-kan* in this case has not been clarified at all; it appears likely that the particle has something to do with the perfective aspect. In addition, the use of *-kan* is obligatory with some verbs, for example *kuen-* 'kill' (cf. sentence (b) in the example in the previous section). The most important work of reference on the spatial particles in Anatolian is Carruba (1969b); see also Carruba (1985). On Hittite in particular there are many other studies, among which attention should be drawn to Boley (1989).

The Anatolian languages make great use of connectives, both prepositive and enclitic. The latter go in the initial chain, where they precede all the other enclitics. Very frequently, especially in Hittite and after the oldest period, we find a connective introducing a sentence; this seems to have no function other than to host the enclitics. From the Hittite texts there emerges an opposition between sentences introduced by the prepositive connective (normally *nu*), which has additive value, and sentences introduced by the enclitic connective -*ma*-, which has adversative value.

Subordinate Clauses

Anatolian makes extensive use of paratactic structures; the widespread employment of different connectives also makes up in part for the scarcity of subordination. Certain types of construction systematically recur with verbs which in other languages govern complement clauses. For example, the verbs of 'saying' normally use the so-called 'reported speech' construction.

Among adverbial clauses, we do not find purpose or consecutive clauses; however, the use of the infinitive of purpose is attested.

The main subordinating conjunctions in Hittite are *takku* (Old Hittite only) in conditional clauses, *man* in temporal or conditional clauses, *maḫḫan* in temporal clauses, *kuitman* in temporal clauses, and *kuit* in causal clauses.

The formation of relative clauses is of particular interest from a comparative point of view (see Raman 1973; Lehmann 1984). Generally, the head of the relative clause does not appear within the main clause (as happens, for example, in English), but within the relative clause itself. Consider the following example:

(a) *nu= za* ^{D}UTU^{ŠI} *kuin* NAM.RA *INA* É LUGAL *uwatenun*
     conn.refl. His Majesty rel.pron.:acc.sg. prisoner in palace I-took
(b) *n= as* 15,500 NAM.RA *esta*
     conn. dem.pron.:nom.sg. 15,500 prisoner was

'The prisoners whom I, the king, took into the palace numbered 15,500.' (lit. '(a) what (number of) prisoners I took into the palace, (b) that (number) was of 15,500 prisoners.'

(*Ḫattušiliš* 86)

This type of relative clause is also attested in Latin, especially in the older texts, and in Greek, where it is referred to as a proleptic relative:

(a) *quos ferro trucidari opportebat,* (b) *eos nondum voce vulnero*
'I cannot even strike with words those who ought to have been killed with arms', lit. '(a) who ought to have been killed with arms, (b) those I cannot even strike with words'
(c) *eis hèn aphíkonto hoi stratiôtai kômēn.* (d) *ou megálē ên*
'the village which the soldiers were approaching was not large', lit. '(c) to which village the soldiers were approaching, (d) was not large.'

The origin of this construction is probably paratactic. The form *kuis* was originally an adjective which did not have the function of subordinating one clause to another but rather of establishing, in the first clause of a pair, a constituent about which something would be said in the second clause. The two clauses were originally independent, linked only by the informative dynamic of the text, the first clause constituting in a sense the 'topic' of the second (Raman 1973).

The Position of Anatolian within the Indo-European Languages

Immediately after Hittite had been deciphered, the obvious differences distinguishing Anatolian from the other IE languages led scholars to wonder exactly what sort of relationship there was between them.

As long ago as 1921, Forrer suggested that Anatolian should be viewed not as a branch of Indo-European, but rather as a linguistic group in its own right, related only marginally to Indo-European. A similar position was supported by Sturtevant (1933), and is known as the 'Indo-Hittite theory'. According to Sturtevant, Anatolian and Indo-European were two branches of one linguistic family, hence his term 'Indo-Hittite'; from this it follows that the relationships within the IE family would not be modified in the slightest by the discovery of the Anatolian languages.

Sturtevant's position has now been abandoned and the term 'Indo-Hittite' is used only sporadically; nevertheless, although returning to a more flexible model of linguistic relationship, most scholars continue to maintain that Anatolian has special status among the IE languages, in that it was the earliest branch to split off from the rest of the family.

However, the notable differences between Anatolian and the other IE languages are explained in different ways. In broad outline there are two contrasting theories: (a) the 'Schwundhypothese', according to which all categories which may be reconstructed using information from the other languages, but which are lacking in Anatolian (feminine gender, aorist, dual, etc.) have been lost; Anatolian would thus be a particularly innovative branch of Indo-European; (b) the 'Herkunfthypothese', according to which those categories absent from the Anatolian languages were formed only after the Anatolian branch split off from the rest of the IE family; Anatolian would thus be particularly archaic.

The issue about which there is no agreement is not so much the chronology as the degree of archaism of Anatolian. According to the second theory, what Anatolian represents is practically tantamount to a sort of pre-Indo-European, while according to the first, its IE nature has been greatly eroded during the centuries of separation from the other languages.

The Anatolian data in this respect offer themselves freely to a dual interpretation. There has been great debate on the verbal system, which lacks, among other things, categories which have always been reconstructed for Indo-European, such as the optative and the aorist. Recently the gender problem has become the subject of frequent discussion (see Chapter 2, p. 63). We saw in **Nouns and Adjectives,** pp. 177–80 that nouns, adjectives and pronouns in Anatolian have only two genders, common and neuter. The common gender has been so termed because it was initially seen as a fusion of the original IE masculine and feminine. In conformity with this theory, Kammenhuber (1963: 253–5) holds that the feminine gender has fused with the masculine in Anatolian through a developing tendency to make grammatical gender coincide with the semantic categories animate and inanimate.

However, it was very quickly pointed out that another, radically different, interpretation was possible. The common gender might well reflect an IE animate gender. It would be possible to reconstruct for Indo-European an opposition animate–inanimate, directly reflected in Hittite; only subsequently would feminine and masculine have become distinguished within the animate gender. Until a few years ago this second theory was greatly favoured. Typological evidence was also adduced in favour of it; for example, it was claimed that, while it is possible for an animate to split up into masculine and feminine, there exist no parallels for a phenomenon whereby a masculine–feminine contrast disappears, leaving no trace even in the pronoun system.

In the past few years, the question of gender in Anatolian has been addressed with renewed interest; attempts have been made above all to adduce data not only from Hittite but also from the other languages. Starke (1982) draws the attention of scholars to the presence of a suffix -*i*- in the Luwian nominal inflection. Oettinger (1987) identifies this suffix with the IE feminine suffix -*ih*$_2$- (as in Skt *vr̥kî* 'she-wolf') and claims, consequently, that Common Anatolian had had a tripartite gender distinction which was subsequently lost in the attested languages. Weitenberg (1987), too, believes that it is possible to distinguish traces of the feminine in the neuter gender in Hittite. According to the data presented in his article, Hittite animate neuters correspond on the whole to IE feminines, while animate nouns of common gender correspond to the masculines. More recently, Melchert (1992a) has claimed that Lycian preserves traces of the distinction between the IE -*o*- and -*ā*- stems. It is extremely difficult to assess these theories. For example, the suffix -*ih*$_2$- could have existed in Anatolian without having yet developed the function of marking feminine derivatives. According to several Littitologists, including Carruba and Neu, this is the only acceptable theory, because it also has the advantage of being simpler and more economical than the theory according to which Anatolian has lost the feminine. As regards Melchert's position, it involves a revision of the Anatolian 'family tree' according to which Lycian can no longer belong to the Luwian group; further arguments for such revision need to be adduced.

The problem of gender is only one of the many unsolved problems which Anatolian linguistics has to confront today.[15]

Notes

1 In the case of the labials and velars, there is less confusion of spelling simply because the voiceless form is usually written, especially in the case of signs of the type CV.

2 The spelling of the vowels in Hittite varies in such a way that it is difficult to establish which vowels were long and which short. Although we note greater consistency in the oldest texts, there are nevertheless still variations in vowel length in different forms of the same word. On exactly this basis, Carruba (1981c) maintains that the so-called *scriptio plena* represents not long vowels but rather stressed vowels. However, his theory is not universally accepted: see recently Melchert (1992b, 1994). According to Melchert, the only function of the *scriptio plena* in Hittite is to indicate vowel quantity. In the case of *a/ā*, Melchert does not restrict himself to Hittite, but reconstructs the two vowels with different quantities for Proto-Anatolian, where */a:/ would be the reflex of IE */o/, */o:/ and */a:/, while */a/ would be the reflex of IE */a/; see also Melchert (1992a) and Chapter 2, p. 49.

3 Perhaps Lyc. *krzz-* should also be added here, cf. Tischler (1983: 518).

4 To assess the exact position of Lycian it would also be necessary to consider the presence of words such as *keruti* 'deer' (or other animal with horns), (see Carruba 1978: 171).

5 'Luwian is by no means unique in exhibiting reflexes of all three guttural series; the surprising thing is that the closely-related Hittite behaves so differently in this respect. This can only be understood if we free ourselves from the idea that Indo-European was uniform until it split up into various groups' (Tischler 1992).

6 A possible trace of h_1 in medial position is examined in Eichner (1973).

7 In Cuneiform Luwian no genitive form is attested, while in Hieroglyphic Luwian, beside the adjectival formations, we also find true genitives. The same is true of Lycian, but there the genitive forms are restricted to proper nouns.

8 In the late Hittite texts, nouns of common gender with animate referents also take the ablative and, occasionally, instrumental, endings, for example, in expressions indicating 'motion away from' or agents with passive verbs. The use of the concrete cases with nouns denoting animate entities seems to have originated within the 'case-attraction' construction in the same way as the ablative forms of the pronouns, see Pronouns.

9 In this example both the first-person pronoun and the noun *ŠU* 'hand' are in the ablative, which since Old Hittite had additionally taken on the functions of the instrumental.

10 The enclitic possessives are attested with certainty only in Hittite; on their possible presence in Luwian, see Carruba (1983). On the reasons for their loss after Old Hittite, see Luraghi (1990b).

11 According to Laroche (1959), in Luwian the participle in *-mi-* has past value and that in *-nt-* has present value; however, some forms in *-nt-* express the past, such as *ulant-* 'dead' (not 'dying'), cf. Meriggi (1981).

12 It is not clear which form is used for the static adverbs. Conceivably, it could be a nominative-accusative neuter singular but this would have no connection with their function (as locatives). It should also be noted that the adverb *andan* seems to go back to an adverbial formation already extant in IE (Gk *éndon*). The static adverbs can be linked to the possessive suffixes (cf. **Pronouns**, p. 180), which in this case exhibit the form of the nominative-accusative neuter singular. It should be noted, however, that the adverb *kattan*, if linked to possessives, has a dative-locative form *katti=* and consistently appears with the dative-locative of the possessive. Moreover, there are some other static adverbs which do not have

corresponding dynamic adverbs, which exhibit a form which seems to be that of a directive (and thus the same as that of the dynamic adverbs!), as for example *istarna* 'between, among' and *menaḫḫanda* 'before'. Of these, *istarna* may be linked to possessives, in which case it appears in the form *istarni=* (dat.-loc.). On this problem see Starke (1977) and especially Boley (1985).

13 Connectives and enclitic conjunctions are not only mutually exclusive, but are also incompatible with the prepositive connectives, on which see **Connectives and Particles**, pp. 188–9.

14 On this etymology, see Pecora (1984); on the development from verbal root to particle, see Luraghi (1983).

15 I should like to thank Professor O. Carruba, who kindly read and commented on an earlier draft of this chapter.

References

This chapter does not aim to provide an exhaustive bibliography of the Anatolian languages, which would require much more space than is available. The works cited are those directly referred to in the discussion; where it has been necessary to cite general reference works, I have favoured more up-to-date ones, which in turn offer a much more complete bibliography on the individual problems than I have been able to provide here.

Boley, Jacqueline (1984) *The Hittite* har(k)- *Construction* (Innsbrucker Beiträge zur Sprachwissenschaft, 44), Innsbruck: Institut für Sprachwissenschaft der Universität.
——— (1985) 'Hittite and Indo-European place word syntax', *Sprache* 31: 231–41.
——— (1989) *The Sentence Particles and the Place Words in Old and Middle Hittite* (Innsbrucker Beiträge zur Sprachwissenschaft, 60), Innsbruck: Institut für Sprachwissenschaft der Universität.
Cambridge Ancient History, 3rd edn, Cambridge: Cambridge University Press, vol. I, i, 1970; vol. I, ii, 1971; vol. II, i, 1973; vol. II, ii, 1975.
Carruba, Onofrio (1969a) 'Zur Grammatik des Lydischen', *Athenaeum* 47: 39–83.
——— (1969b) *Die satzeinleitenden Partikeln der indogermanischen Sprachen Anatoliens*, Rome: Ateneo e Bizzarri.
——— (1970) *Das Palaische. Texte, Grammatik, Lexikon* (Studien zu den Boğazköy-Texten 10), Wiesbaden: Harrassowitz.
——— (1978) 'Il relativo e gli indefiniti in licio', *Sprache* 24: 163–79.
——— (1981a) 'L'anatolico', in Enrico Campanile (ed.), *Nuovi materiali per la ricerca indoeuropeistica*, Pisa: Giardini, pp. 43–67.
——— (1981b) 'Unità e varietà nell'anatolico', *AIΩN* 3: 113–40.
——— (1981c) 'Pleneschreibung und Betonung im Hethitischen', in *Zeitschrift für vergleichende Sprachforschung* 95: 232–48.
——— (1983) 'Die 3. Pers. Sing. des Possessivpronomens im Luwischen', in Harry A. Hoffner and Gary M. Beckman (eds), *Kanissuwar: A Tribute to Hans G. Güterbock* (Assyriological Studies, 23), Chicago: The Oriental Institute, pp. 49–52.
——— (1985) 'Die anatolischen Partikeln der Satzeinleitung', in Bernfried Schlerath and Veronica Ritter (eds), *Grammatische Kategorien: Funktion und Geschichte, Akten der VII. Fachtagung der indogermanischen Gesellschaft*, Wiesbaden: Reichert, pp. 79–98.
——— (1992) *Per una grammatica ittita*, a c. di O.C., Pavia: Iuculano.
Chicago Hittite Dictionary, ed. Hans G. Güterbock and Harry A Hoffner, Chicago: The Oriental Institute, 1980.

Eichner, Heiner (1973) 'Die Etymologie vom heth. *mehur*', *MSS* 31: 53–107.
—— (1975) 'Die Vorgeschichte des hethitischen Verbalsystems', in Helmut Rix (ed.), *Flexion und Wortbildung. Akten der V. Fachtagung der indogermanischen Gesellschaft*, Wiesbaden: Reichert, pp. 71–103.
—— (1980) 'Phonetik und Leutgesetze des Hethitischen', in M. Mayrhofer (ed.), *Lautgeschichte und Etymologie*, Wiesbaden: Reichert, pp. 120–65.
Friedrich, Johannes (1952) *Hethitisches Wörterbuch*, Heidelberg: Winter.
—— (1960) *Hethitisches Elementarbuch*, vol. I, Heidelberg: Winter.
—— (1966) *Entzifferung verschollener Schriften und Sprachen*, Berlin: Springer, 2nd edn.
Giannotta, M. E. *et al.* (1995) La decifrazione del Cario – Atti del primo Simposio Internazionale, Rome: Institute of Mycenaean and Egypto-Anatolian Studies.
Gusmani, Roberto (1964) *Lydisches Wörterbuch; mit grammatischer Skizze und Inschriftensammlung*, Heidelberg: Winter.
—— (1981) 'Il lidio', in Enrico Campanile (ed.), *Nuovi materiali per la ricerca indoeuropeistica*, Pisa: Giardini, pp. 107–16.
—— (1989–90) 'Lo stato delle ricerche sul miliaco', *Incontri Linguistici* 13: 69–78.
Hawkins, David (1986) 'Writing in Anatolia: imported and indigenous systems', *World Archaeology* 17: 363–76.
Held, W. H. (1957) *The Hittite Relative Sentence* (Language dissertations, 55), Baltimore: Linguistic Society of America.
Houwink ten Cate, Philo (1973) 'Impersonal and reflexive constructions of the predicative participle in Hittite', in M. A. Beck, A. A. Kopman, C. Miyland and J. Ryckmans (eds), *Symbolae Biblicae et Mesopotamicae*, Leiden: Brill, pp. 199–210.
Jasanoff, Jay H. (1979) 'The position of the -*hi* conjugation', in Erich Neu and Wolfgang Meid (eds), *Hethitisch und Indogermanisch* (Innsbrucker Beiträge zur Sprachwissenschaft, 25), Innsbruck: Institut für Sprachwissenschaft der Universität, pp. 79–90.
Kammenhuber, Anneliese (1954) 'Studien zum hethitischen Infinitivsystem', *Mitteilungen des Instituts für Orientforschung* 2, I: 44–77, II: 245–65, III: 403–44.
—— (1955) 'Studien zum hethitischen Infinitivsystem', *Mitteilungen des Instituts für Orientforschung* 3, IV: 31–57; V: 345–77.
—— (1963) 'Hethitisch, Palaisch, Luwisch und Hieroglyphenluwisch', in *Handbuch der Orientalistik*, part I, vol. 2, Lieferung 2, *Altkleinasiatische Sprachen*, pp. 119–357.
—— *Materialien zu einem hethitischen Thesaurus* (1973) Heidelberg: Winter.
Laroche, Emmanuel (1959) *Dictionnaire de la langue louvite* (Bibliothèque archéologique et historique de l'Institut français de l'archéologie d'Istanbul, 6), Paris: Maisonneuve.
Lehmann, Christian (1984) *Der Relativsatz*, Tübingen: Narr.
Luraghi, Silvia (1990a) *Old Hittite Sentence Structure*, London and New York: Routledge.
—— (1990b) 'The structure and development of possessive noun phrases in Hittite', in Henning Andersen and Konrad Koerner (eds), *Historical Linguistics 1987: Papers from the 8th International Conference on Historical Linguistics*, Amsterdam: Benjamins, pp. 309–25.
—— (1990c) 'Osservazioni sulla legge di Wackernagel e la posizione del verbo nelle lingue indoeuropee', in M. E. Conte, A. Giacalone Ramat and P. Ramat (eds), *Dimensioni della linguistica* (Materiali Linguistici, 2), Milan: Franco Angeli, pp. 31–60.

———— (1992) 'I verbi derivati in -nu- e il loro valore causativo', in Carruba 1992: 153–80.

———— (1993) 'Verb serialization and word order: evidence from Hittite', in Henk Aertsen and Robert Jeffers (eds), *Papers from the 9th International Conference on Historical Linguistics*, Amsterdam: Benjamins, pp. 267–281.

Marazzi, Massimiliano (1990) *Il geroglifico anatolico: Problemi di analisi e prospettive di ricerca* (Library of Linguistics and Philological Research, 24), Rome: Dipartimento di studi glottoantropologici dell'Università di Roma 'La Sapienza'.

Melchert, H. Craig (1983) *Studies in Hittite Historical Phonology* (Ergänzungshefte zur *Zeitschrift für vergleichende Sprachforschung*, 32), Göttingen: Vandenhoeck & Ruprecht.

———— (1984) 'Notes on Palaic', *Zeitschrift für vergleichende Sprachforschung* 97: 22–43.

———— (1992a) 'Relative chronology and Anatolian: the vowel system', in R. Beekes, A. Lubotsky and J. Weitenberg (eds), *Akten der VIII. Fachtagung der Indogermanischen Gesellschaft*, Wiesbaden: Reichert, pp. 42–53.

———— (1992b) 'Hittite vocalism', in Carruba 1992: 181–96.

———— (1994) *Anatolian Historical Phonology*, Amsterdam and Atlanta GA: Rodopi.

Meriggi, Pietro (1966–) *Manuale di eteo geroglifico*, Rome: Ateneo e Bizzarri.

———— (1981) *Schizzo grammaticale dell'anatolico* (Atti dell'Accademia Nazionale dei Lincei. Memorie – Classe di scienze morali, storiche e filologiche, serie VIII, vol. 24/3).

Neu, Erich (1968) *Das hethitische Mediopassiv und seine indogermanischen Grundlagen* (Studien zu den Boğazköy-Texten, 6), Wiesbaden: Harrassowitz.

———— (1980) *Studien zum endungslosen 'Lokativ' des Hethitischen* (Innsbrucker Beiträge zur Sprachwissenschaft – Vorträge und kleine Schriften, 23), Innsbruck: Institut für Sprachwissenschaft der Universität.

———— (1985) 'Das frühindogermanische Diathesensystem: Funktion und Geschichte', in Bernfried Schlerath and Veronica Ritter (eds), *Grammatische Kategorien. Funktion und Geschichte, Akten der VII. Fachtagung der indogermanischen Gesellschaft*, Wiesbaden: Reichert: 275–95.

Oettinger, Norbert (1978) 'Die Gliederung des anatolischen Sprachgebiets', *Zeitschrift für vergleichende, Sprachforschung* 92: 74–92.

———— (1987) 'Bemerkungen zur anatolischen *i*-Motion und Genusfrage', *Zeitschrift für vergleichende, Sprachforschung* 100: 35–43.

Pecora, Laura (1984) 'La particella -wa(r)- e il discorso diretto in antico eteo', *IF* 89: 104–24.

Pugliese Carratelli, Giovanni and Meriggi, Pietro (1978) 'Seminario sulle scritture dell'Anatolia antica', *ASNSP* 8: 731–915.

Puhvel, Jaan (1984–) *Hittite Etymological Dictionary* (Trends in Linguistics. Documentation, 1), Berlin, New York and Amsterdam: Mouton-de Gruyter.

Raman, Carol F. (1973) 'The Old Hittite relative construction', Ph.D. dissertation, University of Texas, Austin.

Rosenkranz, Bernhard (1978) *Vergleichende Untersuchungen der altanatolischen Sprachen* (Trends in Linguistics – State-of-the-Art Reports, 8), The Hague, Paris and New York: Mouton.

———— (1979) 'Archaismen im Hethitischen', in Erich Neu and Wolfgang Meid (eds), *Hethitisch und Indogermanisch* (Innsbrucker Beiträge zur Sprachwissenschaft, 25) Innsbruck: Institut für Sprachwissenschaft der Universität.

Shevoroshkin, V. (1988) 'Indo-European consonants in Anatolian', in Y. L. Arbeitman (ed.), *A Linguistic Happening in Memory of Ben Schwartz*, Louvain-la-Neuve: Peeters.

Starke, Frank (1977) *Die Funktion der dimensionalen Kasus und Ortsadverbien im Hethitischen* (Studien zu den Bogazköy Texten, 23), Wiesbaden: Harrassowitz.

—— (1982) 'Die Kasusendungen der luwischen Sprachen', in Johann Tischler (ed.), *Serta Indogermanica: Festschrift für Günter Neumann* (Innsbrucker Beiträge zur Sprachwissenschaft, 40), Innsbruck: Institut für Sprachwissenschaft der Universität, pp. 407–25.

—— (1985) *Die keilschriftluwischen Texte in Umschrift* (Studien zu den Boğazköy Texten, 30), Wiesbaden: Harrassowitz.

Sturtevant, Edgard A. (1933) *A Comparative Grammar of the Hittite Language*, Philadelphia: Linguistic Society of America.

Tischler, Johann (1983–) *Hethitisches etymologisches Glossar* (Innsbrucker Beiträge zur Sprachwissenschaft, 20), Innsbruck: Institut für Sprachwissenschaft der Universität.

—— (1992) 'Zum *Kentum-Satem*-Problem im Anatolischen', in Carruba 1992: 253–74.

Weitenberg, J. J. S. (1987) 'Proto-Indo-European nominal classification and Old Hittite', *MSS* 48: 213–30.

8 Armenian

Roberto Ajello

Armenian is nowadays the official language of the southernmost republic of the Commonwealth of Independent States and is spoken by around four million people living in an area of approximately 29,900 square kilometres. A so-called 'Western' variety of the language is known and used not only by small communities still present in the territory of the Republic of Turkey, but also by an unknown number of emigrants or their descendants in various countries of the world. These speakers, although inevitably bilingual, preserve links with the language and culture of their origin. The area where Eastern Armenian is spoken nowadays – the Armenian republic and a small linguistic enclave in north-western Iran – is smaller than the area which was the historical homeland of the Armenian people from the sixth century BC onwards. It is then that we have the first mention of the Armenians, in an inscription of Darius I at Behistūn. Since that time the Armenians have been present in a broad area of Transcaucasia bounded by Mount Ararat, Lake Van and the sources of the Tigris and the Euphrates. This same area had previously been the seat of the Urartian kingdom, which was definitely destroyed by the Medes and incorporated into their kingdom at the end of the seventh century BC.

The proto-history of the Armenian language extends up to relatively recent times, in that classical Armenian or the *grabar* (written language), which is the linguistic phase with which we shall be concerned in this chapter, is documented only from the fifth century AD onwards, after the creation by a priest called Mašt'oc' (also known as Mesrop) of an original alphabet with signs for the vowels, much closer to the Greek model than to the writing systems of Asia Minor. The traditional date of this historical event varies between AD 406 and AD 407, but similar attempts had probably been made previously, at least since the Armenian kingdom had been evangelized and Christianity had become the state religion in AD 301. Tradition also tells of a previous alphabet, created by the Syriac bishop Daniel, which was abandoned because it was not suited to the phonological inventory of the language.

The reasons why Sahak, the Patriarch of Armenia, and the Armenian king Vramšapuh entrusted to Mašt'oc' the task of elaborating an alphabet were essentially of two kinds: on the one hand, a widening gap was forming between the people and their faith, because the liturgy was conducted in

197

Greek or Syriac, according to the area; on the other hand there was a need for effective measures to counter the Mazdaic propaganda from the East which was intensifying and becoming increasingly insistent in the kingdom of Armenia.

The *grabar* appears to be a language without any dialectal differentiation. Even in recent times there has been much debate about this apparent uniformity: Ovsepjan (1976) maintains that administrative, religious and commercial needs in a state with extensive urban development like Armenia had led to the formation, as early as the Hellenistic period, of an inter-dialectal spoken language which had been the model for a literary language prior to the emergence of the written form, that epic poems and legends had been handed down in it and that it had been used for all cultural expression. However, within this uniform language traces have been found of a very few variant phonological elements which may be interpreted as the emergence of dialectal differences; here it will suffice to cite the Armenian dual development *c*/*t* of IE */ĝ/ which may be reconstructed in cases such as *bucanem* 'I forage' as opposed to *but* 'forage, fodder' < IE *$b^h ew\hat{g}$-.[1]

From the point of view of the structure of the language we can speak of a substantially uniform classical language prior to the emergence of Middle Armenian (twelfth to seventeenth centuries AD) because the authors of literary works sought to model their language on that of the authors of the so-called 'Golden Age' literature (i.e. those authors who wrote in the period between AD 407 and 460–70); however, a close analysis of texts written later than the fifth century shows that within the literary output of this period it is possible, on the basis of linguistic features, to distinguish two subperiods, which we term 'post-classical' (sixth to seventh centuries) and 'pre-Middle Armenian' (eighth to twelfth centuries). From the seventeenth century to modern times, although the *grabar* was still the courtly model to imitate, there emerged a language which was closer to the spoken form. Within this there was a notable split into two broad varieties, Eastern and Western Armenian.

The first documents written in Armenian (in addition to the translation of the Bible) were a large number of other translations of Syriac and Greek texts. The originals of some of these have been lost and they are thus known to us only thanks to the Armenian version. On the whole they are ecclesiastical texts, but they also include secular material such as a large part of the works of Aristotle and the Neoplatonist philosophers such as Porphyry, Probus and Diodorus, and the grammatical treatise by Dionysius Thrax. In addition, a great deal of original literary works suddenly appeared after the invention of the alphabet: among the first of these were historical works such as the 'History of the Conversion of Armenia by Gregory the Illuminator' written by Agatʿangelos, the biography of Maštʿocʿ outlined by Koriwn, and religious treatises such as 'Against the Sects' by Eznik of Kołb, which is a valuable source of information about various religious beliefs that threatened Christianity in the early centuries.

Despite the fact that historical Armenia is held by some scholars to be the original homeland of the IE peoples, it seems unlikely that the Armenians have always lived in the Transcaucasian area. If, then, they settled in their historical territory having come from the west in successive waves on the decline of the Urartian power, we know hardly anything about the extremely long formative period of the Armenian language, since we lack attestations of any kind. The language documented in the fifth century AD looks very unusual as a member of the IE family: its phonological structure is very different from those of the other IE languages and much more closely resembles those of the Caucasian languages; almost 40 per cent of its vocabulary consists of borrowings, a large number of which are words of obscure origin; its morphology is much more Indo-European than the two above-mentioned areas might lead us to expect, but in the area of morphology, too, there have been a large number of far-reaching innovations.

Scholars who have wondered about the position of Armenian within Indo-European have always come to conclusions of a rather generic nature. On the basis of a 'pluralist' classification – one which makes use of all available criteria and not just a few arbitrarily chosen ones – it seems possible to claim that the languages with which Armenian shares the most notable and most numerous isoglosses are Greek, Indo-Iranian and Phrygian (what we know of it). Ancient evidence stresses the Phrygian origin of the Armenians, but the sparse attestations of the Phrygian language cannot be of help from the point of view of placing the Armenians historically. However, archaeological data would seem to reduce the importance of the Phrygian element in the origin of the Armenian people, since in eastern Anatolia there are none of the characteristic tumuli typical of the Phrygian kingdom, in particular of Gordium. According to the archaeological theory, the Phrygians were part of a small group of invaders who imposed themselves on a body of people ethnically related to the Hurrians and the Hattians (and thus, indirectly, to the Urartians). After the destruction of Gordium and Midas City, these 'Phrygianized' peoples, who had adopted the language of the Phrygian rulers but had not adopted some of their customs (such as burying their kings and military leaders in tumuli) sought out new lands to the east of the upper Euphrates and gradually came to settle in Urartian territory, driving the original peoples – traditionally the Alarodi – towards the less fertile mountain regions. In this regard we must mention the theory put forward recently by Soviet scholars (Diakonoff and Starostin 1986), according to which there exist obvious correspondences, as regards both the basic lexicon and some morphological characteristics, between the proto-forms which may be reconstructed for around thirty languages spoken in the north-eastern part of the Caucasus by small – sometimes tiny – communities, and the Hurrian and Urartian languages, which are genetically related to each other. However, a current line of research investigating the relationship between Armenian and the Hurro-Urartian languages, although promising, has not yet provided any

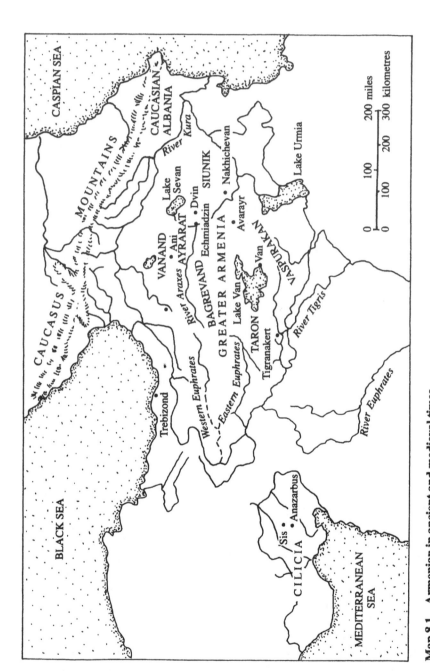

Map 8.1 Armenian in ancient and medieval times
Source: C. J. Walker, *Armenia. The Survival of a Nation*, London and Sydney, Croom Helm, 1984: 22

definite contribution. The great bulk of the vocabulary of obscure origin has not been explained other than minimally: in recent times there has been more detailed work on terms of Mesopotamian and Kartvelian origin (cf. Cardona 1983), but the broad outlines of the linguistic proto-history of Armenian still remain very largely conjectural.

Better known are the lexical borrowings from Greek, Syriac and above all Iranian, which has had a marked influence on Armenian for many centuries. Within the great mass of Iranian borrowings, different layers can be perceived: the oldest, apart from a few doubtful examples attributed to the period of Median domination (end of the seventh to middle of the sixth centuries BC) goes back to the time of the Achaemenids (550–330 BC), when Armenia was under Iranian domination but not completely Iranianized: cf. *Arik'* 'Aryan' < OPers. *Ariya-*; *tšnami* 'enemy' < OPers. **duš-manyu-*; *gušak* 'informer' < OPers. **gaušaka-*. The majority of Iranian borrowings, however, belong to the period during which a branch of the Parthian dynasty of the Arsacids (AD 53–428) was dominant in Armenia; this is demonstrated by the north-eastern dialect characteristics of these words, of which it will suffice here to cite the following:

presence of /s/ instead of /h/: Arm. *vnas* 'wrong, damage, harm', cf. MPers. *wināh*

presence of /z/ instead of /d/: Arm. *yazem* 'I adore', cf. OPers. *yad-*

presence of /rd/ instead of /l/: Arm. *vard* 'rose', cf. MPers. *gul* 'flower'

presence of /r/ (< Parth. /δ/) instead of /y/: Arm. *xoyr* 'diadem', cf. Man. MPers. *xōy*

presence of /(r)h/ instead of /s/: Arm. *parh/pah* 'guard', cf. NewPers. *pās*

A more recent and less obvious layer comprises loans from Middle Persian of the Sasanian epoch. In this period there come in mainly technical terms relating to the military, administrative, legal and commercial spheres, cf. Arm. *sałar* 'chief, general' < MPers. *sālār* < **sardār*.

As well as these dialect areas of Iranian borrowings, another, called Parnian, has been distinguished. This links Armenian with the Eastern Iranian dialects and consists of loans which correspond to terms attested only in Sogdian. These would appear to be elements belonging to the language spoken by those peoples who, moving from the east, conquered Parthia and abandoned their Sogdian-related language in favour of Parthian, which, however, ended up permeated with eastern elements: cf. *margarē* 'prophet', Sogd. *mārkarē* 'magician'; *kari* 'much', Sogd. *k'δy; baw* 'enough', Sogd. *βāw* 'satiety'.

Phonology

Vowels

Armenian is characterized with respect to the IE vowel system by the loss of the quantitative opposition, with the following development:

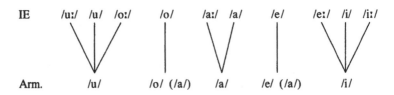

IE   /uː/ /u/ /oː/   /o/   /aː/ /a/   /e/   /eː/ /i/ /iː/

Arm.   /u/   /o/ (/a/)   /a/   /e/ (/a/)   /i/

After the loss of the quantitative opposition, the Armenian vowels underwent further changes consisting of the raising of /e/ to /i/ and /o/ to /u/ before nasals.

Another important change which took place before the written phase was the change of /i/ and /u/ to /ə/ (on the whole not written) in unaccented syllables: this change was caused by the strong stress accent which had become fixed in Proto-Armenian on the original penultimate syllable, perhaps under the influence of Urartian; as well as causing the weakening of /i/ and /u/, this led to the loss of the vowel in the final syllable, regardless of what that vowel was.

IE */a/   Arm. *aɫam* 'grind', Gk *aléō*
IE /aː/   Arm. *bam* 'speak', Dor. Gk *phāmí*
IE */e/   Arm. *es* 'I', Gk *egó*; Arm. *cin* 'birth', Gk *génos*, Ved. *jánaḥ*
IE */eː/   Arm. *mit* 'mind', Gk *mḗdos*
IE */o/   Arm. *ost* 'branch', Gk *ózos*, Goth. *asts*
IE */oː/   Arm. *ul* 'kid', Gk *pô̂los*, Goth. *fula*
IE */i/   Arm. *egit* 'he found', Gk *eîde* < *évide*, Ved. *ávidat*
IE */iː/   Arm. *siwn* 'column', Gk *kîōn*
IE */u/   Arm. *nu* 'daughter-in-law', Gk *nyós*, Lat. *nurus*
IE */uː/   Arm. *mukn* 'mouse', Gk *mŷs*, Lat. *mūs*

Among the Armenian reflexes of the IE vowels, several cases are still unclear; these are:

1   Arm. /a/ instead of expected /e/, cf. Arm. *vaṭsun* 'sixty' beside Arm. *vecʻ* 'six'; Arm. *tasn* 'ten' beside Gk *déka*, Lat. *decem*; Arm. *caɫr* 'laugh' beside Gk *gélōs*;
2   Arm. /a/ instead of expected /o/, cf. Arm. *akn* 'eye' beside Gk *ósse*; Arm. *ateam* 'hate' beside Lat. *odium*.

As regards the phonetic realization in Armenian of */H/ between stops, where a very short vowel is produced before or after the laryngeal, the Armenian reflex is in every case /a/, irrespective of the series to which the above-mentioned laryngeal belonged: cf. *$ph_2tēr$ > Arm. *hayr* 'father'.

On the other hand, according to Kortlandt (1987), different reflexes of the sequences */h_1o-/ and *h_3e-/ may be traceable in Armenian, not as regards the vowel quality (which would be /o/ in both cases because */h_3/, unlike */h_1/, alters the quality of the neighbouring vowel towards backness), but from the presence or absence of Arm. /h-/: *h_1orb^ho- > Arm. *orb* orphan', while *h_3edos > Arm. *hot* 'smell'.

Diphthongs

As with the development of vowels from the IE phase to Armenian, in the case of the diphthongs it is also possible to establish phases of relative chronology. Assuming that Indo-European had the diphthongs */aj/, */ej/, */oj/, */ew/, */ow/, */aw/ (see Chapter 2, p. 50), in the first phase of the development from Indo-European to Armenian original */ej/ and */oj/ would have merged in */ej/, while original */ew/ and */ow/ would have undergone a mirror-image development and merged in */ow/.

Subsequently, after */ow/ had given Arm. /oy/ and new diphthongs had arisen with labial second elements derived from the weakening of stops, as in Arm. *ewtn* 'seven' < *$septm$, or from /-m-/ between sonants, as in Arm. *anun* 'name' < *$anown$ < *$nomn$, a new system of the following type was created:

/aj/ */ej/ /oj/ /aw/ /ew/ /iw/ */ow/

which was finally modified by the closure of */ej/ to /ē/ and of */ow/ to /u/; this latter vowel merged with original /u/ before the spread of the alternation /u/ ~ /ə/ which was linked with the stress accent. This accent-determined alternation also affected /ē/ and /oy/ and the so-called diphthong /ea/ (< */i/ + /a/), which in atonic syllables became /i/, /u/ and /e/ respectively:

IE */aj/   Arm. *ayc* 'goat', Gk *aíx*
IE */ej/   Arm. *edēz* 'he accumulated', Ved. *déhmi* 'smear'
IE */oj/   Arm. *dēz* 'heap, pile', Gk *toîkhos*
IE */aw/   Arm. *awt* 'place to spend the night', Gk *aûlis*
IE */ew/   Arm. *loys* 'light', Gk *leukós*
IE */ow/   Arm. *boyc* 'nourishment', Ved. *bhógaḥ* 'pleasure, delight'

Syllabic Consonants

As is well known, in IE, /m/ /n/ /l/ /r/ between or before stops, before /s/ or /H/, and in absolute final position after most consonants, were realized as allophones with the feature [+syllabic]. Their development into Armenian systematically introduced a supporting vowel /a/; consequently the reflexes were /am/, /an/, /al/ (/al/), /ar/: Arm. *am* 'year' < *$smā$; Arm. negative prefix *an-* < *$n̥$-; Arm. *barjr* 'high' < *$b^h r̥ ĝ^h us$; Arm. *kałin* 'acorn' < *$gwl̥-eno-$.

Consonants

The traditional interpretation posits three series of stops for the common IE phase (a fourth series, consisting of voiceless aspirates, not being attributable to common IE) characterized as (I) voiced, (II) voiced aspirate and (III) voiceless. According to this interpretation, Armenian has innovated greatly. However, the stop series listed above have recently undergone a reinterpretation, due above all to Gamkrelidze and Ivanov (see in particular (1980) and see Chapter 2, **Obstruents**, p. 33), on the basis of typological considerations: from this point of view, the traditional series seem implausible and unrealistic because they go against typologically established phonological universals. Consequently, three series with characteristics very different from the traditional ones have been postulated: (I) glottalic (corresponding to the voiced stops); (II) voiced stops, possibly realized phonetically with aspiration (corresponding to the voiced aspirates); (III) voiceless stops, possibly with aspirated allophones (corresponding to the voiceless stops). If we accept that the IE stops were distinguished from each other in this way (and various factors support the theory, including the fact that series I is still attested in Sindhi, a modern Indo-Iranian dialect), then Armenian, far from having innovated radically, is remarkably archaic in its stop system. Table 8.1 shows the correspondences between the traditional interpretation of phonological characteristics (to which we adhere for convenience in citing examples in the present work) and the more recent interpretation; the reflexes in Classical Armenian are given in the customary transliteration (see the note on transliteration at the end of this chapter).

Examples

Series I

(1) very few, uncertain examples: Arm. *stipem* 'I constrain', cf. Gk *steíbō*

(2) Arm. *tur* 'gift', cf. Gk *dôron*

(3) Arm. *acem* 'I lead', cf. Gk *ágō*, Skt *ájāmi*, with traces of divergent dialectal developments: Arm. *bucanem* 'I forage', but 'forage, fodder'; Arm. *art* 'field', Lat. *ager*

(4) Arm. *kṛunk* 'crane', cf. Gk *géranos*, Lat. *grūs*

(5) Arm. *kov* 'dairy cow', cf. Gk *boûs*, Ved. *gaúḥ*

Series II

(1) Arm. *berem* 'I bear', cf. Gk. *phérō*, Ved. *bhárāmi*; Arm. instr. ending *-w/-v*, e.g. in *azga-w* (nom. *azg* 'people'), but *geto-v* (nom. *get* 'river')

(2) Arm. *durn* 'door', cf. Gk *thýrā*, Lat. *fores*.

(3) Arm. *jiwn* 'snow', cf. Gk *khiṓn*; Arm. *lizem* 'I lick', Gk *leíkhō*, Ved. *léhmi*

Table 8.1 Reflexes of the consonant system in Armenian

Traditional	Recent	Armenian
Series I		
voiced stops	*glottalics*	
1 (/b/)	(/p'/)	(/p/)
2 /d/	/t'/	/t/
3 /ĝ/	/k̂'/ > */č'/	/c/ (/t/)
4 /g/	/k'/	/k/
5 /gʷ/	/kʷ'/	/k/
Series II		
voiced aspirates	*voiced (aspirated)*	
1 /bʰ/	/b/, /bʰ/	/b-/; /-w-/; /-v-/
2 /dʰ/	/d/, /dʰ/	/d-/
3 /ĝʰ/	/ĝ/, /ĝʰ/ > */ʒ(h)/ >	/j-/; /-z-/
4 /gʰ/	/g/, /gʰ/	/g-/
5 /gʷʰ/	/gʷ/, /gʷʰ/	/g-/; /ǰ-/ (before /-e, -i/); /-ž-/
Series III		
voiceless	*voiceless (aspirated)*	
1 /p/	/p/, /pʰ/	/h-/ or 0; /-w-/; /-v-/
2 /t/	/t/, /tʰ/	/tʿ-/ (also after */aw, ow/) /-d/ (after nasal/liquid) */-y-/ (> 0); /-w-/ (before /o/)
3 /k̂/	/k̂/, /k̂ʰ/ > */č(h)/ > */cʿ/	/s/ (/cʿ/)
4 /k/	/k/, /kʰ/	/kʿ-/; /-g/ (after nasal/liquid)
5 /kʷ/	/kʷ/, /kʷʰ/	/kʿ-/; /-g/ (after nasal/liquid); /čʿ/ (before /-e, -i/).

(4) Arm. *meg* 'cloud', cf. Ved. *méghaḥ*

(5) Arm. *gan* 'blow', cf. Ved. *han-* 'to strike', Gk *theínō*; Arm. *ǰerm* 'warm', Gk *thermós*, Ved. *gharmaḥ*; Arm. *iž* 'snake', Gk *ékhis*, Ved. *áhiḥ*, Avest. *aži-*

Series III

(1) Arm. *hayr* 'father', cf. Gk *patḗr*, Ved. *pitár-*; Arm. *otn* 'foot', Gk *póda*, Ved. *pād-*; Arm. *ew* 'and, also', Gk *epí*, Ved. *ápi*

(2) Arm. *faṙamim* 'I wither', cf. Gk *térsomai*, Lat. *torreō*; Arm. *ard* 'order', Gk *artýs*, Ved. *r̥tuḥ*; Arm. *bay* 'word', Gk *phátis*; Arm. *berē* 'he bears' < Proto-Arm. *berey, Ved. *bharati*, Arm. *beraw* 'was borne' < *bʰerato*

(3) Arm. *asełn* 'needle', cf. Gk *akís* 'spur'; Arm. *cʿax* 'branch', Ved. *śā́khā*, Goth. *hōha* 'plough'

(4) Arm. *kʿerem* 'I scratch', cf. Gk *keírō*; Arm. *argel* 'impediment', Gk *arkéō*, Lat. *arceo*

(5) Arm. *elikʿ* 'he left', cf. Gk *élipe*, Ved. *āricat*; Arm. *hing* 'five', Gk *pénte*, Ved. *pañca*; Arm. *čorkʿ* 'four' < Proto-Arm. **čeyorkʿ*, Ved. *cátvāraḥ*, Dor. Gk *tétores*.

As the outline shows, if the starting point is the traditional one, the Armenian consonants appear extremely innovative when compared to Indo-European, but if we accept the interpretation proposed by Gamkrelidze, Armenian seems to have modified only slightly the IE stop system, essentially losing the glottalic feature and undergoing a few other changes of secondary importance. Of particular interest is the development, common to all the satem languages, of the series of palatalized tectals into compact affricates. In Armenian these subsequently develop into diffuse affricates; this phase is maintained in the historic period for the series I and II (but in intervocalic position the reflex of */ǯ(h)/ is sibilant), while */č(h)/ reaches the sibilant stage in all positions, except in a limited number of words where the affricate phase of the voiceless (aspirated) palatalized tectals persists. Those cases hitherto identified, in addition to the above-mentioned Arm. *cʿax* 'branch' < IE **k̂ākʰā* (cf. Ved. *śākhā*, Goth. *hōha*, Slav. *soxa*, NewPers. *šax*), are Arm. *cʿacnul* 'fall' < **k̂ad-snu-*, cf. Lat. *cadere* and OInd. *cad-* 'id.'; Arm. *cʿankl* *cʿang* 'wall, enclosure', *cʿangel* 'to enclose' < **k̂n̥g-*, cf. Gk *kákala*.

Vocalic Prothesis

One phenomenon particularly characteristic of Armenian is the notable development of prothetic vowels: the presence of these vowels in Armenian can be explained partially by allowing the presence in the reconstructed IE form of a laryngeal which in the context ##–[–syll] developed into ##V[–syll], as for example in Arm. *arew* 'sun' < IE **h₂rewō* (cf. the Hittite verb *ḫar-wa-na-iz-zi* 'it is light'), or in Arm. *ayr* 'man' < **h₂nēr*, a nominative form corresponding to Gk *anḗr*, which would have gone through the hypothetical stages **ayyir* < **aynir* < **anir* < **anēr*. The existence of an initial laryngeal in this word allows us to take account both of the correspondence with Greek as regards the development of the initial vowel and of the lengthening of the final vowel in the first element of Vedic compounds of the type *sūnara-*, *viśvānara-*, etc. which have *nara-* as their second element.

Fairly convincing are some reconstructions, such as the two examples mentioned above, in which the initial vowel *a-* of Armenian is taken back to an IE /h₂-/, while the hypothesis of divergent developments within Armenian itself according to the type of laryngeal postulated for the IE form leads to greater complexity. Kortlandt's attempt to pinpoint regular derivations appears problematic (on the basis of these, */h₁/ + [–syll] became Arm. *e-*, Gk *e-*; */h₃/ + [–syll] became Arm. *o-*, Gk *o-*, but became Arm. *a-* in open syllables, as might be deduced form the following correspondences: Arm. *eluzanem* 'I extract', *eleúsomai*; Arm. *erek* 'evening', Gk *érebos*; Arm.

anicanem 'I curse', Gk *óneidos*; Arm. *ołb* 'weeping' Gk *olophýromai*).

If we accept a regular derivation of this type, the deviant cases have to be explained *ad hoc*: thus the correspondence between Gk *ereúgomai* and Arm. *orcam* 'I belch' may be taken back to IE /h₁/ + /C-/ only if we accept that the Armenian form derives from **eruc-* with assimilation of /e-/ to the rounded vowel of the following syllable, even if assimilation of this type is not found in a similar case such as *eluzanem*.

We note, nevertheless, that the Laryngeal Theory takes account of correspondences in words which in Armenian and Greek (see Chapter 9, p. 233) begin with a vowel, while in other languages they can begin with a consonant, irrespective of the type of consonant which followed the initial laryngeal in the reconstructed IE form: not only liquids and nasals, then, but also other consonants.

However, vocalic prothesis in Armenian is a further-reaching phenomenon, on the basis of which a word cannot begin with certain consonants or certain consonantal clusters and has to have a vocalic onset.

The consonant which is systematically avoided in initial position is /r-/, but sporadically the vocalic onset is also used to avoid initial /l-/, /m-/ and /n-/. The antiquity of the phenomenon is notable, since even loan-terms from other languages are subject to this restraint, such as those which come from Iranian: cf. Arm. *erang* 'colour' < MPers. *rang* 'id.'. Arm. *aroyr* 'brass' < MPers. *rōy* 'copper' (< **rōδ*).

In addition, the loans from Iranian also exhibit a phenomenon of vowel prothesis sporadically in the case of initial *sp-*, and systematically in the case of the typically Iranian consonant cluster *xš-* which gives Arm. *šx-*; cf. *ašxarh* 'world' < MPers. Parth. *šahr* (< *xšaeϑra*); Arm. *aspahan*, Gk *Aspadána*, Parth. Man. *'sp'h'n*, NewPers. *Ispāhān*, a toponym derived from *spāda-* 'army', original meaning '(military) field'.

The two initial consonant clusters mentioned above could, however, already have developed the prothetic vowel in their original Iranian dialect, if we accept the hypothesis of Perikhanian (1966; 1971) who, on the basis of attestations in inscriptions from the first half of the second century BC, attributes the prothetic vowel *a-* before *xš-* and *sp-* to the middle phase of the language of the Medes.

The other consonant clusters which determined the Armenian phenomenon of vowel prothesis, with the exception of the cluster **sr-* which developed into Arm. *Vṙ-*, contained an original voiced or voiced aspirated stop in initial position and almost all had the liquid /r/, originally in second position. This /r/ underwent metathesis in Armenian according to the following pattern: **Cr-* > Arm. *VrC-*, cf. **gwrāwōn* > Arm. *erkan* 'millstone', cf. *grāvan-*, OIr. *brau*, OCS *žrunuvi*.

The process of metathesis which changed the cluster **VCr-* > *VrC-* took place systematically even in medial position, cf. **ḱubʰros* > Arm. *surb* 'holy', cf. Ved. *śubhráḥ* 'brilliant'.

Both of these phonetic phenomena, together with others, traditionally controversial, have recently been explained in a particularly brilliant way by Vennemann (1986) on the basis of a theory of syllabic structure which, thanks to few universal rules and one single Armenian-specific syllabification rule, brings apparently disparate phonetic phenomena together within a single explanatory framework. In order to explain the metathesis all we need to say is that, given the Armenian-specific syllabification rule, which states that inter-nuclear consonantal clusters are heterosyllabic (i.e. *VCr > VC#r), a syllabic contact A#B is the more preferred, the lesser the consonantal strength of A and the greater that of B; vice versa, if the relations of consonantal strength are reversed, the greater the tendency to change the syllabic structure until the optimal structure is attained.

Since consonantal strength increases according to the following scheme:

| vowels | central liquids | lateral liquids | fricatives | stops and affricates |

$$\longrightarrow$$

it is clear that the central liquids have less consonantal strength than the occlusives, and consequently the syllable contact *D/T#r is less preferred than the more 'general' heterosyllabic sequence *r#D/T, and it is towards this that Armenian structure tends.

The vowel prothesis fits into this theoretical framework in a fairly convincing manner: before *r- it is interpreted as one of the methods used to eliminate the weaker syllable margins (these are */j/, */w/, */r/) of word-initial syllable onsets. For */w-/ the method adopted consists in the strengthening of the margin, so that the result is Arm. /g/ in all positions (except in word-final postvocalic position, where the result is /-w/ (/-v/), cf. Arm. gayl 'wolf', OIr. fail 'id.' < *wajlo-, while Arm. tiw 'day' < *diwo-, cf. Skt diva 'sky', Lat. tri- duum). On the Armenian reflexes of initial */j-/ there are various theories (/ʃ/ or 0 word-initially, 0 medially, /ʃ/ after a sonant, but if the sonant is preceded by the vowel /a/ there is metathesis of /-j-/: cf. Arm. ǰur 'water', Lith. jûra, pl. jûres 'sea'; denominatives in -em < IE *-eje-, Ved. -aya-, Gk -éō'; Arm. anurǰ 'dream' < *onōrjom, an ablaut form of *onerjom which gives rise to Gk óneiron; Arm. ayl 'other' < *aljo-, Lat. alius, Gk állos). As regards */r-/, the elimination of the weak margin would occur with its transformation into *Vr-, perhaps under the influence of a model with vocalic onset due to the development of the laryngeals into vowels.

Prothesis before consonant clusters would be explained by means of a general rule concerning syllable onsets: in this position all consonant clusters are less preferred than syllable onsets with a single consonant. Unlike previous explanations, which saw the metathesis *Cr- > rC- as preceding the development of prothesis, Vennemann sees the prothesis rather as an event preceding the metathesis. We should thus have: *CrV- > *VC#rV- > Vr#CV-. Vowel prothesis before *Cr- would, then, be only one of the means used to avoid word-initial consonant clusters, while other possible expedients would consist of eliminating a consonantal element or fusing two consonants into a single phoneme: the only clusters tolerated would be sequences of sibilant plus occlusive, where the sibilant could be extra-syllabic.

Prothesis before initial consonant clusters affects not only those clusters containing /r/, but also other sequences, such as IE *dw-, which would become *tw- and according to the syllabic hypothesis would subsequently give *tg because of the strengthening of the semi-vowel, then *tk by assimilation. At this point, in order to avoid the initial cluster, we should have the development of the prothetic vowel: *Vtk, split into two syllables as *Vt#kV and subject to change in the coda of the first syllable to avoid a non-preferred syllable contact. In this case the expedient would consist in the replacement of the stop by the weakest consonantal member of the dental series, which is indeed /r/, with the result that we have the sequence that is in fact attested, Vr#kV: e.g. IE *dwāros > Arm. erkar 'long', cf. Gk dērós, metrically *dvārós, Ved. dūráḥ.

Still unclear in the syllable-based interpretation of the vowel prothesis are the rare cases where the vowel is prefixed to words beginning in /l-/, /m-/ and /n-/, for which it is not always possible to hypothesize an initial laryngeal, as in the case of Arm. amis 'month', cf. Gk mḗn, OIr. mi, Lat. mensis, which allow us to posit a derivation from IE *mēnso-. However, despite the criticisms which have been put forward, particularly by Kortlandt (1989), the syllabic hypothesis makes it possible to interpret many apparently unrelated phenomena on the basis of a small number of general rules. The theory can perhaps be extended to the interpretation of other cases: thus, on the basis of the principle of the simplification of the initial consonantal cluster we can explain why clusters comprising a voiceless stop + /r-/ or /l-/ produce er- and l- respectively: Arm. erekʿ 'three' < *trejes, cf. Skt tráyaḥ, Lat. trēs; Arm. lu 'hearing' < *ḱluto-, cf. Skt śruta- 'heard', Gk klytós. The same motivation lies behind the development from *pt- to Armenian ł: łełi 'elm', cf. Gk pteléa. Certain clusters made up of an IE word-initial voiceless stop followed by */j/, */w/ have monophonematic reflexes with an aspirate, such as:

*kj- > Arm. /čʿ/ (Arm. čʿogay 'I went' < *kjow-ā-)
*tw̌- > Arm. /kʿ/ (Arm. kʿew 'with you (sg.)' < *twe-bʰi

but the reflex is Arm. /k/ medially after /s/, cf. Arm. oskr 'bone' < *ostwer).

The explanation provided by Vennemann of the second case could also be extended to the first; according to this model, the hypothetical developments would be:

(a) a consonantal shift by which */t/ > Arm. /tʿ/ (*tw- > *tʿw-)
(b) strengthening of the semi-vowels: */-w-/ > /-g-/ (*tʿw- > *tʿg-)
(c) assimilation of voicelessness: *tʿg- > *tʿk-

(d) aspiration of the velar, on the basis of which */k/ > */k'/ syllable-initially when a preceding aspirate is lost (/s-/ is also considered to be an aspirate: e.g. Arm. *k'oyr* 'sister' < **swesōr*; the aspirate nature of the sibilant should be clear from the development */s/ > */h/ > 0 in voiced environments, with sporadic retention of the phase /h-/ before vowels: cf. Arm. *ał* 'salt', Lat. *sal*, beside Arm. *hin* 'old', Lat. *senex*).

Probably point (d) can be postulated not only in the case of the velars but also for other voiceless stops (this would be the justification for the dual reflexes of **sp-*, **st-*, giving Arm. *sp-/p'* and *st-t'*; cf. Arm. *spaṙnam* < **sper-*; Arm. *sterĵ* 'sterile' < **ster-*; but also Arm. *p'und* 'pot' < **spond*; Arm. *t'or* 'a dripping' < **ster-*) and also in the case of an affricate */-ĵ-/, the result of the strengthening of the semi-vowel */j-/.

Consequently, in the case of the first phenomenon we can also postulate similar developments, as follows: **kj-* > **k'j*> **k'ĵ-* > **k'č-* > /č-/, since the reflexes of **tj*, **dj*, **k̂j* postulated by Godel (1975), which might contradict the above correlation, are uncertain, as well as occurring in a different position (e.g. Arm. *mucanem* 'I lead in' < **mowd-je-*; Arm. *luc'anem* 'I set light to' < **lowk̂-je-*). The reflex of **-dʰj-*, of which there is only one certain example, is in medial position: *mēĵ* 'middle' < IE **medʰjo-*; this has an unexpected vowel with /ē/ < Proto-Arm. */ey/. normally explained as epenthesis of */y/. However, this case could also be incorporated into the framework of the syllabic hypothesis which would also provide a different explanation of the vowel.

If we accept that the syllabic contact **d#ĵ* deriving from the IE cluster **dʰj* is not optimal and requires a weakening of the coda of the first syllable, we can suppose that */y/, assumed because of the vowel *-ē-*, was not due to epenthesis under the influence of the original */j/, but is the most obvious result of the weakening of */d/ in the series of the weakest syllable margins.

A consonantal weakening analogous to that suggested above is encountered in many of those consonant clusters with an original voiceless stop which we have already examined, when they come to be internal; here the principle of unfavourable syllable contact leads to changes, for example:

*-pn- > Arm. *-wn-*: Arm. *tawn* 'feast' < **dapni-*, cf. OInd. *tafn* 'victim' (< **dapno-*)

*-pt- > Arm. *wt'-*: Arm. *ewt'n* 'seven', Skt *saptá*, etc.

*-tr- > Arm. *-wr-*: Arm. *arawr* 'plough', Gk *árotron*, Lat. *arātrum*, perhaps also **-kr-* > Arm. *-wr-*, if Arm. *mawruk* 'beard' can be made to derive from **smokru-*, attested in Lith. *smākras* 'chin'

*-kt- > Arm. *-wt'-*: Arm. *aławt'- k'* 'prayer' (*pl. tantum*) < **-ak-ti-*

The only clusters which did not alter consonantal strength relations were *st, *sd, which became Arm. st in all positions: Arm. astł 'star', Gk astér, Skt star-; Arm. z-gest 'clothes' < *westu-, cf. Lat. vestis; other clusters were simplified into single-phoneme reflexes even medially: *(-)sk/k̂- > cʿ: Arm. hacʿi 'ash-tree' < *askiā; *(-)k̂/ks- > cʿ: Arm. vecʿ 'six' < *useks; *-kj- > čʿ-: Arm. gočʿem 'shout, cry' < *wok-je, Skt vāc- 'voice'.

Liquids

Indo-European */r/ became Armenian /r/ in all positions without exception, apart from sporadic cases of dissimilation: unlike the stops, /r/ in Armenian is retained also in originally final syllable. Armenian also includes /r:/ (transliterated here as ⟨r̄⟩) in its phonological inventory; this was both the reflex of IE *sr (in part also of *rs) and a contextual variant of /r/ before nasals which was extended beyond its original context by analogy: cf. Arm. aṙu 'stream' < IE *sruti-; Arm. aṙnem 'I do' beside aor. arari 'I did', but aṙnum 'I take' with aor. aṙi 'I took'.

IE */l/ has two reflexes in Armenian, one alveolar and one velar. Greppin (1986) claimed to have established the rules governing this dual development: according to this view, these rules would be disturbed only through deviations which were mainly due to analogical extensions within the flection:

1 IE */l-/ > Arm./l-/ in all cases
2 Proto-Arm. word-final */-l/ > Arm. /-l/: Arm. dal 'yellowish', Gk thállos
3 IE post-consonantal non-final */-l-/ > Arm. /-l-/: Arm. glem 'I turn', Lat. volvo
4 IE post-consonantal final */-l/ > Arm. /-ł/: Arm. astł 'star', Lat. stella
5 IE preconsonantal /-l-/ > Arm. /-ł-/: Arm. ołb 'lament', Gk olophýromai
6 IE intervocalic */-l-/ > Arm. /-ł-/: Arm. ełegn 'reed', Gk élegos
7 Arm. */-l-ł/ > Arm. /-ł-ł/: Arm. kałał 'den, lair', Lith. guõlis

Nasals

The IE initial and medial nasals had the reflexes /(-)m-/, /(-)n-/ in Armenian, except when they were followed by -s: *Ns > Arm. -s, while the inverse sequence *sN > Arm. -N: Arm. us 'shoulder' < IE *omsos, Ved. áṃsaḥ, Gk ômos; Arm. eris 'three (acc.)' < IE *trins; Arm. mi 'one' < IE *smijos; z-genum 'I get dressed' < IE *wesnumi. Note also that */-N-/ between sonants > Arm. /-w-/: cf. Arm. awr 'day', Dor. Gk âmar.

In absolute final position the development of the nasals is linked with the morphological problem of the development of the old inflectional endings; according to the convincing suggestion put forward by Kortlandt (1985), we have the following cases, in chronological order:

1 non-syllabic final nasals > 0 in polysyllables by the following stages: *-VN > *-Ṽ after the fixing of the accent on the penultimate syllable;

subsequently $*-\hat{V} > -V > -0$. As a result of this change the nominative and accusative singular of $-\bar{a}$- stems merged, while $-o$-, $-i$- and $-u$- stems seem to have eliminated the nominative singular sigmatic ending (which ought to give $-k'$, like the nominative plural ending) in favour of the generalization of the accusative singular as the nominative case (which appears as 0 in so far as it derives from $*-\hat{V} < *-VN$). For this reason words such as *jiwn* 'snow' and *siwn* 'column' are to be compared with the Gk accusative singular forms *khíona* and *kíona* and not with the nominative forms; equally the suffix *-tiwn* corresponds not to Lat. *-tiō* but to *-tiōnem*.

2 non-syllabic final nasals gave Armenian /-n/ in monosyllables: Arm. *k'an* Lat. *quam*.

3 final syllabic nasals gave Arm. /-n/: Arm. *ewtn* 'seven'; Arm. *sermn* 'seed'; this development happened after the change $*-VN > -\hat{V} > -V$. When $*N$ became Arm. *-an*, the nasalization of *-VN* was exhausted; for this reason medial $*/-N̦-/$ developed into Arm. *-an-* (cf. *ewt'anasun* 'seventy') while finally the vowel in the final syllable was lost, so that $*-an >$ Arm. /-n/.

Sibilants

As with the nasals, the development of $*/s/$ (whose initial and medial developments have already been discussed) in absolute final position is linked to the morphological problem of the development of the IE flectional endings. In the nominal flection, $-k'$ appears as a plural marker in both the nominative and instrumental of all nouns, pronouns and adjectives: in the verbal flection the same marker appears in the first- and second-person plural. Since almost all the corresponding IE forms ended in $*-s$ (nom. pl.: $*-\bar{o}s$ for $*-o$ stems; $*-\bar{a}s$ for $*-\bar{a}$ stems; $*-es$ for the other stems; instr. $*-b^his$; 1 pl. $*-mes$), we can postulate a special development of $*-s$ in these cases, along the lines of $*-Vh > -(V)k'$. The most contentious point of this theory is the need to accept divergent developments of $*/-s/$, namely to $/k'/$ in the cases mentioned above and to 0 elsewhere, as for example in the nominative singular ($*mr̥tós >$ Arm. *mard*). Among the alternative theories which have been suggested, we note that the most coherent one interprets the ending $-k'$ as a derivational morpheme with collective value, maintaining not the flectional but the derivational nature of the plural marker, which is clear in the syntactic peculiarity whereby the attributive adjective has zero ending in the nominative plural. However, this problem can be overcome by postulating that the adjective had pronominal endings as in the strong adjective declension in Germanic (cf. Goth. *blindai* 'blind (nom. pl.)' beside *dagōs* 'days'): if this were so, the flectional nature of the marker $-k'$ would not be called into question. A further confirmation of the development of $*/-s/ >$ Arm. /-k'/ would also come from the interpretation of the large number of *pluralia tantum* in Armenian as regular phonetic developments of sigmatic nominative singulars which increasingly came to be perceived as nominative plural; in certain cases, for example in the locative, these nouns accompany demonstratives and possessives in the sing., cf. *i keansn k'um* 'in your life' (lit. 'in lives (pl.) your (sg.)').

Morphology

In general terms it can be stated that in certain respects Armenian retains archaic IE characteristics and in others it innovates greatly; however, even when it innovates, it uses morphological material inherited from Indo-European, except in nominal derivation, where many derivative morphemes have been borrowed, mainly from Iranian. These morphemes are:

1 Iranian lexemes which form the second element of compounds in the source language: in Armenian, however, they do not function independently but are taken over, in grammaticalized form, as suffixes, for example -(*a*)*stan*: Arm. *asp-a-stan* 'stable' (lit. 'place of the horse') < Iran. *-stāna-*, Parth. MPers. *-stān*; -(*a*)*ran*: Arm. *ganj-a-ran* 'room of treasure' < Iran. *-dāna-* 'container', Parth. *-dān*

2 elements which are also suffixes in Iranian: these are very productive in both languages: *-ak*, diminutive suffix: Arm. *naw-ak* 'boat' < *naw* 'ship' (+ < Iran. *-aka-*); *-ik*, a diminutive suffix: Arm. *hayr-ik* 'little father' < *hayr* 'father' (+ < Iran. *-ika-*); *-akan*, an adjective suffix indicating 'belonging to': Arm. *mayr-akan* 'maternal' < *mayr* 'mother' (+ < Iran. *-akāna-*); *-ean*, an adjective suffix indicating 'belonging to': Arm. *arewel-ean* 'Eastern' < *arewelk'* 'East' (+ < Iran. *-iyāna-*)

3 prefixal morphemes, not very productive in Armenian: *apa-* < Iran. **apa-/upa-*; *aw-* < Iran. **abi-*; *dž-/t's̆-* < Iran. **duš-*; *ham-* < Iran. *hama-*; *pat-* < Iran. **pati-*.

In its derivation, too, Armenian at times preserves traces of IE morphology, e.g. in the derivatives in **-ti-* and **-tu-* (cf. Arm. *bard* 'heap' < **bʰr̥ti-*; Arm. *ard* 'form' < **r̥tu-*) and in **-mon/-mn̥* (cf. Arm. *erdumn* 'oath' < *erdnum* 'I swear'; Arm. *jermn* 'heat' < *ĵeṙnum* 'heat'); at other times Armenian innovates in that on the whole these same suffixes occur in expanded forms unparalleled in other IE languages (e.g. Arm. *-oyt'*, an abstract suffix from **ow-ti-*; Arm. *-st* < **s-ti-*; Arm. *-awn* < **-a-mn*; Arm. *-umn* < **u-mn*; Arm. *-iwn* < **i-mn*. In other cases, in words of IE derivation, Armenian exhibits suffixes not attested in other IE languages; e.g. Arm. *-s-* < **-k̂-*, as in *lsem* 'I hear' (< **lusem* < **k̂lu+k̂*); Arm. *-or* in *nor* 'new' <**new-or*.

Nouns

Among the principal innovations in Armenian, we may mention the loss of the distinction of grammatical gender even in the pronouns (with subsequent loss of any formal distinction between nouns and adjectives) and the loss of the dual, while as an example of the retention of archaic features we can cite the morphological process of ablaut, clearly preserved above all in the -n- stem declension and to a lesser extent in that of the -r- stems:

Singular		Plural	
Nom. Acc.	*foṙn* 'grandson'	Nom.	*foṙunkʿ*
Gen. Dat. Loc.	*foṙin*	Acc. Loc.	*foṙuns*
Abl.	*foṙnē*	Gen. Dat. Abl.	*foṙancʿ*
Instr.	*foṙamb*	Instr.	*foṙambkʿ*

In the above example, the stem variation between -in, -un and -an (am) reflects the IE alternation *-en/*-on/*-n̥.

Of the -r- stems, only some have a more archaic aspect since they show the zero grade of the final root vowel in the oblique cases of the singular:

Singular		Plural	
Nom. Acc.	*mayr* 'mother'	Nom.	*markʿ*
Gen. Dat. Loc.	*mawr*	Acc. Loc.	*mars*
Abl.	*mawrē*	Gen. Dat. Abl.	*marcʿ*
Instr.	*marb*	Instr.	*marbkʿ*

As regards the other thematic classes, the Armenian vowel stems reflect the IE schema of stems in *-o-, *-ā-, *i and *-u-, but within this schema there is in Armenian a redistribution of nouns and adjectives across the various vocalic declensions: the loss of the gender contrast, which in Indo-European was expressed in many adjectives in the contrast between *-o- stems for the masculine and neuter, and *-ā- stems for the feminine, leads in Armenian to a merger, as a result of which the old adjectives in *-o-/-ā- follow the declension in -o-, while the adjectives in *ijo/ijā- exhibit alternation between endings in -o-/-a- (probably due to a phenomenon whereby the -a- stems underwent expansion). Furthermore, as well as the stems in -a-, there is an expansion in Armenian of the -i- stems, and a moderate expansion of those in -r- and -n-, while stems in -u- decline markedly. The redistribution of nouns and adjectives across the various declensions also affects a large number of Iranian loan words, e.g. Arm. *dat* 'justice' (-i- stem) < Iran. *dāta-*; Arm. *spah/spay* 'army' (-i- stem) < Iran. *spāda-*; Arm. *zēn* 'weapon' (-u- stem) < Iran. *zaina-*; Arm. *pʿut* 'putrid' (-o- stem) < Iran. *pūt-*; Arm. *pet* 'chief' (-a- stem) < Iran. *pati-*. Armenian has lost the stems in stops and in s-: former members of these classes have gone over into the other classes, e.g. *ǰer* 'heat' (-o- stem) < IE *gʷʰeros* (s- stem).

As regards the case endings, Table 8.2 shows some examples of vowel-stem paradigms. The eight cases of Indo-European are reduced to four through a process of syncretism which is different in the singular and the plural. As was mentioned previously, in the singular the nominative and accusative merge formally by means of a complex process which has been reconstructed by Kortlandt (1985):

Table 8.2   Examples of vowel-stem paradigms

	I (-o-)	II (-a-)	III (-i-)	IV (-u-)
Singular				
Nom.Acc.	erg 'poem'	azg 'people'	bay 'word'	gah 'throne'
Gen.Dat	erg-oy	azg-i	bay-i	gah-u
Abl.	erg-oy	azg-ē	bay-ē	gah-ē
Instr.	erg-ov	azg-aw	bay-iw	gah-u
Loc.	erg	azg-i	bay-i	gah-u
Plural				
Nom.	erg-kʿ	azg-kʿ	bay-kʿ	gah-kʿ
Gen.Dat.Abl.	erg-ocʿ	azg-acʿ	bay-icʿ	gah-ucʿ
Acc.Loc.	erg-s	azg-s	bay-s	gah-s
Instr.	erg-ovkʿ	azg-awkʿ	bay-iwkʿ	gah-ukʿ

1   In the *-ā- stems the two cases would have fallen together by regular phonetic development because the non-syllabic nasal of the accusative singular of polysyllables is lost as a result of the changes -VN > Ṽ > V > 0, reducing the form to the root, exactly as happened in the nominative after the loss of the stem vowel caused by the stress accent.

2   The form of the nominative was generalized as the nominative case in the -r- and -n- stems denoting persons (cf. hayr 'father'; mayr 'mother', etc.).

3   The accusative was generalized in the -o-, -i- and -u- stems, which in some cases show the reflex -kʿ from old sigmatic nominative singulars, which is however felt to be a nominative plural ending (e.g. elkʿ 'exit'; xawskʿ 'speech').

The possibility of interpreting the final -n of consonantal stems such as jeṙn 'hand', otn 'foot', jiwn 'snow' as deriving from < *-m̥ makes it possible to postulate that in these stems too the form of the accusative singular was generalized as the nominative case.

More immediate is the derivation of the instrumental ending which appears in vocalic stems as -w/-v (with variation in spelling, while in the -u- stems there is loss of earlier -w) and as -b in nasal and liquid stems. All these forms can be taken back to IE *-bʰi, whose final vowel is still present in the instrumental iwi-kʿ of the indefinite pronoun *i-kʿ. The IE morpheme *-bʰi probably applied to both singular and plural: the Armenian instrumental plural form where -kʿ is added to the singular morpheme is probably to be interpreted as an Armenian innovation formed on the model of the nominative plural.

Another ending which may easily be taken back to Indo-European is the genitive singular -oy of the -o- stems, which reflects *-osjo, while the ending -i of the genitive singular of -a- stems has been borrowed from the -i- stems. For the ablative singular ending -ē (< earlier *ey) we assume a derivation with

an intervocalic voiceless dental; consequently, this ending has been compared
with the Luw. *-ati*, Lyc. *-edi*, *-adi* ablative and instrumental forms, but more
probably the origin of the Armenian form lies not in an inflectional ending but
in a postposed particle **eti*, cf. Gk *éti*, Skt *ati*.

As regards the plural endings, the accusative form *-s* can easily be taken
back to an earlier **-ns*, still attested in Goth. *daga-ns* 'days', *gasti-ns* 'guests',
etc. On the other hand, the *-s* of the locative is to be interpreted in terms of
an extension of function of the accusative. Generally accepted is the
derivation of *-cʿ*, the genitive/dative/ablative ending, from an adjectival suffix
*-sko-, which occurs in many other IE languages. The derived form was
initially used with genitive value and subsequently also underwent an
extension of function to the other cases. We have discussed in **Sibilants**,
pp. 212–13 the possible derivation of the plural marker *-kʿ* from IE **-s* which
is found in the nominative.

Pronouns

The pronouns exhibit stems and endings whose etymologies are often difficult.
As regards the demonstrative stems, they form a coherent deictic system which
makes it possible to distinguish first, second and third persons at the level both of
pronouns and of adverbs: the pronominal stems used, which are recognizable as
Indo-European only if we presuppose irregular phonetic developments, do not
form a system comparable with that of Armenian in any other IE language: *so-*
'this' < **ḱo-*, cf. **ḱi-* in Gk *sémeron* 'today', Lat. *ci-s*; *do-* 'that' (close to the
interlocutor) < **to-*, cf. Gk *to-*; *no-* 'yon' < **no-*, cf. Hitt. *eni-*, *uni-* 'yon', OCS
onŭ. In combination with various particles these stems form other pronouns.
Prefixed with **ay-*, they form *ays*, *ayd*, *ayn* with a demonstrative meaning;
suffixed with *-in* they give rise to *soyn*, *doyn*, *noyn* 'the same'; suffixed with *-a*
they create the anaphoric pronoun *sa*, *da*, *na*. The consonantal element of the
stem on its own, suffixed to a word (not necessarily a noun), is roughly
equivalent to the definite article which occurs in some IE languages: cf. *tag-s*
'this crown', *tag-d* 'that crown', *tag-n* 'yon crown'.

The inflection of the demonstrative stem can be clearly seen for example
in the declension of the anaphoric pronoun in Table 8.3. From the
demonstrative, the following adverbs of place are derived:

ast 'here, in this place'	aydr 'there, in that place'	and 'yonder, in yon place'
aysr 'hither, to this place'	aydr 'thither, to that place'	andr 'to yon place'
asti 'hence, from this place'	ayti 'thence, from that place'	anti 'from yon place'

In the interrogative pronoun there are traces of a stem distinction between
persons and things:

Nom.Acc.	ov/o 'who?'	z-i (z-inčʿ) 'what?'
Gen.	oyr	ēr

Table 8.3 The anaphoric pronoun

Singular			
Nom.Acc.	s-a	d-a	n-a
Gen	sor-a	dor-a	nor-a
Dat.Loc.	sm-a	dm-a	nm-a < *suma, *duma, *numa < *soma, *doma, *noma
Abl.	sm-anē	dm-anē	nm-anē
Instr.	sov-a-w	dov-a-w	nov-a-w
Plural			
Nom.	sokʿ-a	dokʿ-a	nokʿ-a
Acc.Loc.	sos-a	dos-a	nos-a
Gen.Dat.Abl.	socʿ-a	docʿ-a	nocʿ-a
Instr.	sokʿ-awkʿ	dokʿ-awkʿ	nokʿ-awkʿ

Dat.Loc.	um	him/im
Abl.	umē	imē
Instr.	(orov)	iw

The interrogative adjective is *or*, which also takes on the function of a relative pronoun and is inflected like a pronominal stem in *-o-*:

Singular		Plural	
Nom.Acc.	or	Nom.	orkʿ
Gen.	oroy	Acc.Loc.	ors
Dat.Loc.	orum	Gen.Dat.Abl.	orocʿ
Abl.	ormē		
Instr.	orov	Instr.	orovkʿ

The pronominal stem is probably IE *$kʷo$-/$kʷi$-, as in the Slavic languages, and for the interrogative adjective a derivation from *$kʷo(te)ro$- has been assumed. In both cases it is necessary to postulate a special phonetic development by which *$kʷ$- > $kʿ$ > h- > 0.

By means of a suffix -$kʿ$ or a suffix -*mn* which were probably enclitic particles, two indefinite pronoun-adjectives are derived from the interrogative pronouns:

Nom.Acc.	o-kʿ 'someone' (in negative or conditional clauses)	(inčʿ) 'something'
Gen.	urukʿ	irikʿ
Dat.Loc.	umekʿ	
Abl.	umekʿē	
Instr.	(omamb)	iwikʿ

Singular		*Plural*	
Nom.Acc.	omn 'someone' (in affirmative clauses)	Nom.	omankʿ
Gen.	urumn	Acc.Loc.	omans
Dat.Loc.	umemn	Gen.Dat.Abl.	omancʿ
Abl.	umemnē		
Instr.	omamb	Instr.	omambkʿ

In almost all these pronouns the genitive singular ending is - r; this has been interpreted as deriving from an original adjectival suffix *-ro-. As regards the dative singular, the above pronouns have the ending -m, which can easily be taken back to *-smē, cf. Skt tasmai, Goth þamma.

Numerals

The numerals from one to four (mi 'one' < *smijos; erku 'two' < *dwō; erekʿ 'three' < *trejes; čorkʿ 'four' < *kʷetores) are inflected thoroughly in Armenian and agree in number and case with the noun to which they refer, whether they precede or follow it. The numbers from five to ten (hing, vecʿ, ewťn, uť, inn, tasn) are not inflected in the nominative, accusative or locative, but are inflected in the other cases when the noun referred to precedes the numeral. From eleven upwards the numerals are on the whole not inflected, apart from certain instances when the numbered noun precedes the numeral.

The numerals from eleven to sixteen are copulative compounds: metasan, erkotasan, erekʿtasan, čorekʿtasan, hngetasan, veštasan, while those from seventeen to nineteen are juxtapositions of units and tens formed by means of the coordinating conjunction ew 'and'; ewťn ew tasn; uťew tasn; inn ew tasn. The decades from thirty upwards are compounds with the element -sun (< *-ḱomt) in second position.

Personal Pronouns

These pronouns, too, can only be taken back to IE forms by accepting irregular phonetic developments:

The first-person singular pronoun exhibits forms which are difficult to explain phonetically both in the nominative (where es is taken back to *eǵō or *eǵʰom by assuming an irregular development attributable to a Sandhi effect (cf. Chapter 4, p. 107) of the expected consonant, /c/ or /z/ as the case may be) and in the accusative and locative (where is is made to derive from *ins, derived from the stem *em, which is found in the genitive, dative, ablative and instrumental) and from a particle similar to the Greek -ge in emé-ge. However, even for this derivation it is necessary to assume a special phonetic development. The second-person singular pronoun is clearly derived from Indo-European: the nominative du < *tu presupposes an irregular phonetic development, while the derivation of the rest of the flexion is more regular: ḱo < *two-; ḱez, ḱēn, ḱew < *twe-.

Table 8.4 First- and second-person pronouns

	First person	*Second person*
Singular		
Nom	es	du
Gen	im	kʿo
Acc.Loc.	is	kʿez
Dat.	inǰ	kʿez
Abl.	inēn	kʿēn
Instr.	inew	kʿew
Plural		
Nom.	mekʿ	dukʿ
Gen.	mer	jer
Acc.Loc.Dat.	mez	jez
Abl.	mēnǰ	jēnǰ
Instr.	mewkʿ	jewkʿ

In the case of the first-person plural pronoun *mekʿ*, too, there are parallels in other IE languages (cf. Lith. *mēs*, OCS *my*), but for the second-person plural pronoun (except for the nominative, which is derived from the singular with the addition of the plural marker *-kʿ*) there are no parallels in other languages.

Verb Flection

The Armenian verb distinguishes between a present and an aorist stem. These have different aspectual values, the former having an imperfective and the latter a perfective value. The IE perfect has been lost; it remains only in a small number of fossilized forms with present value, such as Armenian *gitem* 'I know' < *wojd-*; Arm. *goy* 'he is' < **wos-*.

From the present stem, which is characterized by one of the stem vowels *-e-*, *-i-*, *-a-*, *-u-*, sometimes with an infixed nasal or *-čʿ-*, the following forms are derived:

Present indicative (e.g. for the class with stem vowel in *-e-*): *gtan-e-m* 'I find' (*-e-s*; *-ē* < **-e-y*; *-e-mkʿ*; *-ēkʿ* < **e-ykʿ*; *-e-n*)
Imperfect: *gtan-ei* (*-e-ir*; *-ēr* < **-e-yr*; *-e-akʿ*; *-e-ikʿ*; *-e-in*)
Present subjunctive: *gtan-icʿ-e-m* (*-e-s*; *-ē* < **-e-y*; *-e-mkʿ*; *-ēkʿ* < *-e-ykʿ*, *-e-n*)
Injunctive: (*mi*) *gtan-e-r*; (*mi*) *gtan-ē-kʿ*
Infinitive: *gtan-el*

From the aorist stem the following are formed:

Aorist indicative: *gt-i* (*gt-ir*; *e-git*; *gt-akʿ*; *gt-ikʿ*; *gt-in*)/middle-passive: *gt-ay* (*gt-ar*; *gt-aw*; *gt-akʿ*; *gt-aykʿ*; *gt-an*)

Imperative: *git* (*gt-ēkʿ*)/middle-passive: *gt-ir* (*gt-aykʿ*)
Aorist subjunctive (which also has future meaning): *gt-icʿ* (*gt-cʿes*; *gt-cʿē*; *gt-cʿukʿ*; *gt-ĵikʿ*; *gt-cʿen*)/middle-passive: *gt-aycʿ* (*gt-cʿis*; *gt-cʿi*; *gt-cʿukʿ*; *gt-ĵikʿ*; *gt-cʿin*)
Participle: *gt-eal*

The Armenian verbal system is remarkably innovative: as well as the loss of the IE perfect, we also have the loss of the optative, whose functions were taken over by the subjunctive; the injunctive, limited to second-person singular and second-person plural and used in negative commands along with the negative particle *mi*: its flectional endings (singular *-r* < Proto-Arm. **-rV*; plural *kʿ* < Proto-Arm. **-yekʿ*) are identical to the secondary endings of the indicative.

As regards number, the opposition is reduced to singular vs plural, the dual having been lost. Extremely innovative is the opposition between active and middle-passive, which is realized incompletely in the verbal flection and by different morphological means from those used by Indo-European to express voice. In the present indicative and subjunctive and in the injunctive, the replacement of the stem vowel *-e-* with *-i-* changes the voice of the verbal form from active to middle-passive. The forms in *-i-* probably derive from IE **-ē-*, which is characteristic of a class of intransitive verbs in the Germanic and Italic languages; these forms would have arisen as present middle indicative morphemes and would have been extended to the present subjunctive and partially to the aorist subjunctive. However, this process does not apply to the other forms derived from the present stem, where the opposition is neutralized in favour of *-e-*. In addition, a contrast in stem vowel is not possible for the other two verb classes, which are characterized respectively by the stem vowels *-a-* and *-u-*. In the forms derived from the aorist stem, the opposition of voice is expressed in the personal endings (although not in all): the first-person plural aorist indicative ending *-akʿ*, first-person plural aorist subjunctive *- ukʿ* and second-person plural aorist subjunctive *-ĵikʿ* are common to both active and middle. The characteristic feature of the middle voice in these forms is *-a-*, which may be compared with the IE **-ā-* to be found in Balto-Slavic and Italic (cf. Lat. *legeram*). In Armenian, this morpheme would have been extended from the indicative to the other moods.

Armenian also turns out to be highly innovative as regards tense formation: only a limited number of Armenian verbs have an aorist form deriving from an IE aorist, whether athematic or thematic (cf. Arm. *edi* 'I put, placed', Gk *é-thē-ka*; Arm. *arari* 'I did', Gk *ēraron*; Arm. *egit* 'he found', Gk *eîdon*; Arm. *elikʿ* 'he left', Gk *élipe*). The majority of the Armenian root aorists go back not to IE aorists, but to imperfects, e.g. *berem* 'I bear' aor. *beri*; *acem* 'I lead', aor. *aci*; *lizem* 'I lick', aor. *lizi*.

As well as those root aorists deriving from IE imperfects, Armenian has aorists with an extension -*c͑* deriving from an IE expansion *-*skelo*- which was suffixed to preterite forms. A close analysis shows that the majority of Armenian aorist forms derive from IE imperfect forms. The most important consequence of this innovation was thus the need to construct a new imperfect form. The origin of the Armenian imperfect is still subject to much debate. One suggestive theory derives the Armenian imperfect from the IE optative, in that Armenian -*i*-, which characterizes many of the endings, could derive from IE *-*jēl-ī*-. Both of the subjunctive forms probably derive from an extension *- *iskelo*-, which can also be traced in Latin and Greek cf. Gk *heurískō, halískomai*, etc. While in the present subjunctive the -*i*- of the extension forms a diphthong with the stem vowel and undergoes regular phonetic development determined by the position of the accent, in the aorist subjunctive the same accent-governed vowel change leads to the weakening of -*i*-. As for the participle, which has the form -*eal* and is inflected according to the -*o*- declension, the suffix which makes it up seems to derive from *-*lo*- and can thus be related to the Indo-European primary adjectives found in various languages, such as Gk *deilós* 'fearful', Lat. *pendulus* 'hanging', etc. The infinitive is also taken back to a suffix *-*lo*- which originally formed nouns of action. As regards the endings of the paradigm, it is not possible here to comment on every point, so it will suffice to mention the fact that Armenian has merged thematic and athematic forms. However, some forms of the personal endings have not yet received satisfactory explanation in terms of their derivation from Indo-European (e.g. -*w* of the 3 sg. aor. mid.; -*ak͑* of the 1 pl. past; -*jik͑* of the 2 pl. aor. subj.).

The presence of the augment, restricted to the monosyllabic forms of the third-person singular of the aorist, should also be mentioned.

Invariable Word Classes
These are conjunctions, adverbs, prepositions and postpositions.

Conjunctions
The main conjunctions are: *ew* 'and' (coordinating); *kam* 'or' (disjunctive); *ayl* 'but' (strongly adversative); *bayc͑* 'but' (delimitative); *isk* 'but' (counter-positive). There are few subordinating conjunctions and each of these has different meanings according to the verbal mood in the subordinate clause: *zi* + indicative has causal value, but when used with the subjunctive it has final value. *T͑ ele͑*, as well as indicating that direct speech follows and introducing indirect interrogative sentences, introduces a final clause if a subjunctive follows and constitutes the protasis of a conditional clause if it is followed by the indicative or subjunctive. Temporal subordinate clauses may be introduced by *ibr(ew)* 'while, after' or by *minč͑(ew)* 'when, until'. The latter conjunction also introduces consecutive clauses.

Adverbs

There are a small number of primary adverbs, e.g. *mišt* 'always', *ard* 'now'. On the whole, however, the adverbs are old inflected forms of nouns, which have become fossilized with adverbial function, e.g. *y-et* 'after', formed with the preposition *i* (in its variant *y* before words beginning with a vowel) and the locative form of the noun *het* 'track, mark, sign' (-*o*- stem), with the loss of *h*-. Adjectives can always be used with adverbial function.

In addition, there exist adverb-specific suffixal formatives which are postposed to nouns, adjectives and adverbs and some of which are of Iranian origin, for example, -(*a*)*pēs*, which in Iranian (but not Armenian) exists as an independent word with the meaning 'manner, method', and -(*a*)*goyn*, which exists independently in both Iranian and Armenian with the meaning 'colour'.

Prepositions

In Armenian almost all the prepositions, with the exception of *cʿ* 'towards' can also function as preverbs; however, the preverb mechanism is no longer productive in Classical Armenian and receives new impetus in the immediate post-classical period from the extremely numerous literal calques formed on Greek. One feature of the Armenian prepositions is their potential for being repeated before each element of a phrase, e.g. *ənd awursn ənd aynosik* 'in those days' (lit. 'in days in those'). In addition, the same prepositions can be used together with different nominal cases, each with a different meaning;

aṙ + acc. = 'towards'
　　 + loc. = 'near'
　　 + gen. = 'because of'
ənd + acc. = 'through'
　　　 + instr. = 'under'
　　　 + loc./dat. = 'with'
　　　 + gen. = 'instead of'
əst + loc./dat. = 'according to'
　　 + abl. = 'after'
z + acc. = governs definite direct complement
　 + abl. = 'because of'
　 + instr. = 'with regard to'
　 + loc. = 'towards'
i/y + acc. = 'in'
　　 + loc. = 'under'
　　 + abl. = 'from'
cʿ + acc. = 'towards'

As well as these prepositions, Armenian has a very large number of adverbs used prepositionally, linked with nouns which are usually in the genitive. Some of these adverbs are used as postpositions.

Word Formation

Of the two methods of word formation which are also found in the other IE languages, derivation and compounding, we linger here on the second, since we have already looked at the process of derivation in Armenian.

As regards nominal compounds, the following types are distinguished (cf. Chapter 4, pp. 121–2):

1   exocentric compounds (also called possessive compounds or *bahuvrīhi*): Arm. *barjr-a-berj* (lit. 'which has a height (*berj*) high (*barjr*)')
2   verb-governed compounds: in this type of compound one element – which is normally in second position, but can also be in first position – is a verb form (corresponding in general to the stem of the aorist), which governs the other term: Arm. *barerar* 'benefactor' < *bari-arar*, lit. '(one) who does (*arar*, aor. stem of *aṙnem* 'I do') good (*bari*)'; Arm. *jerb-a-kal* 'prisoner' (lit. '(one) who is taken (*kal*, aorist stem of *unim* 'have, hold') by the hand (*jerb*, instr. of *jeṙn* 'hand')'); Arm. *yeł-a-mit* 'fickle' (lit. '(one) who changes (*yeł*, aor. stem of *yełum* 'change') (his) mind (*mit*)')
3   preposition-governed compound: in this type of compound a preposition in first position governs the second element: Arm. *c̣erek* 'day' lit. 'until (*c̣*) evening (*erek*)'; *aṙač̣awḳ* 'vision' lit. 'before (*aṙ*) the eyes (*ač̣awḳ*)'
4   determinative compounds (also called *tatpuruṣa*): in these the second element is determined by the first on the basis of a relation which can be of various types: Arm. *get-ezr* 'river bank' (*get* 'river', *ezr* 'bank'); *nor-a-ji* 'unbroken horse' (*nor* 'new', *ji* 'horse'); *mayr-a-k̇ałak̇* 'capital city' (*mayr* 'mother', *k̇ałak* 'city')
5   copulative compounds (also called 'dvandva'): in these neither element is subordinate to the other; rather, they stand in conjunction. This is the case with certain numerals and a few other examples: *hiwf-a-niwf* 'material' (adj. + noun) (*hiwf* 'matter', *niwf* 'substance'); *ayr-ew-ji* 'cavalry' (*ayr* 'man', *ew* 'and', *ji* 'horse')

We note that in all the types of nominal compounding, except the last example, the two elements of the compound are generally joined by means of the linking vowel -*a*- if the second element begins with a consonant.

Very productive in Armenian, unlike the other IE languages, is the process of reduplication, that is the repetition of the whole word, whether a noun or a verb. This repetition of the word cannot be viewed in the same way as compounding because it does not follow the rules of vowel weakening in unaccented syllables: Arm. *bar-baṙ* 'speech', *goyn-a-goyn* 'variegated'.

Syntax

Word order in Armenian is essentially extremely free since the syntactic functions are already clearly indicated in the inflectional elements of the sentence constituents. However, we can establish that the unmarked word order is SVO, while the sequence SOV is marked. The simultaneous presence of direct (O) and indirect (I) objects allows three possible permutations of the elements: SVIO, SVOI and SOVI.

This inflectional indication of the syntactic role played by the individual elements is not provided in a few important instances of phrases which consist of modifier + head noun. The instances listed below share as their common denominator a tendency to view groups formed of modifier + head noun as a whole unit. Functionally relevant is the role of the group within the sentence rather than the indication of the relationship with the sentence established by each element in the group. This syntactic feature, which appears only as a tendency in Classical Armenian, is definitively consolidated in Modern Armenian.

1   Nouns and attributive adjectives agree in case and normally also in number (although the *pluralia tantum* can go with singular adjectives) when the adjective follows the noun (emphatic position), but when the adjective precedes the noun (neutral position) it is on the whole not inflected, except in the case of monosyllabic adjectives: cf. *bazum* 'much' (not inflected) *gorc-s* 'works' (acc. pl.) *bari-s* 'good' (acc. pl.) 'many good works'.

2   In the case of groups formed of two nouns where the first is the head noun and the second the modifier, there are examples of flectional adjustment, where the modifier takes on the same case as the head noun; cf. Deut. 34:9: *lc῾aw hogwov* (instr.) *imastut῾eamb* (instr.), corresponding to Gk *eneplḗsthē pneúmatos synéseōs*, 'was full of the spirit of wisdom'.

Groups composed of modifier + head noun are indicated in various other ways.

3   By means of the repetition of prepositions (including *z-*, a marker of the definite acc.) before every element of the group; cf. Matt. 23:25 *srbēk῾ z-artak̇in z-băzakin*, corresponding to Gk *katharízete tò éxōthen toû potēríou* 'ye make clean the outside of the cup'.

4   By postposing the deictic element (equivalent to the definite article in other IE languages) to the modifier, whatever its position with respect to the head noun; cf. Tit. 2:10: *z- vardapetut῾iwn P῾rkč̇i-n*, corresponding to Gk *tèn didaskalían tèn toû sōtêros* 'the doctrine of the Saviour'.

5   By using the relative pronoun with the function of *izāfat*, perhaps influenced by the Iranian model: cf. 1 Cor. 2:11: *hogi mardoyn or i nma*, corresponding to Gk *tò pneûma toû anthrṓpou tò en autôi* 'the spirit of man which is in him'.

Note

1 The transliteration of the Armenian alphabet corresponds to that used in the *Revue des études arméniennes*, according to which the letters *c*, *c̓* and *ǰ* represent, respectively, voiceless, voiceless aspirated and voiced apical affricates, while *č*, *č̓* and *ǰ* represent, respectively, voiceless, voiceless aspirated and voiced dorsal affricates. The sign ‹'› placed after a consonant indicates aspiration. The phonetic values of the remaining signs are as follows: *š*, *ž* indicate alveolar-palatal grooved fricatives, voiceless and voiced respectively; *x* represents a voiceless velar fricative, *ł* a velarized alveolar lateral, *r̄* a long alveolar trill. As regards the vowels, it should be noted merely that *ē* indicates not a long vowel, but rather a mid-high front vowel, whereas *e* indicates a mid-low front vowel. The IE glottalic stops are represented with the conventional symbol ‹'›.

References

Ačaṙyan, Hrač̓ya H. (1971–9) *Hayeren armatakan baṙaran*, 4 vols, Erevan: Erevani hamalsarani hratarakč̓ut̓iwn.

Benveniste, Emile (1952) 'La construction passive du parfait transitif', *Bulletin de la Société Linguistique de Paris* 48: 52–62.

—— (1959) 'Sur la phonétique et la syntaxe de l'arménien classique', *Bulletin de la Société Linguistique de Paris* 54: 46–68.

—— (1967) 'Le développement des mots composés en arménien classique', *Revue des Etudes Arméniennes*, N.S. 4: 1–14.

Bolognesi, Giancarlo (1954) 'Ricerche sulla fonetica armena', *Ricerche Luinguistiche* 3: 123–54.

—— (1962) 'Studi armeni', *Ricerche Luinguistiche* 5: 105–47.

Bonfante, Giuliano (1942) 'The Armenian aorist', *Journal of the American Oriental Society* 62: 102–5.

—— (1981–2) 'Hayereni dirkə indevropakan lezuneri mēǰ', *Istoriko-Filologiceskij Žurnal Akademii nauk Armjanskoj SSR* 54–67.

Cardona, Giorgio R. (1983) 'Armeno e lingue caucasiche: un bilancio', in: Enrico Campanile (ed.), *Problemi di sostrato nelle lingue indoeuropee*, Pisa: Giardini, pp. 37–75.

Diakonoff, Igor M. and Starostin, S.A. (1986) *Hurro-Urartian as an Eastern Caucasian Language*, Munich: Kitzinger.

Gamkrelidze, Thomas V. and Ivanov, Vjačeslav V. (1980) 'Problema jazykov centum i satem i otraženie "guttural'nyx" v istoričeskix indoevropejskix dialektax', *Voprosy Jazykkoznanija* no. 6: 13–22.

Godel, Robert (1965) 'Les origines de la conjugaison arménienne', *Revue des Etudes Arméniennes*, N.S. 2: 21–41.

—— (1970) 'Questions de phonétique et de morphologie arméniennes', *Revue des Etudes Arméniennes* N.S. 7: 1–7.

—— (1975) *An Introduction to the Study of Classical Armenian*, Wiesbaden: Reichert.

Greppin, John A.C. (1983) 'An etymological dictionary of the Indo-European components of Armenian', ed. Dickran Kouymijan, *Bazmavep* 141: 235–323.

—— (1986) 'The development of Armenian *l* and *ł*', in *Armenian Studies in Memoriam H. Berbérian*, Lisbon: Imprensa de Coimbra, pp. 279–92.

Hübschmann, Heinrich (1883) *Armenische Studien*, vol. I, *Grundzüge der armenischen Etymologie 1*, Leipzig: reprinted in Hübschmann 1976: 152ff.

—— (1897/1962) *Armenische Grammatik*, vol. I, *Armenische Etymologie*, Leipzig and Hildesheim: G. Olms.

——— (1976) *Kleine Schriften zum Armenischen*, ed. R. Schmitt, Hildesheim and New York: G. Olms.

Jahukyan, Gevork B. (1970) *Hayerenə ev hndevropakan hin lezunerə*, Erevan: Haykakan SSH GA hratarakč'ut'iwn.

——— (1980) 'On the position of Armenian in the Indo-European languages (on the areal characteristics of the Armenian language)', in J. A. C. Greppin (ed.), *First International Conference on Armenian Linguistics: Proceedings*, Delmar and New York: Caravan Books, pp. 3–16.

——— (1982) *Sravnitel'naja grammatika armjanskogo jazyka*, Erevan: Haykakan SSH GA hratarakč'ut'iwn.

——— (1987) *Hayoc'lezvi patmut'iwn: naxagrayin žamanakašržan*, Erevan: Haykakan SSH GA hratarakč'ut'iwn.

Jensen, Hans (1959) *Altarmenische Grammatik*, Heidelberg: C. Winter.

Karst, Josef (1901/1970) *Historische Grammatik des Kilikisch- Armenischen*, Strasburg and Berlin: W. de Gruyter & Co.

Kortlandt, Frederik (1985) 'The syncretism of nominative and accusative singular in Armenian', *Revue des Études Arméniennes*, N.S. 19: 19–24.

——— (1987) 'Notes on Armenian historical phonology', *Studia Caucasica* 7: 61–5.

——— (1989) 'The making of a puzzle', *Annual of American Linguistics* 10: 43–52.

Meillet, Antoine (1913) *Altarmenisches Elementarbuch*, Heidelberg: C. Winter, 1980.

——— (1936) *Esquisse d'une grammaire comparée de l'arménien classique*, Vienna: Imprimerie des P.P. Mekhitharistes.

——— (1962) *Etudes de linguistique et de philologie arméniennes*, vol. I, *Recherches sur la syntaxe comparée de l'arménien, suivies de la composition en arménien*, Lisbon: Imprensa nacional de Lisboa.

Morani, Moreno (1981–2) 'Armeno e problema *satem*', *Handes Amsorya. Zeitschrift für armenische Philologie*: 13–30.

Ovsepjan, Liana S. (1976) 'K voprosu o vzaimootnašenii drevnearmjanskogo literaturnogo jazyka i dialektov v V veke', in *Lingvističeskaja geografija, dialektologija i istorija jazyka*, Erevan: Haykakan SSH GA hratarakč'ut'iwn, pp. 369–76.

Périkhanian, Anahit (1966) 'Une inscription araméenne du roi Artašēs trouvée à Zanguézour (Siwnik')', *Revue des Etudes Arméniennes* N.S. 3: 17–29.

——— (1971) 'Les inscriptions araméennes du roi Artachès', *Revue des Etudes Arméniennes*, N.S. 8: 169–74.

Pisani, Vittore (1944) 'Armenische Studien', *Zeitschrift für vergleichende Sprachforschung* 68: 157–77.

——— (1951) 'Studi sulla fonetica dell'armeno', *Ricerche Linguistiche* 2: 47–74.

Schmitt, Rüdiger (1972–74) 'Die Erforschung des Klassich-Armenischen seit Meillet (1936)', *Kratylos* 17: 1–68.

——— (1981) *Grammatik des klassisch-Armenischen mit sprachvergleichenden Erläuterungen*. Innsbruck: Institut für Sprachwissenschaft der Universität Innsbruck.

——— (1983) 'Iranisches Lehngut im Armenischen', *Revue des Etudes Arméniennes*, N.S. 17: 73–112.

Solta, George R. (1960) *Die Stellung des Armenischen im Kreise der indogermanischen Sprachen: Eine Untersuchung der indogermanischen Bestandteile des armenischen Wortschatzes*, Vienna: Mekhitharisten Buchdruckerei.

——— (1963) 'Die armenische Sprache', in *Handbuch der Orientalistik*, I/7, *Armenisch und kaukasische Sprachen*, Leiden and Cologne: E.J. Brill, pp. 80–128.

Tumanjan, Eteri G. (1971) *Drevnearmjanskij jazyk*, Moscow: Nauka.

Vennemann, Theo (1986) 'Syllable-based sound changes in Early Armenian', *Annual of Armenian Linguistics* 7: 27–43.

Vogt, Hans (1930) 'Les deux thèmes verbaux de l'arménien classique', *Norsk Tidsskrift for Sprogmidenskap* 4: 129–45.

——— (1958) 'Les occlusives de l'arménien', *Norsk Tidsskrift for Sprogmidenskap* 18: 143–61.

Winter, Werner (1966) 'Traces of early dialectal diversity in Old Armenian', in H. Birnbaum and J. Puhvel (eds), *Ancient Indo-European Dialects*, Berkeley and Los Angeles: University of California Press, pp. 201–11.

9 *Greek*

Henry M. Hoenigswald

Introduction

Greek is the lone representative of what is perhaps the best known and the second oldest attested subdivision, after Anatolian, of the IE language family. The relationship of Greek to the bits of evidence which we possess for ancient Macedonian, as well as to the language of the neo-Phrygian texts of imperial times, is difficult to judge. Special affinities within the more remote IE fold no doubt linked the dialect or dialects which were destined to become Greek to others. Among the sister languages which have survived, Armenian is sometimes singled out as sharing significant prehistoric innovations with Greek.

Our oldest Greek texts (fifteenth to twelfth century BC) are the 'Mycenaean' documents written in the Linear B *syllabary*, mostly from Pylos, Knossos and Mycenae. After the 'dark' centuries writing emerges once again: while in Cyprus another syllabary was in use from very early days until the Hellenistic age, the 'epichoric' varieties of the Phoenician-based *alphabet* made their appearance in Greece, in the Hellenic West, and among Greeks elsewhere. Not long after the end of the fifth century BC the Ionic alphabet of Miletus superseded other local writings. Aside from inscriptions, our sources are papyri – both utilitarian and literary – from Hellenistic and Roman times, and medieval manuscript copies of ancient literary texts. Material of linguistic interest can be found in works of Greek grammarians and lexicographers, recovered from glosses or loan words in other languages such as Latin, or reconstructed from later forms of Greek.

Alphabetic variation must be kept strictly separate from *dialect* variation. While the disappearance (or transformation) of each reflects the same broad social and demographic history, it does so in different ways and with small but significant chronological discrepancies. In terms of an admittedly idealized tree, even Mycenaean is already the result of diversification, perhaps into South Greek (Mycenaean, Arcado-Cyprian, Ionic(-Attic)) and North Greek (Aeolic (fundamentally Thessalian), Doric/North-west, Pamphylian) (Risch 1955; Schmitt 1977). Other groupings come later; hence the lucidity with which, for example, Attic, the Doric group, or the somewhat hybrid varieties of Aeolic of Lesbos and Boeotia stand out in the first millennium. Even more evident were the stylized uses of dialect in genres of literature: Lesbian in some of melic poetry; varieties of Ionic in the epic and in

Herodotus and the physicians; Doric in choral lyrics; Attic (mitigated or straight) in tragic dialogue and, later, in many other genres. Here and there poets employed their own native form of speech. With few exceptions, the local dialects themselves were supplanted by the Ionic-Attic based *koiné* during a period that extends from the fifth century BC to Roman times (see **Dialects**, pp. 240f.).

Rich though this attestation is, it carries a good deal of unevenness. The Mycenaean texts are only administrative palace records, written in an uncongenial, ambiguous script, something that is true also of the first-millennium texts from Cyprus. The language of the Homeric epic has roots deep in an oral tradition and in concrete metrical practices that must go back beyond Proto-Greek; but its relationship with the Mycenaean, Aeolic and Ionic dialects as we know them is only partly understood. The oldest known alphabetic inscriptions – both metrical – are the 'Dipylon pitcher' from Athens, and the so-called Nestor cup, from an eighth-century grave on Ischia off southern Italy. Archaic and otherwise important material comes from the Doric lands around the Saronic gulf and in some territories colonized from there: Argos, Aegina, Corinth and Corcyra; from Thera, Rhodes and Crete (including the intriguing ποινικαστάς inscription, and the celebrated fifth-century Gortyn Law); from Olympia in Elis; from Boeotia; not much that is outstanding from Thessaly and even less from Lesbos (where the grammar-ians' concern for the literary language makes up for it). More was found in various sites in Arcadia (e.g., a sixth-century dedicatory text from Mantineia); in Cyprus (with the 'Idalion bronze' [early fifth century]); in Athens; and, in great profusion, in the Ionian world, including archaic documents from Kyme, Oropos, Keos, Naxos, Thasos, Miletus (especially the extensive sacrificial calendar).

Foreign Influences

Non-Greek influences are tangible only in the vocabulary. Words without good IE etymologies certainly abound. Only some of these may be unique survivals. Those which have plausible but phonologically aberrant IE etymologies (like, possibly, σῦς 'pig' alongside the regular ὗς) could be borrowed from some shadowy IE sister language. In the remaining instances tell-tale phonological and morphological features – especially derivational suffixes like the 'Aegean' -νθ-(ος) of cultural loan words (e.g. ἀσάμινθος 'bathtub') and place-names (e.g. Τίρυνς, Κόρινθος – make it possible occasionally to distinguish, though not necessarily to identify, the source languages, whether Indo-European or not.

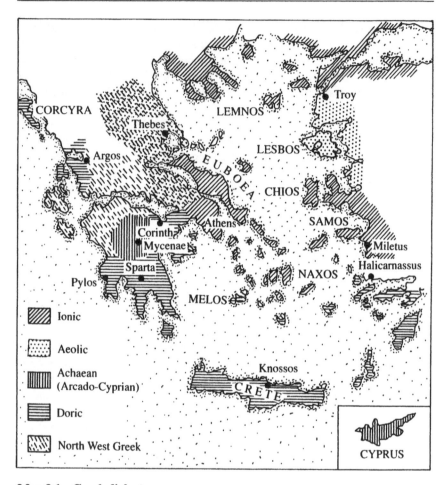

Map 9.1   Greek dialects
Source: L. R. Palmer, *The Greek Dialects*, London: Faber and Faber, 1980

Phonology: Indo-European

At one stage Indo-European possessed:

1   *intonation* morphemes (melodies; mainly in construction with one another)
2   *stress* morphemes (in construction with one another and with other grammatical morphemes) as well as, perhaps,
3   phonological *word-boundary* markers.

Little is known about any of these entities, except that the orthotony of the Greek interrogative τίς τί (with acute even in context) may represent an intonational feature of Indo-European (see also 4 below).

There were also lexical and grammatical morphemes with morphs consisting of

4   a *word accent* of the pitch variety (*´, as well as the largely bimorphemic *~, cf., **Phonology, Accent**, p. 234). The retracted accentuation of several Greek vocatives singular (ἄδελφε 'brother', δέσποτα 'lord', Ἄπολλον) is a remnant of the IE accentuation at the start of a sentence or of enclisis (cf. **Noun and Adjective Paradigms**, pp. 244f.)

5   The *'full-grade' short vowels* (V), *e, *o (*a[?]).

6   The *'lengthened grade'* vowels (V) *ē, *ō (*ā[?]) (see Chapter 2, pp. 52–3), and the long ī and ū and (V) in monosyllabic nouns like ὗς (see p. 237).

7   A set of *resonant* phonemes (R) with both consonantal (non-syllabic; C) and vocalic (syllabic; V) allophones:
     (a) the *semi-vowels* *j [j/i], *w [w/u],
     (b) the *nasals* *n [n/n̥], *m [m/m̥],
     (c) the *liquids* *r [r/r̥], *l [l/l̥].
     (d) here included with the resonants – the *laryngeals* ('*H'), probably, *H_1 [Hᵉ/H̥ᵉ], *H_2 [Hᵃ/H̥ᵃ], *H_3 [Hᵒ/H̥ᵒ]: cf. Chapter 2, pp. 40f.

          Syllabicity largely crops out in such a way as to preclude the accumulation of more than two non-syllabic segments in the flow of speech (with word boundaries playing an uncertain role); hence *Sievers' Law* (*et[j]e, *et[r]e vs *ekt[i]e (*ekt[ij]e), *ekt[r̥]e) as modified by *Lindeman's* (1965) *Law* which regulates word-initial *CR-clusters (cf. Chapter 2, p. 46). On syllabic resonants before consonants and word-end, see pp. 233, 236; on later distinctive syllabicity see also pp. 233, 236, 239f.
     (e) The problematic *schwa secundum* *[ₑ] a transition contiguous to stops and *s, was apparently governed by much the same rules as syllabicity (but see pp. 232, 233).

8   Pure consonants, consisting of:
     (a) the *stops* here traditionally and without prejudice to their phonological properties (see below) symbolized *p, *b, *bʰ, [*pʰ] (labials); *t, *d, *dʰ, [*tʰ] (dentals); *k̑, *ĝ, *ĝʰ, [*k̑ʰ] (palatals); *k, *g, *gʰ, [*kʰ] (velars); *kʷ, *gʷ, *gʷʰ, [*kʷʰ] (labiovelars), as well as
     (b) the *spirant* *s.

9   *Allophonically* the laryngeals colour an adjacent vowel in the way indicated. The divergent yet parallel working of *Grassmann's Law* (see pp. 235) in Greek (where *bʰ ... dʰ ... etc. > π ... θ ...) and in Indic (where *bʰ ... dʰ ... > b ... dh ... etc.) is an indication that the allophones of *bʰ, *dʰ etc. were less than fully 'aspirated' when another aspirate followed in the next syllable. In the 'glottalic' view (Gamkrelidze and Ivanov 1973), our *d, *gʷ ... were glottalized rather than voiced, with plain or aspirated articulation for our *t *kʷ ..., *dʰ

$*g^{wh}$ ...; see Chapter 2, p. 38. While $*s$ was mostly = [s], it was surely = [z] before 'voiced' and 'voiced aspirated' stops, as in $*sd$, $*sd^h$. The nasal, $*n$, before palatal, velar, and labiovelar stops clearly had the appropriate homorganic allophones.

Distributional Gaps: Alternations

Several restrictions stand out because of their morphophonemic aspects.

There was *no hiatus* originally. Full-grade vowels are contracted at morph seams into long vowels or diphthongs and may in the process generate a new accentuation and new vowels – developments for which Greek (e.g. loc. -οῖ < $*$-$o + i$; dat. -ῶι < $*o + ej^\#$ is our best witness.

Stop/spirant (see 8, p. 231) accumulations, when not relieved by $*[_e]$ (see 7(e); p. 231, p. 233), are frequently found simplified by conditioned *consonant deletions* (e.g. $*tk\dm$-$tóm \rightarrow *k\dm tóm$ 'hundred').

Components of stop/spirant (and, in part, laryngeal) clusters do not contrast separately according to their *manner* of articulation; in cases of interest to Greek the final consonant of the cluster prevails, with regressive assimilation across a zeroed vowel or a morph boundary – $*g + t \rightarrow *kt$, $*g[^h]$ + $*s \rightarrow *ks$, $*p + d \rightarrow *bd$ (perhaps also $*p + H_3 \rightarrow *b$, with subsequent application of the rule $*H_3 > 0$, as in Skt *píbati*, OIr. *ibid* 'drinks' [see 7(d), p. 231] if $*H_3$ was indeed voiced).

There are *no geminated* consonants. When they would arise they appear simplified (thus $*es + si$ 'thou art' $\rightarrow *esi$ and Greek εἶ (Hom. ἐσσί is remade; such remakings and otherwise newly created cases of σ + σ generally appear as σ in Ionic-Attic and Arcadian)) except only that $*t + t \rightarrow *tt$ – presumably by an old analogical restoration.

Here, too, belong the rules that express the *compatibility* of consonants at the beginning, with consonants at the end, of 'roots' (see Chapter 2, p. 53).

The velars, $*k$ etc., take the place of the *labiovelars* (see 8(a) p. 231) before $*u$, ($*\bar{u}$, $*uH$?), $*w$.

On *ablaut* see Chapter 2, p. 51.

Word-initially before consonants (perhaps including laryngeals), some roots show interchangeable forms with and without $*^\#s$- (*s movable*).

Phonology, Laryngeals: Proto-Greek

Certain sound changes may belong in the period between Indo-European and Proto-Greek, the common ancestor of the ancient Greek dialects. Foremost are those that in the end *eliminate the laryngeals*. While some of these may be of IE antiquity the whole process was stretched out over a long time, relative chronologies being difficult to determine.

Under appropriate conditions (see 7(d), p. 231; below) $*H_1e$ merges with both $*H_1$ and $*e$, $*H_2e$ with both H_2 and $*a$ (?) and $*H_3e$ with both $*H_3$ and

*o respectively. Before vowels, then, both word-initially and after vowel, *H* > Ø, with the appropriate colouring effect. Before other syllabics that effect is limited.

Word-initial laryngeals before consonants (i.e. before **CV,* especially *RV) seem to develop the Greek prothetic vowels ἐ-, ἀ-, ὀ-, except that *#*Hj*- (though perhaps not *#*H₁j*-; see pp. 248, 259) results in ζ-, as in ζυγόν 'yoke'.

*#*H₁r̥*- > ἐρ-, *#*H₂r̥*- > ἀρ-, *#*H₃r̥*- > ὀρ-, *#*H₁n̥*- > ἐν-, *#*H₂n̥*- > ἀν-, *#*H₃n̥*- > ὀν-, etc., before one more consonant (e.g. in ἔρχομαι 'come', ὀμφαλός 'navel' (*Rix's Law*; Mayrhofer 1986: 129–30); but apparently *#*H₂n̥sV*- > ἀσ- ἄσις 'mud', see pp. 236, 238, 241 (Hoenigswald 1988: 208) as against *# ... *VCn̥sV* ... > *VCαV* ... in ... *V*) δαυλός 'thick', *#*d*)*ansV*- in Hom. Gk δήνεα 'counsels' [cf. p. 241], and *[*H*]*n̥sC*- as in Att. Gk ἡμεῖς 'we' < *[*H*]*n̥sm*-; see p. 247).

Internal *hiatus* due to loss of laryngeal (cf. p. 232) leads to contraction. At compounding seams and, especially, word boundaries this contraction yields to the characteristically Greek phenomenon of *elision* of the morph-final or word-final vowel (cf. p. 238). Internally before a consonant, all three laryngeals lengthen a preceding vowel, thereby creating new instances of *ī, *ū, *ē, *ā, and *ō (cf. 6, p. 231).

Also, *rH₃(= *[*r̥*]*H₃*) in *syllable-final* position seems to end up in Greek as ρω (as against the *īr* [*ūr*] of Sanskrit), *nH₂ as νᾱ etc.

In the positions where the laryngeals are syllabic (*'schwa' vowels*; see p. 231; and above), *H₁ > ε, *H₂ > α, *H₃ > ο.

In environments where laryngeals had contributed to a *consonant accumulation* and had conditioned the syllabicity of nearby resonants, that syllabicity will under certain circumstances survive before a vowel and thereby become phonemic early; thus, in Greek terms, **He-gʷl̥Het* > ἔβαλε 'threw' with the same '... αλε' which otherwise arises from '*... *ekt*][*l̥*]*e*' under *Sievers' Law* (see 7, p. 231). Possibly *i and *j, too, became distinct (... *io ... ≠ * ... *jo* ...) at an early time.

After a full-grade vowel and before a vowel, i.e. in an environment in which a simple *j is lost (cf. (b), p. 235), *jH > ι (e.g. -οια, preserved in Arcadian first-person singular optative ἐξελαύνοια 'may I drive out' < *-*ojHm̥*).

Phonology, Syllabicity, Word-end: Proto-Greek

Aside from their special treatment around laryngeals, the *syllabic nasals and liquids* (**n̥* ..., **r̥* ...) before consonants were still separately in existence in Proto-Greek; on the testimony of certain Homeric scansions they, on a par with *i[i] and *u[u], were the prosodic equivalents of short full-grade vowels. At the same time, the interior allophonics of **r̥*, **l̥* were fixed in some measure (cf. 7, p. 231; (d), p. 235): the dialects tend to agree on the segmentation, though not on the timbre, of the vowels or of the sequences of vowels and non-syllabic liquids, with which *$r̥$ and *$l̥$ ultimately merge (cf. **Phonology, Vowels**, p. 236). It is also likely that *[$e̥$] (see 7(e), p. 231) was on its way to merging with *i into ι (e.g. Aeolic πίσυρες 'four') in certain circumstances.

Although Mycenaean writing is ambiguous, it is best to assume that *word-final stops* were already lost (and that *$m^#$ went to *$n^#$) early in Proto-Greek though after the operation of *Osthoff's Law* (see **Phonology, Other Consonants**, p. 235), thereby imparting a well-defined canonic shape to Greek words and generating alternations like that between ἄνα (voc. sg.), ending-less, and ἄνακτ-(ος) etc. 'lord, king', and incidentally setting in motion the rearrangement of the thematic verb endings which in turn was mostly, though not entirely, Common Greek (see **Analogic Processes, Verbs**, p. 240; **Verb Paradigms: Non-past**, p. 254).

Phonology, Accent: Proto-Greek

Much of the lexical accentuation of Attic is Proto-Greek. It differs from Indo-European (cf. **Phonology: Indo-European**, 4, p. 231) in the *limitation* of the seat of the accent to the last three syllables, including the retracted (i.e. formerly enclitic) accentuation of finite verb forms in main clauses, and in the way in which further limitations are governed by the quantity of the vowels. These limitations operate on the word shapes as they exist before the contractions across *-s- > Ø-, *-j- > Ø, or (later) *-w- > Ø, and before the change ηα, ηο > εᾶ, εω (cf. **Phonology: Dialects**, p. 241). However, syllable weight, not vowel length, is what matters for *Wheeler's Law* whereby dactylically ending oxytones (~ ˘ ˊ) retract their accent to the penult. Otherwise, an accentuation which is neither oxytone nor maximally retracted is limited to a few suffixes (-ίσκος, -ίνδα, -αλέος, -τέος ...). Circumflex and acute are in contrast on diphthongs and long vowels of word-final syllables. Roughly, contractions at old morph boundaries and across lost laryngeals have the circumflex in any case. Contractions more recent than that (see **Phonology: Dialects**, p. 241) show a circumflex only when the first of the two contracted vowels had been accented; this is in keeping with grammarians' descriptions of the circumflex, and also with the retractions in monosyllabic neuters (σκῶρ 'excrement') and vocatives (Ζεῦ vs Ζεὺς (cf. πάτερ vs πατήρ 'father'; cf. 4, p. 231; (cf. (c), p. 235; p. 246) and testifies to the phonetic nature of the (earlier) accent distinction (see **Phonology: Indo-European**, 4, p. 231; **Distributional Gaps**, p. 232). Long vowels and diphthongs with no known history of contraction have mostly the acute (though ἐκποδών 'away' may show the true accentuation of the g.pl. ending, earlier **-όν, against analogical ποδῶν 'feet'; cf. **Alternations, Accent**, p. 239).

Phonology, Other Consonants: Proto-Greek

A good many consonant changes may well be Proto-Greek, sometimes with strong implications for a relative chronology. For example, the '*voiced aspirates*' (cf. **Phonology: Indo-European**, 8(a), 9, p. 231) are devoiced (*$*d^h$ > θ = [t^h] etc.).

Once devoiced, the aspirates lose their aspiration when the next syllable begins with another aspirate. Reduplications of the type *$*b^he$-b^h- *$*b^hi$-b^h- become π ... φ (πέφευγα 'I have fled', τίθημι 'place'). Sequences like *$*b^h$ ... d^h ... etc. become π ... θ ... (*$*b^hu$-n-d^h- > πυνθ(άνομαι) 'inquire'). This is the Greek version of *Grassmann's Law* (9, p. 231 and below). Voiceless aspirates and non-aspirates are neutralized in this environment, and epigraphic spellings like θυφλός alongside the standard τυφλός 'blind', as well as paradigmatically regularized orthographies like παύθητι 'let yourself be stopped!' (not **παύτηθι, cf. ἰ-θι 'go!') or χυθῆναι (cf. παυθῆναι, cp. χέ(F)ω 'pour') arise trivially, presence or absence of aspiration being a property of the entire sequence (cf. above).

*$*tt$ (see **Distributional Gaps**, p. 232) merges with *$*st$ into στ (possibly on the basis of an ancient IE isogloss), cf. Chapter 2, p. 40.

*$*tk(t\hat{k})$, d^hg^h ($d^h\hat{g}^h$), > κτ, χθ (τίκτω 'engender', χθών 'earth' (but see p. 232) and Chapter 2, p. 40.

$*-nsC$- (regardless of antecedent; cf. above) > -σC- ([H]ens tod > ἐς τό 'into the', *$*kent$-tos > κεστός 'pricked'; also σύ-ζυξ 'yoked together' for *$*σύν$-$ζυξ$, one of the indications for ζ = *sda* [zda]; cf. **Phonology: Indo-European**, 9, pp. 231ff.).

*$*\bar{V}nt$ and similar groups > ῦντ etc. (*Osthoff's Law*), prior to the loss of word-final consonants (see **Phonology, Syllabicity**, pp. 233–4) as exemplified by ... ηντ# > ... εν# in the third person plural of passive aorists.

More consequential is the way in which *$*s$ and *$*j$ are affected (see also above).

(a) *After a vowel before a consonant or word-end* ('in diphthong') they remain unchanged (but see **Phonology: Dialects**, p. 241).

(b) Still in Proto-Greek, both go to *h word-initially and between vowels.*
    The clusters which ultimately lead to either compensatory lengthening or gemination (cf. **Phonology: Dialects**, p. 241f.) may have reached a stage with -*h*- in Proto-Greek times.

(c) Apparently only *$*s$, not *$*j$, will suprasegmentally aspirate *a preceding word-initial* *#(H)V; εὕω 'scald' < *$*H_1ews$- but οὐ 'not' if < *$*H_2\acute{o}ju$ (its orthothone shape, a restressed οὐ replacing *οὖ? [cf. **Phonology, Accent**, p. 234]).

(d) *Loan words* already in existence in the Mycenaean texts (e.g. *asamito*; cf. **Foreign Influences**, p. 229), and other developments fill the gap and thereby establish the new *h* (= hiatus once *φερε + ι (3 sg.) had become φέρει (cf. **Verb Paradigms: Non-past**, p. 254, also **Phonology, Vowels**,

p. 237, **Analogic Processes, Verbs**, p. 240, **Phonology: Dialects**, p. 241) as distinct from *s*. The word for 'leek', borrowed by both Greek and Latin (*porrum*) from a source with some [r̥]-like sound, was introduced (πράσον) after the alternation of the old intervocalic **s* but before the disappearance of **r̥* as a short syllabic entity (cf. **Phonology, Syllabicity**, pp. 233f., **Alternations, Analogic Processes**, p. 238).

(e) The new *h* and the '*aspiration*' of stops (both prosodically zero) became associated with each other – a relationship that is further illustrated by the role of *h* in elision (ἐπ' + οὗ → ἐφ'οὗ 'upon which') as well as by its inclusion in *Grassmann's Law* (**seĝʰō > ἔχω* 'hold' but fut. ἕξω (cf. 9, p. 231, **Phonology, Other Consonants**, p. 235; no such cases with **#[H]j- > 0* – or with **#[H]u- > ὑ* [see (g)] seem to be known). The aspiration in **ksn, ksm* is post-Mycenaean (cf. Myc. *aiksma* αἰχμά, 'point of spear'.

(f) Inside some other *triple clusters*, **-s-* for some time > 0 (**H₁r̥ĝjō > *H₁r̥sdō = '*ἔρζω'*, (see 9, p. 231, and below) > ἔρδω 'do').

(g) *Word-initially *#sr-, *#wr- > ρ̇-*; in context, for example, in compounds and after the augment, and to an extent in scansion, there is gemination (ἔρρει from ῥέω 'flow', IE **sr-*). At the beginning of words, **#(H)u- > *#ὑ-*, and possibly also **#r- > *#ρ̇- (*#ῥέζω 'dye': Skt raj-*), in which case every 'prothetic' *#ἐρ-* etc. < **#H₁r̥-* etc.; see **Phonology: Laryngeals**, p. 233.

Non-syllabic *-j- after consonant and before vowel undergoes changes which contribute to the complete elimination of **j* from the inventory: after labials, **-j-* merges with τ (τύπτω 'strike'); **k̂j, *ĝʰj, *kj, *gʰj, *kʷj, *gʷʰj*, yield a long consonantal entity written variously as σσ and in other ways (e.g. ττ in Attic and Boeotian), simplified to σ (or τ) at the beginning of words; **ĝj, *gj, *gʷj*, and also **dj > ζ* (cf. 9, pp. 231f.; and (f) above), **tj, *dʰj*, and similarly **ts*, > σσ (> (-)σ- after long vowels, diphthongs, and consonants and word-initially in some dialects; generally in Attic, etc.).

Phonology, Vowels: Proto-Greek (and earlier)

The full-grade vowels (see **Phonology: Indo-European**, 5, p. 231), the syllabic allophones of the laryngeals as well as '*schwa secundum*' (see 7(d), (e)), which merge with them, and **i, *u* constitute the five *short vowels* of Proto-Greek; shortly thereafter, **n̥, *m̥* before consonants > α (or > o, according to dialect ?), and **r̥, *l̥ > αρ, αλ* (oρ, oλ) after heavy syllables, ρα λα (ρο λο) after light syllables before consonants. Subphonemically, **u* is fronted to [y] though some dialects, like Boeotian, lag behind. Aside from minor local alterations, this part of the system remains stable.

To the five short vowels correspond five *long* ones going back to:

(a) the old *lengthened grade* vowels (see **Phonology: Indo-European**, 6, p. 231),

(b) ῑ and ῡ in ὗς etc. (see 6, p. 231),

(c) vowels *contracted* either across morph boundaries or after the disappearance of intervocalic laryngeals (see **Phonology, Laryngeals**, p. 233),

(d) vowels followed by *syllable-final laryngeals* (see **Phonology, Laryngeals**, p. 233), and

(e) long vowels emerging in situations in which *syllabic nasals and liquids were followed by laryngeals*. The set that results, mostly Proto-Greek, is ᾱ, η(=[ε:]), ῑ, ω (=[ɔ:]), ῡ (the latter largely =[y:]; see above). In Ionic, after the borrowing of Old Persian *māda-* ('Μῆδοι') as well as after certain compensatory lengthenings (see below) and contractions (χώρη 'country', gen. χώρης; ἐμίηνα aorist of μιαίνω 'pollute'), *ᾱ is raised toward η < *ē, though it does not at first merge with it. However, after ε, ι and ρ, Attic merges *ᾱ with some compensatory lengthening and contraction products (χώρᾱ, ἐμίᾱνα; χώρᾱς is both genitive singular and accusative plural). This split-off precedes the loss of ϝ in Att. κόρη < *κόρϝᾱ.

Compensatory lengthenings of all kinds (p. 242) create new occurrences of these long vowels, sometimes in environments in which the latter do not or do no longer occur. In certain dialects, e.g. in Ionic-Attic and in 'mild' Doric, ε and ο are, however, lengthened to new long, higher-mid (rather than lower mid) vowels, written 'spuriously,' EI and OY in the 'Ionic' alphabet: ἔμεινα < *-ens-, Μοῦσα < *-ontj- (see below and **Phonology: Dialects**, p. 241).

The occurrences of *hiatus* that may still exist in Mycenaean (cf. (b), p. 235; **Analogic Processes, Verbs**, p. 240; **Phonology: Dialects**, p. 242) are elsewhere frequently contracted into vowels and diphthongs, according to local rules. In Ionic-Attic, the sequences ηα and ηο, if not contracted, are changed to εᾱ, εω; as πόλεως < πόληος shows, the word accent is no longer adjusted to the new shape (see **Phonology, Accent**, p. 234). The most recent of these hiatuses – the ones created by the loss of ϝ (cf. (a), p. 242 – tend to be contracted later or never (hence, in Attic, γένους < -eso- but ἡδέος < -ewo-). Of the inherited *diphthongs*, '*ei*' (i.e. *ej*), *ew*, *oj*, *ow* etc., *ει, ου are monopthongized to [e:], [o:] in time for merger with the 'spurious' ει, ου (which never were diphthongal; cf. above); 'ου' of both kinds was then raised to [u:], presumably after Indo-European/Proto-Greek *ū had gone to [y:] (see below; special developments in Boeotian and other dialects are here left out of account).

The *accent* of the newly contracted vowels and diphthongs in word-final syllables is set by the accentuation of the antecedent form: x́+ x > x̂, x + x́ > x́ (*εὐγενέ[s]ι > εὐγενεῖ, *πλόϝος > πλοῦς, *ἑσταϝός > ἑστώς (cf. **Phonology, Accent**, p. 234); παϝίδων > παίδων not **παιδῶν as in monosyllabic stems)). A corresponding rule may be recognized for compensatory lengthenings (see p. 237) if πᾶς, εἷς represent the true phonological outcome.

Alternations, Analogic Processes: Proto-Greek

Certain survivals in Greek metrical practice notwithstanding, *words* with their proclitic and enclitic appendages, and to a much lesser degree stems in compounds, stand out as fundamental phonological units. The word is the domain of the (high) accent, at least as written in standard orthography from Hellenistic times on; elision has replaced contraction at the seam, which keeps vocalic (*#HV-?*) word-beginnings intact (cf. **Phonology, Laryngeals**, pp. 232–3); word-beginning and word-end quite routinely function as conditioners of sound change (above, *passim*) – largely no doubt through analogical generalization from the treatment after and before a genuine 'pause'. Sentence sandhi variants, mostly generalized one way or the other, live on feebly in the case of ἐς 'into' (proclitic), -ος, -ας – originally in order before *#C-* (non-laryngeal) – vs ἐνς εἰς, -ονς -ους, -ανς -ᾱς (acc. pl.; the (proclitic) 'article' showing traces of the original distribution), etc. – originally before *#(H)V-*. In Declensional forms like πόλιν 'city', (acc.) [in] < [im] (rather than the expected [ja] < [i̯m̥]), may well be taken as */jm/ with the resonant allophones that are appropriate when *#(H)V-* follows in context; and the accusative singular ending -αν (Cyprian *ijateran* ἰατῆρα, physician', Thessalian κίοναν 'column') as the erstwhile Sievers variant of *m̥ before vowel respectively (see 7, p. 231). These cases may well have had an analogical assist from the -ον, ᾱν of the thematic paradigms (but see also p. 245 on 'first declension' accusatives themselves).

Surviving instances of prehistoric contraction at the compounding seam were reinterpreted, in terms of the new device of elision (see **Phonology, Laryngeals**, p. 233) as compositional *lengthening* (ὁμώνυμος → ὁμ'ώνυμος 'like-named' hence also ἀν-ώνυμος 'nameless'). Other morphological lengthenings (aside from the lengthened ablaut grade (cf. 6, p. 231)) remain odd: in comparatives and superlatives, -ώτερος -ώτατος appears instead of -ότ- if the preceding syllable is light (see **Phonology: Dialects**, p. 242 on στενότερος), and some 'primary' comparatives lengthen their root vowel in Ionic-Attic after the sound change ᾱ > η and after the coming into being of the spurious diphthongs: ἆσσον 'nearer', μείζων 'larger'.

If in some forms of a paradigm a process has eliminated or *de-aspirated* the second of two aspirates, the Grassmann effect (cf. **Phonology, Other Consonants**, p. 235, with data on analogical orthographies in the wake of Grassmann's Law), on the first is cancelled. This results in alternations like θᾶσσων 'more swift' vs ταχύς 'swift', θρίξ vs τριχός; also, ἕξω vs ἔχω (see (e), p. 236).

Alternations, Accent: Proto-Greek

The retracted accentuation of finite verb forms reflects the superimposition of the limitation of the word accent to the last three syllables (see **Phonology, Accent**, p. 234) upon the inherited enclisis which is preserved in paradigms with forms that are sufficiently short, that is, in the verb 'to be' and in φημί 'say'. More recent contractions in verb forms – mostly across *-j- > ∅ – occur after the retracted accent is already fixed (τιμῶμεν). The basic columnarity – the principle whereby the accent stays on the same syllable – in nouns and adjectives set by the masculine nominative singular (except for the retention of accent alternation in monosyllables (πούς ποδός, but also ποδί, in contradiction to the most archaic accentuation seen in Sk. loc. *dyávi'*)), is in part inherited. Here again the recent contractions come later: χωρῶν < *χωρέων < *χωρήων < *χωρά[s]ων, g. pl. of χώρα. However, the contrast of acute in the nominative and accusative against circumflex in the true oblique cases remains alive and productive as witness the analogical accusative λεχώ (instead of **λεχῶ < *λεχόjṃ) and the likewise analogical compensatorily lengthened ἀδούς and the accusative plural forms in -ούς -ᾱς on the one hand; and ποδῶν vs ἐκποδών (see **Phonology, Accent**, p. 234) on the other. The original accent perhaps survives in πᾶς 'all' and εἷς 'one'.

Analogic Processes, Nouns and Adjectives: Proto-Greek

Greek paradigms of all varieties are greatly affected by allomorph loss (*levelling*). This is particularly pronounced in the non-thematic noun and adjective paradigms which retain only traces of the rich inherited diversification by ablaut and accent. Such traces may for instance be seen in the declension of πατήρ (the allomorphs are πατήρ 'father', πατρ'-, πάτερ, πατρά-), ἀρήν 'lamb'. Two opposing forces determine the direction of the levelling: something like:

the *columnar* principle (see **Alternations, Accent**) is visible, for instance, in the instances where the lengthened grade appropriate to the nominative singular is carried through (μνηστήρ 'suitor' → μνηστῆρος, μνηστῆρσιν; ἀγών 'contest' → ἀγῶνος).

But then, *conditioned sound change* has the effect of:

(a) lining up the *sigmatic* nominative singular and 'dative' (see p. 244; p. 247) plural and their inherited or analogically restored sibilant endings against the other case forms and their lucid vocalic endings, and of

(b) exposing the *endingless* variety of the animate nominative singular as well as the endingless vocatives (unless indeed eliminated and replaced by nominatives) and neuters to the loss or alteration of word-final consonants.

These conditions operate in favour of the prevocalic stem being generalized, at least as long as the other allomorph remains phonologically excluded before σ, ς or at word-end. In Mycenaean, the dative of the numeral 'one' is still (*h*)*eme* (< *sem-*), with the neuter > ἕν (**Phonology, Syllabicity**, p. 234); as against ἑν-(ί) elsewhere. In general, the analogical changes affecting noun and adjective declension may be classified into those which serve to make forms in paradigms more uniform (such as the Attic replacement of dative plural -ασι < -ησι by such forms as δαίμοσι 'divine powers'), and those that make different paradigms more uniform.

Analogic Processes, Verbs: Proto-Greek

Verbs may be classified by the allomorphic relationship that exists among their stem forms. Where the present stem differs from the general verb stem ('impure' verbs), the alternations mostly reflect the conditioned *sound changes affecting *j*. Analogic regularization is prominent in contexts where the intervocalic *s of the aorist and the future, as in ἔλῡσα 'freed', λύσω, was restored ((*γεύσ-ω (pres.) > γεύω 'give a taste': (*ἔγευσσα >) ἔγευσα (cf. **Distributional Gaps**, p. 232) :: λύω : ἔλῡσα), or in the replacement of -είω (preserved in Elis; < -έϝjω) by -εύω (ἔγευσα (ἔλῡσα) : γεύω (λύω) :: ἐβασίλευσα : βασιλεύω 'am king'), where the dominance of the general over the present stem is altogether characteristic.

Another typical concatenation of sound change with analogic change, pre-Mycenaean but subsequent to the *loss of word-final -t* (**Phonology, Syllabicity**, p. 234) in ἔφερε(*t*) may explain the active primary endings in thematic paradigms (see **Phonology, Other Consonants** (b) (d), pp. 235ff.; **Verb Paradigms: Non-past**, p. 254).

An example of still another kind of analogic action is seen at work in the verb *'to be'*, where, though generally a high degree of allomorphy is retained, the smooth breathing of ἔστι replaces an expected rough breathing in εἶ (cf. **Distributional Gaps**, p. 232), εἰσί (< *s-enti), etc.

Dialects

As indicated, many developments belong to the several dialects which begin with second-millennium Mycenaean (recorded in the difficult Linear B syllabary) and with the evidence from epic scansion and diction. They are then attested in rich but uneven profusion, both in inscriptions that are written alphabetically (except in Cyprus) in the Greek states and, to an extent, in stylized literary usage. They largely (but not entirely) end with the spread of the Attic *Koiné* in Hellenistic times. The archaic picture is dominated by a twofold division:

1 South Greek, that is, *Mycenaean* (which became extinct) and, in later terms, *Arcado-Cyprian* and *Ionic-Attic*: and

2 the rest, giving rise to *Aeolic* on the one hand and *Doric-North-west* Greek on the other hand. It is difficult to distinguish tentative Proto-Greek reconstructions from the effects of contact among dialects already established.

Phonology: Dialects

In the area of sound change the dialects exhibit some sweeping transformations.

According to the grammarians' statement, as well as to their practice when dealing with texts, word accent becomes generally retracted, hence non-distinctive, in literary Lesbian *Aeolic*. In *Doric*, too, there are modifications.

The *labiovelars*, preserved as such in Mycenaean and indirectly, in one faint trace, in Arcadian, have elsewhere merged with the labials, except that before front vowels they were palatalized into dentals in the non-Aeolic dialects (though the details are not always clear).

The phoneme *h of whichever origin may be considered as having been preserved though not written in Mycenaean, but between vowels it was not in contrast with Ø (hiatus; see **Phonology, Other Consonants** (b) (d), p. 235f.; **Phonology, Vowels**, p. 237). At word beginning this *h* (<ʿ>) is extant as a prosodic feature in many dialects, including Attic whereas it is merged with zero in the many 'psilotic' ones; the aspiration of stops (θ φ χ) is not affected. In the interior of words this loss becomes general.

Word-internal *hiatus* is progressively eliminated through vowel contraction.

Three processes have particular importance for the dialect structure of Greek.

One is the change from *-t(^{h})i- to -si- which is South Greek and thus shared by Mycenaean, Arcadian and Ionic-Attic (e.g. τίθησι 'places', λέγονσι 'they say' > λέγουσι, Myc. *korisio* 'Corinthian', with exceptions that remain unclear).

The other concerns an extensive class of consonant clusters in occurrence before vowels. These sequences lead to *geminate* liquids and nasals in Lesbian and Thessalian Aeolic but to single liquids and nasals with *compensatory lengthening* of preceding short vowels elsewhere; in this way syllabic prosody (length) is preserved in both blocs. The clusters in question are *sr (> ρρ), *sl (> λλ), *sn, *ns (> νν) (in non-psilotic dialects with aspiration on a preceding word-initial vowel; on *-n̥s- see **Phonology, Laryngeals**, p. 233); *-rj- > -ρρ-, *-nj- (as well as *-mj- > *-nj-) > -νν- (and *-wj- > *-j- ?) after *e, *i, *u, while *-arj-, *-anj-, *-amj-, *-orj-, *-onj-, *-omj- (including *-r̥j-, *-n̥j-, *-m̥j-) > αιρ, αιν, οιρ, οιν respectively; *-awj- seems to merge with *-ajw- into -αι(F)- and ultimately Att. ā (Hom. αἰετός 'eagle', Att. ἆετός (but *-lj- remains apart: > -λλ-, except in Cyprus where *-alj- > -αιλ-). The clusters *-sw- and *-ws- (?; see εὔω **Phonology, Other Consonants**, (c), p. 235) are treated like *-sn-, *-ns- (Proto-Gk *naswos 'temple' > Lesbian ναῦος [i.e. -FF-], Lac. νᾱFός, Ion. νηός, Att. νεώς), *-sj- and *-js- apparently in part like -jH- (cf. **Phonology, Laryngeals**, p. 232). Clusters like *-ntj- gave rise to a new -νσ-, which, along with word-final -νς, when retained or restored earlier (cf. **Phonology, Other Consonants**, p. 235; **Alternations, Analogic Processes**, p. 238; see also **Distributional Gaps**, p. 232), remained in being (πάνσα 'all') in Arcadian, Central Cretan, Argive, Thessalian (and possibly Mycenaean) went to -ισ- (παῖσα) in Lesbian and in Cyrenaean, and to 0 with compensatory lengthening (see **Phonology, Vowels**, p. 237) elsewhere, including in Ionic-Attic. Third, w (F) is lost (> Ø) *before vowel* at different times in different dialects (modern Tsakonian preserves it): (a) *intervocalically* (still Myc. *newos*, Cyprian νεϜο- 'νέος'; (b) *after liquid or nasal* (extant in some dialects; lost in Ionic and in some Doric dialects with, elsewhere without, compensatory lengthening of the preceding vowel, (see **Phonology, Vowels**, p. 237) – but it was still intact when *-*rwā* > -ρη in Att. κόρη and when *VCCoteros* → VCότερος (rather than -ώτερος: στενϜότερος 'narrower' > στενότερος, like μεστότερος 'fuller'); see **Alternations, Analogic Processes**, p. 238); and more resistant; (c) initially, except that it was lost in Ionic-Attic (also, #Ϝρ- widely > #ῥ-). It is, however, recognizable by its metrical effects in Homer, and by the failure of certain vowel contractions to take place (see **Phonology, Vowels**, p. 237). Besides, *tw > (σ)σ, (τ)τ, and *k̂w > ππ.

The Ionic-Attic addition of the movable -ν to certain suffixes (-ε[ν], -σι[ν], -θε[ν]), whatever its origin, is not a phonological matter.)

Morphology

Both in *nouns* (and adjectives) and in *verbs*, non-thematic and thematic formations are to be distinguished. The latter are characterized by the presence of an -o/ε-, preceding, and frequently somehow amalgamated with, the inflectional endings. Except for some uncertain traces, thematic conjugation fixes one particular ablaut shape of the stem for the whole paradigm. In a non-thematic paradigm, on the other hand, the stem is in principle subject to gradation. In nouns and adjectives the masculine and neuter o-stems of the second declensions are thematic; the ā/η/ja-stems of the 'first' declension, non-thematic in early IE times prior to the destruction of the laryngeals, were assimilated in several respects to the o-stems, which they provide with parallel feminine paradigms. There is a tendency for the thematic inflections to increase in number; most productive formations are thematic.

Some *pronouns* other than the personal pronouns are thematic in this wider sense (that is, incorporating the first-declension paradigms) – a state of affairs which has facilitated the analogical intrusion of specifically pronominal case endings into thematic noun and adjective paradigms.

Morphology: Noun and Adjective Derivation

Greek has inherited four IE derivational processes for nouns and adjectives, namely *compounding, suffixation, reduplication* and *accent shift* (as when agents (τομός 'cutting') are distinguished by oxytonesis from objects (τόμος 'slice')).

Etymologically, some derivational suffixes are *grammaticalized* from second members of compounds, as in Hom. λυσσώδης 'furious' (built on the likes of θυ-ώδης '*having* the odour (cf. Lat. *odōs*) of incense' – an example of the most common type of compound, *possessive* (or *bahuvrīhi*: see Chapter 4, p. 121; for hypostases, see **Syntax: Trends**, p. 257), though in Greek associated directly with the verb ὄδωδα 'smell'). This works well because synchronically, both compounds and words derived by suffix are overwhelmingly *exocentric*. Examples of endocentric, that is, purely determinative compounds where the meaning of the first member merely narrows down that of the second, are rare and technical in nature, though a few are ancient (e.g. προ-πάτωρ 'forefather'). Suffixes, too, are rarely endocentric; diminutives, for instance, are not yet well established in ancient Greek and are likely to show their exocentric origins (cf. -ίσκος with its English cognate, -*ish*).

Moreover, there prevails a state of quasi-complementarity between compounds and derivatives in the sense that only *primitive* (βαθύ-ζωνος 'deep-girded') adjectives, but not suffixed ones, may function as underlying attributes in compounds (only Hom. θεο-(ειδής) 'having a god's appearance', not **θειο-(ειδής) 'having divine appearance'). Noun and adjectives are built either directly on verb roots ('*primary*') or on existing noun or adjective stems ('*secondary*') that may themselves be derived from roots in turn. It is worth noting that the two comparative and superlative formations are quite different in this respect: while the forms in -ίων (-ων), -ιστος are primary and at best coexist with adjectives based on the same root, those in -τερος, -τατος are derived from adjectives.

An inherited paradigmatic relationship obtains among the *Caland suffixes*: the comparatives and superlatives in -ίων (-*jων*), -ιστος just mentioned are associated with adjectives in -ρός (-ι- in compounds) or -ύς, adverbs in -α, neuters in -ος with adjectival compounds in -ης (ταχύς 'swift', θάσσων τάχιστος; τάχος n. 'swiftness' τάχα 'swiftly'; κῡδρός 'famed', κῡδι-άνειρα 'famous', κῦδος 'fame', n. ἐρι-κῡδής 'glorious', κῡδίων (comp.), κῡδιστος (superl.), κρατύς 'strong', κάρτα, κράτος κρέσσων, κράτιστος). In the Greek period, adjectives in -νος, -ιμος, -αλέος, -εδ(α)νός are added to the list.

Declensional Endings

Since IE times, nouns, adjectives, and pronouns are *inflected* for number (singular, plural, dual) and case. With this framework there intersects the further distinction of gender (animate – that is, masculine and feminine – and neuter) which is semi-*derivational* in nature. These distinctions are defined syntactically. Of an agglutinating structure in which the endings for case and for number are separately segmented there are only the barest hints, and these are disparate: while the animate accusative plural ending *-ns*, -ης suggests, for a remote IE antiquity, the sequence *-m* 'accusative' + *-s* 'plural', the creation in Aeolic, of a new dative plural, (πόδες 'feet':) πόδεσσι (cf. p. 247) after (φίλοι 'friends':) φίλοισι constitutes a much later analogical process implying the reverse order, 'plural' + 'dative'.

Paradigm classes ('*declensions*') differ chiefly (a) because of conditioned *sound changes* (thus, -ν (< *-m) after vowel in λόγο-ν alternates with -α (< *-m̥) after consonant in πόδ-α; (b) because of case *syncretism* combined with the redistribution of suffixes as allomorphs ('dative' sg. λόγωι 'word' < early IE dat. *logo-* + -ej (by an ancient contraction) but 'dative' sg. ποδ-ί < locative *pod-i*); and (c) because of the invasion of noun and adjective paradigms by *pronominal* endings and vice versa (see **Pronouns**, p. 248).

As for the IE inflections for nouns and adjectives see Table 2.10 in Chapter 2, p. 60f.

Noun and Adjective Paradigms: Syncretism

Case syncretism begins in Proto-Greek. The *instrumental* is separately maintained in Mycenaean though written unambiguously in the plural only (*anijapi* ἀνίᾱφι 'with reins', *popi* ποδ-φί (ποπ-φί) 'with the feet'). Aside from this, the earlier *locative*, *dative*, and *instrumental* merge into the Greek 'dative', where the surviving endings, one each for each position in the paradigm, may be those of the earlier locative, or of the dative, or of the instrumental. Similarly, *ablative* (case of 'separation') and *genitive* merge into the new 'genitive' (cf. **Syntax: Trends**, p. 257). The old meanings are recoverable from the distinctions observed in traditional case syntax ('dative of time or place' vs 'indirect object' vs 'instrumental dative'; 'genitive of separation' vs 'attributive genitive', etc.) in so far as these are not merely translational devices.

Noun and Adjective Paradigms: *o*-stems

The *thematic* vowel of the *e/o*-stems ('*second declension*') is -ε- in the vocative singular and anciently in the nominative/accusative/vocative neuter plural; otherwise -o-. The accentuation is columnar (cf. **Alternations, Accent**, p. 239), except for the isolated vocative singular ἄδελφε (see **Phonology: Indo-European**, 4, p. 231). 'Contract' nouns (νοῦς < *νόϜος) and the so-called 'Attic' (i.e., non-Hellenistic) type (ἵλεως) result from late contraction and the treatment of ᾱϜο > ηο respectively, with minor analogical adjustments.

The genitive singular goes back in part to *-o-so* > 'spurious' -ου and its equivalents in the non-Attic dialects, an intrusion from the interrogative pronouns, and in part to *-o-sjo* > -οιο (Myc. *-ojo*), Thessalian (and, alongside -οο = -ου, in Homer), at home, perhaps, in the demonstratives. On the dative singular in -ωι see **Distributional Gaps**, p. 232; in Arcadian, Boeotian etc., the old locative (as in the isolated Attic οἴκοι > *-o + i*) does duty for the 'dative'.

The nominative plural ends in an -οι of pronominal provenience; cf. the 'dative', below. The accusative plural in *-ons* is retained as -ονς in the

Argolid and in Crete, as -οις in Lesbos, and elsewhere as -ως and as -ους, as in Attic. In the nominative/accusative/vocative neuter $*-e-H_2$ is replaced by the -α of the 'third declension'. The genitive plural ends in $*-o-om$ > -ων (Cyprian -ω is obscure) with an IE contraction. 'Dative' plural functions either as an old pronominal locative (with -οι for $*-su$) in the Mycenaean dative-locative '-o-i' = oi(h)i (e.g. 'te-o-i' = theoihi), Lesbian, Old Attic, Homeric etc. -οισι with the intervocalic -s- analogically restored; or as a pronominal instrumental form, Myc. instr. '-o' = -ois (e.g. ku-ru-so = khrusois 'golden'). Similarly, elsewhere -οις, < $*-\bar{o}js$ < $*-o$ + ojs (though Lesbian τοῖς in τοῖς θεοῖσι could be a truncated proclitic locative).

The dual, where it survives (see **Syntax: Trends**, p. 257), ends in -ω, probably < $*-o-H_1$ (inherited at least in the masculine) for the nominative/accusative/vocative, and in Hom. -οιιν (< $*-oisin$?), Arcadian -οιυν, generally > -οιν for the genitive/'dative'.

Noun and Adjective Paradigms: $*\bar{a}$-stems

In the $*\bar{a}$-stems ('*first declension*') an originally derivational H_2 has become amalgamated with preceding and following affixes to form a set of inflectional endings.

The nominative singular feminine -ᾱ, -ῆ (see (e), p. 237) represents $*e-H_2-0$, and -α (-jα, -ια – these variants partly governed by Sievers' Law; see 7, p. 231) < $*-jH_2-0$. The masculines have -ς (νεᾱνίᾱς etc.), analogically from the o-stems. In the accusative singular, -ᾱν, -ην < $*-eH_2-\underset{\circ}{m}$ (generalized from occurrence before a word-initial #(H)V-), and (f.) -αν (-jαν, -ιαν) < $*-jH_2-\underset{\circ}{m}$ (?; cf. **Alternations, Analogic Processes**, p. 238). There are sporadic vocatives in -α: νύμφα 'bride' (Hom.), Att. στρατιῶτα 'soldier', perhaps likewise < $*-eH_2$ when before *#(H)V-; on the accent of δέσποτα etc. see 4, p. 231. The genitive -ᾱς, -ης etc. of the feminines, and rarely for masculines, is best reconstructed as $*-(j)eH_2-s$, with a circumflex accent of possibly analogical origin when accented. More commonly, the masculines have endings transferred from the o-stems: Homeric-Aeolic and Boeotian -ᾱ-ο, Dor. etc. -ᾱ, Ion. -ηο > -εω. In Attic, the analogy, say, στρατηγῶν ('generals (gen. pl.)'): στρατηγοῦ (gen. sg.) :: δικαστῶν 'judges': x has produced the type δικαστοῦ, and further, with appropriate accentuation, πολίτου. The 'dative' (j)ᾱι, -(j)ηι (with Attic -ηι rather than -ει to keep the paradigm orthographically uniform) is < $-(j)-eH_2-ej$; dialects in which o-stems have the old locative -οι as a 'dative' show the locative form -αι, < $*H_2-i$.

The nominative/vocative plural -αι counterpart to the -οι of the o-stems (see p. 245). The accusative plural too, is patterned on the $*-ons$ of the o-stems: Proto-Greek $*(j)-\bar{a}ns$ > $*(j)-ανς$ in Arcadian, Cret. -(j)ανς, Lesbian -(j)αις, Ion.-Att. etc. (j)-ᾱς. The genitive plural, Hom.-Aeolic -(j)άων and Myc. -a-o, Dor. etc. (j)ᾱν, Ion. -(j)έων, Att. -ῶν with accent fixed – except in the adjectives where the accentuation is made uniformly columnar for all three genders – due to the contraction across *s > 0, has the original pronominal ending (Proto-Gk *-$āsōn$). In the 'dative' the foundation is IE *-(j)-eH_2-su, with Gk -οι for *-su, hence Myc. -$ā(hi)$, OAtt., Cret. -$āσι$ (and OAtt. -ησι), with analogically restored -σ-, and then, in further parallelism to the o-stems, -αισι, -αις (see p. 245). True to the non-thematic background of the ā-stems, there is a Mycenaean instrumental, *a-ni-j a-pi* (see p. 244).

The nominative/accusative/vocative dual is at first -ω (Myc. *to-pe-zo* = τορπέζω 'τραπέζᾱ'; Att. μεγάλω 'great (f.)', then -ᾱ (so even in Ionic-Attic!) in analogy to the o-stems. The same relationship exists, *mutatis mutandis*, for the genitive/'dative' (Myc. *wa-na-so-i* 'kings' = Ϝανάσσουν but Att. δραχμαῖν 'drachmas' and Arcadian κράναιυν 'sources').

Noun and Adjective Paradigms: 'Third Declension'

Non-thematic ('*third declension*') nouns and adjectives include stems ending in stops, in -σ-, in ν and Mycenaean -m-, in -ι-, -υ-, -ῡ-, as well as certain heteroclitic nouns. There is much less Greek innovation and Greek productivity here than in the other two 'declensions'. Paradigms have been elaborately and usefully classified according to their accentual behaviour (Rix 1976: 123–4) which represents in-between states between an anciently ablauting and accent-alternating condition on the one hand and the accomplished columnar principle on the other. Monosyllables have retained the alternating accent.

The nominative singular masculine and feminine is of two kinds which may have been very anciently related to one another by a sound change: (a) zero ending with lengthened grade of the final vowel, that is, η or ω in correlation with the accentual type (εὐμενής 'well-disposed', πατήρ; τέκτων 'carpenter'); and (b) ending -ς with antedesinential ablaut variants, again in some relationship to accentuation but with some analogical obscuration. The accusative singular masculine and feminine ending is *-m > -ν after vowels, and, automatically, *-$m̥$ > -α(-αν) after consonants (see 7, p. 231). The vocative singular masculine and feminine, where it has a special form, is endingless (with replacement of the o-grade by the zero grade where the nominative singular has that grade) and may show a retracted accent: πάτερ, μάντι 'seer', ἄνα (with -κτ# > Ø#). The nominative/accusative/vocative singular neuter is endingless as in Indo-European, often with final zero grade (μέλι with -τ# > Ø#, etc.). In the genitive singular, Greek has generalized the ablaut variant -ος. Generally in the oblique cases lengthened-grade or full-grade stem forms intrude; the old zero grade is in retreat (πατρός, χειρός 'hand' < *$ĝʰesrós$, κυνός 'dog', Att. οἰός 'sheep' < *$Howjós$ etc.). The 'dative' singular in -ι is one of the two old locative forms (the other is -0, surviving in such adverbs as αἰέν, αἰές), no longer with full grade in the stem and the zero-grade ending properly unaccented (αἰεί 'always' ἀεί, with acute,

Att. ᾶ may be * < αἰϝεϛ-ί. In Cor. Cyprian ΔιϝεΙ the true dative ending is preserved. In Mycenaean (though not in Mycenae itself) this ending is in normal use for the dative-locative of all classes (*di-we*) except that the *s*-stems show the common *-i* (*we-te-i* ϝέτει 'year').

The nominative/vocative plural masculine and feminine ends in -εϛ, with analogical adjustments in the stem allomorphs which are in part already Indo-European. The accusative plural masculine and feminine ending is *-ns*, *-n̥s*, originally with zero grade on the stem suffix though in Greek full grade (Hom. ἀνέρας) spreads. The nominative/accusative/vocative neuter has generally $-H_2$ > -α (e.g. Hom. γένεα, Att. γένη < $*ĝenH_1esH_2$); whether the type ὕδωρ 'water', an old 'collective' neuter for stems in -*s*, -*n*, and -*r*, is linked to $-H_2$ by a prehistoric sound change is uncertain. The genitive plural ending is *-ōm* (earlier *-om*) with transfer from the *-o-om* > *-ōm* of the *o*-stems; the stem shape is usually that of the genitive singular. The 'dative' plural has the locative ending -οι for *-su* in analogy to singular -ι and to instrumental plural -φι (?); survivals of the original zero grade in the stem include φρασί (< ... n̥ ...), and πατράσι (with accent according to *Wheeler's Law* (see **Phonology, Accent**, p. 234) after *r̥ > ρα). In North-western Greek, -οιϛ is imported from the thematic declension (πάντοιϛ); on -εσσι see **Declensional Endings**, p. 244. These innovations have the advantage of eliminating the effects of the conditioned sound changes affecting *s*-clusters. The instrumental plural in -φι functions as instrumental (and locative) in Mycenaean where it is clearly distinct from the dative(-locative); this is not true of the (artificial) Homeric use (and probably also the Boeotian use in ἐπιπατρόφιον 'patronymic') of -φι as a general oblique not restricted to the plural.

The nominative/accusative/vocative dual masculine and feminine ends in -ε < $*-H_1$; the stem allomorph is that found in the n.pl. The neuter ὄσσε 'eyes' (< $*H_3ek^wjH_1$) shows the inherited *-jH_1*; in other words the masculine and feminine -ε has replaced it. In the oblique dual cases, the thematic -οιν, -οιν has taken over.

Pronouns

The Greek *personal* pronouns contain a core of inherited forms, sometimes enlarged by enclitic particles and modified in other ways. The important elements in the core are first-person singular nominative: ἐγώ < $*(H_1)eĝoH_2$, ἐγών < $*(H_1)eĝH_2-om$; enclitic accusative με < *me*; genitive Hom. μευ, Att. μου, that is, an innovated *me-so* with the ending of the interrogative pronoun; 'dative' μοι < *moj*. Second-person singular nominative: $*tuH_2$ > Hom., Dor. τύ-νη, Ion.-Att. σύ with σ- from the accusative, and $-H_2^{\#}$ > $-\emptyset^{\#}$ by generalization from antevocalic sentence context; in the accusative, *te* competes with *twe*, the latter > σε; the 'datives' τοι and σοι are self-explanatory. First-person plural nominative: $*(H)n̥s-mes$ > Dor. ἁμέϛ,

Lesbian ἄμμες, *(H)n̥s-me-es (?) > Att. ἡμεῖς (see **Phonology, Laryngeals**, p. 233); accusative *(H)n̥s-me > Dor. ἁμές, Lesbian ἄμμε, Hom. ἡμέ-ας, Att. ἡμεῖς (similarly, gen. ἡμέων etc.). The second-person plural forms have analogous explanations, starting, perhaps, from *(H)us- so as to account for Lesbian ὔμμες, Att. ὑμεῖς etc. The antecedents of the dual forms, Att. νώ νῶιν, σφώ σφῶιν are uncertain. The reflexive pronouns (also anaphoric) accusative Fhε (Pamphylian), Lesbian Fε, Hom., Att. ἕ, gen. Att. οὗ, 'dat.' Att. οἷ go back to *sw-. The forms in σφ- (centring around σφι ?) are quite obscure. (Possessive pronouns are either thematized (-o-, -eH₂) or derived by -tero/eH₂ from the personal pronouns, hence Att. σός, ἡμέτερος.)

The other pronouns show many of the pronominal endings (cf. **Declensional Endings** (c), pp. 243f.). The *demonstrative* ὁ ἡ τό (< *so, *seH₂, *tod – the neuter ending is -d > 0 as in ὅ, ἐκεῖνο) with its anomalies is ancient (especially the suppletion between t- and the endingless so in the nominative singular masculine – perhaps a connective particle reinterpreted; in Att. (ἦν δ') ὅς this has been normalized). Particularly striking is the fact that the genitive plural Doric τᾶν (Att. τῶν) tallies exactly with Sanskrit tāsām (*tāsōm). The genitive plural masculine is assimilated, like much else in the paradigm, to the nouns and adjectives but had at one time been *tojsōm; the -oj- recurs in the nominative plural masculine. When ὁ ἡ τό becomes the 'definite article' (see **Syntax: Trends**, p. 257) it is replaced by composites (ὅδε, ὄνε, τῶννι, τόνυ; οὗτος) of varying opacity. There is, however, the stem of Latin is surviving in Cypriot accusative singular masculine and feminine ἴν and in Hom. Myc. μιν, Dor. νιν, if indeed < *(H)im-(H)im with apocope and assimilation.

With *ἴς rimes the *interrogative/indefinite* pronoun τίς τί (with fixed intonational acute), τις τι, accusative singular masculine and feminine in the Οὖτιν of the *Odyssey* (though this is likely to be secondary) once before consonant and once before vowel, οὖτιν(') ἐγώ... ι 369 – an illustration of how the stem τιν- could have started, under the influence of ἕν(') with which it was paired (thus Ζῆν, interpreted in the Homeric text as Ζῆν', gave rise to Ζῆνα and further to Ζηνός etc.). The etymon is *kʷi- (nom. acc.); *kʷe-, kʷo-, hence Attic τοῦ and the like. The allomorphs with π- in πόσ(σ)ος (< *kʷotj-; cf. Lat. quot(idem)) etc. reflect the treatment of the labiovelars.

The *relative* pronoun is ὅς (ἥ ὅ) < *(H)jo- (see **Syntax: Dependent Clauses**, p. 259).

Verb Paradigms

For the *verb*, Greek has increasingly created fully fledged paradigms in which every *root* has, ideally, the *finite* forms which result, through the agency of verb *stems* from the large-scale though not really unlimited intersection of so-called tense and mood with voice, person (in the three numbers), and time reference ('primary' vs 'secondary'), all expressed by (partly segmentable) personal endings. By the same token, it has certain *non-finite* forms which are noun/adjective paradigms derived from verb stems or isolated forms of such paradigms. Verb stems are characterized by ablaut, suffixation, and reduplication, but, except for prefixation by preverbs (see **Syntax: Trends**, pp. 257f.), not by compounding. Past-tense subparadigms in the indicative carry an optional (archaic and poetic) or (later) obligatory prefix, the 'augment' ἐ- (see **Verbs: Augment**, p. 252). Prehistorically, however, the paradigms are not 'complete', and some of the grammatical categories which they are to embody later on are lexical in origin. Aspect differences, for example, were often inherent in particular roots (e.g. (*F*)ιδ- was aoristic or 'punctual') while they are later carried by the stem-forming devices (e.g. the -σ- of the aorist). In such cases, the lexical principle lives on in the guise of suppletion (εἶδον 'saw' vs ἑώρων); no suppletive paradigms are of PIE antiquity. An ancient close and somewhat exclusive relationship between middle voice and perfect tense is visible in the fact that the 'active' perfect, with its special endings, is stative in meaning, often still intransitive like the middle and unlike the active in the other tenses, and that the 'perfect middle' (λέλειμμαι 'have been, am left') is innovated. In Homer, active and middle can be nearly complementary: φημί 'say', but normally φάτο (cf. Chapter 3, **Morphological Categories**, pp. 81–8).

As a rule of thumb for non-suppletive paradigms, aspectually *durative roots* (non-prefixed) form relatively *simple imperfects* and, needing as they do a 'punctualizer', relatively *complex aorists* (mostly σ-aorists), while *punctual roots* have *simpler aorists* and more *elaborate* (e.g. reduplicated or suffixed) *imperfects*. *Aspect*, in other words, is visible in the past ('secondary') indicative. Beyond that, there is great complexity. In the event, Greek has two complements of stems: of 'present stems' (a 'present' being the primary tense that goes with an imperfect in stem formation (see above)), and 'aorist stems'. In addition, there is the perfect system.

Verbs: Present Stems

Root presents, *non-thematic* (type εἶμι 'shall go'): stem equals root; full grade in the singular indicative ipf. and subjunctive, zero grade elsewhere (ἴμεν 1 pl.) except for analogical levelling.

Reduplicated non-thematic presents (reduplication vowel: ι (type τίθημι); same ablaut scheme as above (cf. Chapter 2, p. 56).

Nasal presents, *non-thematic* (cf. Chapter 2, p. 57): (a) νη/να presents (Hom. δάμνημι 'subdue') and (b) νῡ/νυ presents (δείκνῡμι 'show'). These are transformed from the IE presents with nasal infix (full grade -*ne*-; zero grade -*n*-(-*m*-)) between the second and the third consonant of the root (or nasal after the second consonant of the ablauting root; under either interpretation the grades are again distributed as above). In Greek only such instances survive directly in which the third consonant was H_3, so that a present stem *$dm̥$-ne-H_2-* (or $dm̥$-n-eH_2)/$dm̥$-n-H_2- from the root *dmH_2-* (as in ἄδμᾱτος 'untamed') accounts for δάμνᾱμι δάμνημι/δάμναμεν. The -νῡ-/-νυ- presents then go back in principle to *-ne-w-/-n-u from roots ending in -u- (-w-), *-νευ- being replaced by -νῡ- on the analogy -να- : -νᾱ- (< -neH₂-; lengthening substitutes for ancient -e- insertion) :: -νυ- : x. Nasal presents have been made thematic by analogy with the thematic endings (Ion. τίνουσι 'they pay' ← *kʷi-nw-enti (see **Phonology: Dialects** (b), p. 242); similar but less telling ἁμαρτάνω 'fail', ἀπο-λι-μ-πάνω 'leave') and, by some different route, ὀμνύω 'swear'.

e-/o (*thematic*) presents with *e*-grade on the root: φέρω 'carry', ἄγω 'drive' < *H₂eg-, ἔχω < *seĝʰ-, σείω 'shake' < *twejs-, τρέω 'tremble' < *tres-, ῥέω 'flow' < *srew-; frequently inherited. There are no inherited examples in the zero-grade type γράφω 'scratch, write'.

Reduplicated thematic presents with root in zero grade: ἵζω *si-sd- (cf. Lat. -sīdō/sedeō), τίκτω < *ti-tk- (aor. ἔτεκον).

-je/o presents, (a) *primary*, with zero grade on the root except in roots without resonants in which the full grade has done duty instead since IE times (σκέπτομαι 'look' with metathesis, IE *speḱ-j-) and with extensive effects of the sound changes affecting *j*-clusters, e.g. βαίνω 'go' < *gʷm̥-j-; and (b) *secondary*, that is, in verb stems derived from noun or adjective stems (τῑμάω 'honour', φιλέω 'love' (a new type in -όω appears from Mycenaean on), ἀγγέλλω 'report', φυλάσσ/ττω 'guard', < φυλάκ-jω, ἐρίζω 'quarrel' < ἐρίδ-jω etc.; also τελέω 'attain' (< -s-j- ?)). Verbs in -άω, -έω are non-thematic in Arcado-Cyprian, Lesbian (φίλημ[μ]ι 'φιλέω') and Thessalian.

Primary presents in inherited, if semantically ill defined *-sḱe/sḱo- are likewise underlain by zero-grade roots: βάσκω 'come' < *gʷm̥-sḱe/o-, exactly cognate with Skt *gácchati* which serves there as the usual present from the root. The reduplicated variety, as γι-γνώ-σκω, is only Greek.

Verbs: Aorist Stems

There are *root aorists* with full grade in the first- and second-person plural indicative active as well, in contrast to the presents (see **Verbs: Present Stems**, pp. 249f.); full grade also in optative and subjunctive while zero grade prevails otherwise. Examples are Hom. ἔφθιτο 'wasted away' etc.; in Attic, aside from ἔχεα 'poured' < *-ĝʰew-m̥ with analogical replacements in the other persons, the formation is limited to roots ending in -eH: ἔβην, ἔβημεν 'went'. The puzzling indicative singular actives ἔθηκα 'placed', ἔδωκα 'gave', Hom. ἧκα = Att. ἧκα 'let go' (pl. ἔθεμεν etc.), are Indo-European (cf. Lat. *fēcī*).

Non-reduplicated thematic 'second' aorists (ἔβαλε 'threw') seem to be thematizations, via third-person plural (see **Verbs: Present Stems**, p. 249) of root aorists (cf. Hom. βλῆτο).

The *reduplicated* variety seems more genuine: Hom. ἔειπον 'spoke' (< *we-wkʷ- dissimilated to *we-jp-) = Skt *ávocam*.

Sigmatic aorists are on the rise in Greek as elsewhere. Whatever the antecedents, the root vocalism has become identical with that of the present. The *s between vowels is analogically restored. The pervasive quasi-thematic -α- of the indicative (except 3 sg.), optative etc. arose in the first-person singular indicative (> *-s-m̥) and third-person plural indicative.

The η-aorist with suggestions of an inchoative-stative meaning has its possible IE sources with offshoots in Baltic, Slavic, Germanic and Latin in the form of zero-grade presents in *(e)H₁j- (ἐπάγη 'it congealed' (: πήγνῡμι 'fix')). Later, mostly in Attic, it became a 'passive aorist'.

The θη-aorist is likewise inchoative and then passivic. Connection with the preterite of Germanic denominatives (Goth. *salbōdēs* 'anointedst') is uncertain.

Verbs: Perfects

The *perfect* is stative but not inchoative; it denotes a state attained. The Indo-European *'strong'* perfect stem is characterized by *e*-reduplication (except that **wojd-H₂e* 'I know' is unreduplicated). The singular indicative perfect and pluperfect active and the subjunctive (?) has originally the *o*-grade, the other forms have zero grade (Hom. μέ-μον-α 'am eager': μέ-μα-μεν (*-mn̥*-); Hom. δείδω 'fear' (written for, or actually changed from δέδϝω) < **de-dwoj-H₂e* : δεδιτε) – an alternation quite overlaid by analogic levelling. The aspiration of labials and gutturals at root end (τέταχα 'have drawn up' from ταγ- (Att. pres. τάττω)) presumably originated in the middle voice where such aspiration was a matter of conditioned sound change (say, in contact with (σ)θ- in τετάχθαι (inf.)), then spread to the third-person plural middle where the ending -αται was the only one before which manner of articulation was distinctive (cf. **Distributional Gaps**, p. 232) and to the active.

The κ-*perfect*, also with the same reduplication and the same endings as the strong perfect, is a Greek innovation – in Homer competing with the strong perfect with full-grade, root-final η-: ἔσταμεν 'stand', but ἔστηκε. In Attic etc. it partakes of the active and often transitive meaning of which it is the resultative, expressing the state of having acted. Its formal prehistory is probably somehow connected with the aorists of the type **ě-θηκα. In later antiquity the perfect begins to function as a past tense.

Verbs: Futures

As far as the *futures* are concerned, the question is to what extent they are special uses of subjunctives. In ἔδομαι 'shall eat' (Hom. pres. inf. ἔδμεναι) πίομαι etc. this is clearly the case. In the case of ordinary -σε/σο-futures like δείξω this remains the simplest assumption though futures and desideratives in Celtic, Italic and Indic could point to another source as well. Many have a restored intervocalic *s* where the preceding vowel was long as in τῑμήσω 'shall honour', the first-person singular having precisely both functions. Such a state of affairs was altered only by the analogic introduction of the lengthened thematic vowel in the subjunctives (τῑμήσῃς)). After short vowels (mostly < -*H*-), where the consonant preceding them was frequently a liquid or nasal, *s* was lost by sound change and contraction ensued (τεμέω 'shall cut'), and this was then transferred, especially in Attic, to roots and stems ending in nasals and liquids without any laryngeals (ἀγγελέω).

Verbs: Augment

The *augment*, *(*H*)e*-, nearest the verb when in co-occurrence with other prefixes (e.g. προσ-έ-φην 'said'), like other such prefixes marks the point beyond which which finite-verb accent is not retracted inasmuch as those prefixes had borne the accent to which finite verb forms were enclitic in main clauses. The augment is optional in poetry, except in the 'gnomic' aorists expressing sententious truths, and apparently in Mycenaean. It is ἐ- before preserved consonants (ἐδίδουν 'I gave', ἔδωκα, ἐδεδώκειν ...). Both *(*H*₁*)e-HC* ... (by lengthening) and *(*H*)e₁-HV* ... (by ancient contraction; e.g. *(*H*)e-H₃er-to* > *(*H*)o-or-to* > ὧρτο 'arose') will appear as long vowels. Augmented forms from verbs beginning with **se-, *je- > **(h)e*-, and, later, *we- > *e- naturally undergo the more recent contraction into Att. ει-(εἷρπον 'crept' < *(*H*)e-serpom*) unless analogically disturbed. An anteconsonantal augment ἠ- is uncertain. The small class of Homeric and Ionic iterative past tenses in -εσκε/ο- (μαχέσκετο 'battled', στρέψασκε 'twisted'; Hdt. λάβεσκε 'took') is always without augment.

Verbs: Mood

The *subjunctives* are formed by adding the thematic vowel, *-e-/-o-* to the appropriate stem as it appears in the indicative (e.g. Hom. ἴονεν, to match the ind. ἴμεν; sigmatic aorists preserved in certain dialects); if the indicative stem is thematic to begin with, lengthening ensues by ancient contraction (φέρωμεν φέρητε), with some further analogical regularizations. In Attic, aside from remnants like ἔσομαι, ἔδομσι which have become futures, these characteristic long vowels are transferred to non-thematic sub-paradigms as well (e.g. aor. δείξωμεν).

The *optatives* are based on the ablauting suffix *-jeH₁/-iH₁*. In a non-thematic subparadigm this accounts for such forms as *H₁s-jeH₁-t* > εἴη, *H₁s-iH₁-te* > *εἶτε* > εἶτε of the present of the verb 'to be', with full grade of the optative suffix in the active singular and otherwise zero grade, added to this root/stem as it occurs elsewhere in the present. Thematic indicatives are matched by optatives in -οι- (< *-οῑ- < -o-iH₁* (?) in the expected non-ablauting fashion).

Verbs: Personal Endings

The verbal personal endings, of varying segmentability and linked, in part, by ablaut relationships, may be seen at the intersection of the following variables:

(a) *person* (1 to 3)
(b) *number* (sg., pl., dual)
(c) voice (*active, middle*) ...
(d) '*primary*'/'*secondary*'/*imperative*/*perfect* (the voice distinction is neu-tralized in the perfect tense; see **Verb Paradigms**, p. 249). Taken together with stem formation, mood, and augment (see **Verbs: Present Stems**, p. 249 to **Verbs: Mood**, p. 253) there is considerable redundancy; the 'primary'/'secondary' division, for instance, is distinctive by itself only in so far as it serves to keep injunctives – a verbal category for non-temporal statement perhaps still extant in Mycenaean – apart from non-past indicatives: cf. Chapter 4, **Verb Conjugation**, p. 111f. Matters may be tabulated as in Chapter 2, pp. 60–2.

The second-person singular imperative is either endingless (Gk φέρε-∅) or, in non-thematic tense stems, has the ending *-$d^h i$ > -θι. Imperatives could be amplified by affixing the pronominal ablative *to-et > tōt 'from there on forever' (ἔστω). There were further analogical elaborations of these juxtaposi-tions in Greek as in other IE languages.

Verb Paradigms: Past

The tabulation, taken together with the rules of stem formation (see **Verb Paradigms**, p. 249 to **Verbs: Futures**, p. 251; **Verbs: Mood**, p. 252f.), and allowing for modifications by analogy, affecting in particular the verbs εἰμί and εἶμι and imperfects like Attic ἐδίδουν, accounts for most of the actual forms.

In the matter of *past-tense indicatives* it is sufficient to recall that the sigmatic aorists were built up from the first-person singular (*(H)é-dejk-s-m̥ > ἔδειξα)) and third-person plural active with the result of establishing 'alpha-thematic' conjugation (thus 2 sg. *[Hé]-dejk-s-s, was replaced by ἔδειξας etc.). The first-person plural in -μεν (Ion.-Att, Lesbian, Arcadian) against -μες (elsewhere) is obscure. The third-person plural partly ends in -ν (as in -ον < * -o-nt ἔφερον), partly in -αν (< *n̥t with analogical -ν from -ον; ἔδειξαν etc.), partly in -σαν where it is transferred from the sigmatic aorist, with great productivity in a number of dialects and exclusive currency in Attic tense stems ending in (Greek) vowel (ἔδοσαν 'they gave').

The first-person singular middle (ἐφερόμην), a Greek innovation, is without explanation. The second-person singular ending is -(σ)ο (ἐπέπληξο 'hadst struck for thyself' (pluperf.)); σ > 0 after vowel (ἐφέρεο > ἐφέρου; ἐδείξαο (alpha-thematic (see above)) > ἐδείξω), but analogically restored in ἐτίθεσο, ἐπέπαυσο etc.; similarly, the third-person singular has -το. In the first-person plural -μεσθα (Hom.) may be the inherited primary ending (cf. Hitt. *-wasta*), and -μεθα (secondary) the outcome of the relationship *-μες : -με : : -μεσθα : X. The second-person plural in -σθε is puzzling. The third-person plural:

(a) *-nto* in ἐφέροντο;
(b) *-nto* (or *-ento*?) in ἔθεντο (*(H₁)e-dʰH₁-t̥o (-ento*?));
(c) *-n̥to* > -ατο in pluperfects, in the optative, and, fundamentally after consonants or, in Ionic, after *s* > Ø or *j* > Ø (Hom. Ion. ἐκέατο 'lay', but Attic (innovated) ἔκειντο);
(d) 'alpha-thematic' -αντο (ἐδείξαντο).

The dual endings fit the schematic analogies set by the rest of the paradigm.

Verb Paradigms: Non-past

In the non-past subparadigm, endings differ in part from secondary endings by the addition of *-i/j-* (e.g. 2sg., *-s* : *si*). First-person singular active: non-thematic -μι, thematic word-end -ω of whatever origin. Second-person singular: non-thematic -σι in Hom. ἐσ-σί with geminate *-ss-* restored at an early time from other verbs still having this ending; Att. εἶ (see (c), p. 235; **Analogic Processes, Verbs**, p. 240) continuing the genuine form. Third-person singular: non-thematic *-ti* -τι in ἔστι; > -σι after (Greek) vowel in South Greek dialects (τίθησι). The thematic endings of second- and third-persons singular are to be understood as resulting from two analogical processes, first (α) (after the change of *-t#* to Ø#) ἔφερες : ἔφερε : : φέρεσι (> Myc. ****pherehi*) : φέρει (3 sg.) and then (β), say, ἔφερε : ἔρερες : : φέρει : φέρεις see (d), pp. 235f.; **Phonology, Vowels**, p. 237; **Analogic Processes, Verbs**, p. 240). First- and second-person plural: -μεν, -μες and -τε as in the preterite. Third-person plural: *-enti* is recognizable in Myc. *e-e-si* (ἔhενσι) 'they are' with the South Greek change *ti* > *si* (except after *s*). Non-thematic stems in Attic have mostly -ᾱσι (διδόᾱσι) 'they give', presumably from the pluperfect. Thematic stems show *-o-nti* > Dor. -οντι, Myc. Arcadian -ονσι, Lesbian etc. -οισι, Ion.-Att. -ουσι. The dual forms are based on the secondary second-person dual.

In the middle the first-person singular has an intrusive -μ- (imported from -μι) in -μαι instead of -αι. This, in turn, analogically changed second-person singular *-soj* into -σαι: so after consonants (πέπληξαι 'thou hast been (art) struck' perf.); -αι after vowels, with appropriate contraction of thematic *o + aj* into -ει (βούλει, though mostly spelled -ηι) and partial restoration of -σ- (πέπαυσαι, perf.) from there. Third-person singular *-toj* > Myc., Arcadian -τοι; elsewhere replaced by -ται, as above. First-person plural as in the secondary tenses. The third-person plural forms fall in with the examples for the past tense and the active. The endings 1dual -μεθον, 2, 3dual -σθον are based on plural -μεθα and on *-*ton* (2 3dual act.), and transformed after -σθον and -σθε (2pl. mid.), respectively.

Verb Paradigms: Perfect

The *perfect* endings are straightforward: first-person singular -α from *-H_2e (Luv. -*ha*); second-person singular: -θα < *tH_2e in οἶσθα, otherwise replaced by -ας (perhaps on the model of the aorist); third-person singular: -ε from -*e*; first- and second-person plural as generally in the active; third-person plural with the alpha-thematic -α- (Proto-Gk -αντι which surfaces in Dor. -αντι, Arcadian -ανσι, Lesbian -αισι, Ion.-Att. -ᾱσι. The second- and third-person dual (ἕστατον) is part of the same system of paradigmatic innovations as for the other tenses.

The *pluperfect* active is entirely a Greek creation. Some ancient forms are simply like those of the perfect, except that they allow the augment; e.g. Hom, ἐπέπιθμεν 'trusted'). The later paradigm is obscure in origin. The pluperfect middle is likewise due to an analogical build-up; there is no direct connection with parallel entities in Sanskrit and in Anatolian.

Verb: Imperatives

Imperatives compete semantically with *injunctives* – augmentless secondary tenses – (cf. Chapter 4, p. 116) – which explains why some such forms have actually become, or replaced, imperatives: σχές (from ἔχω), and following it, θές and congeners. As for other second-person singular forms, τίθει is due, along with other such crossovers, to imperatives from contract verbs (φίλει < φίλεϳε). Aside from this, -0 prevails in thematic and certain full-grade non-thematic tense stems (Attic in polysyllabic presents like ἵστη), -θι after other non-thematic, zero-grade ones (ἴσθι from οἶδα). Imperatives like δεῖξον are obscure. The second-person plural dual in -τε, -τον is unremarkable. The second-person singular middle of the type φέρου is injunctival in origin; δίωξαι 'pursue' may be an old infinitive (really = διῶξαι, **Verb: Infinitives**, p. 256), suitably reaccented. Third-person singular forms are always reinforced by -τω (in Greek restricted to third person) and its analogical extension for the middle, -σθω. There are further analogical elaborations in the dialects.

Verb: Subjunctives, Optatives

In IE *subjunctives* had both primary and secondary endings. The latter survive in Arcado-Cyprian and sporadically in Doric. Remarkable is the Homeric ἄγηισι (really ἄγησι = Skt *ajāti*).

The first-person singular *optative* found with thematic (φέροιμι) and 'alpha-thematic' stems remains a puzzle; Arcadian ἐξελαύνοια is the last remnant of the expected *-o-iH_1-*m̥* (see **Phonology: Laryngeals**, p. 233).

The third-person plural active in -εν (< *-ent) is at home in non-thematic tense stems as in εἶεν (cf.Lat. *sient*). The third-person plural middle has -ατο < *-n̥to, replaced in Attic by -ντο (φέροιντο).

Verb: Participles

The 'non-finite' participles and infinitives are, at least etymologically speaking, derivational rather than inflectional.

The *active* participles other than those of the perfect are formed, from IE times on, with *-ent/-ont/-n̥t*. Non-thematically it is either the case

(a) that root and tense *stem* suffix have *zero* grade and the *participle* suffix has *full* grade in the 'strong' cases and otherwise zero grade; or

(b) that the *root* is uniformly *full* grade and the *suffix zero* grade (with accent on the root). With thematic tense stems, the suffix is *-nt-*. In Greek the ablauting type has all but disappeared, except for some dialectal traces in the verb 'to be'.

The *perfect* active participle has a suffix *-wos-* (in the 'strong' cases)/-*us-* (in the weak; f. *-usja* > -υῖα). The place of the old accusative singular preserved in Myc. ἀρᾱρϝoha 'fitted together' is taken, already in Homer, by ἀρηρότα with -τ-, perhaps from the other active participles by way of the ambiguous -ώς of the masculine nominative singular (but the neuter in -ός persists).

The *middle* participles in -μενος (accented -μένος in the perfect according to Wheeler's Law; see **Phonology, Accent**, p. 234) have a suffix *-mH₁no/-m̥H₁no-* and Skt -āna-); in Greek the postvocalic and post-laryngeal variety, -μενος, was generalized.

Verb: Infinitives

Etymologically, active infinitives are case forms of verbal nouns, independently incorporated into the verbal paradigm by the several IE daughter languages. Greek examples are typically old *locatives*, either in *-∅* or in *-i* (see p. 246):

Mostly from thematic stems, *-s-en-∅*, Myc. *e-ke-e ekheen*, Att. etc. ἔχειν; from an *s*-stem like γένος, enlarged;

-men-∅: Doric, Boeotian, Thessalian, Hom. (Aeolic) ἔμμεν 'be' < ἔσ-μεν (cf. neuters like εἶμα [< *-mn̥] 'garment');

-(e)naj (see p. 18.3; 245): Arcadian, Cyprian Ion.-Att., Hom.; e.g. εἶναι (< *H₁s-enaj), Cyprian δοϝέναι, Att. δοῦναι 'give' (from a noun of the type Skt *van-ánā-* 'lust' ?).

The analogical developments behind the remaining infinitive formations, Lesbian, Hom. -μεναι (ἔμμεναι), -αι (in -σ-aorists like ἐλάσ[σ]αι 'drive'), and the mid. -σθαι are uncertain.

Syntax: Trends

Literature on Greek syntax is immense and sophisticated but somewhat fragmented. Some topics have already been taken up; e.g. those connected with morphology (see pp. 243–57). Generally it has proved easier to identify sweeping developments affecting the whole language over long periods than to find dialectal diversification and other detail. The 'loss of the dual', the 'rise of the article', the elaboration of prepositional syntax, and the competition between genitival and adjectival attributes are celebrated instances (see also p. 258).

The *dual* number in noun and verb is inherited. Its gradual disappearance is duplicated almost everywhere in Indo-European; duals and plurals merge into new 'plurals'; the morphs are usually the old pluralic ones. The dual is preserved in Mycenaean and in Homer (here overlaid with artificial accretions), in Doric and in Boeotian. True to the inherited state of affairs usage is restricted, overtly or anaphorically, to pairs established as such either semantically (ὄσσε 'eyes'), or by numeral (Hom. υἷε δύω). 'Elliptic' turns such as πατέρε 'father and mother' are survivals and have parallels in other IE languages. In Attic the verbal forms are the earliest to vanish (first persons had been abolished prehistorically). The Atticistic movement of the first century AD gives rise to a contrived revival.

The addition of the definite *article* furnishes a chronological counterpart to the loss of the dual. In the long view the article is a general Greek innovation which anticipates a widespread if not total IE one. Mycenaean, and possibly the poorly known first-millennium dialect of Pamphylia, do not show it. In Homer (and in poetic language later on) the IE demonstrative ὁ, ἡ, το (cf. **Pronouns**, p. 247f.) occurs both in the old and in the new function; expressions abound which, when translated into later prose, require the article (*Iliad* 1.1 Μῆνιν... 'the wrath...', *Odyssey* 1.1 Ἄνδρα... 'the man...'). The shift goes hand in hand with the substitution of new demonstratives to take the place of the old (αὐτόν for τόν etc.). Especially characteristic of Greek is the great device of allowing the article to generalize participial expressions like τῷ ἐξιόντι 'to anyone coming out' or make all kinds of structures into nouns, syntactically speaking: neuters of adjectives (τὸ καλόν 'beauty'), adverbs (τὸ νῦν 'present'), infinitives (τὸ ἐρωτᾶν καὶ ἀποκρίνεσθαι 'questions and answers') etc.

Preverbs (prepositions etc.), too, fit into the larger picture. Their threefold use as adverbs, prefixes, and prepositions proper is a synchronic fact for historical Greek. It is the *adverbial* function which represents the historical centre. As the 'anastrophic', orthotone accentuation indicates, ἔπι 'on top', ἔξ '(on the) outside' are adverbs functioning like other adverbials as independent and somewhat pleonastic elements in the sentence, not tied to any other elements by factors of accentual dependence, selection ('government'), or word order. But this usage is only a relic. New, often more explicit adverbs (ἔξω, ἐκτός...) take over as the basic, short forms

develop mandatory associations with other constituents; thus the archaic
... γῆς ὁποίας ἦλθον '... from what kind of land I came' (Soph.), with
a 'genitive of separation', competes with the innovated (and thenceforth
normal) ἐκ Πύλου εἰλήλουθας 'thou hast come from Pylos' (Hom.) where
the very fact that this kind of unaccompanied genitive is obsolescent causes
the *'preposition'* to be 'governing' the case form. The proclisis in ἐκ, ἐπί
(where the grave is no more than a zero sign) is in keeping with this
shift. By the same token, a phrase like ἐκ δ' ἤγαγε κλισίης Βρισηίδα (*Iliad*
1.346) simply represents the old state of affairs; only later does it split
up, as it were, into ἐκ (τῆς) κλισίης '(led) out of the tent' on the one
hand and ἐξήγαγε 'led out ((from) the tent)' on the other (see also Chapter
13, **Prepositions**, p. 408). In the latter case semantic change giving an
idiomatic meaning to a given adverb + verb construct signals the altered
constituency: from the later point of view, ἀπό μ' ὀλεῖς (Soph.) 'ἀπολεῖς
με, you will destroy me' is a classical example of 'tmesis', or 'cutting
in two' a compound verb – not to mention the ordinary augments in
ἐξ-έ-βαλε 'threw out', ἐξ-ήγαγε. This history is mirrored in the abundant
exocentric *compound* adjectives of the type preverb + noun stem. The
Homeric homonyms ἐπήρετμος$_1$ '*having* oars upon it; equipped with oars'
and ἐπήρετμος$_2$ '(*being*) upon the oars; seated at the oars' illustrate this:
one is 'possessive' with the adverbial ἔπι as a first component (after the
manner of ἔνθεος 'having the god inside, inspired'); the other, a
'hypostasis' presupposing an ἐπί that is already a preposition (cf.
Morphology: Noun and Adjective Derivation, p. 243). Hypostatic
compounds do not, however, militate in favour of exclusively prepositive
word order in the underlying phrase since this ordering only reflects the
circumstance that compounds need to be inflected. In fact, postpositive
word order, in part with 'anastrophic' orthotone accentuation, exists – even
in Attic prose; ἀλλοτρίας γῆς πέρι (Thuc.) 'about a foreign land' – as
another facet of the archaic autonomy of the constituents in the phrase
(see Chapter 4, **Prepositions**, p. 120).

Possessive *genitives* and secondary (see **Morphology: Noun and Adjective Derivation**, p. 243) *adjectives* were in ancient competition with each
other in Indo-European. Generally, the adjective usage is on the wane.
Adjectives of appurtenance show a technical, institutional value, as in the use
of Mycenaean and Aeolic patronymics, which are adjectives in -ιος (e.g.
Thessalian Ἀρχελάειος), when compared with the style 'son *of* ... ' as it
prevails in other dialects. Once again, Homer offers both: Τελαμώνιος Αἴας,
Ἀ. Τελαμώνιος υἱός vs Πηλέος υἱός (alongside the patronymic nouns
Τελαμωνιάδης, Πηληεάδης).

Syntax: Dependent Clauses etc.

Greek has inherited at least one device reserved for *hypotaxis*: the relative pronoun stem, *(H)jo-* (perhaps *H_1j-o-*, built on the zero grade of the demonstrative or anaphoric *($H_1)j$-; see **Phonology, Laryngeals**, p. 233; **Pronouns**, p. 248). Other varieties of subordination have a more clearly paratactic origin in Greek and in other IE languages. Indirect questions go back to direct ones (note the uses of τίς, ὅστις 'who'), conditional periods to juxtapositions of wishes (contrary to fact or otherwise as the case may be; this is reflected both in the way in which the conjunctions are paired (Att. εἴθε 'if only' vs εἰ, ἐάν 'if') and in the use of the tenses and moods), result clauses with ὥστε to coordination with ὥστε, and so on.

For embedding purposes clauses may be transformed into participial constructions, including the 'absolute' genitive (see also pp. 257f.). Mood cannot be preserved in this case but mood-connected devices such as ἄν (κε(ν)) (see below) are.

Syntax: Word Order etc.

Enclitics – and *de facto* enclitics like the oblique cases of αὐτός or like ἄν, the precise cross-dialectal equivalent of enclitic κε(ν) (Chantraine 1968: 82) – take the second place in the phrase regardless of constituency grouping. This ancient, trivial rule (Chapter 2, p. 70), concerning as it does the borderline area between morphology and syntax, is, however, only marginal to the syntax of word order proper. The same is true of *postpositions* (see p. 258). Apropos of word order it has been said that Greek represents a transition from S(ubject)–O(bject)–V(erb) order with its contingent accessories such as the location of attributes and relative clauses. These surface phenomena depend, in turn, on the grammar of the stress morphemes (see **Phonology: Indo-European**, p. 230).[1]

Note

1 Extensive reliance on Helmut Rix, *Historische Grammatik des Griechischen* (Darmstadt: Wissenschaftliche Buchgesellschaft, 1976), is gratefully acknowledged.

References

Baldi, Philip (ed.) (1990) *Linguistic Change and Reconstruction Methodology*, Berlin and New York: Mouton de Gruyter.

Bammesberger, Alfred (ed.) (1988) *Die Laryngaltheorie*, Heidelberg: Winter.

Beekes, Robert S.P. (1969) *The Development of the PIE Laryngeals in Greek*, The Hague: Mouton.

—— (1990) 'The historical grammar of Greek', in Baldi 1990: 305–29.

Cardona, George and Zide, Norman H. (eds) (1987) *Festschrift for Henry Hoenigswald*, Tübingen: Narr.

Chantraine, Pierre (1957) *Grammaire homérique*, 3rd edn, 2 vols, Paris: Klincksieck.
—— (1968–80) *Dictionnaire étymologique de la langue grecque*, Paris: Klincksieck.
Gamkrelidze, Thomas V. and Ivanov, Vjačeslav V. (1973) 'Sprachtypologie und die Rekonstruktion der gemeinindogermanischen Verschlüsse', *Phonetica* 27: 150–6.
Hiersche, Rolf (1970) *Grundzüge der griechischen Sprachgeschichte*, Wiesbaden: Reichert.
Hoenigswald, Henry M. (1988) 'A note on semivowel behavior', in A. Bammesberger (ed.) (1988): 199–211.
Humbert, Jean (1945) *Syntaxe grecque*, 3rd edn, Paris: Klincksieck, 1960.
Lejeune, Michel (1972) *Phonétique historique du mycénien et du grec ancien*, Paris: Klincksieck.
Lindeman, Fredrik O. (1965) 'La loi de Sievers et le début de mot en indo-européen', *New Testament Studies* 20: 38–108.
Mayrhofer, Manfred (1986) *Lautlehre*, vol. 1.2 of *Indogermanische Grammatik*, Heidelberg: Winter.
Meillet, Antoine and Vendryes, Joseph (1945) *Traité de grammaire comparée des langues classiques*, 2nd edn, Paris: Champion.
Morpurgo Davies, Anna (1987) 'Folk-linguistics and the Greek word', in Cardona and Zide 1987: 263–80.
Palmer, L.R., (1980) *The Greek Language*, London: Faber and Faber.
Peters, Martin (1980) *Untersuchungen zur Vertretung der indogermanischen Laryngale im Griechischen*, Vienna: Akademie der Wissenschaften.
Risch, Ernst (1955) 'Die Gliederung der griechischen Dialekte in neuer Sicht', *Museum Helveticum* 12: 61–76.
—— (1974) *Wortbildung der homerischen Sprache*, 2nd edn, Berlin and New York: de Gruyter.
—— (1987) 'Sonderfall Griechisch?', in Cardona and Zide 1987: 329–35.
Rix, Helmut (1976) *Historische Grammatik des Griechischen*, Darmstadt: Wissenschaftliche Buchgesellschaft.
Ruijgh, C.P. (1967) *Études sur la grammaire et le vocabulaire du grec mycénien*, Amsterdam: Hakkert.
Scherer, Anton (1959) *Handbuch der griechischen Dialekte*, 2, 2nd edn, Heidelberg: Winter.
Schmitt, Rüdiger (1977) *Einführung in die griechischen Dialekte*, Darmstadt: Wissenschaftliche Buchgesellschaft.
Wackernagel, Jacob (1950–7) *Vorlesungen über Syntax*, 2nd edn, Basle: Birkhäuser.

10 Latin

Edoardo Vineis

Closely related to Oscan-Umbrian and the Sabellian dialects of central Italy, Latin is considered a member of that important branch of the IE language family traditionally termed 'Italic'. This branch of Indo-European appears, in turn, to share a number of similarities exclusive to itself and Celtic, and together with the latter, Germanic, Greek, Hittite and Tocharian, forms what are called the *centum* dialects. It will not be inappropriate, we believe, to clarify, albeit briefly, this widely held view, commonly found in most current handbooks, which may at first seem puzzling. For instance, an immediate comparison between, say, a Latin text and a text written in another Italic dialect or language will clearly reveal two or more fundamentally different and mutually unintelligible languages. Undoubtedly, the degree of unintelligibility is far greater, for example, than that between Modern Italian and Spanish or Portuguese. In fact, if we look beyond the unmistakable superficial differences, there emerge 'obvious' similarities between Latin and Osco-Umbrian, as identified by the historical-comparative method, including among others the following:

(a) Phonetics: $*\partial > a$, $*ew > ou$, $*l̥$, $*r̥ > ol, or$, $*m̥$, $*n̥ > em, en$, $*-s- > -z-$, $*-t/t- > -ss-$, $*-t > -d$, the word-initial voiced aspirates $*b^h$, $*d^h$, $*g^h$ become voiceless fricatives, and the assimilation of words of the syllabic pattern $*p \ldots k^w > k^w \ldots k^w$.

(b) Morphology: the ablative in -d is extended beyond -o/e- stems, the formation of the dative singular of the personal pronouns, the formation of the imperfect indicative and subjunctive paradigms, the formation of the passive, gerundive and the supine, the fusion of the IE aorist and perfect into a single *perfectum*, and the fusion of the subjunctive and optative moods.

Clearly, many of these phenomena may have developed independently in Latin and Osco-Umbrian, nor do they appear, when considered individually, peculiar and exclusive to these languages alone, inasmuch as they are attested in other IE languages (and must therefore be ascribed to more general phonetic developments, a fact confirmed by typological linguistics). Yet, the fund of common phenomena occurring in both languages leads us to hypothesize, not without reason, that a strong bond once existed between the

261

languages belonging to this group. A similar argument can be put forward to demonstrate the much disputed hypothesis of a common 'Italo-Celtic' unity, within which Latin, in particular, allegedly shares some features with Gaelic, and similarly Osco-Umbrian with Brythonic. The following phenomena would seem to support this view:

(a) Phonetics: the labiovelars $*k^w$, $*g^w$, $*g^{wh}$ show similar treatment in Latin and Gaelic, but become labials in Osco-Umbrian and Brythonic, the previously noted assimilation in the sequence $*p \ldots k^w > k^w \ldots k^w$, giving rise to labiovelars in Latin and Gaelic, but labials in Osco-Umbrian and Brythonic.

(b) Morphology: the genitive singular of -o/e- stems (which ends in -ī in both Latin and Gaulish), impersonal forms of the verb characterized by -r, the future in -b- (attested in Latin and Irish), subjunctive formed by adding -ā- and -s- to the verbal root, the formation of the comparative and superlative by the addition of the suffixes $*-j\breve{o}s-$ and $*-somo-$, respectively.

(c) Vocabulary: the existence of a number of words exclusive to 'Italic' and Celtic, e.g. such Latin words as *terra, harēna, pulvis, seges, dorsum, pectus, tālus, grossus, mītis, vastus, metere.*

Pursuing this line of investigation, it has been further observed that Italic, Celtic and Germanic (and sometimes also Balto-Slavonic) have a number of elements in common, particularly in the field of lexis, which do not appear in Greek, Armenian and Indo-Iranian. Although faced with the difficulties of an admittedly approximate chronology, scholars have been led to postulate that this common fund of words in the above languages reflects a common period of civilization, the so-called 'civilization of the North-west'. However, it can be equally shown how a group of words in the field of lexis, say Latin and Greek, or Latin, Greek and Indo-Iranian, figure to the exclusion of the languages of the '(north-)western group'. The preceding discussion, admittedly couched in very general terms, suffices to demonstrate the inevitable complexity involved in the problem of classifying Latin in relation to the other IE languages. In this area of investigation, all seemingly strong hypotheses are open to reasoned impugnment. One only has to consider the number of coincidences that are presumably due to the independent preservation of a one-time IE legacy, and the number of times the same coincidences have been shown to be totally absent elsewhere. Such discrepancies can be ascribed to nothing more than pure accident.

The Historical Homeland

The historical homeland of the Latin language corresponds exactly to the *Latium vetus* (or *antīquom*), a geographical area considerably smaller than the present-day homonymous Italian region. It was bordered by the Tiber to the north, the lower course of the Anio to the north-east, the Apennine chain to the east, the Volscian territory to the south, and by the Tyrrhenian Sea to the west, with a stretch of coast extending from the Circaeum headland to the mouth of the Tiber. As Roman political and military domination spread, the *lingua Latīna*, which at first did not refer exclusively to the speech of the *urbs Rōma*, came increasingly to be identified antonomastically, so to speak, with the variety spoken specifically in the *Urbs*, as opposed to the varieties of neighbouring areas, themselves originally 'Latin'. Subsequently, the Latin language gradually established itself over the entire Italian territory and beyond, coming to be spoken, as is well known, in much of central and western Europe and on the coasts of north Africa. In fact, despite the fastidious search for standardization in the literary language, Latin exhibited a great deal of dialectal and social variation which simply cannot be dismissed as marginal or irrelevant. Such variation is visible since earliest times in the epigraphic documents and the testimonies of a wide range of authors (and not simply grammarians, historians, or antiquarians). For instance, the Latin spoken in Rome diverged from that spoken in *Falerii* (namely Faliscan) or from the Latin spoken in *Praeneste* or *Lānuvium*. Analogously, one can distinguish between varieties such as the fossilized *sermo* used in religious or legal-administrative practices and the *Umgangssprache* of the aristocracy or the common masses, variously formed by Greek, Italic and Etruscan elements. Moreover, Rome itself originated in a *synoecismus* of cremating Latin and inhuming Sabine folk. If we add to this picture the Etruscan domination and the unquestionable presence *ab antīquō* of Greek (perhaps even Mycenaean) and Italic groups, we are forced to recognize the importance of a linguistic system characterized by a high degree of diversity, which can hardly be termed a single homogenous form of Latin. In accordance with the prescriptions of an admittedly widespread *discrētio*, firmly established in the learned tradition, the immutable normative picture of Latin passed on to posterity through literary texts and grammars represents, in a certain sense, nothing more than the ideal systemization of the *Sprechsprache* diasystem, namely of the combined presence of numerous and mutually intertwining differences in the fields of phonology, morphosyntax and lexis. In the final analysis, the presence of numerous differences is parallel to that which historically characterizes all languages that have experienced a vast territorial expansion.

'Rustic' and 'Urban' Latin: Other Dialectal Influences
In this discussion of Latin we shall not embark upon a detailed examination of the features which distinguished the individual rustic varieties of Latin, which were heavily influenced, in particular, by the neighbouring Italic environment. Suffice it to mention here the ancient inscription found on a cup discovered in the territory of *Falerii* (what is now Civita Castellana), which reads *foied uino pipafo cra carefo* (cf. CIE 8179, see CIE 8180 for an identical

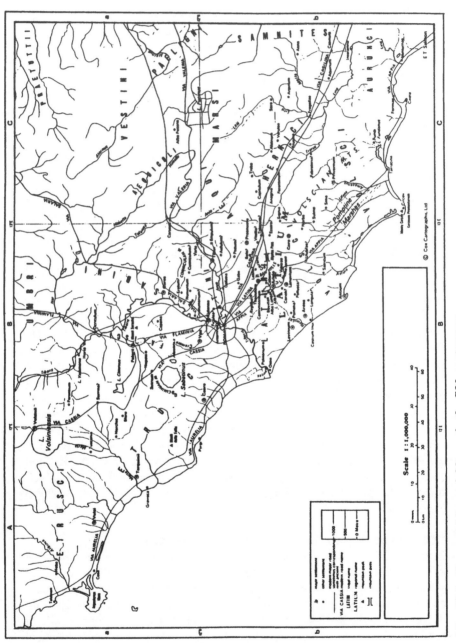

Map 10.1 Rome and her neighbours in the fifth century BC
Source: N. G. L. Hammond (ed.), *Atlas of the Greek and Roman World in Antiquity*, Park Ridgey, NJ: Noyes Press, 1981

inscription, with the exception of *pafo* for *pipafo*, found on another cup from the same area). The same utterance 'translated' in the established Roman standard would almost certainly have read *hodiē vīnum bibam, crās carēbō*. However, as proof of the rapid extraterritorial diffusion of the language of the *Urbs*, one only has to consider the famous Faliscan cooks' slate (cf. CIL I²364), a votive inscription composed in Saturnians, probably dating back to the beginning of the second century BC, where the 'urban' elements outnumber those features of a distinctly more foreign and peripheral nature:

Iouei Iunonei Mineruai I Falesce, quei in Sardinia sunt, I donum dederunt.
magistreis I L(ucius) Latrius K(aesonis) f(ilius),
C(aius) Salu[e]na Voltai f(ilius) coiraueront.

gonlegium quod est	aciptum aetatei age(n)d[ai],
opiparum a[d] ueitam	quolundam festosque dies,
quei soueis aastutieis	opidque Volgani
gondecorant sai[pi]sume	comuiuia loidosque,
ququei huc dederu[nt	i]nperatoribus summeis,
utei sesed lubent[es	be]ne iouent optantis

'To Jove Juno Minerva, the Faliscans stationed in Sardinia made a votive offering. The heads of the guild, Lucius Latrius, son of Caeso, and Gaius Salvena, son of Volta, undertook arrangements. The guild, which makes life agreeable, [and is] rich in gladdening life and feast days, [the cooks' guild] which with their own ability and the help of Vulcan frequently adorn the banquets and games, the cooks dedicated here [their votive offering] to the supreme leaders, in order that they willingly afford their generous help whenever it pleases them.'

Points of note in the first text include the interchange of *f* and *h* at the beginning of words, such that *h*- in the Latin of Rome corresponds to an *f*- in Faliscan (however the reverse may equally occur, as in the case of Fal. *hileo* ~ Lat. *fīliō*, and similarly *haba* ~ *faba*, etc.). This phenomenon is found also in the dialect of Praeneste, as shown by the forms *Fercles, Felena, Foratia*, corresponding to Lat. *Herclēs, Helena, Horātia*. Nor can we rule out the possibility that such variations are of Etruscan origin, in so far as other Etruscan influences have apparently been detected in both the Faliscan and Praenestine varieties.

Furthermore, we should note the presence of -*f*- between vowels as opposed to -*b*-, the loss of final -*m* and -*s* (which, in any case, already characterized the most colloquial registers of the captial), and in the second text, the diphthong -*ei* > -*e*, several cases of *c* voicing (> *g*) both word-initially and word-internally, and a nominative plural in -*eis* for -*ole*- stems. Apart from the two texts just examined, already exemplary *per se*, we should mention here among the many other features typical of rustic Latin the marked tendency to monophthongize diphthongs, the frequent syncope of unstressed vowels, the change *d > r* before [f, w] (and conversely *r > d* in the context [-*r* # *d*-]), the preservation of -*sn*-, the failure of rhotacism to generalize, the nominative plural in -*s* also with -*ā* stems (as well as with -*o/e*- stems, as noted above), the genitive singular in -*osio* of nouns of the II declension, the forms of the genitive singular in -*us* (-*os*) for consonant stems of the so-called III declension (as opposed to -*is* < -*es* in the dialect of Rome; symptomatic in this respect is the parallelism between the verb ending of the second-person singular middle which appears as -*us* instead of -*is*). In vocabulary, too, we have some evidence that the country dialects differed from the dialect of Rome. Of the numerous examples that we could cite here, the well-known testimony of Festus alone will suffice. Based on the latter, we are forced to conclude that, if Roman Latin used the term *rēnēs* for 'kidneys', the Latin dialects of Lanuvium and Praeneste used *nebrundines* and *nefrones*, respectively. Similarly, the Roman *nōsse* and *nōtio* correspond to the Praenestine *tongere* and *tongitio*.

As for particular Italic elements, which not only influenced the Latin country dialects but also left their mark on the dialect of Rome itself, we should mention such words as *būfalus, Mulcifer, rūfus, sīfilō, sīfilus, vafer*, which coexisted alongside their 'authentic' Latin equivalents (which show a medial -*b*- as opposed to -*f*-) *būbalus, Mulciber, ruber, sībilō, sībilus, vaber* (the latter attested in glosses). Hence, such words as *bōs* and *lupus* (where we would expect **vōs* and **luquos*, respectively; note that there is a strong case for ascribing *lupus* to Sabine); and *lacrima, lingua* alongside their expected Roman equivalents *dacruma, dingua* (in the latter example *l*- may, however, be the result of a Latin internal development, if we accept the plausible influence of *lingō*) and similarly *oleō, ūlīgo* as contrasted with *odor, ūdus*, perhaps also *solium* as against *sedeō* (such an alternation, moreover, finds a parallel in Lithuanian). Thus, we have a number of words in which *l* occurs as opposed to the expected Latin *d*, one of the most striking peculiarities repeatedly ascribed to Sabine influence.

If we are indeed justified in postulating that in the linguistic conscience of Latin writers, and particularly grammarians, the apparently general label of *veterēs* or *antīquī* can be frequently and readily taken to refer specifically to a Sabine influence, then we are forced to presume a Sabine origin not only for such words as *cascus* (= *vetus*), *cūris* (= *hasta*), *dīrus* (= *malus*) – recognized and attested by the *auctōrēs* themselves – but also for a whole series of phonetic phenomena such as the interchange of *f*- for *h*- noted above, or the absence of rhotacism (hence *fedus* for *haedus*, *fasena* for *harēna*, etc.). Thus, there is at least a presumption of Sabine origin for those words, to all intents and purposes of Latin stock, that do not exhibit rhotacism of intervocalic -*s*-, such as *Caesar, casa, cāseus*. Today scholars are even more dubious about the presumed Sabine origin of the change *ou > ō* (instead of Latin *ū*, as in *rōbīgo* as opposed to *rūfus*, both from an IE root **rowdʰ-/*

*rewd^h-, which also gives Roman *ruber*), as well as the monophthongization of *ai* and *au* which give *ē* and *ō*, respectively; in this respect we cannot fail to note, in particular, the doublets *aulla* ~ *ōlla*, *cauda* ~ *cōda*, *caudex* ~ *cōdex*, *Claudius* ~ *Clōdius*, *lautus* ~ *lōtus*, *plaustrum* ~ *plōstrum*, etc., and as for the diphthong *ai*, the well-known testimony in Varro *l.L.* 5, 97 illustrates the use of *haedus* ~ *hedus* in accordance with an 'urban' vs. 'rustic' opposition. In fact, the tendency towards monophthongization of the diphthongs generally appears to be, rather, one of the many 'Umbrianisms' that variously influenced the Latin dialects over a long period of time and in a number of ways. In particular, the reductions just examined, namely *ai* > *ē* and *au* > *ō*, are typologically common and widely attested in the most diverse of linguistic systems. This undoubtedly suggests that such phenomena could easily have occurred independently in various registers of the Roman *Umgangssprache*, and are not necessarily the result of a direct 'Italic' influence.

None the less, we cannot fail to observe the well documented pursuit of the educated Roman classes, as early as the second century BC, to impose a standard literary language in which the ideals of *urbānitās* and *ēlegantia* became increasingly established. Thus, there arose a widespread tendency to banish the symbols of *antīquitās*, identified with pure Sabine origin, and those of *rūsticitās*, identified more generally with 'Italic' origin.

Being an argument better suited to a discussion of the history of the Latin language, we limit our discussion to a summary examination of the developments that characterized the vocabulary of the language of Rome. Suffice it to note that Roman vocabulary betrays a significant Greek influence in a number of loan words that arose through direct contact with the Greek, Ionian or Doric colonies and those of southern Italy and Sicily, or, alternatively, through Etruscan intermediacy. In this respect we may list early words like *Achīvī* < Ἀχαιϝοί, *olīva* < ἐλαίϝα (and probably *vīnum* < Ϝοῖνος), and similarly *bal(i)neum* < βαλανεῖον, *calx* < χάλιξ, *camera* < καμάρα, *drach(u)ma* < δραχμά, *māchina* < μαχανά, *menta* < μίνθα, *mina* < μνᾶ, *purpura* < πορφύρα, *tessera* < τέσσαρα, *triump(h)us* < θρίαμβος, and for those words which presumably betray a direct Etruscan intermediacy, we can add *Catamītus* < Γανυμήδης, *cotōneum* < κυδώνιον, *gubernāre* < κυβερνᾶν, *gutturnium/cuturnium* < κωθώνιον, *persōna* < πρόσωπον (via Etruscan intermediacy *φersu*), *sporta* < σπυρίδα (with much uncertainty in rendering both the plosive consonants and the back vowels), hence *cisterna* < κίστη and *lanterna* < λαμπτῆρα (with adjunction of a typical Etruscan suffix to the Greek nominal base).

It appears that the betrayal of an early Greek influence in the Latin and Sabine dialects, following close contact with Greek peoples, is equally confirmed by classical sources which testify to the presence of Arcadians in Latium. On the basis of such sources, it has been possible to postulate that a word such as *Lupercālēs*, which can undoubtedly be traced to the Arcadian settlement on the Palatine Hill, probably represents *wl^uk^w-arkádes,

'Arcadian-wolves', hence the Latino-Sabine transformation of a term probably dating from the Mycenaean period.

Although accidentally or, rather, deliberately absent from the admittedly vast, but none the less normative and puristic, epigraphic and literary documentation of the classical period, an unrelenting and widespread penetration of Greek elements into the most varied registers of the everyday spoken language, and not simply that of the educated classes, is further confirmed by those loan words which betray a popular etymology (such as *aurichalcum* < ὀρείχαλκος, *mīllefolium* < μηλόφυλλον, *caerefolium* < χαιρέφυλλον) and by indirect reconstructions based on the evidence of the Romance languages, or the isolated pieces of evidence that have come to light from the later Latin period.

The Etruscans made remarkably little contribution to the vocabulary of Latin, although there are a number of noteworthy exceptions, as witnessed by the testimonies of grammarians and lexicographers, that we should mention such as *crumīna, fala* 'wooden tower', *fenestra, genista, hister/histrio, lanista* 'trainer of gladiators', *laniēna* 'butcher's shop'.

As for Celtic influence, we should first mention those terms that refer to particular types of carts such as *benna* 'a two-wheeled cart with a wickerwork body', *carpentum* 'a covered wagon, two-wheeled carriage', *carrus* 'a four-wheeled baggage-wagon', *essedum* 'a two-wheeled war-chariot', *petorritum* 'an open four-wheeled carriage', *raeda/rēda* 'a four-wheeled travelling carriage'. We can also include here terms denoting working animals, such as *verēdus* 'a swift horse' (its Low Latin hybrid word, *paraverēdus*, gives Ger. *Pferd*), or weaponry, like *catēia* 'a barbed spear, iron cudgel', *gaesum* 'an iron javelin', *lancea, parma* 'a light shield', *sparus/sparum* 'a short javelin', and, finally, those terms designating clothing, like *brācae* (in turn borrowed by Celtic from Germanic), *sagus/sagum* 'a tunic'. Besides these semantic domains, we can also mention such words as *alauda, betulla* and, in particular, *ambactus* 'serf', used in Ennius and which soon found its way into Germanic (cf. Goth. *andbahti* and present-day Ger. *Amt*).

In light of the obvious complexity involved in the intricate problem of evaluating the linguistic contributions made to Latin by the so-called Mediterranean substratum, we should have to dedicate a separate study to the question. Consequently, we shall limit ourselves to listing some of the uncontroversial cases of Mediterranean influence, such as *plumbum* (for which a vague resemblance with the Greek dialect forms has been noted μόλυβδος, μόλιβδος, μόλιβος, βόλιμος), *vaccīnium* (related to Gk ὑάκινθος), *viola* (Gk Ϝίον), *līlium* (Gk λείριον), *cupressus* (Gk κυπάρισσος), *laurus* (Gk δάφνη/δαῦκον/δαύχνα/λάφνη), *ficus* (Gk σῦκον), *rosa* (Gk Ϝρόδον) and perhaps *bāca/bacca*. In relation to the later example, it will be recalled that, in the absence of any direct evidence, a number of other cases where Latin words presumably descend from a Mediterranean substratum can be reconstructed on the basis of well-founded comparative evidence from Romance.

To conclude, we should finally mention Punic to which we can attribute *māgālia/mapālia* 'the huts of the nomadic peoples', perhaps *tunica* which like the Gk χιτών might have been borrowed from an eastern Semitic language), and above all the greeting *ave*, attested as early as Cicero and Catullus, and directly traceable to the earlier Plautine *avō* (cf. *Poen.* 994, 998, 1001), uttered by the Punic Hanno and glossed as *salūtat* by the slave Milphio.

The Earliest Epigraphic and Literary Records

Among the earliest Latin epigraphic and literary (legal-religious) records, we begin with the *Lapis niger*, the famous mutilated cippus found in 1899, which presumably dates from about the sixth/fifth century BC. On this cippus, there is inscribed vertically boustrophedon a fragmented text, on the extant part of which can be clearly read *quoi* = *quī*, *sakros* = *sacer*, *esed* = *esset*, *recei* = *rēgī*, *kalatorem* = *calātōrem* 'preacher', *iouxmenta* = *iūmenta*, *kapia* = *capiat*, *iouestod* = *iūstō*. Passing over the *fibula Praenestīna*, the falsity of which has already been amply and, dare one say, satisfactorily proven, we cannot forget the inscription written on the so-called Vase of Duenos, found in 1880 in the valley between the Quirinal and the Viminal. The text of the inscription, whose dating may variably fall within the fourth century BC, on more than one occasion has been the subject of *interpretātio*, or rather *dīvīnātio* among many linguists. Once again, we shall limit ourselves to listing only those words that can be clearly made out on the inscription: *iouesat* = *iūrat*, *deiuos* = *deōs*, *qoi* = *quī*, *med* = *mē* (acc.), *mitat* = variant of *mittit*, *nei* = *nī*, *ted endo* = *in tē*, *cosmis* = *cōmis* 'courteous', *uirco* = *virgo*, *sied* = *si(e)t*, *pakari* = *pācārī*, *uois* = *vīs*, *duenos* = *bonus*, *feced* = *fēcit*, *en manom* = *in mānum* (where *mānum* is equivalent to *bonum*), *duenoi* = *bonō*. As for literary evidence, we begin with the few remains of the *Carmina Saliāria*, handed down to us in incomplete form via Varro and Terentius Scaurus, a grammarian of the Hadrian's period. An element of remarkable linguistic interest is the verb form *tremonti* = *tremunt*, precious (and unique) evidence of the original third-person plural 'primary ending' (cf. Chapter 4, p. 113), before the generalization of -*nt* which had long since spread to the entire verbal paradigm. Also of note is the *Carmen Arvāle*, preserved in the record of the proceedings of the *Frātrēs Arvālēs* in AD 218, engraved on stone, whose points of linguistic interest include *Lases* for *Larēs*, the presumed *rues* for the classical *ruīna*, *sins* for *sinās*, the imperative *fu* derived from the root **bʰu-*, which supplied much of the conjugation of the verb 'to be', and *berber* which appears to be a reduplicated form of a demonstrative stem. Other testimonies of early religious formulae appear in Cato's *Dē agricultūrā* and Varro's *Dē linguā Latīnā*. Nor should we forget the admittedly scanty remains of the politico-legal language, closely related to the religious formulae constituted of fragments pertaining to the *Lēgēs XII tabulārum*, the text of which comes to us through quotations or sometimes paraphrases by various *auctōres*, notably

Cicero and the jurists, but not without some obvious modernization. Among the most characteristic features worthy of citation here, we should mention at least those phenomena of considerable relevance to the linguistic history of the Latin language, such as *im* and *em* for the accusative forms *eum* and *sum* of an early deictic **so-* (cf. Gk ό), and, in the field of syntax, the absence of overt marking to signal the change of sentential subject.

Thus, considered as a whole, the earliest epigraphic and literary records examined above (as well as many inscriptions from later periods, inasmuch as they preserve many conservative or distinctly archaizing features) provide us with the means to reconstruct with sufficient approximation many peculiarities of Old Latin.

Suffice it to recall, in the field of phonetics/phonology, the general preservation of original diphthongs (save *eu* which had already evolved into *ou*), of intervocalic *-s-* (which had not yet rhotacized) and of numerous word-internal consonantal groups, which were subsequently simplified (e.g. the reduction of *-sm-* or *-xm-* to *-m-*); as for morphology, we should note in the declension of *-o/e-* stems the consistent distinction between dative and ablative (*-oi/ō* and *-ōd*, respectively), subsequently neutralized in the classical period, and the inherited distinction between primary and secondary endings in the verbal system (*iouesat/mitat* vs. *sied/feced*), equally doomed to extinction with the subsequent generalization of the primary endings. As for points of syntax, these are inevitably scanty in light of the brevity and incompleteness of the texts (particularly illuminating in this respect are later documents like *ēlogia Scīpiōnum* or the *Senātūs cōnsultum dē Bacchānālibus*). We shall, therefore, limit ourselves to mentioning one unmistakable feature of such texts, albeit more relevant to stylistics rather than syntax, namely alliteration, a legacy inherited from the ancient religious formulae and destined to become eternalized as one of the many stylistic devices of the poetic genres.

Accent

Before we proceed to deal with the principal problems of Latin phonetics and phonology, both from an historical perspective and in an ideal synchronic framework, we believe it fitting at this point to touch upon the *vexāta quaestio* of accent, a problem which has notoriously plagued philologists and linguists for decades, leaving them largely divided in their views. At any rate, if IE accent was free and perhaps predominantly a pitch accent (cf. Chapter 2, p. 113), the historical and prehistoric Latin data – both factual and reconstructed – reveal *de facto* a different picture in many respects. Passing over Classical Latin, where the presumed emergence of a pitch accent (used in poetry) can be regarded as a contrived imitation of the Greek, as was prosodic terminology itself which reproduced direct calques of the corresponding Greek terms, it certainly appears difficult to conclude with certainty that Latin once possessed a pitch accent, as undoubtedly was true of Greek. The phenomena of syncope or at least the weakening and subsequent closure of unstressed vowels (suffice it to note the single example *auceps* < **auicaps*, which ideally illustrates both phenomena) undoubtedly bear witness to the existence of a strong stress accent on the initial syllable. The establishment of the so-called 'Penultimate Law' did not significantly change this state of affairs either, as witnessed by the evolution of Latin into Romance which is equally fraught with syllabic reductions, which we would find difficult to account for if we were to accept that Latin exclusively possessed a pitch accent. In this respect, we must remember that Plautine prosody also implies a syllable-initial accent in such words as *fácilius*, *múlierem*, *séquiminī*, as well as in *Phílippus* in certain cases (specifically when the term designates a gold coin, so as to distinguish it from the proper name *Philíppus*, where the Penultimate Law is already operative). Perhaps the only really probative testimony of the Latin grammarians at our disposition is that of the famous passage of Pompeius (cf. GLK V, 126,31–127,11). Unhindered by the traditionally concerted attempts to liken Latin to Greek, the passage appears to depict the Latin situation as it actually was. We cite here the passage *in extēnsō*:

illa syllaba plus sonat in toto verbo, quae accentum habet, ergo illa syllaba, quae accentum habet, plus sonat, quasi ipsa habet maiorem potestatem. et quo modo invenimus ipsum accentum? et hoc traditum est [. . .] finge tibi quasi vocem clamantis ad longe aliquem positum. ut puta finge tibi aliquem illo loco contra stare et clama ad ipsum. cum coeperis clamare, naturalis ratio exigit ut unam syllabam plus dicas a reliquis illius verbi; et quam videris plus sonare a ceteris, ipsa habet accentum. ut puta si dicas orator, quae plus sonat? ra, ipsa habet accentum. optimus, quae plus sonat? illa quae prior est. numquid sic sonat ti et mus, quem ad modum op? ergo necesse est ut illa syllaba habeat accentum, quae plus sonat a reliquis, quando clamorem fingimus

'the most prominent syllable of a word is that which bears the accent; thus the accented syllable has a greater resonance, as if it were pronounced with greater force; and by what method do we ascertain the accent of a word? This has also been passed down to us [. . .] imagine the voice of someone calling someone else far away: suppose for example that someone is standing in front of you at that same distance and that you call him raising your voice. As soon as you begin to call him, you are forced by natural instinct to pronounce one of the syllables of the word with greater stress, and the one you hear resound most loudly is the syllable that bears the accent. Suppose you want to say the word *orator*: which syllable is the most audible? *Ra*, this is the accented syllable. Take *optimus*: which syllable is the most resonant? The first; could it be that *ti* and *mus* are as resonant as *op*? Of course not. Thus the syllable which bears the accent is that which has greater resonance than the others when we imagine we are calling someone.'

Consequently, we conclude that Latin was characterized by a stress accent, whether the latter fell on the first syllable, as our reconstructions of the early linguistic history of Latin lead us to believe, or whether its position was determined by the Penultimate Law, as operative in the classical period. Spurred by the Greek models, the accented syllable in the classical period could at most be pronounced, beside its general increased articulatory force, at a higher pitch than the unstressed syllables. However, the higher pitch played a redundant role, incapable of even preparing the ground for a complete restructuring of a prosodic system which has to all intents and purposes remained intact in the present-day Romance languages.

Phonetics and Phonology
We shall first examine the facts most relevant to historical phonetics, as they now appear to be widely recognized in a large number of studies of comparative reconstruction within the field of Indo-European. Subsequently, we shall proceed to sketch a phonological analysis.

Historical Phonetics
Vowels
We observe the following outcomes and correspondences in initial accented syllables:

IE *a* > Lat. *a*, cf. *agō*, Gk ἄγω; *ager*, Gk ἀγρός, Skt *ajras*, Goth. *akrs*;

IE *ā* > Lat. *ā*, cf. *fāma*, Dor. Gk φᾱμᾱ, *māter*, Dor. Gk μᾱ́τηρ, Skt *mātar-*;

IE *e* > Lat. *e*, cf. *est*, Gk ἐστί, Goth. *ist*, Skt *asti*; *genus*, Gk γένος, Skt *janas*;

IE *ē* > Lat. *ē*, cf. *fēcit*, Gk ἔ-θη-κε; *plēnus*, Gk πλήρης;

IE *i* > Lat. *i*, cf. *videō*, Gk Ϝιδ-εῖν, Goth. *wit-um*, Skt *vid-mas*; **dix, dicis*, Gk δίκη;

IE *ī* > Lat. *ī*, cf. *vīrus*, Gk Ϝῑός; *vīvus*, Skt *jīvas*;

IE *o* > Lat. *o*, cf. *octō*, Gk ὀκτώ, Goth. *ahtau*, Skt *aṣṭau*; *potis*, Gk πόσις, Skt *patis*;

IE *ō* > Lat. *ō*, cf. *dōnum*, Gk δῶρον; *(g)nōtus*, Gk γνωτός, Skt *jñātas*;

IE *u* > Lat. *u*, cf. *iugum*, Gk ζυγόν, Goth. *juk*, Skt *yugam*; *ruber*, Gk ἐ-ρυθρός, Skt *rudhiras*;

IE *ū* > Lat. *ū*, cf. *fūmus*, Gk θῡμός, Skt *dhūmas*; *mūs*, Gk μῦς, OHG *mūs*;

IE *ə* > Lat. *a*, cf. *pater*, Gk πατήρ, Goth. *faðar*, Skt *pitar-*; *status*, Gk στατός, Skt *sthitas*.

Although the presumed original IE vowels generally persist, we should, however, note a whole host of syntagmatically determined innovations characteristic of Latin:

1   *e* > *i* when followed by [ŋ], i.e. the groups [ŋk, ŋg] and [ŋn] < [kn]: **tengō* > *ting(u)ō*, Gk τέγγω; **penkʷe* > *kʷenkʷe* > *quīnque*, Gk πέντε; **dec-nos* > *dignus* [ŋn], cf. *dec-et*;

2   *e* > *o* beside [w]: **newos* > *novus*, Gk νέϜος; **swesōr* > **sosōr* > *sorōr*, Skt *svasar-*, Goth. *swistar*; **swek̑uros* > *socer*, Gk (σϜ)εχυρός; the same phenomenon obtains when *e* is followed by [ɫ], i.e. by the elements [ɫa, ɫo, ɫu, ɫ + conson. ≠ from l]: **welō* > *volō*, **welti* > *volt* (> *vult*); **se-luō* > *solvō*; **elaiwa* > *olīva*, Gk ἐλαί(Ϝ)α, as well as **helus* > *holus*, but in *scelus, gelū* this change was perhaps inhibited by the slight palatization of *c, g*, followed by *e*;

3   *o* > *u* when followed by [ŋ], cf. *uncus* against Gk ὄγχος, *unguis* against Gk ὄνυξ, but note *longus* where *o* remains intact, cf. Goth. *laggs*; also when *o* is followed by [mb], cf. *umbo* against Gk ὀμφαλός, or [mk], cf. *hunc* < *honc* < **hom-ce*, and [ɫ]: *sulcus* against Gk ὁλκός, *ulcus* < **olkos* < **elkos*, Gk ἕλκος, and similarly for *volt* > *vult, colpa* > *culpa, molta* > *multa*;

4   *wo-* > *we* before [r, s, t]: *vorsus, vortex, vortō, voster, votō* > *versus, vertex, vertō, vester, vetō*, a change which seems to have taken place around the middle of the second century BC;

5   *ō* > *ū* when followed by [r]: *quōr* > *cūr, fūr* against Gk φώρ.

As far as *diphthongs* are concerned, the following changes are of interest:

IE *aj* > Lat. *ai* > *ae* (but > *ē* in rustic dialects) from the beginning of the second century BC, hence > [ε:] which, in variations of speech, could undergo 'regularization' to yield [ε] or [eː], cf. **ajdʰ-* > *aedēs* (originally 'fireplace'), *aestus, aestās*, Gk αἴθω, Skt *ēdha-*, OHG *eit* 'stake' (and cf. OLat. *aidīlis*); *laevus* against Gk λαι(Ϝ)ός;

IE *ej* > Lat. *ī*, passing through the intermediate stage *ē*, the latter persisting in the country dialects, cf. **dejk-* > *dīcō*, Gk δείχνυμι; **bʰejdʰ-* > *fīdō*, Gk πείθω; **ej-ti* > *īt*, Gk εἶ-σι; **dejwos* > *dīvus*, but archaic and 'rustic' *dēvos*;

IE *oj* > Lat. *oi* > *oe* > *ū*: **ojnos* > *oinos* > *oenos* > *ūnus*, Gk οἴνη 'one on a dice'; OLat. *comoinem* > *commūnem, coirāvit* > *cūrāvit*, but compare the doublets *poena* (Gk ποινή)/*pūniō, moenia/mūrus* < *moerus* and *mūniō, Poenī/Pūnicus* (Gk Φοῖνιξ) and the isolated *foedus*, which still await an adequate explanation;

IE *aw* > Lat. *au* (but often > *ō* in the country dialects), hence > [ɔ:] which, in variations of speech, could undergo 'regularization' to yield [ɔ] or [oː], cf. **aws-* > **awsis* > *auris*, Goth. *ausō*, Lith. *ausis*; **awg-* > *augeō*, Gk αὔξω, and note the oscillation between forms like *aulla/ōlla, cauda/cōda, plaustrum/plōstrum*, or, conversely, *plōdō/plaudō* (the latter hypercorrect form being an example of a hyperurbanism);

IE *ew* > Lat. *ou* > *ū* as early as the third century BC, cf. **dewk- > doucō > dūcō*, Goth. *tiuhan*; **ewsō > *owso > ūrō*, Gk εὔω; **lewk- > lūx*, Gk λευκός, Goth. *liuhaþ* 'light'; note the intermediate stage *ou > oi* exhibited by Faliscan, and sporadically by urban Latin (subsequently yielding *oi > ei > ī*), where between *l* and a labial consonant (or labiodental consonant, recall, for instance, that Latin *f* was articulated with a high degree of labialization), *ou* presumably underwent dissimilation. Thus given IE **lewdʰro-* 'free', cf. Gk ἐ-λεύθερος, this obviously yields **lowfro-/*lowbro-* and hence **lojfro-/*lojbro-*, as can be inferred from the Faliscan *loifirtato* and the urban Latin *līber < *leibros*;

IE *ow* > Lat. *ou* > *ū*, cf. **lowkos* 'clearing' > *lūcus* (old acc. *loucom*); **lowksno-* 'shining' > *lūna* (Praen. *losna*).

The long diphthongs, which are normally found not only word-initially and word-internally, but also in the desinential case endings, will be discussed in the treatment of Latin morphology.

In unstressed medial syllables, short vowels and diphthongs are subject to particular modifications, which we summarize here in more general terms:

(a) In open syllables all short vowels tend to be systematically raised to *i*, cf. such alternations as *faciō ~ conficiō, cadō ~ occidō* (equally evident in a number of Greek loan words, such as Dor. Gk μᾱχανά́ ~ *māc(h)ina*), *sedeō ~ obsideō, legō ~ colligō, locus (< *stlocos) ~ īlicō (< *en stlocōd), novus < novos ~ novitās, caput ~ capitis, manus ~ manica* (*i* obviously remains unchanged: *video ~ invideō, citō ~ incitō*). Observe, however, that before *l* the vowel appears variously as *i* (as before palatal [l]) or *u* (as before velar [ɫ]): *exilium ~ exulāns, familia ~ famulus, similis ~ simulāre* (the same also holds of Greek loan words: *scutula ~ σκυτάλα, crāpula ~ κραιπάλα, paenula ~ φαινόλης*), and even as *o*, especially following vowels, cf. *fīliolus, viola*. Moreover, before *r* the vowel generally appears as *e*, cf. *cineris < *cinises* (the same can be said of Greek loan words, cf καμάρα > *camera*), although an original *o* persists in many cases or, alternatively, is the result of analogical forces: *memoria, pectoris, temporis* (although the form *temperī* is also attested). Finally, before labial consonants the vowel appears variously as *i* and *u*, as the following alternations illustrate: *incipiō ~ occupō, regimen ~ documentum*.

(b) In closed syllables we generally find the changes *a > e* and *o > u*, whereas *e, i, u* remain unchanged, cf. alternations of the type *castus ~ incestus, arma ~ inermis* (also in Greek loan words like τάλαντον ~ *talentum*), *alumnus < *alomnos, secundus < *sekʷondos* and, in contrast, the unchanging *sessus/*

obsessus, *dictus/addictus*, *ductus/adductus*. Note, however, the development *a > e > i* before [ŋ], cf. *frangō ~ confringō*, *tangō ~ contingō*, or *a > e > u* before [ł]: *calcō ~ inculcō*, *salsus ~ insulsus*, which also explains *e > u*, equally before [ł], cf. *percellō ~ perculsus*.

(c) As for the diphthongs, note *ai > ei > ī*: *aequos ~ inīquos*, *aestimō ~ exīstimō*; *ei > ī*: **feidō* (classical *fīdō*) *~ confīdo*; *oi > ē*: **postmoiriom > pōmērium*; *au > ou > ū*: *claudō ~ inclūdō, fraudō ~ dēfrūdō* (arch.), but *audiō ~ oboediō* remains unexplained; *ou > ū*: *doucō* (arch.) *~ addūcō* (this also holds of *eu* since the latter merged *ab antīquō* with *ou*). Observe that the alternation *plaudō ~ explōdō* confirms that *plaudō* is a hyperurbanism for the original *plōdō*.

Finally, points of note with regard to final syllables:

(a) In open syllables, *a*, *e* and *u* generally persist whereas *i* gives *e*, e.g. **mari > mare*, **anti > ante* (Gk ἀντί), and similarly *o > e*: **sekʷeso > sequere*. Moreover, *-i* may be lost as in the primary endings of the verb, e.g. *tremonti > tremunt*, **esti > est*, **sonti > sunt*, as well as *-e*, e.g. *dīc*, *dūc*, *fac*, *em*, as opposed to the canonical forms of the present imperative like *lege*, *cape* (the same phenomenon can occur when enclitic particles attach to particular verb forms, cf. *vidēsne > vidēn > viden* with *e* for *correptio iambica*).

(b) In closed syllables, the following changes occur: *a > e* e.g. **artifax > artifex*, **tībīcan > tībīcen*, whereas *e* is preserved, except before *-s* and *-t* where it gives *i*: **ages(i) > agis,* aget(i) > agit, dedet > dedit, *rēges > rēgis*; *i* and *u* also persist, in contrast to *o* which develops into *u*, except following [u, w]: *dominus, aliud, istud, illud*, but *exiguos, equos, parvos*.

(c) The treatment of diphthongs in final syllables is parallel to that in unstressed medial syllables, thus *ai/ei/oi > ei > ī*. Compare here the development of the nominative plural desinences of *-o/e-* stems (so-called II declension) and the first-person singular of the active perfect indicative: **lupoi > lupei > lupī*: **wojdai > *weidei > vīdī*.

(d) Finally, long vowels in closed final syllables undergo shortening before *-m, -t, -nt, -l, -r* (e.g. *amēs* against *amem, amet, ament*; *tribūnālis* against *tribūnal*; *amōris* against *amor*, etc.), as well as in open final syllables (in both nominal and verbal inflection), as a consequence of iambic shortening, attested since earliest times.

Semi-vowels
As for the semi-vowels, it is worth noting the following changes:

IE [j] > Lat. [j], which is vocalized following consonants and falls in intervocalic position: ** jugom > iugum*, Gk ζυγόν, Skt *yugam*, Goth. *juk*; **jekʷr̥t > iecur*, Gk ἧπαρ, Skt *yakr̥t*, but **aljos > alius* (trisyll.), Gk ἄλλος,

Goth. *aljis*; **medʰjos* > *medius* (trisyll.), Gk μέσ(σ)ος, Skt *madhya-*, Goth. *midjis*; **trejes* > **trees* > *trēs*, Gk τρεῖς, Skt *trayas*, Goth. *þreis*;

IE [w] > Lat. [w]: **wiro-/*wīro-* > *vir*, Skt *vīras* 'hero', Goth. *wair*; **owis* > *ovis*, Gk ὀ(F)ίς, Skt *avis*; **newos* > *novos*, Gk νέ(F)ος, Skt *navas*; **ekwos* > *equos*, Skt *aśva*; **swādwi-* > *suāvis*, Dor. Gk (σF)ᾱδύς, Skt *svādus*. Note that [w] is vocalized in the word-internal cluster *-tw-*, e.g. **kʷetwor-* > *quattuor* (trisyll.), Skt *catvāras*, and falls entirely in the cluster **swo-* < **swe-*, e.g. **swesōr* > **swosōr* > *sorōr*, **sweḱuros* > **swokuros* > *socer*.

Consonants

We shall now examine the principal phenomena relating to the consonants, beginning, as with tradition, by an examination of the nasals and liquids.

Consonant phonemes prove to be potentially more robust in processes of linguistic change, as a small sample of Latin examples will suffice to demonstrate:

IE *m* > Lat. *m*: **mātēr* > *māter*, Dor. Gk μάτηρ, Skt *mātar-*; **bʰeromes* > *ferimus*, Dor. Gk φέρομες, Skt *bharāmas*;

IE *n* > Lat. *n*: **newos* > *novos*, Gk νέ(F)ος, Skt *navas*; **seno-* > *senex*, Gk ἕνος, 'of the year before', Skt *sana-*;

IE *l* > Lat. *l*: **lewk-* > *lūx*, *lūceō*, Gk λευκός; **klutos* > *(in)clutus*, Gk κλυτός, Skt *śrutas*;

IE *r* > Lat. *r*: **rewdʰ-/*rudʰ-* > *rūfus*, *ruber*, Gk ἐ-ρυθός, Skt *rudhiras*; **bʰer-* > *ferō*, Gk φέρω, Skt *bharāmi*.

As for the sonants, namely the syllabic nasals and liquids, they underwent the following changes in Latin:

IE *m̥* > Lat. *em*: **km̥tom* > **kemtom* > *centum* (with *m* > *n* before *t*), Gk ἑ-κατόν, Skt *śatam*; **deḱm̥* > *decem*, Gk δέκα, Skt *daśa*; **septm̥* > *septem*, Gk ἑπτά, Skt *sapta*;

IE *n̥* > Lat. *en*: **mn̥tis* > *mentis* > *mēns*, Skt *matis*; **tn̥tos* > *tentus*, Gk τατός, Skt *tatas*; **newn̥* > *novem* (with *-m* rather than *-n* by analogy with *septem*, *decem*), Skt *nava*;

IE *l̥* > Lat. *ol*: **ml̥du-* > **moldwis* > *mollis*, Gk ἀ-μαλδ-ύ-νω, Skt *mr̥du-*;

IE *r̥* > Lat. *or*: **mr̥tis* > *mors*, Skt *mr̥tis*; **kr̥d-* > *cor*, *cordis*, Gk καρδία; **pr̥k-skō* > **porc-scō* > *poscō*;

Sonorants also arose when a strong accent on an initial syllable gave rise to syncope; we list the following examples involving *r̥* (> *er*), which was particularly affected by this phenomenon:

*agros > **agr̥s* > **agers* > *ager*, **agrolos* > **agr̥los* > **agerlos* > *agellus*, **tris* > **tr̥s* > **ters* > *ter*.

Without wishing to enter into the problematic area of the IE long sonants, we shall simply mention here the more straightforward examples:

for *n̥̄* cf. **gn̥̄tos* > *gnātus*, Skt *jātas*;
for *l̥̄* cf. **wl̥̄na* > **wlāna* > *lāna*, Skt *ūrṇā*, Lith. *vilna*;
for *r̥̄* cf. **gr̥̄nom* > *grānum*, Skt *jīrṇa-* 'meal, grist', Goth. *kaurnō* 'grain'.

As for the plosive consonants, Latin generally preserved both the voiceless and the voiced series, whereas the voiced aspirates underwent the same changes as those common to most of the IE languages:

IE *p* > Lat. *p*: **ped-/*pod-* > *pēs, pedis*, Gk πούς, ποδός, Skt *pad-*; **spek-* > *speciō*, Gk σκέπτομαι (with metathesis of *p*/*k*); **septm̥* > *septem*, etc.;

IE *b* > Lat. *b*: **belo-* 'strength' > *dē-bilis*, Skt *balam*; **pibeti* '(he/she) drinks' > *bibit* (with non-contiguous assimilation of *p* > *b*), Skt *pibati*;

IE *bʰ* > Lat. *f* and *b* in initial and medial position, respectively: **bʰer-* > *ferō*, Gk φέρω, Skt *bhar-*, Goth. *bairan*; **albʰo-* > *albus*; **orbʰ-* > *orbus*, Gk ὀρφανός; in some country dialects we find *h-* rather than *f-*, cf. *haba* against urban *faba*;

IE *t* > Lat. *t*: **trejes* > *trēs*, Gk τρεῖς, Skt *trayas*; **esti* > *est*, Gk ἐστί, Skt *asti*; cf. also the change *-tl-* > *-cl-*: **pōtlom* > *pōc(u)lum*, **saitlom* > *saec(u)lum*, Gk ἀντλεῖν (*ex-*)*anclāre*, which is also a feature of Late Latin: *vet(u)lus* > *veclus*, *test(u)lum* > *tesclum*. After a consonant, final *-t* is lost, e.g. **lact* > *lac*, and is voiced after a vowel, e.g. the archaic forms *esed*, *feced* (before the generalization of the primary ending *-t* < **-ti*);

IE *d* > Lat. *d*: **domos* > *domus*, Gk δόμος, Skt *damas*; **ed-* > *edō*, Gk ἔδομαι, Skt *admi*. Note that **dw-* > *b-*: *duellum* > *bellum*, *duenos* > *bonus*. Final *-d* falls after long vowels, e.g. *lupōd* > *lupō*, *mēd* > *mē*, and following consonants, e.g. **cord* > *cor*. Note that in certain dialect forms an alternation between *d* and *l* is observed: *dingua* ~ *lingua*, *dacruma* ~ *lacruma*, *odor* ~ *oleō*, *sedeō* ~ *solium*;

IE *dʰ* > Lat. *f* and *d/b* in word-initial and word-medial position, respectively: **dʰūmos* > *fūmus*, Gk θυμός, Skt *dhūma-*; **dʰē-* > *fēcī*, Gk ἔ-θη-κα, but **ajdʰ-* > *aedēs, aestus, aestās*, Gk αἴθω, Skt *ēdha-*. Under certain conditions, *dʰ* becomes *-b-*: (a) before or after *-r-*: **rudʰro-* > **rubros* > *ruber*, Gk ἐ-ρυθρός, Skt *rudhira-*, **werdʰo-* > *verbum*, Goth. *waurd*; (b) before *-l-*: **stədʰlo-* > *stabulum*, with an anaptyctic *-u-* in the cluster *-bl-*; (c) after (*-*)*u-*: **ūdʰer* 'breast, udder' > *ūber*, Gk οὖθαρ, Skt *ūdhar*;

IE *k* > Lat. *k* (as one of the *centum* languages, Latin does not distinguish between pure velars and palatalized velars): **krewəs* > *cruor*, Gk κρέας, Skt *kravis*; **kerd-/*kr̥d-* > *cor, cordis*, Gk καρδία; **ekwos* > *equos*, Skt *aśvas*; **ōku-* 'quick' > *ōcior*, Gk ὠκύς, Skt *āśu-*;

IE *g* > Lat. *g* (same considerations as for *k*): **steg-* > *tegō*, Gk στέγος 'roof'; Lith. *stogas*, 'roof'; **agō* > *agō*, Gk ἄγω, Skt *ajāmi*; **ĝenos* > *genus*, Gk γένος, Skt *janas*; **ĝenu/*ĝonu > genū*, Gk γόνυ, Skt *jānu*;

IE *gʰ* > Lat. *h*: **gʰejm-/*gʰ(i)jem-* > *hiems*, Gk χιών; **gʰem-/*gʰom-* > *homō, humus*, Gk χαμαί, Goth. *guma*; **gʰostis > hostis*, Goth. *gasts*. After the velar nasal [ŋ], *gʰ* appears as *g*, cf. **angʰ- > angō, angustus*, Gk ἄγχω, **dʰejgʰ- > fingō*, and as *f* before *u*, cf. **gʰew-/*gʰu- > fundō*;

IE *kʷ* > Lat. *qu*: **kʷi-/*kʷo- > quis, quod*, Gk τίς, Skt *kas*; **sekʷ- > sequor*, Gk ἕπομαι, Skt *sacatē*; **lejkʷ- > linquō*, Gk λείπω. The labial element is lost before *o* (> *u*), *i* and consonants, while in the context -*CkʷC*- the labio-velar falls: **sekʷondos > secundus, *sokʷjos > socius, *wōkʷs > vōx, coctus* against *coquō, quīntus* (< **-ŋkʷt-*) against *quīnque, tormentum* (< **-rkʷm-*) against *torqueō*;

IE *gʷ* > Lat. *v*: **gʷīwos > vīvus*, Skt *jīvas*; **gʷem- > veniō*, Gk βαίνω, Goth. *qiman*; the *b-* in *bōs < *gʷow-* betrays its dialect origin. Observe also the preservation of *gʷ* after the velar nasal [ŋ], e.g. **ŋgʷēn > inguen*, Gk ἀδήν, and *gʷ > g* (without the labial element) when followed by *l, r*, e.g. **gʷel-n- > glāns, glandis*;

IE *gʷʰ* > Lat. *f* in word-initial position, e.g. **gʷʰe-/*gʷʰormo-* - 'heat' > *formus*, Gk θερμός, Skt *gharma-*; **gʷʰen- > (dē)-fendō*, Gk θείνω, but > *v* in intervocalic position, e.g. **snigʷʰ- > nivem* (whereas in *nix* the velar element is devoiced and the labial falls altogether), and > *gu* after the velar nasal [ŋ], e.g. **sningʷʰeti > ninguit*, whereas before *r, gʷʰ > f*, e.g. **negʷʰro- >* arch. *nefrundines* (and Praen. *nefrones*, but Lanuvian *nebrundines*, further proof of dialectal variation).

Spirants: IE *s* > Lat. *s* initially and finally and also internally before and after voiceless plosives and after *n*: **seno- > senex*, Gk ἔνος 'of the year before', Skt *sana-*; **ĝenos > genus*, Gk γένος, Skt *janas*; **wes- > vestis, vestiō*, and note *sistō, est, vesper, axis, mēnsis*. A notable phenomenon is the rhotacism of intervocalic *s* (> [z]) > *r*, cf. **geneses > generis, *arbosem > arborem, *flōsem > flōrem*, although this change is absent in borrowed or dialect words like *rosa, casa*. Where intervocalic *s* appears in pure Latin words, it is the outcome of the reduction of -*ss*- > -*s*- after long vowels and diphthongs: **vīssos > vīsus, caussa > causa, quaessō > quaesō*. Before voiced sounds [s] > [z] > Ø with compensatory lengthening of the preceding vowel, e.g. **nisdos > *nizdos > nīdus, *prīsmos > *prīzmos > prīmus*, and initially *sr*- > *fr*- and internally -*sr*- > -*br*-: **srīgos > frīgus, *dʰojnesris > fūnebris*.

Apophony

Apophony (alternatively termed 'vowel gradation' or 'ablaut') persists in Latin as a residual and little-productive phenomenon inherited from Indo-European, where it undoubtedly played an important role in the morpho-phonological system and continues as such in Sanskrit, Greek and the Germanic languages. It continues to have an unmistakably marked morphological role especially in the alternations $\breve{V} \sim \bar{V}$ of the verbal system, frequently giving rise to an *īnfectum ~ perfectum* opposition, as well as maintaining some functional distinctions within the nominal declension. Other vocalic alternations, although present in both the nominal and verbal inflection, are, strictly speaking, more pertinent to vocabulary, of which we list the following examples:

e/o: *pendō ~ pondus, tegō ~ toga, terra ~ extorris, eque* (voc.) *~ equos* (nom.), *dīcit* (< **dīc-e-ti*) *~ dīcunt* (< **dīc-o-nti*);
e/Ø: *est* (< **est-ti*) *~ sunt* (< **s-onti*), *ed-ō ~ d-ēns* (old pres. part. of **ed-* 'the eating'), *gen-uī ~ gi-gn-ō, hiems ~ bīmus* (< **bi-himos*, i.e. 'of two winters', hence 'of two years');
o/Ø: *doceō ~ discō* (< **di-dc-scō*);
e/o/Ø: *fīdō* (< **feidō*) *~ foedus* (< **foidos*) *~ fidēs*;
e/ē: *emō ~ ēmī, tegō ~ tēgula*;
o/ō: *fodiō ~ fōdī, odium ~ ōdī, vocō ~ vōx*;
e/ē/o/Ø: *sedeō ~ sēdēs ~ solium* (< **sod-iom*) *~ sīdō* (< **si-sd-ō*);
e/ē/Ø: *occulō* (< **ob-cel-ō*) *~ cēlō ~ clam*;
e/o/ō: *maiestās ~ maius* (< **maios*) *~ maiōrem* (< **maiōsem*);
e/ō: *honestus ~ honōrem* (< **honōsem*);
ō/Ø: *nepōtem ~ neptis, genitōrem ~ genetrīcem.*

Phonetic Development
Of the various phenomena relevant to the historical phonetic development of Latin, it will suffice to note here the most important phenomena, predominantly processes of regressive assimilation:

the non-contiguous consonantal assimilation in the sequence **p ... kʷ > kʷ ... kʷ*: **penkʷe > *kʷenkʷe > quīnque, *pekʷō > *kʷekʷō > *quoquō > coquō* (*c-* with the loss of the labial following dissimilation);
non-contiguous vocalic assimilation: **hemō > homō, *pepugī > pupugī*, and perhaps **memordī > momordī*;
the devoicing of the voiced plosives before voiceless plosives and fricatives: *āctus, rēctus, tēctus* as opposed to *agō, regō, tegō* (note also the lengthening of the short root vowel in accordance with so-called Lachmann's Law, although ultra-short *i*, e.g. *strictus* against *stringō*, and *e* and *o* may sometimes escape this lengthening process) and *nūpsī, scrīpsī* as opposed to *nūbō, scrībō*. Observe furthermore that the spelling in such words as *obtineō, subtīlis, plēbs* and *urbs* does not represent the actual pronunciation, that is [p] for written *b*, but is simply a case of analogy in accordance with the desire to render the preposed element etymologically transparent or to safeguard 'regularity' within the inflectional paradigm;
the voicing of voiceless plosives and *s* before nasals (*s* also before *l, r*: in all such cases the spirant falls with compensatory lengthening of the

preceding vowel): *segmentum* against *secō*, **sobnos* (> *somnus*, see below) against *sopor*, *prīmus* < **prīzmos* < **prīsmos*, *cānus* < **caznos* < **casnos* against *cascus*, *dīruō* < **dizruō* < **disruō*, *prēlum* < **prezlom* < **preslom*;

the complete assimilation of the plosives before the fricative *f*: *officīna* < **op(i)ficīna*, *afferō* < **adferō*;

the complete assimilation of the dental plosives before the spirant *s*: *assum* < **adsum*, *concussī* < **concutsī*; recall also the reduction *ss* > *s* in final position, cf. **mīlets* > *mīless* > *mīles*, **obseds* > **obsess* > *obses*, and after a long vowel or diphthong: **suādsī* > **suāssī* > *suāsī*, **claudsī* > **claussī* > *clausī*;

the nasal assimilation of the plosives before *n*, whereby the plosive becomes the homorganic nasal, namely *p/b* + *n* > *mn*, *t/d* + *n* > *nn*, *c/g* + *n* > *gn* (where *g* stands for [ŋ]): **sopnos* (see *sopor*) > *somnus*, **scabnom* (see *scabellum*) > *scamnum*, **petna* (see *petō*) > *penna*, *adnuō* > *annuō*, **decnos* (see *decet*) > *dignus* [diŋnus], **legnom* (see *legō*) > *lignum* [liŋnum];

the nasal assimilation of labial and dental plosives before *m*: **supmos* > **submos* > *summus*, **caidmentom* > **caemmentum* > *caementum* (with the reduction of *mm* > *m* following a long vowel or diphthong);

the assimilation *d* > *l* before *l*: *sella* < **sedla* against *sedeō*, *lapillus* < **lapidlos* against *lapis*, *lapidis*;

the assimilation of *n* > *l* or > *r*: **conloquiom* > *colloquium*, **corōn(e)la* > *corōlla*, **tign(e)lom* > *tigillum*, **conripiō* > *corripiō*;

the assimilation of *r* > *l*: **perlaciō* > *polliciō*, **agerlos* > *agellus*, **ampor-(e)la* > *ampulla*.

Among the most important cases of progressive assimilation, we can include:

the change *ls/rs* > *ll/rr*, which implies an intermediate phase *s* > [z]: **velse* > *velle*, **colsos* > *collus*, **ferse* > *ferre*, **torseō* > *torreō*; note that *farsī* from *farciō* and *fulsī* from *fulciō/fulgeō* betray an earlier **farcsī* and **fulcsī/*fulgsī*, respectively, and similarly *ars* from an earlier **artis*;

the change *ln* > *ll*: **pelnō* > *pellō*, **tolnō* > *tollō*, **colnis* > *collis*, **pelnis* > *pellis*.

Finally, we shall examine the phenomena of rhotacism and assibilation, namely *dt/tt* > *ss*, passing through the intermediate stage **tst* with bilateral assimilation: **cadtos* > *cāssus* > *cāsus* (with vowel lengthening in accordance with Lachmann's Law and simplification of *-ss-* after a long vowel or diphthong), **pattos* > *passus*, **quattos* > *quassus*, **vidtos* > *vīssus* > *vīsus*, **fidtos* > *fissus*.

Among a number of dissimilation processes, we list here the following:

the change *l* ... *l* > *r* ... *l*: **caeluleus* > *caeruleus*;

the change *l* ... *l* > *l* ... *r* as in the change of the suffix *-ālis* > *-āris* whenever attached to nouns already containing an *l*, e.g. *cōnsulāris, mīlitāris, singulāris*, as opposed to *mortālis, nāvālis, rēgālis*; in the same way, we find *calcar, exemplar* as opposed to *animal, tribūnal*;

the change *r* ... *r* > *r* ... ∅: **agrestis* < **agrestris* (the latter is comparable to *silvestris*);

the change *n* ... *n* > *r* ... *n*: *carmen* < **canmen, germen* < **genmen* (cf. also *canō, genuī*, respectively);

the change *d* ... *d* > *r* ... *d*: **medīdiē* (loc.) > *merīdiē*.

We shall list here, albeit briefly, other noteworthy phonetic phenomena which are essential to an understanding of the linguistic structure of Latin.

First, syncope, caused by a strong initial accent, frequently represents the first stage of later phonetic changes, e.g. **avicaps* > *auceps*, **iovestōd* > *iūstō*, **propiter* > *propter*, **rāvicos* > *raucus*, **brevima* > *brūma*, **biiugai* > *bīgae*, **iuveniōs* > *iūnior*. The underlying tendency of this phenomenon, a truly constant structural factor frequently found in the spoken language of the classical period (cf. such alternations as *calidus* ~ *caldus, balineum* ~ *balneum, porrigō* ~ *porgō, surripiō* ~ *surpiō*) continues unperturbed into Late Latin and is even responsible for a number of Romance changes, e.g. *oculus* > *oclus, vetulus* > *vetlus* > *veclus*, etc.

The tendency to shorten long vowels in closed final syllables, in particular before *-m, -t, -nt* (but not before *-s*) and in polysyllabic words even before final *-l, -r*: *amās, monēs* against *amat, amant, monet, monent*, and *sāl, fūr* against *animal* (gen. *animālis*), *calcar* (gen. *calcāris*). Note that before final *-ns*, vowels are always long, whatever their original quantity (probably because the vowel was liable to nasalization, see below), e.g. *amāns, monēns, legēns, potēns, oriēns*, whereas before *-nt* (even word-internally) vowels are always short, e.g. *amantis* against *amāre, monentis* against *monēre*, etc.

So-called *correptio iambica*, as in *bene, modo, cave, puta* for *benē, modō, cavē, putā*, and the tendency to shorten long vowels in open final syllables, even independently of the iambic structure of the word (at least in the nominative singular of nouns in *-ō, -ōnis* and the 1sg. in *-ō* of the verb paradigm): however, it is difficult to ascertain to what extent these two phenomena were operative within the linguistic system as a whole, or whether, rather, they exclusively characterized the poetic genres.

The loss of final *-d* after a long vowel: **rosād* > *rosā*, **lupōd* > *lupō*.

The lengthening of all original short vowels before *nf/ns*, e.g. *īnfēlīx, īnsānus* and the wide-range of examples quoted in Cicero's *or.* 159. In fact, in accordance with a structural tendency of Latin, the nasal consonant in this position was liable to loss, triggering in this context the nasalization of the preceding vowel which was perceived as long or, at any rate, treated in on a par with long vowels. From the fact that we can easily reconstruct changes in the early history of Latin like *lupons > lupōs, *puppins > puppīs, *manuns > manūs, coupled with well-known variations in the spelling of words like cēsor/cēnsor, cōsol/cōnsul in the early period, we can conclude that the systematic reintroduction of n in the literary language of the classical period is presumably due to the endeavour to standardize and maintain, as is usual, analogical and etymological regularity, with the preceding vowel preserving, in any case, its acquired nasal/(>) lengthening features.

The presence of an anaptyctic vowel in such words as drac(h)uma < drac-(h)ma < δραχμά, pōculum < pōclum < *pōtlom.

The presence of epenthetic consonants such as t in the group *-ssr-, e.g. claustrum < *clausstrom < *claussrom (< *claudtrom), and p in the groups *-ml-, *-ms-, *-mt-, e.g. exemplum < *exemlom, sūmpsī < *sūmsī, prōmptus < *prōmtus.

The change *dw- > b-: *dwis > bis, duenos > bonus, duellum > bellum.

The loss of the labial element in labiovelars before another consonant, e.g. coctus against coquō, nix < *nigʷ(i)s, ūnctio against unguentum.

The change *-sr- > -br-, presumably passing through the intermediate stage s > [θ] and hence > f in word-internal position in the dialects, as opposed to b in the urban dialect, and preserved in such loans as rūfus, scrōfa, vafer, etc., e.g. sobrīnus < *sosrīnos (the latter related to soror < *sosōr), fūnebris < *fūnesris (cf. fūnestus).

The simplification of complex groups consisting of three or four consecutive consonants: *ārdsī > ārsi, *fulcsī > fulsī, *fulgmen > fulmen, *ulctos > ultus, *torkʷmentom > tormentum, *lowksna > lūna, *didcscō > discō, *pr̥kskō > *porcscō > poscō, *en stlocōd > īlicō (recall also *stlītis > arch. stlīs > līs), *skandsla > scāla, etc.

The loss of a whole syllable through dissimilation: *cōnsuētitūdō > cōn-suētūdo, *honestitās > honestās, *portitōriom > portōrium, *sēmimodios > sēmodius, occlusistī > occlūstī, scrīpsistī > scrīpstī, accessistis > accestis, ēvāsistī > ēvāstī, mīsistī > mīstī, cōnsūmpsisse > cōnsūmpse, etc.

Metathesis, for which we shall mention here two examples, recorded, so it seems, even by literary tradition: accersō for arcessō and pristīnum for pistrīnum 'mill'.

Phonological System

Having examined the essentials of historical phonetics, we shall now reconstruct the phonological system of Classical Latin, where the latter is understood to cover a period extending from the end of the Republican Age to the beginning of the Imperial Age. Obviously, Latin being a dead language, all such reconstructions, however cautious one endeavours to be, will inevitably be liable to a considerable degree of arbitrariness. A strictly more accurate approach, taking into account the Latin diasystem and the range of diastratic and diatopic varieties, reveals the following picture.

Twelve vowel phonemes: two central vowels, five front vowels and five back vowels, which considered together exhibit four (but one could just as well argue for five) levels of aperture, namely /a/, /aː/, /ɛː/, /e/, /eː/, /i/, /iː/, /ɔː/, /o/, /oː/, /u/, /uː/.

We should note that (1) the long vowels (except /ɛː/ and /ɔː/) and short vowels, with their presumably characteristic tense and lax pronunciations, respectively, tended in the former case to maintain their original closed quality, whereas the latter (except /a/) progressively acquired a more open quality, ultimately leading to the situation found in Romance; and (2) the long and lax vowels /ɛː/ and /ɔː/ were, as such, extremely unstable sounds and liable to be reinterpreted, in 'educated' or 'popular' speech, in terms of length or laxity, respectively. Hence, in educated speech they were reinterpreted as long and closed, and in popular speech as open and potentially (although not necessarily) short, if it is true that of the two originally concomitant oppositions, long ~ short and tense ~ lax, only the first played a functional role in educated speech. On the other hand, only the tense ~ lax opposition had a distinctive value in popular speech, since vocalic quantity was determined in accordance with the different vocalic structure: $\bar{V}$ in open syllables, $\breve{V}$ in closed syllables. That being said, we can, in addition, think of [e], [ɪ], [ɔ], [ʊ] as frequent allophones of /e/, /i/, /o/, /u/, respectively, and [ɛ]/[eː], [ɔ]/[oː] as probable allophones of /ɛː/ and /ɔː/, respectively. Appropriately, we should recall that /ɛː/ and /ɔː/ were the outcome of the monophthongization of the diphthongs *ae* and *au* (at first limited to the country dialects with subsequent extension to the urban dialect), or the result of foreign influence through a number of Greek loan words containing η or ω, notoriously long vowels and more open than the corresponding original Latin long vowels. Thus it is not by mere chance that such words as Κύμη, σκηνή, σκῆπτρον are transliterated as *Cūmae*, *scaena*, *scaeptrum*, clearly indicating that the digraph *ae* increasingly represented the phone [ɛː], in addition to the diphthong which presumably persisted in the most formal registers.

Whether [y] (and possibly [yː]) should be included in the inventory of vowel phonemes is a problem for which it appears difficult to provide a satisfactory answer. [y], which was undoubtedly an allophone of [i] (the so-called *sonus medius*, continually alluded to by the Latin grammarians), can only be justifiably accorded phonemic status if we take into consideration the numerous Greek loan words where its occurrence was not determined by context. Moreover, given the rarity of minimal (or near minimal) pairs such as *cytī* (dat.) 'kind of precious stone' ~ *citī* and *cytī* ~ *cutī*, *Pylus* ~ *pilus*, *Lȳdus* ~ *lūdus*, etc., and, hence, the low functional load of such oppositions as /y/ ~ /i/, /y/ ~ /u/ (as well as /yː/ ~ /iː/, /yː/ ~ /uː/), it clearly seems dubious whether *y* and *ȳ* can be integrated into the inventory of Latin vowel phonemes.

In addition we could postulate, although this is equally a delicate matter of interpretation, the existence in Latin of a series of long nasalized vowels, namely /ãː/, /ẽː/, /ĩː/, /õː/, /ũː/, occurring in the word-final sequences -am, -em-, -im, -om, -um, and in the word-initial and word-internal monemes in the contexts $\bar{V}$ + nf/ns ($\bar{V}$ + ns also in word-final position). In fact, the phonemic status of /ãː/, /ẽː/, /ĩː/, /õː/, /ũː/ is suggested by: (a) epigraphic documents characterized by the omission of -m and -n- in the contexts quoted above; (b) the testimonies of Cicero and the grammarians regarding the length of the vowel preceding nf/ns, the latter confirmed by the spelling with an *apex* attested in inscriptions; and (c) the treatment of -$\breve{V}$m in poetry which could be entirely integrated into synaloepha or a hiatus on a par with long vowels (and where, in agreement with Quintil. 9, 4, 40 and Vel. Long. GLK VII, 80, 17, we are forced to conclude that the nasal sound was not an autonomous phoneme but, rather, an intrinsic distinctive feature of the vowel). This conclusion is further supported by minimal pairs in which there arise a number of functional oppositions both in vocabulary (cf. such examples as *mōns* ~ *mōs*, *dēns* ~ *dēs*) and especially in nominal and verbal morphology (cf. such examples as *rosam* ~ *rosā*, *rem* ~ *rē*, *puppim* ~ *puppī*, *equom* ~ *equō*, *manum* ~ *manū*, *amāns* ~ *amās*, *monēns* ~ *monēs*, *legēns* ~ *legēs*, *audiēns* ~ *audiēs*, etc.). Furthermore, we know how, in the interests of the usual principles of analogical and etymological standardization and paradigmatic transparency in the field of inflection, nasals tended to be reintroduced in all those positions in which they were signalled by learned spelling. This justifiably casts doubt on the claim that long vowels were generally realized with nasalization. However, in the absence of more concrete evidence, it will suffice to have at least raised the problem.

Two semi-vowels, namely /j/ and /w/, with respective allophones [i] and [u], as witnessed by the poetic genres (cf. for [i] the trisyllabic scansion of *Caius* and the bisyllabic genitives in -*āī/āi*, found as early as Lucretius and Virgil, where we should expect [gajjus] and the diphthong [aj], and for [u] cf. such alternations as *lārva* ~ *lārua*, *silva* ~ *silua*). The phonemic status of /j/ against /i/ appears at least to be assured by such sequences as *iam*- and *iūl*- (cf. the oppositions *iam* [j] ~ *iambus* [i], *Iūlius* [j] ~ *Iūlus* [i]), whereas the phonemic status of /w/ against /u/ is overwhelmingly demonstrated by such oppositions as *alvī* ~ *aluī*, *calvī* ~ *caluī*, *salvī* ~ *saluī*, *servī* ~ *seruī*, *volvī* ~ *voluī* (and, in the case of the voiceless labiovelar realized as [kw], by pairs like *aquās* ~ *acuās*, *sequī* ~ *secuī*). It should be remembered that in some contexts [j] and [w] are allophones respectively of /i/ and /u/ (cf. the bisyllabic scansions of *abiēs*, *ariēs*, *battuō*, or the trisyllabic scansions of *īnsidiae*, *principium*, *fortuītus*, *pītuīta*), and that in intervocalic position /j/, in contrast to /w/, is invariably realized as [+ tense] (e.g. *maior* [majjor], *peior* [pejjor], *cuius* [kujjus]). Note, finally, that on the basis of the testimonies of a few grammarians, it is possible to postulate the existence of the allophone [ɥ] for the phoneme /w/. The semi-vowel *e* [ɛ], as found in the second element of the diphthong *ae* (the latter certainly coexisted alongside *ai* – which was earlier and originally bisyllabic – in the poetic genres and the most formal styles, whereas in the *Umgangssprache* it was being systematically replaced by [ɛː] in accordance with the overwhelming processes of monophthongization), clearly must be classed as an allophone of the phoneme /j/.

Eight plosive phonemes, namely /p/, /b/, /t/, /d/, /k/, /g/, /kʷ/, /gʷ/. Observe that the phonemic status of the labiovelars appears to be assured by minimal pairs like *sequor ~ secor, loquor ~ locor, anguis ~ angis, pinguis ~ pingis* (where the distinctive value is provided, in Jakobsonian terms, by the presence ~ absence of the feature [flat]), which could be realized also as [kw] and [gw], respectively.

Three fricative or spirant phonemes, namely /f/, /s/, /h/, the latter, strictly speaking, an aspirate, also engenders a few problems with respect to its exact classification. Although its phonemic status is assured by such minimal pairs as *haurī ~ aurī, haustrī* (gen.) 'a bucket for drawing water' *~ austrī* (gen.) 'the south wind', *hortus ~ ortus, hōs ~ ōs, hostium, ~ ōstium* (near minimal pair), it should not be forgotten that its 'correct' realization, apart from Hellenized uses and hypercorrect reactions to *rūsticitās*, both typical of *parvenus* such as *Arrius* in Catullus' famous epigram, was increasingly restricted to the educated classes and to strictly formal registers. Yet, in actual fact, *h* was exclusively restricted to occurring in word-initial position (recall, in this respect, that the presence of the word-internal grapheme *h* denotes either a simple hiatus, as in *ahēnus, cohors, trahō, vehō*, or in compound words serves to maintain the 'etymological transparency' of the lexical components, e.g. *cohortārī, exhaurīre, inhūmānus, prohibēre*).

At least two nasal phonemes, namely /m/ and /n/: in consonant clusters it makes more sense to talk of the archiphoneme /N/, since the nasal consonant is homorganic with the following consonant, variously realized as [m], [ɱ], [n] or [ŋ]. Recall in this respect that the graphemic sequence *gn* was pronounced [gn] in word-initial position, as in *gnārus, gnāta*, but [ŋn] in word-internal position, as in *dignus, lignum*. Based on the latter examples, we could justifiably argue for the phonemic status of [ŋ] in Latin, as confirmed by such minimal pairs as *agnus ~ annus, ignēs ~ innēs* (subj.) 'that you may float', *pignus ~ pinnus* 'sharp', *magnus ~ mannus* 'a small horse of Gaulish breed', although, on the whole, the opposition /n/ ~ /ŋ/ has a very low functional yield and a limited distribution.

Two liquid phonemes, namely /l/ and /r/: as recognized by the Latin grammarians, /l/ had a velar allophone [ɫ] (termed *l pinguis* as opposed to *l exīlis*) whenever it was followed by a back vowel or a consonant, in which case it influenced the quality of the preceding vowel: *familia/famulus, Sicilia/Siculus, velle, velim/vult < volt*. As for /r/, there was a tendency in word-internal position for short vowels before /r/ to develop into *e*, cf. the systematic development of **-is- > -er-*, as in *cineris, pulveris* against *cinis, pulvis, lēgerunt* against *lēgistis*, or cases like *reddere, trādere* against *dare, peperī* and *reperiō* against *pariō*.

Here we can only briefly mention the problem of geminate consonants, occurring in nominal and verbal compounds (usually the result of an earlier assimilation process) and in simplex words. In the latter case, this frequently gave rise to alternating doublets, where the sequence VCC coexisted alongside its equivalent V̄C sequence: *bāca/bacca, cūpa/cuppa, lītus/littus*. In fact, the correlation between single and geminate consonants had a certain functional yield in Latin, ensuring the survival of consonantal quantity as distinctive (even though this distinction was far from being as relevant as vocalic quantity), as can be inferred from such oppositions as *ager ~ agger, colis ~ collis, colum* (acc.) 'distaff' ~ *collum, anus ~ annus, ferum ~ ferrum, terās ~ terrās, valēs ~ vallēs, velit ~ vellit*, etc. Note that in the opposition /s/ ~ /ss/, the preceding vowel is invariably short in the latter case but long in the former, such that the change *-ss- > -s-* following a long vowel or diphthong (although we still find *dīvīssio* and *caussa* in Cicero) can bring about near minimal pairs like *cāsus ~ cassus, fīsus ~ fissus*. This situation was not too far removed from that of pre-Romance where vowel quantity was determined by the following single or geminate consonant and, more generally, by syllabic structure, namely long vowels in open syllables and short vowels in closed syllables. Moreover, it should be pointed out that in many cases consonantal gemination presumably had a highly phonostylistic function, carrying certain connotations associated with the uneducated speech of the masses and those varieties characterized as [-formal] and [+affective].

We shall now illustrate with some relevant examples the functional load of those oppositions based on vowel quantity, relevant to both lexis and nominal and verbal morphology.

/a/ ~ /aː/ ~ /ãː/: *malum ~ mālum, plaga ~ plāga, rosa ~ rosā ~ rosam*, and the stem oppositions between present and perfect, e.g. *cav- ~ cāv-, fav- ~ fāv-, lav- ~ lāv-*;

/e/ ~ /eː/ ~ /ɛː/ ~ /ẽː/: *edēs ~ ēdēs ~ aedēs, est ~ ēst, equos ~ aequos, es ~ ēs ~ aes, levās ~ lēvās ~ laevās, arte ~ artē ~ artae ~ artem, rē ~ rem*, and such oppositions between present and perfect as *emit ~ ēmit, legit ~ lēgit, venit ~ vēnit*, or less frequently verb stem oppositions, e.g. *sed- ~ sēd-*;

/i/ ~ /iː/ ~ /ĩː/: *dicō ~ dīcō, fidēs ~ fīdēs, liber ~ līber, is ~ īs, vī ~ vim, vīvis ~ vīvīs*, as well as the usual oppositions between the present and perfect verb stems, e.g. *vid- ~ vīd-*;

/o/ ~ /oː/ ~ /ɔː/ ~ /õː/: *os ~ ōs, colō ~ cōlō, solum ~ sōlum, equos ~ equōs, equō ~ equom, ōris ~ auris, lorīs ~ lōrīs ~ laurīs*, and the oppositions between the present and perfect, e.g. *fodit ~ fōdit*, or less frequently oppositions in the verbal stem, e.g. *fov- ~ fōv-, mov- ~ mōv-, vov- vōv-*;

/u/ ~ /uː/ ~ /ũː/: *ducēs ~ dūcēs, lustrum ~ lūstrum, fructus ~ fructūs, lacū ~ lacum*, as well as the usual oppositions between present and perfect like *fugit ~ fūgit*, or less frequently between verbal stems, cf. *iuv- ~ iūv-*.

To conclude, typologically it is interesting to note that in terms of its phonetico-phonological structure Latin is generally quite conservative, as regards its vowels, with respect to the characteristics and features that presumably distinguished Indo-European, whereas in terms of its consonants, we witness the loss of aspiration and a number of markedly innovatory processes.

Morphology

In the nominal declension Indo-European distinguished eight cases (nominative, vocative, accusative, genitive, dative, ablative, locative and instrumental), which Latin simplified through processes of syncretism to six cases. In addition to its own original functions, the ablative assumed the functions of the instrumental and locative cases, though isolated locative case forms do survive in Latin. Thus, a number of semantic specifications came to be signalled through the use of prepositions, especially in the least formal registers, a process which was to characterize the descendant Romance languages. In addition, the three genders (masculine, feminine and neuter) persist, whereas, within the grammatical category of number, the dual distinction is lost, leaving but only a few traces.

Declension of Nouns

The traditional five Latin declensions are the result of a complex reorganization of the various IE declensional classes, which can be classed into stems ending in -ā, -o/e-, -ej(oj)/i-, -ew(ow)/u-, -ī-, -ū-, -ēj-, -āw-, -ew-, -ow-, and various stems ending in consonants. Without repeating the inflectional paradigms of the so-called five Latin declensions set forth in the standard grammars, we shall restrict ourselves to commenting on the individual case desinences.

As far as singular number is concerned, the nominative of masculine and feminine nouns may end in -s, but may equally be characterized by the absence of any specific desinence. We can, therefore, distinguish between such forms as *parricīdas, lupus, equos* (where, it will be remembered, the presence of the labiovelar, or rather the biphonemic sequence [kw] < IE *-kw-, precluded -o- from raising to -u-, as happened elsewhere), *mōns, collis, fructus, diēs* and such forms as *rosa* (where the generalization of final short -a < *-ā is undoubtedly due to the influence of suffixed stems in -ia, e.g. *audācia, praesentia*, etc. – where presumably the final vowel was short *ab antīquō* – as well as the analogy with the nominative in -us of -o/e- stems, the need to distinguish the nominative from the ablative in -ād following the loss of -d, and *correptio iambica*), *sōl, fūr, cōnsul, soror, homō, liēn* (note also that stems in -ro- end in -er in the nominative in accordance with well-known phonetic processes, e.g. **pueros > *puers > *puerr > puer, *agros > *agr̥s > *agers > *agerr > ager*). As for neuter nouns, the nominative desinence (which is not distinguished from the accusative and vocative) for -o/e- stems ends in -m (only in -s in the words *pelagus, vīrus* and *vulgus*), e.g. *lignum,* whereas for all other stems (except those in *-ā* and *-ē-*, which do not include neuters) there is no one single characteristic nominative desinence, e.g. *genus, caput, nōmen, mare, cornū,* etc.

The vocative usually coincides with the nominative, except for masculine and feminine nouns in *-o/e-* with nominative in *-us,* e.g. *domine,* and the special cases of *fīlī, Pūblī,* etc. which have nominative in *-ius.*

The accusative of masculine and feminine nouns (in neuter nouns, the accusative is not distinguished from the nominative) ends in *-m* in the case of vocalic stems and in *-em* < **-m̥* for consonantal stems, e.g. *rosa-m, lupu-m* (< **lupo-m*), *equo-m, classe-m* (< **classi-m*), *puppi-m, fructu-m, die-m, mont-em, rēg-em.*

The genitive ending in *-ī* (also attested in Celtic) found with *-o/e-*stems (which also had a genitive in *-osio,* cf. the forms *Popliosio Valesiosio* in the inscription of *Satricum* near Anzio and similar developments in Faliscan) had long spread to the *-ā* and *-ē-*stems, whereas the genitive of all other stems ends in *-s/-is* < **-es* (*-os* in certain dialects), e.g. *dominī* (with the loss of the stem vowel *-o-*), *rosae* < *rosai* < *rosā-ī, diē-ī,* but *rēg-is* < **rēg-es, manū-s* < **manou-s* (and the archaic and/or dialect forms *senātu-os, senātu-is*). Observe that *classis* was remodelled analogically on consonant stems like *rēg-is,* since as an *-i-* stem, we should expect **classīs* (< **classei-es*), and that *-s* appears sporadically in *-ā* and *-ē-*stems, cf. the archaic forms *familiās* and *diēs* (Ennius, *Ann.* 413), respectively. It is likely that the extension of *-ī* to *-a* stems began with the masculine nouns of the *-ā* class in phrases like *bonī *agricolās,* which by analogy became *bonī agricolāī* and ultimately > *bonī agricolae.*

As for the dative, we can distinguish two main desinences according to the declension class: stems in *-ā, -o/e-* and *-ē-* form their dative by adding the ending *-i* to the lengthened stem vowel, e.g. *rosae* < *rosai* < **rosā-i* (recall that, in contrast to the genitive, *-ai* is never bisyllabic, except in *aquāi* in Lucr. 1, 453, and that dialect forms in *-ā* are also attested, e.g. *Diānā, fortūnā, Loucīnā*), *lupō* < **lupō-i, diei* (but the forms *dieī, diēī* and *diē* also exist) < **diē-i,* whereas all other stems form their genitive with the ending *-ī* < **-ej,* cf. *rēg-ī, classī* < **classei-ei, manu-ī* < **manou-ei* (but in poetry *manū* is also found, no doubt formed by analogy with *lupō, classī*).

As for the ablative, *-o/e-* stems add *-d* to the long vowel of the stem, e.g. **lupō-d,* with subsequent loss of the final *-d,* yielding the classical *lupō.* This *-d* then spread analogically to the stems in *-ā* (which in Indo-European did not distinguish between the ablative and genitive), e.g. **rosā-d* > *rosā,* and to the stems in *-i/ej-* and *-u/ow-,* e.g. *loucarīd, *classī-d* > *classī, *manū-d* > *manū,* but failed to spread to the stems in *-ē-* (even if the Faliscan *foied,* equivalent to *hodiē,* might not altogether rule out this possibility). In consonant stems the ablative was formed by adding the ending *-e* (without final *-d* which would have been preserved following a short vowel), e.g. *rēg-e,* spreading analogically to the *-i/ej-* stems, cf. the well-documented *classe* alongside *classī* < **classīd* (and almost invariably *colle* for *collī*, etc.).

Finally, the locative was formed by adding the ending *-i* to stems in *-ā* and *-ole-* (in the latter case, by adding *-i* to the stem vowel in *-e-*), e.g. *Rōmae* < **Rōmā-i*, *Tusculī* < **Tuscule-i*, and *-ī* < **-ej* to consonant stems, e.g. *Carthāginī*, *rūrī*, *temperī*.

The plural declension can be summarized as follows: the nominative and vocative of masculine and feminine nouns was signalled by the ending *-ī* < *-ei* < **-oj* in *-ole-*stems (which borrowed this marker from the inflection of the demonstratives, the early ending of these stems and those in *-ā* being **-es*, hence **-oes* > *-ōs*, **-āes* > *-ās*, as witnessed by the Italic languages). The **-oji* phase was equally responsible for the corresponding **-āi* ending, which clearly spread by analogy to the stems in *-ā*, e.g. **rosāi* > *rosai* > *rosae*, **lupoj* > *lupei* > *lupī*; the same phonetic development can be seen in forms like *pilumnoe*, *poploe*, *fesceninoe* (cf. Festus and Paulus Diac.) and in epigraphic evidences such as *foideratei*, *oinuorsei*, *uirei* (cf. *Sen. Cōns. dē Bacchānālibus* and many other inscriptions from the Republican Age). However, traces of the ending *-ās* do persist, as in Pomponius' *laetitiās īnspērātās* 141 and the Pisaurian form *matrona* (CIL I² 378) for *mātrōnās* with 'rustic' loss of final *-s*. It should not be forgotten that in various provincial areas *-ole-*stems sporadically exhibit *-eis*, *-es*, *-is*, e.g. *magistreis*, *coques*, *ministris* (all epigraphic attestations), as a result of the contamination between *-ei/-ī* and the *-s* of the early ending **-ōs*. All other stems have **-es*, which in the case of stems in *-i/ei-* and *-ē-* gave *-ēs*, e.g. *classēs* < **classei-es*, *rēs* < **rē(i)-es*, with the result that *-ēs* was extended analogically to consonant stems, e.g. *rēg-ēs* (originally **rēges*, cf. Gk κήρυκ-ες, Osc. *humuns*). Note furthermore that in the case of stems in *-u/ow-* we should expect **manues* (**manuis*) < **manoues* < **manewes*, whereas the only attested form *manūs* must be explained in relation to the accusative form *manūs*, on which the nominative was remodelled by analogy with the consonant stems, where the ending *-ēs* marked both nominative and accusative. As for neuter nouns, where the nominative coincides with both the accusative and the vocative, we systematically find *-a*, e.g. *templa*, *capita*, *genera*, *maria*, *cornua*, etc. (but with traces of *-ā* – clearly alternating with *-a* and whose derivatives are well attested in the Italic languages – in the now indeclinable numerals *trīgintā*, *quadrāgintā*, etc., more accurately 'three, four sets of ten') which presumably designated a singular collective noun, as in Greek which retains third-person singular verb agreement in such cases.

As for the accusative, masculine and feminine nouns with vowel and consonant stems have respectively **-ns* (with loss of *-n-* and subsequent lengthening of the preceding vowel when short) and **-ṇs* (with the development > **-ens* > *-ēs*), e.g. **rosā-ns* > *rosās*, **domino-ns* > *dominōs*, **duc-ṇs* > **ducens* > *ducēs*, **classi-ns* > *classīs* (then > *classēs* by analogy with *ducēs*), **manu-ns* > *manūs*, **rē(i)-ns* > *rēs*.

The original genitive ending for all stems in *-um* < **-ōm* was replaced in

Old Latin by the pronominal ending *-*sōm* in *-ā* and *-ole-* stems, yielding, with rhotacism of intervocalic *-s-*, the classical endings *-ārum* and, by analogy, *-ōrum* (evidence for the original endings for these stems is provided by the forms *agricolum* and *Grāiugenum*, found respectively in Lucretius and Virgil, as well as *socium*, *Rōmānom*, *deum*, *dīvom*, *līberum*, *virum*, *nummum*, *iūgerum*, etc.). Very early this ending was analogically extended to *-ē-*stems, e.g. *rērum*, *diērum*. Consonant stems thus show *-um*: *duc-um*, *rēg-um*, *classi-um*, *manu-um* (although the forms *manum*, *currum*, *passum*, formed analogically on *nummum* or *rēgum*, are also attested).

Finally, in the dative, ablative and locative cases, the *-ā* stems have *-*ā-is* > *-*ajs* > *-eis* > *-īs*, traceable to the IE instrumental ending, cf. *soueis aastutieis* attested in the famous slate of the Faliscan cooks, *rosīs*, *grātiīs*, etc., and *-ole-* stems have *-*o-is* > *-eis* > *-īs*, cf. *oloes* for *illīs* preserved in Festus' epitome of Paul. Diac., *agreis*, *anneis*, *lūdeis*, *lupīs*, etc. Both stems attest to sporadic forms in *-bus* < *-*bʰos* (cf. *deābus*, *fīliābus*, and *generibus* for *generīs* in Accius), equally visible in the Skt dat./abl.pl. *aśvābhyas* 'equābus' and Skt instr. pl. *aśvābhis*, which are common to all the remaining stems, e.g. *classi-bus* and, by analogy, *rēg-i-bus*, and hence *manu-bus*, *cornu-bus* (with variations presumably due to the need to render the *sonus medius* that could occur in labial contexts, and to simple analogy, e.g. *manibus*, *cornibus* and normally only *fructibus* as opposed to *arcubus*, *artubus*, *partubus*, *quercubus*, *tribubus*), *diē-bus*, *rē-bus*.

Numerous analogical processes appear to have occurred within the Latin nominal declension, especially in the so-called third declension which is a result of the merger of the inflectional paradigms common to the *-i/ei-*stems on the one hand and the consonant stems on the other. When compared against the backdrop of other IE languages, the Latin data reveal a number of undoubtedly innovative and, at the same time, 'regularizing' processes. Additional examples include the fate of the early class of neuter nouns characterized by the *-r/n-* alternation, as in *femur/feminis* (the 'standard' *femoris* was not established until quite late). However, this alternation was analogically 'regularized' in such words as *iecur* (gen. *iecoris* and *iecinoris* [*iocineris*] which must have blended with the original form *iecinis*) or *iter* where the older *itinis* and the analogical *iteris* (attested in early times) combined to produce the genitive *itineris*. Finally, we should remember that there was a tendency, already apparent during the Republican Age, for a certain number of nouns originally belonging to the *-ē-* and *-u/ou-* stems to merge with the large and productive classes of the *-ā* and *-ole-* stems, respectively.

Declension of Adjectives

The declension of adjectives does not readily diverge from that of nouns. Traditionally, the following three classes are distinguished:

(a) a class of adjectives in which the feminine follows the inflectional paradigm of -*ā* stems, and the masculine and neuter that of -*o/e*- stems, e.g. such adjectives as *bonus, -a, -um, līber, -era, -erum, pulcher, -chra, -chrum*, etc.;

(b) a class of adjectives whose inflectional paradigms are identical to those of -*i/ei*- stems, namely such adjectives as *ācer, ācris, ācre, fortis, -e, audāx, -ācis*;

(c) a class of adjectives which follow the inflectional paradigm of the consonant stems, namely adjectives like *inops, -pis, vetus, -eris*, etc.

Present participles such as *amāns, ferēns*, which originally exhibited two distinct inflectional paradigms with the feminine following the pattern of -*i/ei*-stems (**amānti-s, *ferenti-s*) and the masculine and neuter that of the consonant stems (**amānt-s/*amānt, *ferent-s/*ferent*), soon merged with the generalization of the inflectional paradigm of -*i/ei*- stems. The dual form of the ablative singular (in -*ī/-e*), which served to distinguish respectively between the distinct adjectival and verbal values of the present participle, clearly betray, albeit residually, the earlier existence of two distinct inflectional paradigms. More generally, one cannot fail to note the unmistakable Latin tendency to eliminate progressively the masculine ~ feminine distinction from the adjectival declension. This was systematically the case with the present participles, a fact which clearly acquires importance in light of its innovative character. Finally, we should recall that all adjectives in -*ā* and -*o/e*- formed *ab antīquō* their genitive plural (as well as their genitive and dative singular in some cases, as we shall see) from the ending drawn from the demonstrative pronouns, a fact which clearly contributed to the extension of this ending to those nouns with the same stem.

The Degrees of Comparison of the Adjective

Alongside the analytic type of comparative formed by placing *magis* (or *plūs*, attested in earliest times but not commonly used until the Imperial Age) before the adjective in the positive degree, the predominant form found in the Romance languages, the synthetic comparative is well documented in Latin and was formed at first by adding the IE suffix **-jŏs*- directly to the root. This is proven beyond doubt by examples like *maior < *mag-jōs* as opposed to *magnus < *mag-no-s*, and similarly for *nēquior, propior, senior* as opposed to *nēquam, propinquos, senex*. However, the attachment of the suffix to the stem of the positive generalized very quickly. The regular process of rhotacism of the intervocalic sibilant, *-s- > -r-*, was generalized through the declension and analogically extended to the nominative masculine/feminine singular with shortening of the originally long vowel: **mag-jōs-es > maioris*, with analogical nominative *maior < maiōr (< *mag-jōs)*, and neuter *maius < maios < *mag-jos* with preservation of the sibilant and the original short vowel (had the vowel in fact been long, it would have been regularly preserved before final -*s*; observe, incidentally, that early neuter forms in -*r* like *prior, posterior*, used by the early historians and perhaps analogous to neuter nouns like *aequor, marmor*, were short-lived).

Another IE suffix, *-tero- (/*-ero-/*-tro-*), contrastive and separative in function and equally well documented in Greek, survived in Latin in such forms as *īnferus, superus, exterus* (but not **interus*!), *dexter, sinister, posterus*, as well as in *alter, uter, noster, vester* (a number of such forms also survive in the Italic languages, but cf. in particular such Greek examples as ὕπερος, ἔντερον, δεξίτερος, ἀριστερός, ἕτερος, πότερος, etc.: cf. Chapter 2, p. 64) and in the nouns *magister, minister*. That this suffix was no longer associated with any particular value in the linguistic consciousness of speakers is demonstrated by the existence of etymologically double comparative forms like *īnferior, superior, exterior, interior*. It should be observed that originally *minor/minus* was not a true comparative at all, but, rather, gradually acquired its comparative value and function, with respect to *parvus*, through its meaning 'diminishing', closely related to the verb *minuō*.

Finally, it must not be forgotten that originally the Latin comparative in -*ior/-ius* had an 'intensive' value, such that *Aemilius Iūliō doctior est* means that Aemilius is quite educated, he has attained a certain degree of education with respect to Iulius, the standard of comparison, and hence 'Aemilius is more educated that Iulius'.

The Latin superlative is essentially characterized by the suffix **-mo-*, which originally indicated the extreme member of a group, in particular with spatial reference (thus its meaning was closely related to that of the ordinal numbers). It could, however, be preceded by other suffixes, e.g. **-o-mo-*, **-so-mo, *-to-mo-, *-is-so-mo-*, where the penultimate vowel, raised due to a strong initial accent, must have represented the *sonus medius* [y] variously attested by grammarians and apparently confirmed by the variation in spelling between forms with *u* and *i*.

Examples of the suffix **-mo-* include *īmus, dēmus/dēmum, prīmus < *prīsmos, summus < *sup-mos, extrēmus, postrēmus, suprēmus*, respectively derived from the old instrumental forms **extrē-, *postrē-, *suprē-* (for -*ē* cf. adverbs like *certē*, in which the old instrumental desinence can also be observed), and probably *minimus < *minu-mos*. For the suffix **-o-mo-* we can cite *īnfimus* and *postumus*, and for **-so-mo-*, *maximus < *mag-so-mos, pessimus < *ped-so-mos, proximus < *prokʷ-so-mos* (cf. *prope < *prokʷe*), *pulcherrimus < *pulcher-so-mos < *pulchr̥-so-mos < *pulchro-so-mos, ācerrimus < *ācer-so-mos < *ācr̥-so-mos < *ācri-so-mos* (with usual -*o-* > -*i-* in medial unstressed position, the development of -*e-* before -*r̥-*, and the assimilation of -*rs-* > -*rr-*), *miserrimus, pauperrimus, facillimus < *facil-so-mos* (with assimilation of -*ls-* > -*ll-*), *gracillimus, humillimus, simillimus*. As for the suffix **-to-mo-* we can cite *citimus, extimus, intimus, ultimus, optimus* (and *fīnitimus, maritimus*), and for the suffix **-is-so-mo-*, the most typical form of the Latin superlative, such forms as *altissimus, fortissimus*, etc.

Some adjectives have suppletive forms of the comparative and superlative which are not formed on the stem of the positive grade, e.g. *bonus ~ melior ~ optimus*, etc. By close analogy with the comparative periphrasis formed with *magis* (formed from the stem **mag-* with adjunction of **-is-*, the reduced grade of the IE suffix **-jes-/*-jŏs-*) or *plūs* (< **plois*), there exists an analytic superlative formed by placing *maximē* before the adjective in its positive grade.

Demonstrative Pronouns and Adjectives

As is well known, Latin possessed a well-structured system of demonstrative elements: parallel to the Italian *questo*, *hic* indicated proximity to the speaker, while *iste*, corresponding to the Tuscan *codesto*, indicated proximity to the interlocutor, and *ille*, like the Italian *quello*, expressed remoteness with respect to both participants of the speech act. *Is*, which functioned largely like *ille*, cannot be wholly defined as a demonstrative since it is closely related to the relative pronoun *quī*, to which it referred both anaphorically and cataphorically. More generally, these demonstratives tended to assume strengthened forms either by the attachment of deictic elements like *-ī* and *-ce*, or frequently by the combination of reinforcing elements like *ecce*, *eccum*, which give Romance forms like Fr. *cet*, It. *questo*, *quello*, etc. The declension of these elements follows that of *-o/e-* stems in the masculine and neuter and *-ā* stems in the feminine, combining both features of nominal inflection and inflectional features particular to the demonstratives, such as the identical forms of the genitive and dative singular for all three genders.

Let us begin with an examination of the forms *hic*, *haec*, *hoc*: the nominative masculine singular *hic* (also *hec* in many inscriptions) is derived from the stem **hi* to which the particle *-ce* is added with subsequent loss of the vowel, while the feminine *haec* is derived from **hā-ī-ce*. The neuter *hoc(c)* < **hod-ce*, usually written *hoc* but pronounced emphatically with a double consonant before a vowel (as metrics confirm), gives rise to the analogical masculine form [hikk], well attested in classical poetry.

The reconstructed genitive form is not altogether without its problems, possibly having arisen from an original **hoijos* > **hoius* > *huius*, a development paralleled by the genitive of the relative pronoun *quoius* > *cuius*. The dative is less problematic, **hoi-ei-ce* > *huic*, a form which, like the genitive, could be considered monosyllabic. In the masculine and feminine accusative we find respectively **hom-ce* > *honce* > *hunc* and **hām-ce* > *hance* > *hanc*, and in the ablative **hōd-ce* > *hōc*, **hād-ce* > *hāc*. In the plural forms, the masculine nominative has the forms *hei* > *hī* (and *heis*, *heisce*, epigraphically attested, on the model perhaps of *eeis*, *ieis*, *eis* from *is* and (as is the case with nouns with *-o/e-*stems, presumably a compromise between the Latin nominative in *-ei* and that of the Italic dialects in *-ōs*), whereas the usual two deictic particles can be seen in the neuter form *haec* < **ha-ī-ce*, originally used also for the feminine. Note in this respect that the feminine form *hae* was certainly a later analogical creation to distinguish the latter from the neuter *haec*, and that there also existed the form *hās*, widespread in the dialects but also present in Pomponius 151. The genitive *hōrum* and *hārum* can be traced back respectively to **hōsōm* and **hāsōm*, forms, which we have seen, also spread analogically to the nominal declension. Finally, in the dative-ablative *hīs* prevails for all genders, although the form *hībus* is found in Plautus, presumably formed analogically on *ībus* from *is*.

The origin of the final *-e* of the nominative masculine singular forms of *iste/ille* (archaic forms *olle*, *ollus* whose stems are probably related to *ōlim*, *ultra*) remains obscure, although it may derive from the bare stem with *-e-*grade. The neuter desinence *-ud* < **-od* bears similarities with the Gk **τοδ* > τό and also with Latin *quod* and *aliud* (observe that *iste* and *ille* are often subject to apocope or aphaeresis in the language of the *comoedia*).

The inflection of the genitive singular in *-īus* (*-ī-* was subsequently shortened in accordance with the *correptio* of *vōcālis ante vōcālem*) can be traced back to **isteius/*illeius* (cf. also *eius*), and forms like *istīmodī*, typically found in the language of the *comoedia*, must obviously go back to **istī(u)smodī*, with the loss of *-u-* and subsequently *-s-* before a consonant. The dative ends in *-ī* < **-ei*, although forms identical with the *-ole-* and *-ā* nominal stems, like *istō/illō* and the Plautine *istae/illae*, are found very early. Other points of note include, in the plural, an old nominative *illīsce* (cf. *heisce*, *hīsce*) and the genitive in *-ōrum* < **-ōsōm* and *-ārum* < **-āsōm*; the former, which replaced an earlier **-ojsōm* (continued in Sanskrit and Old Slavic), was remade analogically on the latter which shares similarities with Sanskrit *tāsām* and Hom. Gk τάων.

The forms *is*, *ea*, *id* can be traced back to an original **i-/*ej*-stem and an **ejo-/*ejā*-stem, whose distribution throughout the paradigm was determined in accordance with an alternation observable in the pronoun *quis/quī*, *quae*, *quid/quod*. The nominative-accusative neuter singular *id* bears similarities with Skt *id-am* and Gk **τοδ* > τό.

The genitive *eius* implies an earlier **ej-os* with final *-os* (which notably alternated with *-es/-s*, cf. the nominal inflectional paradigm), and, parallel to *huius*, is frequently considered to be monosyllabic. The dative singular *ei* presupposes a form **ej-ei*, attested in the *Lēx Repet*. 1,12. We should also consider the accusative masculine singular forms *im*, *em* which occur in the Twelve Tables for the classical *eum*, and the final *-d* of the ablative singular which is attested in epigraphic records: *eōd*, *eād*. In the nominative masculine plural **ejo-i* > **eje-i* > *iī* > *ī* (cf. *diī* > *dī*), widely attested in the Republican Age, whereas *eī* could have been remade on the analogy of *eōrum*, *eōs*. Similarly, we find forms in *-s* like *eeis*, *ieis*, *eis*, as was seen to be the case for the nominal *-ole-*stems, or alternatively such forms could be traced back to a form **eies*. It would seem that the old genitive *eum* for *eōrum* was remade on the old genitive plural in *-um* of the nominal *-ole-* stems. Finally, for the dative and ablative plural, both **ejois* and **ejāis*, through **ejeis*, gave *iīs* >

īs (cf. *diīs* > *dīs*), while *eīs*, in contrast, was presumably recreated on the analogy of *eōs*, *eās*. Nor should we forget the form *ībus* < **ei-bʰ-os*, found in Plautus and more generally in the earlier period, which also had the dative feminine plural *eābus*, clearly remade on *deābus*.

The forms *īdem*, *eadem*, *idem* were formed by attaching to *is* the invariable particle *-dem*, itself presumably the result of *-de* + *em*. This generalization holds for all cases except the nominative-accusative neuter singular, where we are forced to presume a form *id-em*, in perfect correspondence with Skt *idam*. Alternatively, *idem* may have been falsely analysed as *i-dem*, producing the particle *-dem* which subsequently generalized to the other stems.

The forms *ipse*, *ipsa*, *ipsum* can be retraced to the stem of *is, ea, id* followed by the invariable particle *-pse*, as is confirmed by the old forms *eapse*, *eumpse*, *eampse*, *eōpse*, *eāpse*. These were soon assimilated to *iste/ille*, thus giving rise to the normal declension *ipse, ipsa, ipsum*. The form *ipsus* for *ipse*, frequent in Plautus, perhaps produced the genitive *ipsī* for *ipsīus* and the 'regular' neuter *ipsum*.

Traces of an old demonstrative stem **so-* are to be found in the Latin forms *sam, sōs, sās, sapsa* (= *ea ipsa*), which occurred in the early period and share similarities with Skt *sa, sā*, Gk ὁ, ἁ, Goth. *sa, so*. The same stem can also be seen in the adverb *sīc* < **sei-ce*, whereas the corresponding neuter stem **to-*, cf. Gk τό < **τοδ*, appears only in such adverbs as *tum, topper* < **tod-per*.

The declension of the demonstratives is also shared by the adjectives *alius, alter, uter, neuter, uterque, utervīs, uterlibet, alteruter, ūnus, ūllus* (< **oinolos*), *nūllus, sōlus, tōtus*. Also of interest are the neuter singular in *-um*, except for *aliud*, and the genitive and dative singular in *-īus* and *-ī* (respectively), typical of the entire series. Moreover, alongside *alius* there existed a nominative *alis, alid*, which might derive from an *-i-* stem **ali-s* also detectable in words such as *ali-quis, ali-bī, ali-ter*. Finally, the analogy with nominal stems in *-ā* and *-o/e-* gave rise to early 'regular' genitive and dative forms, e.g. *aliī/aliae, aliō/aliae*, etc.

Relative and Interrogative-indefinite Pronouns

Here we have to go back to two different stems, one in *-o/e-* and the other in *-i-*, **kʷo-* and *kʷi-* respectively, which show obvious similarities with the two alternating stems **ejo-* and **i-* of the demonstratives *is, ea, id*. Over an extensive period of time, these two stems were subject to mutual influence, such that by the classical period the inflectional paradigms of the relative pronoun hardly differed from those of the interrogative-indefinite pronouns, except in the forms of the nominative singular.

A brief examination of the individual cases reveals the following facts: in the nominative singular of the relative pronoun the development **quo-ī* (where *-ī* is the deictic particle also found with the demonstratives) > *quei* > *quī*, and similarly **qua-ī* > *quae*, hence *quod* (which shows the specific neuter pronominal desinence -*d*), whereas the interrogative-indefinite pronouns have masculine and feminine *quis* (as well as the alternative feminine form *qua*) and neuter *quid*. *Quī* and *quod* could also assume an interrogative-indefinite value, when used as adjectives. The genitive of all three genders is presumably the rest of the development *quej-os > *quoios > *quoius* > *cuius*, and similarly the dative *quej-ei > *quoiei* > *quoī* > *cuī*, the latter marked by the tendency to be pronounced monosyllabically on a par with *cuius*. Clearly, the expected accusative *quom would have formally coincided with the homonymous conjunction *quom* > *cum*; in fact only the forms *quem* and *quam*, for the masculine and feminine respectively, are found. In the ablative, *quei* > *quī* occasionally persists, despite the generalization of *quō*, *quā*. In the plural, the nominative masculine and feminine interrogative-indefinite pronoun *quēs* < *quejes (attested in inscriptions and in Pacuvius) soon gave way to the relative pronoun *quoi > *quei* > *quī* and *quai* > *quae*, whereas in the neuter, apart from *quia* which was reduced to a simple conjunction, we find *qua* for the indefinite pronoun and *quae* < *qua-ī for the relative and interrogative pronoun (cf. also a nom. f. *quās*, which reveals the usual Italic and/or dialect influence). The genitive forms *quōrum*, *quārum* supplanted *quium*, found in Cato, whereas the dative-ablative *quibus* all but replaced *quīs* < *queis < *quois/*quāis, except for a few traces in poetry. Among the compounds formed from *quis*, we can cite *quisquis*, *aliquis*, *ecquis*, *quīdam*, *quisnam*, *quispiam*, *quisquam*, (*ūnus-*)*quisque*, *quīvīs*, *quīlibet*, which assume the neuter singular form -*quod*- when used as adjectives. In contrast, *quīcumque* is a compound formed on the stem of *quī*, which equally yielded the interrogative adjectives *cuius*, -*a*, -*um* and *cuiās*, -*ātis*.

The Personal Pronouns
Directly inherited from Indo-European, the personal pronouns do not distinguish for gender and have different stems for singular and plural. The first-person singular *ego* (cf. Gk ἐγώ) shows the usual ending -*o*, in accordance with *correptio iambica* (though there are a number of Plautine examples with -*ō*). By contrasts, the second-person singular *tū* (cf. Gk σύ, Hom. τύνη) usually has a long vowel, which can, however, be shortened when followed by an enclitic (as in *tuquidem*). This suggests that the quantity of the vowel in Indo-European varied somewhat: **tŭ̄*. In the third-person singular and plural, Latin usually made use of the demonstrative pronouns for the subject forms, but made use of the reflexive pronoun in all other cases, singular and plural. The old genitive singular forms *mīs*, *tīs*, found in Plautus, can be traced back to the IE enclitic genitive-dative forms *mej/*moj, **t(w)ej*/**t(w)oj*, and hence *mī, *tī, with the adjunction of the genitive desinence -*s* (recall, in this respect, that *mī* continues as the vocative of *meus*, cf. *fīlī mī*, corresponding to the Gk ὦ τέκνον μοι). In contrast, *meī*, *tuī*, *suī* are simply genitive forms drawn from the series of possessive pronouns/adjectives *meus*, *tuus*, *suus*. As for the dative, the -*hī* of *mihī* and the -*bī* of

tibī and *sibī* presuppose the respective forms *-*hei* < *-*gʰej* and *-*bʰej* (apparently confirmed by the numerous epigraphic attestations of *mihei, tibei, sibei*). The final vowel, the result of the monophthongization of -*ei*, was frequently shortened in accordance with *correptio iambica*, and, in the case of *mihī*, the intervocalic -*h*- gave rise to the expected contracted form *mī*. Following the loss of final -*d*, the Old Latin accusative forms *mēd, tēd, sēd* yielded the predominant classical forms *mē, tē, sē*. Observe that this final -*d* is unrelated to that found in the ablative, but, rather, is a simple particle used to strengthen the pronominal stem, or, alternatively, may be the result of the reduplication of the second-person singular accusative pronoun, *tē-te > *tēt > *tēd*, analogically generalized at a later date to the corresponding first- and third-person forms. Formally identical to the accusative, the ablative certainly appears to exhibit in the old forms *mēd, tēd, sēd* (> the classical *mē, tē, sē*) the same final -*d* that originally characterized the ablative of nominal -*o/e*-stems. Among the facts which merit mention with respect to the forms of the plural personal pronouns, we can cite here the following: the same form for both nominative and accusative, namely *nōs, vōs*, which share similarities with the Skt genitive and accusative plural enclitics *nas, vas* (but with a short vowel), the Hittite accusative and dative plural *nas*, as well as the Goth. *uns* (< **n̥s*). Nothing certain can be said with respect to the form *enos*, attested in the *Carmen Frātrum Arvālium*. The genitive forms *nostrum, vestrum* derive from the stem of the possessive, where final -*um* is open to two possible interpretations: either it represents the neuter form of the possessive, or it is the outcome of the original genitive plural desinence *-*ōm*, found with nominal -*o/e*- stems (forms made on the analogy of the usual genitive desinence -*ōrum*, e.g. *nostrōrum, vestrōrum*, are not infrequent either). On the other hand, *nostrī, vestrī*, also drawn from the possessives, represent without doubt the genitive singular of the neuter *nostrum, vestrum*. In this respect, note that the singular forms were specifically used as the objective genitive, while the plural forms assumed the function of the subjective genitive. The dative and ablative forms *nōbīs, vōbīs* were formed by attaching the inflection -*bīs* < -*beis* < *-*bʰej-s* to the stems *nō-, vō-*, extracted from *nōs* and *vōs*. According to the testimony of Paul. Fest., these forms replaced the older forms *nīs* and (perhaps also) *vīs, which show obvious similarities with the singular forms *mīs, tīs* above.

The possessive adjectives and pronouns follow the same inflectional paradigm as that of the nominal -*ā* and -*o/e*- stems: *meus* < *mej-os (presumably derived from the pronominal enclitic *mei, examined above), *tuus* < *touos* < *towos (/*twos, presumably from the genitive *tu-os of the second-person singular personal pronoun **tŭ̄*, cf. Hom. Gk τε(ϝ)ός, with secondary apophony), *noster, vester* formed by adjunction of the contrastive suffix *-*t(e)ro*-, and, finally, *suus* < *souos* < *sowos/*sewos, cf. Hom. Gk ἑός < **σε(ϝ)ός*, used both in the singular and plural with a reflexive meaning (the original meaning must have been that of '(one's) own' or at least 'belonging to a kind', cf. the IE root *sū- 'to be born'). Furthermore, in Old Latin the genitive plural forms *meum, tuom, nostrum, vostrum*, were frequently found, as well as the following inflectional forms of the reflexive: *sus, sa, sum*. Finally, the personal pronouns could also be strengthened by the adjunction of one of the particles -*pte*, -*met*, -*pse*, -*te*, and, in the accusative-ablative, the reflexive pronoun could be strengthened by the use of the reduplicated form *sēsē*.

Numerals

We begin by noting that the first three cardinal numbers are declinable. The numeral for 'one' *ūnus* < *oinos*, cf. Gk οἴνη 'one on a dice', Goth. *ains*, has the characteristic genitive and dative forms *ūnīus* and *ūnī*, respectively, which are used for all three genders. The plural forms are normally used in conjunction with those nouns which are plural in form but singular in meaning (the so-called *plūrālia tantum*), having replaced the root **sem-*, still visible in *singulī, simplex, semel, semper, simul, similis*. *Duo* continues the old dual, cf. Hom. Gk δύω, hence δύο, Goth. *twai*, of which the following inflections are preserved in Old Latin: masculine accusative plural *duo* (subsequently replaced by *duōs*, in line with the emergence of the feminine accusative plural *duās*, both remade analogically on the plural inflection of nominal -*ā* and -*o/e-* stems of the I and II declension), a feminine *duo*, a genitive plural *duum* and a nominative-accusative neuter *dua*, where usually one has *duae*, *duōrum/duārum* and *duo*, respectively. Similar considerations apply to *ambō*, cf. Gk ἄμφω, with final -*ō* in contrast to the predominant -*o* of *duo*. *Trēs* represents the regular outcome of the nominative plural **trejes*, from a stem in -*i-* **tri-*, cf. Gk τρεῖς, Skt *trayas*. The same stem also turns up in such forms as *tria, trium, tribus* (and the old accusative masculine/feminine plural *trīs*).

Quattuor can be traced back to **kʷetwores* (m.)/ **kʷetwōr* (n.), cf. Gk τέτταρες/τέτταρα, Dor. Gk τέτορες, Skt *catvāras/catvāri* which all continue to be declined, in contrast to Latin which made the numeral indeclinable (probably as a result of the confusion engendered between the masculine and neuter forms following regular phonetic processes). *Quīnque* (with -*ī*- by analogy with *quīntus* < **quinctos*) from **penkʷe* (cf. Gk πέντε) shows the 'Italic' regressive assimilation **p ... kʷ > kʷ ... kʷ*, as seen above. *Sex* (cf. Gk ἕξ) can be traced to a form **seks* rather than **sweḱs* (which is reconstructed on the form of the numeral in Greek, Avestan, Gaulish and Welsh); *septem* (cf. Gk ἑπτά) is the regular product of **septm̥*, while *octō* (cf. Gk ὀκτώ, Skt *aṣṭau*, Goth. *ahtau*) would imply a form **oḱtōw*, the old dual form presumably meaning 'a set of four fingers'. *Novem* is from **newn̥* (cf. Gk ἐννέ(F)α, Goth. *niun* and *nōnus, nōnāgintā*); the expected **noven* was transformed under the influence of *septem, decem* (**-n* > -*m*), the latter derived from **deḱm̥(t)*, cf. Gk δέκα, Skt *daśa*, Goth. *taihun*.

The numerals from eleven to twenty show the innovative forms *duodēvīgintī* and *ūndēvīgintī*, which do not conform to the general pattern of 'unit +

ten', operative in such forms as *ūndecim, duodecim*, etc. (cf. Gk ἔνδεκα, δώδεκα, Hom. δυώδεκα, etc.) The numerals from twenty to ninety, by contrast, are compounds meaning 'two sets of ten', 'three sets of ten', etc. with the individual unit followed by the noun stem **(d)ḱm̥t-* (a form of **dekm̥t-* with zero grade). The dual **ḱm̥tī* is observable in *vīgintī* (< **vīcentī* < **wī-ḱm̥t-ī*, cf. Dor. Gk Ϝίκατι), whereas the remaining numerals of the group preserve the neuter plural **ḱm̥tā*: *trīgintā, quadrāgintā*, etc. *Octōgintā* replaced an older **octuāgintā* (cf. Gk ὀγδο(Ϝ)ήκοντα), which influenced the form of *septuāgintā*. *Centum* presumably goes back to the neuter word **(d)ḱm̥tóm* meaning 'ten sets of ten', which was soon made invariable, cf. Gk ἑ-κατόν. The numerals from 200 to 900 are compounds of the cardinal numerals two to nine and *centum*. Originally indeclinable (cf. *argentī sescentum et mīlle* in Lucilius 1053), they were treated in Latin as plural adjectives, and hence as *bahuvrīhi* compounds, as in Sanskrit and eventually in Greek. As with *vīgintī, trīgintā*, etc., the *-g-* of *quadringentī, quīngentī*, etc. remains obscure, and the forms *quadringentī* and *octingentī* were modelled on the analogy of *quīngentī* and *septingentī*. *Mīlle*, which has no congeners in other IE languages, is an indeclinable neuter (though the ablative *mīllī* is attested in Lucilius 506) which in early times was regularly constructed with the genitive. In contrast, the plural forms *mīlia/millia* are declinable.

As far as the ordinals are concerned, *prīmus* is strictly speaking a superlative, as demonstrated by the presence of the suffix **-mo-*, while *secundus* is a verbal adjective of the verb *sequor* (cf. the verbal adjective *oriundus* from the verb *orior*). *Tertius* from **tri-tjos* shows the development **tri-* > **tr̥-* > *ter-*, whereas *quārtus, quīntus, sextus*, parallel to Greek, show the suffix **-to-*. *Septimus, octāvus, nōnus* and *decimus* are simply made by adding *-o-* to the corresponding cardinal numeral. Observe that **novenos*, which would regularly have produced **nūnus* (on a par with *nūper* < **novi-per*), yields *nōnus* under the influence of *novem*. The suffix *-ē(n)simus*, seen in *trīcēsimus, quadrāgēsimus, centēsimus, ducentēsimus*, etc. derives from *vīcēsimus* which merges the two suffixes **-to-* and **-mo-*, cf. **vīcent-to-mo-s* > **vīcē(n)ssomos* < *vīcē(n)simus*, with assibilation and simplification of *-ss-* after a long vowel.

Finally, the distributive and multiplicative numerals deserve some comment. *Singulī, simplex, semel* show the root **sem-* 'one', which also turns up in *semper, simul, similis*, and in the Gk εἷς, ἕν, < **σεμς, *σεμ*. The second element in *simplex, duplex*, etc. derives from the root **plek-* 'to bend', while *bis, bīnī* derive from **dwis, *dwisnoi*, respectively. *Ter* goes back to *terr* (attested in Plautus) < **ters* < **tr̥s* < **tris* (cf. Gk τρίς), with an adverbial *-s*. All the multiplicative adverbs, like *totiē(n)s, quotiē(n)s*, were formed by attaching the suffix **-iē(n)s* (on the model of *quīnqu-iē(n)s*) to the stem of the various numerals. Similarly, the suffix **-no-* from the multiplicative adverb *bīnī* was used to form the distributive adjectives *ternī/trīnī, quaternī, quīnī, dēnī, vīcēnī, centēnī, mīllēnī*.

Verbs

The Latin verbal system was based on the fundamental opposition between the *īnfectum* and the *perfectum*, the latter combining (also formally) the functions of the original aorist and perfect. For each of these two aspects a complete tense system, present, past, and future developed based on the use of distinct stems (as intuitively observed by Varro): *nōscō, nōscēbam, nōscam* contrasting with *nōvī, nōveram, nōverō*. However, the unmistakable development of a system in which temporal relations were precisely differentiated largely obscured the old aspectual distinction of Indo-European, with the result that such distinctions had to be restored, and then only in part, through the devices of verbal prefixation, e.g. *faciō ~ cōnficiō/perficiō* and similar examples. As for the moods, the indicative, or the mood of fact, contrasts with the subjunctive, the mood of possibility or expectation, whereas the optative, except for a small number of cases, does not survive in Latin, where its functions were taken over by the subjunctive. Of particular note among the indefinite moods are the gerundive and the supine. The ancient-old tradition of dividing Latin verbs into four distinct conjugations proves irrelevant from a historical perspective, as does the division according to thematic and athematic inflection, in light of its overwhelming absence from the Latin verbal system. Consequently, we shall base our analysis on the principal classificatory criteria that are traditionally adopted by the standard handbooks, whereby, as a general principle, such criteria descriptively contrast the stems of the *īnfectum* and *perfectum*. Among the distinctions of voice, we can formally distinguish between an active voice and an impersonal/mediopassive voice which were differentiated by a series of distinct desinences. Among the impersonal/mediopassives, we can further distinguish on the one hand between such forms as *bibitur, ēstur, ītur*, derived both from transitive and intransitive verbs and where the absence of a specific subject presents the verbal action as complete in itself (similarly in the Italic languages), and forms like *cingor, induor* on the other, which function as reflexive-middles when no agent is expressed but as true passives when an agent is expressed. Related are the so-called 'deponent' verbs like *hortor, proficīscor, sequor, vēscor*, which are middle forms showing various grades of 'active' meaning. In fact, parallel to the original active transitives, many of the deponents could govern an object complement or combine with active desinences. However, the opposite process also occurred, especially in Late Latin, whereby the deponents were used as true passives, on account of their belonging formally to the passive voice (which presumably outweighed the fact that they had developed a relatively stable active semantic value). This situation inevitably engendered ambiguity, confusion and hypercorrect forms, as reflected by their absence in Romance.

The inflectional system of the Latin verb comprises, in both voices, distinct morphemes for each of the three singular grammatic persons and their corresponding plural forms, whereas the category of dual, which continues to play a vital role in Greek, does not survive in Latin. With the loss of the original distinction between primary and secondary endings, caused in part by phonetic developments and in part by analogical levelling, the inflectional system of early Latin can be described as follows:

active desinences: *-ō/-m, -s, -t* (sg.), *-mus, -tis, -nt* (pl.);
medio-passive and deponent desinences: *-r, -re/-ris, -tur* (sg.), *-mur, -minī, -ntur* (pl.).

The active desinence *-ō* (which tended to be shortened in possible contexts of *correptio iambica*, cf. Plautine *scio*) represents the generalized ending of the so-called thematic verbs in the first-person singular of the present indicative (cf. Gk λύω), of the futures in *-bō* and *-sō*, and of the future perfect. On the other hand, *-m* can be traced back to the athematic primary ending **-mi*, as in *sum* (cf. Gk εἰμί), and above all to the secondary ending **-m* (cf. corresponding final Gk *-n* in ἔλυον), which specifically occurs in the imperfect and pluperfect indicative, the future in *-am* (an old subjunctive form), and in the present, imperfect, perfect (an old optative form) and pluperfect subjunctives, as well as in *inquam*, an old subjunctive form in *-ā-*. The second-person singular desinence *-s* can be retraced to the primary ending **-si*, as in *es* < *es-s* < **es-si* (cf. Hom. Gk ἐσ-σί), *legis* < **leg-e-si*, and to the secondary ending **-s*, as in the imperfect *erās* (cf. Gk ἔλυε-ς). Similarly, the third-person singular may continue both the primary ending **-ti*, as in *est* < **es-ti* (cf. Gk ἐσ-τί), and the secondary ending **-t*, as in *erat* (cf. Gk **ἔλυε-τ* > ἔλυε). The original opposition *-t ~ -d* (primary vs. secondary), resulting from the development **ti* > *-t* and **-t* > *-d* (cf. the early verb forms *sied* < **siēt, esed* < **essēt, feced* < **fēcet*, etc.), was lost in the second century BC with the generalization of *-t*, in accordance with the tendency of Latin to eliminate the secondary endings to the advantage of the primary endings. In spite of its ablaut grade, the first-person plural desinence from **-mos* shows similarities with the desinence **-mes*, found in Dor. Gk φέρομες. Traces of an old secondary ending **-mo* (?) can perhaps be detected in the mediopassive desinence *-mur* < **-mo-r*. The second-person plural implies a form **-tes*, in which the final *-s* (perhaps by analogy with the second-person singular or the first-person plural) has been attached to *-te* (cf. Gk φέρετε), a desinence which also turns up in the second-person plural of the present imperative. The third-person plural may be a continuation of the primary ending **-nti*, cf. Dor. Gk φέροντι (of which the only direct evidence is the doubtful *tremonti* of the *Carmen Saliāre*) or the secondary ending **-nt*, cf. Gk ἔφερον < **ἔφεροντ*. In contrast with Osco-Umbrian, which distinguished between the primary and secondary endings, the loss of final *-i* inevitably led to the levelling of the two originally distinct endings, with generalization of *-nt*, parallel to what happened in the third-person singular. As for the mediopassive and deponents, the final *-r*, characteristic of the impersonal passive, spread from the third-person singular (in Benveniste's terms the non-person) to the first-person singular and plural and then to the third-person plural. The first-person singular -ōr is formed by simply attaching -r to the desinence of the active, with progressive shortening of the original long vowel, whereas the desinences -ār, -ēr are formed by substituting -r for the secondary ending -m, similarly with gradual shortening of the vowel in the Republican Age. The earlier second-person singular desinence -re from *-se, an old e-grade form of the middle secondary ending *-so (cf. Gk *λύ-ε-σο > λύου), persists only in the imperative, since in all other cases -s was attached on the analogy of the corresponding second-person singular active form: -ris < *-se-s. In addition, the occasional dialect form *-so-s > -rus occurs in epigraphic records: utarus, spatiarus. In the third-person singular -r was attached to the secondary ending *-to, yielding the form -tur. In the first-person plural -r was attached to the desinence of the corresponding active form *-mo-(s), yielding -mur. Decidedly more complex, however, is the case of the second-person plural -minī, whose origin still remains obscure to the present day, despite a number of attempts to throw light on the matter. Among the various explanations put forward is that which retraces the desinence back to a participle form similar to the Gk λεγόμενοι (and hence to an early periphrasis such as λεγόμενοί ἐστε, in which the auxiliary was subsequently lost and the nominative form of the middle participle was morphologically frozen, and ultimately no longer recognized as such), or to an infinitival form in -menai, which, although without any direct congener within the Italic languages, does show obvious similarities with the Greek infinitives in -μεναι, e.g. λεγέμεναι. The third-person plural -ntur, in contrast, proves relatively straightforward in that it arose from the addition of -r to the old middle secondary ending *-nto.

As for the inflectional forms of the active perfect indicative, ideally these deserve to be accorded a study of their own, at least as far as the element -is- (> -er- in intervocalic position) of the second-person singular and plural and the third-person plural is concerned: lēg-is-tī, lēg-is-tis, lēg-ĕr-unt (in fact the same element is systematically found throughout the paradigm of the perfectum, cf. lēg-er-am, lēg-er-ō, lēg-er-im, lēg-is-se, etc.). Specific points of note include the -ī of the first-person singular (-ei in early inscriptions), which can be retraced to a diphthong *-ai, an early middle desinence (also found in Old Slavic) presumably formed by attaching the typical primary ending -i to the original desinence *-a (cf. Skt ved-a, Gk (Ϝ)οῖδ-α). The second-person singular -istī reveals the element -is- to which the desinence -tī (arch. -tei) was added, whereas a comparison with Indo-European would lead us to expect *-ta (cf. Gk οἶσθα). Without excluding the possibility that this -ī was simply added on the analogy of the first-person singular, it would not be unreasonable to presume, instead, an original form *-ta-i, with the typical -i of the primary endings. As for the third-person singular, by contrast, there were two desinences, -ed and -īt (-eit in early inscriptions). The first of these desinences, also found in Osco-Umbrian, is an old secondary ending replacing the original IE desinence *-e of the perfect, cf. Gk λέλοιπε (however, in accordance with the tendency to eliminate the secondary endings to the advantage of the primary endings, -ed > -et > -it, as witnessed by epigraphic records). The second desinence -it, on the other hand, could have been made analogically on the desinence of the first-person singular -ī, or, alternatively, could be the result of attaching the secondary ending -t to the usual primary ending -i, namely *-e-i-t, which would have become confused with the preceding ending -ed after the shortening of syllable-final long vowels before all consonants except -s. In the first-person plural, the desinence -mus is the same as that of the present and the other tenses, but is attached here to the stem of an element -i-, which presumably spread to all verbs on the analogy of a few verbs where -i- (probably < *-ə-) appeared in the root, cf. dedi-mus, steti-mus. The second-person plural, in contrast, is characterized by -is- (see above) which was placed before the desinence -tis < *-tes of the present and all other tenses. The third-person plural proves to be more problematic for there are three desinences: -ĕrunt, -ēre, -ērunt (with -unt < -ont, as witnessed by early inscriptions). -ĕrunt, which is the only form found in Romance and undoubtedly, therefore, the most widely used in the spoken language, clearly shows the element -is- (< *-is-ont), whereas -ēre, which was considerably less used and, on the whole, avoided by classical prose, also turns up in Indo-Iranian and Tocharian. Finally, -ērunt, which was advocated by Cicero and used in dactylic poetry as a device to avoid words of impossible rhythmical pattern such as cretic, is seemingly nothing more than an artificial compromise between the two preceding desinences. As for the perfect of the mediopassive and deponent verbs, it is worth noting that, in contrast to the system of the īnfectum, the perfect is not an inflectional paradigm but, rather, is formed analytically from the adjective in *-to- combined with the inflection of the present or perfect indicative (or subjunctive) of esse. Clearly, this type of periphrastic construction contributed to the development of the analogical periphrasis habeō + verbal adjective in *-to-, which continues in Romance, originally expressing the idea of completed aspect rather than the idea of past time. Note that this latter periphrasis is distinct from the synthetic perfectum, which both formally combined and conveyed the values of the original 'aorist' and 'perfect', before progressively assuming a specific temporal value.

The Infectum
A brief examination of the stems of the īnfectum according to the criteria familiar from standard handbooks reveals the following cases:

(a) a reduced number of athematic root stems, e.g. īs < *ej-si, īt < *ej-ti, vult < volt < *wel-ti, vīs < *wej-si, es(s) < *es-si, est < *es-ti, ēs < *ēd-si, ēst < *ēd-ti, fers < *bʰer-si, fert < *bʰer-ti (as well as some traces in the inflection of *dō*), and the ablaut alternations with full grade appearing in the singular and the weak grade in the plural have essentially been lost;

(b) thematic verbs, radical or otherwise, which in the present indicative place between the verbal stem and its desinence an element generally termed the thematic vowel.

The thematic vowel which appears as *e* or *o* before a nasal (preserved particularly well in Greek, cf. alternations like λέγετε~λέγομεν), has largely been obscured in Latin in so far as *e* and *o* > *i* in open syllables and *o* raises to *u* in closed syllables: **leg-e-si, *leg-e-ti, *leg-o-mos, *leg-e-tes, *leg-o-nti* > *legis, legit, legimus, legitis, legunt*. A more detailed examination of thematic stems reveals the following cases:

1 verb stems showing reduplication (athematic root stems did not survive) in which the root normally appears in the zero grade: *gi-gn-ō, sīdō* < **si-sd-ō, serō* < **si-s-ō*;

2 verb stems with an infixed nasal: *iungō, linquō, rumpō, scindō*;

3 verb stems with a nasal suffix: *cernō, sinō, sternō, pellō* < **pel-n-ō, tollō* < **tol-n-ō*;

4 so-called 'inchoative' verbs in *-scō*: *poscō* (< **pr̥k̂-sk̂-ō*, with zero grade of the root **prek̂-*, cf. *precor*), also with reduplicated forms like *discō* (< **di-dk̂-sk̂-ō*, with zero grade of the root **dek̂-/*dok̂-*, cf. *decet, doceō*);

5 verb stems with the suffix **-jeljo-*: *spec-iō, ven-iō*, a large number which are denominative verbs, e.g. *fugō* < **fugā-jō, albeō, fīniō, gregō, metuō*. This suffix typically had a whole host of functions, attaching to verbal roots, as in *spec-iō, ven-iō*, or, more frequently, to nominal stems (in *-ā*, *-ole-, -i-, -u-, -ē-*, and consonant stems), as in the case of the denominatives *cūrō, dōnō, aequō, fīniō, laudō, aestuō, glaciō*, etc. Alternatively, it was used to form causative verbs such as *doceō, moneō, moveō, spondeō, torreō*, etc., in which the verbal root normally appears in the *o*-grade.

The Tenses and Moods of the īnfectum

The present indicative, which is not distinguished by any specific temporal or modal suffix, presents the following peculiarities:

(a) In verbs with thematic roots like *leg-ō, leg-i-s*, the original alternation of the thematic vowel *-e/o-* (*o* in the first-person singular and first- and third-person plural, and *e* in the second- and third-person singular and second-person plural) is no longer visible. Thus we find *legō*, but **leg-o-mos* > *legimus* (note however the archaisms *quaesumus, volumus*, and the special cases of *sumus* and its compounds, whose original athematic forms were replaced in the first-person singular and first- and third-person plural by thematic forms with the regular *o*), **leg-o-nti* > *legunt*, hence *leg-e-se(s) > legere/legeris (with the preservation of e before r), but *leg-e-si > legis, *leg-e-ti > legit, *leg-e-tes > legitis.

(b) In verbs with vocalic root stems in -ā- and -ē-, e.g. amō, moneō, neither the thematic vowel nor the suffix *-je/jo- are longer visible on account of the loss of -j- in intervocalic position with concomitant vocalic contractions, and on the analogy of the athematic verbs.

(c) In verbs with vocalic root stems in -i-/-ī-, e.g. capiō, capis/audiō, audīs, the thematic vowel has also been obscured, except in the third-person plural where, in contrast to amant, monent, we find respectively capiunt < *capi-o-nti, audiunt < *audī-o-nti, and not the expected athematic forms *capint, *audint.

(d) The archaic suffix -n- found in the third-person plural of some verbs, e.g. da-n-unt, ferī-n-unt, redī-n-unt, nequī-n-unt for dant, feriunt, redeunt, nequeunt, still remains obscure.

Besides the secondary ending -m of the first-person singular, the imperfect indicative reveals the suffix -bā-, in which the element ā originally had a modal value and could be used with a past time function, as witnessed by early forms of the subjunctive and the īnfectum and perfectum preterites, e.g. erās < *es-ā-s, dīxerās < *dīx-is-ā-s. On the other hand, the b of -ba- is from the stem *bhu- 'to be', which gives forms like fuī, etc. Thus, the attachment of the suffix a to the root *bʰu- would have produced the imperfect form of the verb 'to be' *bʰwām, which, in turn, was attached periphrastically to the verbal stem. Consequently, the original meaning of a form like amā-bām can be interpreted as 'I was in the act of loving'. The origin of the first element in this periphrastic combination is a matter of speculation. Presumably, though, amā-, monē-, legē- were verbal nouns similar to infinitives (a similar verbal noun appears in the first element of the compounds ārĕ-faciō, pūtĕ-faciō), although this is not the only possibility, and the explanation of capiē- and audiē- (in capiēbam, audiēbam) remains obscure. The Latin future indicative exhibits three distinct forms: those in -am/-ēs, in -bō and in -sō. In actual fact, the forms in -am/-ēs continue the old -ā- and -ē-subjunctive formants (the former is found in Osco-Umbrian, Old Irish and Tokharian A, and the latter bears similarities with the Greek subjunctive forms with a long thematic vowel). In the -ere and -īre conjugations, the -ā- formant retains its subjective value, whereas the -ē- formant comes to mark the future, with the exception of the first-person singular which uses the subjunctive desinence -am < *-ām (unsurprisingly since the function of the subjunctive is closely related to that of the future), though in Plautus' and Cicero's manuscripts, forms like accipiem, experier, faciem, sinem, do occur alongside such 'canonical' forms as legam, capiam, audiam. In the -āre and -ēre conjugations, the subjunctive was formed respectively from the -ē- and -ā- formants, e.g. amem, amēs/moneam, moneās, such that the -ā- formant could not possibly be used to form the future of verbs of the -āre conjugation, nor the

-ē- formant in verbs of the -ēre conjugation, since these would have coincided with the respective present indicative forms of these verbs. On a par with the imperfect in -bam, the gap was filled by the creation of a new periphrastic future formed on -bō. Specifically, the verbal stems amā-, monē- were combined with a (probable) short-vowel subjunctive form of the verb *bʰu- 'to be', namely *bʰwō, *bʰwes, yielding amā-bō, monē-bō (and with a number of analogical extensions to verbs of the III and, in particular, the IV conjugations). Future forms in -sō, e.g. capsō, dīxō, faxō, can generally be retraced to a stem which is unrelated to that of either the īnfectum or the perfectum. It is traditionally thought that this future is an old desiderative verb form (cf. Gk -σω). This conclusion finds support within Latin itself where this same suffix can be related to the sequence -ssō, as in the desiderative verbs capessō, lacessō (note that forms such as amāssō, indicāssō, servāssō are later analogical creations). On the other hand, we cannot exclude the possibility that these modal forms in -sō uniquely continue the stem of an old aorist subjunctive. It is worth pointing out, in this respect, that the future of sum, erō < *es-ō, eris < *es-e-si, erit < *es-e-ti, etc., is an old subjunctive form with a short thematic vowel, as was normally the case with athematic verbs.

The present subjunctive, to which we alluded above, can be traced partly to the IE optatives and partly to the old subjunctives in -ā- (modal forms) and in -ē- (note that from the old IE subjunctive in -ē/ō-, normally with a lengthened vowel in the case of thematic verbs, Latin generalized -ē- to all persons with the usual shortening of the vowel before -m, -t, -nt). As in the case of the future in -sō above, the subjunctive forms in -ā-, namely duās, crēduās, fuās, abstulās, attigās, advenat, etc., seemingly contain a stem which is not related to either the īnfectum stem or that of the perfectum. Rather, such forms betray a subjunctive-optative suffix -(s)im, which can still be seen in the paradigms of a small number of athematic verbs, e.g. sim/siem, velim, edim, in a number of thematic verbs, e.g. duim, crēduim, perduim, ausim, dīxim, faxim, and presumably in the negative imperative *nē faxīs (> nē fēceris), a reconstructed form supported by such forbidding expressions as the Plautine cave respexīs. The imperfect subjunctive, by contrast, continues the suffix -sē-, with -s- > -r- in intervocalic position, e.g. amārēs < *amā-sē-s, monērēs < *monē-sē-s, forēs < *bʰu-sē-s, but essēs < *es-sē-s, ferrēs < *bʰer-sē-s, vellēs < *wel-sē-s etc.

Finally, we shall look at the imperative for which Latin distinguished between present and future forms. In the present imperative, the second-person singular is formed simply from the athematic or thematic verbal stem with shortening of -V̄ in accordance with correptio iambica in some cases, e.g. es, ēs, fer amā, monē, lege, cape < *capi, audī. In some cases, the imperative has lost the final vowel, e.g. dīc, dūc, em, fac. In the second-person plural the inflection is -te (cf. Gk λύετε). In the passive, the singular and plural desinences -re and -minī, respectively, are identical to those used in the indicative. The future imperative proves slightly more problematic: in the second- and third-person singular active, the inflection -*tō* < *tōd, in origin the ablative of the demonstrative pronoun **to-* (cf. *topper* < *tod-per) with the meaning 'from this/that moment on', was added to the second-person singular form of the present imperative, hence *amātō*, *monētō*, *legitō* < *lege-tōd, *capitō*, *audītō*. On the other hand, the corresponding plural forms were created analogically: *amātōte*, *legitōte* are derived from *amātō*, *legitō* on the analogy of the transparent relationship between *amāte*, *legite* and *amā*, *lege*, whereas *amantō*, *leguntō* were remade on the present indicative forms *amant*, *legunt*. The passive future imperative inflections -*tor* (2 and 3 sg.) and -*ntor* (3 pl.), exhibiting the 'characteristic' attachment of -*r* to the active desinences typical of the mediopassive and deponent paradigms, are a relatively recent creation, inasmuch as the passive future imperative was originally expressed by the corresponding active forms. An alternative second- and third-person singular form in -*minō*, e.g. *profiteminō*, *progrediminō*, attested in the Republican Age, is clearly an analogical creation, e.g. *legite*: *legitō* = *legiminī* : *legiminō*.

As for the non-personal forms of the *īnfectum*, we can note the following. First, the present infinitive, both active and mediopassive/deponent forms, is originally a verbal noun which lacked any specific temporal reference. In fact, an active form such as *agere*, plausibly from *agesi, may be interpreted as the locative singular of a nominal -*s*-stem *agos/*agesos 'the leading', whereby *-*si* (or perhaps in its subsequent form *-*se*) was presumably reinterpreted as a characteristic infinitival marker, systematically attached to all verbal stems (the -*s*- was rhotacized or assimilated according to the phonetic environment, e.g. *es-se*, *fer-se > *ferre*, *vel-se > *velle*, *amā-se > *amāre*, etc.). The endings of mediopassive and deponent infinitives, namely -*ī*/-*rī*, are generally traced to *-*ej*/*-*sej*, hence *leg-ī*, *cap-ī*, *amārī* < *amā-sej, etc. Comparing *agī* with Skt *aje* < **ag̑-ej* would suggest that -*ī* is a dative form (cf. OLat. -*ei*) of the root noun of the so-called III declension (in spite of evidence to the contrary from the Duenos inscription, where the form *pakari* does not exhibit a final diphthong). In this light, -*rī* can be regarded as the merger of -*ī* and the active inflection -*re* < *-*si*. Nothing certain can be said about the early Latin forms of the passive infinitive in -*ier*/-*rier*, exception that the final element -*er* shares similarities with the inflection of the Osco-Umbrian impersonal-passive. The present participle active is formed from the suffix -*nt*-, with the generalization of *e* in thematic verbs (though we cannot rule out -*ent*- < *-*ṇt*-), e.g. *amāns* < *amā-nt-s, *amantis* < *amā-nt-es, *monēns* < *monē-nt-s, *legēns* < *leg-e-nt-s, *capiēns* < *capi-e-nt-s, *audiēns* < *audī-e-nt-s, etc., in contrast to Greek, which systematically shows *o*, e.g. λύων, λύοντος, though isolated traces can be found in Latin, cf. *sōns*, *sontis* 'guilty', or more accurately 'he who is the one', from a root *es-/*s- 'to be', *euntis* < *ej-ontes from a root *ej-/*i- 'to go'. As is well known, Latin had no mediopassive present participle, even if a handful of nouns like *alumnus*, *fēmina*, *Vertumnus* can be compared with the Greek and Avestic participles in -μενος and -*mna*-, respectively. On the other hand, Latin did have a gerundive, or future participle passive, which was formed by attaching the suffix *-ndo- to the stem of the present, generally with the thematic vowel *e* in thematic verbs, on the analogy of the present participle active, e.g. *ama-ndus, mone-ndus, lege-ndus, capi-e-ndus, audi-e-ndus*. However, gerundives with thematic *o* (< *-o-ndos*) do occasionally occur, especially in Old Latin, e.g. *legundus, scrībundus, oriundus, secundus* (note that the last two are also found in all ages as 'standard' forms). Although no satisfactory explanation has been offered for the original value of the suffix *-ndo-* (also found, incidentally, in Osco-Umbrian where it appears to be a Latin loan), we cannot entirely rule out the possibility that it is related to the element *-do-* that appears in verbal adjectives like *timidus*, and more frequently in those in *-bundus* like *moribundus, pudibundus, vagābundus* (in turn comparable to those adjectives in *-cundus* like *fācundus, fēcundus, īrācundus, iūcundus, verēcundus*). The meaning of the gerundives was that of 'involved in the action of . . .-ing', which clearly accounts for how this participle readily came to develop also an active use. Finally, it will be noted that the forms of the gerundive in *-ndum, -ndī, -ndō* are used as declined forms of the infinitive, traditionally termed 'gerunds'. It is still not known, however, whether this use of the gerund emerged from the gerundive, or whether the entire functional paradigm of the gerundive developed from original forms of the gerund.

The Perfectum

Unrelated to the organization and structure of the *īnfectum*, the Latin perfect was formed in several different ways: (a) by reduplication; (b) by modification of the root vowel; (c) by suffixation of *-sī*, corresponding to the sigmatic aorist in other languages; and (d) by the addition of *-vī* to the stem, the so-called 'weak' perfect.

As for the various forms of the perfect exhibited by the various conjugations, we can note the following: *-āre* conjugation exhibits 'weak' perfects in *-āvī/-uī* (with an *īnfectum ~ perfectum* opposition, in the second case, in accordance with the vocalic alternations *ā ~ a* or *ā ~ Ø*), e.g. *amāvī, cubuī < *cuba-uī, secuī < *sec-uī*, and reduplicated perfects, like *stetī < *stest-ai* (with dissimilation of *-s-*); the *-ēre* conjugation has 'weak' perfects in *-ēvī/-uī* (for the latter form see above), like *plēvī, monuī < *mone-uī, docuī < *doc-uī*, and 'strong' perfects, e.g. *mo-mordī* (reduplicated), *sēdī* (root-vowel modification, cf. pres. *sedeō*) and *auxī < *aug-sī* (sigmatic); the *-ere* conjugation shows all the perfect types just examined, e.g. *tutudī, ēgī, sparsī, strāvī, aluī*; the *-īre* conjugation equally exhibits all attested perfect types, e.g. *audīvī, aperuī, repperī, vēnī, vīnxī*.

The stems of the *perfectum* and the *īnfectum* are originally unrelated, as examples like *gen-uī, vīc-ī* against *gi-gn-ō, vi-n-cō* clearly confirm. However, by a process of analogical regularization, the perfect of derived verbs and, more generally, of neo-formations is clearly made, as a rule, on the present stem, e.g. *cūrā-vī, fīnī-vī* on a par with *cūrā-mus, fīnī-mus*, etc. More specifically, we should point out the following with regard to the formations of the perfect: (1) those verbs (radical or otherwise) with consonant stems normally have perfects formed by reduplication, root vowel modifications or sigmatic perfects (*-sī*); and (2) those verbs (radical or otherwise) with vocalic stems, by contrast, generally have 'weak' perfects in *-vī/-uī*. The reduplicated type of perfect, attested in Greek and Sanskrit, usually has the reduplicated vowel *e* in Latin (in contrast to the present where the vowel appears as *i*, cf. *bi-bō, gi-gnō*), e.g. *ce-cidī, fe-fellī, pe-pigī*. As is also occasionally the case in Sanskrit and Old Irish, the vowel of the reduplication may be assimilated to the root vowel, variously yielding *i, o, u*, e.g. *di-dicī, mo-mordī, tu-tudī*. The *o*-grade ~ zero-grade alternation, characteristic of the IE reduplicated perfect distinguishing the singular from the plural persons (as is clearly visible in the Greek alternations μέμονα ~ μέμαμεν < **memn̥men*), left no trace in Latin (except perhaps in *stetimus* < **ste-stə-mos*, cf. Gk ἔ-στα-μεν), since the vowel of the present was generalized to both the singular and plural persons of the perfect, e.g. *poposcī, cucurrī, tetendī*. In other cases, the vowel in syllable-medial position was raised on account of the strong initial accent, e.g. *cecidī, cecinī, cecīdī, fefellī, pepercī, pepulī* (< **pe-pel-ai*, with *u* following regressive assimilation caused by [ł]), etc. Note, however, the preservation of the zero grade in *de-d-ī*. In the perfect type based on root-vowel alternations, there were two principle patterns: the first involves solely a modification of the quantity of the root vowel, a type of IE perfect which is well attested in the Germanic languages (cf. Goth. 1 pl. pret. *sētum, qēmum* as opposed to the pres. infin. *sitan, qiman*), e.g. *ēdī, ēmī, lēgī, sēdī, vēnī, fōdī* (as opposed to *edo, emō, lego, sedeō, veniō, fodiō*), *vīdī, līquī, fūgī* (the product of original diphthongs **-oj-* > **-ej-* and **-ew-* > **-ow-*, as opposed to *-i-* and *-u-* in the present-tense forms *video, linquō, fugiō*). The second type involves a modification of both the quantity and the quality of the root vowel (cf. Greek aorists like ἔθηκα, ἧκα), e.g. *ēgī, cēpī, fēcī, frēgī, iēcī* (as opposed to *ago, capiō, faciō, frangō, iaciō*). The perfect in *-sī* is traceable to an old aorist in *-s-* (cf. Gk ἔδειξα) of which Latin made considerably more use than the other types of perfect formation. In fact, the latter can arguably be regarded as historical residues, rather than functionally productive linguistic devices. Equally in terms of relative chronology, the sigmatic perfect appears to be more recent than the other perfect types, and progressively spread to those compound verbs whose verbal element otherwise exhibited a different type of perfect formation, cf. *cōmpsī, intellēxī* as opposed to *ēmī, lēgī*. Normally, the sigmatic perfects do not exhibit vocalic modifications, except in the cases of *rēxī, tēxī* as opposed to *rego, tego*, which were presumably made on the analogy of their respective participles *rēctus, tēctus*, or, alternatively, underwent the same phonetic process as the latter, namely Lachmann's Law whereby the plosive was devoiced and the vowel underwent compensatory lengthening. Others, however, have rejected this explanation, maintaining that the lengthening of the vowel in the participle arose, rather, on the analogy of the perfect form. Finally, as for the 'weak' perfect in -*vī*/-*uī*, this type is particularly common in denominative verbs and increasingly spread analogically to other verbal stems too, as if driven by a process of paradigmatic regularization. The 'weak' perfect is clearly an early formation (as *sēvī*, with an ablaut grade distinct from that of the present *serō* < **si-s-ō*, would seem to indicate), although there lack any satisfactory explanations for its origin. For instance, it has been proposed that -*vī*/-*uī* may have been extracted from *fuī* (< *fūī* < **bʰow-ej* < **bʰew-ai*), falsely analysed by speakers as **fu-uī* (probably pronounced ['fuwiː]). Nor can we exclude the possibility of tracing its origin to the Sanskrit reduplicated perfects like *ja-jñau*, *pa-prau*, even though, contrary to Sanskrit, their Latin equivalents (*g*)*nōvī*, *plēvī* show a long vowel. Moreover, the -*u*- in Sanskrit appears only in reduplicated perfects, whereas in Latin these two perfect types are mutually exclusive. Examples such as *amāvī*, *audīvī*, *crēvī*, *lēvī*, *pāvī*, *sprēvī* have a long root-stem vowel, as opposed to forms like *cubuī*, *domuī*, *genuī*, *monuī*, *sonuī*, *vetuī* which have a short root-stem vowel, such that *amā-vī*, *audī-vī* must be from *amā-*, *audī-*, whereas *mon-uī* (probably pronounced ['mɔnuwiː]) is from **monu-wī* < **moni-wī* < **mone-wī*.

Between similar vowels -*v*- disappeared with subsequent contraction of the vowels in perfects of this type, e.g. *audīvistī* > *audīstī*. These forms were then extended analogically to forms where the loss of -*v*- was not phonetically motivated, e.g. *amāstī* < *amāvistī*, *dēlēsti* < *dēlēvistī*, etc., as well as to other tenses and moods of the *perfectum*.

Finally, to conclude, we should very briefly mention the problem of the so-called preterite-present forms. Such forms, which are considerably more common in the Germanic languages (cf. Chapter 13, Verb Conjugation, pp. 403–7), are only observable in the three Latin verb forms *meminī*, *nōvī*, *ōdī*, which cannot be readily assimilated into a single formally or semantically coherent category.

Among the various tenses and moods of the *perfectum*, we begin with the pluperfect, corresponding to the imperfect tense of the *īnfectum*, which has both indicative and subjunctive paradigms. In the indicative, the ending in -*eram* is clearly traceable to **-is-ā-m*, which is formed from the characteristic *perfectum* suffix **-is-* and the usual element -*ā*-, originally a modal marker but equally a marker of past tense, followed by the secondary ending -*m*. The pluperfect subjunctive, by contrast, has -*is-sem* < **is-sē-m*, which again is formed from the *perfectum* suffix **-is-*, to which is added the suffix -*sē*-, characteristic of the imperfect subjunctive (cf. *amārem* < **amā-sē-m*), followed by the secondary desinence -*m*. As for the future perfect, its inflection became confused with that of the perfect subjunctive (except in the first-person singular) in the classical period, though in Old Latin it is still possible to detect traces of two quite distinct inflectional paradigms. Note that, as a rule, the opposition between these two tenses is identical to that between *erō* and *sim/siem*, the respective old forms of the subjunctive and optative which came to express, respectively, the future indicative and present subjunctive of the *īnfectum*. Besides the usual element *-is-* (> *-er-* in intervocalic position), the future perfect was characterized by the inflection *-i-* (cf. *eris* < **esis* < **es-e-si*, hence *lēgeris*, *lēgerimus*, *lēgeritis*), whereas the perfect subjunctive was distinguished by the inflection *-ī-* (which continues an old optative, cf. *sīs*, *velīs*, and hence *lēgerīs*, *lēgerīmus*, *lēgerītis*), subsequently shortened for phonetic reasons in final closed syllables before *-m*, *-t*, *-nt*, and eventually throughout the entire paradigm by analogy. Consequently, the distinction between the two paradigms was obscured, except in the first-person singular where the original opposition survived: *lēgerō* ~ *lēgerim*. Finally, the system of the *perfectum* did not possess an imperative form, though there are traces of a perfect imperative in the isolated examples *mementō*, *mementōte*, derived from the preterite-present form *meminī* seen above, the meaning of which also gave rise in Late Latin to the 'present' participle form *meminēns*.

Points of interest regarding the non-personal forms of the *perfectum* include the following. The perfect infinitive was formed by adding to the perfect stem the characteristic suffix *-isse*, containing the usual element *-is-* followed by the infinitival ending *-se*, e.g. *amāvisse*, *monuisse*, *lēgisse*, *audīvisse*. In the latter case, *-vi-* could fall, yielding the contracted form *audīsse*, a pattern which spread analogically giving such forms as *amāsse*, *dēlēsse*, *nōsse*, etc. Although not possessing a morphologized perfect participle active, Latin did nevertheless have a verbal adjective in **-to-*, principally used (except in the case of the deponents and similar cases, e.g. *ausus*, *fīsus*, *gāvīsus*, *solitus*) with a passive value. However, we should not forget examples like cautus, *cēnātus*, *pōtus*, *prānsus*, *scītus* with active meaning and, conversely, deponent examples like *meditātus*, *ratus* with passive meaning. In origin, the suffix **-to-* was added to the weak grade of the verbal root, of which only a few traces are still visible in Latin, e.g. *datus*, *satus*, *status* (where *-a-* < **-ə-*, alternating respectively with *ō*, *ē*, *ā*, e.g. *dō*, *sēvī*, *stāre*), and similarly *dictus*, *situs*, *ductus*, *ustus* (where *-i/u-* alternate with *-ī* < **-ej/ū-* < **ow-* < **ew-*, e.g. *dīcō*, *sīvī*, *dūcō*, *ūrō*). Subsequently, it generalized combining with all types of verbal root, even those with particular infixes or suffixes, although at first these were lost, e.g. *aptus*, *nactus*, *ruptus* as opposed to *apīscor*, *nancīscor*, *rumpō*. It seems appropriate at this point to recall the various phonetic developments affecting the vowels and consonants of the verbal roots and stems to which the suffix **-to-* was attached (cf Chapter 2, **Dental plus Dental**, p. 40), such as vowel lengthening in accordance with Lachmann's Law (as when the root ended in a voiced velar plosive, e.g. *āctus*, *frāctus*, *lēctus*, *pāctus*, *rēctus*, *tāctus*, *tēctus*, with the exception of *strictus*, and occasionally when it ended in a voiced dental plosive, e.g. *cāsūrus*, *ēsus*, *vīsus*, with the exception of *fissus*, *fossus*, *scissus*), the forms in *-sus* created by assibilation *-t/d-* + *-t-* > *-ss-*) and subsequently extended by analogy to the perfects in -*sī*, where their presence was not phonetically motivated, e.g. *mānsus, mulsus, sparsus, tersus*, etc. We should also note the lengthening and nasalization of the vowel in *mēnsus, pēnsus, sēnsus*. As is well known, the perfect participle passive in *-*to*- is also used to form the periphrastic perfect of the mediopassive voice and the deponent verbs in conjunction with *sum*. More rarely, it was combined with *habeō*, as early as Plautus, to form the periphrasis which was later to be developed in all the analytic forms of active paradigms in the Romance languages.

Other active forms are derived from the verbal adjective in *-*to*-, namely the future participle and the so-called future infinitive. The first of these was an adjective in -*tūrus*/-*sūrus* (very occasionally made on the present stem, e.g. *moritūrus, nāscitūrus, oritūrus, paritūrus*, the latter perhaps modelled on *peritūrus*), whereas the second was formed from the future participle combined with *esse* or *fuisse* for the *īnfectum* and *perfectum*, respectively). In Old Latin, however, it could also appear in the invariable form -*tūrum*/-*sūrum*. It may be the case that the forms in -*tūrus* are related to the nouns in -*tūra*, and in spite of their differing vowels, to the desiderative nouns in -*turiō*. Finally, we must examine the supine which was a verbal noun in *-*tu*-, in which the latter suffix, contrary to *-*to*-, was originally attached to the full grade of the root, as confirmed by a few Latin examples, e.g. *genitum* against (*g*)*nātus*, and perhaps *crētum* against *certus* < *kritos. Eventually, as in the case of the perfect participle, the *-*tu*- suffix was attached to the root, whatever its ablaut gradation; in practice the vocalism of the perfect participle and the supine systematically coincided. Of the various case forms in use, the supine was used in the accusative in -*um* after verbs of movement like *īre, venīre* (frequently with a simple periphrastic value, as in *perditum īre* corresponding exactly to *perdere*), in the dative-ablative in -*ū* (but Plautus still distinguishes a dative in -*uī*) with adjectives in such expressions as *mīrābile vīsū, facile dictū*, etc. In addition, a periphrastic construction formed from the supine in the accusative combined with *īrī*/*īrier*, the impersonal form of the infinitive of *eō*, was used to express the future infinitive passive, e.g. *amātum īrī, monitum īrī*, etc. When compared with other Indo-European languages, it is immediately obvious that the Latin supine is related to the datives in -*tavē*, genitives in -*tōs* and the accusatives in -*tum* of the deverbal abstract nouns in -*tu*-, which are frequently attested in Vedic (recall that the accusative in -*tum* < -*tu*- stems becomes the only infinitive in Classical Sanskrit), and share similarities with the corresponding forms in Old Prussian and Old Slavic.

The Invariable Parts of Speech

These include a whole host of elements which are mostly characterized by the fact that their interpretation within Latin, and Indo-European more generally, remains uncertain or at the very least problematic. Consequently, we shall merely undertake a brief examination of such parts of speech.

Adverbs

Among the various types of adverb, many of which subsequently developed into prepositions or conjunctions, we begin with the adverbs of negation, such as *ne-* (cf. Skt *na*) used in compounds like *nefās, nēmō < *nehemō, nequeō, nesciō, nihil(um) < *ne-hīlom* 'not a thread', *nōlō < *ne-volō* (cf. the Plautine *nevīs, nevolt*), *nōn < *ne-oinom, neque*, hence *nē, nī < *nē + i*. As for deictic adverbs with spatial-temporal reference, we can cite *ante* (cf. Gk ἀντί), *circā, circiter, circum, idcircō* (obviously related to *circus*), *post, pōne < *post-ne, prope, propter, praeter, subter* (the latter with the comparative suffix *-ter*), *suprā, īnfrā, ultrā, citrā, simul, usque, versus/versum, adversus*, etc. It will be noted that a number of adverbs continue fossilized case forms of nouns: *parum, prīmum, multum, nimium, minus, plūs, tum, dum, num, cum < quom, tunc < *tum-ce, nunc < *num-ce, ōlim, partim, statim, iam, nam, tam, quam, clam, palam* can all be traced to accusative neuter, masculine or feminine forms, while *prīmō, retrō, extrā, īnfrā, certō* clearly betray an original ablative case form, *noctū, diū, temperī* old locatives, *nox, dius* old genitives, and the class of adverbs in *-ē* probably continues an instrumental desinence. Other adverbs can be retraced to fossilized expressions, e.g. *intereā, hāctenus, scīlicet (< scīre licet), dumtaxat* (with *-taxat < *tag-s-ā-t*, the aorist subjunctive of *tangō*), whereas the widespread type in *-ter* appears to have originated in the adverb *aliter*, with subsequent analogical creations like *pariter, similiter*, etc. (cf. also formations in *-per*, like *parumper, semper, topper*).

Prepositions

From the class of prepositions, we list here, in addition to those adverbs above which developed uses as prepositions (according to a process widely found in the world's languages), the following: *ad, apud, cis, uls, ob, per, inter* (all with congeners in other IE languages), *ergā, penes, trāns* (all governing the accusative), *ab, cum, dē, ex, prae, prō, sine* (all governing the ablative, and with congeners in other IE languages), and *in, sub* (cf. Gk ἐν, ὑπό) which may govern both the accusative and the ablative.

Conjunctions

We list here the following conjunctions: *et*, the enclitic *-que* (cf. Gk τε), *atque > ac, etiam, quoque < *quō + que, neque > nec, aut, vel (< *vell < *vels < *wel-si*, 2 sg. of the pres. indic. of *volō*, or simply the 2 sg. of the imp.), *-ve, sīve > seu, sed, at, autem, tamen, (e)quidem, quīn (< *quī ne* 'how not?'), *immō, nam, enim, quippe < *quidpe, itaque, igitur* (presumably from *agitur*, an enclitic form exhibiting the usual raising of *a > i* in phrases like *quid agitur?*), *ergō < *ē-regōd, cūr < *quōr, ut, utī < utei* (with *-ei* as in *ubĭ < *ubei*, etc.), *nē, cum < quom, quoniam < quom iam, quod, quia, quamquam, quamvīs* (with *vīs* 'you want' 2 sg.), *quandŏ, dōnec, dōnicum, quoad < *quō + ad, sī, sīcut, ceu < *ce-ve*; and a number of interrogative particles like *an, -ne, anne, nōnne, num, utrum* (nom.-acc. n. of *uter*).

Interjections

Finally, we shall look at interjections, most of which are onomatopoeic, like *heu*, *ēheu*, etc.; the form *vae*, however, could be related to the Goth. *wai*. There is also a large number of interjections of Greek origin, such as *ēia/hēia* (cf. Gk εἶα, εἴα), *euoe/euhoe* (cf. Gk εὐοῖ), and others which are fossilized forms of old imperatives, e.g. *em* (< *eme*, cf. It. *to'* 'here you are' from *togli!*), *age*, *ēn* 'here's' (which, combined with *illum*, *illam*, gave the forms *ellum*, *ellam*, frequent in the language of the Roman playwrights), *ecce/eccum* (which, combined with *iste/ille*, form the Italian demonstrative pronouns *questo*, *quello*), *nē* 'truly' (cf. Gk νή). Finally, there exists a number of interjections drawn from the names of gods, e.g. *hercule*, *hercle*, *meherculēs*, *mehercle* (namely, from *Herculēs* and *mē Herculēs* [*iuvet*]), *ēcastor*, *mēcastor* (as before but from *Castor*), *edepol* (presumably from *Pollūx*), etc.

Word Formation

In light of the complex nature of the processes of suffixation involved in the creation of nouns and adjectives, it would be impossible to do justice here to the subject of Latin word formation, as a summary examination of the very large number of morphological formants involved in such processes will confirm, just less than about 100 if we include the numerous amalgams containing two or more suffixes. In contrast to Greek and the Germanic languages, Latin word formation generally exhibits very little evidence of vowel gradation in root syllables (note that cases like *pend-ō ~ pond-us*, *teg-ō ~ tog-a*, *ed-ō ~ d-ēns*, *gi-gn-ō ~ gen-us* cannot be adduced as evidence for paradigmatic alternations). We shall begin with the important class of *nōmina agentis* suffixes in *-tōr-* (f. *-trīc-*), e.g. *genitor* (*genetrīx*), the *nōmina āctiōnis* in *-ti-ōn-* (*-(s)si-ōn-*), e.g. *āctio* (*vīsio*, *mānsio*, *sessio*), and the deverbal suffixes in *-ti-*, *-tu-*, *-tūra*, e.g. *mors* (< *morti-s*), *cantus*, *pictūra*. We may also list the instrumental suffixes in *-tro-*, *-c(u)lo-* (< *-tlo-*), *-cro-*, *-bulo-* (< *-dʰlo-*), *-bro-* (< *-dʰro-*), e.g. *arātrum*, *pōc(u)lum*, *sepulcrum*, *stabulum*, *lavābrum*, nouns in *-men*, *-mentum*, e.g. *carmen* (< *can-men*, with dissimilation), *documentum*, nouns in *-ārium*, e.g. *grānārium*, abstract nouns in *-ia*, *-īna*, *-tāt-(i-)*, *-tūt-*, *-tūdin-*, e.g. *mīlitia* (denominal)/*audācia* (de-adjectival), *medicina*, *vēritās* (< *vēritāt-s*, as opposed to *cīvitās* probably < *cīvitāti-s*), *virtūs* (< *virtūt-s*), *fortitūdo*, adjectives in *-ālis*, *-ārius*, *-ānus*, *-bilis/-ilis*, *-ēnsis*, *-ōsus*, e.g. *annālis*, *argentārius*, *urbānus*, *amābilis/facilis*, *forēnsis*, *herbōsus*, etc. Also of interest are the so-called radical nouns with zero suffixation, such as *dux* (< *duk-s*), *lēx* (< *lēg-s*), *lūx* (< *louk-s*), *nex* (< *nek-s*), *pāx* (< *pāk-s*), *rēx* (< *rēg-s*), *vōx* (< *wōkʷ-s*), etc. A large number of such nouns are not found as autonomous elements but, rather, occur exclusively as the second member of those compounds, termed radical compounds, e.g. *rēmex* (< *rēm(o)-ag-s*) possibly related to Old Indic where the IE root *ag̑-* equally occurs as the second element of a compound, *oscen* (< **obs-can*), *tībīcen* (< **-can*), *auceps, particeps, princeps* (< **-kap-s*), *praecox* (< **-kokʷ-s*, from the root **kʷekʷ-* < **pekʷ-*, and cf. Old Indic *śvapac-* 'that cooks dogs'), *index, iūdex* (< **-dik-s*, weak grade of **dejk̂-*, with *-dex* for the expected **-dix* on the analogy of those compounds in *-fex*), *artifex, aurifex, carnifex, opifex, pontifex* (< **-fak-s*), *coniu(n)x* (< **-iug-s*, with secondary nasal on the analogy of *iungō* which preserves the nasal throughout the paradigm, and a number of parallels in Greek, Old Indic and Gothic), *obses, praeses* (< **-sed-s*, cf. the Old Indic and Avestan compounds in *-sad-* and *-šad-*, respectively), *auspex, extispex, (h)aruspex* (< **-spek-s*; these latter three examples may have influenced those compounds in *-dex* where we should expect **-dix*), etc. When compared with Old Indic, Greek and the Germanic languages, the degree of productiveness exhibited by the Latin devices used to form noun compounds generally appears to be considerably reduced (as well as the fact that many compounds have become opaque, e.g. *hospes* < **hosti-potis*). Moreover, we should not be fooled by the large number of essentially endocentric compounds found in the poetic genres, e.g. *frondifer, frūgifer, armiger, corniger, nāviger, altitonāns, suāviloquēns*, etc., inasmuch as they are to be ascribed, not to factors inherited from Indo-European but, rather, to particular stylistic stimuli which were progressively established as the *auctōrēs* increasingly adopted the norms of *imitātio* and *aemulātio* from the Greek.

Syntactic Overview

In the following overview of Latin syntax we shall confine ourselves to briefly bringing together a number of Latin phenomena which we deem (although a degree of arbitrariness is inevitably involved) to be among the most important.

Syntax of the Cases

In contrast to the stability exhibited by the six canonical cases of the Latin declination, the locative is characterized by a low degree of productiveness. In fact, since the time of our earliest written records, the locative case clearly appears to be already on the way to extinction. However, even the accusative and the ablative cases frequently appear in combination with prepositions, foreshadowing the generalized development of such analytic constructions in the Romance languages. Nor can we forget the vocative case which, since early times, tended to be replaced by the nominative even in the masculine and feminine singular of *-o/e-* stems. Among the various uses of the nominative, we should mention its absolute uses (the so-called *nōminātīvus pendēns*), frequently attested since early times, cf. Plaut. *Poen.* 659: *tu, si te di amant, agere tuam rem occasiost* ('you, if the Gods are in your favour, this is the right time to conclude the matter'), Calp. Pis. 27: *hi contemnentes eum, assurgere ei nemo voluit* ('the latter, despising him, no one wanted to stand up to him'). The Latin accusative case was most suited to generally expressing the goal towards which an action is directed, extent with reference to space and time, and direction of movement. Among the peculiarities of the Latin accusative, we can include here its usage following deverbal nouns in Old Latin, cf. Plaut. *Amph.* 519: *Quid tibi hanc curatio est rem ...?* ('Why do you concern yourself with this matter ...?'), *Truc.* 622–3: *Quid tibi hanc aditio est? / Quid tibi hanc notio est, inquam, amicam meam?* ('Why do you approach her? I say, what reason do you have to know this friend of mine?'), and the accusative after middle verbs of dressing and undressing (*induī, exuī vestem*), cf. Plaut. *Men.* 512–13: *non ego te indutum foras / exire vidi pallam?* ('Did I not perhaps see you go outside dressed in a cloak?'). Examples such as the latter provided the pattern for the so-called (but strictly speaking, incorrectly termed) Greek-style accusative (from the type *nūdus membra* develop such forms as *lacrimīs perfūsa genās*, both found in Virgil), which characterized the classical poetic genres. Nor can we forget traces of a possible ergative use of the accusative in such phrases as *mē pudet, mē taedet*. Apart from the 'subjective' and 'objective' uses of the genitive (whereby a sequence like *Poenōrum bellum* could equally refer, according to context, to either the war waged by the Carthaginians or against the Carthaginians), we shall only mention here the use attested since earliest times of so-called derived adjectives which competed to some extent with the genitive. Such adjectives, inherited from Indo-European and continuing in the Aeolian dialect, in Homeric Greek and in Old Slavic, generally persist in Latin only in those most conservative and archaizing linguistic uses, such as the language of worship or that of the jurists, eventually increasingly equated with oratory and affected styles. Thus, *fīlius erī* is clearly destined to prevail over *erīlis fīlius*. Among the typical uses of the dative, which as a rule expresses the interest or involvement in the verbal action, we can mention its frequent use as a so-called ethic dative, especially in the spoken language as evidenced by early plays, e.g. Plaut. *Mil.* 5: *ego hanc machaeram mihi consolari volo* ('I wish to console this sword'). A Latin usage inherited from Indo-European is that of the dative used for the complement of the verbal adjective in *-*to*-, e.g. Cic. *ad fam. ep.* 5, 19, 2: *mihi consilium captum iamdiu est* ('for me the decision was taken long ago'). Finally, the ablative, a syncretistic case having taken over the functions of the original instrumental and locative cases, indicated, strictly speaking, the origin or point of departure of an action. Here, we shall only mention its specific 'absolute' use, cf. the Plautine *mē praesente, mē vīvō*, which soon became set phrases, or classical examples like Caes. *b.G.* 4, 12, 6: *incitato equo se hostibus intulit* ('having spurred his horse, he pounced on his enemies'), etc.

Tenses and Moods

As far as the use of tenses and moods of the verb are concerned, unmistakably characteristic of Latin is its tendency to maximize the grammatical category of tense, to the detriment of aspectual distinctions, through the development of a comprehensive system of distinct temporal oppositions. This view is supported by an examination of the immutable system of the *cōnsecūtio temporum*, in which the expression of anteriority with reference to the present, past and future plays a central role.

Characteristic of the expressive *Umgangssprache* are the uses of the historic present, the *praesēns prō futūrō*, and the imperfect used, not to express relative time, that is, an action contemporaneous with another action, but, rather, with a 'descriptive' function foreshadowing its development in Romance as the chief tense of narration. One peculiarity that Latin curiously shares with Hittite is the use of the so-called 'epistolary past', of which Cicero, in particular, provides us with a notorious wealth of examples. Although the subjunctive mood was preferably used in dependent clauses, ultimately leading to its characterization as the specific mood of subordination, many of its uses in simple sentences persisted, where it was most apt to expressing will, likelihood and expectation, as well as wish and contingency. Note that the latter two values were originally expressed by the optative mood which did not survive in Latin, having fused with the subjunctive by a process of syncretism, except for a handful of isolated cases examined above. Of particular interest with regard to the imperative is its use in Old Latin in contexts similar to hypothetical clauses clearly recognizable as such notwithstanding the preservation of a paratactic structure consisting of the simple juxtaposition of two main clauses. In such structures, the imperative does the duties of the subjunctive (in the same way that it may also express will and wish), e.g. Plaut. *Rud.* 386: *verbum etiam adde unum: iam in cerebro colaphos apstrudam tuo* ('Say another word, and I'll brain you'), Cic. *Tusc.* 4, 54: *iracundus non semper iratus est; lacesse, iam videbis furentem* 'If you provoke him, you'll see him immediately get angry', etc.

The nominal character of the infinitive is still apparent in Latin in the numerous cases where it functions as the subject or object of a verb. In addition, the infinitive was found since early times used as an imperative, a usage which has survived (also in prohibitions) in Romance. Since Latin could not make use of the infinitive in the oblique cases (unlike Greek where the article made this usage possible), it had to use the gerund in its place. As for the gerundive, we note that in Old Latin it could also be used with intransitive verbs with a meaning not too removed from that of the future active participle, cf. Plaut. *Epid.* 74: *puppis pereunda est probe* ('the boat is about to sink'; cf. *peritūra*), and in phrases like *cupidus urbis videndī*, which appear to confirm the original nominal value of the gerundive (the latter example being equivalent to *cupidus urbis vīsiōnīs*, whereas classical usage would presumably prefer *c. urbis videndae* or *c. urbem videndī*). In contrast to Greek, the absence in Latin of a perfect participle with active meaning (except for deponent participles and a few exceptional forms like *cēnātus*, *pōtus*, *prānsus*, etc., cf. above) led to the use of a wide range of temporal clauses and favoured the extension of the so-called absolute ablative. The supine in *-tum/-sum* was used to express the aim or purpose of an action, e.g. the Plautine *nūptum dare*, *nūptum conlocāre*, and the frequent examples with verbs of motion such as *ambulātum abīre*, *accubitum īre*, *cōmissātum īre*, *cubitum īre*, where, incidentally, the supine found itself in direct competition with the infinitive, e.g. Plaut. *Cas.* 855–6: *eximus ... / ludos visere* ('we are going out ... to see the games'). In addition, in Old Latin the supine, like the *nōmina āctiōnis*, may take a direct object, e.g. Plaut. *Aul.* 247: *si opulentus it petitum pauperioris gratiam* ('if a rich man goes to ask the friendship of one poorer than himself'), Caes. *b.G.* 1, 11, 2: *legatos ad Caesarem mittunt auxilium rogatum* ('they send ambassadors to Caesar to ask for help'), Liv. 3, 25, 6: *venerunt questum iniurias* ('they came to complain about the injustices'), etc.

Subordination

Although we cannot possibly discuss here, even briefly, the vast and complex phenomena relating to Latin subordination, we must at least mention the original paratactic structure typical of a number of constructions which continue in Old Latin and colloquial speech, that became fossilized in the hypotactic structures of classical prose. Such was the fate of *ut* and *nē* (or *ut nōn*) used with the subjunctive in various types of complement or adverbial clauses, where, as a rule, the subjunctive is associated with the same values as those it bears in main clauses: *rogō ut veniās* is readily analysed into *ut veniās*: *rogō* 'may you come somehow or other: (this) I ask', whereas *timeō nē veniat* presumably means something along the lines of 'I am afraid: may he not come!', while *metuō ut redeat* originally meant 'I am worried: may he somehow return!', *suādeō ut caveās* 'I'll give you a piece of advice: may you somehow or other be on your guard!', and so forth. A similar explanation holds also for the uses of *sī* (which clearly betrays a time-old close relationship with *sīc* < **sei-ce*), in that examples like *sī faciās hoc, pereās* clearly reveal a paratactic structure, which may be expressed as 'Do it like that! You could die!', etc. Occasionally, the simple juxtaposition of two verbal constituents, without an intervening conjunction, unmistakably betrays an original paratactic structure, cf. such examples as *hoc volō agās*, *fac sciam*, *cavĕ putēs*, etc. Moreover, a recurrent phenomenon of para-hypotaxis is still observable in the use of the so-called *cum inversum* 'when suddenly ...'. In many other cases, we can only distinguish between a hypotactic and a paratactic structure by means of sentential intonation (irretrievably lost to us), cf. examples such as *nesciō quid agam* or the Plautine *nesciō quis loquitur* (*Persa* 99). Significantly, it has been noted that Plautine examples like *veniat velim* or *sine dem sāvium* can be translated both as 'I would like him to come' or 'may he come: it would please me', and 'let me give you a kiss' or 'allow me: I would like to give you a kiss', respectively. In fact, we could continue extending this line of reasoning to all types of so-called dependent clauses introduced by conjunctions which originally had an adverbial function involving a simple form of clause juxtaposition, and which ultimately came to be fossilized grammatical markers of subordination.

Finally, we shall briefly examine complement clauses. Apart from the privileged status accorded by the literary language to the accusative + infinitive construction, constructions like *dīcō/sciō quod* were presumably in everyday use in the spoken language (nor can we exclude the influence of the corresponding Greek phrase λέγω ὅτι, since the widespread diffusion of diglossia phenomena, if not bilingualism, is attested diastratically and diatopically in the history and prehistory of Latin). The subliminal reappearance of such structures as in the Plautine example (*As.* 52–3) *scio iam filius quod amet meus / istanc meretricem* ('I know that my son loves that prostitute'), rejected and (un)understandably attacked with tenacity by philologists, is unmistakable in less formal styles (like the *Bellum Hispāniēnse*) or those that deliberately imitate the everyday usage of the middle-lower registers of the *Umgangssprache* (cf. especially Petronius' *Satiricōn*).

Word Order

Finally, the word order of Old Latin and the classical period is, as a rule, completely free, all combinations being admissible (and widely attested): SOV, SVO, OSV, OVS, VSO, VOS, even if SOV appears to be the preferred order (as a typological classification of 'standard' Old and Classical Latin would suggest), in so far as it seems to be the non-marked order, leaving aside stylistic and rhythmical considerations. As for dependency relations, the regressive order (dependant/head), that is the so-called right-headed construction, is the most common, e.g. *rēgis solium, summum iūs, bene agitur*, etc. In Late Latin, by contrast, SVO order was gradually established following the 'analytic' development of the left-headed construction, both phenomena continuing in Romance.

References

Adams, J. N. (1976) 'A typological approach to Latin word order', in *IF* 81: 70–99.

Bernardi Perini, G. (1986) *L'accento latino*, Bologna: Pàtron.

Calboli, G. (1987) 'Die Syntax der ältesten lateinischen Prosa', in A. Giacalone Ramat, O. Carruba, G. Bernini (eds), *Papers from the 7th International Conference on Historical Linguistics*, Amsterdam and Philadelphia: Benjamins, pp. 137–50.

——— (ed.) (1989) *Subordination and Other Topics in Latin*, Amsterdam and Philadelphia: Benjamins.

Devoto, G. (1983) *Storia della lingua di Roma*, Bologna: Cappelli (repr. of 1944 edn, with Introduction by A. L. Prosdocimi and Bibliography by A. Franchi De Bellis).

Durante, M. (1982a) *Dal latino all'italiano moderno*, Bologna: Zanichelli.

——— (1982b) 'Il latino preletterario', in Vineis 1982, pp. 65–78.

Ernout, A. (1953) *Morphologie historique du latin*, Paris: Klincksieck.

Ernout, A. and Thomas, F. (1984) *Syntaxe Latine*, 6th edn, Paris: Klincksieck (revised version, with corrections, of 1953 2nd edn).

Hammond, Nicholas G. L. (ed.) (1981) *Atlas of the Greek and Roman World in Antiquity*, Park Ridgey, NJ: Noyes Press.

Haudry, J. (1973) 'Parataxe, hypotaxe et corrélation dans le phrase latine', in *BSL* 68: 147–86.

Hofmann, J. B. (1985) *La lingua d'uso latina*, 2nd edn, Introduction, translation and notes by L. Ricottilli, Bologna: Pàtron (Italian transl. of 1951 3rd edn of *Lateinische Umgangssprache*, Heidelberg: Winter).

Lehmann, Chr. (1979) 'Zur Typologie des Lateinischen', in *Glotta* 57: 237–53.

—— (1989) 'Latin subordination in typological perspective', in Calboli 1989, pp. 153–79.

Leumann, M., Hofmann, J. B. and Szantyr, A. (1963–77) *Lateinische Grammatik*, Munich: Beck.

Marouzeau, J. (1922–53) *L'ordre des mots dans la phrase latine*, Paris: Les Belles Lettres (vols I–IV).

Meillet, A. (1966) *Esquisse d'une histoire de la langue latine*, Paris: Klincksieck (repr. of 1952 6th edn with updated bibliography by J. Perrot).

Negri, M. (1982) *Latino arcaico, latino rustico e latino preromanzo*, Milan: Unicopli.

Niedermann, M. (1985) *Phonétique historique du latin*, 4th edn, Paris: Klincksieck (revised and enlarged version of 1953 3rd edn *Précis de . . .*).

Palmer, L. R. (1961) *The Latin Language*, London: Faber and Faber.

Panagl, O. and Krisch, Th. (eds) (1992) *Latein und Indogermanisch* (Akten des Kolloquiums der Indogermanischen Gesellschaft, Salzburg, 23–26. September 1986), Innsbruck: Innsbrucker Beiträge zur Sprachwissenschaft.

Panhuis, D. G. J. (1982) *The Communicative Perspective in the Sentence: A Study of Latin Word Order*, Amsterdam: Benjamins.

—— (1984) 'Is Latin an SOV language? A diachronic perspective', in *IF* 89: 140–59.

Peruzzi, E. (1990) *I Romani di Pesaro e i Sabini di Roma*, Florence: Leo S. Olschki.

Pinkster, H. (1990) *Latin Syntax and Semantics*, London: Routledge.

—— (ed.) (1983) *Latin Linguistics and Linguistic Theory*, Amsterdam: Benjamins.

Pisani, V. (1974) *Grammatica latina storica e comparativa*, Turin: Rosenberg and Sellier.

Porzio Gernia, M. L. (1982) 'Il latino e le lingue indoeuropee dell'Italia antica', in Vineis 1982, pp. 11–26.

Ronconi, A. (1959) *Il verbo latino. Problemi di sintassi storica*, Florence: Le Monnier.

Safarewicz, J. (1969) *Historische lateinische Grammatik*, Halle a.d.S.: Niemeyer.

Scherer, A. (1975) *Handbuch der lateinischen Syntax*, Heidelberg: Winter.

Sommer, F. and Pfister, R. (1977) *Handbuch der lateinischen Laut- und Formenlehre*, Heidelberg: Winter.

Stolz, F., Debrunner, A. and Schmid, W. P. (1982) *Storia della lingua latina*, 4th edn, Bologna: Pàtron (revised and enlarged by E. Vineis (ed.) 1993; Italian transl., with Introduction and notes by A. Traina, of *Geschichte der lateinischen Sprache*, Berlin: de Gruyter, 1966).

Strunk, K. (ed.) (1973) *Probleme der lateinischen Grammatik*, Darmstadt: Wissenschaftliche Buchgesellschaft.

Szemerényi, O. (1985) *Introduzione alla linguistica indoeuropea*, Milan: Unicopli (Italian transl. of 1980 2nd edn of *Einführung in die vergleichende*

Sprachwissenschaft, Darmstadt: Wissenschaftliche Buchgesellschaft, completely revised and updated by G. Boccali, V. Brugnatelli and M. Negri (eds)).

Tagliavini, C. (1962) *Fonetica e morfologia storica del latino*, Bologna: Pàtron.

Traina, A. (1955) *Esegesi e sintassi. Studi di sintassi latina*, Padua: Liviana.

Vineis, E. (1982) *Alle origini del latino* (Proceedings of the Convegno della Società Italiana di Glottologia, Pisa, 7–8 December 1980), Pisa: Giardini.

11 The Italic Languages

Domenico Silvestri

Introduction

The label 'Italic languages' is nowadays used to refer collectively to a group of IE languages, which does not include Latin (cf. Jones 1950; Beeler 1952, 1966; Jeffers 1973) which are attested exclusively – apart from a restricted handful of glosses and place-names (cf. Pellegrini 1978; Silvestri 1982, 1985, 1986) transmitted via Greek and Latin – in epigraphic *corpora* from ancient Italy which vary considerably with respect to the extent and nature of the texts. The philological and linguistic study of these corpora, as well as the need to place them in a historical framework, requires a great deal of caution regarding the adoption of earlier language-name labels based on the ancient names of tribes whose territory corresponds roughly to that of the epigraphic documentation. Moreover, 'Italic' is also clearly more a political (Social War) concept than a linguistic one, but it is in fact the linguistic evidence which leads us to use this simple term – for want of anything better – to refer collectively to *Oscan, Umbrian, South Picene* (the latter more closely related to Umbrian) and some minor languages, inappropriately termed 'dialects' in handbook practice, and which are identifiable as being located in the territories of the Paeligni, the Vestini, the Marrucini, the Marsi, the Volsci and, perhaps of the Aequi, territories to which the umbrella term 'Central Italic linguistic area' might be applied (for collections of tests and for handbooks, cf., in general, Vetter 1953, Bottiglioni 1954; Pisani 1964 (2nd edn); Poccetti 1979; on South Picene in particular, cf. Marinetti 1985).

However, the languages in this brief list do not exhaustively cover the complex linguistic mosaic of ancient Italy, although they do constitute an essential and pre-eminent part of its make-up. If we leave aside the two major dominant languages, Latin and Greek, and the many important influences they had on the Italic languages (cf. Lazzeroni 1965, 1972; Campanile 1976; Prosdocimi 1976) – yet bear in mind the Latin of ancient Rome and its extra-urban form – and also leave aside a few languages which were certainly imported, but did not undergo a period of prolonged naturalization (*Mycenaean Greek* in early Latium, according to Peruzzi 1980; *Punic* in Sardinia and Sicily, cf. Guzzo Amadasi 1978), we find that the linguistic 'stage' becomes crowded, with a number of 'extras' circling round a few undisputed 'leading lights'. Foremost among the latter, *Etruscan*, with a large number of inscriptions, is the most important of the non-IE languages of ancient Italy.

322

Prominent among the IE languages, are *Venetic* in north-east Italy (cf. Pellegrini and Prosdocimi 1967; Lejeune 1974) and *Messapian* in the south-east (present-day Puglia) (cf. De Simone 1972; Santoro 1982–4), both of which are richly attested. Here, too, the picture may be completed with a list of the 'minor' languages: in northern Italy we have attestations of 'Ligurian', 'Lepontic' and 'Gaulish' (mainly or wholly Indo-European), 'Camunian' and 'Rhaetic' (mainly or wholly non-Indo-European) (cf. Tibiletti Bruno 1978a, 1978b); in central Italy the language of the inscription of Novilara ('North Picene') only vaguely resembles Etruscan (cf. Durante 1978), while *Faliscan* is a Latin idiom with strong 'rustic' connotations (due to Umbrian influence; cf. Giacomelli 1963, 1978); in Sicily, finally, we can recognize the independence of *Sicel* (cf. Zamboni 1978) and, perhaps, of *Elymian* (cf. Ambrosini 1968, 1970, 1971; Agostiniani 1987), both IE languages (the latter tentatively compared with the Anatolian languages), while other epigraphic attestations seem to suggest elements that are Italic (Mendolito; cf. Prosdocimi 1979) and positively Latin (Montagna di Marzo; cf. Ambrosini 1984).

Phonetic Development

In order to pinpoint the prehistoric and proto-historic situation of the Italic languages within the IE language family, it will be useful to stress that the undisputed (and numerous) connections with Latin are largely the result of late processes of convergence and do not therefore bear witness to the existence of any 'intermediate unity' at the prehistoric level. Moreover, certain similar phonetic developments in Latin and Goidelic on the one hand, and Italic and British on the other, invalidate the equally mechanistic theory of a broader intermediate 'Italo-Celtic' unity. In fact all those languages that are related genetically (which do not converge solely by virtue of linguistic 'leagues') may be compared without adopting rigid evolutionary schemes of the vertical type (cf. Silvestri 1981: 165–7). In this sense the Italic IE entity is, primarily, of the Western (more precisely North-western) type, and here we may talk of a 'Old-European' formative phase, certainly earlier than the second millennium. Second, and at a more recent prehistoric level, we must take account of isoglosses with the Germanic languages and with Greek (particularly significant are those of the lexical type, which reflect the rise and spread of definite cultural concepts (cf. Pisani 1952; Delfino 1958)); third and finally, it will be necessary to position the subsequent formative processes of the proto-historical period within the framework (and diverse configuration) of the 'linguistic league of ancient Italy' (cf. Pisani 1978), in which Latin, Greek (of the colonies) and Etruscan play a full part, and with which Messapian, Venetic and other minor languages are by no means unconnected.

The Italic Languages

It is clear that *Oscan* and *Umbrian*, that is, the two Italic languages with the most consistent epigraphic corpora, although closely related, cannot be reduced to diatopic varieties of a single historical language. More difficult (or perhaps simply less clearly defined) is the discussion of the so-called 'minor' languages, which some sort of mental indolence has often led scholars to measure in terms of greater or lesser 'distance' from the two major linguistic poles, in certain cases with theories of the superimposition of the one over the other (and consequent stratification), as if Oscan and Umbrian could be taken to exist out of their historical context and used in dangerous inter-linguistic alchemies, while in fact they represent phenomenologically quite distinct realities. *Umbrian*, in fact, is principally the language of one text (the famous seven tables of Gubbio, which contain around 4,500 words): *Oscan*, on the other hand (and we should not forget that since antiquity the term has been used to refer only to the language) is the gradual result of a process of linguistic homogenization starting from various autonomous languages of central-southern Italy, and is therefore not the language of a single text, but rather that of a complex multipolar process of textual production. We may suppose that the scribes possessed specific awareness of this, as shown by certain Paelignian inscriptions. Anything that falls outside these two different emerging forms and so appears as an idiosyncratic Italic entity is thus very interesting. In such cases it is not by chance that attestations go further back in time, that is to before the processes just referred to as in the case of *South Picene*, which appears to be Italic and which introduces the 'Sabine' dimension into Italic (cf. Marinetti 1981, 1985), a dimension which is neither monocentric, as in Umbrian, nor polycentric, as in Oscan, but which in recent studies has come to be viewed increasingly as thoroughly 'national', that is, corresponding more closely to the oldest form of Italic ethnic self-identification.

Vestinian, *Marrucinian* and above all *Paelignian* are not just direct continuations or localized fragmentations of this 'national' dimension, but later 'replicas' of it, in some cases with archaizing 'temptations', having an 'anti-Latin' function and easily realizable with Oscan linguistic ingredients.

Documentation

The oldest stage of textual documentation in Italic languages (seventh to sixth centuries BC) can be seen in the inscription from Poggio Sommavilla (in the area of ancient Capena), in two 'Proto-Campanian' inscriptions from Nocera and Vico Equense (sixth century BC), and in three South Picene inscriptions from Penna S. Andrea (Teramo). In these we can see the outline of a pre-Oscan, pre-Umbrian Italic entity which it is perhaps not too far-fetched to define as 'Proto-Sabine', when we consider, too, the fact that this ethnic name, which probably represents the 'national' Italic name, indeed appears in first direct attestation in the South Picene inscriptions.

The main documentation of Oscan extends from Messina (where it had been imported by the Mamertini, mercenaries in the service of Agathocles), through Bruttium and Lucania and part of the Apulian area (excluding ancient Calabria, corresponding to the Salentine peninsula), to Campania, Samnium and the territory of the Frentani (South Adriatic Abruzzo). The documentation is substantially uniform, with obvious dialectal features. Amongst the documents or the major groups of inscriptions one might mention the following: the inscriptions of the Lucanian sanctuary at Rossano di Vaglio, the *Tabula Bantina* (Apulia, beginning of the first century BC, the most extensive Oscan document hitherto discovered), the inscriptions of Pompeii (including the 'eituns' inscriptions), the *Cippus Abellanus*, the so-called *iuvilas* from Capua, the texts from Agnone and from Pietrabbondante, and so on. In the Central Italic linguistic area we should mention the *Tabula Veliterna* (Volscian), the Bronze of Rapino (Marrucinian) and the *Herentas* inscription (Paelignian). Finally it will be useful to stress once more the great importance of the South Picene corpus, both from a purely linguistic point of view and for its historico-cultural implications, and, passing over some minor inscriptions, to recognize in the *Tables of Gubbio* (produced between the second and first centuries BC) the most important epigraphic monument not only of Umbrian but of the whole of ancient Italy (cf. Prosdocimi 1984). The content of the seven tables concerns a complex ritual which includes ceremonies with sacrifices and offerings to various deities as well as rules relating to the running of the college of the Atiedian brethren, who are appointed to perform the ceremonies. Texts may be written either in an epichoric alphabet, derived like the Latin one from Etruscan, or in Latin alphabet, or in the 'Magna Graecia' in an ionic-tarantine Greek alphabet.

Common Italic

With the reservations just expressed in relation to a different arrangement of the historical and institutional contexts of the documentation (on these ideas cf. Silvestri 1987), it seems possible to pose here the problem of a Common Italic. However, this is certainly not to be seen as a prehistoric language that can largely be reconstructed, but rather as a set of pre-documentation linguistic features characterized by an undisputed degree of cohesion, to be seen not in a genealogical framework, but as the result of prehistoric and proto-historic processes of convergence. These convergences are exemplified by a number of sound laws, that also occur in Latino-Faliscan, and seem very early. Among these we should mention the development of the diphthong -*eu*- to -*ou*-, the vocalization to *or*, *ol* of the sonants r and l, the formation of a class of voiced fricatives as reflexes of original voiced aspirates (following the traditional formulation of the IE consonant system, but see below), the change

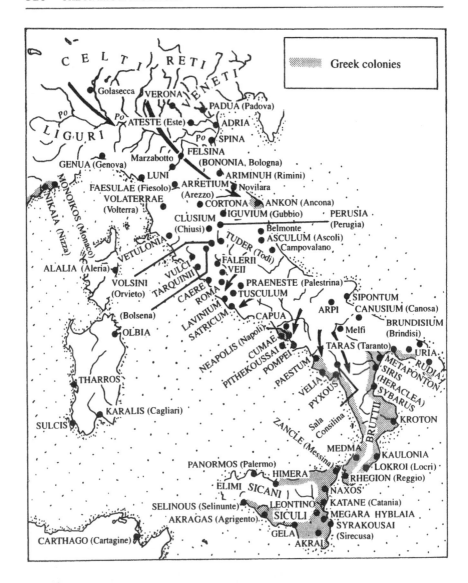

Map 11.1   Population and principal centres of Ancient Italy
Source: *Popoli e civiltà dell'Italia antica*, vol. VI, ed. A. Prosdocimi, Rome: Biblioteca di
storia patria, 12, 1978

of the cluster *-tl-* into *-kl-* word-internally, the assimilation of the sequence *p
... kʷ* to *kʷ ... kʷ*, the voicing of intervocalic *-s-*, etc. It should be made clear
that the phenomena mentioned here have later, specific historical developments in the individual languages. In order to produce an outline of common
Italic (excluding Latin) let us now examine some morphological features,

which will also be useful for a more detailed characterization, although again without any claim to completeness. In the noun we may note the endings *-*rs*, *-*ns* (> -*rr* -*f*) in the nominative singular of -*r* and -*n* stems, the genitive singular ending -*eis* of the *o*- stems and consonant stems (following the *i*-stem paradigm), the accusative singular ending -*om* in the consonant stems (following the *o*- stem paradigm). Also notable are the conservation of the endings *-*ōs*, *-*ās* in the nominative plural of the *o*- and *a*- stems respectively, and the analogical diffusion of these endings in the pronominal declension. Striking features of the pronoun system are the presence of the stem *ek*(*s*)*o*- as against Lat. *hic* and the accusative ending -*om* in Umbro *tiom* 'you', Osc. *siom* 'oneself'. In the verb, finally, we may note the secondary third-person plural active ending in -*ns*, the passive forms in -*r* of the type Osc. *loufir*, Umbr. *ier*, *ferar*, the infinitive ending in -*om* in the active, Umbr. -*fi*, Osc. -*fir* in the mediopassive and the formation of the future with the suffix -*s*- (and of the future perfect with the suffix -*us*-). However, Oscan and Umbrian differ, for example, in the formation of the dative plural of the consonant stems (in Oscan there is levelling on the basis of the *i*-stems, in Umbrian on the basis of the *u*-stems) and in the formation of different types of the perfect of the 'weak' verbs. The features mentioned here show a marked tendency to analogical innovation in the Italic languages and together pose the problem of whether the reconstruction of a Common Italic ('Proto-Osco-Umbrian' as Rix 1983 calls it) is possible. The answer to this question is only partially positive: such a reconstruction is possible only as long as the documented data coincide; otherwise, if we wish to pursue this end, we must have recourse to other IE languages or to reconstructed Indo-European itself, following a procedure which will then no longer consist merely of reconstruction, but also of meta-historical 'integration'.

Also Rix notes the problematical nature of a similar procedure, on defining his Proto-Italic alias 'Proto-Osco-Umbrian',

> the chronological distance between Proto-Osco-Umbrian and Proto-Indo-European is great, around two and a half millennia; equally the grammatical difference is marked. The distance would decrease, and our knowledge of the pre-history of the 'Italic' languages increase, if Proto-Italic had existed and could be reconstructed. This Proto-Italic would have to satisfy two conditions: (a) it would have to be compatible both with Latin and with Osco-Umbrian and (b) it would have to be different from Proto-Indo-European. The decision as to whether such a proto-language can be reconstructed or not depends not on opinions but on the results of a long series of detailed attempts at reconstruction.
>
> (Rix 1983: 104)

The phenomena described here and, in more general terms, the description of the most important phonological, morphological, lexical and syntactic features of the Italic languages present the problem of their periodization or, at least, of the establishment of their relative chronology. Here, too, we must state that opinions (genetic relationship vs affinity through contact) count for less than facts, depending in particular on the amount of documentary evidence there is to support them. For example, some Umbrian phonetic features (palatalization of *k* to *š* [ʃ], *l*- becoming *v*-, monophthongizations, the change of *d* to *ř* [r], etc.) certainly belong to an early chronological stage (by virtue of their presence in Umbrian names which passed into Etruscan at an early point; cf. Meiser 1986: 10), but, being innovations exclusive to Umbrian, they cannot be taken back to a very old prehistoric phase: conversely, the creation of a class of voiced fricatives certainly belongs to such a phase, since the original existence of these may be inferred not only from the common Osco-Umbrian developments, but also from the developments peculiar to Latin. Here we shall therefore refrain from using diachronic labels (of the type 'old', 'middle', 'new/modern/late' and so on) and by refraining from structuring divisions of history in terms of a proto-history and a history that are inevitably incomplete on the documentary level, we shall attempt to introduce such depths of perspective into a comprehensive framework as seem appropriate and possible.

General Phonological Features

Among these, the *accent* is worthy of particular mention, with regard to its nature and its position. It tends to fall on the initial syllable of a word and is always strongly dynamic, as is clear, on the one hand, from the preservation of the long vowel quantity in initial syllables or, indeed, from lengthening phenomena in this position; and, on the other hand, from extensive instances of *syncope* which, in contrast with Latin, involve not only the antepenultimate and the penultimate, but also the final syllables of words: Thus we have, on the one hand, Oscan **faamat fluusaí** (transcription in bold indicates a form written in the epichoric alphabet; **í** = [e]) with the vowel of the initial syllable written twice and an etymological long vowel, a phenomenon which is not encountered in other syllabic positions, the exceptions being Osc. **tristaamentud** and αϝααματεδ (both compounds showing the analysis of the second element) and Osc. **diíviai** with short *i*. On the other hand we have forms such as Oscan nominative plural **akkatus** (cf. Lat. *advocātus*), Umbr. *perca* (cf. Lat. *pertica*), Osc. **húrz** (cf. Lat. *hortus*; **ú** = [o], **z** = [ts]). In reality the three instance of syncope mentioned here cannot all be conditioned by the same initial position; hence the syllabic reduction 'rule' can be reformulated thus: the syllable immediately following the accent is deleted, according to two different manifestations, of which the first – of earlier relative chronology – allows for accent on the penultimate and apocope in the final syllable (of the type **húrz** < *hórtos, cf. also **túvtíks** < *toutikos and, for a later reduction, Umbr. *todco-*, *toce*), while the second, linked to the initial accent, exclusively affects vowels in medial syllables (cf. Prosdocimi 1986: 611–12). Largely connected with these processes of syncope are cases of vocalic *epenthesis* (or anaptyxis), very rare in Umbrian but well represented in Oscan, where they occur mainly in consonant groups containing a liquid or nasal. It does not seem possible, though, to establish any greater or lesser incidence of the phenomenon according to the relative position of the liquid/nasal with respect to the stop (or other articulation) of the consonant cluster. However, it can be stated that the epenthesis occurs regularly only after a short open syllable and that the quality of the epenthetic vowel is the same as that of the vowel of the preceding or following syllable (cf. Schmid 1954). Examples of this are: Osc. **patereí** 'father (dat. sg.)', (but **maatreís** 'mother (gen. sg.)', Osc. **aragetud** 'silver (abl. sg)', **salavs** 'safe (nom. sg.)', etc. There is no doubt that accentual and related phenomena have specific culminative and delimiting functions in the Italic languages; in more general terms, on the behaviour of phonemes in word-initial and final position, see Untermann (1968) (who is very enlightening on this).

Vowels

The IE vowels, at least those in tonic syllables, tend to be preserved intact in Osco-Umbrian, if we disregard a phenomenon whereby $\bar{e}$ < [i] and $\bar{o}$ < [u]. This phenomenon, which is not conditioned by the position of the accent, is evident in cases such as Osc. **patir** > **pətér* (note, incidentally, the development of *ə* to *a*, as in Latin) and Osc. **dunum** (beside Lat. *donum*). However, the variation between $\breve{a}$ and *o* (for example in Umbr. *Tesenocir/Tesenakes*, dat. pl., with old $\bar{a}$ in the penultimate syllable) is conditioned by the accent (not exclusively the initial accent, see above). One consequence of the initial accent is the Pan-Italic development of -$\bar{a}$ to open -$\breve{o}$ (spellings: Osc. **ú**, *o*; Umbr. **a**, **u**, *o*). We can perhaps place the uncertainty between *o* and *a* in initial syllables within the same interpretative framework, if we assume that the quality *a* is tonic and *o* atonic (e.g. Osc. **kahad** beside Lat. *incohāre*, but Umbr. *hostatu* beside Lat. *hastātus*; uncertain – and suspect – is Pael. *hanustu* beside Lat. *honesta*, which could be the result of ethnolinguistic hyper-characterization). A special development of $\breve{u}$ (from the third century BC onwards) after a dental consonant (*t*, *d*, *n*, *s*) is to be seen as a combinatory variant of this phoneme and consists in a process of palatalization (e.g. Osc. **tiurrí** beside Lat. *turrim*). Taking these factors into account, although they do not exhaust the whole range of the vowel phonemes, the Italic vowel system may be represented as a system with seven members.

i		u
í[e]		ú[o]
e[ɛ]		o[ɔ]
	a	

in which quality (the correlation of openness) is clearly more important than quantity (and this seems to fit in with the various vowel phenomena mentioned above and with the subsequent Italo-Romance developments; in general see Lejeune (1975)).

Sonants

The development of the IE sonants (*r, *l, *m, *n-) poses no particular problems, in that it is broadly similar to what happens in Latin. We thus have the reflexes *or, ol* of *r, *l (see above) and *em, en* of *m, *n (*am, an* in initial syllables) while the reflexes of the long sonants are different: they develop into *ra, la, ma, na*.

Diphthongs

The treatment of the original diphthongs, which are by no means negligible as regards vowels and connected phenomena, merits a brief mention, partly for its implications in Romance. Here we note a marked difference between Oscan and Umbrian, apart from the case of the shared early development of *ew* into *ow* which, as we have already seen, also affects Latin. Oscan in fact preserves the old diphthongs (e.g. **kyaístur, deíkum, múíníkú**, etc.), while Umbrian systematically shows monophthongization, by which even *ou*, the reflex of *eu*, becomes *o, u* (in both cases with the value of [o]). The languages of the Middle Italic area occupy a special position: Volscian, for example, exhibits monophthongization of *ai-* in *esaristrom* (from **aisaristrom* 'sacrifice'), while a Marsian form (*i*)*ouies.pucle*(*s*) (dat. pl.) 'to the sons of Jupiter, i.e. the Dioscuri', with monophthongization, contrasts with the Paelignian *iouiois.puclois* 'id.' with preserved diphthong. The South Picene (Penna S. Andrea) attestations are interesting: they show the coexistence of *toúta-* and *túta-*, with undisputed monophthongization in the second case and probably [o].

Consonants

With respect to the traditional framework of IE consonants the most obvious Italic innovation consists in the special development of the voiced aspirate stops (**b^h, **d^h > f, **g^h > h) in all positions. In this case the innovation is shared only in part by Latin, that shows the same development only in initial positions. There has also been much discussion as to whether this development presupposes an intermediate phase with voiceless aspirate stops (the Greek model) or with voiced fricatives as well as in connection with the resolution of problems of linguistic attribution for glosses or isolated forms or, in more general terms, within the context of more or less shared etymological hypotheses (cf. above all Martinet 1950; Szemerényi 1952–3). Less attention has been paid, however, to the fact that here, as also in the case of the vowels, we have a merger phenomenon, perhaps even more extensive if we consider that the phonemes that result (*f, h*) are phonetically similar and in some languages tend to become even closer and sometimes reach the stage of becoming interchangeable (as in the Faliscan and rustic Latin area, perhaps through Etruscan influence); in any case, the manner of production clearly prevails over the place of articulation. Another considerable feature is the shift of the IE labiovelars to labials: hence we have, for example, Oscan **pís** beside Latin *quis* or, with the regressive assimilation already mentioned, Oscan **pompe* (recoverable from the derived form **pumperia-**) beside Latin *quinque*. The other consonants tend to remain unchanged, apart from some very specific cases of conditioned phonetic changes (on these, see below). On the whole (and leaving aside the special case of the labiovelars) the primary Italic developments (the creation of a class of voiceless fricatives alongside the voiceless and voiced stops) are very similar to those of 'Common Germanic' which obviously presuppose a completely different process of development (cf. Chapter 13, **Consonants**, pp. 391–5).

Consonant System
Obviously, it is possible to restate the development of the Italic consonant system (as far as the category of stops is concerned) in terms of the 'New Sound of Indo-European' (cf. Baldi and Johnston-Staver 1989: 97–8). First, this is a question of accepting the notion that the IE consonant system contained glottalic consonants (/p'/, /t'/, /k'/ instead of /b/, /d/, /g/), voiced consonants (possibly aspirated: /b[h]/, /d[h]/, /g[h]/ instead of /b^h/, /d^h/, /g^h/), and voiceless consonants (possibly aspirated: /p[h]/, /t[h]/, /k[h]/ instead of /p/, /t/, /k/), following what is considered to be a more plausible typological framework (Chapter 2, **The Glottalic Theory**, p. 38). Second, it is necessary to take the Italic reflexes back to a scheme of development which may be represented as follows:

p[h]	t[h]	k[h]	>	p		t	k
b[h]	d[h]	g[h]	>		f		h
p'	t'	k'	>	b		d	g

With this new approach to the problem of reconstructing the IE consonant system, it now seems preferable to abandon once and for all the theory of an intermediate 'voiceless aspirate' stage (which as such would have yielded *p, t, k*) as a precursor of the articulations *f, h*. On the other hand, the idea of intermediate voiced fricatives, which might also be (re)converted into voiced stops, finds support not only in some Umbrian reflexes and in some regular Latin developments, but also in the allophonic status of the Germanic voiced fricatives beside the voiced stops deriving from the IE voiced aspirates (according, of course, to the traditional framework).

Phonetic Development in Consonants
Other consonantal phenomena worthy of mention are a number of unusual conditioned phonetic developments. Most notable are cases of palatalization under the influence of a following *j*, attested above all in the *Tabula Bantina*, by which *l, r, t, d, k* become *ll, rr, s, z, x* (= *š*); the spelling with double consonant, in the case of the liquids, may be taken to indicate a phenomenon

already realized or, at least, in the process of development. Moreover, the phenomenon spreads throughout the entire Italic area (starting from an undoubtedly southern focal point) and is certainly old, because there are already traces of it in the South Picene texts: hence, for example, in Umbrian *k* and *g* (followed by *e*, *i* and *j*) palatalize to *ç*, *š* (= [ʃ]) and *j* respectively; something similar is probably suggested by the Paelignian spelling *pellegie* 'read through' (if it is correctly read); more obscure, at first sight, is Umbr. **îiuvînas**, *iouina* beside *ıkuvina* (cf. Lat. *Iguvium*), but perhaps here the cause lies in the influence of the preceding *i*, rather than in any para-etymological assimilation to the name of Jove. The list could be extended (cf. Pisani 1954, Orioles 1972). Another conditioned phenomenon is the voicing of inter-vocalic *s* in Oscan, while in Umbrian (as in Latin) this combinatory variant is rephonologized to *r* (even in word-final position in the latter period). The intervocalic position is, moreover, the cause of a shift of *-d-* to *-ř-*, to *-rs-* (= [r]) in Umbrian, while an earlier stage of this process is no doubt represented by a special fricative *d* which can be seen in the Paelignian documentation. Finally we should mention some processes of assimilation (*nd* < *nn*, pan-Italic; *mb* < *m*, confined to Umbrian) which, together with the cases examined previously, clearly show how the necessary preconditions of various historical sound changes in the Italo-Romance dialect area are clearly present in Italic.

Morphology

In the Italic noun declension we see a simplification of the IE morphology, but this is not as radical as in other languages (e.g. Germanic). In fact, in the singular at least, the nominative, accusative, genitive, dative, ablative, locative and vocative survive (with only the instrumental being lost). Moreover, the tripartite gender distinction (masculine, feminine and neuter) is preserved, while the tripartite number distinction is reduced to the opposition of singular and plural through the almost total elimination of the dual.

Nouns

The IE stem classes (at least those of the older period) must all have had distinct semantic functions and we can still perceive traces of this at the level attained by comparison and reconstruction. However, these functional distinctions must already have been on the point of collapse in late IE and appear almost totally obscured in the Italic languages. Here we speak – as in Latin – of five declensions, but it should be made clear that the fourth (*-u*-stems) and above all the fifth (*-ē*-stems) are sparsely attested, while in the third, as in Latin, *-i-* stems and consonant stems fall together, although they preserve a greater independence. Table 11.1 gives some inflectional para-digms. Note that these show the presumed (later) IE antecedents, beside which the inflected Italic forms with their special phonetic developments are shown (note the rhotacism of Umbrian final *-s*).

Table 11.1   First declension: -ā- stems

Singular						
Nom.	IE	-ā	Osc. víú.	touto	Umbr. **muta,**	**mutu**
Voc.		-ă			Tursa	prestota
Acc.		-ām	**víam,**	toutam	**tuta,**	totam
Dat.		-āi	**deívaí**		**tute,**	tote
Abl.		-ād	**eítiuvad,**	toutad	**tuta,**	tota
Gen.		-ās	**vereias,**	eituas	**tutas**	totar
Loc.		-āi	**víaí,**	Bansae	**tafle**	tote
Plural						
Nom.		-ās	**aasas,**	scriftas	**pumperias**	iuengar
Acc.		-āns	**víass,**	eituas	**vitlaf**	uitla
Dat.-Abl.		-āis	**kerssnaís**		**tekuries**	dequrier
Gen.		-āsōm	**eehiianasúm**	egmazum	**urnasiaru**	pracatarum

Table 11.2   Second declension: -o- stems

Singular			Osc.		Umbr.	
Nom.	IE	-os	**húrz**	Bantins	**Ikuvins**	ager
Voc.		-e	**Statie Silie**		Serfe	Tefre
Acc.		-om	**húrtúm**	dolom	**puplu(m)**	poplo(m)
Dat.		-ŏi	**húrtúí**		**kumnakle**	pople
Abl.		-ōd	**sakaraklúd**	dolud	**puplu**	poplu
Gen.		-eis	**sakarakleís**		**katles**	popler
Loc.		-ei	**tereí**	comenei	**kumne**	pople
Plural						
Nom.		-ōs	**Núvlanús**		**Ikuvinus**	Iouinur
Acc.		-ons	**feíhúss**		**vitluf**	uitlu
Dat.-Abl.		-ōis	**Núvlanúís**		**veskles**	uesclir
Gen.		-ōm	**Núvlanúm**		**pihaklu**	pihaclo

We should also mention the Paelignian dative singular in -a, probably influenced by Latin (cf. Lazzeroni 1965).

Note that the genitive singular ending Osc. **-eís**, Umbr. **-es**, -er is formed analogically on that of the -i-stems of the third declension. This phenomenon could have been favoured by the reflexes of nominative -is and accusative -im of original -jo-stems. The second declension also includes neuter words with predictable reflexes (Osc. nom. acc. sg. **sakaraklum** from -om, pl. **prúftú** from -ā, cf. Umbr. **persklum** and **veskla**, **vesklu**, uatuo). In the third declension (-i-stems and consonant stems) one final analogical phenomenon should be mentioned: the inflection of the accusative singular of the consonantal stems has been re-formed on that of the -o-stems (hence Osc. **aitatum**, **leginum**, Umbr. **erietu**, **abrunu**). Notable, finally, is the change of -u- stems to -i- stems in some forms of the fourth declension (e.g. Osc. acc. sg. manim, abl. sg. castrid, Umb. abl. sg. **mani**, although in the case of the ablative forms we cannot preclude the possibility of a regular phonetic development; cf., for a reconstruction of the oldest phase of this declension, Lejeune 1972).

Adjectives

From a purely formal point of view, it is possible to take the Italic adjective back on the one hand to the first and second declensions (e.g. Osc. *túvtiks* 'publicus (nom. sg.')), and on the other hand to the third declension *-i-* stems e.g. Osc. **sakrím**, m. and f. acc. sg.; but cf. also Umbr. *sakra*, f. acc. pl., Osc. **sakrvist** 'sacra est', etc.). The formation of the comparative and superlative does not differ greatly from familiar Latin-morphological processes (cf. Chapter 10, **Degrees of Comparison of the Adjective**, pp. 291–3). We note, however, in some cases, the accumulation of two suffixes: e.g. Osc. *minstreis* 'minoris', Umbr. *mestru* 'maior' from **min-is-tero-* and **ma(g)-is-tero-* respectively. In the superlative there occur almost exclusively terms denoting place or time, starting from pre- and postpositional elements (e.g. **pos-*: Osc. **pús-tr-eí** 'in postero', **pus-tm-as** 'postremae'; **sub-*: Osc. **sup-r-uis** 'superi', Umbr. **sub-r-a** 'supra', Umbr. *somo* from **sup-m-o* 'summum').

Determiners

Of the IE deictic elements used either purely as determiners or as anaphoric pronouns, the best represented in the Italic languages is *i-*, *e-*, *eo-/eā-* (corresponding to Latin *is*), which in the oblique cases exhibits various consonantal extensions (*-s-*, *-sm-*), and is in some cases redetermined, as a deictic, by the enclitic particle **-k**, *-c* (similar cases exist in Latin). The extended form Umbrian *-ont -unt* (and variants), marking identity, is also very interesting, while Oscan **ísídum** (from **is-id-um*; on this last morph cf. Umbr. *on-t*, *un-t*, mentioned above) shows the same semantic specialization; cf. also Lat. *idem*. Table 11.3 shows the paradigm of the attested forms, with the caveat that this *reductio ad unum* does not exclude the possibility that the speakers may have been conscious rather of a sort of pronominal 'family' with distinct semantic specializations by virtue of specific morphological arrangements.

We may note, amongst other features, the thematization in *-i-/-í-* in the Oscan masculine and neuter nominative forms, in *-e-* in the corresponding Umbrian forms, with non-homogeneous extension to the other forms of the paradigm, where it competes with the thematization in *-o-* (in *-ā-* in the feminine). This fact is worthy of attention since we have already noted other cases in which the second and third declension stems exhibit inter-paradigmatic interference. It will suffice here to give a mere indication of the other demonstrative pronouns (all with stems in *-o*, *-ā-*): we have Osc. *eko-* (redetermined from *ekso-*, cf. Umbr. *eso*, Marrucinian *esu-c*) with the meaning 'hic'; Umbr. **uru**, abl. sg., Osco. **úlleis**, gen. sg., cf. OLat *olle* (of identical etymological origin, if we accept that *-l > -r-* in Umbrian, cf. Pael. *firata* 'line, row') with the meaning 'ille'; Umbr. *esto-*, with the meaning

Table 11.3   Determiners/anaphoric pronouns

	Oscan			Umbrian		
	Masculine	*Neuter*	*Feminine*	*Masculine*	*Neuter*	*Feminine*
Singular						
Nom.	iz-i-k	**íd-i-k**	**íú-k**	**ere**, ere	**eř-e-k**	———
		id-i-k	**iiu-k**	**er-e-k**	erse-e	
		id-i-c	io-c	er-e-c		
Acc.	ion-c	- hom.	**ía-k**	———	- nom.	eam
Dat.		———		esmei		———
				esmi-k		
Abl.	**eísúd**	———	**eísa-k**	**eru(-ku)**		**era-k**
	eizu-c		eiza-c	eru(-com)		
Gen.	**eiseis**		———	erer, irer		erar
	eizeis			**erer-e-k**		
Loc.	**eíseí**		eisai	esme		———
	eizei-c					
Plural						
Nom.	**íus-su**	———	———	eur-ont	———	———
	(íusu)					
	ius-c					
			(Marrucinian)			
Acc.	———	ioc	**iaf-**	———	**eu**, eo	**eaf**, eaf
			c			
Dat. Abl.	eizois		———	erir-ont		**erer-unt**
Gen.	**eisun-k**		eizazun-c	**eru**, ero(m)	———	

(on this summary, cf. Pisani 1964: 18–19)

'iste'; Osc.-Umbr. *esso-* (cf. Osc. **essuf**, Umbr. *esuf*) with the meaning 'ipse'. It should be understood that the meanings assigned here are based on the etymological evidence and in every case require precise textual verification.

Interrogative, Relative and Indefinite
The single morph *pi*, *po-/pa-* unites the IE functions of interrogative and indefinite, to which the Italic languages (like Latin and – among the Germanic languages – English and German) add the function of a relative. It is probable, however, that the ability to merge these functions goes back to IE times, since it is also reflected in some Sanskrit pronoun forms (e.g. *kas-cid* from $*-k^wid$ with the meaning 'quisque'). Also notable in this context is Osc. **pútúrús-pid** 'utrique (nom. pl.)', in which *-pid* (from $*-k^wid$) appears as a form in competition with *-pe* (from $*ke^we$) in Umbr. **putres-pe** 'utriusque gen. sg.'. For the formation of the indefinite the Italic languages have recourse to the addition of *-um* (Osc. *pis-um*, **píd-um**, cf. Osc. **ísídum** and see above) or to the particle *-i*. As in Latin, finally, the interrogative function in the nominative singular is covered by the form Osc. **pís**, *pis*, **pid** 'quis, quid', while the relative function competes with the form Osc. **pui**, m., **pai**, f., **púd**, *pod*, nt., corresponding exactly to Lat. *qui, quae, quod*.

Numerals

The cardinal numerals from one to four are declinable (with some uncertainty in the case of four, unless we are willing to accept the idea that the form *petora* in Fest. 226 L (206 M.) is neuter, contrasting with Osc. *pettiur* ('quattuor', m. and f.)). In this case Italic would be, like Greek and Germanic, more conservative than Latin. 'One' is not continued directly in the cardinals (Umbr. **unu** has been wrongly taken to be 'one' since it means 'ovinum, ovillum'); the attested ordinal form is Umbr. **prumum**, *promom* (but cf. also Pael. *prismu*, a feminine forename, in reality an adjective in the superlative degree meaning 'first'). As regards 'two', as well as the obvious suppletion in the form of the ordinal (cf. Umbr. *etru*), it will suffice to cite the Umbrian forms nominative. *dur*, accusative **tuf**, neuter **tuva** and to note the alternative forms *u/i* in the compounds Umbr. *du-pursus*, dative plural 'bipedibus' and *di-fue*, neuter accusative singular 'bifidum'. For 'three' the situation is as in Latin (cf. Osc. **tris**, Umbr. acc. **trif, tref**, n. **triia** and the Umbr n. abl. sg. ordinal *tertiu*). 'Four' has already been discussed. We do not have direct attestation of the numerals from five to ten: 'five' is **pompe*, cf. the derivatives Osc. **púmperia-**, Umbr. **pumpeřias**; 'six' is in the derivative Umbr. **sestentasiaru** (gen. pl.); 'seven' does not appear to be attested even indirectly; 'eight' is, as an ordinal, in **Uhtavis**; 'nine' is, as a cardinal, in the Marsian *novesede* 'Novensides' cf. the ordinal Umbr. **nuvim**); 'ten' is in the compound Umbr. *desen-duf* 'twelve', as well as in the derivatives Osc. **dekkviarím**, Umbr. **tekvias**, etc. (Osc. **dekmanniúís** seems to be derived from the ordinal form.) We have no attestation of 'eleven', while 'twelve' is Umbr. *desen-duf* with significant reversal of the order of constituents with respect to the Greek and Latin models. Other forms of numerals are not attested.

Personal Pronouns

The documentation is sparse, in that it is limited to the first two persons singular (1 sg.: Osc. **íív** 'ego'; Umbr. *mehe* 'mihi'; 2 sg.: Osc. **tiium, tiú** (nom. sg.) 'tu', Umbr. *tiom, tio,* **tiu** acc. sg.) 'te', as well as Osc. **tfei,** Umbr. **tefe,** *tefe* (dat. sg.) 'tibi', while the third-person singular, in its function as a reflexive pronoun, is attested in Osc. **sífeí** 'sibi', Pael. *sefei*; Osc. *siom* 'se'; Umbr. *seso* 'sibi'. We note in *tiom* etc. and in *siom* the recurrence of the ubiquitous accusative singular reflex of the *-o-* stems. Paelignian *uus* 'vos' or 'vobis' is an isolated form. On the forms of the possessive pronouns, which are derived from personal pronouns, it is enough to say that they do not differ significantly from the morphological situation in Latin.

Verb Conjugation

In the Italic languages the IE system of verb morphology appears greatly simplified and is on the whole very similar to that of Latin. On the temporal axis there is a present tense, from which the future is formed by means of the morpheme *-s(e)-* and a perfect (formed in a variety of ways, see below), from which the future perfect is derived by means of the morpheme -*us*(*e*)-. However, controversy surrounds the possible existence of an imperfect, since the form Oscan **fufans** (attested in the *Cippus Abellanus*) is still a matter for debate (cf. Pisani 1963) and could in fact be a pluperfect (cf. Lejeune 1964). On the axis of mood the opposition is between the indicative, with zero morpheme, and the subjunctive (with the morpheme -*a*- in the present in all conjugations other than the first, where -*ē*- occurs, as in Latin; the morpheme -*se*- in the imperfect; and the morpheme -*e*- in the perfect). Umbrian *si*, *sins*, and so on, forms of the verb 'to be' show the use of ancient optative in the function of subjunctive. The imperative, which has the same endings as Latin (apart from Umbr. 2 pl. and 3 pl. -**tuta**, -**tutu**, -*tuto* where -*ta* is morphologically difficult to interpret), is based on the present stem. Finally, there are two voices, active and mediopassive (the latter not corresponding exactly to the situation found in Latin).

In the active conjugation we have to distinguish between primary endings (1 sg. -*o*, 2 sg. -*s*, 3 sg. -*t*; 3 pl. -*nt*), used in the present, future and future perfect indicative; and secondary endings (1 sg. -*m*, 2 sg. -*s*, 3 sg. -*d*; 3 pl. -*ns*), used in the imperfect (or pluperfect, see above) and perfect indicative, as well as in all the tenses of the subjunctive. In the mediopassive conjugation we see the morpheme with -*r*- typical of 'peripheral' Indo-European Tocharian, Indo-Iranian, Armenian, Hittite, Celtic and Latin; this occurs in the present forms and, in part, those of the perfect (e.g. 3 sg. pres. -*nter*; also notable are the Umbrian forms in -*ntur*, restricted to the subjunctive only). Compare also forms such as Oscan **sakrafír** 'to be consecrated', Umbrian *ferar* 'may it be carried', etc.

Something must also be said about the substantival forms of the verb. The active infinitive is formed with the morpheme -*om* (markedly different from Latin and comparable specifically with some Greek endings of the Doric type); moreover, in Umbrian the forms *pihafi*, *herifi*, *cehefi* are very notable; these represent old prehistoric middle infinitives (cf. Gusmani 1966; Rix 1977), starting from an ending *-d^hjōj, which is also continued in Sanskrit and Avestan. The gerundive (with -*nn*- from -*nd*-) is borrowed from Latin. The supine, present participle active (on the inflection of this cf. Lejeune 1986) and past participle passive do not differ from the Latin processes of formation. Finally, the two forms Oscan *sipus* 'sciens' and *facus* 'factus', rather than being perfect participles with active value, go back to the category of IE adjectives with 'participial' value (derived, by means of the suffix -*u*-, from verbal roots, cf. Gusmani 1970).

A separate discussion is necessary for the various forms of the perfect, which for good reason represents the best-attested verbal form (we must remember that our knowledge of forms is determined by the nature of the epigraphic evidence and what typically occurs in these texts). Notwithstanding numerous detailed studies, it is still not possible to claim that absolute clarity has been reached on the question. (There is essentially no adequate explanation of the multiplicity of forms alongside their presumed uniformity of function.) In any case, the forms of the Italic perfect are as follows: perfects with reduplication (Osc. **deded**, Umbr. **dede**, cf. Lat. *dedit*); perfects with lengthening of the root vowel (Osc. **upsed** 'operavit', **uupsens** 'operaverunt' from *ōps-* beside Osc. *upsannum* 'operandum' from *ŏps-*, cf. Lat. *uēni*, *fēci*); perfects in *-f* (Osc. **aíkdafed**, **aamanaffed**, Umbr. **a-tera-f-us-t** 'circumdederit', fut. perf.); perfects in *-tt-*, typical of the Oscan first conjugation (e.g. **prúfatted** 'probavit'), but present also in Paelignian *coisatens* 'curaverunt', while absent from Umbrian; perfects in *-nki-*, attested only in some Umbrian forms, with palatalization (cf. e.g. Umbr. *purdinsiust* 'porrexerit', fut. perf.); perhaps, similar to this, a perfect in *-k-* (Osc. λιοκα-κ-ειτ, **kella-k-ed**); finally, a presumed perfect in *-s-* (but Umbr. *sesust* 'sederit' is not decisive and Pael. *lexe*, rather than a past infinitive, could be a reduced form corresponding to Lat. *legistis*). On the problems of interpretation relating to the various perfect forms cf. Olzscha 1958; Diels 1959; Olzscha 1963; Parlangeli 1972; Pisani 1975; Negri 1976; Markey 1985).

Invariable Parts of Speech

These are conjunctions, adverbs, pre- and postpositions, but note that in the case of the latter the prepositions function mainly as preverbs, while in the noun phrase the postpositions are undisputedly a special characteristic.

Conjunctions

We can enumerate about twenty forms, almost all of pronominal origin. The great majority of these are those connected with the interrogative-relative pronoun (compare, e.g. Osc. **puf**, Umbr. *pufe* 'ubi' with the adverbial ending *-dʰe* or *-dʰi* and apocope of the final vowel; the same morphological structure can be found in the Paelignian adverb *ecuf* 'hic', but this has a different pronominal stem; on the productivity of this formation compare the adverbial forms Umbrian *esuf* and South Picene *estuf* with further pronominal stems). Other interesting formations are those composed of fossilized verbal forms (of the type Umbr. *heri* ... *heri* ... 'vel ... vel ...' or Osc. *loufir*, 3 sg. passive, with the same impersonal value as Lat. *libet*. Belonging among well-known Latin and Greek features are Umbr. **et** 'et', Osc. **iním**, etc.; Umbr. *enem*, etc., with the value of 'et', as well as Osc. *auti*, *aut*, **avt**, Umbr. *ote*, **ute** 'aut', etc. Finally Oscan **svaí**, *suae*, Umbrian **sve**, *sue* 'si' is an old locative corresponding to Latin *si* (from **sei*), which exhibits a different pronominal stem.

Adverbs

As well as the aforementioned adverbs formed with **-dʰe/-i* with locative value, we should mention old ablative forms (with which the functions of the instrumental merge) with the reflexes *-ēd*, *-ē* (e.g. Osc. *amprufid* 'improbe',

Umbr. *prufe* 'probe'), *-ōd*, *-ō* (e.g. Pael. *ecu-c* 'huc?' with enclitic *-c*, Umbr. *supru* 'supra'), *-ād*, *-ā* (e.g. Umbr. **subra** and cf. Osc. **ehtrad** 'extra', with propositional value), and finally *-īd* (e.g. Osc. **akrid**, which may mean 'acriter', but also 'a culmine'). Another morphological problem is posed by some cases of original neuter accusatives (e.g. Umbr. *promom* 'primum', *tertim* 'tertium'). Notable, finally, are adverbial forms such as Umbrian **akru-tu** 'ab initio', 'de integro', *scalse-to* 'ex patera', which imply old ablatives with the postposition *-tu/o*, *-ta* (perhaps from older *-tā*; for an alternative form in *-tus* cf. Lat. *funditus* and similar).

Prepositions and Postpositions
The former, when they are not functioning as preverbs (e.g. *prai-* in Umbr. **prehabia**, 3 sg. pres. subj. 'prae(hi)beat', *pru-* Umbr. *pruhipid*, 3 sg. perf. subj. 'prohibuerit', etc., in line with a well-known Latin system cf. also Untermann 1973), have a construction with the accusative (e.g. Osc. **ant** in **ant púnttram** 'usque ad pontem', Osc.-Umb. **pert** in Osc. **pert víam** 'trans viam', Umbr. **pert spinia** 'trans spinam'); with the ablative (e.g. Osc. **up**, *up* 'apud' in Osc. **úp eísud sakaraklúd** 'apud id templum') or with the locative (e.g. Umbr. **super** in Umbr. **super kumne** 'super comitio'). Postpositions, much more frequent than in Latin, are represented in cases such as Oscan *petiro-pert* 'quarter' (with *-pert* from **per-ti* just as Osc. *post* is from **pos-ti*), Umbrian **vuku-kum** 'ad lucum', Umbrian *tota-per* 'pro civitate' and above all, in Oscan *-en*, Umbrian *en*, *-e* 'in', which can follow both forms of the accusative and forms of the locative (evidently with the same relationship that links Latin *in* with both the accusative and the ablative); hence, for example, Umbrian **vukum-en** 'in lucum', *amglom-e* 'ad angulum' (motion), but Oscan **hurtín** 'in horto', Umbrian **arven** 'in arvo' (rest). Notable are the expressions Oscan **imad-en** 'ab imo', *eisuc-en ziculud* 'ab eo die' with ablative forms, which could be interpreted, by virtue of the first above-mentioned meaning of *-en* (namely, the idea of movement) as 'starting from', 'from (a certain moment) onwards'.

Word Formation
On this important aspect, which is part of the morphosyntactic level, it can be said that the Italic languages do not differ greatly from Latin, with which they share the basic processes of derivation (but it is difficult to identify a typically Italic suffix or, at least, one which is typically productive in Italic), while nominal compounding is much less well represented (there are few examples and all can be taken back to Latin models, even as regards compounds with adverbs or prepositions in first position). In the case of root apophony, too, which is rightly part of the study of word formation and is a typical IE process, Italic is particularly lacking in documentary evidence. In any case, as in Latin – indeed more so – the phenomenon is residual (on quantitative apophony in one of the forms of the perfect, see above).

The Syntactic Type of the Italic Languages

As regards case syntax (see above for the purely morphological aspects and see also Berrettoni 1971), it can be said that the Italic languages are almost completely identical to Latin. In Umbrian, however, we do see an early and profound alteration of the case system at the morphological level as the result of syncope and weakening of final syllables (largely due to the accent) and of homophony (a result of individual phonetic developments, particularly instances of monophthongization). Cases of allomorphy consequently arise (many 'signifiers' for the same case morpheme) and, on the other hand, the same morph has to fulfil different functions (different case morphemes with a single form). Umbrian, unlike Oscan, which tends to strengthen the inflectional case system, with the influence of the -o stems on the other declension (cf. Gusmani 1965), thus undergoes an early topological change (cf. Porzio Gernia 1983) which takes it in the direction of 'incipient' agglutinization. Another aspect of this is the use of postpositions, which are much more vital and differentiated in Umbrian than in Oscan (remember that the latter only has the morpheme -in/-en which, in this sense, is clearly residual). It is difficult to say whether these typologically innovative impulses came into Umbrian from Etruscan by virtue of some ancient ethnolinguistic contiguity, but it is certainly true that in this central area of the peninsula, phenomena which are, broadly speaking, typological began to arise which come to fruition in late or pre-Romance Latin.

As regards Greenbergian typology of the basic ordering of elements (relative position of S = subject, O = object, V = verb and of N = noun, A = adjective, G = genitive; presence or absence of prepositions and postpositions, etc.), it can be said that Italic (and in particular Umbrian) is of the type SOV, which indeed predicts postpositions (on the relative position of A, N and G and, in more general terms, on word order in the Italic sentence, cf. Berrettoni 1967, 1969). The syntax of the moods, known to us mainly via the Umbrian documentation, exhibits a difference between indicative and infinitive on the one hand ('affirmation') and subjunctive on the other ('command', 'doubt'), whenever the embedded clause acts as a subject or object complement clause (for further details, see Rix 1976; for a distinction between the use of the imperative and that of the 'iussive' subjunctive in Umbrian, cf. Jones 1962).

Finally, worthy of note is the fact that the Italic, especially in Umbrian (as at times in Latin), subordinate clauses can occur without a conjunction (e.g. Pael. *upsaseter coisatens* 'operaretur curaverunt', Umbr. **esunu fuia herter** 'sacrificium fiat oportet') and that in these cases, both in Umbrian and in Oscan, asyndeton is very common, probably under the pressure of official and formal situational contexts.

References

Aoliego Lujara, Ignacis-Javier (1990) 'Der Archaismus des Südpikenischen', *HS* 103: 69–80.

—— (1992) *Protosabelio, Osco-Umbro, Sudpiceno*, Universitas 20, Barcelona: PPU.

Agostiniani, Luciano (1987) *Le iscrizioni anelleniche della Sicilia: Le iscrizioni elime* (Lingue e Iscrizioni dell'Italia Antica, 1) Florence: Olschki.

Ambrosini, Riccardo (1968) 'Italica o anatolica la lingua dei graffiti di Segesta?' *Studi e saggi linguistici* 8: 160–72.

—— (1970) 'A proposito di una recente pubblicazione sulla lingua dei graffiti di Segesta', *Studi e saggi linguistici* 10: 232–7.

—— (1971) 'Problemi e ipotesi sulla lingua dei graffiti di Segesta', *Atti delle Accademia Nazionale dei Lincei, Rendiconti della Classe di scienze, storiche e filologiche*: 461–74.

—— (1984) 'Lingue nella Sicilia pregreca', in Adriana Quattordio Morschini (ed.), *Tre millenni di storia linguistica in Sicilia*, Atti del Convegno della Società Italiana di Glottologia, Palermo, 25–27 March 1983, Pisa: Giardini, pp. 13–35.

Baldi, Philip and Johnston-Staver, Ruth (1989) 'Historical Italic phonology in typological perspective', in Theo Vennemann (ed.), *The New Sound of Indo-European: Essays in Phonological Reconstruction*, Berlin and New York: de Gruyter, pp. 85–101.

Beeler, Madison S. (1952) 'The relation of Latin and Osco-Umbrian', *Language* 28: 435–43.

—— (1966) 'The interrelationships within Italic', in Henrik Birnbaum and Jaan Puhvel (eds), *Ancient Indoeuropean Dialects*, Berkeley and Los Angeles: University of California Press, pp. 51–8.

Berrettoni, Pierangiolo (1967) 'Ricerche sulla posizione delle parole nella frase italica', *Annali della Scuola Normale Superiore di Pisa* 36: 31–81.

—— (1969) 'Il rapporto tra determinazione aggettivale e genitivale nelle lingue italiche', *Studi e saggi linguistici*: 139–84.

—— (1971)'Due note di sintassi osco-umbra dei casi', *Studi e saggi linguistici* 11: 200–9.

Bottiglioni, Gino (1954) *Manuale dei dialetti italici: Osco, umbro e dialetti minori. Grammatica, testi, glossario con note etimologiche*, Bologna: Società Tipografica Editrice Bolognese.

Campanile, Enrico (1976) 'La latinizzazione dell'osco', in *Scritti in onore di Giuliano Bonfante*, I. Brescia: Paideia Editrice, pp. 109–20.

De Simone, Carlo (1972) 'La lingua messapica: tentativo di una sintesi', in *Le genti non greche della Magna Grecia* (Atti dell'XI Convegno di studi sulla Magna Grecia, Taranto, 10–15 October 1971), Naples, pp. 125–201, 221–2.

Delfino, Maria Giovanna (1958) 'Il problema dei rapporti linguistici tra l'osco e il latino', in *Serta Eusebiana* (Pubblicazioni dell'Istituto di Filologia Classica, Università di Genova, 11), pp. 27–86.

Diels, Paul (1959) 'Zur umbrischen Konjugation', *Münchener Studien zur Sprachwissenschaft* 15: 17–22.

Durante, Marcello (1978) 'Nord-piceno: la lingua delle iscrizioni di Novilara', in Prosdocimi 1978a: 393–400.

Etter, Annemarie (ed.) (1986) *Festschrift für Ernst Risch zum 75. Geburtstag*, Berlin and New York: Walter de Gruyter.

Giacomelli, Gabriella (1963) *La lingua falisca*, (Istituto di Studi Etruschi e Italici Biblioteca di 'Studi Etruschi', 1), Florence: Olschki.

—— (1978) 'Il falisco', in Prosdocimi 1978a: 505–42.

Gusmani, Roberto (1965) 'Note marginali sulla declinazione osco-umbra', *Rendiconti dell'Istituto Lombardo di Scienze e Lettere, Classe di lettere e scienze morali e storiche* 99: 380–8.

—— (1966) 'Umbrisch *pihafi* und Verwandtes', *Indogermanische Forschungen. Zeitschrift für Indogermanistik und allgemeine Sprachwissenschaft* 71: 64–80.

—— (1970) 'Osco *sipus*', *AGI* 55: 145–9.

Guzzo Amadasi, Maria Giulia (1978) 'Il punico', in Prosdocimi 1978a: 1013–28.

Hamp, Eric P. (1990) 'On the Oscan-Umbrian *f*-perfect', *Glotta* 68: 211–15.

Jeffers, Robert J. (1973) 'Problems in the reconstruction of Proto-Italic', *Journal of Indo-European Studies* 1: 330–44.

Jones, D. M. (1950) 'The relation of Latin to Osco-Umbrian', *Transactions of the Philological Society*: 60–87.

—— (1962) 'Imperative and jussive subjunctive in Umbrian', *Glotta* 40: 210–19.

Lazzeroni, Romano (1965) 'Il dativo "sabellico" in -*a*. Contributo alla conoscenza della latinizzazione dei Peligni', *Studi e saggi linguistici* 5: 65–86.

—— (1972) 'Contatti di lingue e di culture nell'Italia antica: elementi greci nei dialetti italici', *Studi e saggi linguistici* 12: 1–24.

—— (1993) 'Latino e osco-umbro fra unità genetica e affinità acquisita', *Incontri Linguistici* 16: 61–9.

Lejeune, Michel (1964) 'Osque *fufans*', *Bulletin de la Société Linguistique de Paris* LIX: 77–81.

—— (1972) '*Aisu- "dieu" et le quatrième déclinaison italique', *Bulletin de la Société Linguistique de Paris* 67: 129–37.

—— (1974) *Manuel de la langue vénète*, Heidelberg: Winter.

—— (1975) 'Réflexions sur la phonologie du vocalism osque', *Bulletin de la Société Linguistique de Paris* 70: 233–51.

Marinetti, Anna (1981) 'Il sudpiceno come italico (e come "sabino"?): Nota preliminare', *Studi Etruschi* 49: 113–58.

—— (1985) *Le iscrizioni sudpicene*, vol. 1, *Testi* (Lingue e Iscrizioni dell'Italia antica 5), Florence: Olschi.

Markey, T. L. (1985) 'Some Italic perfects revisited', *Word* 6: 26–41.

Martinet, André (1950) 'Some problems of Italic Consonantism', *Word* VI: 26–41.

Meiser, Gerhard (1986) *Lautgeschichte der umbrischen Sprache*, Innsbruck: Institut für Sprachwissenschaft der Universität (IBS 51).

—— (1987) 'Pälignisch, Latein und Südpikenisch', *Glotta* 65: 106–25.

Negri, Mario (1976) 'I perfetti oscoumbri in -*f*-', *Rendiconti dell'Istituto Lombardo di Scienze e Lettere, Classe di lettere e scienze morali e storiche* 110: 3–10.

Nocentini, Alberto (1982) 'Preposizioni e posposizioni in oscoumbro', *AGI* 77: 196–292.

Olzscha, Karl (1958) 'Das umbrische Perfekt auf-*nki*', *Glotta* 36: 300–4.

—— (1963) 'Das *f*-Perfektum im Oskisch-Umbrischen', *Glotta* 41: 290–9.

Orioles, Vincenzo (1972) 'Su alcuni fenomeni di palatalizzazione e di assibilazione nelle lingue dell'Italia antica', *Studi Linguistici Salentini* 5/1: 67–100.

—— (1993) 'Lega Linguistica italica e palatalizzazioni', *Incontri Linguistici* 16: 71–8.

Parlangeli, Oronzo (1972) 'Isoglosse italiche: perfetti in -*k*- e in -*v*-', *Rendiconti dell'Istituto Lombardo di Scienze e Lettere, Classe di lettere e scienze morali e storiche* 106: 234–41.

Pellegrini, Giovanni Battista (1978) 'Toponimi ed etnici nelle lingue dell'Italia antica', in Prosdocimi 1978a: 79–127.

Pellegrini, G. B. and Prosdocimi, A. L. (1967) *La lingua venetica*, vol. I, *Le iscrizioni*, ed. G. B. Pellegrini and A. L. Prosdocimi; vol. II, *Studi*, ed. A. L. Prosdocimi, Padua: Istituto di Glottologia dell'Università; Florence: Circolo Linguistico Fiorentino.

Peruzzi, Emilio (1980) *Mycenaeans in Early Latium*, with an archaeological appendix by L. Vagnetti (Incunabula Graeca, 75), Rome: Ateneo.

Pisani, Vittore (1952) 'Über eine pälignische Inschrift (Co. 208 bis, Pl. 246d) und die Herkunft des Oskisch-umbrischen', *Rheinisches Museum für Philologie* 95: 1–22.

——— (1954) 'Palatalizzazioni osche e latine', *AGI* 39: 112–19.

——— (1963) 'Oskisch *fufans*', *Zeitschrift für vergleichende Sprachforschung* 78: 101–3.

——— (1964) *Manuale storico della lingua latina*, vol. IV, *Le lingue dell'Italia antica oltre il latino*, 2nd edn, Turin: Rosenberg & Sellier.

——— (1975) 'Intorno al suffisso umbro di perfetto *-nc-, -ns-*', *AGI* 60: 220–2.

——— (1978) 'Le lingue preromane d'Italia: origini e fortune', in Prosdocimi 1978a: 15–77.

Poccetti, Paolo (1979) *Nuovi documenti italici* companion to the handbook of E. Vetter (Orientamenti linguistici, 8) Pisa: Giardini.

Porzio Gernia, Maria Luisa (1983) 'Tipologia linguistica e crisi della declinazione italica', in *Scritti linguistici in onore di Giovanni Battista Pellegrini*, Pisa: Pacini, pp. 1443–52.

Prosdocimi, Aldo Luigi (1976) 'Sui grecismi dell'osco', in *Scritti ... Bonfante* (q.v.), vol. II: 781–866.

——— (ed.) (1978a) *Lingue e dialetti*. Popoli e civiltà dell-Italia Antica, vol. 6. Rome Biblioteca di Storia Patria.

——— (1978b) 'Contatti e conflitti di lingue nell'Italia antica: l'elemento greco', in Prosdocimi 1978a: 1029–88.

——— (ed.) (1978c) *Popoli e civiltà dell'Italia antica*, vol. IV, Rome: Biblioteca di Storia Patria.

——— (1979) 'Le iscrizioni italiche. Acquisizioni, temi e problemi', in *Le iscrizioni prelatine in Italia*, Rome, 14–15 March 1977 (Atti dei Convegni Lincei 39): 119–204.

——— (1984) *Le tavole iguvine*, I (Lingue e iscrizioni dell'Italia antica, 4), Florence: Olschki.

——— (1986) 'Sull'accento latino e italico', in Etter 1986: 601–18.

Prosdocimi, Aldo Luigi and Marinetti, Anna (1993) 'Appunti sul verbo italico (e) latino', in Rix 1993: 219–79.

Rix, Helmut (1976) 'Subjonctif et infinitif dans les complétives de l'ombrien', *Bulletin de la Société Linguistique de Paris* 71: 221–40.

——— (1977) 'Die umbrischen Infinitive auf *-fi* und die urindogermanische Infinitiv-endung *-d^hiōi*', in Anna Morpurgo Davies and Wolfgang Meid (eds), *Studies in Greek, Italic, and Indo-European Linguistics offered to Leonard Palmer*, Innsbruck: Institut für Sprachwissenschaft der Universität Innsbruck (IBS, 16): 319–31.

——— (1983) 'Umbro e Proto-Osco-Umbro', in Edoardo Vineis (ed.), *Le lingue indoeuropee di frammentaria attestazione: Die Indogermanischen Restsprachen*, Atti del Convegno della Società Italiana di Glottologia e della Indogermanische Gesellschaft. Udine 22–24 September 1981 (Biblioteca della S.I.G., 7), Pisa, Giardini, pp. 91–107.

——— (1986) 'Die Endung des Akkusativ Plural commune im Oskischen', in Etter 1986: 583–97.

———— (1993) 'Oskisch-Umbrisch. Texte und Grammatik', Working party of the Indogerman Society and the Italian Glottological Society, 25–28 September 1991, Freiburg, edited by Helmut Rix, Wiesbaden: Reichert.

Santoro, Ciro (1982–4) *Nuovi studi messapici*, vols I–III, Galatina: Congedo.

Schmid, Wolfgang (1954) 'Anaptyxe, Doppelschreibung und Akzent im Oskischen', *Zeitschrift für vergleichende Sprachforschung* 72/1–2: 30–46.

Silvestri, Domenico (1981) 'La posizione linguistica dell'indoeuropeo. Genealogie, tipologie, contatti', in Enrico Campanile (ed.), *Nuovi materiali per la ricerca indoeuropeistica* (Testi linguistici, 1) Pisa: Giardini, pp. 161–201.

———— (1982) 'Identificazione e interpretazione linguistiche di etnici e toponimi nell'Italia antica', *AIΩN* 4: 65–74.

———— (1985) 'Etnici e toponimi di area osca: problemi di stratigrafia e di storia onomastica', in Enrico Campanile (ed.), *Lingua e cultura degli Oschi* (Testi linguistici, 9) Pisa: Giardini, pp. 67–87.

———— (1986) 'Il progetto del DETIA (Dizionario degli Etnici e dei Toponimi dell'Italia Antica) e i dati etno-toponomastici della Campania', in Domenico Silvestri (ed.), *Lineamenti di storia linguistica della Campania antica*, vol. I, *I dati etnotoponomastici*, (*AIΩN*, Series Minor, Quaderno 1), Naples: Istituto Universitario Orientale, pp. 7–14.

———— (1987) 'Storia delle lingue e storia delle culture', in Romano Lazzeroni (ed.), *Linguistica storica* (Studi Superiori NIS/25 Lettere), Rome: La Nuova Italia Scientifica pp. 55–85.

Szemerényi, Oswald, (1952–3) 'The development of the Indo-European mediae aspiratae in Latin and Italic', *ArchL* 4: 27–53, 99–116; 5: 1–21.

Tibiletti Bruno, Maria Grazia (1978a) 'Ligure, leponzio e gallico', in Prosdocimi 1978a: 129–208.

———— (1978b) 'Camuno e dialetti retico e pararetico', in Prosdocimi 1978a: 209–55.

Untermann, Jürgen (1968) 'Merkmale der Wortgrenze in den altitalischen Sprachen', *Word* 24: 479–90.

———— (1973) 'The Osco-Umbrian preverbs *a-*, *ad-*, and *an-*', *Journal of Indo-European Studies* 1: 387–93.

Vetter, Emil (1953) *Handbuch der italischen Dialekte*, vol. I, *Texte mit Erklärung, Glossen, Wörterverzeichnis* (Indogermanische Bibliothek, Reihe I), Heidelberg: Winter.

Zamboni, Alberto (1978) 'Il siculo', in Prosdocimi 1978a: 949–1012.

12 The Celtic Languages

Patrick Sims-Williams

Introduction

The surviving Celtic languages fall into two groups: (a) the *Brythonic* (or Brittonic or British) group; (b) the *Gaelic* (or Goidelic or Irish) group. The two are very distinct and may have been mutually unintelligible for as long as two millennia. To the Brythonic group belong Welsh, spoken widely in Wales, and Breton, spoken in the west of Brittany. Cornish, the language of Cornwall, which was very similar to Breton, died out as a natural language in the eighteenth century. To the Gaelic group belong Irish (or Irish Gaelic), spoken mainly in the west of Ireland, and Scottish Gaelic, spoken mainly in the west of Scotland. Manx, the Gaelic language of the Isle of Man, died out as a natural language in the twentieth century. Celtic languages are also spoken in the Americas, as a result of the modern diaspora of Celtic-speaking peoples, so that, for example, there are Welsh/Spanish bilinguals in Patagonia in Argentina, and Scottish Gaelic/English bilinguals in Nova Scotia in Canada.

All these surviving Celtic languages (including Breton!) are known collectively as *Insular Celtic* languages, as opposed to the ancient *Continental Celtic* languages, e.g. Gaulish, Galatian, Celtiberian, etc., which were all dead by AD 500 and mostly much earlier. The term 'Insular' refers to the two islands of Ireland and Britain. From these the Gaelic and Brythonic languages spread: in about the fifth century AD Scotland was settled by emigrants from Ireland (the *Scotti*), while Armorica was settled by emigrants from southern Britain, becoming known as Brittany (Breton *Breiz* < *Brettia*). The theory that the Breton language includes a substratum of indigenous Armorican Celtic is unproven but not impossible.

The Brythonic dialects began to diverge into West British (> Welsh) and South-West British (> Cornish and Breton) in about the fifth century AD, but probably remained mutually intelligible for several centuries. The Gaelic dialects began to diverge in about the tenth century AD, but there was a common literary language to the end of the Middle Ages, and even today Irish and Scottish Gaelic are much more similar than are Breton and Welsh, which have long been mutually unintelligible. The geographical reason is obvious: there has always been easy travel between Scotland and northern Ireland. Another factor is that Welsh has been in contact with English, whereas Breton has been in contact with French. These contacts have influenced the syntax, morphology and phonology of the languages; for example, there are nasal vowels in Breton and French, but not in Welsh and English.

Within most individual surviving languages there are marked dialectal differences, so that Breton speakers from north and south may find it easier to communicate in French, while Gaelic speakers from north and south may prefer to talk English together. Nearly all adult Celtic speakers are bilingual.

A general impression of the divergence of the Celtic languages may be gained from comparing the ordinal numerals in Gaulish (Schmidt 1983: 81, Lambert 1994: 131, McCone 1994: 208) with those in Old Irish (OIr.) and Middle Welsh (MW):

Table 12.1   Comparison of the ordinal numerals

	Gaulish (first century AD)	Old Irish (eighth century)	Middle Welsh (thirteenth century)
1	cintuxo(s)	cétn(a)e	kyntaf
2	al(l)os	tán(a)ise, aile	eil
3	trito(s), tr(itios)	tris	trydyd, f. tryded
4	petuar(ios)	cethramad	pedwyryd, f. pedwared
5	pinpetos	cóiced	pymhet
6	suexos	se(i)ssed	chwechet
7	sextametos	sechtmad	seithvet
8	oxtumeto(s)	ochtmad	wythvet
9	namet(os)	nómad	nawvet
10	decametos	dechmad	decvet

Celtic

The term 'Celtic', as applied to the Insular Celtic-speaking peoples and their languages, is a modern one. These peoples did not refer to themselves and their languages as 'Celtic' until recently. For example, the medieval Irishmen were *Goídil* (an opprobrious name derived from Brythonic cf. W. *gŵydd* 'wild') and their language was *Goídelach*, and medieval Welshmen regarded themselves as *Brython* (< Lat. *Brittones*) or *Cymry* (< **kom-brogī* 'co-countrymen') and their language was *Cymraeg*. (The Welsh themselves do not use the English name *Welsh* < Old Eng. *w(e)alh* 'foreigner, or slave, mostly speaking a Romance or Gallo-Brythonic language'. This may derive ultimately from the Continental ethnic name *Volcae*.) There is no evidence that medieval Brythonic and Gaelic speakers recognized their special linguistic kinship; this was discovered by early comparative philologists such as the Welshman, Edward Lhuyd (in his *Archaeologia Brittanica*, 1707). The modern Romantic idea of a pan-Celtic ethnic unity and 'Celtic national character' has had some influence even in the Celtic-speaking countries, but really derives from foreign works such as Ernest Renan's *La Poésie des races celtiques* (1854) and Matthew Arnold's *The Study of Celtic Literature* (1866).

The linguistic term 'Celtic' derives from the usage of ancient and early medieval Greek and Latin writers, who only use it of *Continental* Celtic languages; for example, as late as the ninth century Heiric of Auxerre, *Vita S. Germani* I.353, explains the place-name *Augustidunum* as meaning 'Augusti mons' in *Celtica lingua*. *Celtica lingua*, in fact, seems to have been equivalent to *Gallica lingua*, the term used, for example, in the sixth century by Venantius Fortunatus, who explained the old Gaulish place-name *Vernemetis* as 'fanum ingens' (great temple) (*Carmina* I.ix.9–10). Because close ethnic and linguistic similarities between Gaul and Britain had been noted by writers from Tacitus (*Agricola*, 11) down to the Renaissance, it seemed reasonable to early modern scholars to apply the term 'Celtic' to Brythonic as well. Thence it was extended to the languages of Ireland and Scotland, on comparative philological grounds, even though the Insular Celtic languages may never have been called 'Celtic' in Antiquity.

Despite its dubious origin, the term 'Celtic' remains a useful label for a distinct family of IE languages. The phonological and lexical similarities between Gaulish, Brythonic and Gaelic are illustrated by the above forms *Augustidunum* (i.e. Gaulish **-dūnon*) and *Vernemetis* (i.e. Gaulish **Wernemeton*). With the first compare OIr. *dún* 'fort', Old Breton *din* gl. 'arx', Cornish *dyn*, OW *din* (note /uː/ > /yː/ > /iː/ in Brythonic). These Celtic cognates are distinct from the Germanic cognates such as Engl. *tūn* (> Modern Eng. *town*) in not showing the effect of Grimm's Law (/d/ > /t/; see Chapter 13, **Consonants**, pp. 391–5). With the intensive prefix *Ver-* 'ingens' compare OIr. *for* < **wor-* < **wer-* and OWCB *guor-* < **wor-* < **wer-* (**Subdivision**, pp. 352–3). These cognate forms differ from IE cognates such as Gk *hyper* in showing the well-known Common Celtic loss of IE /p/, i.e. **uper* > **wer-*. Lastly, Gaul. *nemeton* 'fanum' is probably related to Lat. *nemus*, Gk *némos* 'grove', but the dental formation is only paralleled within Celtic, for example, OIr. *nemed* [nʲeμʲəð] (where μ represents a nasal bilabial fricative and cf. p. 362) gl. *sacellum* < **neμeþan* < **nemeton*, and OBret. personal names in *-nemet* [neμed] < South-West British **-neμedon* and Old Welsh ones in *-nimet* [nəμed] < West British **-niμedon*, both < Early British **nemeton*. This formation is already seen in the Celtic name **Nemetios* in an Etruscan inscription of the fifth century BC at Genoa: *MI NEMETIEŚ* 'I am [the tomb] of Nemetios' (de Simone 1980).

Origins

The original 'homeland' of the Celtic speakers is unknown – but in any case the simplistic concept of a 'homeland' is of limited validity, both in terms of ethnogenesis and in terms of language origins: a people may comprise diverse ethnic elements, and a language may derive from various sources (e.g. the English are ethnically both Celtic and Germanic, and the IE element in

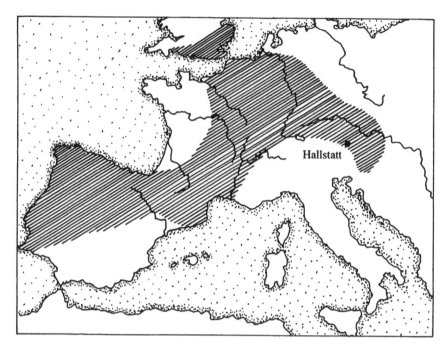

Map 12.1   Extent of the 'Hallstatt Culture' at the opening of the fifth century BC
Source: T. G. E. Powell, *The Celts*, London: Thames and Hudson, 1980

English comes via Latin and French as well as from Germanic). There are three main approaches to the problem.

Archaeologists have often associated Celtic speech with either the so-called Hallstatt Iron Age Culture or the later, so-called La Tène, Iron Age Culture (or with both); see, for example, the following maps (Figures 12.1, 12.2) from a classic work on the Celts (Powell 1980: 48, 115; cf. Mallory 1989: 96–107).

While it is likely that Celtic speakers were found in these areas, as in later centuries, we cannot equate language with material remains: there may have been non-Celtic speakers within these areas and Celtic speakers outside them. Hence we should *not* deduce from these maps that, for example, Celtic was spoken in Spain during the Hallstatt period, but did not reach Ireland until the late La Tène period. The fact is that we do not know for certain when Celtic was first spoken in Britain and Ireland (cf. Evans 1988). Even the extreme view is possible, that a form of Indo-European was already spoken in north-west Europe by 4000 BC and gradually developed into Celtic *in situ* (Renfrew 1987: 249; cf. Meid 1989; Mallory 1989: 274), *provided that* (it is a massive proviso) we can believe that communications over the four millennia BC

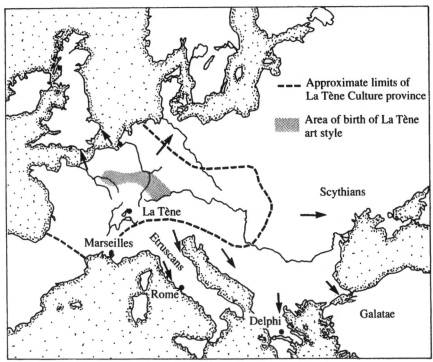

Map 12.2   The expansion of the Celts between the late fifth and the mid-third century BC
Source: T. G. E. Powell, *The Celts*, London: Thames and Hudson, 1980

would have allowed many parallel developments to take place in the Late IE and Early Celtic dialects. In short, archaeology cannot locate the first speakers of Celtic.

A second approach to the problem is to examine the references to *Keltoi*, *Celtae*, *Galatae*, etc. by Greek and Latin writers. There are several problems here: (a) these ethnic labels, which are of uncertain etymology (Evans 1967: 332–3), may not always correspond to our modern linguistic use of the term *Celtic* (see pp. 346–7 above). (b) Mediterranean observers may not have distinguished clearly between barbarian peoples such as *Celtae* and *Germani*, and probably simplified the true situation, especially at first (just as even today the French tend apply the term *Anglais* to all the inhabitants of Britain). (c) There are very few references to 'Celts' before 400 BC, the period when their violent expansion into Italy, the Balkans, Greece and Turkey began to bring them to the serious attention of Mediterranean writers. Earlier Greek writers associate them variously with Spain (the Marseilles *periplus* in the sixth century BC, if correctly reported in Avienus' *Ora maritima*), with the hinterland of Marseilles (*Massilia*) and with *Nyrax* = (?) Noreia in Austria

(Hecataeus of Miletus, *c.* 500), and with the far west of Europe, including the source of the Danube (!) in the *Pyrene* = (?) Pyrenees (Herodotus, *c.* 450). (See Powell 1980: 11–15; Schmidt 1986a: 15; Tovar 1986: 79–80.) Obviously these Greek writers were chiefly familiar with the Celts nearest to them; but there may well have been peoples calling themselves 'Celts', or who were called 'Celts' by others, in northern Europe too. As we cannot prove this, however, the early ethnographical testimonies are of limited help in defining the 'Celtic' area of Europe before 400 BC. It is probably significant, however, that Avienus' names for the inhabitants of Ireland (*Hierni*, see **Consonant-ism**, p. 357) and Britain (*Albiones* cf. MW *elvyd* 'world' < **albjo-*) have specifically Celtic etymologies (Koch 1990; Meid 1990). We cannot be sure, however, that these names originated in the British Isles.

The third approach to the problem is to examine the distribution of apparently Celtic personal, place- and ethnic names and that of Celtic-language inscriptions, coin legends, graffiti and so on. Here, too, there are insuperable obstacles: (a) such data are of course chiefly recorded in the vicinity of Mediterranean cultures, where writing systems developed; and (b) they mostly belong to the period shortly before the Christian era or still later, that is, too late to shed light on the areas in which Celtic speech originated. (On the orthographies of the Celtic languages see Russell 1995: 197–230.)

Position within IE

The position of Celtic among the IE languages has been approached in various ways during the twentieth century (cf. Schmidt 1979: 197). (1) Pokorny, Wagner, and other emphasized Celtic's divergence from the IE model, and explored the possibilities of substratum or 'areal' influences from non-IE languages, for example, Semitic and Hamitic, mostly on the vague basis of typology (see Greene 1966; Schmidt 1986b: 209). Regrettably, too little is known about the early history of the non-IE languages with which Celtic-speakers were in contact, for example, Pictish in Scotland (Jackson 1980) or Basque in Spain. (2) In reacting to this trend, Dillon, Watkins, Meid and others stressed the degree to which Celtic could be explained by 'forward reconstruction' from Indo-European (C. Watkins 1962: 7); but at the same time they regarded Celtic as particularly archaic, preserving hypothetical IE features lost in other less 'marginal' IE dialects (e.g. the original distribution of primary and secondary verbal endings, **Personal Endings**, pp. 369–70). (3) Reacting in turn to this, scholars such as Rix and Cowgill have argued that the peculiarities of Celtic can mostly be explained as internal developments and do not require significant modification of the traditional IE model reconstructed on the basis of Indo-Iranian and Greek (see McCone 1986: 222–3). (4) Other linguists still insist 'on the high importance of Old Irish and other genetically western branches for the reconstruction of proto-Indo-

European' (Hamp 1987). Probably there is truth in all these approaches, although inevitably the third has the best chance of leading to testable conclusions.

Celtic cannot be grouped with any other branch in an IE subdialect. For a while the possibility of 'Italo-Celtic' unity seemed tempting, but is now out of favour (see C. Watkins 1966; Schmidt 1991). Some of the similarities, such as the retention of the mediopassive in -r (shared with Hittite and Tocharian), can be regarded as shared archaisms. Others, such as the apparent equivalence of the Latin future in -bo and the Old Irish f-future, may be illusory (**Future Stem**, p. 372). Others, such as the o-stem genitive singular in -ī (also in Messapic, but not found in Celtiberian (p. 355) or Osco-Umbrian), and superlatives of the type Oscan nessimas 'proximae': Gaulish neδδamon (gen. pl.), OIr. nessam, OBr. nesham 'nearest', may be due to contamination over the long period during which Italic and Celtic speakers lived side by side. (In fact, the Italic influence on Celtic has never ceased, owing to continual borrowings from Latin, which have had a fundamental influence on Celtic word formation, as well as supplying many loan words.) The lack of significant Italo-Celtic phonological developments is a strong argument against the Italo-Celtic theory.

There is even less evidence for any deep connection between early Celtic and Germanic, despite the fact that they were spoken in close proximity by the time of Julius Caesar and Tacitus. There are no shared innovations in phonology and morphology, and the number of significant lexical correspondences was formerly exaggerated (see Campanile 1970; Evans 1981; Polomé 1983; Schmidt 1984; 1986b: 205–6). According to the minimal approach of Evans (1981: 248), only about a dozen early Germanic words are certainly borrowed from Celtic, for example, Goth reiks 'ruler': Gaul. -rīx < IE *rēĝs (cf. Chapter 1); Goth. eisarn 'iron': Gaul. Isarnus (personal name), OIr. iarnn, W haearn (< *(h)əi(h)arn-) < *isarno-; OHG ledar 'leather': OIr. lethar, W lledr < Celtic *letro- < IE *pl(e)-tro- (cf. Lat. pellis, etc.). The Insular Celtic languages were, of course, influenced by Germanic through English at a later stage, and there is also a slight Old Norse element.

The fact is that Celtic shares some isoglosses with almost all other IE languages, and these can be selected to support many different theories (cf. Schmidt 1985, 1986b: 202–6; Stalmaszczyk and Witczak 1995). Similarly, scholars wishing to stress the peripheral and/or archaic nature of Celtic can and have noticed certain remarkable retentions, for example, masculine and feminine forms of the numerals 'three' and 'four' in Modern W: tri chi 'three dogs', tair cath 'three cats'; pedwar ci 'four dogs', pedair cath 'four cats'. Generalizations about the affiliations of Celtic and about its archaic or innovative tendencies are usually subjective, lacking a statistical basis. Statistical attempts to compare the IE languages on the basis of 'core vocabulary' (Elsie 1990: 318) or of occurrences under Pokorny's roots (Bird 1982: 119–20) are open to objections, but do agree on Celtic's closeness to Germanic and (to a lesser extent) to Latin/Italic.

Some form of the hypothesis of 'Late Western Indo-European' (Meid 1968: 53) could explain this lexical convergence.

Subdivision

The internal subdivision of the Celtic languages has not yet been agreed by scholars; either the data are inadequate or the reality is more complex than a simple genetic model would allow.

A traditional division distinguishes 'P Celtic', in which IE *k^w > * p, and 'Q Celtic', in which *k^w remained: Gaelic and Celtiberian are Q Celtic, whereas Brythonic, Lepontic and most (but not all) Gaulish material is P Celtic. In view of the originally allophonic nature of the *k^w/*p alternation in Celtic (**Consonantism**, p. 358), most linguists would now agree that 'the "isogloss" between P-Celtic and Q-Celtic is structurally trivial' (C. Watkins 1966: 32 n. 7, following Hamp 1958: 211). Nevertheless, the P/Q division has had a great influence on archaeological speculation, and 'P' and 'Q' remain useful labels for the important and valid distinction between Brythonic (or possibly 'Gallo-Brythonic') and Gaelic.

Some linguists use the term 'Insular Celtic' (see **Introduction**, p. 345) in a more than geographical sense, emphasizing a special relationship between Gaelic and Brythonic (Greene 1966; McCone 1986: 262; cf. Evans 1988: 219). It is true that these groups share certain important developments – such as the development of morphophonemic mutations of initial consonants (**Consonantism**, p. 359) and the system of absolute and conjunct verbal endings (**Personal Endings**, pp. 369–70) – but it could be argued that these developments might also have occurred in Gaulish if this were attested after AD 500 (Sims-Williams 1984: 147–8). Logically, it is impossible to establish a genetic relationship between two dialects on the basis of a shared innovation occurring after all other dialects have died out. An opposing approach, which still leads to the same negative conclusion, is to argue that a feature like the absolute/conjunct system occurs in Insular Celtic but not (apparently) in Continental Celtic because the Continental dialects were less archaic, having drifted towards Greek and Latin or even Late IE innovations (Meid 1986: 120–1). The fundamental problem, however, is the chronological disjuncture between our evidence of Insular and Continental Celtic. A single example illustrates this. We noted above (**Introduction**, p. 347) that *wer (< *uper) became *wor in Brythonic and Gaelic, whereas Ver- is attested in Gaulish. Is this innovation an Insular Celtic isogloss (Schrijver 1995: 129, 464)? The change *wer > *wor (due to influence of *wo < *upo 'under' or simply to rounding after /w/, cf. Evans 1967: 279) must in fact be late in Brythonic, since in 725 Bede, *Chronica maiora* 434, records the name of a fifth-century Briton as *Uertigernus* (> later *Uortigern*, *Gwrtheyrn*). As the change *wer > *wor did not occur before the fifth century AD in Brythonic, it is possible that it would also have occurred in fifth-century Gaulish as well, if this was attested – for there *is* evidence of shared phonetic developments between British and Late Gaulish (Fleuriot 1978). Moreover, /wer/ > /wor/ might occur quite independently; for example, there is evidence for it in Spain (Tovar 1986: 89).

The term 'Gallo-Brythonic' emphasizes the similarities in language (e.g. name formations) between Gaulish and British which were already noted by ancient writers (**Introduction**, p. 347). It is debatable whether these similarities are due to the many ethnic movements across the English Channel (already mentioned by Julius Caesar) or go back to a genuine 'Gallo-Brythonic' dialect of Celtic, genetically distinct from Gaelic, Celtiberian, Lepontic, and so on (cf. Evans 1988: 220; Fleuriot 1988; Lambert 1994: 17–19; Schrijver 1995: 463–5).

The most ambitious attempt at a Celtic family tree (Schmidt 1988: 235) combines the ideas of 'P Celtic' and 'Gallo-Brythonic' with a distinction between an '*em/en*-language' (i.e. Gaelic), which diverged very early, and the '*am/an*-languages' (i.e. Celtiberian and most or all the P Celtic languages). This distinction, which has not convinced everyone (e.g. Tovar 1986: 84 n. 3; Evans 1983: 29–31; McCone 1991a: 22, 48–50, 161), is based on the treatment of IE /m̥/ and /n̥/ in initial position and before plosives, e.g. IE *mb^hi 'about' > Celtiberian *amPi*-, Gaul. *ambi*-, W *am*: OIr. *imb* (see further De Bernardo Stempel 1987: 38, 51, 121). A secondary Gaelic development of /-an/ > /-en/ has been suggested (Cowgill 1975: 49), and some scholars postulate a Proto-Celtic phoneme /æ/ before nasals (e.g. Hamp 1965: 225, Joseph 1990: 126 n. 10). McCone (1991b) argues convincingly that /m̥, n̥/ gave CC /am, an/ and that raising of the /a/ to /e/ or /i/ occurred in Primitive Irish (cf. Schrijver 1993).

Documentation

The earliest connected written material in Celtic languages comes, as would be expected, from the Mediterranean world – Italy, France and Spain – in the second half of the first millennium BC (possibly slightly earlier in the case of some north Italian inscriptions: Russell 1995: 5, 205, 229; Schmidt 1995: 252). For other areas at this period there are only place-, personal and ethnic names (e.g. Billy 1993), but even these are of some value. For example, judging by the onomastic evidence, the language of the Galatians in Asia Minor was similar to Gaulish (Mitchell 1993; Schmidt 1994). Again, there is obvious Celtic material in the 'Thracian' onomastic corpus (Orel 1987; cf. Ködderitzsch 1993). Here, however, I shall concentrate on the Celtic languages from which more than names and odd words are known (see also Eska and Evans 1993).

Lepontic is the not uncontroversial name given to the language of inscriptions first found within a 50 km radius of Lugano, in north-west Italy and Switzerland (Lejeune 1970). They date from at least the fourth century (probably earlier) to the first century BC and are written in the Lugano alphabet.

This alphabet does not distinguish between /p t k/ and /b d g/ and avoids double letters; for example, the Lepontic personal name *ANOKOPOKIOS* corresponds to Gaulish *Andocombogios*. Here /nd/ > /nn/ is a Lepontic peculiarity, but the suppression of the nasal in *KO(m)P* may be purely graphic. Like Gaulish **(Consonantism**, p. 358), Lepontic distinguishes between two sibilants, both seen in *IŚOS* [ʔiˈsos] < **istos* 'that (man)' in an inscription from Vergiate, now in the archaeological museum in Milan (Lejeune 1970: 444–52): *PELKUI PRUIAM TEU KARITE IŚOS KALITE PALAM* = ? *Belgui bruwyam Dēwū garite, iˈsos kalite palam* = ?'Dēwū enclosed the construction for Belgos; he erected the stone.' The word for 'construction', accusative of **bruwyā*, recalls Gaulish *brīvā* 'bridge' < **bʰrēwā*, but the closest cognates are in Germanic, for example Old Saxon *bruggia* 'bridge' < **bʰruw-jo-*. The word possibly meaning 'stone', *palā*, which is common in Lepontic inscriptions, is of unknown etymology. The verbal stem **gar-* may derive < **gr̥-*: IE **ǵʰer-* 'to enclose', as in OIr. *gort* 'field', W *garth* 'enclosure' (but cf. Hamp 1991); and **kal-* may derive < **kl̥-*: IE **kelH-* 'to raise, rise', cf. Gaul. *celicnon* 'building', Lat. *collis*, OEng. *hyll* 'hill', and possibly *Celtī* '?exalted ones'. The dental preterites are obscure (cf. Schmidt 1990: 596, Eska 1990a, Eska and Evans 1993: 37, 42, 46), but seem to be confirmed by the Gaulish verbs *KarniTu* (3 sg.), *KarniTus* (3 pl.) found farther south in Gaulish inscriptions in Lugano script at Todi and at San Bernadino di Briona (unless *KarniTus = karnintus* cf. Lambert 1994: 64, 73; De Hoz 1995). In the Todi inscription, which is bilingual, *KarniTu* corresponds to *LOCAVIT ET STATVIT.*

Celtiberian is the only Hispano-Celtic language known from inscriptions as well as proper names. (The Celtic nature of Lusitanian is dubious.) The 'Celtiberian' inscriptions come from north-eastern Spain, in exactly the same region that the *Celtiberi* are located by ancient writers (De Hoz 1988). The earlier inscriptions, such as the best known of the two from Botorrita 20 km south of Zaragoza (*c.* 100 BC), are written in the native Iberian script (Eska 1989, Eichner 1989: 23–55, Meid 1994a). This did not distinguish voiced and voiceless stops, like the Lugano alphabet, and it had the added ambiguity of using syllabic characters for these sounds (*Pa, Ca, Ta, Pe, Ce, Te*, etc.); e.g. the *Ti* symbol could denote /ti/, /di/, /t/ or /d/. Its *ś* = /s/, but *s* = /z/ or /ð/ by lenition of **s* and **d* (Villar 1995). Later inscriptions are in the Roman alphabet, like the following of the first or second century AD from Peñalba de Villastar (Ködderitzsch 1985; cf. Eska 1990b; Villar 1991; Meid 1994a and 1994b): *ENIOROSEI VTA TIGINO TIATVNEI ERECAIAS TO LVGVEI ARAIANOM COMEIMV ENIOROSEI EQVEISVIQUE OGRIS OLOGAS TOGIAS SISTAT LVGVEI TIASO TOGIAS* = ? 'To Enior(o)sis and to Tiatū of Tiginos we bestow furrows, and to Lugus a field; to Enior(o)sis and to Equaesos, Ogris submits the protections of the fertile-land, to Lugus the protections of the scorched-land.' *If* the etymologies are correct (Meid's interpretation is completely different from Ködderitzsch's), notable phonological points here include:

1   the loss of /p/ in (a) *er(e)caia-* 'furrow' < IE *$perk̑$- (cf. W *rhych*, Lat. *porca*, Eng. *furrow*); in (b) *ol(o)ga-* 'fertile-land' < *IE *polĝ(^{h})ā*, *polk̄ā* (cf. Gallo-Latin *olca* > Fr. *ouche*, Eng. *fallow* < Gc *falgō*); and in (c) *tiaso* 'burnt land' < *teposo-* (cf. OIr. *tee* 'hot' < *tepe-*, Lat. *tepeo*);

2   the retention of IE /k^w/ in *-que* 'and' (Lepontic *-pe*, arch. OIr. *-ch*);

3   the apparent (orthographical?) retention of IE /ej/ in *com-(m)ei-mu* 'we bestow' < IE *mej-* (cf. Skt *máyate* 'exchanges', Lat. *mūnus* < *moj-nes-*, OIr. *moín* 'treasure' < *moj-ni-*, MW *mwyn* 'value' < *mej-no-*);

4   the retention of final /m/ (not > /n/) in the acc. sg. *ar(a)ianom* 'field' (for the stem cf. OIr. *airim*, MW *ardaf* 'I plough' < *arjomi*);

5   in *sistat* 'puts' < *sistati* the apocope of *-i*, as in Lat. *sistit* (**Personal Endings**, pp. 368–9).

In morphology note the *o*-stem genitives in *-o* (*Tigin-o*, *tias-o*) rather than the *-ī* found elsewhere in Celtic and Italic (**Position**, p. 351; cf. McCone 1994: 96; Eska 1995; Schmidt 1995: 252–3).

Gaulish inscriptions begin in about the third century BC, but the bulk of material comes from the first century BC and the first century AD (Lambert 1994). The earlier material is mostly written in Greek script, with a few texts in the Lugano script from Cisalpine Gaul. The later material is mostly in Roman letters. To the inscriptions on stone which have long been known can now be added important long texts on metal plates, notably from Chamalières and Larzac; these are transforming, and confusing, understanding of the Gaulish language(s). The following example of Gaulish is a stone inscription from Alise-Sainte-Reine (first century BC): *MARTIALIS DANNOTALI IEVRV VCVETE SOSIN CELICNON ETIC GOBEDBI DVGIIONTIIO VCVETIN IN ALISIIA* (Lambert 1994: 98–101; differently Szemerényi 1995) 'Martialis [son] of Dannotalos offered to [the god] Ucuetis this edifice, and to the smiths who honour (?) Ucuetis in Alisia'. Note here *-e* < *-ei* in the dative *Ucuete* and *-n* < *-m* in the acc. sg. *celicnon* (the source of Goth. *kelikn* 'tower'). Morphological points of interest include genitive singular in *-ī* in *Dannotali*, dative (or instrumental?) plural in *-bi* in *gobedbi*, third-person singular preterite in *-u* (cf. Lepontic), and indeclinable relative particle *jo* in *dugiionti-io* (**Pronouns**, p. 366).

British and its successors, Primitive Welsh, Primitive Cornish and Primitive Breton, are known only from proper names in inscriptions and Latin texts, which provide, nevertheless, detailed information about phonological developments (Jackson 1953; Sims-Williams 1990, 1991). From *c*. AD 800 onwards we have manuscript glosses, memoranda, and so on in Old Welsh, Old Cornish and Old Breton. (In addition some Welsh poetry may be as early as the sixth century, although transmitted in late manuscripts.) The orthography of Old Welsh, Old Cornish and Old Breton is based on a pronunciation of Latin found in Britain, the main feature of which was that medially Latin consonants underwent the native sound change called 'lenition' (**Consonantism**, p. 360), so that Latin words like *medicus, decimatus* were pronounced [meðigəh], [degiμaːdəh]. Consequently similar values were assigned to letters in writing OWCB; for example [degμed] ('tenth' < **dekametos* (see Table 12.1 on p. 346)) would be written *decmet*.

Primitive Irish (McCone 1994) is known from proper names in inscriptions and Latin texts. Most Irish inscriptions of the fifth, sixth and seventh centuries AD are in the Ogam (or Ogham) alphabet (McManus 1991, Sims-Williams 1992, 1993, Ziegler 1994). This is well suited to carving on wood and stone, since only straight strokes are used, e.g. ///// = /kʷ/, //// = /k/. The phonology of the earliest Ogam inscriptions is archaic, for example, distinguishing between /k/ and /kʷ/ and (probably) between /g/ and /gʷ/, and showing the old case endings. The earliest extant manuscripts containing *Old Irish* (glosses and short texts) are eighth century, but it is probable that some texts extant in late manuscripts were written down towards the end of the sixth century. Most Old Irish material is written in an orthography based on the British pronunciation of Latin described above (for exceptions see Harvey 1989; Russell 1995: 224); hence medial and final [b d g] are written *p t c*, and medial and final [β ð γ μ] are written *b d g m*. Medially and finally double consonants may be used to avoid ambiguity, e.g. [b] may be written *bb* and [k] may be written *cc*. Palatalized consonants are indicated by flanking vowels, e.g. *macc* [mak], *maicc* [makʲ], *beirid* [bʲerʲəðʲ], *feraib* [fʲerəβʲ]. In modern edited texts, diphthongs are generally distinguished by placing the length mark on the *i*; e.g. *aí* and *uí* are diphthongs, but *ái* and *úi* denote [aː] and [uː] followed by palatalized consonants (in the phonetic transcription ʲ marks a palatalized consonant, as in OIr. [nʲeμʲəð], **Introduction**, p. 347).

The Phonology of Common Celtic (CC)

The following features would generally be accepted as defining 'Celtic'. For ease in consulting handbooks (e.g. Lewis and Pedersen 1961), I give IE sounds in their traditional reconstructions without prejudice to the actual phonetic reality of /bʰ/, /ə/, etc. Also not much attention is paid to laryngeals, for which Celtic provides little independent evidence (cf. Hamp 1965; Joseph 1982; Ringe 1988; Lindeman 1988, 1989: 291–3; McCone 1994: 71–3). Almost nothing certain is known about the fate of the IE free accent in Celtic nor about the development of the very different initial and penultimate stress accents of Gaelic and Brythonic respectively (cf. Koch 1987). There is already evidence for penultimate accentuation in Continental Celtic (De Bernardo Stempel 1995).

Vocalism

The IE short vowels /i e a o u/ remained in Common Celtic, and /ə/ (= /H/) > /a/, e.g. **pətḗr* > Gaul. *atir* (Larzac inscription), OIr. *athair* 'father' [aþərʲ]. The IE long vowels /iː aː uː/ remained in Common Celtic but IE /eː/ > /iː/, e.g. **rḗĝs* (: Lat. *rex*) > Gaul. *-rix*, OIr. *rí*, W *rhī*, and IE /oː/ > /aː/, e.g.

dōnom (: Lat. *dōnum*) > OIr. *dán* 'gift', W *dawn* (with /au/ < /ɔː/ < /aː/) 'gift', except when IE /oː/ occurred in final syllables, where it became CC /uː/, e.g. *$b^h erō$ > *$birū$ > OIr. *-biur* 'I carry' and Gaul. *delgu* 'I hold' (cf. Eska 1995: 34). One gap in the resulting Common Celtic system of vowels

ī ĭ   ŭ ū

ĕ   ŏ

     ă
     ā

was filled by the development /ei/ > /eː₂/ (cf. Gk *steíkhein* 'to walk': Early OIr. *-tēgot* [tʲeːɣōd] 'they go' = Later OIr. *-tíagat* [tʲiəɣəd]); but /ei/ > /eː/ may not have been completed in Common Celtic. (See p. 355 for Celtiberian *ei*, and note dative *-ei* in Lepontic as well.) The other gap was filled in Gaelic by /eu au ou/ > /oː₂/ (later alternating with /uə/) and in Brythonic by /eu ou/ > /oː₂/ (later > /tː/); but in Common Celtic /eu ou au/ remained diphthongs, as did /ai/ and /oi/. There was, however, an early tendency, seen already in Lepontic and Gaulish, for /eu/ > /ou/, e.g. *teutā* 'people' > *touta* (> OIr. *túath* [tuəþ], MW *tut* [tʉːd]).

The semi-vowels /w/ and /j/ remained in Common Celtic, and indeed survive to this day in Welsh. Vocalic /m̥, n̥, r̥, l̥/ developed as vowel + consonant (/am, em, an, en, ar, al/) or consonant + vowel (/ri, li/), depending on context (see De Bernardo Stempel 1987; McCone 1991a: 15–19); there is often apparent divergence between /em en/ in Gaelic and /am, an/ elsewhere (**Subdivision**, p. 353). The so-called 'long resonants', that is, vocalic /m̥, n̥, r̥, l̥/ + laryngeal /H/, developed mostly as /maː, naː, raː, laː/, e.g. IE *$ĝr̥H-no-$ > OIr. *grán*, W *grawn* 'grain' (: Lat. *grānum*). The derivation of reflexes with short /a/ is debated: for example, does OIr. *tarathar*, W *taradr* 'auger' < *$tara-tro-n$ come from *$tr̥H-$, or is *tara-* due to vowel harmony in *$tera-tro-n$ coming from *$terH-$? The latter is probable. (See Joseph 1982; De Bernardo Stempel 1987: 43–5; Lindeman 1988; Schrijver 1995: 87.)

Consonantism

/m, n, r, l, s/ remained basically unchanged. Final *-m* became *-n* in most Celtic languages, but not in Lepontic, Celtiberian (pp. 354–5) and some Gaulish. As in other IE languages, /s/ had an allophone [z]; this is not differentiated from *S* in Continental Celtic writings, but in Insular Celtic [z] > [ð], e.g. Gaul. *TASGO-*: Ir. *Tadg* (personal name). As in Armenian, IE /p/ was completely lost (perhaps via /f/); it had already been reduced to /h/ or /zero/ when classical writers borrowed the names of Ireland (**Origins**, p. 350: Skt *pīvarī*, Gk *píeira* 'fat, rich') and of the *Hercynia silva* in central Germany (: IE *$perk^w us$ 'oak', cf. Evans 1979: 531–2). Among the plosives there is no trace of an original palatal series (Gaelic palatalization arose much later, p. 362), and the only trace of the aspirate/unaspirate distinction is between the labiovelars /gʷ/ > CC /b/ and /gʷʰ/ > CC /gʷ/ (Cowgill 1980; Sims-Williams 1981, 1995). For IE /gʷ/ note OIr. *béo*, W *byw* 'living': Lat. *uīuus*; OIr. *imb* 'butter': Lat. *unguen*; the only *certain* exception is before /j/ which delabialized /gʷ/, e.g. OIr. *nigid* [nʲiɣʲəðʲ] 'washes' < *nigʷ-je-ti* and W *gïau* 'sinews': Ved. *j(i)yā-*'bowstring', Avest. *ǰiiā-* 'bowstring, sinew', Gk *biós* 'bow'. For IE /gʷʰ/ note OIr. *gonaid* 'wounds', W *gwanaf* 'I wound': Gk *phónos* 'murder', *theínō* 'I strike', Hitt. *kuenzi*, Skt *hanti* 'kills'. By the time of Old Irish, /gʷ/ was delabialized, but there is probably an old symbol for /gʷ/ in the Ogam alphabet (p. 356). In Brythonic, initial /gʷ-/ > /gw-/, probably directly and not via /w-/ in view of the early Welsh inscription *GVANI* which predates the general change of IE /w-/ > W /gw-/ (Sims-Williams 1995). In Gaulish /gʷ-/ > /w-/ is possible, *if* the first singular verb *uediiumi* (? *uediiu mi*) in the Chamalières inscription is cognate with W *gweddi* 'prayer', OIr. *guide* 'prayer' < ?*gʷedjā, Gk *pothéō* 'I wish', Avest. *ǰaiδiia-* etc. (Cowgill 1980). The fate of non-initial /gʷ/ < /gʷʰ/ is debated; the Welsh words *nyf* 'snow' and *deifio* 'to burn' (*f* = [v]) are probably wrongly cited in the handbooks as reflexes of IE intervocalic /gʷʰ/ (Sims-Williams 1995).

The above data are best explained by the following chronology (cf. Sims-Williams 1981: 227): starting from the system

(p)	t	k	kʷ
b	d	g	(gʷ)
bʰ	dʰ	gʰ	gʷʰ

Common Celtic merged /gʷ/ and /b/ as /b/. Then de-aspiration, occurring throughout the system (/bʰ/ > /b/, /dʰ/ > /d/, etc.), created a new /gʷ₂/ < /gʷʰ/. The relative chronology of /p/ > /zero/ is uncertain, but it was the gap in the system resulting from the loss of /p₁/ which made possible the allophonic alternation between 'Q Celtic' with [kʷ] and 'P Celtic' with [p₂] < [kʷ] (**Subdivision**, p. 352):

[p₂]	t	k	[kʷ]
b	d	g	gʷ₂

The most interesting combinatory change among the consonants was the development of a new dental phoneme, written δδ, *ss*, and so on, in Gaulish (and apparently with special symbols in Lepontic, p. 354), from /d/ + /t/, /t/ + /t/, /t/ + /s/, etc. (Evans 1967: 410–20). Note also a general development of /xt/ < /pt, kt/. Structurally, a more important development was the widespread rise – as in Germanic – of intervocalic geminate consonants contrasting with single consonants in the same position (Kuryłowicz 1960: 259–73, De Bernardo

Stempel 1989). Such geminates are often shown in Gaulish, but are excluded by the scripts used for Lepontic and Celtiberian. In Insular Celtic geminates developed differently from single consonants, for example, OIr. *maicc* [mak^j] 'of a son' < Ogam *MAQQI* = *$mak^wk^w\bar{\imath}$, but MW *meib* 'sons' < *$map\bar{\imath}$ < *$mak^w\bar{\imath}$; the single /p/ is 'lenited' (i.e. voiced) but the geminate /k^{w}k^w/ is simplified. In addition to the *phonemic* distinction between /VCV/ and /VCCV/, there arose, probably already in Common Celtic, an *allophonic* distribution of [C] and [CC] in other environments (Harvey 1984). The evidence for this comes partly from the phonemicization of reflexes of these allophones in Insular Celtic (**Consonantism**, p. 360; p. 362), partly from the analogy of Romance, which may reflect Celtic substratum influence here (Martinet 1952; cf. Villar 1995). Ultimately, this was of great importance in external sandhi, giving rise to the Insular Celtic system of *initial mutations* (Russell 1995: 231–57). For example, **esjo kattos* 'his cat' > OIr. *a chatt* [ə xat] (lenition), MW *y gath* [ɨ ga:þ] (lenition), but **esjās kkatus* 'her battle' > OIr. *a cath* [ə kaþ] (no mutation), MW *y chat* [ɨ xa:d] (spirant mutation). A further set of mutations was produced after old nasals (**Consonantism**, pp. 361–2), e.g. OIr. *a catt* [ə gat] 'their cat', MW *vyg cath* [və ŋa:þ] 'my cat'. These initial mutations, which began as sandhi phenomena (cf. Chapter 4, **Sanskrit Phonology**, p. 107), were grammaticalized in Insular Celtic, for example, as markers of relative clauses (Ó hUiginn 1986).

The Phonology of Early Brythonic

The accent in British fell on the penultimate syllable, which became the ultimate syllable after the loss of final syllables *c.* 500. A full range of vowels was therefore preserved in the final syllables of OWCB words, whereas pretonic vowels tended to have been shortened, reduced, or syncopated. (Much later, in about the eleventh century, the accent shifted from the ultimate to its present position on the penult, except in the Vannetais dialect of Breton.) Schrijver (1995) is the most up to date handbook.

Vocalism

Indo-European vowel quantity was at first retained, but by the sixth century AD a new quantity system applied automatically even in stressed syllables; according to this, Primitive Welsh, Cornish and Breton vowels were short in [VCC] syllables and long in [V(C)] syllables (Sims-Williams 1990: 250–60). In *stressed* syllables, the Common Celtic vowels and diphthongs developed mainly as follows:

/i/ > Pr. W /ɨ(:)/ (written ⟨y⟩ in later W), Pr. Cornish, Pr. Breton /ɪ(:)/
/e/ > Pr. WCB /e(:)/
/a/ > Pr. WCB /a(:)/
/o/ > Pr. WCB /o(:)/
/u/ > Pr. WCB /u(:)/ (later written ⟨w⟩ in Welsh, ⟨ou⟩ in Cornish and Breton)
/i:/ (< IE /e:/ and /i:/) > Pr. WCB /i(:)/
/e:/ (< /ej/) > Pr. WCB /ui/

/aː/ (< IE /aː/ and /oː/) > British /ɔː/ > Pr. W /au/, Pr. CB /ɵ(ː)/
/uː/ (< IE /uː/ and /-oː/) > British /ʉː/ > Pr. WCB /i(ː)/
/au/ > British /ɔː/ > Pr. W. /au/, Pr. CB /ō(ː)/ (see Schrijver 1995: 195)
/ou/ (< /ou/ and /eu/) > British /oː/ > /uː/ > Pr. WCB /ʉ(ː)/
/ai/ > British /ɛː/ > Pr. WCB /oj/
/oi/ > British /uː/ > Pr. WCB /ʉ(ː)/

The semi-vowel /w/ had become /gw/ in absolute anlaut by the time of the earliest OWCB (*c*. 800). Medial /j/ sometimes developed to /ð/.

Consonantism

/s/ tended to become /h/ or /j/ or to disappear. /z/ became /ð/ and /x/ was vocalized as /j/. (On /gʷ/ see p. 358 above.) Most other consonants suffered the change known as 'lenition' in positions where their weaker allophones occurred (cf. p. 359), and there was later a tendency for unlenited voiceless consonants to be spirantized (except in absolute anlaut):

[pp]	>	[p]	>	[f]	(Spirantization)	
[p]	>	[b]	(Lenition)			
[tt]	>	[t]	>	[þ]	(Spirantization)	
[t]	>	[d]	(Lenition)			
[kk]	>	[k]	>	[x]	(Spirantization)	
[k]	>	[g]	(Lenition)			
[bb]	>	[b]				
[b]	>	[β]	(Lenition)		([β] later > [v])	
[dd]	>	[d]				
[d]	>	[ð]	(Lenition)			
[gg]	>	[g]				
[g]	>	[ɣ]	(Lenition)		([ɣ] later lost, or > [j] or [w])	
[mm]	>	[m]				
[m]	>	[μ]	(Lenition)		([μ] later > [v])	

These changes probably took place in three stages: (a) spirantization of /b, d g, ?gʷ, m/ (before *c*. AD 400?); (b) voicing of /p, t, k/ (fifth century?); (c) spirantization of /p₂, t₂, k₂/ (sixth century?) (see Sims-Williams 1990 cf. Russell 1995: 245). Since they occurred in external sandhi, they led to 'lenition' (e.g. /k ~ g/) and 'spirantization' (e.g. /k ~ x/) as initial mutations (p. 359). The above simplifications of double consonants (except [mm], which followed the pattern of [nn]) were completed before the advent of the new quantity system (**Vocalism**, p. 359), hence, for example, W *crēd* 'belief' < *krĕdd-* (versus *măm(m)* 'mother' < *mămm-*).

The Phonology of Gaelic

The accent in Gaelic fell on the initial syllable of stressed words. A full range of vowels was therefore preserved in this syllable, whereas post-tonic vowels tended to be shortened, reduced, or syncopated. For example, in Old Irish there were only two short vowels in closed unstressed syllables, [ə] and [ö] (although the spelling system seems to disguise this). Because Brythonic stress developed very differently (p. 359), the evidence of the two branches is of complementary importance in reconstruction.

Vocalism

Indo-European vowel quantity was retained in stressed syllables; in unstressed syllables long vowels were shortened in Primitive Irish, except in final syllables before final /h/ < /þ ð x s/, and even in these syllables the vowel was eventually shortened, e.g. Celtic *teutās 'tribes' > Pr. Ir. *tōþāh > OIr. túatha [tuəþǎ]. In *stressed* syllables, the Common Celtic vowels and diphthongs developed mainly as follows:

/i/ > OIr. /i/ (if not lowered to /e/ by following low vowel)
/e/ > OIr. /e/ (if not raised to /i/ by following high vowel)
/a/ > OIr. /a/
/o/ > OIr. /o/ (if not raised to /u/ by following high vowel)
/u/ > OIr. /u/ (if not lowered to /o/ by following low vowel)
/iː/ (< IE /eː/ and /iː/) > OIr. /iː/
/eː/ (< /ei/) > OIr. /eː/ alternating with /iə/ (written ‹ía›)
/aː/ (< IE /aː/ and /oː/) > OIr. /aː/
/uː/ (< IE /uː/ and /-oː/) > OIr. /uː/
/au/ > OIr. /oː/ alternating with /uə/ (written ‹úa›)
/ou/ (< /ou/ and /eu/) > OIr. /oː/ alternating with /uə/ (written ‹úa›)
/ai/ and /oi/, though still distinct in most Ogam inscriptions, merged in OIr.
    as a diphthong of uncertain value (/oi/?), written ‹áe›, ‹aí›, ‹óe›, ‹oí›.

The semi-vowel /w/ became /f/ in absolute anlaut and /v/ after nasals, for example, *wiros > fer 'man', *banwos > banb [banv] 'pig' (: Gaul. Banuus, W banw); in other positions /w/ was lost, as was /j/, e.g. *jowankos (: W ieuanc) > *(j)o(w)εgah > OIr. oac [oəg] 'young'.

Consonantism

/s/ tended to become /h/ or to disappear. /z/ became /ð/, but /x/, written *ch*, remained in Old Irish. In the Ogam inscriptions /kʷ/ and (probably) /gʷ/ were still distinct from /k/ and /g/, but they had been delabialized by the Old Irish period. Even before the Ogam inscriptions the combinations /nt, nk, nkʷ, ns/ had become /dd, gg, gʷgʷ, ss/, with compensatory lengthening of a preceding /a/ or /e/ to /εː/, e.g. *sentus (: Breton *hent*, OHG *sind* 'road') > */sεːddus/ > OIr. *sét* [sʲεːd] 'road' (cf. Ogam personal name *SEDANI* > OIr. *Sétn(a)i*); *kʷenkʷe* (: Latin *quinque*) >/kʷεːgʷgʷe/ > /koːgʲe/ > *cóic* [koːg] 'five' (the rounding was due to the labiovelars); *Br(i)g(a)ntī* (: Skt *bṛhatī* f. 'exalted one') > /brigεːddiː/ > /briγεdi/ > *Brigit* [bʲrʲiγʲədʲ] (personal name). These changes after nasals also took place in external sandhi, giving rise to the *initial* *nasal mutation*, e.g. gen. pl. **wiran trumman* > **wira ddrumman* > OIr. *fer tromm* [fʲer drom] 'of heavy men'. (This mutation was not usually shown in writing.) As in Brythonic, most consonants underwent 'lenition' in positions where their weaker allophones occurred (cf. p. 359), but lenition of /t/ and /k/ took a different form in Gaelic:

[tt]	>	[t]	
[t]	>	[þ]	(Lenition)
[kk]	>	[k]	
[k]	>	[x]	(Lenition)
[bb]	>	[b]	
[b]	>	[β]	(Lenition)
[dd]	>	[d]	
[d]	>	[ð]	(Lenition)
[gg]	>	[g]	
[g]	>	[γ]	(Lenition)
[mm]	>	[m]	
[m]	>	[μ]	(Lenition)

Gaelic lenition probably took place in two stages: (a) spirantization of /b, d g(ʷ), m/; (b) spirantization of /t k k(ʷ)/; they cannot be dated precisely, but (b) occurred later than the (fifth-century?) voicing of /p t k/ in British (see Sims-Williams 1990: 233; McCone 1994: 74). In external sandhi, lenition resulted in an initial mutation (**Consonantism**, p. 359). Internally, lenited consonants were often lost with compensatory lengthening, for example, Ogam *SAGRAGNI* (gen. sg.) > OIr. *Sáráin* [saːraːnʲ]; Pr. Ir. **eþn-* (: W *edn* < **petnos*) > OIr. *én* 'bird'. Note that this gave rise to new long vowels in unstressed syllables. Phonemically, the most important other change was the growth of palatalized consonants before front vowels in certain environments (Greene 1973), e.g. **aljos* (: Lat. *alius*, MW *eil*) > Pr. Ir. **alʲijah* > **alʲejah* > OIr. *aile* [alʲe] 'other'. Contrast **kaletos* (: W *caled* 'hard') > Pr. Ir. **kaleþah* > OIr. *calad* [kaləð] 'hard', and note that palatalization had become phonemic at the point when [alʲejah] was opposed to [kaleþah]. All consonants could be palatalized. On the spelling of palatalized consonants see **Old Irish**, p. 356.

The typical development of consonants in Insular Celtic can be exemplified by IE **t* and **th* as follows: IE **t*, **th* > Celtic /t/; Celtic /t/ allophonically = [tt] and [t]; in Brythonic [tt] > /t/ (absolute anlaut) and /þ/ (elsewhere), but [t] > /d/; in Gaelic [tt] > /t/ and /tʲ/, but [t] > /þ/ and /þʲ/.

The Morphology of Common Celtic

This cannot be fully recovered, since the Continental Celtic evidence is incomplete and the Insular Celtic languages seem to derive from different dialects and to have selected differently from the morphs available in the parent language.

In nominal morphology the threefold distinctions in gender (masculine, feminine, neuter) and number (singular, plural, dual) survived from late Indo-European. The neuter was lost in Middle Irish and only traces remain in Brythonic. The dual is always reinforced by the numeral *dá* 'two' in Old Irish and is merely residual in Brythonic, where it is formally identical with singular or plural, for example, W *y gafl* 'the fork' (< **sindos gablos*), *y geifl* 'the forks', *Yr Eifl* (mountain-name) 'the (two) forks': the last two forms imply **sindī gablī* (not dual ***sindōu gablōu*), but whereas the masculine plural has dropped lenition by analogy with non-lenition after the feminine plural article *y* < **sindās*, the lenition remains in the dual. This is an illustration of 'the eviction or replacement of a morph by a new morph only in the former's primary or secondary function' (Kuryłowicz 1964: 14).

The number of cases is reduced to five in Old Irish, with a 'dative' case subsuming the functions of the dative, ablative, locative and instrumental. (Some of these distinctions remain in Celtiberian and Gaulish.) Owing to syncretism, the endings of the 'dative' may derive not only from the IE dative, but also from the IE ablative, locative, or instrumental. In Insular Celtic, inflected forms began to be 'hypercharacterized' (Schmidt 1974), owing to the functions of the case endings being increasingly subsumed by fixed syntactic structures such as preposition + noun, VSO word order (**Syntax**, p. 374), noun + dependent genitive (in prose texts), noun + qualifying adjective. It is not surprising, then, that case endings were often allowed to remain ambiguous in Old Irish and disappeared altogether in Brythonic, apart from a few fossils, for example, the dative of *penn* 'head' (*o*-stem) in MW *erbyn* 'against, to meet' < **are pennū* = OIr. *ar chiunn* (+ gen.) 'id.' < **are kʷennū*. In Brythonic, nouns (and some adjectives) have only singular and plural. Some plurals are historical, for example, MW *mab* 'son', pl. *meib* (form used after numerals) < **mapos, -ī* (cf. OIr. *macc*, pl. *maicc*), but many are analogical, e.g. *meib(i)on* 'sons', with -(*i*)*on* from the old *n*-stem pl. **-ones*. Ahistorical plurals were inevitable in Brythonic wherever there would have been no distinction of number; for example, **donjos*, pl. **donjī* 'man' (< **gdonjos*: Gk *khthónios*, **Word Formation**, p. 373) gave *duine*, pl. *duini* in Old Irish, but *dyn*, pl. ***dyn → dynion* in Welsh; plural *dyn* only survived after numerals, where it came to be regarded as singular. Many Brythonic plurals were old collectives, which may account for the use of singular verbs with plural subjects in Welsh.

The case system survived the loss of final syllables in Old Irish because the latter left traces in vowel affection, palatalization and following mutations. The paradigm of the masculine *o*-stem **wiros* 'man' (: Latin *vir*) illustrates this. (L = + lenition, N = + nasal mutation.) Parallel endings are given here (and for *ā*-stems below) from Gaulish, Lepontic, and Celtiberian (Evans 1967: 420–6; Lejeune 1970: 467; 1985a, 137–8; 1985b; Tovar 1986: 91–2;

Table 12.2   Nominal stems in -o-

Singular				
Nom.	*fer*	[-r]	< **wiros*	cf. Gaul. *-os*, Lep. *-os*, CI *-oś*
Voc.	*fir*^L	[-rʲ]	< **wire*	cf. Gaul. *-e*(?)
Acc.	*fer*^N	[-r]	< **wiron*	cf. Gaul. *-om*, *-on*, Lep. *-om*, CI *-om*
Gen.	*fir*^L	[-rʲ]	< **wirī*	cf. Gaul. *-ī*, Lep. *-ī*, *-oiso*, ?*-ū*, CI *-o*
				(see Celtiberian on p. 355)
Dat.	*fiur*^L	[-r]	< **wirū*	cf. Gaul. *-ūi*, *-ū*; Lep. *-ūi*, CI *-ūi*, *-ei*
				(loc.), *-us* (abl.)
Plural				
Nom.	*fir*^L	[-rʲ]	< **wirī*	cf. Gaul. *-oi*, *-ī*, Lep. *-oi*, CI ?*-oi*
Voc.	*firu*	[-ru]	< **wirūs*	
Acc.	*firu*	[-ru]	< **wirū(n)s*	cf. Gaul. *-ŏs*, *-ūs*, CI *-ūś*(?)
Gen.	*fer*^N	[-r]	< **wirŏn*	cf. Gaul. *-on*, CI *-ŭm*
Dat.	*feraib*	[-rəβʲ]	< **wirobis*	cf. Gaul. *-obo*, Lep. *-oPos*, CI *-uPoś.*

Eska 1989: 160–3; 1995; Prosdocimi 1989; Lambert 1994: 49–58; Eska and Evans 1993: 32–5, 41–6; Villar 1995); the quantities of vowels in these scripts are sometimes guesswork.

The dative singular *-ū(i)* may derive from the IE dative **-ōi*, instrumental **-ō* or ablative **-ōd*. The old nominative/vocative plural **-ōs* > **-ūs* has been replaced by **-ī* (< pronominal **-oi*?) in the nominative but survives in its secondary function as vocative. The Old Irish palatalization in the dative plural points to **-b*^(h)*is*, an instrumental ending; cf. Gaul. *gobedbi* (p. 355). The genitive plural *fer*^N points to **-ŏm*, not ***-ūm* < **-ōm*; possibly all long vowels before final nasal were shortened very early in Celtic, before the five long vowels were reduced to three (Cowgill 1975: 49; Jasanoff 1989: 139), although CI *-um* (*if* = /uːm/ < /oːm/) may tell against this (cf. Evans 1983: 34).

The Old Irish *ā*-stem is also quite well paralleled in Continental Celtic (see Table 12.3). The most problematic Old Irish ending here is the accusative singular with palatalized *-th*. Possibly the development was **-ām* > **-ăm* (cf. above) > **-æn* causing palatalization (cf. **Subdivision**, p. 353). Alternatively, the Irish *ā*-stems may have borrowed **-en* (< **-m̥*) from the consonantal stems, while late Gaulish borrowed *-im* from the *i*-stems. There is clear indication of syncretism in the genitive singular, where both Irish and Late Gaulish have replaced **-ās* with **-(i)jās*, the pronominal and *jā*-stem ending (cf. Lat. *pater familiās*), which developed via Ogam *-EAS* to OIr. *-e*. The original **-ās* was retained in the irregular paradigm of OIr. *ben* 'woman'. This also preserved an old ablaut pattern, for example, nominative/vocative/accusative plural *mná* (= Gaul. *mnās* < **bnās*) and genitive plural *ban*^N (< **banom* cf. Gaul. *bnanom* = ?**bn-ānom* or < ?**banom*, De Bernardo Stempel 1987: 83, 1995: 27). The singular is as follows:

Table 12.3 Nominal stems in -ā-

Singular

Nom.	túath^L	< *teutā	cf. Gaul. -ā, Lep. -ā, CI -ā
Voc.	túath^L	< *teutā	cf. Gaul. -ā
Acc.	túaith^N	< ?	cf. Gaul. -an, -im, Lep. -ăm, CI -ăm
Gen.	túaithe	< *teut(i)jās	cf. Gaul. -ās, -iās, CI -āś
Dat.	túaith^L	< *teutī	cf. Gaul. -ai, -ī, Lep. -ai, CI -ai

Plural

Nom./Voc.	túatha	< *teutās	cf. Gaul. -ās (?), CI -āś
Acc.	túatha	< *teutā(n)s	cf. Gaul. -ās, CI -āś
Gen.	tuath^N	< *teutŏn	cf. Gaul. -ānom, CI ?-āūm
Dat.	tuathaib	< *teutābis	cf. Gaul. -ābo, -ābi

Nom.	ben^L	< *bena	< *bena	< *g^{w}énH$_2$
Acc.	bein^N	< *bencæn?	< *benam	< *g^{w}énH$_2$m
Gen.	mná	< *mnās	< *bnās	< *g^{w}néH$_2$s
Dat.	mnaí^L	< *mnāi	< *bnāi	< *g^{w}néH$_2$(e)i

In Old Irish there is also bé^N 'woman', and it has been suggested that this derives < *ben < *g^{w}ĕn < *g^{w}ēn < *g^{w}énH$_2$, whereas ben < *benă (or *benā) is analogical (Jasanoff 1989). This depends, however, on the correctness of the doctrines that IE /-VRH/ > IE /-V:R/, and that CC /V:/ > CC /V/ before /-m/ and /-n/ (p. 364).

The only other Old Irish paradigm which may preserve ablaut in the oblique cases is the n-stem cú (= Brythonic ki < *kū), in which oblique con- may partly continue *kwon- and may partly represent the weak grade *kun- with regular lowering of /u/ before following /o/ (see Joseph 1990 and Table 12.4).

Most other Indo-European declensional classes, for example, i-stems, u-stems, various consonantal stems, and even heteroclitic r-/n- stems (Lambert 1979), are represented in Insular Celtic, but much less completely on the Continent; for reasons of space they are omitted here. Adjectives belong to a more restricted range of declensions, mostly vocalic stems. Celtic retained the IE degrees of comparison – the comparative, mostly in -(i)u in OIr. < *-jōs, e.g. siniu 'older' (: Lat. senior), also residually in Brythonic, e.g. W hŷn 'older' < *senjōs (De Bernardo Stempel 1989), and the superlative, in -em, -am in Old Irish, -sam in Old Welsh, < *-isamo/ā (Gaul. Marti Rigisamo, cf. **Position**, p. 351). Celtic also added the equative, in -ithir, -idir in Old Irish, but -(h)et in Brythonic; its etymology is uncertain (cf. C. Watkins 1966: 37; McCone 1994: 125).

Table 12.4 Nominal stem in -*n*-

Singular						
Nom.	*cú*[L]	< **kū	< **k̂wō*	cf. Skt	*śvā́*	
Acc.	*coin*[N]	< **konæn?*	< **k̂wonm̥*	cf. Skt	*śvā́nam*	
Gen.	*con*	< **kunos*	< **k̂unos*	cf. Skt	*śúnas*	
Dat.	*coin*[L]	(from acc.)	(**k̂unei, -i*)	cf. Skt	*śúnā* (instr.)	
Plural						
Nom.	*coin*	< **kones*	< **k̂wones*	cf. Skt	*śvā́nas*	
Acc.	*cona*	< **kunās*	< **k̂unn̥s*	cf. Skt	*śúnas*	
Gen.	*con*[N]	< **kunŏn*	< **k̂unōm*	cf. Skt	*śúnām*	
Dat.	*conaib*	< **kunobis*	< **k̂wn̥bʰis*	cf. Skt	*śvábhiṣ* (instr.)	

Pronouns

Pronouns are not well attested in Continental Celtic, and in Insular Celtic they have evolved through analogical levelling, through interaction with verbal endings, and through phonetic attrition, especially when unstressed.

The demonstratives mostly derive from IE **so* + clitics, e.g. Gaul. *sosin celicnon* (acc.), *sosio* < ?**sosiod* 'this' (p. 355; **Syntax**, p. 374), OIr. *suide* < **sodjo-*. Demonstratives recalling Latin *iste* occur in Lepontic *iśos* (p. 354) and in Celtiberian *iśTe*, *śTena* (n. pl.) (Eska 1989: 165). In Insular Celtic the definite article comes from **sindos*, **sindā*, **sen*. Demonstrative **so* may mark the relative in the Old Irish third-person singular relative *beires* 'who carries, which he carries' < ?**beret-so-*, while *(s)a*[N] < **sen* appears as antecedent in for example, OIr. *for(s)a*[N] 'on which'; but the usual relative marker was uninflected **jo* (: Hitt. *ya* 'and'): for example, **esti-jo* 'who is' > OIr. *as(a)*, MW *yssyd*; **welesi-jo* '**whom thou seest' (Sims-Williams 1984: 153–4) > OIr. *file* 'who is'; **beronti-jo* 'who carry, which they carry' > OIr. *berte*; cf. Gaul. *dugiiontiio* (p. 355). In compound verbs **jo* was infixed, causing lenition, e.g. *do-ceil* 'hides', relative *do-cheil* < **di-jo-kelet(i)* (McCone 1980; Ó hUiginn 1986). The interrogative stem **kʷej-* (OIr. *cía*, OW *pui* 'who?') is rarely used to express the relative. The connective particles **kʷe* (: Latin *-que*, Celtiberian *-Cue*) > OIr. *-ch* ('and') and **de* (: Gk *dé*) > OIr. *-d-* may serve as relative markers in Old Irish, by a secondary development (Vendryes 1911, C. Watkins 1963).

In the personal pronouns the distinction between nominative and accusative in the first and second person seems to have been lost in Celtic, and in Insular Celtic 'dative' pronouns occur, in greatly reduced form, only in combination with other words, for example OIr. *duit* 'to you' < ?**to tī* < ?**to toi*. First-person singular OIr. *mé* and OBret. *me* suggest **mĕ*, so OW *mi* may be influenced by second-person singular *ti*, rather than deriving from **mī* < **mē* (but cf. *mi* in Gaulish, below). OIr. gen. *mo*[L] 'my', stressed *muí* 'mine', imply **mowe* < **mewe*, whereas MW *vy*[N] 'my' implies **men* < **mene* (cf. Avest. *mana*, Slav. *mene*), so the Old Irish forms (and Middle Welsh stressed *meu* 'mine') may be analogical to the second-person singular **tewe*. The Old Irish second-person singular *tú* and Old Welsh *ti* together imply CC **tū*. Its genitive forms, OIr. *do*^{L}, stressed *tuí*, *taí*, and MW *dy*^{L}, stressed *teu*, imply Celtic **tewe* (: Skt *táva*). The first-person plural forms, OIr. *sní*, MW *ni*, Gaul. *sni*, suggest **snīs* < **(s)nēs*, and the second-person plural, OIr. *sí*, MW *chwi*, suggest **swīs* < **(s)wēs*; the **s-* may be due to the first-person plural verbal ending: **-mos nīs* > **-mos snīs*. The Old Irish genitive forms *nathar*, *nár* 'ours' (unstressed *ar*^{N}, MW *an*), *sethar*, *sár* 'yours' (unstressed *far*^{N}), are obscure but have been compared with Latin *noster*, *vester*, Gothic *unsara-*, *izwara-* etc.

The third-person pronouns are problematic. The Old Irish subject pronouns, singular *é* (m.), *sí* (f.) (W *hi*), *ed* (n.) plural *é* (W *wy*), may derive from **es*, **sī*, **edā*, **ei*. Welsh *ef* 'he' may come from accusative **emem*, while an unreduplicated accusative **em* lies behind the masculine infixed object pronouns OIr. *-a*^{N}-, Breton *-en-*. Old Irish accusative feminine *-s*^{N}-, *-e*^{N}, implies **(s)iyam*, and the neuter accusative singular *-a*^{L}- implies **e* < **ed*. (In Gaulish *id* may occur, but OIr. *beirthi* 'carries it' implies **bereti-e(d)*, not ***bereti-id*.) The accusative plural *-s-* (also *-s*^{N}-) comes from **sūs* < **sō(n)s* (cf. Gaul. *sos* 'them'). Most of the above forms cannot be traced *directly* back to Indo-European. By contrast, the unstressed genitive forms OIr. *a*^{L} (m. n.) (MW *y*^{L}), *a* (f.) (MW *y*^{S}), *a*^{N} (pl.) (W *eu h-*) can be derived regularly from IE **esjo*, *esjās*, **ejsōm*; the /j/ survives as /ð/ in the stem of the Middle Welsh stressed forms m. *eidaw*, f. *eidi*.

Subject pronouns seem to occur after verbs in Gaulish (*uediiu mi* **Consonantism**, p. 358, unless *-mi* is an added athematic ending as in Skt *bhárāmi*), and they perhaps lie behind OIr. 1 sg. *-mm* in for example *benaimm* 'I strike' < ?**binam-me*. Some Old Irish 'emphasizing pronouns' are pronominal, for example, *laimir-sni* 'we dare', *ní-bir-siu* 'you do not carry' < **nīs-beres-tū* (cf. MW *kereist* 'you loved' with *-t* < **tī*); most of them, however, are demonstratives in origin, for example, *beirid-som* 'he carries' (: Goth. *sama* 'the same', Gk *homós*), earlier *-sa* (< IE **so* 'this'). Old Irish object pronouns are suffixed to simple verbs, for example, *beirthi* 'carries it' < **bereti-e* (above), but infixed within compound verbs and after particles, for example, *da-chèil* 'hides it' < **di-e-kelet(i)*, *ra-mbèrt* 'has carried him' < **pro-em-berst(i)*. They are often combined with the particle **de*, for example, *fordom-chàin* 'he teaches me' < **wer-de-me-kanet(i)*. The Old Irish stress (`) regularly *follows* infixes and the latter cause sandhi mutations. Deuterotonic compound verbs without visible infixes or sandhi, for example, *do-cèil* 'hides' have been attributed either to a meaningless sandhi-inhibiting particle, for example **di-(e)s-kelet(i)* (Cowgill 1985, Schrijver 1994: 180–6), or to analogical creation by 'infix deletion', for example, **di-e-kelet(i)* > **d(i)-e-xèle(þ)* → **di-kèle(þ)* > *do-cèil* (McCone 1985 – the *-c-* is not spirantized because it arose after the period of lenition, p. 362, *pace* Russell 1995: 54). The sentence-initial position of such deuterotonic verbs in Old Irish (**Syntax**,

p. 374) implies the former presence of infixes, standing in second position according to Wackernagel's Law (Vendryes 1911; Chapter 2, p. 70). The deleted particles may have been mainly proleptic/redundant neuter pronouns (e^L, $d(e)$-e^L), whose deletion would have avoided confusion with relative verbs of the type *do-chèil* (**Pronouns**, p. 366) (Sims-Williams 1984). For *prototonic* verbs (e.g. *dìchil* < **di-kelet(i)*) see **Syntax**, p. 374; such forms occur when a proclitic particle precedes, with or without an infix, e.g. *ní-dìchil* 'does not hide', *ním-dìchil* 'does not hide me'.

The Celtic Verbal System

This simplified semantic distinctions carried by inflections in Indo-European. For example, the IE aorist and perfect merged in a single 'preterite' tense, and the subjunctive and optative moods merged as a single 'subjunctive' mood; instead aspectual differences were expressed syntactically by the use of preverbs and particles, for example OIr. *ro*, MW *ry* < **pro* (Schmidt 1990). The inflectional system survives most fully in Old Irish. In Old Irish, verbs express the active *voice* with either active *inflection* or deponent *inflection*, and for the passive/impersonal *voice* a passive *inflection* evolved which was similar to but distinct from the deponent inflection; both probably resulted from a late split in the IE mediopassive: e.g. *suidigidir* 'places' differs from *suidigthir* 'is placed' only in lacking syncope. Syncope patterns would vary according to the syllable-count of the base, and this variation was probably exploited in order to differentiate deponent and passive (McCone 1986: 240). Already in Gaulish deponent verbs (i.e. verbs with active meaning and mediopassive inflection) are apparent, e.g. *marcosior* 'I shall (*or* may I) ride' (Lejeune 1985a: 138; Lambert 1994: 125).

Personal Endings

The personal endings of the Celtic verb derive mainly from:

(a) the primary endings of the IE present/aorist system (**ō/*mi*, **si*, **ti*, etc.), which probably fell together with the secondary endings (**m*, **s*, **t*, etc., Chapter 4, p. 113), partly through early loss of **-i* as in Italic (Cowgill 1975, 1985; Lambert 1994: 63; Schrijver 1994; Villar 1995) and possibly through a still earlier expansion of the domain of primary endings;
(b) IE imperative endings;
(c) IE mediopassive endings in *-r* (as in Hittite, Italic, Tocharian: cf. Chapter 11, **Verb Conjugation**, pp. 336–8);
(d) IE perfect endings (see Chapter 2, p. 57).

In Insular Celtic there are also obscure 'imperfect' endings in the imperfect indicative, conditional, and past subjunctive. They are identical in both active and deponent verbs and are perhaps of mediopassive origin (cf. Ahlqvist 1993; McCone 1994: 161).

Like other IE languages, Celtic came to prefer 'thematic' inflection, with a thematic vowel alternating between *e* and *o* before the personal endings, to 'athematic' inflection, without *e/o* but often with ablaut variation in the root in the present (full grade in singular, weak grade in plural). A survivor of the athematic type is the 'copula' (the form of the verb 'to be' expressing equivalence rather than existence): third-person singular OIr. *is*, MW *ys* < **és-ti*, third-person plural OIr. *it*, MW *ynt* < **s-énti*. Celtic tended to thematicize athematic verbs and to generalize a single grade of ablaut, usually the zero grade of the plural: thus IE **mélk-ti*, **mlg-énti* 'milks' → CC **mlig-e-ti*, **mlig-o-nti* > OIr. *mligid*, *mlegait* (C. Watkins 1962: 141–2; McCone 1986: 228; 1991a: 29). The **e/o* spread wherever it helped to avoid awkward consonant clusters; hence it was not inserted after roots with final laryngeal, which gave Celtic /a/ and remained athematic, e.g. **skérH-ti*, **skrH-énti* > **skarati*, **skaranti* > OIr. *scaraid*, *scarait* 'separate(s)' (cf. C. Watkins 1962: 189).

(a) *Primary endings* occur in Old Irish active verbs in the present indicative, present subjunctive, future indicative, and in such preterite indicatives as derive from the IE aorist (i.e. not those which derive from the IE perfect). In Insular Celtic this type of ending has two forms: (a) 'absolute', in simple verbs in absolute initial position without preceding particle; and (b) 'conjunct', in all compound verbs and in simple verbs in non-initial position: e.g. (a) OIr. *beirid* 'carries', MW *trenghit* 'dies'; (b) *ní-beir* 'does not carry', *ny threingk* 'does not die'. It is now agreed that 'absolute' and 'conjunct' endings have a single origin, and do not derive from the IE primary and secondary endings respectively (see Sims-Williams 1984; Cowgill 1985; McCone 1985; Koch 1987; Russell 1995: 49–55; cf. C. Watkins, 1963). Accepting an early apocope of **-ĭ* (**Personal Endings**, p. 368 cf. *sistat* p. 355), the *conjunct* forms of *beirid* 'carries' can be derived from primary forms as follows:

1 sg.	-*biur* [bʲiur]	< **birū*	< **bʰerō*
2 sg.	-*bir* [bʲirʲ]	< **biris*	< **bʰeresi*
3 sg.	-*beir* [bʲerʲ]	< **beret*	< **bʰereti*
1 pl.	-*beram* [bʲerəμ]	< **beromos*	< **bʰeromosi*
2 pl.	-*beirid* [bʲerʲəδʲ]	< **berete*	< **bʰerete*
3 pl.	-*berat* [bʲerəd]	< **beront*	< **bʰeronti*

The Old Irish *absolute* forms are longer than the conjunct forms, and it appears that they originally included some additional element which protected final **-i* from apocope. Since absolute verbs always occur at the head of clauses, the position of the additional element must be due to Wackernagel's Law (cf. p. 368). Various particles have been proposed (cf. p. 367), but the most likely candidate (Sims-Williams 1984) is a redundant or proleptic neuter object pronoun **e(d)*:

1 sg.	*biru* [bʲiru]	< **birū-e*
2 sg.	*biri* [bʲirʲi]	< **birisi-e*
3 sg.	*beirid* [bʲerʲəðʲ]	< **bereti-*
1 pl.	*bermai* [bʲermi]	< **beromosi-e*
2 pl.	*beirthe* [bʲerʲpʲe]	< **berete-e*
3 pl.	*berait* [bʲerədʲ]	< **beronti-*

In the third persons (or all persons according to McCone 1994: 141, who posits analogical developments) the additional element was dropped before the general apocope by a process of 'suffix deletion' presumably contemporary with 'infix deletion' in compound verbs (p. 368).

(b) The *imperative endings* were mostly similar to the conjunct of the present indicative except the second-person singular, e.g. OIr. *gaib* 'get!', Gaul. *gabi*, and the third-person singular, e.g. OIr. *gaibed* < **gʰabʰjetou?* (cf. Goth. *-dau*); the need for distinct indicative endings in absolute initial position may have encouraged the generalization there of the absolute (rather than conjunct) indicative endings of simple verbs (Sims-Williams 1984: 171; Eska 1991). Similarly the imperative of compound verbs was distinguished from the (deuterotonic) indicative by its protonic stress (cf. pp. 367–8).

(c) The *passive/impersonal* inflection has third-person singular and third-person plural endings only. (The absolute forms, with palatalized final consonant, are probably based on the analogy of active absolute forms like third-person plural *berait*.) In the present tense there are two inflections in the singular, with or without a dental consonant (cf. Umbrian pres. subj. *ferar* vs Latin *feratur?*), as seen in the following conjunct forms:

3 sg.	*-berar*	< **beror*	(absolute *berair*) 'is carried'
	-marbthar	< **marwător*	(absolute *marbthair*) 'is killed'
3 pl.	*-bertar*	< **berontor*	(absolute *bertair*)
	-marbtar	< **marwăntor*	(absolute *marbtair*)

Infixed pronouns indicate the first and second persons, e.g. *nom-berar* 'I am carried'.

The passive preterite paradigm, however, was built up on the basis of the IE verbal adjective (Sims-Williams 1984: 183), e.g. MW *llas* 'he was slain' < **slad-tos*, OIr. *nom-breth* 'I was carried' < **nu-me-britos* (< **bʰr̥tos*).

The *deponent* conjunct endings may be illustrated with OIr. *-fograigedar* 'sounds'. The irregular syncope outside the third-person singular and third-person plural of this five-syllable base presumably follows the pattern of four-syllable bases (**The Celtic Verbal System**, p. 368).

1 sg.	-fograigiur	< *wogaro-sagī-ōr	(absolute fograigim)
2 sg.	-fograigther	< *wogaro-sagī-ter	(absolute fograigther)
3 sg.	-fograigedar	< *wogaro-sagī-tor	(absolute fograigidir)
1 pl.	-fograigmer	< *wogaro-sagī-mor	(absolute fograigmir)
2 pl.	-fograigid	< *wogaro-sag-edwe(?)	(absolute fograigthe)
3 pl.	-fograigetar	< *wogaro-sagī-ntor	(absolute fograigitir)

The first-person singular and second-person plural absolute endings are borrowed from the athematic active, and the palatalized consonants in the absolute third-person singular, first-person plural and third-person plural are by analogy with passive absolute forms like *gaibthir, gaibtir.*

(d) Some IE *perfect endings* survived in the OIr. 'suffixless preterite', e.g. 1 sg. -*gád* 'I prayed' < *g^wāda*, 3 sg. -*gáid* < *g^wāde*, 3 pl. -*gádatar* < *g^wādontVr* – the last a blend of the IE *r*-ending (cf. Skt *vid-úr*) and the *nt*-ending of the present/aorist (cf. Lat. *uidē-r-unt*).

Present Stem
The present stem (used to form the present and imperfect indicative and the imperative) was formed with various suffixes, which merged to give the following Old Irish conjugations according to the numeration of Thurneysen 1946:

AI: -*ā*- (cf. Lat. -*āre*) and -*ă*- < root-final *-*H*, e.g. *scaraid* (**Personal Endings**, p. 369)

AII: *-*eje/ejo*- (denominative and causative), also *-*ī*- (partly < stative *-*ē*-, e.g. -*ruidi* 'blushes' cf. Lat. *rubēre* 'to be red, blush')

AIII: miscellaneous verbs with hiatus, e.g. *baïd* 'dies' < *ba-eti* (McCone 1986: 228)

BI: *-*e/o*- (e.g. *beirid* **Personal Endings**, p. 370)

BII: *-*je/jo*- (3 sg. -*gaib*, not **-*gaibi* < *g^hab^{h}jet(i)*, is probably on the analogy of BI, although a *-*ĭ/jo*- suffix has been suggested (cf. Sims-Williams 1981: 211–16)

BIII: *-*e/o*- with nasal infix, e.g. *bongid* 'reaps', passive pret. -*bocht*, cf. Lat. *ta-n-go, tac-tus* (cf. Joseph 1990; McCone 1991a: 41–7);

BIV: *-*nă*-, e.g. *crenaid*, pl. *crenait* 'buys' < *k^wri-nă-ti, *k^wri-nă-nti* (? ultimately from *k^wri-né-H_2-ti, *k^wri-n-H_2-énti*, with nasal infixed in the root *k^wr(e)iH_2-*, seen without infix in the Old Irish subjunctive stem *cria-*) (McCone 1986: 225; cf. 1991a: 11–54);

BV: supposedly *-*n(e)u*- (but see McCone 1986: 225–7; Campanile 1990; Hamp 1991; McCone 1991a: 13–15, 22–3).

AI and AII are the only productive formations in Old Irish, and lie behind the Brythonic regular verbs, MW *caraf* 'I love' < *karāmi, kenif* 'I sing' < *kanīmi* (unless the latter is < *kanū-mi*).

Subjunctive Stem

The subjunctive stem (used for present and past subjunctive) is divided into two classes: (a) the unproductive s-subjunctive, e.g. OIr. *geiss, -gé* 'may pray' < *$*g^wed$-s-t(i)*, MW *gwnech* 'may do' < *(g)wrex* < *wrek-s-et(i)*; (b) the productive so-called *ā*-subjunctive, e.g. *beraid, -bera* 'may carry' < ?*ber-ā-t(i)*. It is semantically difficult to derive (a) from the IE s-aorist indicative (with C. Watkins 1962), and derivation from the s-aorist subjunctive is difficult unless *$*g^wed$-s-t(i)* replaced the expected *$*g^wed$-s-et(i)* under the influence of the s-preterite inflection (McCone 1986: 245–6), which is against the normal Celtic athematic → thematic tendency (cf. Hamp 1987; McCone 1991a: 57, 73, 79–80). Subjunctives in *-se-Tī* may occur in Celtiberian (Eska 1989: 170). (b) The *ā*-subjunctive, traditionally derived, with that of Latin, from an Italo-Celtic optative suffix *-ā-* (cf. OLat. *aduenat*, subj. of *aduenio*), is now often analysed as *-ă-se/o-* or *-ā-se/o-*, with *ă, *ā originally from roots in *-H, -RH* (McCone 1986: 260; 1991a: 85–113, but cf. Schmidt 1991: 17–19).

Future Stem

There are three main types of Old Irish future stem (used for indicative future and conditional): (a) the *f*-future, e.g. *rannfa, -rannub* 'I shall divide'; (b) the reduplicated s-future, e.g. *gigis, -gig* 'will pray' < *$*g^wi$-g^wed-s-t(i)*; (c) the reduplicated so-called *ā*-future, e.g. *cechnaid, -cechna* 'will sing' < *ki-kană-se-t(i)*, and its subtype the *ē*-future, e.g. *célaid, -céla* 'will hide' < ?*ki-klă-se-t(i)* (with *kikl-* > *kexl-* > *cēl-*). (a), the *f*-future, is traditionally compared with the Latin future in *-bo*. This is phonetically controversial – normally /f/ is < *sw* – but because the *f*-future occurs only in Old Irish, where it is very productive, it is difficult to avoid the conclusion that it is a late, parallel innovation, based on a periphrasis involving the root *$b^h(e)w$-* 'to be' (Quin 1978; Bammesberger 1979; on /bw/ cf. McManus 1991: 122). However, McCone (1991a: 17 and 82) suggests that it spread from a verb in which reduplicated *si-sw-* > *si-f-*; Russell (1995: 20 and 49) rejects this. (b–c), the two reduplicated futures, run parallel to the corresponding subjunctives and their suffixes must be explained similarly. They are originally desideratives (semantically cf. English 'he *will* pray') and are comparable with Sanskrit desideratives, e.g. *títrpsati* < *tí-trp-se-ti* (root *terp-* 'enjoy') (Thurneysen 1946: 414–15; McCone 1986: 248–55). Unreduplicated futures in *-sje/o-* have been identified in Continental Celtic, Indo-Iranian and elsewhere (e.g. Schmidt 1988: 241, Lambert 1994: 63).

Active Preterite Stem

The Old Irish active preterite stem (to which 'deponent' as well as 'active' inflections could be added) derived, for most verbs, from the IE aorist, but for others from the IE perfect.

With few exceptions the aorists were originally athematic and sigmatic, e.g. *$*skerH$-s-t, *ber-s-t*. Such third-person singular forms developed

regularly via *skarass(i), *bert(i) to -scar, -bert (cf. OIr. tart < *tr̥stu-
'thirst'), and these third-person singular forms formed the basis for the whole
paradigms, e.g. first-person singular *skarass-ū > -scarus (the s-pret.), *bert-
ū > -biurt (the t-pret.). Cf. MW 1 sg. kereis, keint < *karassū, *kantū, 3 sg.
(*)caras, cant < *karassit(i), *kant(i). Other stem vowels before *ss were
partly influenced by present stems (McCone 1986: 232, Joseph 1988). The
third-person singular Brythonic termination of Middle Welsh absolute
keressyt < *karass-iti, conjunct (*)caras < *karass-it is an innovation
paralleled in Gaulish legasit < ?*legast + -iti versus more archaic prinas <
*kʷrinast (Sims-Williams 1984: 188; cf. Eska and Evans 1993: 42; Lambert
1994: 64, 68). For other Continental Celtic preterites see p. 354.
   Some of the Old Irish 'suffixless preterites' based on old perfects
employed reduplication (cf. Lat. tango, te-tigi), e.g. OIr. cechain 'he sang' <
*ke-kan-e (a rare MW example is kigleu 'he heard'); others replaced *ĕ in the
root with Celtic *ā (probably < *ō), e.g. OIr. do-feid < *-wedet 'leads',
do-fáid < *-wāde 'led', MW godiwawd < *-wāde 'overtook'. The origin of
the ā-preterite is obscure (cf. Germanic comparison in McCone 1986: 235–8;
1994: 168) and it is unclear whether it is attested in Continental Celtic: a
possible precursor, perhaps with /ŏ/ as in the IE perfect, is Gaulish AVVOT(E)
'FECIT' = ? /aw-wŏd(e)/ < *a(p)o-wŏd(ʰ)-e 'led away, carried out,
produced' (Lambert 1987, 1994: 122; cf. Hamp 1973).

Word Formation

Despite much work on Celtic name formation (e.g. Uhlich 1993), the vast
subject of Celtic word formation is only beginning to be studied in detail, for
example Joseph (1987) on denominative verbs in *-sag- 'seek' (e.g.
fograigedar: fogur 'sound', **Personal Endings**, pp. 370–1), and Russell
(1990) on the productive velar suffixes such as *-ākos. Most IE types of
composition survive in Celtic, at least residually (cf. McCone 1994: 126–32),
including dvandva-compounds such as OIr. gaisced < *gaiso-skeitom 'spear-
and-shield' or TEVO-XTONION (gen. pl.) = DEIS ET HOMINIBUS in a
bilingual Gaulish inscription at Vercelli (Schmidt 1983: 81, cf. p. 363). Like
other IE languages, Celtic developed the use of preverbs to modify verbal
bases aspectually (**The Celtic Verbal System**, p. 368) or semantically, e.g.
OIr. fo-reith 'helps < *'runs under' < reithid 'runs' (: MW gwaret 'helps';
Lat. subcurro, succurro < curro). Large numbers may be strung together (e.g.
OIr. intururas 'incursion' < *ind-to-are-uks-ret-), and they tend to appear in
a particular hierarchy (McCone 1987: 94) which has parallels elsewhere, e.g.
ro < *pro tends to occur close to the root as did Vedic prá, Homeric pró
(Sims-Williams 1984: 190). Despite similarities, the system of preverbs and
prepositions in Celtic and Italic cannot be reduced to a unity (C. Watkins
1966: 36). As in other IE languages, e.g. OLat. ob uos sacro (→ obsecro uos),
preverbs may be divided by tmesis (see **Syntax** below; McCone 1985: 267).

Syntax

The most important development in Celtic is in the position of the verb. Whereas the normal order is SOV in Celtiberian (e.g. p. 354) and in some Gaulish (e.g. *Buscilla sosio legasit in Alixie Magalu* 'B. placed this in Alisia for Magalos'), Insular Celtic favours VSO (p. 363), with most apparent exceptions, such as SVO (Lewis 1989), being explicable either as *nominativus pendens* or as cleft sentences with [copula] + S + relative verb (T. A. Watkins 1987; Fife and Poppe 1991; Russell 1995: 292–300). The most important exception is the archaic Old Irish construction known as Bergin's Law (Binchy 1979), by which the verb, instead of appearing initially in *absolute* (**Personal Endings**, pp. 369–71) or *deuterotonic* (p. 367) form (e.g. **Loiscis Lugaid trebthu* 'Lugaid burnt dwellings', **Ad-rími maicni nAilb* 'You reckon the sons of Alb'), appears finally/medially in *conjunct* or *prototonic* form, e.g. *Lugaid loisc trebthu, Maicni nAilb áirmi*. This construction is probably a relic of the SOV/SVO syntax seen in Continental Celtic. The key to the development of VSO was identified by Vendryes (1911; cf. C. Watkins 1963; Eska 1994; Russell 1995: 13, 303) in the phenomenon that certain clitics were closely tied to verbs in Celtic and therefore drew either the verb or its first preverb to the head of the clause by Wackernagel's Law (p. 368; **Personal Endings**, pp. 369–70), e.g. verb + relative **jo* in Gaulish *dugiiontiio Ucuetin* 'who honour Ucuetis' (p. 355), preverb *imm + -a* < **jo* in archaic OIr. *imma- lanna -lig* 'which lies about lands' (with tmesis (**Word Formation**, p. 373), later → **imma-lig lanna*). This phenomenon must surely be linked with the fact that absolute and deuterotonic verbal forms, which are required in VSO order, seem originally have included clitic elements subject to Wackernagel's Law (see **Pronouns**, pp. 367–8, **Personal Endings**, pp. 369–71 and Sims-Williams 1984).

References

Ahlqvist, Anders (1993) 'The Old Irish imperfect indicative', in B. Brogyanyi and R. Lipp (eds), *Comparative-Historical Linguistics: Indo-European and Finno-Ugric. Papers in Honor of Oswald Szemerényi*, vol. III, Amsterdam: Benjamins, pp. 281–9.

Bammesberger, Alfred (1979) 'On the origin of the Irish *f*-future', *Bulletin of the Board of Celtic Studies* 28: 395–8.

—— (ed.) (1988) *Die Laryngaltheorie und die Rekonstruktion des indogermanischen Laut- und Formensystems*, Heidelberg: C. Winter.

Billy, Pierre-Henri (1993) *Thesaurus Linguae Gallicae*, Hildesheim: G. Olms.

Binchy, D. A. (1979) '"Bergin's Law"', *Studia Celtica* 14–15: 34–53.

Bird, Norman (1982) *The Distribution of Indo-European Root Morphemes*, Wiesbaden: Harrassowicz.

Campanile, Enrico (1970) 'Sulle isoglosse lessicale celtogermaniche', *AIΩN* 9: 13–39.

—— (1990) 'A note on the classification of some Old Irish verbs', *Celtica* 21: 99–103.

Cowgill, Warren (1975) 'The origins of the insular Celtic conjunct and absolute verbal endings', in H. Rix (ed.), *Flexion und Wortbildung*, Wiesbaden: Reichert, pp. 40–70.

—— (1980) 'The etymology of Irish *guidid* and the outcome of *g^wh in Celtic', in M. Mayrhofer, M. Peters and O. Pfeiffer (eds), *Lautgeschichte und Etymologie*, Wiesbaden: Reichert, pp. 49–78.

—— (1985) 'On the origin of the absolute and conjunct verbal inflexion of Old Irish', in B. Schlerath (ed.), *Grammatische Kategorien: Funktion und Geschichte*, Wiesbaden: Reichert, pp. 109–18.

de Bernardo Stempel, Patrizia (1987) *Die Vertretung der indogermanischen liquiden und nasalen Sonanten im Keltischen*, Innsbruck: Institut für Sprachwissenschaft der Universität.

—— (1989) 'Britannischer Komparativ und Konsonantenverdoppelung', *Indogermanische Forschungen* 94: 207–33.

—— (1995) 'Gaulish accentuation: results and outlook', in Eska, Gruffydd and Jacobs 1995: 16–32.

de Hoz, Javier (1988) 'Hispano-Celtic and Celtiberian', in MacLennan 1988: 191–207.

—— (1995) 'Is -*s* the mark of the plural of the preterite in the Gaulish verb?', in Eska, Gruffydd and Jacobs 1995: 58–65.

de Simone, Carlo (1980) 'Gallish **Nemeti̯os* – etruskisch *Nemetie*', *Zeitschrift für vergleichende Sprachforschung* 94: 198–202.

Eichner, Heiner (1989) 'Damals und heute: Probleme der Erschließung des Altkeltischen zu Zeußens Zeit und in der Gegenwart', in B. Forssman (ed.), *Erlanger Gedenkfeier für Johann Kaspar Zeuß*, Erlangen: Univ. Bibl., pp. 9–56.

Elsie, Robert W. (1990) 'Proto-Brittonic Celtic and dispersion in the Indo-European Lexicon', *Ollodagos* 1: 279–321.

Eska, Joseph F. (1989) *Towards an Interpretation of the Hispano-Celtic Inscription of Botorrita*, Innsbruck: Institut für Sprachwissenschaft der Universität.

—— (1990a) 'The so-called weak or dental preterite in Continental Celtic, Watkins's Law, and related matters', *Zeitschrift für vergleichende Sprachforschung* 103: 81–91.

—— (1990b) 'Syntactic notes on the great inscription of Peñalba de Villastar', *Bulletin of the Board of Celtic Studies* 37: 104–7.

—— (1991) 'First person emphatic and imperative in Early Irish', *Bulletin of the Board of Celtic Studies* 38: 87–92.

—— (1994) 'On the crossroads of phonology and syntax: remarks on the origin of Vendryes' Restriction and related matters', *Studia Celtica* 28: 39–62.

—— (1995) 'Observations on the thematic genitive singular in Lepontic and Hispano-Celtic', in Eska, Gruffydd and Jacobs 1995: 33–46.

Eska, Joseph F. and Evans, D. Ellis (1993) 'Continental Celtic', in Martin J. Ball and James Fife (eds), *The Celtic Languages*, London: Routledge, pp. 26–63.

Eska, Joseph F., Gruffydd, R. Geraint and Jacobs, Nicolas (eds) (1995) *Hispano-Gallo-Brittonica: Essays in Honour of Professor D. Ellis Evans*, Cardiff: University of Wales Press.

Evans, D. Ellis (1967) *Gaulish Personal Names*, Oxford: Oxford University Press.

—— (1979) 'The labyrinth of Continental Celtic', *Proceedings of the British Academy* 65: 497–538.

—— (1981) 'Celts and Germans', *Bulletin of the Board of Celtic Studies* 29: 230–55.

—— (1983) 'Continental Celtic and linguistic reconstruction', in G. Mac Eoin (ed.), *Proceedings of the Sixth International Congress of Celtic Studies*, Dublin: Institute for Advanced Studies, pp. 19–54.

—— (1988) 'Celtic origins', in MacLennan 1988: 209–22.

Evans, D. Ellis et al. (eds) (1986) Proceedings of the Seventh International Congress of Celtic Studies, Oxford: Oxbow Books.

Fife, James and Poppe, Erich (eds) (1991) Studies in Brythonic Word Order, Amsterdam: Benjamins.

Fleuriot, Léon (1978) 'Brittonique et gaulois durant les premiers siècles de notre ère', Étrennes de septantaine: travaux de linguistique et de grammaire comparée offerts à M. Lejeune, Paris: Klincksieck, pp. 75–83.

—— (1988) 'New documents on ancient Celtic and the relationship between Brittonic and Continental Celtic' in MacLennan 1988: 223–30.

Greene, David (1966) 'The making of Insular Celtic' in Proceedings of the Second International Congress of Celtic Studies, Cardiff: University of Wales Press, pp. 123–36.

—— (1973) 'The growth of palatalization in Irish', Transactions of the Philological Society 127–36.

Hamp, Eric P. (1958) 'Consonant allophones in Proto-Keltic', Lochlann 1: 209–17.

—— (1965) 'Evidence in Celtic', in W. Winter (ed.), Evidence for Laryngeals, The Hague: Mouton, pp. 224–35.

—— (1973) 'Some a-preterites', Celtica 10: 157–9.

—— (1987) 'The athematic s-subjunctive', Ériu 38: 201.

—— (1991) 'Varia', Celtica 22: 33–47.

Harvey, Anthony (1984) 'Aspects of lenition and spirantization', Cambridge Medieval Celtic Studies 8: 87–100.

—— (1989) 'Some significant points of early Insular Celtic orthography', in: D. Ó Corráin, L. Breatnach and K. R. McCone (eds), Sages, Saints and Storytellers: Celtic Studies in Honour of James Carney, Maynooth: An Sagart, pp. 56–66.

Jackson, Kenneth Hurlstone (1953) Language and History in Early Britain, Edinburgh: Edinburgh University Press.

—— (1980) 'The Pictish language' in F. T. Wainwright (ed.), The Problem of the Picts, 2nd edn, Perth: Melven Press, pp. 129–66, 173–6.

Jasanoff, Jay H. (1989) 'Old Irish bé "woman"', Ériu 40: 135–41.

Joseph, Lionel S. (1982) 'The treatment of *CRH- and the origin of CaRa- in Celtic', Ériu 33: 31–57.

—— (1987) 'The origin of the Celtic denominatives in *-sag-', in C. Watkins (ed.), Studies in Memory of Warren Cowgill, Berlin: de Gruyter, pp. 113–59.

—— (1988) 'Rethinking the Celtic s-preterite', in MacLennan 1988: 608.

—— (1990) 'Old Irish cú: a naïve reinterpretation', in A. T. E. Matonis and Daniel F. Melia (eds), Celtic Language, Celtic Culture: A Festschrift for Eric P. Hamp, Van Nuys, Calif.: Ford & Baillie, pp. 110–30.

Koch, John T. (1987) 'Prosody and the Old Celtic verbal complex', Ériu 38: 143–76.

—— (1990) 'New thoughts on Albion, Ierne, and the Pretanic Isles', Proceedings of the Harvard Celtic Colloquium 6: 1–28.

Ködderitzsch, Rolf (1985) 'Die große Felsinschrift von Peñalba de Villastar', in H. M. Ölberg, H. Bothien and G. Schmidt (eds), Sprachwissenschaftliche Forschungen: Festschrift für Johann Knobloch, Innsbruck: Institut für Sprachwissenschaft der Universität, pp. 211–22.

—— (1993) 'Keltisch und Thrakisch', in Martin Rockel and Stefan Zimmer (eds), Akten des ersten Symposiums deutschsprachiger Keltologen, Tübingen: Niemeyer, pp. 139–57.

Kuryłowicz, Jerzy (1960) Esquisses linguistiques, Wrocław and Cracow: PAN.

—— (1964) The Inflectional Categories of Indo-European, Heidelberg: C. Winter.

Lambert, Pierre-Yves (1979) 'Restes de la flexion hétéroclitique en celtique?', in

Étrennes de septantaine: travaux de linguistique et de grammaire comparée offerts à M. Lejeune, Paris: Klincksieck, pp. 115–22.

—— (1987) 'Notes linguistiques gauloises', in *Mélanges offerts au Docteur J.-B. Colbert de Beaulieu*, Paris: Le Léopard d'Or, pp. 527–34.

—— (1994) *La Langue gauloise*, Paris: Editions Errance.

Lejeune, Michel (1970) 'Documents gaulois et para-gaulois de Cisalpine: Lepontica', *Études Celtiques* 12: 357–500.

—— (ed.) (1985a) 'Le plomb de Larzac', *Études Celtiques* 22: 95–177.

—— (1985b) 'La première déclinaison celtique', *Études Celtiques* 22: 88–93.

Lewis, Henry (1989) *Die kymrische Sprache*, Innsbruck: Institut für Sprachwissenschaft der Universität.

—— (1990) *Handbuch des Mittelkornischen*, Innsbruck: Institut für Sprachwissenschaft der Universität.

Lewis, Henry and Pedersen, Holger (1961) *A Concise Comparative Celtic Grammar*, 2nd edn, Göttingen: Vandenhoeck & Ruprecht.

Lewis, Henry and Piette, J. R. F. (1990) *Handbuch des Mittelbretonischen*, Innsbruck: Institut für Sprachwissenschaft der Universität.

Lindeman, Fredrik Otto (1988) ' Some remarks on "laryngeals" and Celtic', in M. A. Jazayery and W. Winter (eds), *Languages and Cultures: Studies in Honor of Edgar C. Polomé*, Berlin: de Gruyter, pp. 397–400.

—— (1989) review of *Die Laryngaltheorie und die Rekonstruktion des indogermanischen Laut- und Formensystems*, ed. Alfred Bammesberger, *Zeitschrift für vergleichende Sprachforschung* 102: 268–97.

McCone, Kim (1980) 'The nasalizing relative clause with object antecedent in the glosses', *Ériu* 31: 10–27.

—— (1985) 'The absolute and conjunct verbal inflection in Old Irish', in B. Schlerath (ed.), *Grammatische Kategorien: Funktion und Geschichte*, Wiesbaden: Reichert, pp. 261–70.

—— (1986) 'From Indo-European to Old Irish: conservation and innovation in the verbal system', in Evans *et al.* 1986: 222–66.

—— (1987) *The Early Irish Verb*, Maynooth: An Sagart.

—— (1991a) *The Indo-European Origins of the Old Irish Nasal Presents, Subjunctives and Futures*, Innsbruck: Institut für Sprachwissenschaft der Universität.

—— (1991b) 'The PIE stops and syllabic nasals in Celtic', *Studia Celtica Japonica* 4: 37–69.

—— (1994) 'An tSean-Ghaeilge agus a Réamhstair', in K. McCone, D. McManus, C. Ó Hainle, N. Williams and L. Breatnach (eds), *Stair na Gaeilge in ómós do Pádraig Ó Fiannachta*, Maynooth: St Patrick's College, pp. 61–219.

MacLennan, Gordon W. (ed.) (1988) *Proceedings of the First North American Congress of Celtic Studies*, Ottawa: Chair of Celtic Studies.

McManus, Damian (1991) *A Guide to Ogam*, Maynooth: An Sagart.

Mallory, J. P. (1989) *In Search of the Indo-Europeans: Language, Archaeology and Myth*, London: Thames & Hudson.

Martinet, André (1952) 'Celtic lenition and western Romance consonants', *Language* 28: 192–217.

Meid, Wolfgang (1968) 'Indo-European and Celtic', *Scottish Studies* 12: 45–56.

—— (1986) 'The Celtic languages', in Schmidt 1986a: 116–22.

—— (1989) *Archäologie und Sprachwissenschaft*, Innsbruck: Institut für Sprachwissenschaft der Universität.

—— (1990) 'Über *Albiōn, elfydd, Albiorīx* und andere Indikatoren eines keltischen Weltbildes', in M. J. Ball, J. Fife, E. Poppe and J. Rowland (eds), *Celtic*

Linguistics: Festschrift for T. Arwyn Watkins, Amsterdam: Benjamins, pp. 435–9.

———— (1994a) *Celtiberian Inscriptions*, Budapest: Archaeolingua.

———— (1994b) 'Die "große" Felsinschrift von Peñalba de Villastar', in R. Bielmeier and R. Stempel (eds), *Indogermanica et Caucasica: Festschrift für Karl Horst Schmidt*, Berlin: de Gruyter, pp. 385–94.

Mitchell, Stephen (1993) *Anatolia: Land, Man and Gods in Asia Minor*, vol. I, *The Celts in Anatolia and the Impact of Roman Rule*, Oxford, Clarendon Press.

Ó hUiginn, Ruairí (1986) 'The Old Irish nasalizing relative clause', *Ériu* 37: 33–87.

Orel, Vladimir E. (1987) 'Thracian and Celtic', *Bulletin of the Board of Celtic Studies* 34: 1–9.

Polomé, Edgar C. (1983) 'Celto-Germanic isoglosses (revisited)', *Journal of Indo-European Studies* 11: 281–98.

Powell, T. G. E. (1980) *The Celts*, 2nd edn, London: Thames & Hudson.

Prosdocimi, Aldo L. (1989) 'L'iscrizione gallica del Larzac e la flessione dei temi in *-a, -i, -ja*', *Indogermanische Forschungen* 94: 190–206.

Quin, E. G. (1978) 'The origin of the *f*-future: an alternative explanation', *Ériu* 29: 13–25.

Renfrew, Colin (1987) *Archaeology and Language*, London: J. Cape.

Ringe, Donald A. (1988) 'Laryngeal isoglosses in the western Indo-European languages', in Bammesberger 1988: 415–41.

Russell, Paul (1990) *Celtic Word-Formation: The Velar Suffixes*, Dublin: Institute for Advanced Studies.

———— (1995) *An Introduction to the Celtic Languages*, Harlow: Longman.

Schmidt, Karl Horst (1974) 'Zur Vorgeschichte des keltischen Kasussystems', *Bulletin of the Board of Celtic Studies* 25: 402–7.

———— (1979) 'On the Celtic languages of Continental Europe', *Bulletin of the Board of Celtic Studies* 28: 189–205.

———— (1983) 'Grundlagen einer festlandkeltischen Grammatik', in E. Vineis (ed.), *Le lingue indoeuropee di frammentaria attestazione*, Pisa: Giardini, pp. 65–90.

———— (1984) 'Keltisch und Germanisch', in J. Untermann and B. Brogyanyi (eds), *Das Germanische und die Rekonstruktion der indogermanischen Grundsprache*, Amsterdam: Benjamins, pp. 113–53.

———— (1985) 'Keltisch, Baltisch und Slavisch', in José L. Melena (ed.), *Symbolae Ludovico Mitxelena septuagenario oblatae*, Instituto de Ciencias de la Antigüedad/ Aintzinate-Zientzien Institua, Universidad del Pais Vasco Euskal Erriko Unibertsitatea, vol. I, Vitoria, pp. 23–9.

———— (ed.) (1986a) *Geschichte und Kultur der Kelten*, Heidelberg: C. Winter.

———— (1986b) 'The Celtic languages in their European context', in Evans *et al.* 1986: 199–221.

———— (1988) 'On the reconstruction of Proto-Celtic', in MacLennan 1988: 231–48.

———— (1990) 'On the prehistory of aspect and tense in Old Irish', *Celtica* 21: 593–603.

———— (1991) 'Latin and Celtic: genetic relationship and areal contacts', *Bulletin of the Board of Celtic Studies* 38: 1–19.

———— (1994) 'Galatische Sprachreste', in Elmar Schwertheim (ed.), *Forschungen in Galatien*, Bonn: Rudolf Habelt, pp. 15–28.

———— (1995) Review of *Études celtiques* 28–29, *Zeitschrift für celtische Philologie* 47: 248–54.

Schrijver, Peter (1993) 'On the development of vowels before tautosyllabic nasals in primitive Irish', *Ériu* 44: 33–52.

———— (1994) 'The Celtic adverbs for "against" and "with" and the early apocope of *-i*', *Ériu* 45: 151–89.

—— (1995) *Studies in British Celtic Historical Phonology*, Amsterdam: Rodopi.

Sims-Williams, Patrick (1981) 'The development of the Indo-European voiced labiovelars in Celtic', *Bulletin of the Board of Celtic Studies* 29: 201–29, 690.

—— (1984) 'The double system of verbal inflexion in Old Irish', *Transactions of the Philological Society*: 138–201.

—— (1990) 'Dating the transition to neo-Brittonic: phonology and history, 400–600', in A. Bammesberger and A. Wollmann (eds), *Britain 400–600: Language and History*, Heidelberg: C. Winter, pp. 217–61.

—— (1991) 'The emergence of Old Welsh, Cornish and Breton orthography, 600–800: The evidence of archaic Old Welsh', *Bulletin of the Board of Celtic Studies* 38: 20–86.

—— (1992) 'The additional letters of the Ogam alphabet', *Cambridge Medieval Celtic Studies* 23: 29–75.

—— (1993) 'Some problems in deciphering the Early Irish Ogam alphabet', *Transactions of the Philological Society* 91: 133–80.

—— (1995) 'Indo-European $*g^{wh}$ in Celtic, 1894–1994', in Eska *et al.* 1995: 196–218.

Stalmaszczyk, Piotr and Witczak, Krzysztof T. (1995) 'Celtic-Slavic language connections: new evidence for Celtic lexical influence upon Proto-Slavic', *Linguistica Baltica* 4: 225–32.

Szemerényi, Oswald (1995) 'Loan relations between Gaulish, Gothic, Latin and Greek', in H. Hettrich *et al.* (eds), *Verba et structura: Festschrift für Klaus Strunk*, Innsbruck: Institut für Sprachwissenschaft der Universität, pp. 303–15.

Thurneysen, Rudolf (1946) *A Grammar of Old Irish*, Dublin: Institute for Advanced Studies.

Tovar, Antonio (1986) 'The Celts in the Iberian peninsula: archaeology, history, language', in Schmidt 1986a: 68–101.

Uhlich, Jürgen (1993) *Die Morphologie der komponierten Personennamen des Altirischen*, Witterschlick and Bonn: M. Wehle.

Vendryes, J. (1911) 'La place du verbe en celtique', *Mémoires de la Société de Linguistique de Paris* 17: 337–51.

Villar, Francisco (1991) 'Le locatif celtibérique et le caractère tardif de la langue celtique dans l'inscription de Peñalba de Villastar', *Zeitschrift für celtische Philologie* 44: 56–66.

—— (1995) *A New Interpretation of Celtiberian Grammar*, Innsbruck: Institut für Sprachwissenschaft der Universität.

Watkins, Calvert (1962) *Indo-European Origins of the Celtic Verb*, vol. I, Dublin: Institute for Advanced Studies.

—— (1963) 'Preliminaries to a historical and comparative analysis of the syntax of the Old Irish Verb', *Celtica* 6: 1–49.

—— (1966) 'Italo-Celtic revisited', in J. Puhvel and H. Birnbaum (eds), *Ancient Indo-European Dialects*, Berkeley and Los Angeles: University of California Press, pp. 29–50.

Watkins, T. Arwyn (1987) 'Constituent order in the Old Welsh Verbal sentence', *Bulletin of the Board of Celtic Studies* 34: 51–60.

Ziegler, Sabine (1994) *Die Sprache der altirischen Ogam-Inschriften*, Göttingen: Vandenhoeck & Ruprecht.

13 The Germanic Languages

Paolo Ramat

All the Germanic languages spoken in the world today may be divided into two subgroups: (a) North Germanic, or Scandinavian, comprising Danish, Norwegian (both *bokmål* and *nynorsk*), Swedish, Icelandic and Faroese; (b) West Germanic, comprising English, Frisian, Dutch and Afrikaans and German. As a result of colonial expansion, which has led to the introduction of Germanic languages – especially English – into every continent, these languages are among the most widely spoken in the world today. In total there are around 440 million first-language speakers of Germanic, and many more second-language speakers: consider for example the part played by English as a language of international communication, and those states where English is an official language, such as Pakistan, Hong Kong and Puerto Rico.

Of particular importance from the point of view of Indo-European studies is a third subgroup, now extinct, namely (c) East Germanic. This group comprised Gothic, which has left us the first Germanic text of any length (cf. **Documentation**, pp. 386–7), and also the languages of the Herulians, the Burgundians, the Vandals and the Gepids, all of whom were tribes originally from Scandinavia like the Goths (cf. the Swedish place-name *Göta-land* and the name of the island *Got-land* in the Baltic) who migrated on to the Continent at the beginning of the Christian era (cf. *Gdansk < Gotiscandza*), moving progressively south-eastwards. Around AD 250 the Goths settled in Moesia (now Bulgaria). During the period of the so-called 'barbarian invasions' all these tribes, under pressure from the Huns, moved westwards, crossed the boundary (*limes*) of the Roman Empire and established a number of more or less ephemeral Romano-Barbarian kingdoms. Linguistically, these were soon absorbed into the Romance-speaking area. Apart from Gothic, the only remains of these languages are place-names (e.g. *Andalucía < Vandalicia* 'land of the Vandals', *Bourgogne < Burgundia*, etc.); a large number of personal names of the type *Federico, Ferdinand, Guglielmo/Guillaume/ Guillermo* etc.; and a considerable number of borrowings into the Romance languages such as Italian *guerra, guardia* and *guardare, tregua*, etc.

The Homeland of the Germanic Tribes

The original homeland of the Germanic tribes (*Germani*) may be identified as the southern part of the Scandinavian peninsula, Jutland and the southern shores of the Baltic, between the rivers Elbe and Oder. It is probable that in this area tribes speaking an IE language replaced previous non-IE peoples, since a great deal of the Germanic vocabulary, in particular items pertaining to the environment, cannot be traced back to an IE root: Eng. *sea*, Ger. *See*, Swed. *sjö*, Goth. *saiws*, originally 'marsh, pool'; Eng. *ebb*, Ger. *Ebbe* 'low tide', OI *efja* 'mud'; Eng. *eel*, Ger. *Aal*, Icel. *áll*; Eng. Swed. Dan. *stork*, Ger. *Storch*; Ger. *Hafer*, Dutch *haver*, Dan. Norw. Swed. *havre* (> Eng. *haver*) 'oats', etc. However, it should not be thought that the *Germani* as such arrived from other areas and simply replaced the other peoples. Wherever the original homeland of the Indo-Europeans may have been, the *Germani* may be regarded as having originated in the area around Scandinavia and Jutland indicated above: that is to say, a distinctly Germanic people and culture became established in that area through a gradual process of elaboration and diffusion which may be dated roughly between 1200 and 900 BC, on the basis of archaeological data such as the megalithic tombs and funnel-shaped pottery of the oldest period, the introduction of the battle axe from the south and the spread of the urnfields (see Hutterer 1975: 43ff. and cf. Map 13.1).

Germanic tribes began to spread out from this original territory, probably from the eighth century BC onwards, and by 500 BC the *Germani* had already reached and crossed the Rhine to the west; to the east they had advanced as far as the Vistula, while to the south they had occupied roughly the whole of the Low German plain; cf. Map 13.2.

Map 13.3 reproduces the classic map by R. Much of *Germania* at the time of Tacitus (AD *c*. 55–*c*. 117), author of the valuable ethnological descriptive work *De origine et situ Germanorum*.

At this time Germanic was bounded to the north by Finnish, a non-IE language in which there are significant borrowings from Germanic: Finn. *kuningas* 'king', *kana* 'hen', *niekla* 'needle', *pelto* 'field'; cf. Eng. *king*, Ger. *König*, Ger. *Hahn*, Dan. Swed. *hane*; Eng. *needle*, Ger. *Nadel*; Eng. *field*, Ger. *Feld*. To the west and south-west of the Germanic area lay Celtic, from which there derive important cultural terms such as OHG *rīhhi* (> Ger. *Reich*), OEng. *rīce* (cf. Eng. *bishop-ric*), etc.; Goth. *andbahts* 'servant' and *andbahti* 'service', OHG *ampaht(i)* (> Ger. *Amt* 'office'); OEng. *īse(r)n* (> Eng. *iron*) and OHG *īsa(r)n* (> Ger. *Eisen* 'iron'), etc.; to the east of the Germanic area lay the Baltic languages (with many borrowings from Germanic: Lith. *kiēmas* 'village', Latv. *gatva* 'street, way'; cf. Eng. *home*, Ger. *Heim*; Eng. *gate*, Ger. *Gasse*) and, partially, the Slavic languages, which had been pushed further to the east. To the south-east there may have been Venetic and 'Illyrian' tribes. Germanic belongs to the Western IE group – to which Latin and Italic, and to a much lesser extent Greek, also belong – called *alteuropäisch* by Krahe (1954), one characteristic of which is a relatively homogeneous hydronymy

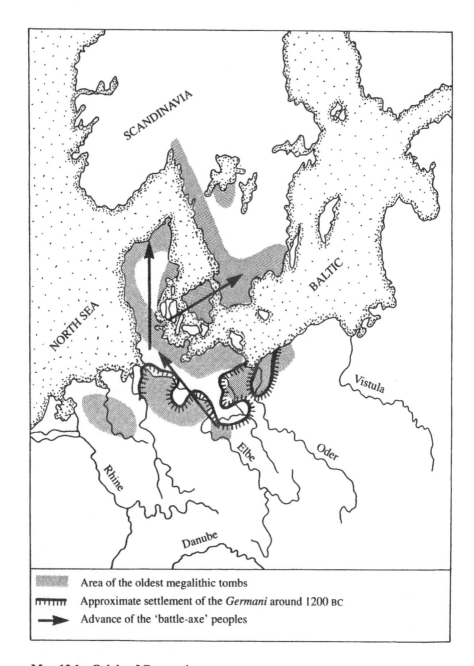

Area of the oldest megalithic tombs

Approximate settlement of the *Germani* around 1200 BC

Advance of the 'battle-axe' peoples

Map 13.1   Origin of Germanic
Source: Claus Jürgen Hutterer (ed.), *Die germanischen Sprachen. Ihre Geschichte in Grundzügen*, Munich: C. H. Beck, and Budapest: Akadémiai Kiadó, 1975

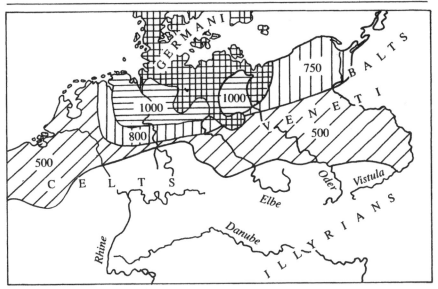

Map 13.2 Expansion of Germanic (1000–500 BC)
Source: Claus Jürgen Hutterer (ed.), *Die germanischen Sprachen. Ihre Geschichte in Grundzügen*, Munich: C. H. Beck, and Budapest: Akadémiai Kiadó, 1975

(perhaps a remnant of a pre-IE layer: see Vennemann 1994). The social structure of these 'European Indo-Europeans', according to Krahe, consisted of semi-nomadic tribal groupings known as *teutās*, cf. Osc. *touto*, Umbr. *totam* (acc.) 'state, community of citizens, *civitas*', OIr. *túath*, Breton *tut*, Lith. *tautà*, Latv. *tàuta* 'people' and, within the Germanic languages, Goth. *þiuda*, OI *þjōd*, OEng. *þēod*, Old Frisian *thiād*, OSax. *thiod(a)*, OHG *thiota* 'people', whence the adjective *þiudisk*, OEng. *þēodisc*, OSax. *thiudisc*, OHG *diutisg* 'of the people, popular, German' which became the ethnic name *Deutsch, Dutch*. These tribal groupings, as is also shown by the case of *Deutsch*, progressively gave way to subsequent broader ethnic groupings such as the Celts, the Balts, the Slavs, the Veneti, and the Germani.

There has been much discussion of the position of Germanic within Indo-European as a whole, and at various times greater emphasis has been placed on Germano-Celtic, Germano-Italic and Germano-Balto-Slavic isoglosses (see the discussion by Polomé in Van Coetsem and Kufner 1972: 43–69). In the light of what has been said above, the question is probably badly formulated, since it considers Indo-European (but of which variety, which period?) as a single entity within which the future Celtic, Slavic, Germanic, and so on, peoples already existed side by side, waiting, as it were, for the break-up and subsequent diffusion to take place.

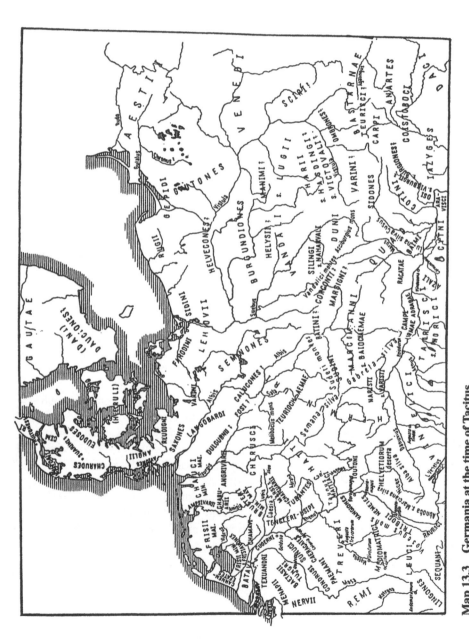

Map 13.3 Germania at the time of Tacitus

Source: R. Much, *Die Germania des Tacitus*, third edn, Heidelberg: Universitätsverlag C. Winter, 1967

The Subdivision of the Germanic Languages

As far as the internal subdivision of the Gmc. group is concerned, the tripartite division into Northern, Western and Eastern Germanic is purely for convenience and its inflexible nature reflects the sort of ahistorical schematism typical of a 'family tree' model, taking account only of points where languages split up but not of those where they come closer together or, in the most extreme case, where neighbouring languages actually merge. In reality the different Germanic languages have gone through different periods of coming closer together and moving further apart over time, depending on geographical shifts and historical events among the various peoples. Figure 13.4 provides a non-chronological overall view of the relationships between the different subgroups of Germanic from roughly the Common Germanic (CGmc) period to around AD 800.

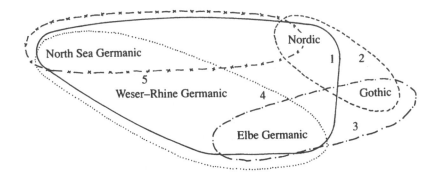

Figure 13.1 Contact among the old Germanic dialects
Source: Van Coetsem, Frans-Kufner and Herbert, *Toward a Grammar of Proto-Germanic*, Tübingen: Max Niemeyer, 1972: 74

Line 1 of Figure 13.1. reflects the fact that until the fifth century AD it does not seem possible to identify individual dialectal differences, apart from the divergence shown by the Goths and the other 'East Germanic' tribes.

Line 2 is intended to indicate the particular links between Gothic and 'North Germanic' which are due to the northern origin of the Goths ('Gotho-Nordic'), whilst line 3 is intended to indicate the links which arose between Gothic and 'Elbe Germanic' ('Elbgermanisch') while the Goths were situated along the middle and lower reaches of the Vistula.

Line 4 groups together the dialects of 'West Germanic'. Line 5 is intended to indicate what has been termed 'North Sea Germanic' ('Nordseegermanisch') or 'Ingvaeonic': in the course of the fifth century, after the Angles and Saxons had settled in Britain, a kind of linguistic alliance slowly started to develop along the coasts of the North Sea as a result of intensive commercial and cultural contact. The languages involved in this 'linguistic alliance'

(*Sprachbund*) were the early stages of Anglo-Saxon and Frisian (whence also the name 'Anglo-Frisian' which has been given to this grouping), Old Saxon and, to a much lesser extent, (Western) Norse, but not German. Progressively, during the eighth and ninth centuries, Old Saxon was more and more attracted into the sphere of influence of its southern neighbour, High German, and moved away from North Sea Germanic. Nowadays Old Saxon is continued more or less directly by 'Low German', spoken in the north of Germany, which has become more or less a dialectal variant of High German. This division into 'High' and 'Low' German is discussed below, p. 393.

Documentation

The oldest documents in Germanic, apart from place-names, personal names and single words documented in Greek and Latin writers, are the runic inscriptions. These texts, usually short, are incised (the original meaning of *wrītan* > Eng. *write* is 'scratch, incise') using an alphabet derived from those of the Mediterranean region, on to a variety of different materials – wood, bone, stone and metal. The oldest inscriptions go back to the third century AD and are mainly concentrated in what are now Denmark and Norway. These reflect a form of Germanic which still showed relatively little dialectal variation (cf. Line 1 in Figure 13.4): the famous inscription on one of the two golden horns of Gallehus (Denmark, *c.* 400) *ek Hlewagastiz Holtijaz horna tawido* ('I, Hl., son of Holt, made [the/this] horn', or, perhaps better, 'I, Hl., son of Holt, made [these] two horns': see Vennemann 1990) in (Late) Common Germanic reconstructed by means of comparison (see **Common**

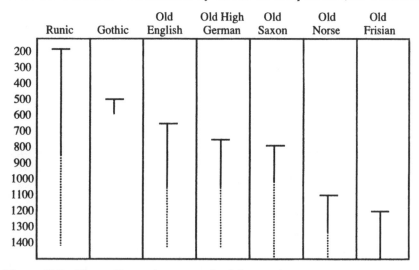

Figure 13.2   The earliest written records of Germanic

Germanic, below) would be *ek(a")* *hlewagastiz hultijaz hurnan tawidō"* (cf. with slight differences, Penzl 1988: 6), while in Old High German, for example, it would be something along the lines of *ih Hliugast Helzi horn teta*.

The second oldest document is the translation of the Bible into Gothic made by Wulfila (*c.* 311–*c.* 383), (Aryan) bishop of the 'Gothi minores' of Moesia (Bulgaria). This is the first text of any length written in a Germanic language, and is therefore of particular importance for the process of linguistic comparison and reconstruction (see **Common Germanic** below).

Some considerable time later there follow the first documents in Old English (Anglo-Saxon), then Old High German, Old Saxon, Old Norse and finally (Old) Frisian.

Common Germanic

By comparing the different Germanic languages, particularly their earliest attested forms, it is possible to reconstruct a form of Germanic which has been termed 'Common Germanic'. The further back in time we go, the greater are the similarities among the Germanic languages: Middle English *while* 'interval of time' and Middle German *wīle* are more similar to each other than are the modern forms *while* ['wail] and *Weile* ['vailə] 'moment', and in their turn OEng. *hwīl* and OHG *hwīla* are more similar than *while* and *wīle*. At its greatest extent, this process of convergence may lead back to a common starting point, in this case **hwīlō*. The reconstructed forms tend towards a uniform whole which is referred to as 'Common Germanic' (*Gemeingerma-nisch*); see Ramat (1988: 26). Some scholars have also introduced terms such as 'Pre-Germanic' (*Vorgermanisch*), 'Proto-Germanic' (*Urgermanisch*), 'Early Proto-Germanic' (*Frühurgermanisch*) and 'Late Common Germanic' (*Spätgemeingermanisch*); see Van Coetsem (1970: 12ff). These are suggestions motivated by a real need to cover the period of time from (late) IE (*c.* 2000 BC?) to the first attestations of the Germanic languages. It is of course unthinkable that over such a long span of time there would have been no profound linguistic changes or that these would have occurred suddenly. But it must be stressed that anything we succeed in reconstructing from comparison within Germanic can only be – by definition – Common Germanic. Comparison with reconstructed Indo-European and a variety of internal features of Germanic itself than permit us to establish, at least to some extent, a relative internal chronology for 'Common Germanic' and therefore allow its approximate *periodization*.

It is possible to postulate an older phase in which the IE movable accent, which may have been predominantly musical in nature, was still in force. Traces of it remain in Verner's Law (see p. 394). Gradually, this phase was succeeded by another, in which the accent (by this time strongly dynamic or expiratory) tended to be fixed on the root syllable. As a transitional stage between the first and second phases, around the second or first centuries BC, may be placed the so-called '*e–a* period', characterized by a change in vowel quality: IE *o > Gmc *a*; IE *$\bar{a}$ > Gmc *$\bar{o}$*: see Van Coetsem (1970: 16f). This change may be related to a type of accent which was still predominantly musical, with a contrast between high and low tones. The 'Consonant Shift' (**Consonants**, p. 391) seems, however, to be linked with a strong expiratory accent. On the other hand, a fairly late date for the Consonant Shift (400–200 BC?) is indicated by external evidence, such as Germanic words in Greek and Latin authors (e.g. *ganta* 'wild goose', cf. Ger. *Gans*, Eng. *goose* < IE *$\hat{g}^h ans$-; *medus* 'mead', cf. Ger. *Met*, Eng. *mead* < IE *$med^h u$*); old loan words with on the one hand, shifted consonants such as the above-mentioned Gmc *$r\bar{\imath}kja$-, Goth. *reiki*, OEng. *r\bar{\imath}ce*, Ger. *Reich* < Celtic *r\bar{\imath}giom*, and, on the other hand, the lack of shifted consonants, as in Latin terms pertaining to viticulture which were introduced into Germanic areas by the Romans around the end of the first century BC: OHG *kellari* 'cellar' < Lat. *cellarium*, *trihtere* 'funnel' < Lat. **trajectorium*, Dutch *perse* 'press' < Lat. *pressa*, etc.). These contradict the supposed succession of accentual types. The problem has not yet been resolved.

There follows a summary description of the principal characteristics of 'Common Germanic' at the phonological, morphological, syntactic and lexical levels. It must be noted, however, that this is not, and obviously cannot be, an exhaustive description, but merely an outline of the most distinctive traits.

Phonology of Common Germanic

Vowels (in Tonic Syllables)

In relation to Indo-European, the principal change in Common Germanic was the above-mentioned qualitative merger of /o/ and /a/: IE *o > a, *$\bar{a}$ > $\bar{o}$, cf. Goth. *hva*, OI *hvat*, OEng. *hwæt* (> Eng. *what*), OSax. *hwat*, OHG (*h*)*waz* (> Ger. *was*) < IE *$k^w od$*, cf. Lat. *quod*; Goth. *brōþar*, OI *brōðer*, OEng. *brōðor* (> Eng. *brother*), OHG *bruoder* (> Ger. *Bruder*) < IE *$b^h r\acute{a}t\bar{e}r$*, cf. Lat. *frāter*. IE *a and *$\bar{o}$ remained unchanged: IE *$a\hat{g}ros$* > Goth. *akrs*, OI *akr*, OHG *ackar* (> Ger. *Acker*) OEng. *æcer*; IE *$b^h l\bar{o}$-men* 'flower' > Goth. *blōma*, OEng. *blōma*, OHG *bluoma* (> Ger. *Blume*). In the absence of an opposition (a(ː)/ ~ /o(ː)/, there remained a quantitative opposition rather than one of height and backness; in other words, /aː/ could have been realized as back, rounded and raised with no risk of encroaching on the phonological space of /oː/; consequently, /eː/ could have been lowered and centralized (= [æː]), without encroaching on the phonological space of /aː/.

The IE vocalic triangle:

/i(ː)/   (u(ː)/

   /e(ː)/   /o(ː)/

       /a(ː)/

was transformed into two quadrangles:

short vowels: /i/   /u/   long vowels: /iː/   /uː/

       /e, æ/   /a, å/   /eː, æː/ /oː, ɔː/

These quadrangular systems very soon acquired a tendency to change back into triangular ones in the individual languages, as would be expected from the point of view of 'natural phonology': a new /aː/ (distinct from /oː, ɔː/) arose from the cluster [aŋχ]: e.g. *paŋχto^n 'I thought' (< root *teng-/tong, cf. Lat. tongeo) > Goth. þāhta, OI þátta, OEng. þōhte (> Eng. thought, cf. Ger. dachte). Similarly, a new /o/ arose, either from the lowering of /u/ before an /a/ in the following syllable ('umlaut', 'mutation', 'metaphony'): cf. OHG and OFrisian wolf, joh cited below; or as a result of other phonetic conditioning environments in the individual languages (e.g. Gmc *burg- > Goth. baurgs 'town', where ‹au› has the value [ɔ]; OI borg).

In the long vowel system there also occurred an important innovation, the appearance of a new /eː/. This probably took place after the 'Common Germanic' period since it is absent from Gothic and from some of the Old English dialects (Anglian and Kentish). It is conventionally termed '$\bar{e}^2$', to distinguish it from the /eː/ of IE origin. The origin of this new long vowel is controversial (for bibliography, see Ramat 1988: 42); whatever its origin, it seems to have been less open than the original [eː]. The original long vowel system of those Germanic languages where '$\bar{e}^2$' occurs thus appears as follows:

/iː/   /uː/

   /eː/ (= '$\bar{e}^2$')

   /ɛː/ (= '$\bar{e}^1$')   /ɔː/

In this system there is still no /aː/. As we have seen, /aː/ had become /ɔː, oː/; this made possible a very open realization of /ɛː/. In Norse, Old High German, Old Saxon and Old English (West Saxon dialect), /ɛː/ was realized as [æː, aː]; compare Goth. ga-dēþs, Anglian, Kentish and Frisian dēd 'deed' with OI dāð, OHG tāt, OSaxon dād, OEng. dǣd.

Indo-European schwa /ə/ became /a/ in Germanic: IE *pətér (cf. Lat. pater) > Gmc *fader (Goth. fader, Runic fadiz, faþir, OEng. fæder, OHG fater 'father'); *stətis (cf. Lat. statio) > Gmc *staþiz (Goth. staþs, OI staðr, OHG stat 'place, town'); cf. Chapter 2, p. 40.

The IE sonants which could form a syllabic peak (/r̥ l̥ m̥ n̥/) developed a supporting vowel /u/ in Germanic: IE *bʰr̥tís 'action of carrying' (< root

*$b^h er$-; cf. Lat. *fortis*, gen.) > Gmc *$burđis$ (Goth. *ga-baurþs*, OI *burđr*, OFrisian *berth*, OEng. *ge-byrd*, OHG *gi-burt* 'birth, offspring'); IE *$w[k^w os$ (cf. Lat. *lupus*) > Gmc *$wulfaz$ (Goth. *wulfs*, OI *ulfr*, OHG and OFrisian *wolf*, OEng. and OSax. *wulf* 'wolf'); IE *$g^w mtis$ (< √ *$g^w em$- 'move', cf. Lat. *uenire*) > Gmc *$qumþiz$ (Goth. *ga-qumþs*, OHG *cumft* 'arrival'), etc.

The IE semi-vowels /w/ and /j/ retained their value as the first elements in diphthongs: IE *$wiros$ (cf. Lat. *uir*) > Gmc *$weraz$ (Goth. *wair*, OI *verr*, OEng. OFrisian OSax. OHG *wer* 'man'; IE *$jugom$ (cf. Lat. *iugum*) > Gmc *$jug-a^n$ (Goth. *juk*, OI *ok*, OEng. *geok*, OSax. *juk*, OHG *joh* 'yoke' (note the lowering of /u/ to /o/, mentioned above).

Indo-European diphthongs were typically made up of a vowel (/a/, /e/, /o/) plus a semi-vowel (/j/, /w/) or semi-consonant (/r̥/, /l̥/, /m̥/, /n̥/): see p. 404) below on ablaut in the strong verbs. In general, the Germanic diphthongs retain the values of their two constituent elements: they are bi-phonematic. The following diphthongs may be reconstructed for 'Common Germanic':

	/iu/ (< IE *iw, *ew)
(/ei/) (< IE *ej)	/eu/ (< IE *ew)
/ai/ (< IE *oj, aj)	/au/ (< IE *ow, aw)

/ei/ is listed in parentheses because it became /iː/ at a very early stage. /eu/ appears very early as /iu/.

Characteristic of the development of vowels in the individual languages, particularly in Anglo-Saxon and Norse, are the phenomena of umlaut and vowel breaking: see e.g. Runic *-gastiz* (**Documentation**, pp. 386–7) and Goth. *gasts* 'guest' but OI *gestr*, OEng. *giest* with *a* > *e* because of the presence of *-i-* in the following syllable (< IE *$g^h ostis$, cf. Lat. *hostis* 'enemy'); Gmc *$eđuraz$ 'wild boar' (cf. Ger. *Eber*) > OEng. *eofor*, OI *jǫfurr*: the initial tonic *e-* has 'broken' into two distinct vowels under the influence of *-u-* in the following syllable. Many English words such as *heart*, *earth*, *eight*, *seal*, show the end result of a breaking process which occurred in Anglo-Saxon. Umlaut and breaking manifest themselves in different and complex ways in the different Germanic languages: in each case there is a change in the (tonic) vowel under the influence of particular phonetic environments, which are, as it were, attracted towards the vowel of the tonic syllable (assimilation, mostly regressive). The syllable boundary is in fact weakened in relation to the strong expiratory accent, which falls heavily on the root syllable. A wide variety of different vocalic elements may then occur in this root syllable (cf. the diphthongs in the English examples mentioned above) and these may then be in a position partially to compensate for the weakening and loss of the endings (atonic syllables following the tonic root syllable): e.g. Eng. *foot* (sg.), *feet* (pl.), Ger. *Vater* (sg.), *Väter* (pl.), *wir kamen* (1 pl. pret. ind. of *kommen* 'to come'), *wir kämen* (1 pl. pret. subj.). The present-day Germanic languages, which have a richer and more complex vowel system than that which may be reconstructed for 'Common Germanic', have the linguistic information that they convey concentrated in the root syllable (even – at least in part – where morphological information is concerned, as in the above examples; see also the so-called 'strong verbs' (pp. 403–7) such as Eng. *sink/sank/sunk*, Swed. *sjunka/sjönk/sjunken*) (cf. Ramat 1988: 44f).

After what has been said above, it should come as no surprise that after the Common Germanic period, atonic vowels show a clear tendency to be reduced and even to disappear, although in principle it may be said that the IE atonic vowels undergo the same treatment in their development to Germanic as do the tonic vowels: see the above-mentioned IE **ghostis* > Gmc **gastiz*, with *-i* still retained (it tended to disappear later in the individual Germanic languages, see above); IE **peḱu-* 'cattle' (cf. Lat. *pecus*) > Gmc **fehu* > Goth. *faihu*, OHG *fihu* (> Ger. *Vieh*), OSax. *fehu* (this *-u*, too, was to disappear: cf. OI *fé* (> Norw. *fe*, Swed. *fä*), OEng. *feoh* (> Eng. *fee*), OFrisian *fiāh*); IE **bʰeromes* 'we carry' (cf. Dor. Gk. *phéromes*, Lat. *ferimus*) > Gmc **beram(i)z* > Goth. *bairam*, OI *berom*, OHG *berumēs*. As can be seen from this last example, even when vowels in atonic syllables are preserved they are subject to many changes in the individual languages. However, in the Germanic period there is a tendency for atonic vowels to disappear when short and to become short when long: cf. IE **dʰug(ʰ)ətér* 'daughter' (cf. Gr. *thygátēr*) > Gmc **duhter* > Runic *dohtriz* (pl.), Goth. *dauhtar*, OEng. *dohtor* (> Eng. *daughter*), OHG *tochter* (= Ger.); IE **pətér* > Gmc **fađer* (see above) (cf. Krahe and Meid 1969: vol. II, 64f).

Consonants

Germanic is distinguished from IE by a regular shift of all the occlusive consonants. This is the so-called (First) Consonant Shift ((*erste*) *Lautverschiebung*), as a result of which the IE occlusives are shifted by one degree in Germanic:

	Voiceless stops	Voiced aspirates	Voiced stops
IE ↓	/p/ /t/ /k/	/bʰ/ /dʰ/ /gʰ/	/b/ /d/ /g/
Gmc	/f/ /þ/ /x/ (> /h/)	/b, ƀ/ /d, đ/ /g, ǥ/	/p/ /t/ /k/
	voicless fricatives	voiced stops/fricatives	voiceless stops

The original labiovelars are treated in Germanic as sequences of velar + /w/ and thus their development does not differ from that of the simple velars. From the point of view of Germanic it is immaterial whether they are reflexes of IE velars (**k*) or front palatals (**ḱ*); cf. Chapter 2, **The Tectals**, p. 38f.

/p/ > /f/: IE *penk^we 'five' (cf. Gk pénte, Lat. quinque) > Gmc *finfe > Goth. fimf, OHG fimf (> Ger. fünf), OEng. fīf (> Eng. five), QI fimm (> Norw. Dan. Swed. fem)

/t/ > /þ/: IE *trejes 'three' (cf. Gk treîs, Lat. trēs) > Gmc *þrijiz > *þrīz > OIr. þrīr (> Norw. tri, Dan. Swed. tre), OEng. þrī (> Eng. three), OHG drī (> Ger. drei)

/k/ > /x/ (later /h/, with a shift from true velar fricative to glottal fricative): IE *dekm̥ 'ten' (cf. Gk déka, Lat. decem) > Gmc *tehun > Goth. taihun, OSax. tehan, OHG zehan (> Ger. zehn), OEng. tīen (> Eng. ten)

/bʰ/ > /b, ƀ/: IE *bʰer- 'carry' (cf. Gk phérō, Lat. ferō) > Gmc 1 sg. pres. ind. *bero > Goth. baira, OI ber, OEng. bere (> Eng. bear), OHG biru; IE *nebʰelā 'mist, cloud' (cf. Gk. nephélē, Lat. nebula) > Gmc *neƀ(u)la > OHG nebel (= Ger.), Dutch nevel, OSax. nebal.

/dʰ/ > /d, đ/: IE *dʰur- 'gate, door' (cf. Gk thyrā, Lat. foris) > Gmc *dur- > Goth. daur, OI dyrr, OEng. dor (> Eng. door), OHG turi (> Ger. Tür); IE *medʰjos 'middle' (cf. Lat. medius) > Gmc *miđja- > Goth. midjis, OI miðr, OEng. midd (> Eng. mid-st, middle). OHG mitti (> Ger. Mitte).

/gʰ/ > /g, ǥ/: IE *gʰostis 'foreigner' (cf. Lat. hostis 'enemy', OCS gostĭ 'guest') > Gmc *gastiz > Goth. gasts, OI gestr (> Eng. guest), OHG and OSax. gast (= Ger.); IE *stejgʰ- 'to advance, go up' (cf. Gk steíkhō) > Gmc (inf.) *steiǥanaⁿ > Goth. steigan, OI OFrisian stīga, OEng. OSax. OHG stīgan (> Ger. steigen).

/b/ (not frequent) > /p/: IE *dʰewb- 'deep' (cf. Lith. dubùs) > Gmc *deupa- > Goth. diups, OI djūpr, OSax. diop, OEng. dēop (Eng. deep), Dutch diep, OHG tiof (> Ger. tief).

/d/ > /t/: IE *dekm̥: see above.

/g/ > /k/: IE *eĝō(m) 'I' (cf. Skt ahám, Gk egṓ, Lat. egō) > Gmc *ek(aⁿ) > Goth. ik, OI ek, OEng. ic (> Eng. I), OSax. ik, OHG ih (> Ger. ich).

From the above examples the consonants of German can be seen to be (in part) very different from those of the other Germanic languages: this is because of the phenomenon of the so-called 'Second Consonant Shift' (High German Consonant Shift); see p. 393.

As can be seen from the examples, the IE voiced aspirates exhibit two allophonic variants in Germanic. In initial position they appear as simple voiced stops; intervocalically and after /l r m n/ they become voiced fricatives (spirants): IE *orbʰ-o- 'lacking' (cf. Gk orph(an)ós, Lat. orbus, orfanus) > Gmc *arƀ- > Goth. arbj, Runic arbija, OFrisian erve, OSax. erƀi, OHG erbi (> Ger. Erbe) 'inheritance'. These voiced fricatives subsequently became voiced stops in many languages.

The original voiceless occlusives remain in Germanic if preceded by Germanic *s, *f, *h: cf. IE *ster- 'star' (cf. Gk astér, Lat. stēlla) > Gmc *stern-/-r > Goth. stairno, OI stjarna (> Swed. stjärna, Dan. stjerne, Norw. stjerna), OEng. steorra (> Eng. star), OSax. OHG sterro (Ger. Stern); IE *kap-tos* 'captive, prisoner' (cf. Lat. *captus*) > Gmc *hafta* > Goth. *-hafts*, OHG *haft* (> Ger. *Haft*), OEng. *hæft*; IE *$nok^w t$-s* 'night' (cf. Gk gen. *nyktós*, Lat. gen. *noctis*) > Gmc *nahts* > Goth. *nahts*, OEng. *neaht* (> Eng. *night*), OHG *naht* (> Ger. *Nacht*).

Among the other IE languages, only Armenian exhibits a consonant shift like that of German (cf. Chapter 8, **Consonants**, pp. 204–6). This shift is not restricted to particular positions or any phonetic conditioning environment and it is found fully implemented since the earliest documents (cf. p. 387–8).

A recent proposal by Theo Vennemann (1984, 1988) accepts the reconstruction of the IE consonant system with the glottalic consonants posited by Gamkrelidze and Ivanov (1973): the starting point would thus be an IE system comprising (1) glottalic consonants; (2) voiced (aspirated) stops; (3) voiceless (aspirated) stops (cf. Gamkrelidze 1979: 289; see above, Chapter 2, **The Glottalic Theory**, p. 38):

1	2	3				
(/p'/)	/b[h]/	/p[h]/	instead of	/b/	/bʰ/	/p/
/t'/	/d[h]/	/t[h]/	instead of	/d/	/dʰ/	/t/
/k'/	/g[h]/	/k[h]/	instead of	/g/	/gʰ/	/k/

In the Proto-Germanic phase, this system would then have changed as follows:

1	2	3
/p'/	/ƀ/	/f/
/t'/	/đ/	/þ/
/k'/	/g̣/	/h/

where /p', t', k'/ represent fortis plosives with glottalic closure, /ƀ, đ, g̣/ lenis plosives and /f, þ, h/ fortis fricatives.

Gradually this Proto-Germanic phase would have given way to two distinct but concurrent treatments of the fortis plosives ('bifurcational theory'); for example in the dental series:

$$t^h > t \qquad \text{('Low Gmc')}$$
$$/t'/ \bigg\langle$$
$$t^s > tz-,\ -ss-,\ -s \qquad \text{('High Gmc')}$$

The first treatment corresponds to the Germanic or First Consonant Shift, the second to the High German or Second Consonant Shift: compare, for example IE *$t'ek^h m$* (*dek̂m̥* in the traditional reconstruction): Eng. *ten* vs Ger. *zehn* (see above); IE *wot'ōr* (*wodōr* in the traditional reconstruction) 'water' (Gk *hýdōr*) > PGmc *waťōr > 'Low Gmc' *wathar, whence OSax. *watar*, OEng. *wæter* (> Eng. *water*), Dutch and Low Ger *water*, OI *vatn* (> Norw. Icel. Far. *vatn*, Swed. *vatten*), Goth. *wato* as opposed to 'High Gmc' *watsar whence OHG *wazzar* (Ger. *Wasser*); IE *kʰʷoť (*kʷod in the traditional reconstruction): Eng. *what* vs Ger. *was* (see above). There is thus a bifurcation of Germanic into 'Low Germanic' and 'High Germanic'. Without wishing here to intervene in the discussion about the reconstruction of the IE consonant system by Gamkrelidze and Ivanov, Vennemann's hypothesis has the advantage for Germanic of presenting the consonantal phenomena as a single event, whereas the facts of German (Second Shift) do not always allow us to establish a centre or direction of the diffusion of these phenomena with respect to the Germanic situation (First Shift). On the other hand it must be noted that the consonant systems in the Germanic languages show a certain tendency to repeat phenomena which have already characterized their earlier development: a large number of the modern Germanic languages have, for example, a voiceless aspirated stop at the beginning of tonic syllables (cf. Eng. *cup* [kʰʌp], *pit* [pʰɪt]; intervocalic voiceless occlusives are again showing a tendency to become voiced (fricatives) (cf. American Eng. *city* ['sɪdɪ]). This theory of the repetition of phenomena in successive chronological phases does not pose insuperable problems (for a critique of Vennemann's theory see Polomé (1992), with the latest bibliographical references, and Van Coetsem 1990: 55f)).

As long ago as 1877, the Danish linguist Karl Verner outlined the circumstances under which the First Consonant Shift (also known as Grimm's Law) does not apply. Verner's Law states that the IE voiceless stops, along with the voiceless (sibilant) fricative /s/, rather than becoming fricatives in Germanic according to Grimm's Law, became voiced fricatives in voiced environments when the original accent did not fall on the immediately preceding syllable: thus we have

IE   /p/   /t/   /k/   /kʷ/   /s/
↓
Gmc   /ƀ/   /đ/   /ǥ/   /ǥʷ/   /z/

In the various Germanic languages these voiced fricatives then underwent the same developments characteristic of the other voiced fricatives, which are allophones of the voiced stops that derived from the original voiced aspirates as a result of the Consonant Shift. Compare for example IE **upér(i)* 'above' (cf. Skt *upári*, Gk *hypér*) > Gmc *uƀer > Goth. *ufar*, OI *yfir*, OEng. *ofer* (> Eng. *over*), OSax. *oƀar*, OHG *ubar* (> Ger. *über*); IE *patér (cf. Gk *patér*, Skt *pitár-*) > Gmc *fađer > Goth. *fadar*, OI *fađer*, OEng. *fæder*, OFrisian *fader*; IE **sweḱrú-* 'mother-in-law' (cf. Lat. *socer, socrus*) > Gmc *sweǥur > OEng. *sweger*, OHG *swigar* (> Ger. *Schwieger*); IE *(d)ḱm̥tóm 'hundred' (cf. Skt *śatám*, Gr. *ekatón*) > Gmc **hund-* > Goth. OSax. OEng. *hund*, OI *hund-rað* (> Eng. *hundred*); IE **snusós* (cf. Skt *snuṣā́*, Lat. *nurus*) > Gmc **snuzo* > OI *snor*, OEng. *snoru*, OHG *snur(a)*.

In practice this is a weakening (lenition) of the voiceless stops (and of /s/), which thus escape the effects of Grimm's Law, which in its turn may be seen as a process of 'fortition' (strengthening) of the consonants (e.g. /d/ > /t/). Verner's Law depends on the position of the original movable accent and precedes the Consonant Shift, which was probably triggered off by the strong expiratory accent (perhaps of the type *p, t, k´* > *pʰ, tʰ, kʰ´* (fortition) (then *f, þ, χ*): see the discussion and bibliography in Ramat 1988: 59ff.).

The effects of Verner's Law are of consequence for the morphophonological phenomenon referred to as Grammatical Change: see pp. 403–7.

From the point of view of phonetic typology it may be claimed, paradoxically, that unlike the vowel system, the Germanic consonant system is on the whole remarkably conservative when compared with the IE point of departure, in spite of the changes wrought by the Consonant Shift: its phonemes appear in bundles of distinctive features of equal complexity to those of the IE phase. This may be contrasted with a language such as Latin, where a tripartite division is retained only in the labial series /p/:/f/:/b/, while there are only two dentals (/t/:/d/, with */dʰ/ → /f/- !) and only two velars (/k/:/g/).

Morphology of Common Germanic

In the nominal declension there is a remarkable reduction of the extremely rich morphology which may be reconstructed for the IE phase: as in many other languages, the three numbers of the nominal declension (singular, dual, plural) are reduced to two, with the exception of some sporadic remains of the dual; the eight cases (nominative, accusative, genitive, dative, ablative, instrumental, locative and vocative) are reduced to four (nominative, accusative, genitive, dative) in Common Germanic. The vocative is absorbed into the nominative, the instrumental and the locative into the dative; some uses of the ablative are taken over by the genitive, others by the dative.

This syncretism may be regarded as a suspension of functional oppositions, whether of form or of content; indeed, this occurs where cases are semantically similar (for example, there is never syncretism of the nominative and dative, while syncretism of the two 'direct cases' (nominative and accusative) does occur). The semantic information which was conveyed primarily by the case system is increasingly taken over by the prepositional system (see **Prepositions**, p. 408).

However, the three genders of (late) Indo-European, masculine, feminine and neuter, do remain.

Nouns

Indo-European had an extremely complex nominal declension system (including adjectives, pronouns and numerals), in which it is still possible to glimpse a functional opposition at the semantic level: thus we have a class of sigmatic neuters in *-es/-os expressing deverbal abstract nouns: root *$\hat{g}enH_1$- 'create, produce, → *$\hat{g}enos$ 'creation, that which is created, family, race' (Gk *génos*, Lat. *genus*) and a class of irregular stems in *-r/n grouping together the names of natural physical entities (nom. *$wédor$, gen. *ud-n-$és$ 'water'; nom. *$péwor$, gen. *pu-n-$és$ 'fire': cf. Gk *hýdōr*, *pŷr*). No trace remains of this functional distinction in Germanic, where the different classes survive as mere formal categories; in other words, the fact that a noun belongs to the class in -n- or to the class in -i- is of no relevance to its semantic value. In the subsequent development of the individual languages some flectional types disappear and others are extended (notably the stems in -n-, the so-called 'weak declension').

Table 13.1. shows the Common Germanic paradigm of a masculine noun in -a- (< IE -o-) as far as it can be reconstructed from a comparison of the oldest Germanic languages (it is to be remembered that Germanic *o* is always long). For comparison, Table 13.2. shows a masculine -i- stem. As it clear from a comparison of these paradigms with the IE declension, not only has there been considerable syncretism of the eight original cases in the Germanic languages, but as the result of regular phonetic developments (reduction of atonic syllables) there has been a great reduction in the original formal differences between declensions (see e.g. Goth. acc. sg. *wulf* like *gast*; OHG *wolf* like *gast*; OI gen. pl. *ulfa* like *gesta*, etc.), culminating in the complete disappearance of all differences (now purely formal, non-functional) between flectional classes: in English, umlaut plurals – with what

Table 13.1   Nominal stems in -a-

	CGmc	Gothic	Old Icel.	Old English	Old Saxon	Old High German
Singular						
Nom.	*wulfaz	wulfs	ulfr	wulf	wulf	wolf
Acc.	*wulfa[n]	wulf	ulf	wulf	wulf	wolf
Gen.	*wulfiza, -aza	wulfis	ulfs	wulfes	wulƀes	wolfes
Dat.	*wulfai, -ē	wulfa	ulfi	wulfe	wulƀe	wolfe
Instr.	*wulfo	——	——	wulfe	wulƀu	wolfu
Plural						
Nom.	*wulfos, -oz	wulfos	ulfar	wulfas	wulƀos	wolfã
Acc.	*wulfanz	wulfans	ulfa	wulfas	wulƀos	wolfã
Gen.	*wulfo[n]	(wulfē)	ulfa	wulfa	wulƀo	wolfo
Dat.	*wulfamiz	wulfam	ulfom	wulfum	wulƀum	wolfum

Note: This table does not indicate the numerous variants of the individual forms in the different languages. The Gothic genitive plural cannot derive from -$\bar{o}^n$.

Table 13.2   Nominal stems in -*i*-

	CGmc	Gothic	Old Icel.	Old English	Old Saxon	Old High German
Singular						
Nom.	*gastiz	gasts	gestr	giest	gast	gast
Acc.	*gasti^n	gast	gest	giest	gast	gast
Gen.	*gastiza	gastis	gests	giestes	gastes	gastes
Dat.	*gastai	gasta	gest	gieste	gaste	gaste
Instr.	*gastī	———	———	gieste	gasti	gast(i)u
Plural						
Nom.	*gastijiz	gasteis	gester	giestas	gesti	gesti
Acc.	*gastinz	gastins	geste	giestas	gesti	gesti
Gen.	*gastio^n	(gastē)	gesta	giesta	gestio	gestio
Dat.	*gastimiz	gastim	gestom	giestum	gestium	gestim

may simply be considered as an internal flection from a synchronic point of view – such as *feet, geese* (< OEng. *fēt* < **fotiz*, OEng. *gēs* < **gansiz*, vs sg. *foot, goose* < OEng. *fōt, gōs*: cf. p. 390f.) are fossilized remains and are no longer productive. The earlier plural form *beech* (< **bokiz*) has been replaced with the regular, generalized form *books*. Analogical processes also took place among the cases: since in the singular the nominative and accusative came to coincide as a result of the regular loss of the unstressed final part of the word, in Old English the ending of the nominative plural was extended to the accusative; the opposite happened in Old High German. The end result of this process, which has been reached by English, but not by German, is that there remains only a number distinction (sg. vs pl.), but no longer any case distinction.

Adjectives

Like the other noun determiners (demonstratives, participles and numerals) these are characterized, as they were in Indo-European, by agreement in gender, number and case with the noun to which they refer. The adjectives fall into the same classes as the nouns (classes in -*a*-, -*i*-, etc.), and again there is no longer any functional contrast. However, Germanic develops a contrast between 'weak' and 'strong' forms in the adjectival declension. The 'weak' flection is the same as that of the *n*-stems (of the same type as Lat. *homō, hominis*; *Catō, Catōnis*; Gk *Plátōn, Plátōnos*). It has a particularizing, determining function (to such an extent that it can itself be made into a noun: Goth. *sa dumba* (weak) 'the mute' vs *jah ⟨ga⟩was dumbs* (strong) 'and he remained silent' – or even into a proper name as in the Latin and Greek examples); from the very earliest texts onwards, the adjective with this function is often accompanied by a demonstrative (> article): Goth. *sa auhumista gudja* 'the highest priest'; *ik im hairdeis sa goda* 'I am the good shepherd' (literally 'I am shepherd the/that good'); cf. still in Ger. *ich bin der gute Hirt* (vs *ein guter Hirt*, indefinite); (cf. Ramat 1988: 103f).

The 'strong' inflection of the adjective 'blind' is shown in Table 13.3. The forms in *italics* are those which clearly correspond to those of the nominal declension. Those in plain type, on the other hand, have been borrowed from the demonstrative flection (to some extent this also occurred in Latin, cf. *totīus, unīus* declined like *illīus, eius*. On the demonstratives, see below). Given the variation among the individual languages as far as the use of nominal and demonstrative forms is concerned (cf. the accusative and dative plural), it is not always possible to reconstruct the Common Germanic form with any certainty: as is the convention, the forms here are based on Gothic. The Old Icelandic and Old Saxon dative singular is given in brackets because it goes back not to an old dative but to an instrumental.

Table 13.3   The 'strong' inflection of the adjective

	CGmc	Gothic	Old Icel.	Old Saxon	Old High German
Masculine					
Singular					
Nom.	**blinđaz*	*blinds*	*blindr*	blind	*blint*, -ēr
Acc.	**blinđano^n*	blindana	blindan	blindon	blintan
Gen.	**blinđez(a)*	*blindis*	*blinds*	*blindes*	*blintes*
Dat.	**blinđ^e/$_a$sm^e/$_ā$*	blindamma	[blindom	blindum(u)]	blintemu
Instr.	**blinđō*	———	———	*blindu*	*blintu*
Plural					
Nom.	**blinđai*	blindai	blinde-*r*	blinde	blinte
Acc.	**blinđanz*	*blindans*	*blinda*	blinde	blinte
Gen.	**blinđaizo^n*	(blindaizē)	blindra	blindero	blintero
Dat.	**blinđaimiz*	blindaim	*blindom*	*blintum*	blintēm
Feminine					
Singular					
Nom.	**blinđo*	*blinda*	*blind*	blind	*blint*, -iu
Acc.	**blinđo^n*	*blindai*	*blinda*	*blinda*	*blinta*
Gen.	**blinđezoz*	blindaizos	blindrar	blindera	blintera
Dat.	**blinđai*	*blindai*	blindre	blinderu	blinteru
Plural					
Nom.	**blinđoz*	*blindos*	*blindar*	*blinde*	blinto
Acc.	**blinđoz*	*blindos*	*blindar*	*blinda*	blinto
Gen.	**blinđaizo^n*	blindaizo	blindra	blindero	blintero
Dat.	**blinđaimiz*	blindaim	*blindom*	*blindum*	blintēm
Neuter					
Singular					
Nom.-Acc.	**blinđa^n*	*blind*		blind	*blint*
and	**blinđat(ō)^n*	blindata	blindet		blintaz
Plural					
Nom.-Acc.	**blinđo*	*blinda*	*blind*	blind	blint(i)u

Note: In the other cases the neuter inflection does not differ from the masculine.

Table 13.4   The 'weak' inflection of the adjective

	CGmc	Gothic	Old Icel.	Old Saxon	Old High German
Singular					
Nom.	*blinđano	blinda	blinde	blindo	blinto
Acc.	*blinđana^n	blindan	blinda	blindon	blinton
Gen.	*blinđeniz	blindins	blinda	blindon	blinten
Dat.	*blinđeni	blindin	blinda	blindon	blinten
Plural					
Nom.	*blinđaniz	blindans	blindo	blindon	blinton
Acc.	*blinđaniz?	blindans	blindo	blindon	blinton
	*blinđanunz?				
Gen.	*blinđano^n	(blindanē)	blindo	blindono	blintōno
Dat.	*blinđanmiz	blindam	blindom	blindon	blintōm

Table 13.4. shows the masculine forms of the 'weak' inflection of the adjective. This inflection corresponds in every respect to that of the nouns in -n-, which, as mentioned above, takes on an extraordinary development in Germanic.

The comparison of the adjective in Germanic is still synthetic in nature – that is, it is carried out by adding a flectional suffix to the adjectival stem (the analytical type (Eng. *more intelligent – (the) most intelligent*) is a later development): in the comparative, *-iz-a^n- < IE *-is-on- (cf. Slav. -$i\check{s}$-), and in the superlative, *-is-ta-z/-is-ta-n < IE *-is-to- (cf. Skt -$isthah$, Gk -$istos$), beside a new formation *-oz-a^n, *os-ta-z/-os-ta-n: Gmc *harđuz 'hard', *harđiza^n, *harđistaz/-istan, whence Goth. harđiza, hardists/-ista and OHG hertiro, hertisto (Ger. härter, härtest: note the mutation of the root vowel), beside OI harđare, harđastr; OEng. heardra, heardost.

Determiners

There existed in Indo-European a series of deictic forms which, like the adjectives, could be used with nouns with a demonstrative function ('this/that old man') as well as having a pronominal function ('I want this one, not that one'). These forms are retained in Germanic.: m. *sa (< IE *so-, cf. Skt $sáh$ 'this (man), he', Gk ho 'the'); f. *so (< IE *$s\bar{a}$, cf. Skt $s\bar{a}$ 'this (woman), she', Gk $h\bar{e}$ 'the'); n. *pat (< IE *tod, cf. Skt $tád$ 'this one, this', Gk $tó$ 'the', Lat. is-tud 'that'). The inflection is shown in Table 13.5.

It is not possible to take account here of individual variants, of which there are many in the different languages as a result of various analogical processes. From the point of view of Common Germanic it should be noted that the forms of this inflection have spread in part to the declension of adjectives, which share with the demonstratives the characteristic of being noun phrase constituents, namely noun determiners. It is obvious that, as in Greek, the article has developed from this deictic; the article is now obligatory in the noun phrase (Eng. *the old man, the three nice girls*). In English (partially) and German it also assumes the function of a relative pronoun (Eng. *that*, Ger. *der die das*, same plural *die* for all three genders): but the NP type 'determiner + noun' was not yet obligatory either in the oldest Runic inscriptions (cf. *horna tawido* above) or in the Gothic text, though this is a translation from New Testament Greek, where the article has become widespread (on the origin of the category 'article' see Ramat 1988: 106ff.).

sa, so, þat is not the only Germanic deictic. From à demonstrative stem *hi-* (< IE *k̂i-*, cf. Gk *e-keî-nos* 'this (man)') comes the third-person singular

Table 13.5   Demonstrative pronoun

	CGmc	Gothic	Old Icel.	Old English	Old Saxon	Old High German
Masculine						
Singular						
Nom.	*sa	sa	sā	se	se, the	der
Acc.	*þe/an-on	þana	þann	þone	thena	den
Gen.	*þes(a)	þis	þess	þæs	thes	des
Dat.	*þe/asmo	þamma	þeim	þām, þǣm	them(u)	demu
Instr.	*þio	———	———	———	thiu	———
Loc.	*þī	———	———	þȳ (þon)	———	———
Plural						
Nom.	*þai	þai	þeir	þā	the, thia	die
Acc.	*þans	þans	þā	þā	the, thia	die
Gen.	*þezon	(þizē)	þeira	þāra, þǣra	thero	dero
Dat.	*þemiz, þaimiz	þaim	þeim	þām, þǣm	them	dēm
Feminine						
Singular						
Nom.	*so	so	sū	sēo, sīo	thiu	diu
Acc.	*þon	þo	þā	þā	thea	dea
Gen.	*þezoz	þizos	þeirar	þǣre	thera	dera
Dat.	*þezai	þizai	þeire	þǣre	theru	deru
Plural						
Nom.	*þoz	þos	þǣr	þā	the, thia	die
Acc.	(As nom. pl. in all the Germanic languages)					
Gen.	*þaizon	þizo	þeira	þāra, þǣra	thero	dero
Dat.	*þaimiz	þaim	þeim	þām, þǣm	them	dēm
Neuter						
Singular						
Nom. Acc.	*þat	þata	þat	þæt	that	daz
Instr.	*þē	þē	———	———	thiu	diu
Loc.	*þī	———	þ(u)ī	þȳ (þon)	———	———
Plural						
Nom. Acc.	*þo, þio	þo	þau	þā	thiu	diu

pronoun Eng. *he*, Swed. m. *han*, f. *hon*. In addition we have **jainaz* > Goth. *jains*, OEng. *geon* (> Eng. *yon*), OHG *jener* (= Ger.) 'that man'. From the fusion of two deictic stems **þe-sa-* there then arises the demonstrative seen in Eng. *this*, Ger. *dieser*.

Interrogative

The interrogative, too, derives from the old IE interrogative/indefinite stem **kʷo-/kʷe-* (also **kʷi-* : cf. Gk *tís*, Lat. *quis*) > Gmc **hwaz* 'who?', whence Goth. *hvas*, OE *hwa* (> Eng. *who*), OHG (*h*)*wer* (> Ger. *wer*); and **hwat* 'what?', whence Goth. *hva*, OI *hvat*, OEng. *hwæt* (> Eng. *what*), OHG (*h*)*waz* (> Ger. *was*). Note that from this stem, English and German form a relative pronoun *who*, *which* (beside *that*) and *welcher* (beside *der*), exactly as Latin has done with *qui quae quod* (Ramat 1988: 133).

Numerals

The numerals from one to four were still declinable for each gender in Germanic, as in Indo-European:

*ojnos (cf. Lat. *unus*) > Gmc **ainaz* > Goth. *ains*, OI *einn*, OEng. OFrisian *ān*, OHG *ein*; the inflection is that of the strong adjective

*dwo- (cf. Gk *dúo*, Lat. *duo*) > Gmc **twa* (originally a dual, this then came to be inflected like a plural in the three genders): Goth. *twai twōs twa*, OI *tveir tvǣr tvau*, OEng. *twēgen twā twā*, OHG *zwēne zwō zwei*

*trejes (cf. the discussion of the Consonant Shift above)

*kʷetwor- (cf. Lat. *quattuor*) > Gmc **fiðwor* > Goth. *fidwor*, OI *fjōrer*, OEng. *fēower*, OHG *fior*; only Norse has retained the inflection in the three genders

The cardinal numerals from five to ten, which are indeclinable, faithfully reflect the IE state of affairs. Eleven and twelve constitute on the contrary a peculiarity of Germanic (shared in part with Baltic) which has led to the postulation of an original duodecimal system:

Gmc **ain-lif*, literally 'one left over' (with root *-likʷ-* 'to leave'), whence Goth. *ainlif*, OI *ellefo* (> Swed. *elva*), OEng. *endleofa* (> Eng. *eleven*), OHG *einlif* (> Ger. *elf*)

Gmc **twa-lif* > Goth. *twalif*, OI *tolf* (> Swed. *tolv*), OI *twelf* (> Eng. *twelve*), OHG *zwelif* (> Ger. *zwölf*)

The numerals from thirteen to nineteen are still formed according to the old system of copulative compounding: thus fourteen, for example, would be 'four-ten': Goth. *fidwortaihun*, OI *fiogortan*, OEng. *fēowertȳne*, OHG *fiorzehan*, etc.

Personal Pronouns

The personal pronouns directly continue the IE state of affairs, without distinction of gender in the first and second person, and with different stems for singular and plural (with traces of the dual).

'I': *$ek(a^n)$ (cf. above)

'you (sg.)': *$p\breve{u}$ (< IE *$t\breve{u}$, cf. Gk *sý*, Lat. *tū*, Lith. *tù* etc.), whence Goth. *þū*, OI *þū̆*, OE *þū̆* (> MEng. *thou*), OHG *dū̆*

'we two': *wit > Goth. *wit*, OI *vit*, OEng. *wit*

'you two': *jit > OI *it*, OEng. OSax. *git*

'we': $w\bar{i}(z)$ (< IE *wei, cf. Skt *vayám*), whence Goth. *weis*, OI *vēr*, OHG *wir*, OEng. OSax. OFrisian *wi, we*

'you (pl.)': *$j\bar{u}z$ (< IE *$j\bar{u}s$, cf. Skt *yūyám*, Lith. *jūs*) whence Goth. *jūs* and, with analogical vowel from the 1 pl., OI *ēr*, Eng. OSax. OFris. *gi*, OHG *ir*.

The genitive is in fact a form of the possessive: *$mein(a^n)$ 'my, mine', *$pein(a^n)$ 'your, yours' (sg.), *$uns\text{-}era\text{-}$ 'our, ours', *$i(z)w\text{-}era\text{-}$ 'your, yours' (pl.), whence Goth. *meina, þeina, unsara, izwara*, and corresponding forms in the other languages.

For the third person the Germanic languages use three pronominal stems, all clearly deictic in origin (cf. **Determiners**, pp. 399–401), although it is not possible to reconstruct one single original form: Goth. *is* and OHG *er* (cf. Lat. *is* 'he'), OI *hann* and OEng. OFrisian OSax. *he* (in Saxon with suppletion, as in the case of 'I'). These are inflected according to the pronominal declension seen above for the deictic determiners. We give as an example the Old Saxon paradigm (in one sense a halfway stage between English and German) in Table 13.6. The table shows that in the plural the gender difference has disappeared.

Table 13.6   Third-person pronoun

	Masculine	Feminine	Neuter
Singular			
Nom.	he, hie, hi	siu, sea, sia	it, et
Acc.	ina, -e	sia, sea	it, et
Gen.	is, es	ira, iru, -o	is, es
Dat.	im(u), -o	iru, -o, ira	im(u), -o
Plural			
Nom.	sia, se(a)	sia, se(a)	sia, se(a)
Acc.	sia, se(a)	sia, se(a)	sia, se(a)
Gen.	iro, -a	iro, -a	iro, -a
Dat.	im	im	im

Verb Conjugation

In the Germanic verb system there is again a great reduction in relation to the morphological system we reconstruct for Indo-European, which was based on threeway oppositions of mood (indicative, injunctive, optative), tense (present, aorist, perfect), voice (active, middle (passive)) and number (singular, dual, plural). In Germanic there is basically a two-way opposition of mood and tense:

	present	preterite
indicative	+	+
subjunctive	+	+

The so-called subjunctive continues the forms of the original optative. The imperative is restricted to the second-person singular present (in the plural, except in Gothic, the same forms occur as in the indicative). As far as voice is concerned, there is again a two-way opposition, active vs passive (in Gothic still in the synthetic form of the original middle, in the other languages in a periphrastic form: for example, OHG *kawīhit sī namo dīn* as in English *hallowed be Thy name* vs the original Latin *sanctificetur nomen tuum*. The analytic construction 'auxiliary + past participle' also has intransitive and impersonal middle values: OHG *wart ... birenkit (Merseburger Zauber-sprüche* b 2:) 'was dislocated', OSax. *sint ... cumana (Heliand* 2027) 'they have come', Goth. *qiþan ist* (Matt. 5:21) 'it has been said'. The infinitive, gerund and participle (present and past) are the nominal forms of the verb. Only Gothic preserves a separate dual; elsewhere there is only the binary opposition of singular vs plural.

On the functional level a basic opposition may be perceived between the real (= indicative) and the unreal (= subjunctive), between the present (= present) and the past (= preterite). The so-called 'preterite-presents' form a group on their own (see further, below). The idea of future is expressed by the present. Periphrastic forms with an auxiliary (as in Eng. *shall* and *will*, Ger. *werden*), originally having more a modal than a temporal value, are subsequent innovations in the individual languages. The opposition of verbal aspect (perfective vs imperfective), important from the IE point of view, is not represented morphologically; nevertheless, prefixes such as Ger. *ver-*, Goth. OHG *ga-* can serve to convey this opposition: *ver-brauchen* 'to use to the end > to consume' vs *brauchen* 'to use'; Goth. *ga-sat* 'sat down' vs *sat* 'was sitting', OHG *gaswīgan* 'to silence' vs *swīgan* 'to be silent'. As a result of its perfectivizing value (cf. the related Latin prefix *cum-* in *con-ficio, com-pello*, etc.), the preverb *ga-* (> *ge-*) became a morphological marker of the past participle in German.

At a formal level two verbal types are distinguished: the 'strong' and the 'weak' conjugations. The former continues and extends the IE system based on ablaut (apophony, vowel gradation) of the root vowel (as in Eng. *sink/ sank/sunk*, see above); the latter is a Germanic innovation with a preterite suffix containing a dental element and without root ablaut (Runic *tawido*, Eng. *love, loved*).

On the basis of the different types of ablaut, seven classes of strong verbs are traditionally distinguished. The following are examples of the third and the sixth classes:

Class III
pres. inf. **benđana^n* 'tie' (< root **b^{h}end^h*-. cf. Skt *badhnāti* 'he ties')
1 sg. pret. **banđa* (< **b^{h}ond^h-a*)
1 pl. pret. **bunđume* (< **b^{h}ņd^h-mé*)
past part. **bunđanaz* (< **b^{h}ņd^{h}onós*).

Cf. Goth. *bindan/band/bundum/bundans*; OI *binda/batt/bundo/bundenn* (Swed. *binda/band/bundo/bunden*); OEng. *bindan/band/bundon/bunden* (> Eng. *bind/bound/bound*), OHG *bintan/bant/bundun/gibuntan* (> Ger. *binden/band/gebunden*). Apart from the elimination of the singular/plural opposition in the preterite (except in Norse), these forms are still preserved today.

Class VI
pres. inf. **hafjana^n* 'lift' (< root **kap-*, cf. Lat. *capiō* 'I seize')
1 sg pret. **hofa*
1 pl. pret. **hoƀum*
past part. **haƀanaz*.

Cf. Goth. *hafjan/hof/hofun/hafans*; OI *hefja/hōf/hōfo/hafenn*; OEng. *hebban/hōf/hōfon/haben*; OSax. *hebbjan/hōf/hoƀun/-haƀan*; OFrisian *heva/ hōf/hōvon/heven*; OHG *heffen/huob/huobun/gihaban* (*ha-* > *he-* by umlaut through the presence of *j* in the following syllable: this also caused gemination of *-f-* in 'Western Germanic').

It is clear that the third class directly continues the IE ablaut series **en/*on/*ņ* (with **ņ* > *un*: cf. p. 389). The sixth class, however, develops an ablaut series **a/o/o/a* based on quantitative oppositions (note: Germanic *o* is long), which Indo-European used only sporadically (cf. Lat. *sedeō/sēdi*).

Note the 'grammatical change' in **hofa/hoƀum*, in other words the voicing of the voiceless fricative by Verner's Law (p. 394f.) because of the final position of the original accent in the preterite plural and past participle. In many cases this alternation was abandoned in favour of a more regular paradigm: in our example it appears clearly only in Old Saxon and Frisian.

A small but important group of verbs are the so-called 'preterite-presents': these are verbs which often have a modal value, such as 'can', 'must', 'fear', 'dare'; they have the form of a (strong) preterite but the meaning of a present. For example, one of the members of the third class mentioned above is the verb *kann 'I know, am able to' (< root *ĝenH-/ĝnē-/ĝnō-, cf. Gk gi-gnó-skō, Lat. gnōscō) > Goth. OI OHG kann, OSax. can; plural: Goth. OHG kunnun, OI kunno, OEng. cunnon, OSax. cunnun, while the fourth class contains *skal 'I must', plur. *skulum > Goth. OI OSax. skal, OEng. sceal, OFrisian skel, OHG scal, plur. Goth skulum, OI skolom, OSax. skulum, OEng. sculum, OFrisian skilun OHG sculum.

Many of the 'preterite-presents' are directly derived from Indo-European and seem to express aspect more than tense: e.g. Goth. wait, OI veit, OEng. wāt, OSax. wēt, OHG weiz 'I know' and Skt véda, Avest, vaēδa, Gk (w)oîda 'I have seen' (cf. Lat. vīdī) > 'I know', as a resultative. But after they assumed the temporal value of a present, these verbs could then develop a new (weak) preterite: thus we have Goth. kunþa and þaurfta, OI kunna and þurfta, OEng. cūðe and ðorfte, OFrisian kūthe and thorste, OSax. consta and thor(f)ta, OHG konda and dorfta, Goth. skulda, OI skylda, OSax. skolda, OEng. sc(e)olde, OFrisian skolde, OHG scolta.

This leads on to the discussion of weak verbs. These are in general secondary formations, derived by means of a suffix from nouns and adjectives (see e.g. Goth. stain-ja-n 'to stone' from stain-s 'a stone'). Four classes of weak verb are distinguished, according to the derivational suffix employed (e.g. those in -jan represent the first class). The main difference with respect to the strong verbs is the formation of the preterite with a dental suffix *-đo/-đē, about the origin of which there is still much debate (see Ramat 1988: 208). Because the derivational suffix is retained throughout the conjugation and because there is no root ablaut, these verbs have a much more regular paradigm than that of the strong verbs, and in the development of the individual Germanic languages we see the spread of the weak paradigm at the expense of original strong verbs (e.g. Ger. wob, buk (from weben 'weave' and backen 'bake') > webte, backte), although there are many examples of movement in the opposite direction (e.g. Dutch sande, clink(e)de > zond 'sent', klonk 'sounded').

It remains to draw attention to the sparse traces of the athematic conjugation in *-mi (cf. Gr. dídōmi), particularly the verb 'to be', IE *es-mi (cf. Skt ásmi, Gr. eimí, Lith. esmi) > Goth. im, OI em, OEng. (b)ēo(m), OSax. bium, OHG bim, all clearly irregular from the point of view of Germanic.

Table 13.7 shows the main forms of a verb such as *berananⁿ 'bear, carry' (> Eng. bear, Norw. bera; strong, class IV). It is not possible here to comment on the forms of the paradigm. However, these clearly continue the paradigms that we reconstruct for IE (e.g. Gmc 1 pl. pres. ind. *berum(i)z < IE *bʰeromes, cf. Gk phéromes, Lat. ferimus; 2 sg. pret. ind. *bart < IE *bʰortha, cf Skt bi-bhartha). Note the second-person singular preterite indicative in OI, Old Saxon and Old High German: this does not continue the old IE perfect, but rather an injunctive form (*bʰēres ?): this is a classic case of the impossibility of reconstructing a uniform 'Common Germanic' starting point (see Ramat 1988: 21).

Table 13.8 shows the preterite of a weak verb such as *salƀona^n 'anoint' or Norse *kalla* 'call' (-*o*- suffix, class II).

Table 13.7   The strong preterite

	CGmc	Gothic	Old Icel.	Old English	Old Saxon	Old High German
Present indicative active						
1 sg.	*bero	baira	ber	bere	biru	biru
2 sg.	*beris(i), -z(i)	bairis	berr	bires	biris	biris
3 sg.	*beriþ(i), -đ(i)	bairiþ	berr	bireþ	biriđ	birit
1 dual	*beraw(i)z	bairos				
2 dual	*beraþ(i)z	bairats				
1 pl.	*beram(i)z	bairam	berom	berađ	berađ	berumēs
2 pl.	*beriþ(i), -đ(i)	bairiþ	bereþ	berađ	berađ	beret
3 pl.	*beranþ(i), -đ(i)	bairand	bera	berađ	berađ	berant
Preterite indicative active						
1 sg.	*bara	bar	bar	bær	bar	bar
2 sg.	*bart	bart	bart	bære	bāri	bāri
3 sg.	*bare	bar	bar	bær	bar	bar
1 dual	*bēru	bēru				
2 dual	*bēruþ(i)z	bēruts				
1 pl.	*bērum	bērum	bǫrom	bæron	bārun	bārum
2 pl.	*bēruþ(i), -đ(i)	bēruþ	bǫroþ	bæron	bārun	bārut
3 pl.	*bērun(þ)	bērun	bǫro	bæron	bārun	bārun
Present subjunctive active						
1 sg.	*beraju^n, -ai^n	bairau	bera	bere	bere	bere
2 sg.	*berais, -z	bairais	berer	bere	beres	berēs
3 sg.	*berai(þ, -đ)	bairai	bere	bere	bere	bere
1 dual	*beraiwē	bairaiwa				
2 dual	*beraiþ(i)z	bairaits				
1 pl.	*beraimē	bairaima	berem	beren	beren	berēm
2 pl.	*beraiþ(i), -đ(i)	bairaiþ	bereþ	beren	beren	berēt
3 pl.	*berain(þ)	bairana	bere	beren	beren	berēn
Preterite subjunctive active						
1 sg.	*bēri^n	bērjau	bæra	bære	bāri	bāri
2 sg.	*bēris, -z	bēreis	bærer	bære	bāris	bāris
3 sg.	*bēri(þ, -đ)	bēri	bære	bære	bāri	bāri
1 pl.	*bērīmē	bēreima	bærem	bæren	bārin	bārīm
2 pl.	*bērīþ(i), -đ(i)	bēreiþ	bæreþ	bæren	bārin	bārīt
3 pl.	*bērin(þ)	bēreina	bære	bæren	bārin	bārīn
Infinitive	*berana^n	bairan	bera	beran	beran	beran
Present participle	*berand	bairands	berande	berende	berandi	beranti
Past participle	*buranaz	baurans	borenn	boren	giboran	giboran

Table 13.8   The weak preterite

	CGmc	Old Icel.	Old English	Old High German
1 sg.	*salƀoðon	kallaþa	sealfode	salbōta
2 sg.	*salƀoðēz	kallaþer	sealfodes(t)	salbōtos(t)
3 sg.	*salƀoðē(þ)	kallaþe	sealfode	salbōta
1 dual	*salƀoðun			
2 dual	*salƀoðuþ(i)z			
1 pl.	*salƀoðum(i)z	kǫlloþom	sealfodon	salbōtum
2 pl.	*salƀoðuþ(i)	kǫlloþoþ	sealfodon	salbōtut
3 pl.	*salƀoðun(þ)	kǫlloþo	sealfodon	salbōtun

Gothic, however, has reduplicated forms of the dental ending: dual *salbo-dēdu*, *-dēduts*, pl. *-dēdum*, *-dēduþ*, *-dēdun*. In the present, infinitive and participles the endings are the same as those of the strong verbs: thus we have Goth. 1 sg. pres. ind. *salbo*, pres. pt. *salbonds*, past pt. *salboþs*, with retention of the characteristic class suffix.

The Invariable Word Classes

Conjunctions
Only the following conjunctions may be attributed with certainty to the common linguistic phase:

endi, *undi* 'and' (> Eng. *and*, Frisian Dutch *en*, Ger. *und*)
auk 'also, and' (> Norw. Dan. *og*, Eng. *eke*, Dutch *ook*, Ger. *auch*)
þ^e/$_a$ + *uh* (< IE *-k^{w}e*, cf. Lat. *-que*) > *þauh* 'but' (> Eng. *though*, Ger. *doch* > Dan. *dog*, Swed. *dock*)
iƀa, *uƀa* 'if' (> Icel. *ef*, Eng. *if*, Frisian Dutch *of*, Ger. *ob*).

Only the last of these is clearly a subordinating conjunction; the others can also be coordinating conjunctions. Germanic therefore seems to have had relatively few subordinating conjunctions. The forms meaning 'because, while, when, after', etc. (such as Swed. *för att* 'in order that', Eng. *so that*, Ger. *nachdem* 'after') developed subsequently in the individual languages with the development of a subordinating syntax. On the whole these originated, as in the examples given, in deictic pronominal stems, which is in keeping with their anaphoric function in the sentence: *bis das es alles geschehe* (Luther, Matt. 5: 18), literally 'until that it all happen', 'donec omnia fiant'.

Adverbs

In general we find nominal forms fossilized in an adverbial function, such as Goth. *gistradagis* 'tomorrow', actually 'the next day' (gen.), OEng. *geostran day* (> Eng. *yesterday*); Goth. *galeiko*, OI *līka*, OHG *gilīcho* (> Ger. *gleich*) 'equally' from an old IE ablative in *-ōd* (cf. also the adverbs in *-ly* in English, *-lich* in German < Gmc *-līko*, ablative of the noun for 'body'). On the adverbs of place, such as Goth. *iup*, OSax. *upp(an)*, OI OEng. *upp*, OHG *ūf* 'up'; see the following discussion of prepositions.

Prepositions

As indicated above, with the great reduction in the inflectional system, the prepositions take on a heavy functional load in the Germanic languages. Some examples of prepositions attributable to Common Germanic are:

frama 'from' (agentive) > Goth. OSax. OHG *fram*, OEng. *from*
med̄(i) 'with' (agentive) > Goth. *miþ*, OI *međ*, OEng. *mid*, OHG *mit(i)*
under 'under' > Goth. OSax. *undar*, OEng. OFrisian *under*, OHG *unter*
to, ta 'towards' > OEng. OSax. OFrisian *tō*, OHG *zuo*
ūt 'out of' > Goth. OI OEng. OFrisian OSax. *ūt*, OHG *ūz* etc.

It is clear that these prepositions have been retained in the modern languages. They are lexemes which have an adverbial function when used independently, a prepositional function when linked with a noun and a verb specifying function (as preverbs) when linked with a verb: *sōkead fadar iuwan upp* (adv.) *te* (prep.!) *themu ēwinom rīkea* (*Heliand* 1795) 'look for your father up in the eternal kingdom' vs *bīdan uppan* (prep.) *themo berge* (*Heliand* 4733) 'wait on the mountain'. Thus we have Goth. *af-gaggan* 'go away', OEng. *forð-bringan* 'bring forth', OHG *untan-gangan* (> Ger. *untergehen*) 'go under', etc.; Goth. *faur-biudan*, OEng. *for-bēodan* (> Eng. *forbid*), OHG *fir-biotan* (> Ger. *verbieten*) 'forbid', and so on. As English *to bring forth* and German *ich gehe unter* still demonstrate, these preverbs were separable and had a marked semantic independence, as adverbial modifiers of the basic meaning expressed by the verb (and in this, too, Germanic is not alone among the IE languages: cf. Chapter. 2, p. 68, and Chapter 3, **Word Classes**, p. 79). Note finally that in prepositional phrases, too, the 'preposition' can in fact be postposed: OEng. *ūs betwēonan*, *him beforan* (Eng. *between us*, *before him*). Therefore, it would be more correct to speak of verbal and nominal adpositions instead of prepositions.

Word Formation

This subject often tends to be omitted from descriptions of Germanic; but it too is clearly subject to precise morphological (or morphosyntactic) rules of formation. Every 'part of speech' – noun, adjective, pronoun, verb etc. – has its own unambiguous formal (i.e. morphological) characteristics. In an inflecting language like Common Germanic a noun does not appear without indication of the nominal class to which it belongs, nor does a verb appear without specification of tense, mood or person; in other words, there are no undifferentiated lexemes such as English *like* (noun, verb, adjective and adverb).

An important area of word-formation rules is derivation: suffixes such as *-ingo/-ungo* serve to form denominal and verbal abstracts (cf. OI *þrenning* 'trinity' < *þrennr* 'triple', OEng. *leornung* 'knowledge' < *leornian* 'to learn', Eng. *learning*; Ger. *Verachtung* 'scorn' < *verachten* 'to scorn'); suffixes such as *-þla-/-đla-* serve to form the names of concrete entities (cf. OEng. *stađol*, Ger. *Stadel* 'barn' < root *steH₂-* 'to stand'), and so on; these suffixes are very numerous.

A much less common means of word formation, but also one which goes back to Indo-European, is root ablaut: cf. Lat. *toga*, Gk *phygḗ* 'flight' beside *tegere* 'to cover', *pheúgein* 'to flee', Ger. *Bund* 'tie', *Trunk* 'drink, draught' beside *Band* 'band', *Trank* 'drink', with the same roots as *binden* 'to tie', *trinken* 'to drink'; Norw. *song* and Eng. *song* vs *syngja* and *sing*, etc. (On the variation in the root vowel, see pp. 403–7). The examples just given have zero suffixation, but there are also cases of derivation by means of ablaut + suffix: IE *pér-tu-* > Gmc *fer-þuz* > OI *fjǫrðr* (> Eng. *firth*) 'inlet' vs IE *pr̥-tú-* > Gmc *fur-đuz* > OEng. *ford*, OHG *furt*, Dutch *voort* 'ford', from the root of *faran* 'go, pass, cross'.

The preceding paragraphs concerning word classes belong more to morphology, but the rules concerning nominal compounds have more to do with syntax. In a two-part compound the first term is usually a plain stem; the second conveys that information about gender, number and case which is typical of a noun. The functional relationship of the first to the second term may be accusatival (e.g. Goth. *mana-maurþrja* 'men-killer > murderer'), genitival (e.g. OHG *brūti-gomo* (> Ger. *Bräutigam*) 'bride's-man > husband'), instrumental (e.g. Goth. *handu-waurhts*, Eng. *handmade*), locatival (e.g. Ger. *Nachtigall*, Eng. *nightingale* 'night-singer', etc.) (see Krahe and Meid 1969: vol. III, 16). The compound is thus equivalent to a full phrase (prepositional or otherwise). Germanic is here continuing and developing a technique already present in Indo-European.

Three semantic types of compound are distinguished (see Chapter 4, p. 121f.):

1   copulative ('dvandva'), in which the two elements stand in equal relation, neither subordinate to the other: a typical example are the numbers 'thirteen' to 'nineteen' (cf. **Numerals**, p. 401);
2   determinative ('tatpuruṣa'), in which the first element usually modifies or limits the second, as in the case of *manamaurþrja*, *brūtigomo* etc.;
3   exocentric ('bahuvrīhi'), in which the compound refers to an entity external to the compound itself: OEng. *bærfōt* (> Eng. *bare-footed*),

MHG *barfuoz* (Ger. *barfuß*); Goth. *fidur-dogs*, OEng. *fēower-dōgor*, OHG *fior-tagig* 'four-day, lasting four days')

The compounding of verbs with prefixes has already been covered in the discussion of prepositions (cf. **Prepositions**, p. 408).

The Syntactic Type of Common Germanic

In dealing with the morphology we have inevitably had to make reference more than once to syntactic information (see syncretism of the cases, weak and strong adjective declensions, word-formation rules, etc.). In fact it would be more appropriate to deal with both jointly under the heading of 'morphosyntax'. However, let us outline some phenomena directly relevant to sentence structure.

In the discussion of the conjunctions (**Conjunctions**, p. 407) it was seen that Germanic cannot have had a greatly developed subordinating syntax (hypotaxis). In fact, even in late medieval texts there are numerous examples of coordination (parataxis) and simple juxtaposition: *de konnynck heft dat ordel ghegeven, Reynke schal nich lenger leven* (*Reineke de Vos*, 3271) 'the king has passed the verdict, R. shall live no longer', *ja se ropen alle, men schal ene hangen* (*ibid.*, 3910) 'all cry out, he should be hanged' (see Behaghel 1928: vol. III, 616). In place of subordinate clauses we often find nominal forms as participles (such as Goth. *sēhvum sumana ... usdreibandan unhulpons*, Mark 9: 38, 'we saw one casting out devils'), as gerunds (OSax. *ik iuhu ... sweriannias endi liagannias*, literally 'I confess perjuring and lying' > ' ... that I have perjured and lied' and as infinitives (Goth. *urrunnun wiþragamotjan imma*, John 12:13, 'they went forth to meet him'; in the Greek text this is conveyed by a prepositional phrase: *exêlthon eis hypántēsin* 'they went out to the meeting'!).

This ties in with the fact that 'Common Germanic' retained from Indo-European a predominantly inflectional character, as well as with the fact that Proto-Germanic, like its ancestor Indo-European, was an OV-type language, that is, had the object preceding the verb in unmarked linear order. Indeed, subordination is, in general, more characteristic of (S)VO languages (S = subject; see Lehmann 1978: 195).

The conclusion that 'Common Germanic' was an SOV language is reached not so much because of the order in which these basic components occur in the oldest documents as from other typical characteristics of (S)OV languages. In fact, because 'Common Germanic' was still a heavily inflected language, each constituent of the sentence carried its own information (case, person, voice) relating it syntactically to the rest of the sentence. The order of S, O and V is thus substantially free from syntactic constraints and can serve for discourse strategies (pragmatical goals): e.g. in the oldest Runic inscriptions *ek ... horna tawido* (SOV) vs *hApuwolAfA sAte stAbA þria* 'Haþ.

set staves three' (*Gummarp*: SVO) vs *hAidʀ runoronu fAlAh-Ak* 'bright runes-sequence hid-I' (*Björketorp*: OVS) (cf. Chapter 3, **Constituent Order**, p. 89f.).

However, other facts clearly indicate an (S)OV order, above all the structure of compounds such as the above-mentioned *mana-maurþrja*, OHG *heri-zogo* 'leader of the army' (> Ger. *Herzog*) in which the first element stands in accusative relation to the verbal noun of the second element; also, in more general terms, *handu-waurhts*, *brūti-gomo* (already mentioned), OI *vind-augi* (> Eng. *window*) 'wind-eye > window', where the first element determines the second (i.e. its 'head').

Among the other syntactic structures of the type Determiner + Determined characteristic of OV languages are the following (cf. Ramat 1988: 218ff.):

1   The Genitive and Adjective tend to precede the noun: *Manne sums* (Lk.15:11) 'of-men one > a man', *Hariwulfs stainaz* (*Rävsal*) 'Hariwulf's stones', *mahtiges mōder* (*Heliand* 1998) 'might-one's mother', *afar ni managans dagans ... sa juhiza sunus* (Luke 15:13) 'after not many days ... the youngest son', *um langan veg* (*Locasenna* 6.3) 'after [a] long way', *lēof lēod-cyning* (*Beowulf* 54) 'beloved of-the-people's-king'.

2   The term of comparison tends to precede the comparative form of the adjective: *mergi smæra* (*Locasenna* 45.4) 'of-the-marrow finer' > 'more delicate/softer than marrow', *dhemo neowiht nist suozssera* (*Isidor* 32.5f) 'of-this nothing (not-) is sweeter', *ther ist mir strengiro* (*Tatian* 13.23) 'that-man is than-me stronger > he is stronger than me'.

3   The indirect object precedes the direct object: *and hie him friþ wiþ nāmon* (Anglo-Saxon Chronicle, AD 866) 'and they to-him [O_i] peace [O_d] with took > and they made peace with him', *dat ih dir it nū bi huldī gibu* (*Hildebrandslied* 35) 'that I to-you [O_i] it [O_d] now in friendship give', *hann hafði būit āsom ǫl* (*Locasenna, Prose* 1) 'he had prepared for the Aesir [O_i] the beer [O_d]'.

4   The adverbial determiners of the verb can follow it (postpositions, cf. **Prepositions**, p. 408) instead of preceding it: *ec kom þessar hallar til* (*Locasenna* 6.1 f.) 'I came this room to > ... to this room', *him cōm micel eāca tō* (Anglo-Saxon Chronicle, AD 868) 'to-them came great reinforcements towards', *die pringent sia sār ūf / in himilo rīhi* (*Muspilli* 13) 'they bring it [the soul] immediately up / into heaven's kingdom'. Postpositions also occur in 'prepositional phrases': *Scoedelandum in* (*Beowulf* 19), *Frēslondum on* (*Beowulf* 2358).

5   In subordinate clauses especially, the finite element of the verbal complex ('auxiliary') tends to occur at the end of the clause: *hausideduþ þatei qiþan ist* (Matt. 5: 27) 'you have heard that said is', *... sīn tac piqueme, daz er towan scal* (*Muspilli* 1) ' ... his day came, that he die must', *oft forgeaton þone þe hie him to hihte habban scealdon* (*Christ and Satan*, 640f.) 'often they forgot the one in whom they ought to have had hope',

Dat gafregin ih ... dat ero ni was (Wessobrunn 1f.) 'That learned I ...
that earth not was'.

Some of these characteristics, such as (2) and (5) (the latter with the
exception of German and Dutch) have now disappeared in all the Germanic
languages, and for each, numerous counterexamples can be quoted from as
far back as the oldest attestations; but it is really the cumulative evidence
they provide which allows us to conclude that Germanic must have had an
OV phase and the linguistic type Determiner + Determined, with a
subsequent shift to VO, which is clearly exemplified in the change from
John's Bible (Determiner + Determined) to *The Bible of John* (Determined
+ Determiner).

According to Hopper (1975: 82), the Germanic simple declarative sentence
may be represented by this ideal sequence of elements:

Particles–Pronouns–Pronominal Adverbs–Nominal Subject–Indirect Nom-
inal Object/Nominal Complement–Direct Nominal Object–Heavy Adverbs–
Verbal Complex #

Naturally it is difficult to find examples where all the theoretically possible
elements occur: cf. the Anglo-Saxon Chronicle, AD 867: *and hie þēah micle*
fierd gegadrodon 'and (particle) they (subj. pron.) nevertheless (adv.) great
troop (dir. nom. obj.) gathered (verb)'. Lehmann (1972: 267f.) quotes the
following case where the syntax of the subordinate clause is also apparent
(Anglo-Saxon Chronicle, Parker MS, AD 418):

Her   Romane   gesomnodon al þa gold hord   þe on Bretene
in this year [the] Romans collected   all the gold-hoards that in Britain

wæron 7   sume on eorþan   ahyddon þæt   hie   nænig mon siþþan
were   and some in [the] earth [they] hid [so] that them no   man since

findan ne meahte, 7   sume mid him   on Gallia læddon
find   not could, and some with them to Gaul   [they] carried

'In this year the Romans collected all the gold-hoards that were in Britain, and
some they hid in the earth so that no man has been able to find them since,
and some they carried with them to Gaul.'

To sum up, 'Common Germanic' appears: (a) with clear characteristics of
the (S)OV type, but already with hints of the shift SOV → SVO; (b) as a
language that is still heavily inflected – although there are also cases of
analytic structures, as in the use of pre-/postpositions, the middle/passive/
intransitive expressed by means of an auxiliary + past participle and some

examples of agglutination such as *fAlAh-Ak*, quoted above; (c) as a 'nominative-accusative' language – here, too, with traces of possible instances of ergativity, cf. the constructions, analogous to those in Latin of the sort *me pudet* 'I am ashamed', such as Goth. *mik huggreiþ*, OI *mik hungrar*, OEng. *me hungrað*, OHG *mik hungirit* (> Ger. *mich hungert*) 'I am hungry'; OEng. *me þincþ*, OHG *mih dunchit*, in which the only agent involved in the action occurs in the 'accusative' case (subsequently regularized in constructions with 'unspecified subjects' and the dative personal pronoun: *es dünkt mir* 'it seems to me': see Hirt 1934 : vol. III, 161).

References

Althaus, Hans Peter, Henne, Helmut and Wiegand, Herbert (eds) (1980) *Lexikon der Germanistischen Linguistik*, 2nd edn, Tübingen: Niemeyer.

Behaghel, Otto (1923–32) *Deutsche Syntax*, 4 vols, Heidelberg: Winter.

Branmüller, Kurt (1982) *Syntaxtypologische Studien zum Germanischen*, Tübingen: Niemeyer.

Calder, Daniel G. and Christy, T. Craig (eds) (1988) *Germania: Comparative Studies in the Old Germanic Languages and Literatures*, Wolfeboro, NH: Brewer.

Gamkrelidze, Thomas V. (1979) 'Hierarchical relationships of dominance as phonological universals and their implications for Indo-European reconstruction', in *Festschrift for Oswald Szemerényi*, ed. Béla Brogyanyi, Amsterdam: Benjamins, pp. 283–90.

Gamkrelidze, Thomas V. and Ivanov, Vjačeslav V. (1973) 'Sprachtypologie und die Rekonstruktion der gemeinindogermanischen Verschlüsse', *Phonetica* 27: 150–6.

Hirt, Hermann (1931–4) *Handbuch des Urgermanischen*, 3 vols, Heidelberg: Winter.

Hopper, Paul J. (1975) *The Syntax of the Simple Sentence in Proto-Germanic*, The Hague and Paris: Mouton.

Hutterer, Claus Jürgen (ed.) (1975) *Die germanischen Sprachen. Ihre Geschichte in Grundzügen*, Munich: C.H. Beck, and Budapest: Akadémiai Kiadó.

Krahe, Hans (1954) *Sprache und Vorzeit*, Heidelberg: Quelle & Mayer.

Krahe, Hans and Meid, Wolfgang (1969) *Germanische Sprachwissenschaft*, vol. I, *Einleitung und Lautlehre*; vol. II, *Formenlehre*; vol. III, *Wortbildungslehre*; Berlin: De Gruyter ('Sammlung Göschen').

Lehmann, Winfred P. (1972) 'Proto-Germanic syntax', in van Coetsem and Kufner 1972: 239–68.

—— (1978) 'English: a characteristic SVO language', in Winfred P. Lehmann (ed.), *Syntactic Typology*, Austin, Tex. and London: University of Texas Press, pp. 169–222.

Meillet, Antoine (1930) *Caractères généraux des langues germaniques*, 3rd edn, Paris: Hachette.

Penzl, Herbert (1988) 'Can Proto-Germanic be reconstructed as a "natural" language?', in Calder and Christy 1988: 1–8.

Polomé, Edgar C. (1992) 'Zur Chronologie des Germanischen', in Robert S.P. Beekes, Alexander Lubotsky and Jos Weitenberg (eds), *Rekonstruktion und relative Chronologie*, Proceedings of the 8th Special Conference of the Indogerman Society, Leiden, 31 August–4 September 1987, Wiesbaden: Reichert, pp. 55–73.

Ramat, Paolo (1988) *Introduzione alla linguistica germanica*, Bologna: Il Mulino (repr. of the 1986 edition).

Rösel, Ludwig (1962) *Die Gliederung der germanischen Sprachen nach dem Zeugnis ihrer Flexionsformen*, Nuremberg: H. Carl.

Swan, Toril, Mørck, Endre and Westvik, Olaf J. (eds) (1994) *Language Change and Language Structure: Older Germanic Languages in a Comparative Perspective*, Berlin and New York: Mouton de Gruyter.

Van Coetsem, Frans (1970) 'Zur Entwicklung der germanischen Grundsprache', in Ludwig Erich Schmitt (ed.), *Kurzer Grundriß der germanischen Philologie bis 1500*, vol. I, *Sprachgeschichte*, Berlin: de Gruyter, pp. 1–93.

—— (1990) 'Grimm's Law: a reappraisal of Grimm's formulation from a present-day perspective', in Elmer H. Antonsen (ed.), *The Grimm Brothers and the Germanic Past*, Amsterdam and Philadelphia: Benjamins, pp. 43–59.

Van Coetsem, Frans and Kufner, Herbert L. (eds) (1972) *Toward a Grammar of Proto-Germanic*, Tübingen: Niemeyer.

Vennemann, Theo (1984) 'Hochgermanisch und Niedergermanisch. Die Verzweigungstheorie der germanisch-deutschen Lautverschiebungen', *Beiträge zur Geschichte der deutschen Sprache* 106: 1–45.

—— (1988) 'Systems and changes in early Germanic phonology: a search for hidden identities', in Calder and Christy 1988: 45–65.

—— (1990) 'Wer hat das andere Horn gemacht? Zum Numerus von *horna* in der Gallehus-Inschrift', *Beiträge zur Geschichte der deutschen Sprache* 111: 355–68.

—— (1994) 'Linguistic reconstruction in the context of European prehistory', *Transactions of the Philological Society* 92 (2): 215–84.

14 Slavic

Henning Andersen

Introduction

The modern Slavic languages are traditionally divided into three groups. East Slavic (ESlav.) comprises Russian (Russ.), Belorussian (Bel.) and Ukrainian (U); the South Slavic (SSlav.) languages are Bulgarian (Bulg.), Macedonian (Mac.) in the East and Serbo-Croatian (SC) and Slovenian (Sn) in the West; the West Slavic (WSlav.) group comprises three subgroups, Slovak (Sk) and Czech (Cz.), Upper and Lower Sorbian (US and LS), and Lechitic, represented by Polish (Pol.) and Kashubian (Kash.), formerly including also Polabian (Pb.), extinct since the eighteenth century and Slovincian (Slov.), which died out in the early twentieth century.

Old Church Slavonic (OCS) is the language of the mostly ecclesiastical, oldest Slavic texts written between 863, the date of the Byzantine mission to the Principality of Moravia, and the mid-900s. This written language was created by Constantine the Philosopher, the later Saint Cyril, who devised the first Slavic alphabet and translated essential sacred and administrative texts into Slavic prior to his and his brother, the monk Methodius' mission to Moravia. It is based on the South Slavic dialect native to the missionary brothers, who hailed from Thessaloníki in Greece. This language is reflected, with modifications, in copies dating back to the tenth century. It was earlier called Old Bulgarian. Later texts in this language show deviations in spelling and grammar which betray their place of origin. The earliest of these are recognized as local (e.g. Moravian, East Slavic) recensions of Old Church Slavonic. Later texts are referred to simply as Russian (Bulgarian, Serbian, etc.) Church Slavonic (Ch.S).

The Original Homeland and Geographical Expansion of the Slavs

The area from which the Slavs expanded during the first centuries of our era can be approximately inferred from two kinds of linguistic evidence, appellatives and toponyms.

The shared, inherited vocabulary of the modern Slavic languages includes no detailed terminology for physical surface features characteristic of the mountains or the steppe, nor any relating to the sea, to coastal features, littoral flora or fauna, or salt water fishes. By contrast it includes a well-developed terminology for inland bodies of water (lakes, rivers, swamps) and kinds of forest (deciduous and coniferous), for the trees, plants, animals and birds indigenous to the temperate forest zone, and for the fish native to its waters. It thus points to a broad zone stretching from modern-day eastern Germany eastward to the middle Dnieper, a zone lying to the north of the foothills of the Sudetes, the Beskids and the Carpathians in the west and the steppe and

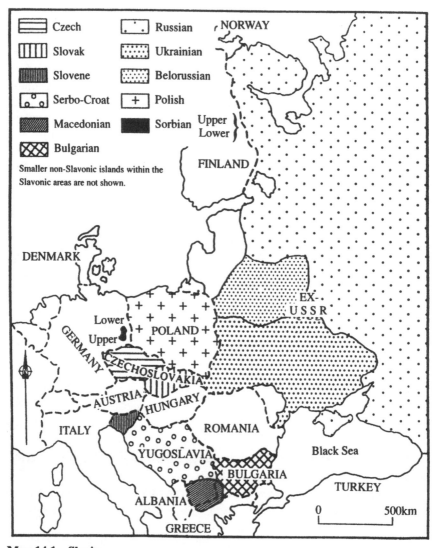

Map 14.1   Slavic
Source: B. Comrie (ed.), *The World's Major Languages*, London and Sydney: Croom Helm, 1987: 323

parklands (forest-steppe) in the east (cf. Filin 1962: 114–22).

Within this very large area the Slavs seem to have occupied areas to the east of the trade routes connecting the Baltic Sea with the Mediterranean world, roughly from the upper Vistula in the west to the middle Dnieper in the east. This latter area exhibits a high density of hydronyms representing archaic Slavic patterns of word formation. On the eastern flank of this area there is a predominance of Iranian hydronyms. To the north of it, the river names have Baltic etyma (cf. Toporov and Trubačev 1962).

In the area between the upper Vistula and the middle Dnieper archaeologists find apparent cultural continuity going back to the emergence of the corded ware type in the second millennium BC and a gradual differentiation *vis-à-vis* the contiguous areas to the north, where several Baltic cultural subtypes are defined (cf. Gimbutas 1971; Sedov 1979; Mallory 1989: 76–84).

During the first few centuries after the beginning of our era, the Slavs begin to expand their territory. In the east, they move northward, infiltrating the Baltic-speaking areas of what is now Belarus', founding colonies around Ladoga, Pskov, and Novgorod, in the border regions between Balts and Finns, in time establishing first a predominance and then the monopoly of Slavic speech through a combination of colonization and assimilation of local populations in what is now Belarus' and Russia. In the west, the Slavs expand northward toward the Baltic Sea, as well as westward, crossing the Oder *c.* 400 and reaching their westernmost extension, defined by the Elbe and Saale rivers, about 700. During the same period, they expand southward into the Balkan peninsula along several routes, east of the Carpathians across the lower Danube, across the Carpathians into the Hungarian Plain, and into Bohemia and Bavaria and across the Julian Alps, establishing themselves in Macedonia, Thessaly, Epirus, Attica and the Peloponnesus around 600, smaller numbers reaching Crete, the Greek Islands and the coast of Asia Minor.

Subsequent centuries see a curtailment of the Slavic presence in these vast areas. They are in part absorbed in local populations (thus in Greece, Albania and Romania), in part displaced by other ethnic groups, Magyars in Hungary (896), Germans in Bavaria and Austria and in what is now northern and middle Germany. Only in the east does the expansion continue through the Middle Ages and, after the rise of Muscovy in the fourteenth to sixteenth century, to the recent past (Alaska, northern California).

Baltic and Slavic

Among the IE languages, Slavic shows special genetic relations with Germanic and Italic in the west and with Indo-Iranian, Armenian and Tocharian in the east. But the Slavic languages are particularly closely related to the Baltic languages.

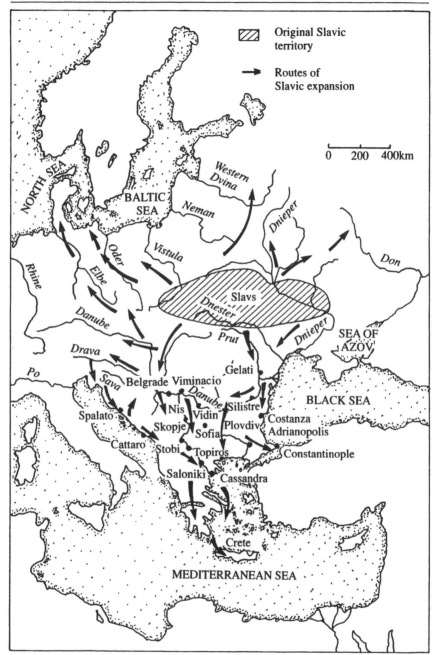

Map 14.2   Slavic expansion in Europe in the sixth and eighth centuries
Source: F. Conte, *Gli Slavi*, Turin: Einaudi, 1991: 25

Map 14.3   Slavic from the eighth to the tenth century
Source: F. Conte, *Gli Slavi*, Turin: Einaudi, 1991: 91

The nature of this relationship has been the subject of much controversy during this century, but has now been clarified to such an extent that genuine progress can be made. Stang (1964: 1–21) has demonstrated that West Baltic (Old Prussian) and East Baltic (Lithuanian and Latvian) do not provide the basis for reconstructing a single Baltic proto-language, and that Slavic bears very different relations to West Baltic and to East Baltic. From this it follows that Slavic and the three attested Baltic languages should be understood as the sole surviving, originally discontinuous, fragments of a former Slavic–Baltic dialect continuum which was established, probably, in the second millennium BC, and which during the subsequent two thousand years developed a mosaic of internal isoglosses, formed in periods of gradual differentiation and presumably shifted and levelled in intermittent periods of convergence.

During their period of expansion, the Slavs overlaid Baltic varieties of speech in Poland, Belarus and Russia, which can be identified now mainly on the basis of toponyms, but perhaps also through their substratum effects on local dialects of Polish, Belarusian and Russian (cf. e.g. Lekomceva 1981, 1982). Pressured by the expansion of the eastern Slavs, the Latvian and Lithuanian speech communities were partly displaced towards the west and, in their turn, submerged dialects spoken by other Baltic tribes mentioned by name in medieval chronicles and discernible through place-names and dialect vocabulary in modern Lithuania and Latvia (cf. Buga 1961: 85–282; Volkaitė-Kulikauskienė 1987: 157–60). The net result of these displacements of communities was the disappearance of large portions of the original Slavic–Baltic dialect continuum. But pale reflections of it appear to remain in local speech forms. The task of the comparative study of Baltic and Slavic, therefore, is not the theoretically straightforward (but practically impossible) one of establishing Schleicherian Stammbaum relations, but the more subtle (and moderately feasible) one of elucidating the prehistoric spatio-temporal differentiation of a Schmidtian dialect area.

In the Slavic segment of this prehistoric dialect continuum no long-established internal divisions have been convincingly reconstructed on the basis of the attested Slavic languages.

The phonological and morphological differences among the modern Slavic languages form isoglosses of two geometric types, chords and circles. The chords bisect the language family one way or another, separating an innovating segment from a non-innovating one or separating from each other two alternative innovations. The circular isoglosses separate peripheral dialects from more central ones, reflecting differences in the rate of development, which generally was greater nearer the centre than on the periphery of the speech area during the period of territorial expansion. As an illustration, consider the development of (low vowel) diphthongs ending in a liquid: a chord separates East Slavic vowel epenthesis from West and South Slavic, which show metathesis (contrast PS uĀRNĀ- 'crow' > Russ. voróna, but US wróna, Pol. wrona, Cz. vrána, SC vr̀ana, Bulg. vrána); but both on the north-western and on the southern periphery liquid diphthongs remain unchanged (cf. Pb. *Wôrnó* 'crow', Bulg. *Várna* (toponym)).

It is clear that the circular isoglosses arose during the period of expansion. Apparently the chord-like isoglosses did so too. But it is possible that some lexical isoglosses can be projected back into the period before the expansion (Martynov 1981) and that one can eventually form a coherent account of the pre-expansion Slavic dialects and their relations to the lost intermediate dialects between Slavic and Baltic; cf. Andersen 1996.

Periodization of Common Slavic

In a realistic account of the prehistory and early history of Slavic, it is useful to distinguish three broad periods, Pre-Slavic, Common Slavic, and historical Slavic.

First, there is an initial period between the chronological stages associated with Proto-Indo-European and Proto-Slavic. This is a period characterized by developments the later Slavic dialects share with other IE dialects. These changes collectively constitute Slavic as distinct from the other branches of Indo-European. This period may be called Pre-Slavic.

Second, there is a Common Slavic period characterized by innovations that are specifically Slavic, and which are shared by all or several of the historically documented Slavic languages.

Developments occurring in Early Common Slavic appear to be shared by all the prehistoric dialects, whereas Late Common Slavic developments typically either affect only part of the Slavic speech area or yield different results in different parts of this area. But in reality there is no clear-cut boundary between these two phases of the Common Slavic period.

When it is necessary to refer to individual parts of the Common Slavic speech area, this may be done with such designations as 'the Pre-East Slavic dialects', 'the Pre-Serbo-Croatian-Slovenian dialects' or 'the Pre-Polish dialects' of Common Slavic.

Finally there is the historical period, which begins at different times in different parts of the Slavic language area. In purely linguistic terms, this period is not clearly separate from the Common Slavic period. Certain developments that began in prehistory, and which are Common Slavic in the sense that they are common to several of the individual Slavic languages, continue well into the historical period, even while the dialectal differentiation of all parts of the Slavic speech area continues. But what defines the historical period is the emergence and formation, besides the spoken medium, of written standards, local and regional, and the gradual establishment of the historical traditions of the modern national languages, one after another.

Slavic and IE handbooks traditionally cite prehistoric Slavic word forms in a very shallow reconstruction, which ignores theoretical advances and factual discoveries made in the twentieth century. Forms in this purely conventional notation will here be labelled Late Common Slavic (LCS). When such forms are phonologically identifiable with forms attested in OCS, they will not be asterisked (e.g. LCS *žena* 'woman' = OCS *žena*, LCS *jĭmę* 'name' = OCS *imę*); if they are identical to forms attested early outside the OCS corpus, their provenience will be specified (e.g. LCS (ORuss.) *jablŭko* 'apple'). When conventionally written LCS forms differ from the attested dialects, they will be asterisked and contrasted with relevant attested forms (e.g., LCS *vĭlkŭ*, OCS *vlĭkŭ*, ORuss. *vŭlkŭ*, Pol. *wilk* 'wolf'). In addition, reconstructed forms will be cited in terms of the Proto-Slavic (PS) phoneme inventory; these will be written in small capitals and not asterisked. Proto-Slavic is understood as the most distant stage(s) of Slavic that can be reached by the methods of comparative and internal reconstruction from within Slavic. In reconstructing individual Proto-Slavic word forms information from the other IE languages will naturally be used. This is especially so, for instance, with regard to many grammatical morphemes which cannot be reconstructed on the basis of Slavic data alone.

The Oldest Attestation

The textual attestation of Slavic begins with the creation of Old Church Slavonic in the mid-800s (cf. p. 415). Some of the extant (copies of) OCS texts are written in the glagolitic alphabet (Russ. *glagolica*) designed by Constantine (St Cyril), others in an adaptation of the Greek alphabet misnamed Cyrillic (Russ. *cirilica*).

The East Slavic written traditions reach back to the eleventh century (earliest dated texts *c.* 1050), consisting of texts in a rich variety of genres, written in Church Slavonic with widely varying degrees of Old Russian admixture in different genres. Local writing traditions develop into early forms of Russian (the language of Novgorod from the eleventh century, the chancellery language of Muscovy from the fourteenth century on), Belarusian (the administrative language of the Grand Duchy of Lithuania, fifteenth to seventeenth century) and Ukrainian (sixteenth to seventeenth century).

There is a rich, continuous attestation of Polish going back to the fourteenth century, but copies of earlier texts document the existence of a literate culture before that date. Old Czech is established as a language of literature *c.* 1300. The native tradition is eclipsed in the seventeenth century due to the spread of German, but resurrected at the end of the eighteenth century. At this time, too, Slovak is established as a separate language. Kashubian and the two Sorbian languages are first reduced to writing in the sixteenth century in connection with the Lutheran Reformation.

This is true of Slovenian as well, though there is one isolated text from the tenth century (the so-called Freising Fragment). Croatia and Serbia continue Church Slavonic traditions with notable local developments along the Croatian coast in the twelfth to sixteenth century in Ragusa (Dubrovnik) from the sixteenth century on, and since the eighteenth century with a growing tendency toward a unified Serbo-Croatian written language. Bulgaria and Macedonia, too, continue Church Slavonic traditions through Middle Bulgarian (eleventh to fifteenth centuries) into modern times, with the earliest texts intended to reflect the spoken language dating only from the eighteenth to nineteenth century. (Cf. Schenker and Stankiewicz 1980.)

Phonology: The Pre-Slavic Period

The Proto-Slavic phoneme inventory comprises the following segments:

Vowels		Sonorants		Obstruents				
I Ī	U Ū	M	N	P B	T D	K G		
E Ē	A Ā		L R		S Z	X		

The short high vowels have non-syllabic variants before a vowel; they eventually turn into LCS /j/ and /v/. Syllable peaks are simple or complex. Simple peaks consist of a single vowel. Complex syllable peaks consist of a low vowel followed by a short high vowel (oral diphthongs), or of any vowel followed by a nasal consonant (nasal diphthongs) or by a liquid consonant (liquid diphthongs). Obstruents and obstruent clusters occur both as syllable onsets and as syllable codas.

The following set of regular obstruent correspondences sums up the Pre-Slavic changes enumerated in the following five sections.

PIE	p	b	b^h	t	d	d^h	$\hat{k}$	$\hat{g}$	$\hat{g}^h$	k	g	g^h	k^w	g^w	g^{wh}	s
PS	P	B	B	T	D	D	S	Z	Z	K	G	G	K	G	G	X, S

The Labiovelar Stops

The labiovelar stops lose their labialization.

> PIE *$k^w ejh_1$- 'rest' > PS PA-KĒI-TĒI (LCS *počiti* 'to rest')
> PIE *kes- 'comb' > PS KES-Ā-TĒI (LCS *česati* 'to comb')
> PIE *$g^w en$- 'woman' > PS GEN-Ā- (LCS *žena* 'woman')
> PIE *$gerh_2 ōw$- 'crane' > PS GERĀU-IA- (LCS *žeravjĭ*, Ch.S *žeravlĭ*, Russ. *žurávl'* 'crane')
> PIE *$g^{wh} er$- 'hot' > PS GAR-Ē-TĒI (LCS *gorěti* 'to burn; intr.')
> PIE *$g^h osti$- > PS GAST-I- (LCS *gostĭ* 'guest').

The RUKI-change

Proto-Indo-European /s/ develops a marked allophone after PIE /i u r k g g^h/; the marked allophone (approximately [ṣ] is subsequently phonologized (cf. next section) and retracted, yielding PS /x/.

PIE *pejs- 'crush' > PS PIX-EN-IK-Ā- (LCS pišenica 'wheat')
PIE *saws- 'dry' > PS SAUX-A- (LCS suxŭ 'dry')
PIE *wer-s- 'high' > PS UIRX-U- (LCS (ORuss.) vĭrxŭ, OCS vrĭxŭ 'top, peak')
PIE *lejkʷ- 'leave', *lejkʷ-so- > PS LEIK-X-A- (LCS lixŭ 'excessive')
PIE *s preceding a sonorant:
PIE *gʷʰejh₁-, *gʷʰih₁-sl-eh₂ 'vein, sinew' > PS GI-XL-Ā- (LCS žila 'vein, sinew')
PIE *lewk- 'light', *lowk-sn-eh₂ > PS LAUK-XN-Ā- (LCS luna 'moon')

For initial /x/, see Gołąb (1973). Before a stop, the [ṣ]-allophone merges with the spirantized allophone of PIE /k̂/, eventually yielding PS /s/; hence the /x/ ~ /s/ alternations in the sigmatic aorist illustrated in **The Aorist**, p. 446. For other morphophonemic consequences of this change, see next section.

The Satəm Assibilation

The PIE palatal stops are affricated and then spirantized and merge with the [s] and [z] allophones of PIE /s/ (cf. **Sequential Constraints**, p. 425), yielding PS /s z/. For example, PIE *k̂lew- 'hear' > PS SLAU-XA- (LCS sluxŭ 'hearing, rumour'), PIE *ĝneh₃- 'know' > PS ZNĀ-TĒI (LCS znati 'to know'), PIE *ĝʰej-mn- 'winter' > PS ZEIM-Ā- (LCS zima 'winter') (cf. Trubačev 1973).

In a number of etyma, PS has irregular reflexes of PIE palatal stops, e.g. PIE *k̂erh₁- 'horn' > PS SIR-N-Ā- 'roe-deer' and KĀR-U-Ā- 'cow' (LCS *sĭrna, *korva, ORuss. sĭrna, korova); PIE *ĝʰerdʰ- > PS ZARD-A- 'stake' and GARD-A- 'enclosure' (LCS *zordŭ, *gordŭ, Russ. dialect (o-)zoród 'drying rack', Russ. górod 'town'). For some etyma such irregular correspondences (traditionally called Gutturalwechsel) involve Baltic and/or Indo-Iranian as well. Compare PIE *k̂lew- 'hear' > PS SLAU-XA- (LCS sluxŭ 'hearing, rumour'), Li. šlóvė 'fame' and klausýti 'listen', Skt śrávaḥ 'fame'; PIE *ĝʰan-s- > PS GANS-I- (LCS (Ch.S) gǫsĭ 'goose'), Li. žąsìs, Skt haṃsáḥ. These irregular correspondences may be due to early culturally motivated borrowing from kentum dialects (cf. Trubačev). Some may reflect a (Pre-)Proto-Indo-European neutralization rule replacing palatals with plain velars in certain environments (cf. Gamkrelidze and Ivanov 1984: 109ff.).

Since PIE *k̂ merges with the [s]-allophone of PIE /s/, the /s/ ~ /x/ alternations that result from the RUKI-change are synchronically derivable from underlying /x/; subsequently the /x/-alterant is consistently generalized so that it follows any vowel (cf. Andersen 1968). Hence, besides such aorist forms as LCS pixŭ 'I drank' (< PS PĒI-X-AM, PIE *peh₁i- 'drink'), LCS byxŭ 'I was' (< PS BŪ-X-AM, PIE *bʰewh₁- 'be'), we find LCS znaxŭ 'I knew' (< PS ZNĀ-X-AM, PIE *ĝneh₃- 'know'), LCS mĭněxŭ 'I thought' (< PS MIN-Ē-X-AM, PIE *men- 'think'), etc. Within the Old Church Slavonic corpus, older forms of the types jęsŭ 'I took' (< PS IM-S-AM, PIE *h₁em- 'take'), jasŭ

'I ate' (< PS ĒD-S-AM, PIE *h_1ed- 'eat') are replaced by the younger *jęxŭ*, *jaxŭ*, etc. The same analogical levelling in favour of /x/ can be assumed in word-final position for certain desinences, cf. **Nominal Morphology**, p. 437.

The Loss of the Aspirates
The PIE voiced aspirates merge with their unaspirated counterparts:

PIE *b^her- 'carry' > PS BER-ĀM (LCS *berǫ* 'I gather')
PIE *bel- 'more' > PS BAL-IIX-I (LCS *bolı̌ši* 'bigger (nom. sg. f.')
PIE *d^heh_1- 'put' > PS DĒ-TĒI (LCS *děti* 'to put')
PIE *dem- 'build' > PS DAM-U- (LCS *domŭ* 'house')
PIE *g^host-i- > PS GAST-I- (LCS *gostı̌* 'guest')
PIE *gal-so- 'call' > PS GAL-SA- (LCS *golsŭ, OCS *glasŭ* 'voice')
PIE *$g^{wh}er$- 'hot' > PS GAR-Ē-TĒI (LCS *gorěti* 'to burn intrans')
PIE *g^wow- 'ox' > PS GAU-INA- (LCS *govı̌no, Russ. *govnó* 'dung').

In postvocalic position, this merger appears to leave a difference in quantity in the preceding vowel. Contrast the short vowels before aspirates in PIE *neb^h-os- 'cloud' > PS NEB-AS- (LCS *nebo* 'sky'), PIE *wed^h- 'lead' > PS UED-ĀM (LCS *vedǫ* 'I lead'), with the long vowels before plain voiced stops in PIE *ab-l- > PS ĀBL-UKA- (LCS (ORuss.) *jabl̆ŭko* 'apple'), PIE *sed- 'sit' > PS SĒD-Ē-TĒI (LCS *sěděti* 'to sit'), PIE *b^heg^w- 'flee' > PS BĒG-Ē-TĒI (LCS *běžati* 'to flee').

The merger of the two obstruent series is shared with Baltic, which shows the same vowel lengthening before voiced stops, as discovered by Winter (1978). Viewed in terms of the glottalic theory, the change can be interpreted as the transfer of the glottalic feature from stops to preceding vowels (e.g. PIE /-ed-/ vs /-et'-/ is rephonologized as /-ed-/ vs /-e'd-/; Pre-Slavic /-e'd-/ subsequently yields long vowel with acute accent); thus Kortlandt (1978), Gamkrelidze and Ivanov (1984: 76f). The articulatory and perceptual aspects of this putative change are in need of clarification.

Sequential Constraints
Proto-Slavic obstruent clusters are voiced or voiceless throughout depending on the last segment:

PIE *mis-d^ho- 'wage' > PS MIZD-Ā- (LCS *mı̌zda* 'wage')
PIE *$we\hat{g}^h$- 'convey' > PS UEZ-ĀM, UES-TĒI (LCS *vezǫ, vesti* 'to convey (1sg., inf.)').

PIE clusters of dental stops are dissimilated to /s/ + stop:

PIE *wed^h- 'lead' > PS UED-ĀM, UES-TĒI (LCS *vedǫ, vesti* 'to lead (1sg., inf.)')
PIE *$(s)k^wejd$- 'separate' > PS KĒIS-TA- (LCS *čistŭ* 'pure')

cf. Chapter 2, **Dental plus Dental**, p. 40.

PIE clusters *sr, *zr change to PS str, zdr, for example, PIE *srew- 'flow' > PS AB-STRAU-A- (LCS *ostrovŭ* 'island'); PIE *swe-sr- 'sister' > PS SESTR-Ā- (LCS *sestra* 'sister'); PIE *ak̂-ro- 'sharp' > PS AST-RA- (LCS *ostrŭ* 'sharp').

Laryngeals

Laryngeals become syllabic only after an obstruent in initial consonant sequences, where they are identified with PS A; for example, PIE *sph₁-ro- 'prospering' > PS SPA-RA- 'abundant' (LCS *sporŭ*), PIE *sth₂- 'stand' PS STA- (I)Ē-TĒI 'to stand' (LCS *stojati*). Medial between consonants they are lost, for example, PIE *dʰugh₂-ter- 'daughter' > PS DUK-TER- (LCS *dŭtjer-*, OCS *dŭšter-*). Laryngeals are lost, leaving compensatory length and acute accent on any preceding syllable peak, for example, PIE *speh₁- 'prosper' > PS SPĒ- TĒI 'succeed' (LCS *spěti* 'progress'); PIE *steh₂- 'stand' > PS STĀ-TĒI (LCS *stati* 'go and stand, arise'). The resulting difference between long and short diphthongs is evidenced only in the metathesized initial liquid diphthongs, for example, PIE *arh₁- 'plough' > PS AR-Ā-TĒI 'to plough', but ĀR-DLA- 'plough' (LCS *oráti, *órdlo*, Russ. *orát', rálo*, Pol. *orać, radło*), contrast PIE *horbʰ- 'orphaned' > PS ARB-A- 'slave' (LCS *õrbŭ*, ORuss. *robŭ*, Pol. *robek*), and only in the north Slavic languages (cf. OCS *orati, ralo, rabŭ*). In other diphthongs and in non-initial liquid diphthongs quantity is lost, and only the difference between acute and non-acute accent remains (cf. **Prosody**, p. 428).

Syllabic Sonorants

Proto-Indo-European syllabic sonorants (*R̥) change to PS *ıR and *uR. The conditioning of the two different outcomes has not been determined; perhaps it is basically phonological, but obscured by dialect interference; Baltic shows a similar diversity. Examples of PIE /r̥ l̥/:

> PIE *k̂r̥d- 'heart' > PS SIRD-IKA- (LCS (ORuss.) *sĭrdĭce*, OCS *srĭdĭce* 'heart')
>
> PIE *ĝr̥h-nó- 'ground' > PS ZIRN-A- (LCS (ORuss.) *zĭrno*, OCS *zrĭno* 'grain')
>
> PIE *wl̥kʷo- 'wolf' > PS UILK-A- (LCS *vĭlkŭ*, ORuss. *vŭlkŭ*, OCS *vlĭkŭ*, Pol. *wilk*)
>
> PIE *wl̥h-n-eh₂ 'wool' > PS UILN-Ā- (LCS *vĭlna*, ORuss. *vŭlna*, OCS *vlĭna*, Pol. *wełna*)
>
> PIE *gʷerh- 'swallow' > PS GŪR-DLA- (LCS (WSlav.) *gŭrdlo*, Cz. *hrdlo*, ORuss. *gŭrlo* 'throat').

The diphthongized syllabic nasals (PIE /n̥ m̥/) develop into nasal vowels in Common Slavic, (cf. p. 430) PS /ĭ/ + nasal being reflected as LCS, OCS /ɛ/ and PS /ū:/ + nasal as LCS (OCS) / > for example, PIE *(d)n̥ĝ-uh₂- 'tongue' > PS INZŪ-KA- (LCS *językŭ* 'tongue'); PIE *h₁em- 'take' > PS IM-TĒI

(LCS *jęti* 'to take'); PIE *b^hewh_1- 'be' > PS BŪ-N-D-ĀM (LCS *bǫdǫ* 'I shall be'). The expected reflex of a nasal is missing before consonant in a few lexemes, for example PIE *(d)ḱṃtó- 'hundred' > PS SUT-A- (LCS *sŭto* 'hundred') and word-finally in certain desinences (cf. p. 430; Tables 14.1 and 14.2).

Like Baltic, Germanic, Greek and Armenian, Slavic has reflexes of syllabic sonorants also before vowels:

PIE *stelh- 'spread' > PS STEL-IĀM, STIL-Ā-TĒI (LCS *steljǫ, stǐlati* 'to spread (1sg., inf.).')

PIE *b^her- 'carry' > PS BER-AM, BIR-Ā-TĒI (LCS *berǫ, bǐrati* 'to gather (1sg., inf.)')

PIE *$d^hwṛ$- > PS DUIR-I- (LCS *dvǐrǐ* 'door')

PIE *g^when- 'strike' > PS GEN-ĀM, GUN-Ā-TĒI (LCS *ženǫ, gŭnati* 'to drive, chase (1sg., inf.)').

Vowel Correspondences

Here is a summary of the regular vowel correspondences between Proto-Indo-European and Proto-Slavic:

PIE	i	ī	e	ē	a	ā	o	ō	u	ū
PS	I	Ī	E	Ē	A	Ā	A	Ā	U	Ū

PIE *o, *a merge in PS A, PIE *ō, *ā merge in PS Ā. PS A and Ā are differentiated as /o/ and /a/ in the Second CS Vowel Shift (cf. **The Earliest Vowel Shifts**, p. 429):

PIE *to- 'that' > PS TA (LCS *to*)

PIE *sal- 'salt' > PS SAL-I- (LCS *solǐ*)

PIE *ĝneh₃- 'know' > PS ZNĀ-TĒI (LCS *znati*)

PIE *$b^hrā$-ter- 'brother' > PS BRĀ-TR-A- (LCS *bratrŭ*).

These mergers are similar to vowel mergers in Baltic and in Germanic and for this reason have been thought of as shared areal innovations.

Some changes affecting vowels before non-syllabic /i u/ may belong to the Pre-Slavic period: (a) /e/ > /i/ before [j], for example, PIE *trej- 'three' > PS TRII-ES, TRI (LCS *trǐje, tri* 'three; (nom. m., n.-f.)'). (b) With certain limitations, subsequently obscured by analogical levelling, /e/ > /a/ before non-syllabic /u/, whereas tautosyllabic /ẽw/ > /iau/ (see further p. 431): PIE *newo- 'new' > PS NAU-A- (LCS *novŭ*); PIE *plew- 'float' > PS PLAU-E-TI, PLAU-TĒI, PLAU-T-IĀ- (LCS *plovǫ, pluti* 'to float (1sg. pres. inf.)', LCS *plutja*, OCS *plušta*, Pol. *płuca* 'lungs', but PLIAU-T-IĀ- in SC *pljuća* 'liver', ORuss. *pluča*, Cz. *plíce*). The changes affecting /ẽw/-sequences have parallels in Baltic (cf. Arumaa 1964: 86ff.).

Prosody

Proto-Slavic inherits from Proto-Indo-European a free and mobile accent, and from Pre-Slavic developments such as those mentioned in **The Loss of the Aspirates**, p. 425 and **Laryngeals**, p. 426, also a distinction between acute (glottalized or high-toned) and circumflex (not so characterized) syllabics. In the Pre-Slavic period, several phonetically motivated changes in the place of accent occur, and the distinction between acute and circumflex syllabics is lost in unaccented syllables (Dybo *et al.* 1990). The outcome of these changes is the state reconstructible for Proto-Slavic in which there is a distinction between unaccented morphological words (enclinomena) and accented (orthotonic) morphological words; a distinction between two accents, the acute (a high-toned syllabic followed by a low-toned one) and the neo-acute (a high-toned syllabic followed by another high-toned one), and rules assigning prominence (ictus) to phonological words and phrases, making particular reference to the presence of enclinomena and clitics (enclitics or proclitics) (cf. Jakobson 1971b).

Phonology: The Common Slavic Period

During the Common Slavic period, the reconstructed phonology of Proto-Slavic goes through a series of developments which diversify the expanding Slavic language area.

The developments have traditionally been recognized as manifestations of two universal tendencies. The first of these ('the Law of Open Syllables' or 'the Law of Rising Sonority') includes the loss of syllable codas (p. 429), the monophthongization of oral diphthongs (p. 429) and of nasal diphthongs (p. 430), the elimination of liquid diphthongs through vowel epenthesis, metathesis and monophthongization (p. 430), the elimination of glides in complex syllable onsets (p. 431) and the development of prothetic glides before initial vowels (p. 431). The second tendency (traditionally, 'the Law of Syllabic Synharmonism') includes not only intra-syllabic tonality assimilations, such as the palatalization of velars before front vowels (p. 429) and the fronting of back vowels after palatal consonants (p. 432), but also inter-syllabic assimilations, progressive as well as regressive (p. 432). The actualization of these two drifts is punctuated by three Common Slavic vowel shifts with which they interact intricately (cf. Andersen 1986).

Although these developments occur in all the Slavic dialects, they result in great dialect diversity, for some changes affect only parts of the language area, some are in part incompletely carried through, and some yield different results in different areas, in part because of geographic differences in relative chronology. The following brief survey includes only the most important generalities.

The Earliest Vowel Shifts and Velar Palatalizations

In the *First Velar Palatalization*, PS к, г, х > /č ž š/ before (PS) front vowels (including non-syllabic /i/); for example, PS кеѕ-ā-теі (PIE *kes- 'comb') > LCS *česati* 'to comb', PS гіu-а- (PIE *$g^w ih$-wo-) > LCS *živŭ* 'alive', PS хід-l-а- (PIE *sed- 'sit, ride') > LCS *šĭdlŭ*, OCS *šĭlŭ* 'gone (m. sg.)'; PS дauх-ıā- (PIE *$d^h wes$- 'breath') > LCS *duša* 'soul'. The later merger of CS /ē/ with /ā/ after palatals, for example, PS ѕта-(ı)е-теі (PIE *sth_2- 'stand') > LCS *stojati* 'to stand'; PS лег-е-теі (PIE *leg^h- 'lie') > LCS *ležati* 'to lie', is thought to be connected with the First Velar Palatalization.

In the *First CS Vowel Shift*, PS ʊ > /ȳ/ [ɨː] and the oral diphthongs are monophthongized and in part merge with existing long vowels: PS еі, ɛі > /ī/, аі, āі > /ē/, еu, ɛu > /(j)ū/, аu, āu > /ū/; but аі, āі > /ī/ after non-syllabic /i/ (umlaut; see examples in the next paragraph; cf. p. 432) and in certain desinences (see PIE *t-oi below and Table 14.1, p. 435; Table 14.8; p. 445). The new vowel system: /ī i ȳ ū u ē e ā a/.

In the *Second CS Vowel Shift*, the difference between long and short vowels is reinterpreted as a (qualitative) distinction between tense (i y u ě a/ and lax vowels /ĭ ŭ e o/ (see further **Third CS Vowel Shift**, p. 432). Note the alternations conditioned by syllable boundaries in such examples as CS *t-a^{s}i-ām^s, *t-ai^s-mi^s, *t-ai^s (PIE *t-oi 'those') > LCS *tojǫ, těmĭ, ti* 'that (instr. sg. f., m., nom. pl. m.)', CS *j-a^{s}i-ām^s, *j-ai^s-mi^s, *j-ai^s (PIE *i-s, *jos 'he, it') > LCS *jejǫ, jimĭ, ji* 'he, it (instr. sg. m., nom. pl. m.)'; CS *sē^{s}u-e^{s}ra--x^s, *sēu^s-ia-x^s (PIE *$seh_1 w$- 'left; north') > LCS *sěverŭ* 'north, north wind', *šujĭ* 'left (side)'; CS *ab^s-stra^{s}u-a-x^s, *strau^s-iā^s (PIE *srew- 'flow') > LCS *ostrovŭ* 'island', *struja* 'stream'.

The *Second Velar Palatalization* occurs after the First CS Vowel Shift. In it, CS /k g x/ > /ć з́ ś/ (approximately IPA [c ɟ s], later mostly [t͡s] z s]): (a) before front vowel (the reflexes of PS аі, āі, /ī ē/, and in borrowings), but not in northern East Slavic dialects, for example, PS каіл-а- (PIE *kaj-lo-) > LCS (ONovg. dialect) *kělŭ*, OCS *cělŭ*, Sn, Russ. *cel*, Cz. *celý*, Pol. *cały* 'whole, healthy', Gmc *kirkō* (OHG *chirihha*) > LCS *kĭrky*, OCS *crĭky* 'church'; (b) before non-syllabic /u/ followed by any front vowel, for example, PS куаіт-а- > LCS *květŭ*, OCS *cvětŭ*, SC, Sn, Russ. *cvét*, but not in West Slavic and some parts of East Slavic, cf. Cz. *květ*, Pol. *kwiat*, U *kvit* 'flower' beside *cvit* 'bloom', NR dialect *kv'et*. The outcomes of this change are not uniform: (a) PS /x/ yields /s'/ (IPA [s^j]) and /s/ in East Slavic and South Slavic, but /š/ (IPA [ʃ] in West Slavic, for example, PS хаір-а- (PIE *(s)koj-ro- 'grey') > LCS (ONovg. dialect) *xěr-*, OCS *sěrŭ*, Sn, Russ. *sér*, but Cz. *šerý*, Pol. *szary* 'grey'; (b) the palatalized reflex of PS г is lenited (to /z'/ or /z/) everywhere except in some Lechitic dialects and in Old Church Slavonic (cf. p. 432).

Changes in Syllable Structure

Syllable-final obstruents are lost, for example, PS греб^s-теі, гре^{s}б-āм, греб^s-ѕ-ам (PIE *$g^h reb^h$- 'dig') > LCS *greti, grebǫ, grěsŭ* 'to dig (inf., 1sg.

pres., aor.)', PS UIRT-É-TÉI, UIRT-NŪ-TÉI, UERT-MEN- (PIE *wert- 'turn') > LCS
*vĭrtěti, *vĭrnǫti, *vermę, OCS vrĭtěti 'to turn', Ch.S vrĭnǫti 'to return', OCS
vrěmę 'time', PS PEK-ĀM, PĒK-X-AM, PAK-TA- (PIE *pekʷ- 'cook') > LCS
*pekǫ₁ *pěxŭ 'to bake (1sg. pres., aor.)', potŭ 'sweat' (but before front vowel,
PS -KT- merges with prevocalic PS -TI-, LCS /tj/; see p. 431); PS GI-XL-Ā-
(PIE *gʷʰih₁-sl-eh₂) > LCS žila 'vein, sinew', PS LAUK-XN-Ā- (PIE *lowk-
sn-eh₂) > LCS luna 'moon'. Areal diversity: PS -TL-, -DL- are simplified
to -l- in South Slavic and East Slavic but not in West Slavic, for example,
PS KIT-L-AI (PIE *(s)kʷejt- 'consider') > LCS *čĭtli, OCS čĭli, Russ. -čli
vs Cz. čtli, OPol. cztli 'to read (result. pcpl., m. pl.)', PS UED-L-AI (PIE
*wedʰ- 'lead') > LCS *vedli, OCS veli, Russ. velí vs Cz. vedli, Pol. wiedli
'led (result. pcpl., m. pl.)'. In northern East Slavic, these clusters are replaced
by -kl-, -gl- (cf. Russ. NW-dialect so-čkle, vegli) in conformity with the
Baltic substratum.

Nasal diphthongs: in (CS ĭn ĭm ěn ěm ŭn ŭm ăn ăm/), the /n/ vs /m/
distinction is lost and nasality transferred to the vowel. Later /ĭ/ merges with
/ę/ and /ŭ/ with /ą/, yielding LCS (OCS) /ę ǫ/, for example:

PS INZŪ-KA- (PIE *(d)ņ ĝʰ-uh₂-) > LCS językŭ 'tongue'
PS DENT-SN-Ā- (PIE *h₁d-ent- 'tooth') > LCS *dęsna (Pol. dialect dziąsna
'gum')
PS BŪ-N-D-ĀM (PIE *bʰewh₁- 'become') > LCS bǫdǫ 'to be (1 sg. fut.)'
PS ZAMB-A- (PIE *ĝombʰo- 'peg') > LCS zǫbŭ 'tooth'.

In final syllables the developments are different and in part inscrutable (cf.
pp. 435–6, p. 434). Areal diversity arises as the nasal vowels are denasalized
(e.g. Sn jézik, zôb), mostly after a low/high differentiation of the front and
back nasal vowels (SC jèzik, zûb, Cz. Sk. jazyk, zub, U-Bel.-Russ. jazýk, zúb).
The Lechitic languages retain nasal vowels, but with diverse secondary
qualitative changes, and diphthongized before stops, for example, Pol. język,
dziąsna, będę, ząb [jĕzɨk ʒʲɔ̃sna bɛndɛ zɔmp].

Liquid diphthongs: There is no uniformity in the development of the liquid
diphthongs.

(a) Word-initially, liquid diphthongs are metathesized. The distinction
    between long and short diphthongs is reflected in most of West Slavic and
    in East Slavic (PS ĀRT-: ART- > CS RāT-: RaT- > LCS RăT-: RoT-), but
    South Slavic loses it before the metathesis (PS ĀRT-: ART- > ART- > CS
    RĀT > LCS RĀT-) and preserves only an accentual difference. Compare
    PS ĀR-MA- (PIE *arh-mo- 'arm') > LCS *órmo, ORuss. ramo, OCS
    ramo, SC rȁmo 'shoulder', PS ARS-TA- (PIE *h₂erd- 'tall, grow') > LCS
    *õrstŭ, ORuss. rostŭ, OCS rastŭ, SC rȁst 'stature, growth' (cf. **Laryn-
    geals**, p. 426).

(b) In medial position, low-vowel liquid diphthongs are metathesized after the loss of quantity in diphthongs, before the Second CS Vowel Shift in South Slavic and in Czech–Slovak (TᴀRT > CS TRāT > LCS TRǎT), but after the Vowel Shift in the rest of West Slavic (TᴀRT > LCS TōRT > TRŏT), whereas East Slavic develops its so-called 'pleophony' (TᴀRT > ToRoT). Compare PS ᴋᴀʀʟ-ɪᴀ- (< Gmc *Karl* 'Charlemagne'), ᴍᴀʟᴛ-ᴀ- (PIE *mel-* 'crush') > SC *krâlj, mlât*, Cz. *král, mlat*, Pol. *król, młot*, Russ. *koról'* 'king', *mólot* 'hammer'. But in some peripheral areas these liquid diphthongs remain partly or completely unchanged (cf. p. 421).

(c) The areas that metathesize low-vowel diphthongs at first change high-vowel diphthongs to syllabic liquids, but later diverse secondary developments occur. Compare PS ᴜɪʀx-ᴜ- (PIE *wer-s-* 'high') > LCS *vǐrxǔ* 'top'; PS ɢᴏʀ-ᴅʟᴀ- (PIE *gʷerh-* 'swallow') > LCS *gǔrdlo* 'throat'; PS ᴜɪʟᴋ-ᴀ- (PIE *wl̥kʷo-* 'wolf') > LCS *vǐlkǔ* 'wolf'; PS sᴜʟɴ-ɪᴋᴀ- (PIE *seh₂w-el/n-* 'sun') > LCS *sǔlnǐće* 'sun': SC *vr̂h, gr̂lo, vûk, sûnce*, Cz. *vrch, hrdlo, vlk, slunce*, Pol. *wierzch, gardło, wilk, słońce*. In East Slavic, these diphthongs remain (ORuss. *vǐrxǔ, gǔrlo, vǔlkǔ, sǔlnǐce*, Russ. *vérx, górlo, vólk, sólnce*), but in northern East Slavic they develop parallel to the low-vowel diphthongs (e.g. Russ. *vérx, sólnce*, Russ. dial *v'er'óx, pó-solon'* 'from east to west, clockwise').

Glides in onset clusters: After the First CS Vowel Shift, non-syllabic PS ᴜ and ɪ are glides, /w j/; their LCS reflexes are /v j/. But after labials, /w/ is lost and /j/ changes to /ľ/ (IPA [ʎ] misnamed 'epenthetic *l*', for example, PS ᴜᴇɪᴅ-ᴇ̄-ᴛᴇ̄ɪ, ᴀʙ-ᴜᴇɪᴅ-ᴇ̄-ᴛᴇ̄ɪ (PIE *wejd-* 'see') > LCS *viděti* 'to see', *obiděti* 'offend'; PS ʙᴜᴅ-ᴇ̄-ᴛᴇ̄ɪ, ʙᴇᴜᴅ-ᴀ̄ᴍ, ʙᴀᴜᴅ-ɪ-ᴛᴇ̄ɪ (PIE *bʰewdʰ-* 'observe') > LCS *bǔděti, bĺudǫ* (cf. **Vowel Correspondences**, p. 427), *buditi* 'to wake, I watch, to waken'. Dentals become palatal before /j/, and then /j/ is lost after all palatals, including the reflexes of the First Velar Palatalization; /s z n l r č ž š/ + /j/ uniformly yield LCS /š ž ń ĺ ŕ č ž š/. Late Common Slavic *tj* (which also continues PS -ᴋᴛ- before front vowel, see p. 429) and *dj* have diverse reflexes, compare PS sᴜᴀɪᴛ-ɪᴀ- (PIE *ḱwejt-* 'light') > LCS *světja* 'candle'; PS ɴᴀᴋᴛ-ɪ- (PIE *nekʷ-* 'night') > LCS *notjǐ*; PS ᴍᴇᴅ-ɪᴀ- (PIE *medʰi-* 'middle') > LCS *medja*: OCS *svěšta, noštǐ, mežda* 'road', SC *svéća, nôć, mèđa* 'balk', Sn *svéča, nòč, méja*, Cz. *svíce, noc, meze*, Pol. *świeca, noc, miedza*, Russ. *svečá, nóč', mežá*.

Prothetic glides: initial vowels develop prothetic glides at different times in the Common Slavic period and later, for example, PS ɪx (PIE *i-s*) > LCS *jǐ*, OCS *i* 'he (nom. sg. m.).'; PS ɪɴᴢᴏ-ᴋᴀ- (PIE *(d)n̥g-uh₂* 'tongue') > LCS *językǔ* 'tongue'; PS ᴜɴ (PIE *n̥-* 'in') > LCS *vǔ(n)-* 'in'; PS ᴏᴅ-ᴍᴇɴ- (PIE *uhdʰ-* 'udder') > LCS *vymę*, ORuss. *vymä* 'udder'; PS ᴇs-ᴍɪ (PIE *h₁es-* 'be') > LCS *jesmǐ* 'I am'; PS ᴇ̄s-ᴛᴇ̄ɪ, ᴇᴅ-ᴍɪ (PIE *h₁ed-* 'eat') > LCS *jěsti, jěmǐ* 'to eat (inf., 1sg. pres.)'; PS ᴀ̄ʙʟ-ᴜᴋᴀ- (PIE *ab-l-* 'apple') > LCS (ORuss.) *jablǔko* 'apple'.

Late Common Slavic Tonality Assimilations

The First and Second Velar Palatalizations (p. 429) are intrasyllabic, regressive assimilations. At the same time as the Second Palatalization, velars undergo an intersyllabic, progressive assimilation, traditionally termed the *Third Velar Palatalization*: /k g x/ > /ć ʒ ś/ between a high front vowel (/i ī į/) and a low back vowel (/a ā/, for example PS AU-IK-Ā- (PIE *h_3ew- 'sheep') > LCS *ovĭća, OCS ovĭca 'sheep'; PS STIG-Ā- (PIE *stejg^h- 'tread)' > LCS *stĭʒa, OCS stĭʒa 'path'; PS UIX-A- (PIE *wis- 'all') > LCS *vĭsĭ, OCS vĭsĭ 'all.' The outcomes are the same as for the Second Palatalization, that is, (a) PS x > /s/ s'/ or /š/: OCS vĭsĭ, Sn vès, Russ. vés', but OCz. veš, OPol. wszy [fši]; (b) /ʒ/, the palatalized reflex of Proto-Slovic G, is eventually lenited everywhere except in parts of Lechitic: PS KUNING-A- (< Gmc *kuning-az 'king') > LCS *kŭnęʒĭ, OCS kŭnęʒĭ, SC knêz, OCz. knēz, Russ. knjáz' 'prince', Pol. ksiądz [kʃɔnts] 'priest'; but unlike the Second Palatalization, the Third Palatalization does occur in northern East Slavic.

Umlaut: after the Third Palatalization, back vowels are fronted after any palatal consonant (an intrasyllabic, progressive assimilation). This change creates allomorphs (in inflection and derivation) of all suffixes beginning with a back vowel, for example, PS T-A-X, NĀS-IA-X, UIX-A-X, T-A, NĀS-IA, UIX-A > LCS t-ŭ vs naš-ĭ, vĭš-ĭ, t-o vs naš-e, vĭš-e 'that, our, all (nom. sg. m., n.)' (cf. umlaut in p. 429 and the 'twofold declensions' in **Nominal Morphology**, p. 434). But the change is not limited to affixes; compare PS IUG-A- (PIE *jug-o- 'yoke') > LCS jĭgo 'yoke'; PS SIŪ-TĒI (PIE *sewh- 'sew') > LCS šiti 'to sew'.

Dental and labial consonants become *sharped* (palatalized, as a secondary manner feature) before all front vowels, remaining plain before back vowels. This intrasyllabic regressive assimilation develops into phonemic sharping (palatalization as a secondary manner feature) in West Slavic and East Slavic (cf. **Third CS Vowel Shift** below).

Front vowels develop back-vowel off-glides (allophonic *breaking*) unless followed by a sharped consonant (an inter-syllabic, progressive assimilation). Later, dialectal reinterpretations of these allophones produce a variety of vowel alternations such as SC dialect *viditi ~ videl*, Pol. *widzieć ~ widział* (LCS *viděti, viděl* 'to see; (inf., result. ptcpl. m. sg.)'), Cz. *přítel ~ přátel*, *pět ~ pátý* (LCS *prijatelĭ, prijatelŭ* 'friend (nom. sg., gen. pl.)', LCS *pętĭ, pętŭ* 'five, fifth'), Russ. *žénskij ~ žóny*, Pol. *żeński ~ żona* (LCs *ženĭskŭ, žena* 'female, woman').

Third CS Vowel Shift

This is traditionally called 'the Fall of the Jers'. The two lax high vowels (known by their Old Church Slavonic spelling names *jerĭ* and *jerŭ* as 'jers') cease to be identified as the lax counterparts of (LCS) /i u/. In some dialects they are reinterpreted as /ə/, in others as /e o/, but only in certain environments, termed strong; in all other environments, termed weak, they are lost; generally, jers are weak when word-final, or when the following syllable contains a vowel other than a jer (e.g. LCS *kŭnęʒĭ, ORuss. kŭnäʒĭ > Russ. knjáz' /knʲazʲ/ 'prince'), and they are strong when the following syllable contains a weak jer (e.g. PS DI-N-I- (PIE *di-n-), LCS (ORuss.) dĭnĭ > Russ. dén' /dʲenʲ/ 'day'; PS SUP-NA- (PIE *swep-no-) LCS (ORuss.) sŭnŭ > Russ. són 'sleep').

The vowel shift has widely different outcomes in different dialects depending on the presence or absence of nasal vowels, on differences in quality among oral vowels, on the presence or absence of phonemic sharping in consonants, and on the development of prosodic features, quantity as well as accent. It seems typologically significant that sharping becomes phonemic in the East Slavic and West Slavic languages, which give up the inherited pitch accent, but not in the South Slavic languages, where pitch accent (at least initially) persisted (cf. Jakobson 1971a).

Prosody
From the time of the Second CS Vowel Shift on, one can reconstruct notable differences among the Slavic dialects in word rhythm and tonal contours, which eventually lead to phonemic differences in the distribution of long and short vowels and in the value assigned to different prosodic dimensions. Russian, for instance, abandons phonemic quantity and the accent opposition, developing phonemic stress as the reflex of the Proto-Slavic acute, the neo-acute and the automatically assigned ictus of enclinomena. Czech, on the other hand, gives up phonemic accent, retaining phonemic quantity and automatic ictus on the first syllable of the word. Serbo-Croatian, again, preserves accent and quantity, but the difference between the two accents is reinterpreted as a difference in quantity. The great diversity of outcomes and their considerable regularity makes the accentual data of the Slavic languages quite reliable for reconstruction.

Inflectional Morphology
Proto-Slavic maintains the PIE nominal categories of gender (masculine, neuter and feminine) and number (singular, dual and plural), and of the original cases only the ablative is lost, having merged with the genitive. The diversity of declensional classes has been reduced, more so in adjectives than in substantives, and there is a growing correlation between gender and declensional class, which continues to strengthen in the individual Slavic languages. Umlaut produces new subparadigms (the twofold declensions; cf. **Nominal Morphology** below) in the Common Slavic period, but this allomorphy is greatly reduced or entirely lost in the historical languages. At the beginning of the attested period, the Slavic dialects innovate a morphological expression for animacy in certain substantival and adjectival paradigms: where nominative and accusative have syncretized through sound change, animate nouns (and their determiners and modifiers) in accusative

function take a genitive ending. Like Germanic and Baltic, Slavic grammaticizes a category of definiteness in the adjective, expressed (as in Baltic) by an enclitic pronoun.

Verb morphology, by contrast, is thoroughly different from the PIE state of affairs. Although many of the morphological means survive, the categories of aspect, tense, voice and mood have been recast.

Nominal Morphology: The Substantive

The comparison of Late Common Slavic with the other early IE languages permits the reconstruction of several Proto-Slavic declensional classes characterized by a vocalic stem formative (traditionally called *o/jo*-stems, *u*-stems, *ā/jā*-stems, *i*-stems) or a consonantal one (stems in PS -EN-, -MEN-, -ENT-, -ER-, -E/AS- or -O/-U^{S}U-/-UĀ- < PIE *-uh_2/-weh_2).

A number of PIE stem types have been fitted into these classes either directly or by means of productive derivational processes; compare PIE *$g^w en$- > PS GEN-Ā- (LCS *žena* 'woman'), PIE *$wodōr$- > PS UAD-Ā- (LCS *voda* 'water'), PIE *$pont$- > PS PANT-I- (LCS *pǫtĭ* 'road'), PIE *$h_3 nh_3 m$-en- > PS I-MEN (LCS *jĭmę* 'name'); and PIE *$swel/n$- > PS SUL-N-IKA- (LCS (ORuss.) *sŭlnĭće*, OCS *slŭnĭce* 'sun'); PIE *$ḱerd$- > PS SIRD-IKA- (LCS (ORuss.) *sĭrdĭće*, OCS *srĭdĭce* 'heart'); PIE *wlk^w-i-h > PS UILK-I-KĀ- (LCS *vĭlčĭća*, Russ. *volčica* 'she-wolf'), PIE *meh_1- 'measure' > PS MĒS-IN-KA- (LCS *měsęćĭ* 'moon, month'), PIE *$(d)ņĝ^h$-uh_2- 'tongue' > PS INZŌ-KA- (LCS *językŭ* 'tongue'); cf. Birnbaum (1972).

One cardinal change is the shift of the morphological boundary between stems and desinences, which is shown below. Due to the Common Slavic umlaut changes (**The Earliest Vowel Shifts**, p. 429, **Late Common Slavic Tonality Assimilations**, p. 432), *o*-stems and *jo*-stems develop different desinences (e.g. OCS *-ŭ/-ĭ*, *-ĕ/-i*, *-omĭ/-emĭ*, *-y/-ę*, *-ĕxŭ/-ixŭ*, *-y/-i*); similarly *ā*-stems and *jā*-stems. These so-called twofold declensions are unified in different ways in the historical languages and will not be discussed here. The class of *o/jo*-stems comprises masculines and neuters. The latter have special endings in the nominative-accusative singular (LCS *sel-o* 'village' with *-o* from PS T-A, LCS *to* 'that' or from the PIE *-e/os*- formative as in PS SLAU-AS-0, LCS *slov-o* 'word', for PIE *-om* (PS -AM) regularly yields LCS *-ŭ*; see below); also in the nominative-accusative dual (PS SEL-AI, LCS *sel-ě*) and nominative-accusative plural (PS SEL-Ā, LCS *sel-a*). The original neuter nominative-accusative singular desinence (PIE *-o-m*) was renewed (yielding LCS *-o*) only after neuters with final accent merged with the masculine *o*-stems (e.g. PIE *$dwor$-$ó$-m (n.) > PS DUAR-AM > LCS *dvorŭ* (m.) 'court, yard'). In the earliest attested Slavic, the class of *u*-stems is small; it includes only masculines (cf. PIE *$med^h u$-, PS MED-U, LCS *medŭ* 'honey (m.)') and is merging with the *o*-stems. The *ā/jā*-stems are feminine, except those that denote male humans. The class of *i*-stems is almost exclusively feminine with only a few handfuls of masculines, which gravitate

Table 14.1 Examples of vowel-stem paradigms

	o-stems		u-stems		ā-stems	
Singular						
Nom.	STAL-A~X >	stol-ŭ	DAM-U~X >	dom-ŭ	GEN-Ā >	žen-a
Acc.	STAL-A~M >	stol-ŭ	DAM-U~M >	dom-ŭ	GEN-Ā~M >	žen-ǫ
Gen.	STAL-A~AT >	stol-a	DAM-AU~X >	dom-u	GEN-? >	žen-y
Loc.	STAL-A~I >	stol-ě	DAM-ĂU~0 >	dom-u	GEN-Ā~I >	žen-ě
Dat.	STAL-? >	stol-u	DAM-AU~EI >	dom-ovi	GEN-Ā~I >	žen-ě
Instr.	STAL-Ă ≠	stol-omĭ	DAM-U~MI >	dom-ŭmĭ	GEN-Ā~M ≠	žen-ojǫ
Dual						
Nom.-Acc.	STAL-Ā >	stol-a	DAM-0 >	dom-y	GEN-AI >	žen-ě
Gen.-Loc.	STAL-0~AU >	stol-u	DAM-AU~AU >	dom-ovu	GEN-0~AU >	žen-u
Dat.-Instr.	STAL-A~MĂ >	stol-oma	DAM-U~MĂ >	dom-ŭma	GEN-Ā~MĂ >	žen-ama
Plural						
Nom.	STAL-0~AI >	stol-i	DAM-AU~EX >	dom-ove	GEN-Ā~? >	žen-y
Acc.	STAL-A~NS >	stol-y	DAM-U~NS >	dom-y	GEN-Ā~NS >	žen-y
Gen.	STAL-0~AM >	stol-ŭ	DAM-AU~AM >	dom-ovŭ	GEN-0~AM >	žen-ŭ
Loc.	STAL-AI~XU >	stol-ěxŭ	DAM-U~XU >	dom-ŭxŭ	GEN-Ā~XU >	žen-axŭ
Dat.	STAL-A~MAX >	stol-omŭ	DAM-U~MAX >	dom-ŭmŭ	GEN-Ā~MAX >	žen-amŭ
Instr.	STAL-AIS? >	stol-y	DAM-U~MĪX >	dom-ŭmi	GEN-Ā~MĬX >	žen-ami

Table 14.2 *i*-stem paradigms; consonantal stem paradigms

	i-stems		C-stems		Other C-stems types (nominative singular and genitive singular)
Singular					
Nom.	KAST-I-X >	kost-ĭ	SLAU-AS-0 >	slov-o	——
Acc.	KAST-I-M >	kost-ĭ	SLAU-AS-0 >	slov-o	KÁM-ĀN-S > kam-y
Gen.	KAST-EI-X >	kost-i	SLAU-ES-EX >	slov-es-e	KÁM-EN-EX > kam-en-e
Loc.	KAST-EI-0 >	kost-i	SLAU-ES-E >	slov-es-e	
Dat.	KAST-(EI)-EI >	kost-i	SLAU-ES-EI >	slov-es-i	UERT-MEN-0 > vert-mę
Instr.	KAST-EI-ĀM >	kost-ĭjǫ[1]	SLAU-ES-E-MI >	slov-es-emĭ	UERT-MEN-EX > vert-men-e
Dual					
Nom.-Acc.	KAST-I >	kost-i	SLAU-ES-Ā >	slov-es-a	
Gen.-Loc.	KAST-EI-ĀU >	kost-ĭju	SLAU-ES-ĀU >	slov-es-u	TEL-ENT-0 > tel-ę
Dat.-Instr.	KAST-I-MĀ >	kost-ĭma	SLAU-ES-? >	unattested	TEL-ENT-EX > tel-ęt-e
Plural					
Nom.	KAST-EI-X >	kost-i[2]	SLAU-ES-Ā >	slov-es-a[3]	
Acc.	KAST-I-NS >	kost-i	SLAU-ES-Ā >	slov-es-a	MÁ-TER-0 > mat-i
Gen.	KAST-EI-AM >	kost-ĭjĭ	SLAU-ES-AM >	slov-es-ŭ	MÁ-TER-EX > mat-er-e
Loc.	KAST-I-XU >	kost-ĭxĭ	SLAU-ES-E-XU >	slov-es-exŭ	
Dat.	KAST-I-MAX >	kost-ĭmŭ	SLAU-ES-E-MAX >	slov-es-emŭ	SUEKR-0-0 > svekr-y
Instr.	KAST-I-MIX >	kost-ĭmi	SLAU-ES-? >	slov-es-y	SUEKR-UU-EX > svekr-ŭv-e

Notes: [1]'Feminine *kost-ĭjǫ* 'bone', but masculine PANT-I-MI > *pǫt-ĭmĭ* 'road'. [2] Feminine *kost-ĭ*, but masculine PANT-II-EX > *pǫt-ĭje*. [3] Neuter *slov-es-a* 'word', but masculine KÁM-EN-EX > *kamene* 'stone', feminine MÁ-TER-EX > *matere* 'mother'.
Glosses: *kostĭ* 'bone', *slovo* 'word', *kamy* 'stone', LCS *vertmę* 'time', OCS *vrěmę* 'time', *telę* 'calf', *mati* 'mother', *svekry* 'mother-in-law'.

towards the *o/jo*-stem declension. The consonant stems are changing declension, masculines and neuters taking on *o/jo*-stem endings, feminines joining the *i*-stem declension.

Some LCS desinences have transparent PIE etyma; others can easily be reconciled with PIE etyma if one assumes a number of natural sound changes limited to final position (all these are marked with '>' above); a few desinences have plausible morphological origins within Slavic (marked '≠' above); others must be outcomes of unknown morphophonemic or morphological innovations (the PS forms of these are marked with '?' above). The last two categories are exemplified in the next paragraph.

The difference between PIE *-*os* in LCS *stol-ŭ* and *slov-o* points to a Proto-Slavic difference -A-X vs -AS-, with the -X 'nom. sg.' generalized from an earlier /s/ ~ /x/ alternation in this (and other) case endings (cf. **The Satəm Assibilation**, p. 424), but the non-alternating /s/ in *-e/os-* preserved. The inherited *o*-stem instrumental singular desinence PIE *-*o-h*. PS -A is preserved in adverbs (LCS *vičera* 'yesterday'), but is otherwise replaced: the *u*-stem desinence PS -U-MI serves as model for a new *o*-stem desinence in South Slavic, but is generalized for both stem classes in East Slavic and West Slavic, compare OCS *stol-omĭ, dom-ŭmĭ* vs ORuss. *stol-ŭmĭ, dom-ŭmĭ*, Russ. *stolóm, dómom*, Cz., Pol. *stolem, domem*. The *ā*-stem instrumental singular is pronominal, as is also the *o*-stem nominative plural and locative plural. The identity of the *ā*-stem genitive singular and nominative-accusative plural -*y* is difficult to understand; the umlauted counterpart, ESlav. and WSlav. -*ě* 'gen. sg., nom.-acc. pl.' but SSlav. -*ę* 'gen. sg., nom.-acc. pl.', likewise. Similarly inscrutable are the *o*-stem dative singular and instrumental plural. Note in the dative plural and instrumental desinences the characteristic Slavic -M- for PIE *-*bʰ*-.

Adjectives

The adjective agrees in case, number and gender with its head noun, *o/jo*-stem desinences showing agreement with masculines and neuters, and *ā/jā*-stem desinences with feminines, for example, LCS *nov-ŭ* (m.), *nov-o* (n.) (PS NAU-A-) vs *nov-a* (f.) (PS NAU-Ā-) 'new'. A few indeclinables in Old Church Slavonic are the remains of *i*-stem adjectives. Other *i*-stem and *u*-stem adjectives have been replaced by *o*-stem/*ā*-stem derivatives, for example, OCS *udobĭ* (indecl.) (PS AU-DAB-I-) beside LCS *udob-ĭn-ŭ, udob-ĭn-o, udob-ĭn-a* (PS AU-DAB-I-NA-/-Ā-) 'easy, simple', LCS *glad-ŭk-ŭ* (PS GLĀD-U-KA-, cf. Li. *glodùs*) 'smooth'. A few athematic desinences remain in some forms of comparatives (see below) and of present and past active participles.

Like the Baltic languages Slavic has developed a grammatical category of definiteness, expressed by the enclitic pronoun PS I-A-X (m.), I-A-M (n.), I-Ā- (f.) (PIE *-*i-s, jo-s*; LCS *jĭ, je, ja*) in noun phrases containing adjectives or participles, for example, OCS *slěp-ŭ* 'a blind [man]', *slěp-ŭ-j-ĭ* 'the blind [man]'. In Old Church Slavonic definiteness occasionally is expressed only once with conjoined attributes (e.g. *slyš-ę–j-ĭ slovesa moja i tvor-ę ja* 'he who hears my words and does them', alternatively: *slyš-ę–j-ĭ . . . i tvor-ę–j-ĭ . . .*), which shows the definite marker's original status as a phrase clitic; but the earliest attested forms of the definite adjective already contain numerous shortened or otherwise remodelled desinences, which indicate fusion of the original clitic with the preceding endings. In the paradigms in Table 14.3, [] indicates omitted segments, Y indicates an interfix /y/ that has replaced the original nominal desinence before the pronominal enclitic.

Several of the desinences occur in variant shapes in the most archaic texts and early undergo additional contraction.

The PS comparative continues a PIE formation with *-jes-/-jos-*. It has regular *jo*-stem and *jā*-stem desinences except for some of the nominative forms, compare LCS *nov-ě-jĭ* 'nom. sg. m.' (PS -IIX–0 ?), *nov-ě-je* 'nom. acc. sg. n.' (PS -IAS–0), *nov-ě-jĭš–i* 'nom. sg. f.' (PS -IIX–I), *nov-ě-jĭš–e* nom. pl. m.' (PS -IIX–EX), *nov-ě-jĭš–i* 'nom. pl. n.' (PS -IIX–I, beside *nově-jĭš–a*, PS -IIX–IĀ), but *nov-ě-jĭš–a* 'gen. sg. m. n.' (PS -IIX–IĀT). The productive, accented (LCS acute) interfix *–ě-* (PS –Ɛ-, of adverbial origin) occurs regularly with derived adjectives and with underived adjectives that have fixed accent on the stem (LCS acute accent) or desinence. But underived adjectives with no inherent accent (LCS circumflex, that is, enclinomena), as well as all of the suppletive formations, omit this interfix and accent the stem in the comparative (cf. LCS **dôrgŭ – *dórž-e*, SC *drâg – drȁž-e*, Russ. *dórog – doróže* 'dear – dearer').

Table 14.3 The definite adjective

	Masculine	Neuter	Feminine
Singular			
Nom.	nov-ŭ–j-ĭ	nov-o–j-e	nov-a–j-a
Acc.	nov-ŭ–j-ĭ	nov-o–j-e	nov-ǫ–j-ǫ
Gen.		nov-a–j-ego	nov-y–j-[ ]ę
Loc.		nov-ě–j-emı	nov-ě–j-[ ]i
Dat.		nov-u–j-emu	nov-ě–j-[ ]i
Instr.		nov-Y–j-imı	nov-ǫ–j-[ ]ǫ
Dual			
Nom.-Acc.	nov-a–j-a	nov-ě–j-i	nov-ě–j-i
Gen.-Loc.		nov-u–j-u	
Dat.-Instr.		nov-y̶–j-ima	
Plural			
Nom.	nov-i–j-i	nov-a–j-a	nov-y–j-ę
Acc.	nov-y–j-ę	nov-a–j-a	nov-y–j-ę
Gen.		nov-y–j-ixŭ	
Loc.		nov-y̶–j-ixŭ	
Dat.		nov-y̶–j-ixŭ	
Instr.		nov-y̶–j-imi	

An absolute superlative (elative) is formed from the comparative with the prefix OCS *prě-* (PS PER- 'over, through'), and a relative superlative with the prefix LCS *najĭ-* (PS NĀ, identical to the preposition 'on', plus a particle, PS I).

Numerals

Proto-Slavic numerals have the appearance of recent renewal: the syntactic relations of phrasal numerals are transparent and many of the numeral lexemes are morphological innovations.

'One' to 'four' are adjectives: LCS *jedinŭ* with a doublet stem *jedĭn-* (PS ED-EIN-A-, ED-IN-A-, composed of PS EIN-A-, LCS *inŭ* 'someone, another' and a proclitic deictic (cf. Lat. *ecce* < *ed-ce*?), the two dualia tantum *dŭva* 'two (m,), *dŭvě* '(n., f.)' (PS DUU-Ā, DUU-AI) and *oba* 'both (m.)', *obě* '(n., f.)' (PS AB-Ā, PIE *amb^h-ō*), and the pluralia tantum *trĭje* 'three (m.)', *tri* '(n., f.)' (PS TR-EI-EX, TR-I) and *četyre* 'four (m,)' *četyri* '(n., f.)' (PS KETŪR-EX, KETŪR-I). The corresponding ordinals are LCS *pĭrvŭ*, OCS *prĭvŭ* 'first' (PS PĪR-UA-), *drugŭ* 'second' (PS DRAUG-A- 'companion, other'), *tretĭjĭ* 'third' (PS TRE-TI-IA-), LCS *četvĭrtŭ*, OCS *četvrĭtŭ* 'fourth' (PS KETUĪR-TA-).

'Five' through 'nine' are feminine *i*-stem substantives derived from the (previously derived) ordinals: LCS *pętĭ* from *pętŭ* 'fifth' (PS PENK-TA-; for /kt/ + front vowel, cf. **Changes in Syllable Structure**, p. 431), *šestĭ* from *šestŭ* 'sixth' (PS XES-TA-, with /x-/ from Pre-Slavic **şekş* for **sekş* < PIE **s(w)eks*), *sedmĭ* from *sedmŭ* 'seventh' (PS SEBDM-A-), *osmĭ* from *osmŭ* 'eighth' (PS AST-MA-), *devętĭ* from *devętŭ* 'ninth' (PS DEUIN-TA-, with /d-/

Table 14.4 Demonstrative pronoun

	Proto-Slavic			Late Common Slavic		
	Masculine	Neuter	Feminine	Masculine	Neuter	Feminine
Singular						
Nom.	T-A-X	T-A	T-Ā	t-ŭ	t-o	t-a
Acc.	T-A-M	T-A	T-Ā-M	t-ŭ	t-o	t-a
Gen.	T-A-GA		T-AI-ANS	t-ogo		t-oję
Loc.	T-A-MI		T-AI-ÊI	t-omĭ		t-oji
Dat.	T-A-MAU		T-AI-EI	t-omu		t-oji
Instr.	T-AI-MI		T-AI-ĀM	t-ěmĭ		t-ojǫ
Dual						
Nom.-Acc.	T-Ā	T-AI	T-AI	t-a	t-ě	t-ě
Gen.-Loc.		T-AI-AU			t-oju	———
Dat.-Instr.		T-AI-MĀ			t-ěma	———
Plural						
Nom.	T-AI	T-Ā	T-ANS	t-i	t-a	t-y
Acc.	T-ANS	T-Ā	T-ANS	t-y	t-a	t-y
Gen.-Loc	T-AI-XU				t-ěxŭ	
Dat.	T-AI-MAX				t-ěmŭ	
Instr.	T-AI-MĪX				t-ěmi	

Table 14.5 The relative pronoun

	Proto-Slavic	Late Common Slavic
Animate		
Nom.	K-A-X TA	k-ŭ-to
Acc.	K-A-GA	k-ogo
Gen.	K-A-GA	k-ogo
Loc.	K-A-MI	k-omĭ
Dat.	K-A-MAU	k-omu
Instr.	K-AI-MI	ć-ěmĭ
Inanimate		
Nom.	KI(-D) TA	č-ĭ-to
Acc.	KI(-D)TA	č-ĭ-to
Gen.	KI-ESA	č-eso
Loc.	KI-A-MI	č-emĭ
Dat.	KI-A-MAU	č-emu
Instr.	KI-AI-MI	č-imĭ

from 'ten'). The masculine LCS *desętĭ* 'ten' is a consonant stem except in the nominative singular (PS DESIMT-I-), *sŭto* 'hundred' is a neuter *o*-stem (PS SUT-A-), and LCS *tysętji*, *tysǫtji*, OCS *tysęšti*, *tysǫšti* 'thousand', an *ī*-stem turned *jā*-stem (PS TŪ(X)-SIMT-, TŪ(X)-SAMT- < PIE *tewh-* 'swell' and *(d)ḱm̥t-* 'hundred').

Phrasal numerals are of several types. In 'eleven' to 'nineteen' addition is expressed by the preposition *na* 'on', for example OCS *oba na desęte učenika* 'the twelve disciples' (lit. both $_{nom.\ du.}$ on ten $_{loc.\ sg.}$ disciples $_{nom.\ du.}$). In the decades (twenty to ninety), the syntactic relation is dictated by the part of speech of the smaller factor, e.g. *dva desęti* 'twenty' (lit. two$_{nom.\ du.}$ tens$_{nom.\ du.}$ Noun$_{gen.\ pl.}$), *tri desęte* 'thirty' (three$_{nom.\ pl.}$ tens$_{nom.\ pl.}$ Noun$_{gen.\ pl.}$), *pętĭ desętŭ* 'fifty' (five$_{nom.\ pl.}$ tens$_{gen.\ pl.}$ Noun$_{gen.\ pl.}$), but any unit numeral added (with the conjunction *i* 'and', for example, *dŭva desęti i pętĭ* 'twenty-five') will control the case and number of the quantified noun. From the earliest attestation on, different Slavic dialects introduce different simplifications in numeral syntax tending towards univerbation of the phrasal numerals denoting teens and decades.

Pronouns

Common Slavic developed a special pronominal declension with back- and front-vowel subparadigms analogous to the twofold substantival declensions. The front vowel subparadigm is the result of umlaut (cf. **The Earliest Vowel Shifts**, p. 429; **Late Common Slavic Tonality Assimilations**, p. 432) in LCS *jĭ* 'he; who' (OCS *i*, PS I-X, IA-X, PIE *is*, *jos*; cf. *onŭ*, **Personal Pronouns**, p. 441), in the possessive pronouns LCS *mojĭ* 'my', *tvojĭ* 'thy', *svojĭ* 'own', *našĭ* 'our', *vašĭ* 'your' (e.g. PS MA-IA-, NĀ-S-IA-), in *čĭto* 'what' (PS KI-, PIE *kʷi-*), and in *vĭsĭ* 'all' (PS UIX-A-, PIE *wis-*); there is an amalgamation of *jo/jā*-stem and *i*-stem desinences in *sĭ* 'this' (PS SI-, PIE *ki̯*-). This paradigm is exemplified by *čĭto* here and by the anaphoric pronouns in Table 14.6, below. The basic (back-vowel) paradigm combines *o*-stem and *ā*-stem desinences with desinences added to a pronominal 'theme' PS -AI-, an extension of the PIE nominative plural desinence *-oi*. This is the paradigm of *tŭ* 'this near you' (PIE *to*-), *ovŭ* 'that close by', *onŭ* 'that over there', *kŭto* 'who', *samŭ* 'self', *inŭ* 'another', and the numerals *jedinŭ* 'one', *dŭva* 'two', *oba* 'both' (cf. **Numerals** above).

LCS *čĭto* 'what' alone preserves the inherited PIE genitive desinence *-eso* ('cf. Goth. *þis*, OHG *des*), elsewhere replaced by the unexplained PS -GA (the PIE emphatic particle *ge* or the adjective suffix, PIE *-gʰo*- of LCS *dĭl-g-ŭ* 'long', comparative *dĭlě*, cf. Gk *doli-kho-s*?).

Personal Pronouns
The personal pronouns show partly inherited relations of suppletion between nominative and oblique stems and partly opaque allomorphy among oblique stems.

The first-person singular nominative, LCS *azŭ*, *a* (OCS *azŭ*, ORuss. (*j*)*azŭ*, *ja*, similarly elsewhere) points to Proto-Slavic by-forms AZ-AM, AZ (the former like Skt *aham*, the latter like Li. *aš*, *eš*, Goth. *ik*, PIE *eĝ-om*) with long vowel quantity from Winter's Law; cf. **The Loss of the Aspirates**, p. 425). In the oblique cases there are enclitic forms LCS *me*, *mę* 'acc.' (PS, PIE *me*, with an additional -*m* 'acc.') and *mi* 'dat.' (PS MAI, PIE *moj*) and orthotonic forms with longer stems. The second-person singular nominative is PS, PIE *tū*; its oblique forms, enclitic and orthotonic, have LCS *t*- for expected *tv*- and a stem extension as in Latin *ti-bi*, *nō-bi-s*, to which substantival and pronominal desinences have been added, just as in the first-person singular. The reflexive pronoun '(my-, your- etc.)self' is entirely parallel to the second-person singular pronoun (cf. LCS *sebě*, Lat. *sibi*, OPr. *sebbei*), but lacks the nominative.

The first-person plural nominative LCS *my* has the root of the first-person singular oblique forms and, like the second-person plural *vy*, possibly original accusative plural desinences (PS M-ANS, N-ANS, U-ANS, cf. OPr. *mans* 'us', *wans* 'you'). The identical genitive and locative *nasŭ* (and similarly *vasŭ*) may present PS NĀ-S-AM, respectively NĀ-SU, PIE *nō-s-om*, *nō-su*). The dative and instrumental forms in both dual and plural again show the characteristic Slavic -M- (contrast Lat. *nō-bis*, *vō-bis*).

The third-person pronoun continues both PIE *is* and *jos*. Its nominative forms (LCS *jĭ*, *je*, *ja*, *ji*, etc.) occur only with the enclitic *že* (PS, PIE *ge*), in the function of relative pronoun. In anaphoric function its oblique forms are supplemented with nominative forms of the demonstrative *onŭ*, which also has oblique forms. The desinences of *jĭ* are umlauted allomorphs (cf. **The Earliest Vowel Shifts**, p. 429) of those of LCS *tŭ*; see below.

Table 14.6 Personal pronouns

	First-person singular	Second-person singular	First-person dual	Second-person dual	First-person plural	Second-person plural	Third-person singular m.	n.	f.	Third-person dual m.	n.-f.	Third-person plural m.	n.	f.
Nom.	azŭ	ty	vě	va	my	vy	on-ŭ	on-o	on-a	on-a	on-ě	on-i	on-a	on-y
Acc.	me, mę	te, tę	na	va	ny	vy	j-ĭ	j-e	j-ǫ	j-a	j-i	j-ę	j-a	j-ę
Gen.	mene	tebe	naju	vaju	nasŭ	vasŭ	j-ego	j-ego	j-eję	j-eju	j-eju	j-ixŭ	j-ixŭ	
Loc.	mĭně	tebě	naju	vaju	nasŭ	vasŭ	j-emĭ	j-emĭ	j-eji	j-eju	j-eju	j-ixŭ	j-ixŭ	
Dat.	mi, mĭně	ti, tebě	nama	vama	namŭ	vamŭ	j-emu	j-emu	j-eji	j-ima	j-ima	j-imŭ	j-imŭ	
Instr.	mŭnojǫ	tobojǫ	nama	vama	nami	vami	j-imĭ	j-imĭ	j-ejǫ	j-ima	j-ima	j-imi	j-imi	

The Verb

The morphology of the Proto-Slavic verb has changed considerably from the reconstructed PIE state of affairs.

The morphological category of voice has been lost. Proto-Slavic expresses the passive with the auxiliary verb 'to be' and verbal adjectives (passive participles), present tense in -M– and past in -N–, -EN– or -T– (cf. **The Imperfect**, p. 446), for example, LCS *nes-om-ŭ jestŭ* 'he is being carried' (PS NES-A-MA-X), *nes-en-ŭ jestŭ* 'he has been carried' (PS NES-E-NA-X). But passive and middle senses are expressed also with the reflexive pronoun, for example, *nes-e-tŭ sę* 'he is carried', *dviž-e-tŭ sę* 'he moves', *styd-i-tŭ sę* 'he is ashamed'.

The aspect and tense system has gone through several shifts between Proto-Indo-European and Proto-Slavic. In Proto-Slavic, aspect is expressed by derivation: preverbs are used to derive perfective, telic verbs from imperfective, atelic verbs (e.g. LCS *tvori–ti* 'do': *prě-tvori–ti* 'change', *ras-tvori–ti* 'undo, dissolve', *sŭ-tvori–ti* 'make'); all action verbs, whether underived (e.g. *da–ti* 'give') or derived (e.g. *konĭč-i–ti* 'finish', cf. *konĭc-ĭ* 'end'), are basically perfective and allow the derivation of synonymous imperfective counterparts through suffixation (e.g. *da-ja–ti*, *konĭč-a–ti*, *ras-tvaŕ-a-ti*, with PS -IĀ–; cf. **Stem Formation** below).

The tense system comprises a recent distinction between simple tenses (non-retrospective: present, aorist, imperfect) and compound tenses (retrospective: perfect, pluperfect I, pluperfect II); the latter set utilizes the simple tenses of the auxiliary 'to be' and the resultive participle of the given lexical verb. Within the (older) system of simple tenses the imperfect has the appearance of an innovation.

Present	*nesetŭ* (< NES-E–TI)	Perfect	*neslŭ jestŭ* (< NES-LA-X ES-TI)
Aorist	*nese* (< NES-E-T)	Pluperfect I	*neslŭ bě* (< NES-LA-X-BU-Ê-T)
Imperfect	*nesěaxŭ* (< NES-Ê-ĀX-E-T)	Pluperfect II	*neslŭ běaše* (< NES-LA-X BU-Ê-ĀX-E-T)

The IE mood system has been recast. Apart from the indicative, only the forms of the (present) optative remain, with several functions (cf. **Sentence Modality**, p. 449). One optative paradigm of 'to be' functions as imperative (PIE *-oj-*, PS BŪ-N-D-AI–, LCS *bǫd-ě-mĭ, bǫ-d-i, bǫ-d-i* '1, 2, 3 sg.', *bǫd-ě-mŭ, bǫ-d-ě-te, bǫd-ǫ*, '1, 2, 3 pl.'), another serves as auxiliary with the resultative or a passive participle of a main verb to express an irrealis (PS BU-I–, cf. Lat. *fī–ō, fī–s, fī–t: b-i-mĭ, bi, bi* '1, 2, 3 sg.'; *b-i-mŭ, bi-s-te, b-ǫ* '1, 2, 3 pl.'), for example, LCS *stydilŭ sę bi* 'he would be ashamed'. Old Church Slavonic documents the renewal of the optative: it has isolated inflected forms with optative sense (e.g. *otŭ-pad-ě-mĭ* 'may I fall away') beside a newer, analytic expression with the proclitic *da* (PS DĀ < PIE *deh₃- 'give)' and the present tense, e.g. *da ne po-styžd-ǫ sę v[ǔ] věkǔ* 'may I never be ashamed'.

Stem Formation

Verbs are traditionally classified by the formation of the present tense stem into thematic verbs (PIE: I: *-e/o, II: *-ne/o-, III: *-je/o-), semithematic verbs (IV: LCS -i-, PS -EI-), and athematic verbs (V); they are subclassified by the formation of the aorist stem (see **The Aorist**, p. 446). Class I includes root verbs, a few suffixed verbs (e.g. PS EI–TÊI, I-D-E-TI 'to go (inf., 3 sg. pres.)' > LCS *i-ti*, *jǐd-e-tǐ*, OCz. *jíti, jde*) and a few verbs with a nasal infix (cf. PS SÊ-N-D–E-TI, SÊD-E-T 'to sit down (3 sg. pres., aor.)' > LCS *sęde-t-ǔ, sěd-e*; cf. also PS BŪ-N-D–E-TI 'to be (3 sg. fut.)' > *bǫd-e-tǔ*); some verbs have a suffixal aorist stem in PS -A-; some have apophony between present and aorist stems, for example PS KUEIT-/KUIT- > LCS *cvis-ti, cvǐt–e-tǔ* 'to bloom (inf., 3 sg.)', PS BIR-/BER- > LCS *bǐr-a-ti, ber–e-tǔ* 'to gather'. Class II contains nasal stems, which have a second stem in PS -NŪ-, LCS -ny- (reflected in Pb., US, Sn and western SC, changed to -nǫ- everywhere else, cf. US *mi-nǫ-ć*, OCS *mi-nǫ-ti, min-e-tǔ* 'to pass'). Some of these form the aorist from the suffixed stem, the remainder have thematic aorists (cf. **The Aorist**, p. 446). Class III comprises several types of root verbs (e.g. PS ZNĀ-TÊI, ZNĀ-IE-TI > LCS *zna-ti, znaj-e-tǔ* 'to know', PS KĀL-TÊI, KAL-IE-TI > LCS *kól-ti*, OCS *kla-ti, kolě-tǔ* 'to pierce') and some productive suffixal formations, especially the deverbal, imperfectivizing suffix PS -IĀ- which is accompanied by root vowel lengthening (PS PER-TUĀR-IĀ-TÊI, -TUĀR-IĀ-IE-TI > LCS *prě-tvaŕa-ti, -tvaŕaj-e-tǔ* 'to change'; cf. **The Verb** above) and the

Table 14.7 Verbal classes

	Present	Aorist	Imperfect	Result.ptcpl.	Infinitive
Class I					
A	nes–ǫ	ně-s–ǔ	nes-ě-ax–ǔ	nes-l-ǔ	nes-ti
B	ber–ǫ	bǐr-a-x–ǔ	bǐr-a-ax–ǔ	bǐr-a-l-ǔ	bǐr-a-ti
Class II	dvig-n-ǫ	dvig–ǔ	dvign-ě-ax–ǔ	*dvig-ny-l-ǔ	*dvig-ny-ti[1]
Class III					
1.A	*kol-j-ǫ	*kol-x–ǔ	*kol-j-ě-ax–ǔ	*kol-l–ǔ	*kol-ti[2]
B	*pis-j-ǫ	pǐs-a–x–ǔ	pǐs-a-ax–ǔ	pǐs-a-l–ǔ	pǐs-a-ti[3]
2	děl-a-j-ǫ	děl-a-x–ǔ	děl-a-ax–ǔ	děl-a-l–ǔ	děl-a-ti
Class IV					
A	*bud-j-ǫ	bud-i-x–ǔ	*bud-j-ě-ax–ǔ	bud-i-l–ǔ	bud-i-ti[4]
B	*vidj–ǫ	vid-ě-x–ǔ	vid-ě-ax–ǔ	vid-ě-l-ǔ	vid-ě-ti[5]
Class V	*dad–mǐ	da-x–ǔ	dad-ě-ax–ǔ	da-l–ǔ	da-ti[6]
	jes-mǐ	b-ě-x–ǔ[7]	b-ě-ax–ǔ	by-l-ǔ	by-ti
	bǫ-d-ǫ[8]	by-x–ǔ[9]			

Note: The asterisked forms are in OCS: (1) *dvignǫ dvignǫti*; (2) *kolǫ, klaxǔ, kołaaxǔ, klalǔ, klati*; (3) *pišǫ*; (4) *buždǫ, buždaaxǔ*; (5) *viždǫ*; (6) *damǐ*. (7) Imperfective. (8) Future. (9) Perfective.

unrestricted suffix PS -AU- (PS UĒR-AU-Ā-TĒI, UĒR-AU-IE-TI > LCS věr-ov-a-ti, ver-uj-e-tŭ 'to believe', cf. LCS věra 'belief'). Class IV includes statives with a suffixal aorist in PS -Ē- (e.g. PS BUD-Ē-TĒI, BUD-EI-TI > LCS bŭd-ě-ti, bŭd-i-tŭ 'to wake') and verbs with an aorist stem in PS -I-, which include several productive types, for example, denominal (e.g. PS GAST-I-TĒI > LCS gostiti 'to visit', cf. LCs gostĭ 'guest'), causative (e.g. PS BAUD-I-TĒI > LCS buditi 'to awaken', cf. LCS bŭd-ě-ti 'to wake') and iterative verbs (e.g. PS NAS-I-TĒI > LSC nositi 'to carry', cf. LCS nes-ti 'to carry'). Class V comprises the four verbs PS BŪ-TĒI, ES-MI > LCS byti, jesmĭ 'to be', DĀ-TĒI, DĀD-MI, DĀD-INTI > LCS dati, damĭ, dadętĭ 'to give', PS UAID-Ē-TĒI, UAID-MI > LCS věděti, věmĭ 'to know', PS IM-Ē-TĒI, IM-Ā-MI > LCS jĭměti, jĭmamĭ 'to have'.

Personal Endings
The thematic verbs have generalized the e-grade except for first-person singular and third-person plural. The personal desinences are identical for all verbs – except the first-person singular, which is -ǫ in Classes I–IV (PS -Ā-M with the secondary -M added to the PIE *-eh_3), but -mĭ in Class V (PS, PIE *-mi); however, beside the younger vě-mĭ (PS UAID-MI) Old Church Slavonic and Old Russian have věd-ě 'I know' (PS UAID-AI, similar to Gk (w)oid-a), with a problematic ending. The Late Common Slavic first-person plural is -mŭ (OCS, Russ. Bel.), -mo (SC, Sn, some Slov., U) (suggesting an analogical CS *-max beside *-mas < PS -MAS < PIE *-mos), -me (Bel., Mac., Cz., Slov.; analogical to -te '2 pl.'), and -my (US, LS, Pol., Kash., Slovincian, Pb.; identical to my 'we'). The first-person dual is LCS -va (OSerb., ORuss., OCz., OPol.; PS -UĀ, cf. Li. -vo-), but Old Church Slavonic has -vě (like the 1 du. pronoun vě, PS UĒ). Second-person singular is PS -XEI alternating with -SEI after consonant (cf. **The Satəm Assibilation**, p. 424 < PIE *-s + *-e-i?); second-person plural is -te (PS, PIE *-te); second-person dual is -ta (PS -TĀ, cf. Li. -to-). The third person is -tĭ in Old Russian (< PS, PIE *-ti) but -tŭ in Old Church Slavonic (possibly PS, PIE *-t with paragoge), the third-person plural is LCS -ǫ-tĭ (PS -A-NTI in Classes I–III) and -ę-tĭ (PS -I-NTI in Class IV, PS -INTI < PIE *-nti in Class V), respectively -ǫ-tŭ and -ę-tŭ in Old Church Slavonic. The third-person dual is LCS -te, varying with a younger -ta.

Table 14.8   Present tense formation

	Present Thematic	Semi-thematic	Athematic	Imperative
1 sg.	ved-ǫ	*vidj-ǫ	es-mĭ	bǫd-ě–mĭ
2 sg.	ved-e-ši	vid-i-ši	e-si	bǫdi
3 sg.	ved-e-tĭ	vid-i-tĭ	es-tĭ	bǫdi
1 pl.	ved-e-mŭ	vid-i–mŭ	es-mŭ	bǫd-ě–mŭ
2 pl.	ved-e-te	vid-i-te	es-te	bǫd-ě–te
3 pl.	ved-ǫ-tĭ	vid-ę-tĭ	s-ę-tĭ/s-ǫ-tŭ	bǫd–ǫ

The Aorist

The aorist is expressed by four different formations. Several dozen Class IA and Class II verbs have a thematic aorist, for example *mog-ŭ, mož-e* 'could (1/sg., 2/3 sg.)' (PS MAG-A-M, MAG-E-S/T). Over a dozen Class IA verbs have a sigmatic aorist with lengthened root vowel (*vṛddhi*), but this has (asigmatic) thematic forms in the second and third-person singular (*nese* 'carried (2 sg., 3 sg.)' < PS NES-E–S/T) and (sigmatic) thematicized first-person singular and first-person plural (e.g. *něsŭ* 'carried (1 sg.)' < PS NES-S–A-M, PIE *-s- + *-o-m); similarly *basŭ, bode* 'pierced (1 sg., 2/3 sg.)' (PS BĀD-S–A-M, BAD- –E-S/T). Both types compete with a younger extended formation with different dialect variants, for example, OCS, ORuss. *nesoxŭ, nesoše* 'carried: (1 sg., 3 pl.)' (Early CS *nes-a–x-a-m, *a–x-in-t), but Pre-WSlav. *nesexŭ, *nesexǫ (OCz. *nesech, nesechu,* OPol. *niesiech, niesiechǫ*; Early CS *nes-e–x-am, *-e–x-a-nt). The different aorists show the same generalization of /x/ (< PIE *s) after vowel as the second-person singular desinence and the same set of personal endings, PS -(A)-M '1 sg.', -(E)-S '2 sg.', -(E)-T '3 sg.', ·(A)-MAX '1 pl.', -(E)-TE '2 pl.', -(A)-NT or -INT (PIE *-ṇt) '3 pl.'

Table 14.9 Aorist formation

	Aorist Thematic	Sigmatic	Extended	Suffixal	Imperfect
1 sg.	mog–ŭ	ně–s–ŭ	nes-o-x–ŭ	bĭr-a-x–ŭ	ved-ě-ax–ŭ
2 sg.	mož–e	nes–e	nes–e	bĭr-a	ved-ě-aš-e
3 sg.	mož–e	nes–e	nes–e	bĭr-a	ved-ě-aš-e
1 pl.	mog-o-mŭ	ně–s–o-mŭ	nes-o-x–o-mŭ	bĭr-a-x–o-mŭ	ved-ě-ax-o-mŭ
2 pl.	mož–e-te	ně–s–te	nes-o-s-te	bĭr-a-s-te	ved-ě-aš-e-te
3 pl.	mog–ǫ	ně–s–ę	nes-o-š–ę	bĭr-a-š–ę	ved-ě-ax-ǫ

The Imperfect

The imperfect seems to represent a fusion of a deverbal stem with forms of a defunct tense paradigm of PS ES- 'to be' PS Ā-X- followed by the theme vowel and (secondary) endings, the original /s/ changed to /š/ ~ /s/ by analogy with the aorist (see **Personal Endings** above).

Nominal Forms

The nominal forms of the verb comprise the adjectival participles and the substantival infinitive and supine and verbal noun. The present participles are exemplified by the passive LCS *nes-o-mŭ* 'being led' (PS NES-A-M-A-/Ā- with PIE *-mo-) and active *nes-y* (ESlav., WSlav. *nes-a*), *nes-ǫtj-* 'carrying (nom. sg. m. oblique stem)' (OCS *nesǫšt-*, ORuss. *nesuč-*; PS NES-ANTS, NES-ANT-IA-/IĀ-, with PIE *-nt-), the latter with athematic nominative forms (cf. **Adjectives**, p. 438). The past participles are exemplified by active *nes-ŭ, nes-ŭš-* 'having carried (nom. sg. m., oblique stem)' (PS -UX-IA-/-IĀ-, PIE *-wes-), also with athematic nominative forms, and passive *nes-en-ŭ* 'carried', *vŭz-ę-t-ŭ* 'taken', *pĭs-a-n-ŭ* 'written' (PS NES-EN-A- /-Ā-), the -T- and -N- suffixes in complementary distribution. The resultative participle in PS -LA-/-LĀ- (LCS *nes-l-ŭ* 'having carried') plays a special role in the retrospective tenses (cf. the Armenian participial turn *ekeal em* 'I have come'), cf. **The Verb**, p. 443).

The infinitive in PS -TEI (LCS *-ti) is an original *i*-stem locative, the supine (**Syntax**, p. 449) in PS -TU-M (LCS, OCS -tŭ) is an original *u*-stem accusative. Like the resultative participle, these are mostly formed from the aorist stem. The neuter verbal noun (in PS -IIA-M, LCS -ĭje) is formed from both transitive and intransitive verbs with the suffixes used for the past passive participle, cf. *nes-en-ŭ* 'carried'–*nes-en-ĭje* 'carrying', *vŭz-ę-t-ŭ* 'taken'–*vŭz-ę-t-ĭje* 'taking', *pĭs-a-n-ŭ* 'written'*pĭsa-n-ĭje* 'writing'.

Uninflected Words

Adverbs

De-adjectival adverbs are regularly singular neuter accusative (e.g. LCS *mal-o* 'little', *mŭnog-o* 'much' from *mal-ŭ*, *mŭnog-ŭ*) or locative (*dobr-ě* 'well', *zŭl-ě* 'ill', *krotŭć-ě* 'mildly' from *dobr-ŭ*, *zŭl-ŭ*, *krotŭk-ŭ*). Many other adverbs are lexicalized case forms, for example, accusative (*vŭnŭ* 'outside', *nizŭ* 'down', *utro* 'morning (acc. sg.); in the morning'), locative (*vŭně* 'outside', *gorě* 'mountain (loc. sg.); above'), dative (*gorě* 'mountain (dat. sg.); up'), *domovi* 'house (dat. sg.); home(ward)'), instrumental (*jedĭnojǫ* 'one (instr. sg. f.); once', **notjĭjǫ*, OCS *noštĭjǫ* 'night (instr. sg.); at night').

There is an extensive set of correlative pronominal adverbs, including (1) *tu, sĭde, onŭde, inŭde* 'there, here, yonder, elsewhere', *vĭsĭde, nikŭde* 'everywhere, nowhere', *jĭde* 'where', *kŭde* 'where?'; (2) *tamo, sěmo, onamo, inamo* 'to that, this, yonder, another place', *vĭsěmo, nikamo* 'to all places, no place', *jamo* 'to where', *kamo* 'where to?'; (3) *togda, ovogda, inogda* 'at this, that, another time', *vĭsegda, nikogda* 'always, never', *jegda* 'when', *kogda* 'when?'; (4) *tako, sice, inako* 'thus, this way, otherwise', *vĭsěko, nikako* 'in every, no way', *jako* 'in the manner that', *kako* 'how?'

Prepositions

The Proto-Slavic inventory of prepositions contains several chronological layers of transitive adverbs. There are recent, transparent formations like *krom-ě* 'rim (loc. sg.); outside, except', **medju* (OCS *meždu*) 'border (loc. dual.); between', **perdje* (OCS *prěžde* < PS PER-D-IAS- (comp.) cf. **Adjectives**, p. 437) 'earlier; before', opaque derivational relationships like *na* 'on to, on'–*nadŭ* 'above', *po* 'after, up to'–*podŭ* 'under', **per* (OCS *prě-*, US *pše*, OPol. *prze*) 'over' –**perdŭ* (OCS *prědŭ*) 'in front of', comparable to formations in Old Prussian (cf. Stang 1957), apparent case forms such as this **per* 'over' and *pro* 'for ... sake', *pri* 'near' (PIE, PS **per-/pr-*, + *-o*, *-ej* 'loc.'), and evidently archaic items like *vŭ(n)* 'into, in' (PS UN < PIE **ṇ*), *sŭ(n)* 'with, off' (PS ѕᴜɴ < PIE **sm̥*), *jĭz* 'out of' (PS ɪᴢ, cf. Li. *iš*, La. *iz*, Lat. Gk *ek(s)*), *ob(ĭ)* 'against' (PS ᴀʙɪ, PIE **obʰi*), *ot* 'away from' (PS ᴀᴛ, PIE **et*), *vŭz* 'along' (PS ᴜᴢ, cf. Li. *už* 'behind'), *u* 'by, near' (PS, PIE **aw*), *za* 'beyond' (PS ᴢᴀ̄, cf. Arm. *z*, Goth. *ga*). All but the youngest of these layers of formations are proclitic.

Conjunctions

Parataxis is commonly asyndetic in the Slavic languages, and hypotaxis in early Slavic is regularly expressed through nominalization (participial constructions; cf. **Subordination**, p. 451), but there is a basic Proto-Slavic repertory of conjunctions. The coordinating conjunctions include the copulative LCS *i* 'and' (< PIE **ej*) beside dialectal (OCS) *ti*, (U, SSlav.) *ta*, (ESlav. SSlav.) *to*, (< PIE **to-*), the disjunctive *i-li* 'or' (cf. Li., La., OPr. *lai* 'permissive'), the adversative *a* 'and, but', *nŭ* 'but' (< PIE **no*), and the explicative *bo*, *i-bo* 'for' (< PIE **bʰehₐ-*). Among the subordinating conjunctions, the relative LCS *jĭ-že*, *je-že*, (< PIE **jos*, **jo(d)*, **jā* plus contrastive **ge*) competes with indefinite (interrogative) pronouns (LCS *kŭ-to* 'who', *čĭ-to* 'who, which', *ko-tor-ŭ*, *kŭ-ter-ŭ* 'which (of two)', *kŭ-jĭ* 'which, who'). To introduce adverbial clauses of place, time, manner, and so on, the adverbs derived from PIE **jo-* (e.g. *jĭ-de* 'where', *je(g)da* 'when', *jeli* 'until, when', *jako* 'as, how, that, so that'; cf. **Adverbs** above) are similarly renewed with derivatives based on PIE **kʷo-* (*kŭde*, *kogda*, *koli*, *kako*). Declarative object clauses are marked with *jako* 'that', interrogative ones with the question participle *li* 'whether' (polarity questions) or indefinite (interrogative) pronouns or adverbs.

Word Formation

Word formation plays an enormous role in all periods of the Slavic languages and cannot be adequately characterized here. Three major patterns, all well known from the other IE languages, will be mentioned.

The non-suffixal derivation of nouns (*o-* and *ā-*stems) from verbs is in the older vocabulary accompanied by apophony (*o-*grade or less frequently lengthened grade) serving to denote actions, results and places of actions, and agents, for example, LCS *vŭ-xodŭ* 'entering; entrance', *u-xodŭ* 'fugitive' (PS xɪᴅ-/xᴀᴅ- 'go', PIE **sed-* 'sit, ride'?). With the use of preverbs this allows for the creation of thousands of richly differentiated terms. The process remains productive in the modern languages – for instance, Russian has twenty-three derived substantives in *-xod*, sixteen in *-tes* from *tesati* 'to hew' (PS ᴛᴇѕ-ᴀ̄-ᴛᴇɪ, PIE **teḱs-*), eighteen in *-nos* from *nes-ti* 'to carry' (PS ɴᴇѕ-, PIE **hneḱ-*), and so on (Vaillant 1974: 32–291).

There is an extensive repertory of derivational suffixes, including several dozen productive ones and scores of transparent, non-productive formations in Late Common Slavic, for example, from *l̓ubiti* 'to love' (PS ʟᴇᴜʙ- < PIE **lewbʰ-*): the substantives *lub-ĭć-ĭ* 'lover', *lubl̓-en-ik-ŭ* 'loved one', *lubl̓-*

en-ĭje 'loving', *l̦ub-y* 'love, lust', *ne-l̦ub-ĭstv-o* 'hate' and the adjectives *l̦ub-ŭ* 'dear, expensive', *l̦ub-iv-ŭ* 'loving', *l̦ub-ĭn-ŭ* 'dear', *l̦ub-ĭzn-ŭ*, 'full of love', *l̦ub-ŭv-ĭn-ŭ* 'pertaining to love', and so on.

Compounding is commonly accompanied by suffixation as an explicit means of indicating the semantic and syntactic properties of the compound, for example, *rǫko-vod-ĭn-ik-ŭ* 'guide (lit. hand-lead-er)', *věnĭc-e-nos-ĭc-ĭ* 'wreath-bear-er', but an older, exocentric pattern is non-suffixal, for example, *voj-e-vod-a* 'war-lead-er' (cf. LCS *voj-in-ŭ* 'warrior', *vesti, ved-ǫ* 'to lead (inf., 1 sg.)'), *vod-o-nos-ŭ* 'water container' (cf. *voda* 'water', *nesti, nes-ǫ* 'carry'). This pattern includes examples that are older than the generalization of the interfix *-o-* (e.g. LCS (ORuss.) *medvědĭ* 'bear' < PS MEDU-ED-I- 'honey-eater', *gumĭno* 'threshing floor' < PS GAU-MIN-A- 'ox-crush(ing place)'). But it continues to be productive, compare Russ. *neb-o-skreb*, SC *neb-o-der* 'skyscraper'. The same process forms compound verbs (mostly with incorporated objects, e.g. OCS *blag-o-dar-i-ti* 'give thanks' (*blago* 'good', *dar-i-ti* 'give') and especially adjectives of the type LCS *mal-o-věr-ŭ* 'of little faith' (*mal-ŭ* 'little', *věra* 'faith'), Ch.S *sŭt-o-nog-ŭ*, Russ. *stonóg* 'with a hundred feet, centipede' (*sŭto* 'hundred', *noga* 'foot, leg').

Syntax

The reconstruction of the IE heritage in Proto-Slavic syntax is to some extent problematic. The early corpus of texts in Old Church Slavonic, which was extensively adapted to translation from the Greek, is not a wholly reliable witness. Influences from other recent IE languages can be suspected also in Old Czech (Latin, German) and in Old Russian (Baltic and Balticized West Finnic). As a consequence comparative Slavic syntax weighs evidence not only from the documented histories of the Slavic languages but also from their oral traditions. Here only a few salient features can be mentioned.

Sentence Modality

Among interrogative sentences, constituent questions are introduced by an interrogative pronoun or adverb; for example, OCS *Kŭde estŭ věra vaša* 'Where is your faith?' (Luke 8: 25: Ποῦ ἡ πίστις ὑμῶν;). Polarity questions are marked with the enclitic *li*, which follows the focused constituent; compare *Kŭto sŭgrěši, sĭ li, ili roditelě ego* 'Who did sin, this man or his parents' (John 9: 2: τίς ἥμαρτεν, οὗτος ἢ οἱ γονεῖς αὐτοῦ;) and *Ty li esi carĭ ijudějĭskŭ* 'Art thou the King of the Jews?' (Matt. 27: 11: Σὺ εἶ ὁ βασιλεὺς τῶν Ιουδαιων;). Directive sentences use forms of the original optative, with the first person in hortative, the second in imperative function, and the third in optative or desiderative function, OCS *Po věrě vaju bǫdi vama* 'According to your faith be it unto you' (Matt. 9: 29: κατὰ τὴν πίστιν ὑμῶν γενηθήτω ὑμῖν), but directives may also use the present tense and, occasionally, the infinitive; for example, *Ne preljuby sŭtvoriši* 'Thou shalt not commit adultery' (Matt. 5: 27: Οὐ μοιχεύσεις), *I ne klevetati i ne zaviděti, sĭ že jedinŭ xraniti obyčajĭ* 'And [you are] not to slander and not to envy; this one custom [you are] to keep', cf. ORuss. *A gostja ne prinevoliti, no kuda xočet', tudy poidet'* 'Do not constrain (inf.) a visitor, but where he wishes, there let him go (lit. he goes)'. In negative sentences the negation *ne* is proclitic to the negated constituent; if a sentence contains a negative pronoun or adverb, its predicate is often negated ('double negation') in Old Church Slavonic e.g., OCS *Nikŭtože dajaše mu* 'No one gave to him', var. *Nikŭtože dajaše mu*. The modern languages are more consistent in this usage.

Sentence Types

In the modern languages pronominal subjects remain omissible to different degrees, but the suppression of pronouns may be used to signal an unspecified subject, for example, Russ. *Vas prosjat* (lit. 'they are asking for you') 'There is someone to see you', or a generalized subject, for example, Russ. *Tebja ne ubediš'* 'One (lit. you) cannot convince you'. The first of these constructions is current already in the earliest texts, for example, OCS *Blaženi jeste jegda ponosętŭ vamŭ* 'Blessed are ye, when men shall revile you' (Matt. 5: 11: μακάριοί ἐστε, ὅταν ὀνειδίσωσιν ὑμᾶς). Proto-Slavic has several categories of subjectless verbs, denoting forms of weather, involuntary bodily events, modal states and the like, intransitive (OCS *mrŭče* 'it got dark (3 sg. aor.)', *ašte dostoitŭ vŭ sǫbotǫ dobro tvoriti* 'Is it lawful on the sabbath days to do good' (Luke 6: 9: εἰ ἔξεστιν τῷ σαββάτῳ ἀγαθοποιῆσαι) and transitive (Russ. *menja*$_{acc.}$ *tošnit* 'I$_{acc.}$ am nauseous'). In addition, several de-agentivized constructions are found, exemplified by Russ. *Lodku*$_{acc.}$ *uneslo volnoj*$_{instr.}$ 'the boat$_{acc.}$ swept away$_{trans.}$ by the wave$_{instr.}$' or *Paxnet senom*$_{instr.}$ 'There is a smell of hay$_{instr.}$' (contrast *Volna*$_{nom.}$ *unesla lodku*$_{acc.}$ 'The wave$_{nom.}$ swept away the boat$_{acc.}$' *Seno*$_{nom.}$ *paxnet* 'The hay$_{nom.}$ smells'). Existential sentences (which include possessive sentences) are notable by the fact that a partitive or negated subject is in the genitive, for example *ne bě ima*$_{dat.}$ *čęda*$_{gen.}$ 'they had no child(ren)' (Luke 1: 7: οὐκ ἦν αὐτοῖς τέκνον).

Participant Roles and Cases

In the historical period prepositional syntax has expanded greatly at the expense of absolute case usage. The prepositionless locative (of time or place) is infrequent in Old Church Slavonic, but still used productively in Old Russian, for example, *Samŭ že Izäslavŭ kŭnäzĭ pravl'aaše stolŭ ... Kyjevě*$_{loc.}$ 'Prince I. himself held the throne ... in Kiev' (Ostromir, 1056; later *vŭ Kyjevě*). Similarly the prepositionless dative (of direction), for example, *ustremiša sä bojevi*$_{dat.}$ 'they rushed into battle', *ide Jurĭi Rostovu*$_{dat.}$ 'George went to Rostov' (Kievan Chronicle), later replaced by prepositional turns (*vŭ bojĭ*$_{acc.}$, *kŭ Rostovu*$_{dat.}$). In the medieval Slavic languages the genitive had a number of functions which have since developed other expressions. It was the regular complement of verbs of perception (OCS *slušati* 'to hear', *sŭmotriti* 'to see'), striving and attainment (*iskati* 'to seek', *žĭdati* 'to wait for', *do-iti* 'to reach'), separation and limit (*otŭlǫčiti* 'to separate', *běžati* 'to flee', *bojati sę* 'to fear'), and it denoted the partitive or negated subject (cf. **Sentence Types**, p. 450) and direct object; in some of these functions one can discern traces of the original functions of the PIE ablative (cf. **Nominal Morphology**, p. 435). The genitive also expresses the direct object of the supine, for example, *pride ... viděti groba*~gen.~ '[they] came to see the sepulchre' (Matt. 28: 1: ἦλθεν ... θεωρῆσαι τὸν τάφον), where it reflects the substantival origin of the supine (lit. 'to the seeing of the sepulchre'). The instrumental expresses circumstances of means, time, place, manner, comparison and capacity, and in the last mentioned use is extended to the nominal predicate, compare ORuss. *ta dŭva*~nom.~ *byla poslŭmi*~instr. sg.~ *u Rizě* 'those two were (as) ambassador[s]~instr.~ in Riga' (Smolensk Treaty 1229) and OCS *děvojǫ*~instr.~ *bo bě Eŭa*~nom.~ 'for Eve was a virgin~instr.~'.

Word Order

In the earliest Slavic, as in the modern Slavic languages, word order primarily expresses the information structure of the utterance, the basic principle being that the constituents of the sentence and their subconstituents are arranged from left to right in order of increasing rhematicity. Although the basic word order is SVO, this word order is realized only when it conforms to the pragmatic perspective applied in the individual speech act. In the noun phrase, basically, agreeing attributes precede the head, non-agreeing attributes follow it; but again the speaker's presuppositions regarding the information value of the individual constituent will be expressed in deviations from this basic order (inversion, extraposition).

An important exception to this free word order is the class of atonic words comprising proclitics and enclitics. Proclitic conjunctions (OCS *i* 'and', *a* 'but'), negations and prepositions are obligatorily at the beginning of the constituents they are part of. Enclitic conjunctions (OCS *li* 'whether', *bo* 'for'), modal particles (OCS *li* 'interrogative', *že* 'emphatic'), and inflected forms of personal pronouns are placed after the first orthotonic word of the clause (Wackernagel's position), e.g., *kogda že tę*~acc.~ *viděxomŭ stranĭna*~acc. animate.~ 'When saw we thee a stranger' (Matt. 25: 38: πότε δέ σε εἴδομεν ξένον), *čto ti*~dat.~ *sę*~acc.~ *mĭnitŭ* 'What thinkest thou (lit. 'what thinks itself to you')' (Matt. 17: 25: τί σοι δοκεῖ), *vŭzdastŭ bo ti*~dat.~ *sę*~acc.~ 'thou shalt be recompensed' (Luke 14: 14: ἀνταποδοθήσεται γάρ σοι). Wackernagel's Law continues to be productive in the modern languages, particularly in West Slavic and South Slavic.

Subordination

Subordination is expressed in Proto-Slavic either with finite clauses introduced by conjunctions (**Conjunctions**, p. 448) or with nominalized clauses. The rich participial syntax of the Old Church Slavonic and other Church Slavonic texts is evidence that, prior to the creation of the bookish style of these texts, Common Slavic made extensive use of participial constructions as attributes and appositions. Both attributive and appositive participials serve as alternative expressions equivalent to restrictive and appositive relative clauses; for example OCS *běaxǫ že edini* ... *glagolǫšte* ... 'and there were some that ... said ...' (Mark. 14: 4: ἦσαν δέ τινες ἀγανακτοῦντες πρὸς ἑαυτούς·), *se estŭ tělo moe daemoe za vy* 'this is my body which is given for you' (Luke 22: 19: τοῦτό ἐστιν τὸ σῶμά μου τὸ ὑπὲρ ὑμῶν διδόμενον). But they also occur as unmarked equivalents of circumstantial clauses, for example, *šĭdŭše vŭ gradŭ vŭzvěstišę vĭse* 'they went their ways into the city and told everything' (or: 'after going ...') (Matt. 8: 33: ἀπελθόντες εἰς τὴν πόλιν ἀπήγγειλαν πάντα). When the subjects of the circumstantial and the main clause are not identical, both subject and participial of the circumstantial clause are in the dative ('dative absolute'), for example, *mŭnogu*dat. sg. *sǫštu*dat. sg *narodu*dat. sg *i ne imǫštemŭ*dat. pl. *česo*gen. *ěsti* ... *Isusŭ glagola* 'the multitude being very great, and having nothing to eat, Jesus ... said ...' (Mark. 8: 1: πολλοῦ ὄχλου ὄντος καὶ μὴ ἐχόντων τί φάγωσιν ... λέγει).

References

Andersen, Henning (1968) 'IE *s after *i, u, r, k* in Baltic and Slavic', *Acta Linguistica Hafniensia* 11: 171–90.

—— (1986) 'Protoslavic and common Slavic: questions of periodization and terminology', in Michael S. Flier and Dean S. Worth (eds), *Slavic Linguistics, Poetics, Cultural History: In Honor of Henrik Birnbaum on his Sixtieth Birthday* (*International Journal of Slavic Linguistics and Poetics* 31–2), Columbus, Ohio: Slavica, pp. 67–82.

—— (1996) *Reconstructing Prehistoric Dialects. Initial Vowels in Slavic and Baltic*. Berlin: Mouton de Gruyter.

Arumaa, Peeter (1964) *Urslavische Grammatik* vol. I, *Einleitung, Lautlehre*, Heidelberg: Carl Winter Universitätsverlag.

—— (1976) *Urslavische Grammatik*, vol. II, *Konsonantismus*, Heidelberg: Carl Winter Universitätsverlag.

—— (1985) *Urslavische Grammatik*, vol. III, *Formenlehre*, Heidelberg: Carl Winter Universitätsverlag.

Birnbaum, Henrik (1972) 'Indo-European nominal formations submerged in Slavic', in Dean S. Worth (ed.) *The Slavic Word*, The Hague: Mouton, pp. 142–68.

—— (1985) 'Indo-Europeans between the Baltic and the Black Sea', *Indo-European Studies* 12: 235–59.

Comrie, Bernard (ed.) (1987) *The World's Major Languages*, London and Sydney: Croom Helm.

Conte, Francis (1986) *Les Slaves*, Paris: Albin Michael.

Dybo, V. A. (1981) *Slavjanskaja akcentologija. Opyt rekonstrukcii akcentnyx paradigm v praslavjanskom*, Moscow: Nauka.

—— (1990) *Osnovy slavjanskoj akcentologii*, Moscow: Nauka.

Endzelīn, Jānis (1971) *Jānis Endzelīn's Comparative Phonology and Morphology of the Baltic Languages*, trans. William R. Schmalstieg and Benjamiņš Jēgers, The Hague: Mouton.

Filin, F. P. (1962) *Obrazovanie jazyka vostočnyx slavjan*, Moscow and Leningrad: Akademija nauk.

Gamhrelidze, Thomas V. and Ivanov, Vjačeslav V. (1995) *Indo-European and the Indo-Europeans*, Berlin: Mouton de Gruyter.

Gimbutas, Maria (1971) *The Slavs*, New York and Washington: Praeger.

Gołąb, Z. (1973) 'The initial *x*- in Slavic: a contribution to prehistorical Slavic-Iranian contacts', in Ladislav Matejka (ed.), *American Contributions to the Seventh International Congress of Slavists*, vol. I, The Hague: Mouton, pp. 129–56.

Jakobson, Roman (1971a) 'Remarques sur l'évolution du russe comparée à celle des autres langues slaves', in his *Selected Writings*, vol. I, *Phonological Studies*, 2nd edn, The Hague: Mouton, pp. 7–116.

—— (1971b) 'Opyt fonologičeskogo podxoda k slavjanskoj akcentologii', in his *Selected Writings*, vol. I, *Phonological Studies*, 2nd edn, The Hague: Mouton, pp. 664–89.

Kortlandt, Frederik (1978) 'Comment on W. Winter's paper', in Jacek Fisiak (ed.), *Recent Developments in Historical Morphology*, Berlin: de Gruyter, p. 447.

Lekomceva, M. I. (1981) 'K rekonstrukcii fonologičeskix sistem jazykov goljadi i dneprovsko-dvinskix baltov (I)', *Balto-slavjanskie issledovanija 1980*, Moscow: Nauka, pp. 52–60.

—— (1982) 'K rekonstrukcii fonologičeskix sistem jazykov goljadi i dneprovskodvinskix baltov (II)', *Balto-slavjanskie issledovanija 1981*, Moscow: Nauka, pp. 88–96.

Mallory, James (1989) *In Search of the Indo-Europeans: Language, Archaeology and Myth*, London: Thames & Hudson.

Martynov, V. V. (1983) *Jazyk v prostranstve i vremeni. K probleme glottogeneza slavjan*, Moscow: Nauka.

Schenker, Alexander M. and Stankiewicz, Edward (eds) (1980) *The Slavic Literary Languages: Formation and Development*, New Haven: Yale Concilium on International and Area Studies.

Sedov, V. V. (1979) *Proisxoždenie i rannjaja istorija slavjan*, Moscow: Nauka.

Stang, Christian (1957) 'Eine preussisch-slavische (oder baltisch-slavische?) Sonderbildung', *Scando-Slavica* 3: 236–9.

—— (1964) *Vergleichende Grammatik der baltischen Sprachen*, Oslo: Universitetsforlaget.

Toporov, V. N. and Trubačev, O. N. (1962) *Lingvističeskij analiz gidronimov verxnego Podneprov'ja*, Moscow: Akademija nauk.

Trubačev, O. N. (1973) 'Leksikografija i ètimologija' in S. B. Bernštejn *et al.* (eds), *Slavjanskoe jazykoznanie*, vol. VII, *Meždunarodnyi s'ezd slavistov*, Moscow: Nauka, pp. 294–313.

Vaillant, André (1950) *Grammaire comparée des langues slaves*, vol. I, *Phonétique*, Lyons: Edition IAC.

—— (1958) *Grammaire comparée des langues slaves*, vol. II, 1–2, *Morphologie*, Lyons: Edition IAC.

—— (1966) *Grammaire comparée des langues slaves*, vol. III, 1–2, *Le Verbe*, Paris: Klincksieck.

—— (1974) *Grammaire comparée des langues slaves*, vol. IV, *La Formation des noms*, Paris: Klincksieck.

—— (1977) *Grammaire comparée des langues slaves*, vol. V, *Syntaxe*, Paris: Klincksieck.

Volkaitė-Kulikauskienė, R. (ed.) (1987) *Lietuvių etnogenezė*, Vilnius: Mokslas.

Winter, Werner (1978) 'The distribution of short and long vowels in stems of the type Lith. ĕsti : vèsti : mèsti and OCS jasti : vesti : mesti in Baltic and Slavic languages', in Jacek Fisiak (ed.), *Recent Developments in Historical Morphology*, Berlin: de Gruyter, pp. 431–46.

15 The Baltic Languages

William R. Schmalstieg

The Baltic languages are usually divided into East and West Baltic. The East Baltic languages include the contemporary spoken Lithuanian, Latvian and the extinct Curonian, Zemgalian and Selonian. With minor exceptions the boundaries of the contemporary Lithuanian and Latvian republics correspond to the speech areas of these two languages. The Curonians lived along the coast of the Gulf of Riga (except for the very northern tip which was inhabited by the Finnic Livonians) and south almost to the mouth of the Nemunas (Ger. Memel) on the Baltic. Until the end of the sixteenth century historical sources state that the Curonian language differs from neighbouring languages. In the seventeenth century, however, we encounter testimony that the Curonians speak Latvian (Kabelka 1982: 68). A part of the Curonians adopted the Lithuanian language and there are traces of Curonian in Lithuanian Samogitian (Low Lithuanian) dialects just as there are traces of the original Curonian language in the Latvian Curonian dialect. East of the Curonians in the lowlands of the river which is known in Lithuanian as Mūša (and in Latvian as Lielupe) lived the Zemgalians. Most probably their language became extinct in the second half of the fifteenth century (Kabelka 1982: 77). The Selonians lived to the east of the Zemgalians and it is generally assumed that the northern part was Latvianized and the southern part Lithuanianized before the middle of the fourteenth century (Kabelka 1982: 83).

The West Baltic languages, all extinct, include Galindian, Jatvingian (also known as Sudovian) and Old Prussian (sometimes known simply as Prussian). The second century AD Greek astronomer and geographer Claudius Ptolemaeus in his work *Geōgraphikè hyphégēsis* mentions the *Galíndai kaì Soudinoí*, but we learn little from him except that their neighbours were Slavs, Germans and Finns. In the fourteenth century, the chronicler of the Order of the Cross, Peter Dusburg in his *Chronicon terre Prussie* wrote that the *Galindians* lived in the southern part of the Prussian land and that in the East the *Sudovians* were their neighbours (Kabelka 1982: 27–8).

A Slavicized form of the name *Goljadь* (< Balt. **Galind-*) is found in the Russian chronicles. The Laurentian chronicle under the year 945 contains the first mention of a Jatvingian, namely, *Jatvjagŭ, Gunarevŭ* 'Jatvingian for

454

Gunnar'. Since the Poles were the southern neighbours of the Jatvingians the name of the latter frequently occurs in Polish sources written in Latin, for example, *Jaczwingi, Jazuingi, Jathwingorum natio*. In German sources the name is encountered less frequently, but to refer to the same people we encounter Latin *Sudowite, Sudowenses, Sudowienses*, German *Sudawen, Sudawiter*, etc. It is assumed that this is the same name as the name *Soudinoí* used by Ptolemaeus mentioned above. The identity of the Sudovians and Jatvingians is posited because we find this stated directly in various historical

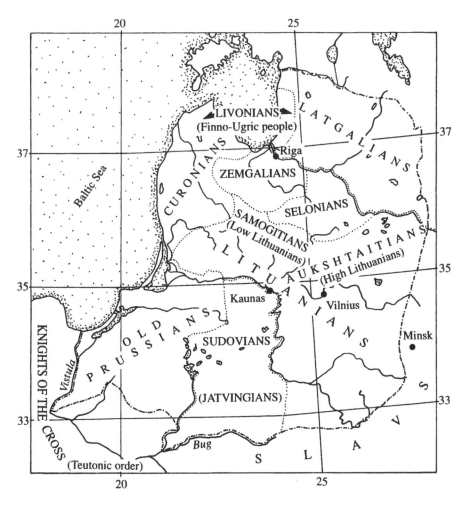

Map 15.1   Baltic tribes at the beginning of the second millennium AD
Source: *Lithuanian Encyclopedia*, Boston: Lithuanian Encyclopedia Press, Inc., vol. II, 1954: 148

sources, for example, *Per terram vocatam Suderland alias Jattuen*, etc. (Kabelka 1982: 29–32; see Map 15.1).

In the twelfth and thirteenth centuries the boundaries of the Prussian people were approximately the following: in the north the Nemunas and the Baltic Sea, in the west the Vistula, in the south unstable borders with the Poles (Cassubians and Mosurians) and in the east Jatvingian–Sudovian and Lithuanian borders (Kabelka 1982: 42). In the beginning of the seventeenth century the Old Prussian language began to die out, but Mažiulis (1966: 26), thinks that there may have been a few speakers here and there until the very beginning of the eighteenth century.

The Baltic People

The Baltic people as a separate IE ethnic and cultural group was formed in the second millennium BC and spread to large areas of south-eastern and eastern Europe along the Baltic Sea, the Dnieper and in the upper reaches of the Volga and the Oka rivers. At this time the Finno-Ugric peoples were their neighbours in the east and north-east and the Iranians (Scythians) and Slavs were their neighbours to the south-east and the south. In the Bronze Age (sixteenth to sixth centuries BC) and in the early Iron Age (fifth to first centuries BC) the separate East and West Baltic cultural areas began to be delineated. One encounters characteristic West Baltic burial mounds of a certain structure with certain stone-covered burials and characteristic East Baltic castle hills (Lith. *piliakalniai*) with finds of the so-called brushed pottery. The territory inhabited by the West Balts included more or less an area bounded in the south-west by the lower reaches of the Vistula (Ger. *Weichsel*) and in the north-east by the lower reaches of the Nemunas (Ger. *Memel*) and the East Balts lived more to the north and espcially to the east. According to Toporov and Trubačëv (1962: *passim*), the prehistoric eastern boundary of the Balts is to be drawn through the upper reaches of the Volga, Moscow and Oka rivers and the southern boundary along the River Seim. In the west one encounters Baltic place-names even to the west of the Vistula. The northern boundary of the Balts and Finns has undergone no substantial changes (Kabelka, 1982: 15–18 see Map 15.2).

Documentation

Apparently the earliest written document in any Baltic language is the Basel epigram discovered by Sephen P. McCluskey in folio 63ra of MS Basel, Öffentliche Bibliothek der Universität Basel, F.V. 2. The text immediately follows the *Quaestiones super quattuor Libros Methodorum* of Nicole Oresme, dated 1369, and immediately precedes – and was clearly written prior to – the undated *Registrum quartium* [sic!] *librorum Methodorum*, which lists all the questions treated by Oresme. The two-line text bisected by

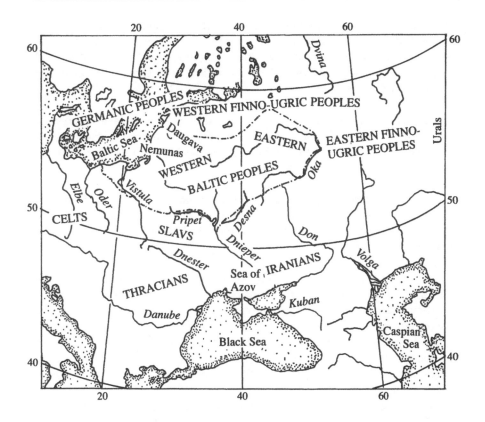

Map 15.2   Areas inhabited by Baltic peoples between the second millennium BC and the first millennium AD
Source: *Lithuanian Encyclopedia*, Boston: Lithuanian Encyclopedia Press, Inc., vol. II, 1954: 147

a standing figure with a balloon has been tentatively transcribed as follows (with a tentative interlinear translation):

Kayle rekyse [figure with balloon] *thoneaw   labonache thewelyse*
Health sir   you are not good   fellow

Eg koyte   poyte [figure with balloon] *nykoyte pēnega doyte*
If   you want to drink   you do not want money to give

'To your health, sir! You are not a good fellow, if you want to drink and do not want to pay money.'

Inside the balloon (in German) one reads the inscription: 'Jesus, ich leid.' In the Middle Ages it was common to insert some short comment with humorous intent following a serious discussion. (Facsimile copies made from the microfilm are published in Schmalstieg 1974: ii; McCluskey, Schmalstieg and Zeps 1975: 160; Mažiulis 1975: 126.) According to McCluskey, Schmalstieg and Zeps (1975: 164–5):

> an analysis of the text of Oresme's *Quaestiones super Methodorum* ... indicates that the portion of Basel F.V.2 that contains the epigram can be associated with a group of codices that emanated from the University of Prague in the last third of the 14th c.

Since at that time Prague drew students from the whole of Bohemia, Germany, Poland and beyond, the presence of a scribe who knew Old Prussian is not problematic. It should be remarked, however, that although the text seems to be in Old Prussian it may actually be in some other now extinct Baltic language.

Also in Old Prussian is the Elbing vocabulary occupying pp. 169–85 of the so-called *Codex Neumannianus*, which dates from around 1400 and is apparently a copy of an original which was composed at the beginning of the fourteenth or the end of the thirteenth century. The Elbing vocabulary containing 802 German words and their Old Prussian glosses is typical of the conceptual dictionaries found in medieval Latin and German manuscripts according to Marchand (1970: 112). Its whereabouts is now unknown (Mažiulis 1966: 27).

Simon Grunau's Vocabulary consists of about 100 German words with their Old Prussian glosses put by Grunau in his *Preussische Chronik* written between 1517 and 1526 to illustrate the Old Prussian language of which he claimed to have a small knowledge (Mažiulis 1966: 31). The original has been lost but several different copies of the vocabulary have survived. Valentin Kiparsky (1970: 219) described the recent discovery of another version of Simon Grunau's Vocabulary in Helsinki, but the unusual feature of this version is that glosses of the Old Prussian words occur in Latin rather than German.

The main source of our knowledge of Old Prussian, however, derives from the three catechisms. The 1st Catechism was published in the press of Hans Weinreich in Königsberg in 1545 in an edition of about 197 copies. Luther's Smaller Catechism published in 1531 in Wittenberg served as the basis for this translation. In the introduction to the 2nd catechism, printed in an edition of 192 copies also in Königsberg, we find the claim that this is a corrected version, presumably a corrected version of the 1st Catechism. The 3rd Catechism (or *Enchiridion*) published in 1561 in Königsberg at the press of Johann Daubman was translated into Old Prussian by Abel Will, the pastor of Pobeten (Lith. *Pabečiai*) on the basis of the German Small Catechism or Enchiridion.

Except for place-names and personal names and a few fragments there are no other sources for Old Prussian. For place-names see Gerullis: (1922) and for personal names see Trautmann (1925). Recent works on Old Prussian include Toporov (1975–), Mažiulis (1981 and 1988).

The first known writings in Lithuanian (in the eastern Dzukish dialect) are a hand-written Lord's Prayer, Hail Mary and Creed discovered in 1962 in a copy of the book, *Tractatus sacerdotalis* published in 1503. This text was written no later than the beginning of the sixteenth century and is probably a copy made of an older version translated from Polish. The first printed book in Lithuanian is Martin Mosvidius' (= Lith. Mažvydas) *Katekizmusa prasti žadei, makslas skaitima rašta yr giesmes* 'The Simple Words of the Catechism, the Art of Reading, Writing and Hymns' published in 1547 in Königsberg in the press of Hans Weinreich (Kabelka 1982: 120–1). Although there may have been between 200 and 300 copies of this book (Ročka 1974: 54) the only known copy was kept in the Königsberg University Library and was bound together with various other books and entitled *Catechismi varii*. In 1956 another copy was discovered in Odessa and then transferred to the University of Vilnius where it is now.

The Latin book *Origines Livoniae* compiled around 1220 by Henry of Livonia contains Latvian place-names and one common noun *draugs* (*draugum suum. id est consocium*) according to Rūķe-Draviņa (1977: 28). The first printed book in Latvian, a translation of Peter Canisius' Small Catechism is the *Catechismus Catholicorum* published in Vilnius in 1585. Although the translator is not indicated in the text it is most likely E. Tolgsdorf (Kabelka 1982: 99).

In spite of the apparent relative simplicity of the Baltic phonological systems and their development, there are significant differences of opinion about them. One of the major problems is the interpretation of the orthographic evidence of Old Prussian. Germans, writing a language that they did not know very well, were prone to interpret the Old Prussian phonemes in terms of their native German speech habits. Since the Old Prussian–German cultural situation is similar to that of Latvian–German it would seem useful to draw a parallel here (Sabaliauskas 1986: 100–1).

Phonology of Common Baltic

The Common Baltic vocalic system seems to have varied little from that of Indo-European which can be set up in the following way:

(I) /i i:/   /u u:/
     /e e:/   /o o:/
           /a a:/

(see Chapter 2, p. 46 and cf. also Chapter 13, p. 388). After this IE system Balticists agree on only one change, namely the merger of (short) */o/ and */a/

producing the following Common Baltic vocalic system which I represent as:

(II)   /i i:/   /u u:/
       /e e:/   /o:/
              /a a:/

In other words short */o/ no longer exists in this system. (Other Balticists picture the Common Baltic system differently, e.g., Kazlauskas 1962: 24).

Any apparent diphthongs which may have existed at period II can probably better be analysed as sequences of */e/ or */a/ (possibly */e:/, */a:/ or */o:/) plus semi-vowel */j/ or */w/, or plus sonant */r l m n/. The canonically possible diphthongs with an initial short element were, consequently: */ej ew er el em en; aj aw ar al am an/. Possibly in early times the sequence */ew/ merged with */jaw/ . If the long diphthongs */ēj ēw ēr ēl ēm ēn; āj āw ār āl ān ām/ ever existed, they were soon shortened and merged with the corresponding short diphthongs. If the long diphthongs */ōj ōw ōr ōl ōm ōn/ (posited by some scholars) ever existed, in my view the initial element was shortened and these merged with */aj aw ar al am an/. Differently from many specialists I do not see a contraction of Common Baltic */ōj/ > E Balt. */uoi/ > /ui/ or a contraction of */ōn/ > E Balt. */uon/> */un (Schmalstieg 1968: *passim*).

The long vowels and the diphthongs could have either an acute or circumflex intonation, so that theoretically possible sequences included the following: */í ế á ố ú; ĩ ẽ ã õ ũ/ and */éj éw ér él ém én; eĵ eŵ eȓ eĺ eɱ eñ; áj áw ár ál ám án; aĵ aŵ aȓ aĺ aɱ añ/. In Proto-Baltic, as in Proto-Slavic, the acute intonation was a rising intonation and the circumflex intonation was a falling intonation; this is almost exactly the opposite of the situation in contemporary Lithuanian where the acute is falling (*tvirtaprādė*, i.e. with a strong beginning) and the circumflex is rising (*tvirtagãlė*, i.e. with a strong ending). Some scholars think that Old Prussian gives evidence of the original situation in the representation of the diphthongs where sometimes the old **circumflex is represented with a macron on the initial vowel of a diphthong**, cf. OPr. acc. sg. *rānkan* 'hand' vs Lith. *rañką* (corresponding to the Latvian falling intonation, cf. *ròku*). The old acute may be represented in Old Prussian by a macron over the second element of a diphthong, compare acc. pl. *kaūlins* 'bones' vs Lith. nom. sg. *káulas* 'bone'. In Latvian the old acute is represented either by the rising intonation (thus Latv. *liêpa* 'linden tree' = Lith. *líepa*), or, if the stress is shifted to an originally unstressed initial acuted syllable, by the 'broken intonation' (thus Latv. nom. sg. *galˆva* 'head' = Lith. *galvà* (acc. sg. *gálvą*)). According to Saussure's Law the ictus is said to be shifted from an originally short or circumflex syllable to a following acuted syllable, thus *r'añkấ > *rañk'ấ. In Lithuanian in word-final position original long acuted vowels (including the diphthongs /uo ie/) were shortened by one mora: (*rank'ấ > rankà, *galvấ > galvà, *nešõ > *nešúo > nešù 'I carry,' etc. In principle the ictus is always on the initial syllable in Latvian.

The vocalic system described in II above could be that of Old Prussian. There is much, however, that is unclear about Old Prussian phonology, particularly the existence of */ō/ might be disputed since the usual reflex of the IE root for 'to give' is found in the Old Prussian 3rd Catechism in the infinitive form *dāt* or *dātwei* (see Burwell 1970: 11–21). On the other hand in the same catechism we encounter *no* 'on' as the apparent cognate of Lithuanian *nuõ* 'from' which must derive from *nō*. It is reasonable to suppose that the phonology of the Pomesanian dialect represented by the Elbing Vocabulary was different from that of the Samland dialect represented by the three catechisms.

Under circumstances which are not completely clear (possibly in stressed syllables[?]) the diphthongs */ej/ (and possibly */aj/[?]) were monophthongized to */ē$_2$/ creating the Common East Baltic vocalic system:

(III) */i, i:/   /u, u:/
       /e:$_2$/ < */ej aj[?]/   /o:/
       /e e:$_1$/   /a a:$_1$/

(Levin 1975: 151)

The above vocalic system lies at the base of all of the contemporary Lithuanian dialects, including standard Lithuanian which is closest to the southern variety (Kauniškiai) of Western High Lithuanian (Vakarų aukštaičiai) (Zinkevičius 1978: 25). The first step in the formation of this latter dialect was the creation of a new long /e:$_3$/ in the sequence */ens/ (cf. *kẽsti* 'suffer' < *kensti) and a new long /a:$_2$/ in the sequence */ans/ (cf. e.g. *sãsaja* 'connection' < *sansaja). The new /e:$_3$/ pushed the old /e:$_1$/ into the position of the old /e:$_2$/ which in turn caused the old /e:$_2$/ to diphthongize to /ie/. In brief:

*/en[s]/ > /e:$_3$/
*/e:$_1$/ > */e:$_2$/
*/e:$_2$/ > /ie/

The new /a:$_2$/ pushed the old /a:$_1$/ into the position of the old /o:/ which in turn caused the old /o:/ to diphthongize to /ua/ (usually written as *uo*). In brief:

*/an[s]/ > /a:$_2$/
*/a:$_1$/ > */o:/
*/o:/ > /ua/

Although many of the slots have different origins from that of Common East Baltic, the resulting vocalic system of standard Lithuanian is much like that of its predecessor:

/i i:/　　　　　　　　　　　　　　　　　/u u:/
/ie/ < */e:₂/ < **/ej ai[?]/　　　　　　/ua/ (usually written *uo*) < */o:/
/e:/ (usually written *ė*) < */e:₁/　　　/o:/ < */a:₁/
/e/ and /e:₃/ (often written *ę*) < */en[s]/　/a/ and /a:₂/ (often written *ą*) < */an[s]/

In Standard Lithuanian the /e:₃/ above may also derive under unclear circumstances from a simple short */e/, compare *mẽs* 'we' (< *mes*) thereby contrasting with *mès* '(he) will throw'. Similarly the /a:₂/ may derive under unclear circumstances from a simple short */a/, compare *mãno* 'thinks' (< *mano*) which contrasts with *màno* 'my, mine'.

The vocalic development from Common East Baltic to standard Latvian is somewhat similar, but in Latvian a new mid vs low vowel contrast deriving from earlier */e e:/ was conditioned by the following vowel. If there was an */i i: e e:/ or the diphthongs */ei ie/ in the following syllable, then earlier */e ē/ received a higher or closer pronunciation, otherwise they had a lower or more open pronunciation, usually written as (short) *ę*, or (long) *ę̄:*, thus with high *e* we have *vecis* 'old man', *vecene* 'old woman', vs *vęcs* < *vecas* 'old' with low *ę*. The higher *e:* vowel (derived from the allophone preceding a high vowel or diphthong) caused the diphthongization of the old Common Baltic */e:₂/ to Latvian /ie/, giving a similar result to the Lithuanian (although for apparently different phonological reasons). Since Common East Baltic */o:/ was the back partner of */e:₂/, this */o:/ underwent the same diphthongization in Latvian as in Lithuanian, that is, it passed to /uo/ or /ua/. Any unmonophthongized long /o:/ actually existing in modern Latvian is encountered only in loan words. Unfortunately the modern Latvian orthography uses the letter *o* to denote both the etymological */o:/ which was diphthongized to /uo/ and to denote the new borrowed long /o:/. Therefore a word written as *jods* can denote either [juods] 'devil' or [jo:ds] 'iodine' (Rūķe-Draviņa 1977: 56). The Proto-Baltic sequence */en/ merged with Latv. */e:₂/ and was diphthongized to /ie/ (cf. Latv. *pìeci* 'five' beside Lith. *penki*) and the Proto-Baltic sequence */an/ merged with /o:/ and was diphthongized to /uo/ (but still written as *o*; cf. Latv. *ròka* 'hand, arm' beside Lith. *rankà*).

Examples below show the IE reconstruction first and then related words in some Baltic and other IE languages (some words illustrate the development of several phonemes):

(a) **likʷ-*: Lith. *lìk-ti* 'to remain, to stay', Latv. *lik-t* 'to put', Skt *rik-táḥ* 'empty', Lat. *re-lic-tus* 'left', Gk *é-lip-e* 'he left'
(b) **gʷīw-*: Lith. *gýv-as* 'alive' (Lith. orthographic *y* denotes phonemic /i:/), OPr. acc. pl. *gijw-ans*, Latv. *dzîv-s*, Lat. *vīv-us*, OCS *živъ*, Skt *jīv-áḥ*
(c) **medʰu*: see (m), p. 464.
(d) **sēd-*: see (i), p. 464.

(e) *$d^h\bar{u}m$-: Lith. *dúm-ai* 'smoke', Latv. *dūm-i*, OPr. *dum-is*, Lat. *fūm-us*, Skt *dhūm-áḥ*, Gk *thūm-ós* 'soul'

(f) *$lejk^w\bar{o}$: see (c), p. 464.

(g) *$d\bar{o}$-: Lith. *dúo-ti* 'to give', Latv. *dô-t*, OPr. *dā-t*, Skt *dá-dā-mi* 'I give', Gk *dí-dō-mi*, Arm. *ta-m*

(h) *$m\bar{a}t\bar{e}(r)$: Lith. *mótė* 'mother', Latv. *mãte*, OPr. (3rd Catechism) *mūti*, (Elbing Vocabulary) *mothe*, OCS *mati*, Lat. *māter*, Skt *mātá̄*, OIr. *māthir*, Gk (Ion.) *mḗtēr*, (Dor.) *mā́tēr*, etc.

(i) *ok^w-: Lith. *ak-ìs* 'eye', Latv. *acs*, OPr. nom. *ackis* 'eyes', Skt *ak-ṣi* 'eye', Lat. *oc-ulus*, Gk nom. dual *ósse* 'two eyes'

(j) *$ak\hat{s}$-: Lith. *aš-ìs* 'axle', Latv. *as-s*, OPr. *ass-is*, Lat. *ax-is*, Gk *áks-ōn*, Skt *aks-áḥ*

(k) *$lewd^h$-: Lith. *liáudis* 'people', Latv. *ḷáudis*, OCS *ljudƀje*, OHG *liut*

The syllable bearing IE sonants */r̥ l̥ m̥ n̥/ for the most part developed the support vowel /i/ (but occasionally apparently /u/) in Baltic (as in Slavic). Thus beside Skt *mṛtáḥ* 'dead' we encounter Lith. *mir̃ti* 'to die', beside Skt *vṛkáḥ* 'wolf', Lith. *vil̃kas* 'id.', beside Goth. *ga-gumþs* 'assembly, synagogue', Lith. *gìmti* 'to be born', beside OHG *gund-fano* 'war-flag', Lith. *giñti* 'to chase'. The circumflex stress in these sequences reflects the etymological short sonant, but an acute stress would apparently reflect an etymological long sonant or short sonant plus laryngeal, compare Lith. *pìlnas* 'full' (*i* is a way of writing the acute in sequences of *i* or *u* plus sonant) beside Skt *pūrṇáḥ*, Goth. *fulls* < *$p\underset{.}{l}n$ or *$pl\underset{.}{H}$-n*; cf. Chapter 14, **Laryngeals** and **Syllabic Sonorants**, p. 426.

The Proto-Baltic consonantal system is presented in the following schema:

	Labial	*Dental*	*Alveopalatal*	*Velar*
Stops				
voiceless	p	t		k (< IE *k and *k^w)
voiced	b	d		g (< IE *g and *g^w)
Continuants				
voiceless		s	š (< IE *$\hat{k}$)	
voiced	v	z	ž (< IE *$\hat{g}$)	
nasal	m	n		
Other resonants j, r, l				

Latvian has merged Proto-Baltic */š/ and */ž/ with /s/ and /z/ respectively, see below. The Proto-Baltic voiced stops seem to derive both from the IE voiced aspirates */bh dh gh ghw/ and the plain voiced stops */b d g gw/ (or in terms of the glottalic theory proposed by Gamkrelidze and Ivanov the plain voiced stops */b[h] d[h] g[h] gw[h]/ and the glottalized consonants */p' t' k' k'w/).

Examples below show the IE reconstruction first and then related words in

Baltic and other IE languages (some words illustrate the development of several phonemes):

(a) *$penk^we$*: Lith. *penkì* 'five', Latv. *pìeci*, OPr. *penckts* 'fifth', Gk *pénte* 'five', Goth. *fimf*, etc.

(b) *$trejes$*: Lith. *trỹs* 'three', Latv. *trîs*, Gk *treîs*, Lat. *trēs*, Skt *tráyas*, Goth. *þrija*, etc.

(c) *$lejk^w\bar{o}$*: Latv. *lieku* 'I put', Lith. *liekù* 'I leave', Gk *leípō*, Goth. *leiƕa* 'I lend', etc.

(d) *$krewə$-*: Lith. *kraū-jas* 'blood', OPr. *kraw-ia*, cf. Skt *kravya-m*, OCS *krъvь*, Lat. *cruor*

(e) *d^hub-*: Lith. *dub-ùs* 'deep', Latv. *dub-t* 'to sink, to become hollow', OCS *dъb-rъ* 'gorge, ravine', (with *-e-* grade ablaut) Goth. *diups* 'deep' (< *d^heub-*)

(f) *$dek\d{m}(-t-)$*: Lith. *dēšimt-s* 'ten', Latv. *desmit* (note merger of Common Baltic */š/* with /s/ and metathesis of /i/ and /m/), OPr. *dessimt-s* 'tenth', Skt *dáśa*, Gk *déka*, Lat. *decem*, Goth. *taíhun*, etc.

(g) *$g^w\d{m}$-*: Lith. *gìm-ti* 'to be born', OPr. acc. sg. *gim-senin* 'birth', Goth. *ga-gum-þs* 'assembly, synagogue', Skt *ga-táh* 'gone', Gk *ba-tós* 'passable'

(h) *awg-*: Lith. *áug-ti* 'to grow', OPr. *aug-innons* 'having grown', Lat. *aug-ēre* 'to increase', Gk *aúk-sein*, Goth. *auk-an*

(i) *$sēd$-*: Lith. *séd-éti* 'to sit', Latv. *sēd-ēt*, OCS *sěd-ěti*, with *-e-* grade root *sed-*, cf. Goth. *sit-an*, Lat. *sed-ēre*, etc.

(j) *$\hat{k}\d{m}t$-*: Lith. *šìmt-as* 'hundred', Latv. *sìmt-s*, Skt *śat-ám*, Gk *he-kat-ón*, Lat. *cent-um*, Goth. *hund*, etc.

(k) *$weĝ$-*: Lith. *vež-ù* 'I transport', Latv. *vęz-ums* 'cart-load', OCS *vez-etъ* 'transports', Skt *váh-ati*, Lat. *veh-it*

(l) *$nizd$-*: (with substitution of *l* for original *n*) Lith. *lìzd-as* 'nest', OHG *nest*, Lat. *nīd-us*, Skt *nīd-á-*, etc.

(m) *med^hu*: Lith. *medù-s* 'honey', Latv. *mędu-s*, OPr. *meddo*, OCS *medŭ*, Skt *mádhu*, Gk *méthu* 'intoxicating drink'

(n) *$nās$-*: Lith. *nós-is*, 'nose', OPr. *noz-y*, Latv. *nãs-s* 'nostril', Skt (dual) *nās-ā* 'nostrils, nose', Lat. *nār-is* 'nostril', etc.

(o) *$j\bar{o}s$-*: Lith. *júos-ta* 'belt', Latv. *jôs-ta*, OCS *po-jas-ъ*, Avest. *yās-ta* 'belted', Gk *dzōs-tós* 'girded'

(p) *rug-*: Lith. *rug-iaî* 'rye', OPr. *rug-is*, OCS *rъž-i*, Old Icelandic *rug-r*

The shift of *$\hat{k}$ > $š$* and *$ĝ$ > $ž$* may not be thoroughgoing, compare such Lithuanian doublets as *klùbas* and *šlùbas* 'lame', etc.

In a sequence of two dental stops inherited from IE times the first dental becomes a sibilant and in regard to voicing (or lack thereof) is assimilated to the second dental: *$ved+tei$* is represented by Lith. *vès-ti* 'to lead' (1 sg. pres. *ved-ù* 'I lead'), Latv. *ves-t*, OPr. *wes-t*; *$met+tei$* is represented by Lith. *mès-ti* 'to throw', (1 sg. pres. *met-ù*), Latv. *mest*, OPr. *met-is* 'a throw' (see Chapter 2, **Dental plus Dental**, p. 40).

The Proto-Baltic sequences */tl dl/ are represented in East Baltic by /kl gl/ respectively (although the Old Prussian evidence is ambiguous), cf. Avest. *aoθrəm* 'footwear', but Lith. *auklė̃* 'cord', Latv. *àukla*, OPr. *auclo* 'collar harness'. On the other hand, one encounters Lith. *žénklas* 'sign' vs OPr. *ebsentliuns* 'designated', and OPr. *addle* 'fir tree', Pol. *jodła* correspond to Lith. *ēglė̃* 'spruce', Latv. *egle*.

The Proto-Baltic sequences of consonant plus */j/ plus non-front vowel led to various types of palatalizations in Lithuanian and Latvian. In Old Prussian the results of such sequences are ambiguous. In the Lithuanian sequence of labial plus */j/ the /j/ is pronounced in word-initial position, but elsewhere merely palatalizes the preceding labial (in Lithuanian the vowel letter *-i-* denotes the palatalization of the preceding consonant if it occurs before a non-front vowel). Thus, for example, Lithuanian *bjaurùs* (= /b^j jaurùs/) 'ugly', but *kópiu* (= /'kop^j u/) 'I climb'. In Latvian in word-initial position an epenthetic /ļ/ is inserted, but elsewhere the /j/ is retained. Cognate with the Lithuanian words given above we encounter Latvian *bļaũrs* 'angry, evil' and *kâpju* 'I climb'. The pronunciation of Old Prussian *piuclan* 'sickle' (cf. Lith. *pjúklas* 'saw') is unknown.

Proto-Baltic */tj dj/ are represented by Lithuanian /č dž/ and Latvian /š ž/ respectively, thus Lith. *vókiečiai* 'Germans' = Latv. *vãcieši* (< *vākietjai*) and Lith. nom. pl. *bríedžiai* 'deer' = Latv. *briêži* (< *briedjai*). The pronunciation of Old Prussian words seeming to presuppose this sequence is not known, for example, *median* 'forest', cf. Latv. *mežs* 'forest', Lith. *mēdžias* 'wood'.

Proto-Baltic */s š ž/ plus */j/ plus non-front vowel resulted in palatalized versions of /s š ž/ in Lithuanian, whereas in Latvian both voiceless spirants gave /š/ and the voiced one gave /ž/. Proto-Baltic */š/ merged with */s/ and Proto-Baltic */ž/ merged with /z/ in Latvian. Then Latvian */sj/ > /š/ and */zj/ > /ž/. Thus *sjū-tei* is represented by Lith. *siú-ti* 'to sew' and Latv. *šū-t*. Compare Old Prussian *schuwikis* 'shoemaker' which may reflect a pronunciation with initial /š/. Note also Latvian first-person singular present *kãšu* (< *kāsju* < **kāšju*) 'I filter' = Lith. *kóšiu*. Thus from Lith. *ežỹs* 'hedgehog', Latv. *ezis*: the respective genitive singular forms are Lith. *ēžio* (< *ežjo*) and Latv. *eža* (< *ezjā* < *ežjā*).

Proto-Baltic */n l r / plus */j/ gave the Latvian dorsal /ļ, ņ/ and palatalized /ŗ/, and Lithuanian palatalized consonants (where the palatalization of the preceding consonant is rendered orthographically by a following letter *-i-*), compare the *-jo*-stem genitive singular forms Lith. *žìrnio* '(of the) pea', *brólio* '(of the) brother', *pavãsario* '(of) spring' = Latv. *ziŗņa, brāļa, pavasaŗa*, respectively. These same phonological sequences are apparently represented in the following Old Prussian words, but it is not known how they were pronounced: *brunyos* 'armour', *kelian* 'spear', *garian* 'tree'.

The Proto-Baltic sequences */kj gj/ and */ k g/ before a front vowel are rendered by palatalized /k̂ ĝ/ in Lithuanian but in Latvian by /c dz/ respectively. The Old Prussian pronunciation of the reflexes of these sequences is unknown. Compare Lith. *tikiù* 'I believe', *regiù* 'I see' = Latv. *ticu, rędzu*. Old Prussian *dragios* 'yeast' seems to contain an etymological sequence with */-gj-/. Lith. *ākys* 'eyes', OPr. *ackis* = Latv. *acis*; Lith. *gérvė* 'crane', OPr. *gerwe* = Latv. *dzẽrve*.

In the Proto-Baltic sequence of consonant plus */j/ plus front vowel the */j/ was lost, compare the Lithuanian vocative singular *svetè* < *svetje. The */j/ is assumed here because the noun is etymologically a *jo-stem noun, compare nom. sg. *svẽčias* 'guest' < *svetjas.

Morphology of Common Baltic

The contemporary Baltic languages have a nominal declension, in which the following cases derive from IE: nominative, genitive, dative, accusative, instrumental, locative and vocative. In addition Latvian and Lithuanian have cases created in Baltic times, namely, an illative, allative and adessive. Lithuanian also has an optional dual number, only traces of which are known in Latvian. The masculine and feminine genders are distinguished in the adjective and noun and there is a vestigial neuter in the Lithuanian and Old Prussian pronoun and adjective.

Substantives

The IE noun was characterized by a root (bearing the lexical meaning), a derivative suffix or suffixes (the meaning(s) of which may or may not be clear now) plus an inflectional ending (showing the function of the noun in the sentence). There are a number of different suffixes or stems used in the formation of the noun as there are in all the conservative IE languages. Here we have chosen for our example an *o-stem noun. This *o-, the meaning of which is no longer clear, is also called the 'thematic vowel' and is represented by Proto-Baltic *a-. Typically the nominative singular of these nouns ended in **-s* and the accusative singular in **-N* ($N = n$ or *m). Sample declensions of *o-stem masculine nouns in the three Baltic languages are given in Table 15.1.

There is fairly general agreement that certain cases derive from certain IE proto-forms: nom. sg. **-os*, acc. **-oN*, instr. **-ō*, voc. **-e*; nom. dual **-ō(u)*; nom. pl. **-oi* (originally a pronominal ending), loc. **-ōse*. The Lithuanian-Latvian genitive singular seems to derive from an etymological ablative **-āt*, cf. Skt abl. sg. *vr̥k-āt* 'from the wolf', whereas the Old Prussian genitive singular may derive from **-os*, cf. Hitt. gen. sg. *antuḫš-aš* 'of the man'. The Lithuanian dative singular may derive from **-ō* (< **-uo* > **-u*) with the addition of *-i* from other dative forms, whereas the Latvian dative singular is taken from the pronominal stems. The Lithuanian locative singular may derive from **-en*, whereas the Latvian is taken from the *ā-stem loc. sg. If the reconstruction is correct the Old Prussian locative singular derives from **-oi*, also represented in some Lithuanian adverbs, for example, *nam-iẽ* (< *ē₂

Table 15.1   Nominal stems in -o-

	Lithuanian	Latvian	Old Prussian
Singular			
Nom.	vil̃kas 'wolf'	vìlks	Deiws (Deiwas 1x) 'God'
Gen.	vil̃ko	vìlka	Deiwas
Dat.	vil̃kui	vìlkam	*Deiwu (?)
Acc.	vil̃ką	vìlku	Deiwan
Instr.	vilkù	vìlku	?
Loc.	vilkè	vìlkā	*Deiwai
Voc.	vil̃ke	vìlk(s)	Deiwe
Dual			
Nom.-Acc.	vilkù	(divu dārzu 'two gardens')	(austo 'mouth'?)
Dat.	vilkám	———	———
Instr.	vilkam̃	———	———
Plural			
Nom.	vilkaĩ	vìlki	*Deiwai
Gen.	vilkų̃	vìlku	*Deiwan
Dat	vilkáms	vilkēm	*Deiwamans
Acc.	vilkùs	vìlkus	Deiwans
Instr.	vilkaĩs	vîlkiēm	?
Loc.	vilkuosè	vìlkōs	?

< *-oi) 'at home', compare Gk oĩk-oi 'id.' (see p. 245). The genitive plural may derive from *-on which passed to Proto-East Baltic *-un under certain conditions, but to *-an in Proto-West Baltic. The Lithuanian dative plural derives from *-omus and the Latvian form is derived from the pronominal stems. The origin of the Old Prussian dative plural is unclear. The accusative plural may derive from *-ons which passed to Proto-East Baltic *-uns under certain conditions, but to *-ans in Proto-West Baltic. The Lithuanian instrumental plural -ais is usually compared with Sanskrit -āiḥ, whereas the Latvian form comes from the Latvian dative plural. Although the *o-stem noun is best attested in Baltic in the masculine gender, many think that there were *o-stem nouns of neuter gender, quoting usually Old Prussian assaran 'lake' (cf. Russ. ozero 'id.'), but this word, ending in -an may merely be the accusative singular of a masculine noun.

The Lithuanian and Latvian singular ending -n and the Lithuanian plural endings -sna, -sne, -sen, -sin, -sn are used for the illative case which usually denotes the final point of some motion, although sometimes the place where something is located. Compare Lith. eĩti laukañ 'to go outside', Latv. kounan tapt 'to come into disgrace' (see p. 475). These have their origin in the accusative singular case followed originally by some postposition which has disappeared. An example of the illative plural is Lith. líeposna 'into the linden trees'. The allative was formed by adding the postposition -p(i) to the genitive case and was normally used with verbs of motion, compare Lith. jaũ vìskas *eĩna velnióp* 'already everything is going to the devil'. The adessive was formed by adding the postposition *-p(i)* to the etymological locative case and denoted a place near something, compare Lith. *Dievíepi* 'in the presence of God' (Endzelīns 1971: 166–7).

Adjectives

These agree in case, number and gender with the substantives which they modify and many of the stems known in the noun classes are known in the adjectives also.

An example of a Lithuanian **o*-stem adjective is given below:

	Singular	*Dual*	*Plural*
Nom.	mãžas 'small' (<*-os)	mažù (<*-uo < *-ō)	mažì (< *-ie < *-ē₂ < *-oi)
Gen.	mãžo (<*-ā[t])	like pl.	mažū̃ (< *-un < *-on)
Dat.	mažám (<-ãmui)	mažíem	mažíem(u)s
Acc.	mãžą (< *-an < *-on)	mažù (< *-uo < *-ō)	mažùs (*-uns < *-ons)
Instr.	mažù (< *-uo < *-ō)	mažiẽm	mažaĩs (< -āis?)
Loc.	mažamè, mažam̃	like pl.	mažuosè (< -*ōsen?)

The **o*-stem adjectives can be masculine in all the Baltic languages and traces of a neuter **o*-stem have been retained in Lithuanian and Old Prussian; compare, for example, the predicative use of the neuter adjective in the Lithuanian sentence: *mán šálta* (< **-o*) 'I am cold' and the nominative singular neuter pronoun and adjective in Old Prussian *sta wissa wargē mien* 'this all bothers me'. The Latvian cognate *mazs* 'small' is declined exactly like *vilks* in **Substantives**, p. 466 above. In Lithuanian and Latvian masculine adjectives the endings of the demonstrative pronouns have been adopted in the dative and locative singular, the nominative and dative plural and the dative and instrumental dual.

In addition to the simple adjective there is also a definite adjective in the Baltic languages. Etymologically this was formed by the addition of the appropriate case ending of the third-person personal pronoun to the simple adjective. Thus one derives *mažàsis* Lithuanian 'the small ...' by adding **-is* 'he' to *mãžas*. For the declension of **-is* see **Pronouns** below. Note then the following definite declensional forms:

	Singular	*Dual*	*Plural*
Nom.	mažàsis	mažúoju	mažíeji
Gen.	mãžojo	like pl.	mažū̃jų
Dat.	mažá(m)jam	mažíe(m)jiem	mažíe(m)siems
Acc.	mãžąjį	mažúoju	mažúosiu(o)s
Instr.	mažúoju	mažiẽ(m)jiem	mažaĩsiais
Loc.	mažãjam(e)	like pl.	mažiuõsiuos(e)

The Latvian definite adjective derives etymologically from the same principle, but since word-final syllables are more reduced in that language the etymological origin is not as immediately clear.

According to one theory the development of the Avestan relative pronoun into a definite pronoun is parallel to the Baltic (and Slavic) development. Thus in Avestan the phrase *daēvo yō apaošō* 'demon which (is) Apaoša' came to mean 'the demon Apaoša' (for this and other theories see Schmalstieg 1987: 304–9).

Demonstrative Pronouns

The demonstrative pronouns nominative singular Lith. m. *tàs*, f. *tà* 'that', Latv. m. *tas*, f. *tā* are cognate with the suppletive IE pronoun which has the nominative singular m. **so*, f. **sā* (cf. Goth. *sa*, *sō*, Gk *ho*, *hē*) but for which the stem in other cases is **t-* (cf. Goth. m. sg. gen. *þis*, Skt *tasya*, Gk *toũ*). In East Baltic the *t*-stem has been generalized to all the cases. The Old Prussian definite article *stas* 'the' may represent a contamination of the stems **s-* and **t-*. Lithuanian *šis* 'this', Latvian *šis*, cognate with OCS *sǐ*, Proto-Gmc **hi* (cf. Eng. *he*), and Lat. *cis* 'on this side' (< **ḱis*) have a declension very similar to that of *tas*. Since IE **/ḱ/* passes to Latv. /s/, the stem of the Latvian nominative singular must be analogical on the basis of some oblique case; compare, for example, the genitive singular masculine Proto-E **ḱjā* > Balt. **šjā* (cf. Lith. *šiõ*) > Proto-Latv. **sjā* > Latv. *šà*. Lithuanian also has the pronoun *anàs* 'that (one over yonder)' denoting a more distant point of reference; this is cognate with Slavic *onъ* 'that' and perhaps somehow connected with Proto-Gmc **jainaz* > Goth. *jains*, Ger. *jener*, Eng. *yon*. Various combinations of these pronouns are also known, for example from *šìs* and *tàs* one encounters Lithuanian *šìtas* 'this', and so on.

Interrogative Stem

The IE interrogative stem **kʷo-* is represented in Lith. *kàs* 'who, what', Latv., OPr. *kas* (= Skt *kaḥ*, Goth. *ƕas*). Lith. *katràs* (also *kataràs*) 'which one of two' is cognate with Skt *kataráḥ*, Gk *póteros*, Goth. *ƕaþar*, OCS *kotoryjь* 'which'. Lith. *kuris* 'which', Latv. *kuŗš* is formed by adding the third-person singular nominative pronoun *jis* 'he' to the adverb *kur* 'where'. These pronouns may also have indefinite and relative meaning.

Old Prussian *ains* 'one' seems to derive from IE **ojnos* and to correspond to Goth. *ains*, OIr. *óin*, Lat. *ūnus*, whereas Lith. *víenas* 'one', Latv. *viêns* 'one' may derive from **ojnos* with an excrescent initial **v-*. The words for 'one' are declined like regular adjectives and agree with the word quantified in case number and gender. Lithuanian masculine *dù* 'two' probably derives from **dvuo* < **dvō*, cf. Skt *dvā(u)*, Gk *dúo*, Lat. *duo*, Goth. *twai*, etc.; Lithuanian feminine *dvi* probably derives from **dvie* < **dvai*, cf. Skt *dvē*, OPr. m.-f. *dwai*. Latvian masculine-feminine *divi* probably derives from **duvi*. For Lithuanian *trỹs* 'three', etc. see (b), p. 464. Latvian *četri* 'four' (beside Lith. *keturì* 'four') is to be ascribed to Slavic influence, cf. OCS *četyre*, Skt *catvãraḥ*, Lat. *quattuor*, etc. For Lithuanian *penkì* 'five,' etc. see (a), p. 464. The second consonant of Latvian nominative *seši* 'six' seems to derive from some oblique case (e.g. gen. *sešu* = Lith. *šešiū̃*), whereas Lithuanian *šešì* has assimilation of the initial consonant to the second consonant, cf. Lat. *sex*, Gk *héks*, etc. Lat. *septem* 'seven', Gk *heptá*, Skt *sapta* seem to presuppose an IE **septṃ* which would give Lith. and Latv. **septin*. The long -*y*- of Lith. *septynì* is probably analogical on the basis of the long vowel of *aštuonì* 'eight'; the -*n* of Latv. *septiṇi* derives from some oblique case, compare Latv. *seši* above. Skt *aṣṭa(u)* 'eight', Gk *oktṓ*, Lat. *octō* suggest a Proto-Baltic **aštō*. Actually encountered are Lithuanian *aštuonì* and Latvian *astôṇi* with the final syllable on analogy with the number for seven or nine. Lith. *devynì* 'nine', Latv. *deviṇi* seem to have replaced an earlier **devin*, in which the initial *d*- has replaced **n*- (as in OCS *devętь*), cf. Skt *náva*, Lat. *novem*, etc. under the influence of the initial **d*- of **dekṃ(-t-)* 'ten' for which see (f), p. 464. The Lithuanian and Latvian numbers from two to ten are declined.

The Lithuanian numerals *vienúolika* 'eleven', *dvýlika* 'twelve', *trýlika* 'thirteen', *keturiólika* 'fourteen', *penkiólika* 'fifteen', *šešiólika* 'sixteen', *septyniólika* 'seventeen', *aštuoniólika* 'eighteen', *devyniólika* 'nineteen' are declined like regular etymological **ā*-stem nouns, except that the accusative case is like the nominative. The second element of the numeral is derived from the root encountered in the verb *lìk-ti* 'to leave' see (a), p. 462, so that a form like *vienúolika* etymologically means 'one left over (after ten)' and so on, cf. Goth. *ainlif*, Eng. *eleven* (cf. Chapter 13, **Numerals**, p. 401).

Pronouns

The first- and second-person singular and plural personal pronouns have no gender distinction, but they do have a full declension: Lith. *aš*, *eš* 'I', Latv. *es*, OPr. *as*, *es* derive from IE **eǵʰ(-om)*, cf. Gk *egṓ*, Lat. *ego*, etc.; Lith. *tù* 'thou, you (sg.)', Latv. *tu*, OPr. *tu*, *tū* derive from IE **tū*; Lith., Latv. *mēs* 'we' derive from Common Baltic **mes*, cf. Arm. *mekʼ*; Lith., Latv. *jūs* 'you', OPr. *ioūs* are cognate with Avest. *yūš* and Goth. *jūs*. An old dual is represented in Lith. *mù-du* 'we two' and *jù-du* 'you two'. A reflexive pronoun Lith. (acc. sg.) *savè*, Latv. *sevi*. OPr. (dat. sg.) *sebbei* which refers in principle to the subject of the sentence is known in all the Baltic languages.

The IE **is* 'he' functions as the third-person personal pronoun in Lithuanian.

Note that the dual forms in Table 15.2 are followed by declined forms of the numeral *dù* 'two'. The Latvian third-person pronoun (m. nom. sg.) *viņš*, (f.) *viņa* is still sometimes used in deictic function and may be connected with OPr. *winna* 'out' and OCS *vъně* 'outside'. The Old Prussian third-person pronoun (m. nom. sg.) *tānas*, (f.) *tannā* is probably derived from a contamination of **tas* and **anas*.

Table 15.2   Third-person personal pronoun

	Masculine Singular	Dual	Plural	Feminine Singular	Dual	Plural
Nom.	jìs	juõ-du	jiẽ	jì	jiẽ-dvi	jõs
Gen.	jõ	———	jũ	jõs	———	jũ
Dat.	jám(ui)	jíem-dviem	jíems	jái	jó-dviem	jóms
Acc.	jĩ	juõ-du	juõs	ją̃	jiẽ-dvi	jàs
Instr.	juõ	jiẽm-dviem	jaĩs	jà	jõ-dviem	jomìs
Loc.	jamè	———	juosè	jojè	———	josè

Verbs

The Baltic simple present and future tenses continue the IE present and future, but in Baltic we encounter a simple preterite instead of an imperfect, aorist, perfect and pluperfect tense (known, e.g. in Greek). Lithuanian also has a newly formed imperfect tense. In addition to an indicative and imperative mood there is also a conditional. The forms of the old middle voice have been lost, but various middle meanings are expressed in the newly created reflexive forms. In addition to the infinitive (ending in *-tie > Lith. -ti, Latv. -t, OPr. -t, -twei) and the supine (*-tum > Lith. -tu) there are many participial formations, which may be used with auxiliary verbs to form various tenses. The dual number has been retained in Lithuanian.

The first-person singular is expressed by one of two possible endings, namely, *-ō > Lith. -uo (still written as -ō in Latvian) (for the 'thematic' verbs) and -mi (for the 'athematic' verbs). In both Lithuanian and Latvian the final *-uo was shortened to -u, giving us such first-person singular present forms as Lith. velk-ù 'I drag', Latv. vèlk-u, but the diphthong was retained when the ending is followed by the reflexive particle, thus Lith. velk-úo-si 'I drag myself along', Latv. vèlk-ô-s. IE *-ō is well represented in Gk phér-ō 'I carry', Lat. fer-ō, OHG bir-u, etc. The athematic ending -mi is encountered in Old Lithuanian es-mi 'I am' (= contemporary standard thematic es-ù). A contamination of the athematic and thematic endings gives Lith. dialect es-mu and Latv. ęs-mu. Old Prussian as-mai 'I am' is unclear. Some think, however, that it results from a contamination of the active ending *-mi and the middle ending *-ai. The Lithuanian second-person singular ending (velk)-ì, encountered in all verb classes, may derive from the athematic verbs, for example, Lith. es-ì 'you (sg.) are' (< root *es- + athematic ending *-si (with simplification of the sequence of two *s's)). There is no distinction of number in the third person, the same form serving to denote singular, dual and plural. Although the usual ending is zero (third person Lith. velk-a 'drags' (thematic vowel -a)) traces of the original ending third-person singular ending *-ti have been retained in athematic Lith. ẽs-ti 'there is, there are' (cf. OPr. ast 'is', Gk es-tì, Skt ás-ti) and was well represented in Old Lithuanian. The Common

East Baltic first- and second-person plural and dual endings were probably those represented in the contemporary Lithuanian thematic verb (1 pl.) *vel̃k-a-me* 'we drag', (2 pl.) *vel̃k-a-te*, (1 dual) *vel̃k-a-va*, (2 dual) *vel̃k-a-ta*; the long vowels attested in the endings of the respective reflexive forms *vel̃k-a-mẽs* (< *-mḗ-s*), *vel̃k-a-tẽs* (< *-tḗ-s*) *vel̃k-a-vos*, (< *-vā-s*), *vel̃k-a-tos* (< *-tā-s*) probably have some analogical origin (Schmalstieg 1961: 371).

In Indo-European the thematic vowel had *-e- grade vocalism in the third-person singular, second-person dual and plural (reflected, e.g. in Gk 3 sg. *phér-e-i* 'carries,' 2 pl. *phér-e-te*, Goth. 3 sg. and 2 pl. *bair-i-þ*) as opposed to the *-o- grade in the first plural (reflected, e.g. in 1 pl. Gk *phér-o-men*, Goth. *bair-a-m*). The generalization of Baltic -a- is connected with the fact that in the sequence of consonant plus */j/ plus */e/ (see p. 466) the */j/ was lost such that before the thematic vowel *-e- there could be no contrast between simple thematic verbs and *-j-stem thematic verbs, thus first-person plural *leid-j-ame (> Lith. *léidžiame* 'we let'), but third-person *leid-j-e > *leid-e. In order to re-establish the *-j-stem the thematic vowel was changed to -a- throughout the conjugation giving *leid-j-a (> Lith. *léidžia*). The thematic vowel -a- was then substituted in the simple thematic verbs also since the old form *ved-e was ambiguous with regard to its derivation (appearing to come either from *ved-e or *ved-je).

Some thematic verbs show root ablaut variation, frequently with *-e-grade ablaut in the present and zero grade in the infinitive stem (also in the preterite and future conjugations), thus, for example, *-e-grade present Lith. *velk-ù*, etc. but inf. *vil̃k-ti*, Latv. *vilk-t* (*vl̥k-tei, see p. 463). Thematic verbs employ either the *-ā- or the *-ē- suffix in the preterite, thus Lithuanian preterite 1 sg. *vilk-aũ* (< *vilk-ā-u (with addition of primary ending -u and shortening of the suffix vowel *-ā-)), 2 sg. *vil̃k-aĩ* (< *vilk-ā- (with addition of primary ending -i and shortening of the suffix vowel *-ā-)), 3 (all numbers) *vil̃k-o* (< *vilk-ā (with zero ending)), 1 pl. *vil̃k-o-me* (< *vilk-ā- (with ending -me)), 2 pl. *vil̃k-o-te* (< *vilk-ā- (with ending -te)), 1 dual *vil̃k-o-va* (< *vilk-ā- (with ending -va)), 2 dual *vil̃k-o-ta* (< *vilk-ā- (with ending -ta)); from *vèsti* 'to lead' Lith. preterite 1 sg. *vedž-iaũ* (< *ved-ja-u < *ved-ē-u (with addition of primary ending -u and shortening of the suffix vowel *-ē-) see p. 460), 2 sg. *ved-eĩ* (< *ved-ē- (with addition of primary ending -i and shortening of the suffix vowel *-ē-)), 3 (all numbers) *vẽd-ė* (< *-ē (with zero ending)), 1 pl. *vẽd-ė-me* (< *ved-ē- (with ending -me)), 2 pl. *vẽd-ė-te* (< *ved-ē (with ending -te)), 1 dual *vẽd-ė-va* (< *ved-ē (with ending -va)), 2 dual *vẽd-ė-ta* (< *ved-ē (with ending -ta)). Possibly this Baltic ending is connected with the thematic aorist ending *-e (Schmalstieg 1965).

In addition to the thematic and athematic verbs there exist verbs with an -i-stem present and *-ē-stem infinitive (preterite and future) and frequently with a zero-grade ablaut of the root. This class of verbs, usually stative in meaning, shares much in common with Slavic verbs in *-i-/-ě- (Leskien's Class IVB). Compare Lith. *minė́ti* 'to mention', Latv. *minét* (= Slav. *mьněti*),

Lith. 1 sg. *min-iù* (< **mn̥-j-ō*), 2 sg. *min-ì*, 3 (all numbers) *mìn-i*, 1 pl. *mìn-i-me*, 2 pl. *mìn-i-te*, 1 dual *mìn-i-va*, 2 dual *mìn-i-ta*, pret. 1 sg. *minė́-j-au*, 2 sg. *minė́-j-ai*, etc. like *vilk-aũ, vilk-aĩ* above.

A third class of verbs has an etymological **-ā*-stem in the present, usually **-ī*- in the infinitive and usually **-ē*- in the preterite. Compare Lith. *prašý-ti* 'to ask', Latv. *prasî-t*, Lith. 1 sg. *praš-a-ũ*, 2 sg. *praš-a-ī̃*, 3 (all numbers) *prãš-o*, 1 pl. *prãš-o-me*, 2 pl. *prãš-o-te*, 1 dual *prãš-o-va*, 2 dual *prãš-o-ta*, pret. 1 sg. *praš-iaũ*, 2 sg. *praš-eĩ*, like *vedž-iaũ, ved-eĩ* above.

The sigmatic future is formed on the infinitive stem and conjugated as follows: from *dúo-ti* 'to give' we encounter the fut. 1 sg. *dúosiu* 'I shall give', Latv. *došu* (< **dōs-j-ō*, cf. Skt *dās-y-ā́-mi*, Gk *dṓsō*), 2 sg. *dúosi*, 3 (all numbers) *duõs*, 1 pl. *dúosime*, 2 pl. *dúosite*, 1 dual *dúosiva*, 2 dual *dúosita*.

A specific Lithuanian imperfect is formed with the suffix *-dav-* plus the **-ā*- preterite endings, thus 1 sg. *vilk-dav-au* 'I used to drag', 2 sg. *vilk-dav-ai*, etc.

The East Baltic conditional mood is derived by the addition of some form of the root **-bi-* 'be' to the supine ending, thus Lithuanian **būtum-biau* 'I would be' contracted to modern *bū́čiau*.

Latvian has a special debitive mood formed by prefixing *jà-* (probably the singular genitive or ablative of the pronoun **is*, see **Pronouns**, p. 470) to the third-person present, the noun subject being in the dative and the object in the nominative: *man* (dat.) *bḗrni* (nom. pl.) *jà-mâca* 'I must teach children' (Endzelīns 1971: 241).

The Indo-European optative in **-oi-* (cf. Gk 2 sg. *phér-oi-s*, pl. *phér-oi-te* 'may you carry', Goth. *bair-ai-s, bair-ai-þ*) is represented in the imperative OPr. 2 sg. *wed-ais* 'lead', Lith. (usually with the prefix *te-*) 3 sg. *te-sãk-ai* 'may he say', *te-dirb-iẽ* 'may he work' (< **-ē₂ < *-aj < *-oj*), Latv. 2 pl. *es-ie-t* 'be' (< **-ē₂- < *-aj- < *-oj-*). The usual Lithuanian second-person imperative, however, is an innovation formed by the addition of (2 sg.) *-k*, (2 pl.) *-kite* to the infinitive stem, thus *saký-k, saký-kite* 'say!'. In modern Latvian the second-person singular imperative is identical with the second-person singular indicative, for example, *es-i* 'be!' (also 'you (sg.) are').

The Baltic languages have retained participles from Indo-European and have created some of their own. Thus one encounters (all forms in the nominative singular masculine unless otherwise specified):

1 Present passive participle, Lith. *vĕd-am-as* 'being led', Latv. *vęd-am-s*, OPr. (f. pl.)*paklausīmanas* 'heard'
2 Future passive participle, Lith. *bùs-imas* 'future'
3 Past passive participle, Lith. *dúo-tas* 'given', Latv. *dôts*, OPr. *crixti-ts*'christened'
4 Special active participle in (Lith.) *-damas*, (Latv.) *-dams*, Lith. *dar-ýdamas* 'doing', Latv. *darîdams*

5   Participle of necessity in -tinas only in Lithuanian, e.g. *abejótinas* 'doubtful, which must be doubted'
6   Present active participle in -nt-, Lith. *vedąs* 'leading' < **vedants*, Latv. dial *vędus*, OPr. (nom. pl.) *skellāntai* 'owing'
7   Future active participle, Lith. *dúosiąs* '(will be) giving', Latv. dialect *došus* (cf. Skt *dāsyan*)
8   Past active participle, Lith. *lìkęs* 'having left', Latv. *licis* 'having put', OPr. *īduns* 'having eaten'

Participles can be used to express reported speech (the indirect mood), compare Lith. *jìs mán pasākė, ką̃ sūnùs dãrąs (dãręs, darýdavęs)* 'he told me what his son is doing (did, used to do)' (with pres., past and impf. act. participles respectively), Latv. *kâdam tȩ̄vam bijuši trîs dȩ̄li* 'a certain father (it is said) had three sons' (Endzelīns 1971: 246).

A wide variety of compound tenses can be formed from various tenses of the copula plus the participles, thus Lith. pres. perf. *esù dìrbęs* 'I have worked', pluperf. *buvaũ dìrbęs* 'I had worked', frequentative perf. *būdavaũ dìrbęs* 'I had worked (at intervals)', fut. perf. *bū́siu dìrbęs* 'I shall have worked', OPr. perf. *kas ast teikūuns dangon bhe Semmien* 'who has created heaven and earth', Latv. perf. *viņš ir aizmidzis* 'he has fallen asleep'.

The Lithuanian passive voice can be expressed only by participles (Ambrazas 1979: 17), for example, with the present passive participle masculine (pres.) *esù mùšamas* 'I am being beaten', (pret.) *buvaũ mùšamas* 'I was being beaten', (frequentative past) *būdavau mùšamas* 'I used to be beaten', (fut. perf.) *bū́siu mùšamas* 'I shall be beaten', (perf.) *esù bùvęs mùšamas* 'I have been beaten', (pluperf.) *buvaũ bùvęs mùšamas* 'I had been beaten', (fut. perf.) *bū́siu bùvęs mùšamas* 'I shall have been beaten'. All of the same tenses can also be formed with the past passive participle *mùštas*, for example, pres. *esù mùštas* 'I am beaten', etc. Latvian also has compound passive preterite forms, for example, pres. *es ęsmu mâcîts* 'I am taught', etc. With a form of the auxiliary *wirst* a compound passive is apparently known in Old Prussian also, for example ... *kas pērwans dāts wirst* '... which is given for you'.

The aspectual system of Lithuanian is complex, frequently a prefix deriving a perfective from an imperfective, for example, *jìs daũg dãrė, bèt niẽko ne-pa-dãrė* 'he did a lot, but accomplished nothing'.

Parts of Speech

The invariable parts of speech consist of conjunctions, adverbs, prepositions and postpositions.

The conjunctions Lith. *ir̃* 'and', Latv. *ir* 'also', OPr. *ir* may be cognate with Slavic *i* 'and, even' if the latter can be derived from **ь(r)*. For the old *ir* contemporary Latvian has substituted the borrowing *un* for the meaning 'and'.

A different ablaut grade of the same particle is Lith. *ař* and Latv. *àr* which mean first of all 'also, in addition to', but also can be used as an interrogative particle, compare Lith. *ař girdéjai* 'did you hear?' Latv. (older) *àr tu jūti* 'do you feel?' It can also mean 'or', compare Lith. *šiaĩp ař taĩp* 'this way or that way' (Endzelīns 1971: 287). These conjunctions are probably cognate with Gk *āra* 'then'. Lith. *õ* 'but', Slav. *a*, are possibly cognate with Skt *āt* 'then'. Lith. *bèt* 'but', Latv. *bet* may be related to OPr. *bhe* 'and', Lith. *be, be-ĩ*. Lith. *be-* may also be used as a prefix to mean 'still, yet', for example, *ař besveĩkas, ař begývas*? 'Is he still healthy, still alive?' Lith. *jeĩ*, Latv. *jā* 'if' are probably derived from the pronominal stem **jo-*.

The Lithuanian subordinating conjunction *kàd* 'that' is derived from the adverb *kadà* 'when', whereas Latv. *ka* 'that' may reflect an old singular nominative-accusative of the interrogative pronoun *kas*.

Adverbs may be derived from fossilized case forms of nouns, for example nominative singular, Lith. *tiesà* 'truly' (lit. 'truth'), Latv. dat sg. *mûžam* 'eternally', acc. sg. Lith. *šiañdien* 'today', Latv. *šòdien*, Lith. instr. sg. *staigà* 'suddenly', loc. sg. *namiẽ* 'at home', illative sg. Lith. *laukañ* 'outside', Latv. *āran* (see **Substantives**, p. 466). The locative singular of the neuter adjective ending in Lith. and OPr. *-ai*, Latv. *-i* also supplies adverbs, for example, Lith. *labaĩ* 'very', OPr. *labbai* 'well', Latv. *labi*. Adverbs are frequently formed from pronominal roots, for example, OPr. *kadan* 'when', Lith. *kadà*, Latv. *kad* (Baltic root **ka-* < IE **kʷo-*), Lith. *kituř* 'elsewhere', Latv. *citur* (cf. Lith. *kìtas* 'other', Latv. *cits*), OPr. *kai* 'as', Lith. *kaĩ*, Latv. dialect *kaî* (loc. sg. n. of *kas*?) (Endzelīns 1971: 259–62).

Many Baltic prepositions are cognate with prepositions in other IE languages, for example, OPr. *en* 'in', Lith. *į̃*, (= Gmc *in*), cf. OPr. *en wissans nautins* 'in all troubles', Lith. *eĩti į̃ miẽstą* 'to go into the city', OPr. *no, na* 'on', Lith. *nuõ* 'from', Latv. *nò* (= Slav. *na* 'on'), cf. OPr. *na semmey* 'on earth', Lith. *nulìpti nuõ árklio* 'to dismount from a horse'; OPr. *per* (translates Ger. *für* 'for' in the catechisms), Lith. *peř* 'through', Latv. *par* 'about, for' (= Lat. *per* 'through'), cf. OPr. *dīnkaumai per twaian labbasegīsnan* 'we thank (thee) for thy kindness', Lith. *eĩti peř laũką* 'to go through a field', Latv. *domāt par ko* 'to think about something'. Frequently the same words can function as verbal prefixes, for example, Lith. *į-eĩti į̃ stõtį* 'to enter (into) the station', OPr. *en-imt* 'to accept', Latv. *ie-brist ūdenī* 'to wade into the water'; Lith. *pér-eiti peř gãtvę* 'to cross the street', Latv. *pār-vilkt* 'to drag over'.

Word Formation

As in all the conservative IE languages word formation plays an important role in the morphology of the Baltic languages.

One morphological category may be derived from another by suffixation, for example, the suffix **-tājo-* (m.) **-tājā(-)* (f.) derives agentive nouns from verbal stems, thus Lith. *giedótojas, -a* 'choir-boy, -girl' < *giedóti* 'to sing hymns', Latv. *dziêdâtãjs* 'singer' < *dziêdât* 'to sing'. A procedure dating from IE times is the formation of etymological **o-* and **ā-*stem nouns from verbal stems by means of the etymological **-o-* (> Balt. *-a-*) ablaut grade of the root, for example, Lith. *brādas* 'ford' (Latv. *brads*) derives from the verb *brìsti* 'to ford' (from the zero grade root form **bṛd-tei*), 1 sg. pres. *bred-ù* (from the *-e*-grade of the root); Lith. *rank-à* 'hand, arm' shows the root vowel *-a-* deriving it from the verb *riñk-ti* 'to gather' (from the zero grade root form **rṇk-tei*), 1 sg. pres. *renk-ù* (from the *-e*-grade of the root).

Like other IE languages the Baltic languages have copulative (*dvandva*), determinative (*tatpuruṣa*) and exocentric (*bahuvrīhi*) compounds (see Chapter 4, p. 121). Copulative compounds are exemplified in Latv. *kurlmḛms* 'deaf and dumb' (Latv. *kurls* 'deaf', *mḛms* 'dumb'), Lith. *plaučkepeniai* 'lungs (heart) and liver' (Lith. *plaūčiai* 'lungs', *kēpenys* 'liver'). In the determinative compounds one element (usually the first) determines the other (usually the second): OPr. *laucagerto* 'partridge' (OPr. *laucks* 'field', *gerto* 'hen'); Lith. *viēškelis* 'highway' (Lith. *viēšas* 'public', *kēlias* 'road, path'); Latv. *trešdiena* 'Wednesday' (Latv. *trešais* 'third', *diena* 'day'). The exocentric compounds refer to something outside of the compound itself: nominative singular feminine Lith. *juodākė* 'dark-eyed', Latv. *mḛlnace* (Lith. *júodas* 'black, dark', Latv. *mḛlns*, Lith. *akìs* 'eye', Latv. *acs*). For verbal prefixation see pp. 474–5.

On Syntax

We can learn little about word order from Old Prussian which shows, with some exceptions a slavish translation of German word for word.

For Lithuanian Ambrazas (1986: 98) writes that for the most part the word order shows that the modifier precedes the element modified, thus adverb + verb, adjective + noun, genitive + noun, particle + verb. The only exceptions are when a noun is modified by an instrumental and when the order is preposition + noun. The usual word order is S(ubject) V(erb) O(bject): *Svēčias nusivil̃ko káilinius* 'The guest took off the fur.' On the other hand the object may precede the verb thereby emphasizing the object: *Mykoliùkas laimḛs nemãtė* 'Mike didn't have any luck.' If the object is a pronoun, its position before the verb is predominant: *Vìsas miēstas manè geȓbė* 'The whole city respected me.' In the folk language and folklore the (S)OV order is more frequent: *Dárbas dárbą vēja* 'Work chases away work.' The more modern unmarked order (S)VO arose in literary Lithuanian after the preposition + noun constructions had already been established, seemingly giving rise to a certain disharmony according to the predictions of word-order typology.

Reflexes of very conservative IE case usage are well represented in the Baltic languages, as exemplified by Lithuanian examples in this paragraph. The nominative case is typically the case of the subject of the sentence: *Màno nãmas* (nom.) *yra dìdelis* 'My house is big.' Typically the genitive case denotes possession: *brōlio stãlas* 'brother's desk'. The genitive also expresses the partitive as in many IE languages: *Mokinỹs padãrė klaidū̃* (gen. pl.) 'The pupil made (some) mistakes.' In addition to such well-attested functions, one encounters the genitive as the object of a supine, or even an infinitive replacing a supine: *Jìs atėjo kárvės* (gen.) *piȓktų* (supine) (*piȓkti* (inf.)) 'He came to buy a cow.' Probably it is the suppression of the supine (or infinitive) in such sentences which has led to the creation of a genitive of goal: *atėjaũ dvìračio* (gen.) 'I came for the bicycle.' The genitive case also expresses the agent of a passive verb and sometimes competes with an instrumental to denote the instrument: *Žẽmė ẽsti sniẽgo* (gen.) or *sniegù* (instr.) *nuklotà* 'the earth is covered by (with) snow.' The genitive case interprets the snow as the agent covering the earth, whereas the instrumental case interprets the snow as the instrument with which the earth is covered. This use of the genitive is well attested in other conservative IE languages: Skt *pátyuḥ* (gen.) *krītá̄ satí* 'the wife bought by the spouse', Lat. *attonitus serpentis* 'astonished by the serpent', etc. The dative case functions with the meaning of the indirect object: *Tévas dãvė vaĩkui* (dat.) *óbuoli* 'Father gave the child an apple' as in many other IE languages. An ancient syntactic feature is the use of the dative as the object of an infinitive to express purpose: *Pirkaũ dal̃gį šiẽnui* (dat.) *pjáuti* 'I bought a scythe in order to mow the hay'. A similar construction is encountered in Old Czech: *Kúpichu pole pútníkóm* (dat.) *hřésti* 'They bought a field to bury the pilgrims in.' Compare also Hitt. *nu* SAL.MEŠ *ukturiya haštiyaš* (dat.) *leššuwanzi pānzi* 'The women go to the *ukturiya* 'to collect bones'. A dative absolute construction is also known: *Sáulei* (dat.) *tēkant, jìs atsikélė* 'When the sun rose, he got up.' The accusative case functions as the direct object of a verb: *Rašaũ laĩšką* (acc.) 'I am writing a letter.' Typically the instrumental case denotes the instrument with which something is done: *Rašaũ pieštukù* (instr.) 'I am writing with a pencil.' The instrumental case may be used as the predicate of the copulative verb when it means 'to become': *Jìs bùvo prezidentù* (instr.) 'He was president.' The locative case, as its name implies, expresses location: *Mẽs gyvẽname miestè* (loc.) 'We live in the city.' The vocative case is used to address someone: *Tė́ve mū̃su . . .* 'Our Father . . .'.

Similar case usages are encountered in Latvian: *Zirgs* (nom.) *ir mežā* (loc.) 'The horse is in the forest'; *nama* (gen.) *jumts* 'the roof of the house'; in Latvian the dative is used with the copula to express possession: *Saimniekam* (dat.) *ir zirgs* 'The farmer has a horse' (lit. 'to the farmer is a horse'); dative absolute: *Saulei rietot, mēs braucām mājās* 'As the sun set, we drove home'; *Es lasu grāmatu* (acc.) 'I am reading a book' (Fennell and Gelsen 1980: 5, 11, 787, 39); *skaties abām acīm* (instr.), *klausies abām ausīm* (instr.) 'look with both eyes, listen with both ears'. The vocative of *māte* 'mother' is *māt* 'Oh, mother!'

One can conclude then that the Baltic case syntax is quite conservative, probably retaining more archaisms than any other contemporary IE language.

Note

I should like to thank herewith my colleagues Professor A. Klimas and Professor A. Sabaliauskas for commenting on an earlier version of this paper.

References

Ambrazas, Vytautas (1979) *Lietuvių kalbos dalyvių istorinė sintaksė*, Vilnius: Mokslas.

—— (1986) 'Dabartinės lietuvių kalbos žodžių tvarkos modeliai', *Lietuvos TSR Mokslų Akademijos darbai*, 3(96): 92–102.

Burwell, Michael (1970) 'The vocalic phonemes of the Old Prussian Elbing vocabulary', in Magner and Schmalstieg 1970: 11–21.

Dambriūnas, L., Klimas, A., and Schmalstieg, William R. (1980) *An Introduction to Modern Lithuanian*, 3rd edn, New York: Franciscan Fathers (361 Highland Blvd, Brooklyn, NY 11207).

Endzelīns, Jānis (1971) *Comparative Phonology and Morphology of the Baltic Languages*, The Hague and Paris: Mouton (English translation by Benjamiņš Jēgers and William R. Schmalstieg of Endzelīns, *Baltu valodu skaņas un formas*, Riga, 1948).

Fennell, T. G. and Gelsen, H. (1980) *A Grammar of Modern Latvian*, The Hague, Paris and New York: Mouton.

Fraenkel, Ernst (1962–65ff.) *Litauisches etymologisches Wörterbuch*, Heidelberg: Carl Winter; Göttingen: Vandenhoeck & Ruprecht.

Gerullis, Georg (1922) *Die altpreussischen Ortsnamen*, Berlin: Walter de Gruyter.

Kabelka, Jonas (1982) *Baltų filologijos įvadas*, Vilnius: Mokslas.

Kazlauskas, Jonas (1962) 'K razvitiju obščebaltijskoj sistemy glasnyx', *Voprosy jazykoznanija* 4: 20–4.

Kiparsky, Valentin (1970) 'Das Schicksal eines altpreussischen Katechismus II', *Baltistica* 6(2): 219–26.

Korsakas, Kostas (ed.) (1974) *Pirmoji lietuviška knyga*, (facsimile edition of Martynas Mažvydas' Catechism; Biography of Mažvydas by K. Korsakas [pp. 7–45]; Evaluation of Mažvydas writings by M. Ročka [pp. 46–82]), Vilnius: Vaga.

Levin, Jules (1975) 'Dynamic linguistics and Baltic historical phonology', *General Linguistics* 15(3): 144–58.

Lithuanian Encyclopedia (1954) vol. II, Boston: Lithuanian Encyclopedia Press, Inc.

McCluskey, Stephen C., Schmalstieg, William R. and Zeps, Valdis J. (1975) 'The Basel epigram: a new minor text in Old Prussian', *General Linguistics* 15(3): 159–65.

Magner, Thomas F. and Schmalstieg, William R. (eds) (1970) *Baltic Linguistics* University Park and London: The Pennsylvania State University Press.

Marchand, James (1970) 'Some remarks on the German side of the Elbing vocabulary', in Magner and Schmalstieg 1970: 109–17.

Mažiulis, V. (1966) *Prūsų kalbos paminklai*, Vilnius: Mintis.

—— (1975) 'Seniausias baltų raštų paminklas', *Baltistica* 11(2): 125–31.

—— (1981) *Prūsų kalbos paminklai*, vol. II, Vilnius: Mokslas.

—— (1988) *Prūsų kalbos etimologijos žodynas*, Vilnius: Mokslas.

Ročka, M. (1974) in Korsakas (ed.) (1974) *Pirmoji lietuviška knyga*.

Rūķe-Draviņa, V. (1977) *The Standardization Process in Latvian: 16th Century to the Present*, Stockholm: Almqvist & Wiksell International.

Sabaliauskas, Algirdas (1986) *Mes Baltai*, Kaunas: Šviesa.

Schmalstieg, William R. (1961) 'Primitive East Baltic *-uo-, *-ie- and the 2nd sg. ending', *Lingua* 10(4): 369–74.

—— (1965) 'Again the Lithuanian preterite in -ė', *Annali, Istituto orientale di Napoli* 6: 123–6.

—— (1968) 'The development of Common East Baltic word-final *-an', *Baltistica* 4(2): 185–93.

—— (1974) *An Old Prussian Grammar: The Phonology and Morphology of the Three Catechisms*, University Park and London: The Pennsylvania State University Press.

—— (1987) *A Lithuanian Historical Syntax*, Columbus, Oh.: Slavica.

Toporov, V. N. (1975–) *Prusskij jazyk* (5 vols to date), Moscow: Nauka.

Toporov, V. N. and Trubačev, O. N. (1962) *Lingvističeskij analiz gidronimov verxnego Podneprov'ja*, Moscow: AN.SSSR., Institut Slavjanovedenija.

Trautmann, Reinhold (1925) *Die altpreussischen Personennamen*, Göttingen: Vandenhoeck & Ruprecht.

Zinkevičius, Z. (1978) *Lietuvių kalbos dialektologija*, Vilnius: Mokslas.

16 Albanian

Shaban Demiraj

Preliminary Notes

Albanian, which has been recognized as an IE language since the last century (Bopp 1854), has undergone a continuous process of development which has caused far-reaching changes at all levels of its linguistic structure. However, it has also preserved many features which are characteristic of Proto-Indo-European and which are also to be found in the other IE languages. Like Greek and Armenian, Albanian is a separate branch of Indo-European. In the course of its development it has also evolved a number of features that are characteristic of the Balkan languages as well as its own particular features, which are covered briefly in the following sections.

Although it is one of the oldest Balkan languages, Albanian – like Rumanian and Lithuanian – is attested relatively late in writing. The earliest printed book in Albanian hitherto discovered is John Buzuku's *Missal* (1555). This was written in the northern dialect (Gheg), while *The Christian Doctrine* (1592) by Matranga was written in the dialect of the *arbëresci* of Italy and exhibits characteristics of the southern dialect (Tosk).

Buzuku's book cannot have been the first written in Albanian. Some references indicate that the language must have been committed to writing at least as early as the fourteenth century. The French monk Broccardus, who for a time was archbishop of Antivari (nowadays in Montenegro) claims in a Latin work of 1332, 'Although the Albanians have another language, totally different from Latin, they still use Latin letters in all their books.'

However, no trace has been found of such books. Only a few short sentences dating from the fifteenth century have been found, among which the most notable is the *Baptism Formula* (1462) of the Archbishop of Durazzo, Paolo Angelo: *Un të paghësont pr emënit Atit e t birit e t spertit senit*, 'I baptize you in the name of the Father and of the Son and of the Holy Spirit.'

A number of shared orthographical features in the works of Buzuku and Matranga also bear witness to the existence of a written Albanian tradition before the time of these two writers, who had no contact with each other. Among such features we may mention in particular the fact that both Buzuku and Matranga indicate long vowels by doubling the letters in question (see **The Vowel System**, p. 483).

Albanian is currently spoken in Albania (over three million speakers), in the former Yugoslavia – in Kossovo, Macedonia, Montenegro, etc. – (over two million), in Greece (to the south of the Albanian border), as well as by a large number of immigrants in Turkey, the United States, Canada, France, Syria, Egypt, Australia and so on, who have left Albania for economic reasons.

There are also many settlements of *arbëresci* (*arvanites*) in southern Greece, in the Peloponnese and on some of the Aegean islands, as well as a large number *arbëresci* villages in southern Italy and Sicily. Those in Greece were founded during the fourteenth century, while those in Italy and Sicily date from the fifteenth to seventeenth centuries. In these settlements the *arvanites* or *arbëresci*, who still preserve their mother tongue, speak an old form of Albanian which they call *arbërisht*. (Note that *ë* is similar to French -*e*- in unstressed syllables and *sh* is equivalent to English *sh* in *she*, etc.)

The ethnic name *arbër-esh* (*arbën-esh* in the northern dialect) is derived from *Arbër* < *Arbën*, the old name for Albania, which has its origins in the name of an Illyrian tribe, the *Albanoi* (in central Albania), mentioned by Ptolemy in his *Geography* (second century AD). This old name for the Albanians also survives in the words *albanenses/arbanenses* (Lat.), *albanese* (It.), *arvanitis* (Gk), *arnaut* (Turkish), etc. But over the past few centuries, the ethnic name *arbën-esh/arbër-esh* has been replaced in modern Albania by the word *shqip-tar*, and the name of the country by *Shqip-ni/Shqip-ë-ri*; these forms derive from the adverb *shqip* (= [ʃʲkʲip]) 'Albanian', whose original meaning seems to have been 'clear', 'frank'. Thus we are dealing with a phenomenon similar to that of the German word *deutsch* < *diutisc* < *deot* 'people', if indeed it is connected with *deuten* 'to interpret' (see Paul 1959: vol. I, 81). The adverb *shqip* in Albanian has replaced the old adverb *arbën-isht/arbër-isht*.

The division of Albanian into two main dialects, northern and southern, separated roughly by the River Shkumbin in central Albania, goes back to the first millennium AD (see Hamp 1966: 98). This dialectal division took place during the gradual transition from the 'parent language' to Albanian (see below).

The differences between the two dialects are mainly phonetic in character. The principal differences are: rhotacism of intervocalic -*n*- to -*r*- (cf. *arbën-esh* > *arbër-esh*), rise of a tonic vowel /ë/ in the southern dialect (see p. 485) and nasalization of tonic vowels before nasal consonants in the northern dialect (see Demiraj 1988: 229ff.). Within each of these two main dialects further subdialectal divisions have been noted; these are characterized by certain innovations which are beyond the scope of the present chapter.

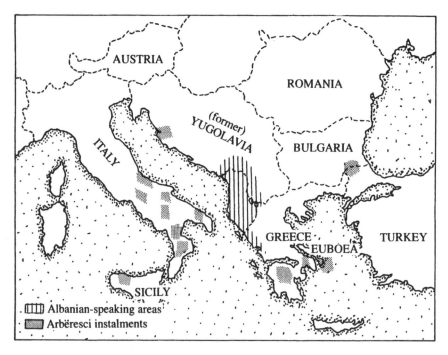

Map 16.1 · Albanian and arbëresci settlements
Source: *Dialectological Atlas of the Albanian Language*, Institute of Linguistics and
Literature, Tirana (unpublished)

Origins

The relatively old dialectal division of Albanian once again poses the question
of the ancient homeland of the Albanians, as well as the problem of the origin
of the language. These two closely related problems have given rise to heated
debate which is still continuing. (For a synopsis of these discussions, see
Demiraj 1988: 146f.)

As regards the ancient homeland of the Albanians, everything seems to
confirm the prevailing opinion that their ancestors in the Graeco-Roman
period lived on the coasts of the Adriatic. However, we may follow Hamp
(1966: 106) in claiming: 'Of course, in any event we could only prove the
Albanians did, and never that they did *not*, precede the Slavs.'

Given such circumstances we may adopt the most plausible view, that
Albanian represents a later stage of development of Ancient Illyrian, or more
precisely of one of the ancient Illyrian dialects (Meyer 1888: 804). But some
linguists maintain that Albanian derives from Thracian or from 'Daco-
Mysian' (on all of these views see Demiraj 1988: 147ff.).

The changes that characterize the gradual emergence of Albanian may be
assigned to the fifth and sixth centuries AD (see Demiraj 1988: 197ff.).

The reconstruction of the oldest stages of Albanian presents great difficulties, which are due not only to the fact that it is attested late (see p. 480), but also to the fact that there remain very few traces of the ancient Balkan languages, apart from Greek. Thus, whether we accept the theory that Albanian is of Illyrian origin, or we take a different view (see above), the problem under investigation exhibits many unknown factors.

But despite such difficulties, Albanian studies in the past two centuries have helped towards a clear identification of the IE heritage in Albanian at all levels of structure, as well as the peculiarities of its development during the prehistoric and historical periods. Thus, for example, scholars have been successful in establishing, amongst other facts, that Albanian is part of the 'Eastern' (*satəm*) group of IE languages (cf. Chapter 2, **The Tectals**, p. 38), which are distinguished by the development of the labiovelars (see pp. 487f. and Chapter 2, **Obstruents**, p. 33f.).

The following sections give a brief outline of the most notable findings in relation to the IE origins of Albanian and to its development at all levels of structure.

The Phonological System

The phonological system of attested Albanian is evidently the result of a continuous process of development which began in the most ancient period, that is at a time when we assume that the different IE tribes spoke related dialects. A comparison of the modern phonological system with that reconstructed for Proto-Indo-European will show that radical changes have taken place. As will become clear from the following outline, certain changes which have occurred in the Albanian phonological system help to confirm its IE origin and to shed light on questions surrounding certain characteristics of Proto-Indo-European as reconstructed by means of the comparative method.

For example, it has generally been accepted that one of the features which characterized the phonological system of Proto-Indo-European at a certain stage of its development was the opposition between short and long vowels (see Szemerényi 1980: 31; Mayrhofer 1986: 171). This contrast was also characteristic of the phonological system of Albanian (or rather of its 'parent language') at an ancient stage (see below and p. 485). The old opposition between short and long vowels is also confirmed by the ablaut alternations *a* ~ *o* and *e* ~ *o* in the verb system (see p. 495).

In certain cases, such as the gutturals, the development of the Albanian consonant system also demonstrates that the language was characterized at an ancient stage by certain oppositions typical of the IE languages in general (see pp. 487f.).

The Vowel System

As mentioned above, the IE languages had at a certain ancient stage of their development evolved a system of five vowels, */a e i o u/, both long and short (cf. Mayrhofer 1986: 168). It is outside the scope of this chapter to examine in detail the process which led to this situation.

In attested Albanian seven vowels (/a i u e o y ë/) are indicated. These occur both long and short in the works of the oldest writers, for example, Buzuku: *pat baam* 'had done', *nee* (acc.) 'us', *hiirplota* 'full of grace', *syytë e tuu* 'your eyes', etc.; Matranga: *ndë dheet* 'on earth', *u bëë* 'was done', *trij* 'three', etc. (see p. 485).

In attested Albanian, three of the five short vowels of Proto-Indo-European, namely */a i u/, have generally preserved their quality in tonic syllables (unless they have been affected by some phonetic or morphophonological process such as umlaut, q.v. p. 490), for example:

> *i athët* 'acid' < **aḱidus*, *kap* 'to grasp' (cf. Lat. *capio*), *gji(n)* breast' (cf. Lat. *sinus*), *lidh* 'to tie' (cf. Lat. *ligare*), *gju(n)* < *glu(n)* 'knee' (cf. OIr. *glun*), *ngul* < **n-kul ~ sh-kul* 'to thrust in ~ root out' (cf. Lith. *kuliù*)

However, short */o/ has regularly become /a/, as in Germanic, Lithuanian and so on, for example:

> *na* (nom.) 'we' < **nos*, *natë* 'night' (cf. Lat. *nox*, Lith. *naktìs* etc.), *darkë* 'supper' (cf. Gk δόρπον) etc.

This change, not found in loan words from Ancient Greek and Latin, took place before these words were borrowed into the Albanian 'parent language'.

Short */e/ in turn originally gave /e/, for example, *mb-ledh* 'to gather' (cf. Lat. *legō*, Gk λέγω), *pesë* 'five' < **penkʷe*, *dredh* 'to twist' < **dreĝʰ-* etc. But in most cases short /e/ became /ie, ié (je)/ and in some cases /ja/, for example:

> *bie(r)* 'to bear' < **bʰerō*, *nier* (modern *njer-i*) 'man' < **ner*, *vjet* 'year' < **wetos* etc.; *mjal-të* 'honey' < **meli-*, *jetër/jatër* (modern *tjetër/tjatër*) 'other' (cf. Gk. ἕτερος) etc.

See Meyer 1892: 83ff.; Çabej 1970: 105f.

The other two Albanian vowels, /y/ and /ë/, have arisen during the course of development of the language.

The front, rounded, very close vowel /y/ arose from the development of a vowel /u:/ (see pp. 485f.), or under the influence of another /y/, for example in the first syllable of *fytyrë* 'face' < Lat. *factūra*, etc.

The central half-close vowel /ë/ (= /ə/) is also a result of innovation within Albanian. But, unlike the other vowels, which occur in both stressed and unstressed syllables over the whole Albanian-speaking area, the vowel /ë/ occurs in tonic position in the southern dialect only, while in atonic position it is characteristic of the whole of Albanian. In atonic position it has arisen as a result of the reduction of another vowel brought about by the strong stress accent (see p. 486).

The stressed vowel /ë/ arose mainly as a result of the evolution of the vowel /a/ and also in part from the vowel /e/ before a nasal. This type of change is a result of the influence of the following nasal consonant, which first through the nasalization of /a/ led to the vowel being pronounced with a gradual raising of the tongue, that is, increasingly close, so that its pronunciation went beyond the limits of the vowel /a/. A similar phenomenon also occurred in the case of the vowel /e/ under the same phonetic conditions. But in the northern dialect the process of nasalization of /a/ and /e/ did not in either case give rise to the vowel /ë/; this is one of the main differences between this dialect and that of the south. Compare, for example, *nánë ~ nënë* 'mother', *e áma ~ e ëma* 'his mother', *bánj > bënj* (modern *báj ~ bëj*) 'to do', etc.

It should be noted that in Albanian the vowel /ë/ in tonic syllables occurs only in native words and Latin loans but not in loans from Slavic. It must therefore have developed during the first half of the first millennium AD.

It should also be noted that a similar vowel in stressed (and unstressed) syllables also arose in Rumanian (on which see *ILR*: vol. II, 191; Sala 1970: 33f.).

The long vowels of attested Albanian bear no relation to the long vowels of the ancient IE period (see p. 483). As indicated below, the other IE long vowels, with the exception of long */i/, changed early in Albanian, or more precisely in the 'parent language'. Thus the long vowels of attested Albanian are a result of the independent historical development of the language. In most cases we see a process of compensatory lengthening as a result of the reduction and loss of unstressed vowels or syllables, or due to the contraction of two vowels. For example, *bë* 'oath' < **beë* < **bédā* (Meyer 1891: 30), (*ti*) *lë* 'you left' < *lae*, *ngë* 'leisure' < *ngae*, etc. Compare also the Latin loans *mjēk* (modern *mjek*) 'doctor' < *medicus*, *kūt* (modern *kut*) 'yard' < *cubitus*, etc.

The IE long vowels developed as follows in Albanian:

Long */a:/ became /o/, e.g. **māter > motër* 'sister', **tās > a-to* 'those' (f.), etc.

Long */e:/ also became /o/, e.g. *dorë* 'hand' < **ĝʰērā*, *mot* 'year' (cf. Lith. *mētas*), *plot* 'full' < **plētos* (cf. Lat. *im-plētus*), etc.

Long */o:/ in turn became /e/, e.g. *ne* (acc.) 'us' < **nōs* (cf. Lat. *nōs*), *pelë* 'mare' (cf. Gk πῶλος), *té-të* 'eight' (cf. Gk ὀκτώ, Lat. *octō*, etc).

Long */i:/, being a vowel of maximum closure, could not undergo such a change, and thus has preserved its quality. But when the system of opposition between long and short vowels broke down, even */i:/ could hardly have preserved its old length. Thus in any attested form such as *pī* 'to drink' (cf. Gk πίνω) the length of the /i:/ must have been reintroduced at a later stage.

Long */u:/ became either the front rounded vowel /y/, or /i/. The latter reflex seems to be the more recent (Meyer 1892: 80), but Pedersen (1900: 340) maintains that the opposite is true. Examples are *dyllë* 'wax' < **ĝʰūd-los*, (*h*)*yll* 'star' < *sūl-, *mi* 'mouse' < *mūs, *thi* 'pig' < *sūs, etc. (see Meyer 1892: 81).

It should be noted that in some Latin loans long /u:/ also became /y/, for example, *iunctūra* > *gjymtyrë* 'joint' (of the body), *factūra* > *fëtyrë* > *fytyrë* 'face'.

To round off these notes on the Albanian vowel system, it should be noted that some traces of qualitative and quantitative ablaut are preserved in the language. As regards qualitative ablaut, we have the contrast */e ~ o/ (cf. Gk λείπω ~ λέ-λοιπα). There are very few traces of this type of ablaut in Albanian, but we do find the words *bie*(*r*) ~ *bar* 'to bear' < *bʰerō ~ *bʰorejō (cf. also *barrë* 'burden' < *bʰorno-), *vjer* ~ *var* 'to hang' < *ver- ~ *vor (see Meyer 1891: 35, 475; Çabej 1970: 119). Note that in attested Albanian the forms *bar* and *var* function as present (indicative).

On quantiative ablaut see p. 483 and p. 495.

As mentioned on p. 484 the rise of the vowel /ë/ in unstressed syllables is a result of the reduction of another vowel caused by the stress accent. This vowel appears in native Albanian words as well as in loans from Ancient and Medieval Greek and from Latin, while in the Slavic loans, in general, no such phenomenon occurs. This supports the claim that the Albanian accent, at least from Graeco-Latin antiquity onwards, was dynamic rather than quantitative in character. No conjecture can be formed about the oldest stages.

Another peculiarity of the Albanian accent is the fact that it is fixed on a certain syllable of the stem. In the case of verbs it regularly falls on the ultimate syllable of bisyllabic or polysyllabic words, while with nouns it can fall on any syllable. In the case of the oldest nouns, however, it most frequently falls on the initial syllable, for example, *émën*(*ë*)/*émër*(*ë*) 'name', *dimën*(*ë*)/*dímër*(*ë*) 'winter', etc. Note also the loan word *mókën*(*ë*)/*mókër*(*ë*) < Ancient Gk μᾱχανά.

Albanian has therefore not preserved the IE feature of accent mobility within the paradigm of one and the same word, a phenomenon which is still alive in Greek, in the Slavic languages in general, and so on.

The Consonant System

The Albanian consonant system, with 29 consonants, is even more complex. Some of these consonants have arisen in the course of the development of the language, e.g. the affricates ‹c› (= /ts/), ‹x› (= /dz/), ‹ç› (= /tʃ/), ‹xh› (= /dʒ/), etc. But since an explanation of all the consonants of Albanian would be beyond the scope of an overview like this, we shall briefly examine here some of the questions surrounding the development of certain oppositions in the consonant system reconstructed for Indo-European; we shall also examine some particular consonants.

Albanian, like the other IE languages, has preserved the contrast *voiceless ~ voiced* in the case of guttural, palatal, dental, labial, etc. consonants, but the opposition between aspirate and non-aspirate consonants was neutralized at an early stage. The old threeway contrast (*voiceless ~ voiced ~ voiced aspirate*) of certain consonants (see for instance Szemerényi 1980: 47ff., 134ff.; Mayrhofer 1986: 91ff.) has thus been reduced to a twoway opposition (*voiceless ~ voiced*). The old oppositions */ p ~ b ~ bʰ; k ~ g ~ gʰ; t ~ d ~ dʰ/ etc. have been reduced to the oppositions /p ~ b; k ~ g; t ~ d/ etc., with the aspirates being lost. For example: *pī* 'to drink' (cf. Gk πίνω etc.), *bānj/bënj* 'to do' < **baniō, bathë* 'bean' < **bʰakā* (cf. Gk φακός, φακή); *ti* 'you' < **tū ~ darkë* 'supper' (cf. Gk δόρπον) ~ *djeg* 'to burn' < **dʰegʷʰō*, etc.

The loss of the voiced aspirates, which also occurred in other IE languages, must have taken place very early in Albanian. This is supported by the fact that loans from Ancient Greek containing an aspirate consonant appear in Albanian with a simple voiceless consonant (e.g. *mokën(ë)/mokër(ë)*, cf. p. 486). Note also that in Ancient Greek the aspirate consonants were voiceless (cf. Chapter 9, (6), p. 235), while in native Albanian words the old aspirate consonants appear as (unaspirated) voiced consonants.

As regards the evolution of the IE *gutturals* (or *tectals*), Albanian corresponds only partially with languages of the *satəm* type, because it has to some extent undergone developments of its own. Albanian thus provides further evidence to support the view that at a certain ancient stage of Indo-European three types of guttural had developed, namely *velars* */k g gʰ/, palatals* */k̂ ĝ ĝʰ/ and *labiovelars* */kʷ gʷ gʷʰ/ (cf. Bezzenberger 1890: 235, 244; Pisani 1961: 43ff.; Szemerényi 1980: 137ff.; Mayrhofer 1986: 102ff.; cf. also Chapter 2, **The Tectals**, p. 38 above).

The *velars* */k g gʰ/ gave /k g/ in Albanian. However, at a later stage, these consonants underwent palatalization before a front vowel to ‹q› (= /kʲ/) and ‹gj› (= /gʲ/) respectively, e.g.

> *ka* 'ox' < **kav-* (pl. *qe* < **kié*); *shteg* 'path' < **stega-* (pl. *shtigj-e*); *gardh* 'hedge' < **gardas* < **gʰordos* (pl. *gjerdhe-e* < **gierdh-e*) etc.

The *palatals* */k̂ ĝ ĝʰ/ produced, respectively, ‹th› (/θ/ as in English *thin*) and ‹dh› (/ð/ as in English *this*) or /d/ (word-initially). According to Pedersen 1900: 340, they changed at an early stage to *[ć, dź], then to *[ś, ź] and finally to ‹th, dh›. Examples of these are:

> *thanë* 'cornel' < **k̂ongā, tho-m/the-m* 'say' < **k̂ens-mi, dimën(ë)/dimër(ë)* 'winter' (cf. Gk χειμών, OCS *zima*)
> *dorë* 'hand' < **ĝʰerā, dhandër/dhëndër* 'son-in-law' < **ĝʰent-* (cf. Lith. *žéntas*)
> *lidh* 'to tie' (cf. Lat. *ligare*)
> *i madh* 'large' < **maĝʰ-* or **moĝʰ-*, etc.

The *labiovelars* */kʷ gʷ gʷʰ/ became /s/ and /z/ respectively before a front vowel /i/ or /e/. In other phonetic environments they became /k/ and /g/

respectively, that is, they behaved like the pure *velars* (see above). Examples:

pesë 'five' < **penkᵂe* (cf. Gk πέντε), *sa* 'how much' < **kᵂo-*, *se* 'what' < **kᵂōd*, *zjarm* 'fire' (cf. Skt *gharmá-s*, Arm. *jerm* 'warm', Gk θερμός 'hot, burning'), etc.

ujk < *ulk* 'wolf' (cf. Lith. *vilkas*, Skt. *vŕka-* etc.), *darkë* 'supper' (cf. Gk δόρπον), *djeg* 'burn' < **dʰegᵂʰō*, etc.

It should be mentioned that the development of the *labiovelars* before a front vowel in Albanian has followed a different course from that of the *satəm* languages in general, where the labiovelars underwent a development similar to that of the *velars*. Note also that in Greek (a language generally included in the *centum* language group) the *labiovelars* have also undergone a different development from that of the other *centum* languages (see Rix 1976: 85f.).

As regards the development of the *labiovelars* before a front vowel in Albanian, we must bear in mind the fact that the consonants /s/ and /z/ represent the final stage of this development. The preceding stages are not attested and so remain uncertain, although some views have been expressed on the matter (see Pedersen 1900: 340). It should be stressed, however, that the /s/ and /z/ stage was reached in a period where /s/ would no longer become ‹sh› (= /ʃ/) in Albanian, in other words towards the end of the tenth century AD (see Jokl 1935: 292).

The development /s/ > /sh/, mentioned above, again raises the problem of the fate of IE */s/ in Albanian. Since this is a relevant question and one which is still open to discussion, we shall go into it in rather more detail.

According to the general opinion, */s/ had the following reflexes in Albanian: ‹sh›, ‹gj›, ‹th› and ‹h›.

1   /s/ > ‹sh› (i.e. [ʃ]): *shi* 'rain' < **sū-*, *shta-të* 'seven' < **septṃ̆*, *ásht* 'bone' < **ost-* etc.

2   /s/ > ‹gj›: *gjak* 'blood' < **sok-*, *gjarpën/gjarpër* 'snake' < **serpono*, *gji(n)* 'breast' < **sin-*, *gjash-të* 'six' < **sex*, etc.

3   /s/ > ‹th› (i.e. [θ]): *thi* 'pig' < **sūs*, *tha-j* 'to dry' < **sausniō* (cf. Lith. *saũsas* 'dry', OCS *suchъ*), etc.

4   /s/ > /h/: *hyll/yll* 'star' < **sūl-* (cf. Lat. *sol-*, etc.), *heq < helq* 'to carry off' < **selkō* (cf. Gk ἕλκω, Lat. *sulcus-*), etc. this last reflex is debatable.

It is currently very difficult to specify precisely the circumstances which have led to these different reflexes of */s/ in Albanian. It should, however, be stressed that this phenomenon is a result not only of the phonetic environment in which the */s/ was found, but also of the fact that its different reflexes could not have arisen in the same period. It should also be stressed that the most general reflex was /s > sh/, which also affected loans from Ancient Greek (e.g. *presh* 'leek' < πράσον) and from Latin (e.g. *shpërej* 'to hope' < *sperare*, *shkallë* < *scala*), as well as the older stratum of Slavic loans (e.g. *grusht* 'fist' < *g ъrstъ* etc., on which see Seliščev 1931: 143).

It is not possible, given the scope of this chapter, to go into greater detail about the complex problem of the reflexes of */s/ in Albanian, on which the reader could consult, among others, Meyer (1892: 40–63), Pedersen (1900: 278) and Çabej (1970: 136–9).

Grammatical Structure

Like the phonetic system of the language (see **The Vowel System**, pp. 483f.), the grammatical structure of Albanian is also the result of a prehistoric and historical process of evolution. Thus, alongside some features inherited from an ancient IE stage of development, there also occur new features which have developed in different periods of the development of Albanian and of its 'parent language'. It should be emphasized that both old and new features have been adjusted to the needs of the linguistic system of Albanian and have thus led to the formation of a comlex but unitary grammatical structure.

In keeping with the introductory scope of the present article, we shall concentrate here on the main IE features and on some relevant innovations in the grammatical structure of Albanian.

The Noun System

In the noun system we find the following features, which are basically Indo-European:

1 traces of neuter gender
2 traces of the old declensional system, which has undergone extensive reorganization.

The Albanian neuter gender is distinguished only in the singular definite declension, where the nominative and accusative have the same ending, unlike nouns of the other two genders, where these two cases are distinguished clearly. Compare for example, masculine *mal-i* ~ *mal-in* 'the mountain', feminine *fush-a* ~ *fushë-n* 'the field', neuter *ballë-të* 'the forehead'.

The gradual reduction of the three-gender system through the gradual loss of the neuter is a very old phenomenon in Albanian. The number of neuter nouns appears extremely reduced even in the works of Albanian writers of the sixteenth and seventeenth centuries, as well as in all the dialects of the language. In the modern language the neuter has become a residual gender (see Demiraj 1986: 198ff.)

In the plural the attested neuters behave in gender as if they were feminine. This phenomenon of dual gender has also affected certain inanimate masculine nouns over the past few centuries (see Hamp 1958; Demiraj 1986: 206ff.).

Even older is the loss of the old threefold opposition between singular, dual and plural. Traces of the dual are not attested.

However, already prior to the sixteenth century the opposition between singular and plural had become more marked. The plural is distinguished by means of a special *stem*, contrasting with that of the singular, and the plural case endings are added to this special stem. Compare *ujk ~ ujq, ujq-ve, ujq-i-sh* etc. 'wolf ~ wolves, to wolves, of wolves'. This phenomenon, which also occurred for example in Rumanian (cf. *om ~ oameni, oameni-lor* 'man ~ men, to the men') and in German (cf. *Mann ~ Männer, den Männer-n*), goes back to the pre-literary period of Albanian (see Demiraj 1986: 213f., 1988: 71).

In the plural of certain masculine nouns a number of phonetic phenomena with morphophonological repercussions also took place, such as the umlaut /a ~ e/ and the palatalization of certain stem-final consonants; for example *dash ~ desh* 'ram ~ rams', *plak ~ pleq* 'old (sg.) ~ old (pl.)' etc. These two phenomena are a result of the old masculine nominative plural ending *-i < *-ī < *-oi (of pronominal origin), which is also attested in other IE languages, such as Greek, Latin, the Balto-Slavic languages, and so on.

The umlaut, a process of regressive assimilation, took place at a time when the ending *-i had not yet been reduced to the semi-vowel *-j, while the palatalization of the final consonant of the stem of certain nouns took place while the ending was *-j; this then vanished completely from the Albanian noun system.

The umlaut took place before Albanian came into contact with Balkan Slavonic, that is before the seventh to eighth centuries AD (see Demiraj 1986: 111f.). A similar phenomenon also occurred in the Germanic languages (see Paul 1959: vol. I, 111, 248ff.; cf Chapter 13, p. 390.

Although the old IE declensional system has undergone considerable change, it has also left behind clear traces in Albanian. Thus, for example, nouns on the whole distinguish both formally and functionally such cases as the nominative, accusative, genitive, dative and the so-called ablative, particularly in the definite declension, where the forms of the postposed article (p. 492) have merged over time with the indefinite forms of the noun cases. Table 16.1 shows, by way of example, the indefinite and definite declension of three Albanian nouns: masculine *mal* 'mountain', feminine *fushë* 'field' and neuter *ujë* 'water':

The endings attested for the indefinite declension are *-i (-u) ~ -e* in the genitive-dative singular, *-v-e* in the genitive-dative plural and *-sh* in the so-called ablative plural.

The ending *-i* goes back to the old IE dative singular ending *-ej. The ending *-v-e* (with *-v-* to prevent hiatus) goes back to the old IE genitive plural ending *-ōn (see Pedersen 1894: 254) and the ending *-sh* goes back to the old IE locative ending *-su (see Pedersen 1900: 280).

Diachronic analysis of the definite declension has made it clear that the accusative singular element *-në* originates from the development of the old

Table 16.1 Examples of indefinite and definite declension

	Singular						Plural					
	Indefinite	Definite	Indefinite	Definite	Indefinite	Definite	Indefinite	Definite	Indefinite	Definite	Indefinite	Definite
Nom.	mal	mal-i	fushë	fush-a	ujë	ujë-të	male	male-t	fusha	fusha-t	ujëra	ujëra-t(ë)
Acc.	mal	mal-në	fushë	fushë-në	ujë	ujë-të	male	male-t	fusha	fusha-t	ujëra	ujëra-t(ë)
Gen	i ... mal-i	i mali-t	i ... fush-e	fushë-së	i ... uj-i	uji-t	i ... male-ve	i maleve-t	i ... fusha-ve	i fushave-t	i ... ujëra-ve	i ujërave-t
Dat.	... mal-i	mali-t	... fush-e	fushë-së	... uj-i	uji-t	... male-ve	maleve-t	... fusha-ve	fushave-t	... ujëra-ve	ujërave-t
Abl.	mal-i	mali-t	fush-e	fushë-së	uj-i	uji-t	male-sh	malesh-i-t	fusha-sh	fushash-i-t	ujëra-sh	ujërash-i-t

Note: The definite forms of the ablative plural have become archaic and are replaced in the modern language with those of the dative plural.

accusative ending *-n plus the corresponding form of the definite article *-të, i.e. *-n + *të > *-ntë > *-ndë > -në. Thus the old IE masculine and feminine noun ending is also attested in Albanian (see Demiraj 1986: 346ff.).

All the attested case endings have preserved the old characteristic of indicating case and number (and in the singular the masculine ~ feminine gender too) at the same time.

In the course of its development Albanian has also come to use a new means of distinguishing the genitive from the dative. This is the so-called 'preposed article', which is declined according to the case, gender and number of the noun modified. For example, *libri i nxënësit ~ librit të nxënësit ~ librat e nxënësit* 'the pupil's book ~ to the pupil's book ~ the pupil's books', etc.; *fletorja e nxënësit ~ fletores së nxënësit ~ fletoret e nxënësit* 'the pupil's exercise book ~ to the pupil's exercise book ~ the pupil's exercise books', etc.

The definite forms of the cases are distinguished from the corresponding indefinite forms by means of the postposed article. This has preserved the inflectional morphology (naturally in reduced form) of the anaphoric demonstrative pronoun from which it originated at a very early stage of development (see Demiraj 1986: 329ff.).

In its use of the postposed definite article, Albanian is in line with Rumanian, Bulgarian and Macedonian. A similar phenomenon also occurred in Armenian and the Scandinavian languages. But in the course of its development Albanian has also created a preposed article, which serves *inter alia* to distinguish the genitive from the dative (see above) and also functions as an integral part of the adjectival group (see below) etc. A similar phenomenon also occurs in Rumanian; for further details on this point see Demiraj 1986: 326f.

Over the course of time the indefinite case forms have generally lost their ability to be used without a preposed determiner or a preposition. However, some are still used on their own with certain functions (see Demiraj 1986: 398f.). More frequently used without a preposed determiner are the definite forms of the noun. It will suffice to bear in mind the fact that the indefinite forms of the genitive and dative cannot be used without a preposed determiner, while the definite forms of these two cases are usually used without such a determiner.

It should also be noted that the use of prepositions with the different cases has been increasing, and, what is most striking, that even the nominative is being used with certain prepositions (see p. 497).

Adjectives have generally preserved their grammatical agreement with the noun. However they have lost the old system of inflectional declension, but in order to express grammatical agreement some adjectives use the forms of a preposed article which has become an integral part of them. These form the 'pre-article' group of adjectives, which contrast with the other group of adjectives; compare *i mirë* 'good ~ *besnik* 'faithful'.

The preposed article in adjectives of the type *i mirë* is declined according to the case, gender and number of the noun it modifies, for example, *djali i mirë* 'the good boy' ~ *djalit të mirë* 'to the good boy' ~ *djalin e mirë* 'the good boy (acc.)' ~ *djemtë e mirë* 'the good boys'; *vajza e mirë* 'the good girl' ~ *vajzës së mirë* 'to the good girl' ~ *vajzën e mirë* 'the good girl (acc.)', etc.

This phenomenon, which also occurred in the genitive (see p. 492), gave way to a notable Albanian innovation distinguishing it from Indo-European, namely a system of word-initial inflection, a phenomenon also characteristic of the possessive pronouns (see below).

Pronouns

In the pronoun system too there are considerable IE remnants, as well as notable innovations. Among the inherited elements, the following should be noted.

The personal pronouns of the first two persons: *u-unë* 'I', *na* 'we', *ti* 'you (sg.)', *ju* 'you (pl.)'. These have their own special declension, as in the other IE languages.

U-në, on the origin of which see Demiraj (1986: 447f.), has suppletive forms in its other cases: *mua* 'me', *me-je* '(from) me'. Compare also *ti* ~ *ty* ~ *te-je* 'you (nom.) ~ you (acc.) ~ (from) you' etc. In the dative and accusative, alongside with the tonic forms, there appear also clitic (generally reduced) forms like *më* for *mua*, *të* for *ty*, etc. Such clitic forms, which arose in other IE languages (e.g. in the Romance languages, etc.) are also used in the third-person personal pronouns, which are of demonstrative origin (and which still retain this function). Compare for example *a-i* ~ *a-tij/i* ~ *a-të/e* etc. 'that ~ to that ~ that (acc.)', etc.

This is a widespread phenomenon in the IE languages, where the third-person pronoun is generally of demonstrative origin. In Albanian the demonstratives in question go back to the IE demonstratives **so, sā, tod* (see Pedersen 1900: 312; Demiraj 1986: 465ff. and cf. Chapter 2, p. 65). But at some stage of the development of Albanian the prefixes *a-* and *kë-* were added to these demonstratives to indicate objects 'far away from' and 'close to' the speaker respectively (e.g. *a-i/a-y, a-ta* etc. 'that, those', *k-y, kë-ta* etc. 'this, these', etc).

It seems that Albanian has lost at an early date the other demonstratives attested in languages such as Latin (cf. *is, hic, ille*) etc. The Albanian demonstratives have preserved their own special declensional system, obviously reduced in the number of its forms (see Demiraj 1986: 463ff.).

Another inherited pronominal form is the interrogative *ku-sh* 'who?' < **kʷu-* (?) (acc. *kë < kā < *kʷon*, dat. *ku-i-t*), corresponding to Latin *quis*, Greek *tis < *kʷis* etc. Among the Albanian pronouns there are also other inherited forms, on which see Demiraj (1986: 504ff.).

A large number of new pronominal forms have appeared during the course of the development of Albanian. We should mention in particular the first- and second-person possessive pronouns and some indefinite pronouns, which are agglutinated forms.

The first- and second-person possessives were formed by means of the merger of two elements, the first of which was a demonstrative or a preposed article and the second a personal pronoun form. Compare, for example, *i-m* 'my' < *a-i* + *m(ua)*, *y-t* 'your' < *a-y* + *t(y)*, *y-në* 'our' < *a-y* + *ne*.

In these agglutinations the first element is declined regularly (e.g. *i-m* ~ *ti-m*). Their declension, once extremely complex, has been reduced considerably over the past few centuries (see Demiraj 1986: 481f.).

Among the indefinite pronouns agglutinated forms have also arisen, for instance, *kush-do* 'whoever', *cili-do* 'anyone, anybody', *çfarë-do* 'whatever'. Such words were formed by means of the agglutination of two elements in a subordinate clause. Thus, from constructions of the type *Këtë e bën kush do* (lit. 'Does this who will') there was a move to constructions of the type *Këtë e bën kushdo* 'Does this who will' (lit. 'Who will does this'), i.e. 'anybody does this'.

From the point of view of their formation, these agglutinated pronouns are similar to Rumanian pronoun forms of the type *cine-va*, *care-va* 'whoever', etc. For further details see Demiraj (1988: 104f.).

The Verb System

The Albanian verb system as compared with the noun system is more complex both in terms of IE inheritance and in terms of innovation. However, in order to gain a clearer impression of the IE traces, it should be stressed that they are grammatical phenomena and forms which are generally attributed to many IE languages at an ancient stage of evolution.

Attested Albanian has preserved very few traces of the athematic conjugation in *-mi* (only three verbs: *ja-m* 'to be', *ka-m* 'to have' and *tho-m* 'to say'), while the type of conjugation in *-ō/-jō* has become very productive. This is particularly true of the *-jō* conjugation, whose first element in certain cases caused the palatalization of the final consonant of the verb stem; for example *bānj/bënj* 'to do' < **banjō* (for the morphological type cf. Gk φαίνω, Lat. *faciō* etc.).

Albanian still clearly preserves the contrast in tense between the present, imperfect and past definite. However, it should be noted that not only forms of the old sigmatic and asigmatic aorist but also forms of the old synthetic perfect have been merged in the so-called past definite. It should also be noted that Albanian, like most of the IE languages, has over time also developed analytic forms of the perfect and pluperfect, formed using the auxiliary verbs *to have* and *to be* (for the active and the middle voice respectively) with the past participle.

Traces of the sigmatic aorist, attested in Greek (cf. ἔ-λυ-σ-α etc.), Latin (cf. the so-called perfect of the type *scrip-s-i*) etc., have been preserved only in the first person of certain native verbs, such as *ra-sh-ë* 'I fell', *qe-sh-ë* 'I was', *tha-sh-ë* 'I said', *la-sh-ë* 'I left', etc. In such cases the formant -*sh*- goes back to the sigmatic element *-*s*- (see Brugmann and Delbrück 1913: 390ff.; Watkins 1969: 44).

Albanian has also preserved traces of the quantitative ablaut which in certain verbs characterized the opposition between the present and (synthetic) perfect (cf. Lat. *venio ~ vēni, lego ~ lēgi*, etc.). These traces are visible in many verbs of the type *dal ~ dol-a* 'I go out ~ I went out', *bredh ~ brodh-a* 'I run ~ I ran', *dredh ~ drodh-a* 'I twist ~ I twisted', etc. In such cases the *o* of the old synthetic perfect was a result of the development *$\bar{a}$ > *o* or *$\bar{e}$ > *o* (see p. 485).

There are also traces of suppletion (cf. Lat. *sum ~ fui, fero ~ tuli* etc., English *I go ~ I went* etc.), for example *ja-m ~ qe-sh-ë* 'I am ~ I was', *jap ~ dha-sh-ë* 'I give ~ I gave', *ka-m ~ pat-a* 'I have ~ I had', *shoh ~ pa-sh-ë* 'I see ~ I saw', *rri ~ ndenj-a* 'I sit ~ I sat', etc.

Albanian has also preserved some verbal endings inherited from an old stage of Indo-European.

The plural endings -*më*, -*të*, -*në*, which have been preserved in particular in the past definite (cf. *qe-më, qe-të, qe-në* 'we were, you were, they were'), but also in the present (with the exception of the second person) and the imperfect (with occasional lengthening) go back to the old IE endings *-*mes/ -mos*, -*tha/-ta*, -*e/onti* respectively.

The ending -*m*, which appears only in the present (first-person singular) of a very small number of verbs (*ja-m* 'I am', *ka-m* 'I have', *tho-m* 'I say'), goes back to the old -*mi* conjugation verb ending *-*mi* (cf. Gk εἰ-μί, Lat. *su-m*, Skt *as-mi* etc).

The ending -*sh*, which appears in the second-person present subjunctive (e.g. *të je-sh* 'that you be', *të shko-sh* 'that you go', etc.) goes back to the old ending *-*si* (cf. Skt *bhara-si*, Lat. *amā-s*, etc.).

The ending -*të*, which occurs in particular in the third-person present subjunctive of -*mi* conjugation verbs (cf. *të je-të* 'that he be', but also *ësh-të* 'he is', *të ke-të* 'that he have', *të tho-të*, but also *tho-të* 'that he say' and 'he says'), goes back to the old IE ending *-*ti* (cf. also Lat. *es-t, habe-t*, etc., Ger. *is-t* etc).

However, there are also endings which have arisen in the course of the development of Albanian, on which see Demiraj (1986: 685ff.).

It can be claimed that the system of inflectional endings in Albanian, as in the other IE languages, has undergone a continuous process of formal reshaping. But all the Albanian endings, whether inherited or innovatory, have preserved one characteristic of Indo-European in that they are multifunctional morphs. In fact, they indicate not only the person but also the number, tense and in certain cases also the mood of the verb. For example, the ending -*sh* in *të je-sh* 'that you be' indicates that the verb is second-person singular present subjunctive.

The forms in -*m*, -*në*, -*rë*, -*të* which appear in the past participle and in certain adjectives (mainly those derived from verbs) were also inherited from an ancient IE stage of development. Compare, for example, in Buzuku: *bā-m* 'done', *ble-në* 'bought', *bā-të* 'done', etc. These forms go back to IE mediopassive participles in *-*mo*/-*meno*- and verbal adjectives in *-*to*/no*- (cf. *lauda-tus*, Gk λυό-μενος, Ger. *ge-schriebe-n*, *ge-hab-t* etc.).

In modern Albanian the form -*në* is more frequent; this is realized as -*rë* in the southern dialect (with the development -*n*- > -*r*- discussed on p. 481).

Among the important innovations in the verb system of Albanian we should note above all certain phenomena which also appear in other Balkan languages. These are *inter alia*:

1   the appearance of a preposed particle in the subjunctive (cf. Alb. *të bëj* 'that I do', Gk νὰ κάνω, Rum. *să fac*, Bulg. *šte pravja* < *šte* + indicative form)
2   the formation of the future by means of a fossilized form of the auxiliary verb *to want* (cf. Alb. *do të bëj* 'I shall do', Gk θὰ κάνω, Bulg. *šte pravja*, Rum. *o să fac*, but also *voiu face*)
3   the frequent use of the subjunctive in place of the infinitive (cf. *dua të bëj* 'I want to do', cf. Gk θέλω νὰ κάνω, Rum. *voiu să fac*, Bulg. *šta da pravja*). (See Sandfeld 1930: 182, Banfi 1985: 58f.).

As regards the infinitive, which since early times has developed independently in the IE languages (cf. Lat. *lauda-re*, *es-se* etc., Gk λύειν, λύσειν etc.), it remains unclear whether such a form ever existed in Albanian, where we find an analytic form functioning as an infinitive, namely the form of the type *me tha-në* 'to say', formed with the preposition *me* 'with' and the substantivized past participle. It is not certain whether this form, which is better attested in the northern dialect, has replaced a synthetic infinitive (see Demiraj 1986: 1010ff.).

Invariable Elements

Albanian adverbs of IE extraction tend to be of pronominal or adjectival origin. They include the interrogative adverts *ku?* 'where?' (cf. the pronoun *ku-sh* on p. 493), *si?* 'how?' < *$k^w ei$* etc., *mirë* 'well' (cf. *i mirë* 'good'), *zi* 'darkly' (cf. *izi* 'dark'). In the latter cases the adverb is distinguished from the corresponding adjective by the absence of the preposed article.

Most of the adverbs in Albanian are fairly old creations. Among these we should mention the very old fossilized and reduced forms such as *sot* 'today' < **so dite* 'of this day', *sonte* 'tonight' < **so nate* 'of this night', *sivjet* 'this year' < **si vjeti* 'of this year'.

Albanian has also preserved some old prepositions, some of which are of IE origin, such as *ën* 'of' (attested in Buzuku); *ndë*/*në* 'in, at', *mbi*/*mbë* 'on, above', etc. (see Demiraj 1986: 630ff. for bibliography).

Many prepositions are of adverbial origin. These include *gjatë* 'along', *afër* 'near', *larg* 'far from'.

The prepositions in Albanian govern the accusative (e.g. *në*, *mbi* etc.) or the dative–ablative (e.g. *prej* 'from, by', *gjatë* 'during', etc.). However, as mentioned on pp. 492, there are also prepositions (*nga* 'from' and *tek* 'near') which govern the nominative, a phenomenon which is not attested in other IE languages.

Similarly very few of the conjunctions have been inherited from the ancient IE period. One might mention here the coordinating conjunction *dhe* 'and', the subordinating conjunctions of pronominal origin *se* 'that' < *$k^w j\bar{o}d$, *si* 'as' < *$k^w ej$, *sa* 'scarcely' < *$k^w o$- (see Pedersen 1900: 317). However, the use of the latter forms as conjunctions very probably dates from a later period. With the development of society the use of conjunctions also became increasingly common and more complex, resulting in the creation of new conjunctions, such as *megjithëse* 'although', *sadoqë* 'though', *kurse* 'while'.

Specific Syntactic Features

As is known, it is very difficult to establish with any degree of certainty which syntactic features were characteristic of Indo-European. Anything that can be deduced from the oldest attested IE languages, such as Greek and Sanskrit, could at least in part be the result of independent developments in these languages. However, it has been possible to establish with some confidence certain rules of sentence construction in Indo-European. These include Wackernagel's Law (Wackernagel 1892: 342, 402), according to which the IE sentence in general could not begin with a clitic word. Moreover, it is generally accepted that there was greater freedom of word order, although the speaker's choice of word order would obviously be dictated by stylistic and pragmatic considerations. It has also been generally agreed that in a stylistically neutral sentence the verbal endings made it unnecessary to express the subject of the clause where this could readily be deduced from the context.

Attested Albanian shows that the language has in part preserved IE-type syntactic features and in part developed features found only in some languages, particularly Balkan languages.

As Albanian has preserved the system of verb endings, the expression of the subject (S) in a stylistically neutral sentence tends to be redundant, particularly when this would have to be expressed using a first- or second-person personal pronoun. In such a sentence the normal word order is (S)VO + other elements, but word order is freer in Albanian than in other languages, e.g. English, German.

However, even in Albanian certain constituents have a fixed position within the clause. This is the case, for example, with certain determiners (see next paragraph) as well as the clitic forms of the personal pronouns (see below).

Determiners are generally placed beside the noun they modify. However, while in certain IE languages (e.g. the Germanic and Slavic languages) there is a tendency to place determiners before the noun, in others we see the opposite tendency. Thus, for example, in Albanian and Rumanian certain determiners (the cardinal numerals, the demonstratives, the interrogatives, the indefinite pronouns), which are also used alone, are placed before the noun, whereas certain others (e.g. adjectives, ordinal numerals, possessive pronouns), which can be used alone only predicatively or as nouns, are regularly placed after the noun. This post-substantival position is the result of a relatively old tendency in the two languages to postpose 'non-self-sufficient' determiners. This is borne out by the postposing of the definite article, which was originally an anaphoric demonstrative (see p. 492).

Clitic forms of the personal pronouns (see p. 493) are placed immediately before the verb in stylistically neutral sentences. They can also be placed in sentence-initial position; this use must be relatively old, pre-dating by at least a few centuries the work of Buzuku (1555). A similar phenomenon has also taken place in Rumanian and the Romance languages in general, as well as in (modern) Greek and Western Macedonian (but not in Bulgarian or the Slavonic languages in general).

The clitic forms, created by the phonetic reduction of their respective 'full' forms in sentences where they did not represent the 'rheme' of the utterance, serve both to express the direct and indirect objects and to reiterate them. Compare for example *Ai më ftoi* (lit. 'he me invited') ~ *Ai më fioi mua* (*e jo ty*) (lit. 'he me invited me (and not you)) 'he invited me ~ he invited *me* (and not *you*)'. The reiteration of the indirect object now tends to be a general phenomenon in modern Albanian, while the direct object (in the first two persons) is only reiterated when it represents the 'rheme' of the utterance (see Demiraj 1986: 584ff., 1988: 64ff.).

The reiteration of the object complement, a relatively old phenomenon in Albanian (having appeared at least several centuries before Buzuku), has also taken place in the other Balkan languages (Rumanian, Macedonian, Bulgarian and Greek), as also in Spanish, Italian dialects, and so on (see the relevant references in Demiraj 1986: 602ff.).

In Albanian, as mentioned on p. 496, the subjunctive is also used with the characteristic function of an infinitive. This phenomenon, which also occurred in the other Balkan languages (see Sandfeld 1930: 7f., 176f.; Banfi 1985: 58ff.) is more widespread in the southern Albanian dialect and goes back to a relatively old period. The phenomenon, which has given rise to heated debate, is extremely complex and in the case of Albanian needs to be considered in close conjunction with the problem of the infinitive (see p. 496).

The Native Vocabulary

Although it has undergone significant changes in the course of its development, the vocabulary of Albanian has also preserved many words of IE origin. These may be identified by comparison with the corresponding words in other IE languages and are in general words which have undergone ancient phonetic changes such as ablaut, the development of the short and long vowels and of the gutturals, and so on, as discussed above. They may also have undergone semantic change, as for example in the case of the noun *motër* 'sister' < **māter* (see p. 485).

With regard to those words of IE origin, it is important to remember that many have been lost in the course of the centuries, having been replaced in part by foreign borrowings or having gone out of use for a number of reasons. It will suffice to remember, by way of example, the noun *mang-u*, which is found once only in the work of Buzuku with the meaning 'male'. This word, which has been compared with Arm. *manr* 'small, thin' (see Çabej 1976a: 1, 331) has been replaced by the Latin borrowing *mashkull* < *masculus*.

Among the ancient native Albanian vocabulary, other than those words already mentioned above, we should mention *inter alia* the cardinal numerals, which, with the exception of *qind* 'hundred' and *mijë* 'thousand' from Latin *centum* and *milia*, are all native Albanian words deriving directly from Indo-European. In this regard it is also important to note that the numerals eleven to nineteen in Albanian were formed by inserting the preposition *mbë* < *mbi* 'on, above' between the unit and the 'ten', for example, *një-mbë-dhjetë* 'eleven', *dy-mbë-dhjetë* 'twelve'. A similar means of forming these numerals can also be found in the Balto-Slavic languages and Rumanian (cf. Rum. *un-spre-zece*, *doi-/două-spre-zece*).

Moreover, it should be mentioned that in the Albanian number system there are also a few traces of the (pre-IE?) vigesimal system which is so prevalent in Basque (cf. also French *quatre-vingts*). Thus in Albanian we have *një-zet* 'twenty', *dy-zet* 'forty' and in certain archaic dialects also *tre-zet* 'sixty' and *katër-zet* 'eighty'.

The IE origin of the Albanian numerals is demonstrated clearly by their development, which is in keeping with the old sound laws of the language. This has led to a situation whereby some of these words have become phonetically very different from the corresponding forms in the other IE languages. Compare, for example, the numeral *gjash-të* 'six' with Lat. *sex*, Gk ἕξ, Skt *śaś*. The Albanian numeral appears lengthened with the suffix *-të*, deriving, most probably, from the ordinal numerals (see p. 500), as in *shta-të* 'seven', *te-të* 'eight', *nën-të* 'nine'. The form *gjash-*, as compared with **s(w)eks*, exhibits the following changes: *s-* > *gj-* as in **serpens* > *gjarpën/ gjarpër* (see p. 488), *-e-* > *-a-* (see p. 484) and *ks* > *sh* (= [ʃ]).

A special position in the native Albanian vocabulary is held by those words which have cognates in Rumanian, namely a large number of words which Rumanian has inherited from the substrate. These include: *baltë*, Rum. *baltă* 'mud', *bollë*, Rum. *balaur* 'snake', *bredh*, Rum. *brad* 'fir-tree', *gropë*, Rum. *groapă* 'ditch', *gushë*, Rum. *gușă* 'bird's crop, throat', *nepërkë*, Rum. *năpîrcă* 'viper', *mal* 'mountain', Rum. *mal* 'bank' (see Brâncuș 1983: *passim*).

The presence of such words in both Albanian and Rumanian, which also have other mutual corespondences, has given rise to discussions about their origin, on which see Demiraj (1988: 100ff.).

In the course of its development Albanian has also been enriched with a large number of derived words, some of which are very old. These include the ordinal numerals, which, with the exception of *i parë* 'first', are formed from the corresponding cardinal numerals with the suffix *-të* of IE origin (see Xhuvani and Çabej 1962: 91) and with the preposed article (see p. 492), for example *i dy-të* 'second', *i tre-të* 'third', *i ghjash-të* 'sixth'. However, *i parë* 'first' is from IE **por-* (see Meyer 1891: 321).

Of the native derived words in Albanian, we can also cite by way of example the verbs *n-gul < *n-kul* 'to thrust in', *sh-kul* 'to uproot', *për-kul* 'to fold'. The root *-kul*, which Meyer (1891: 307) compares with Lithuanian *kuliù kulti* 'to thresh', only occurs in the above-mentioned derivatives.

In the course of its development the vocabulary of Albanian has also been enriched by a large number of compound words, as well as by many loans from Greek (ancient, medieval and modern), from Latin and the Romance languages, from the Balkan Slavonic languages, from Turkish etc. (on which see Demiraj 1988: 105ff.).

References

Banfi, Emanuele (1985) *Linguistica balcanica*, Bologna: Zanichelli.

Bezzenberger, Adalbert (1890) 'Die indogermanischen Gutturalreihen', *Beiträge zur Kunde der indogermanischen Sprachen* 6: 234–60.

Bopp, Franz (1854) 'Über das Albanesische in seinen verwandtschaftlichen Beziehungen', paper presented to the Royal Academy of Science, 18 May 1854.

Brâncuș, Grigore (1983) *Vocabularul autohton al limbii române*, Bucharest: Edit, Știinţifică și enciclopedică.

Brugmann, Karl and Delbrück, Berthold (1913) *Grundriss der vergleichenden Grammatik der idg. Sprachen* 2nd edn, vol. 2, Strasburg: Trübner.

Buzuku, Gjon (1555) *'Meshari' i Gjon Buzukut* (critical edition prepared by Eqrem Çabej), second part, Universiteti Shtetëror i Tiranës. Instituti i Historisë dhe i Gjuhësisë, Tirana, 1968.

Çabej, Eqrem (1970) *Hyrje në historinë e gjuhës shqipe. Fonetike historike e shqipes*, 2nd edn, Prishtinë: Universiteti i Prishtinës (repr. of the 1960 Tirana edition).

——— (1972) 'Problemi i vendit të formimit të gjuhës shqipe', *Studime filologjike* 4: 5–23.

——— (1976a) *Studime gjuhësore*, vol. I, Prishtinë: Rilindja.

——— (1976b) *Studime etimologjike në fushë të shqipes*, vol. II, Tirana: Akademia e Shkencave e Shqipërisë, Instituti i Gjuhësisë dhe i Letërsisë.

——— (1987) *Studime etimologjike në fushë të shqipes*, vol. III, Tirana: Akademia e Shkencave e Shqipërisë, Instituti i Gjuhësisë dhe i Letërsisë.

Demiraj, Shaban (1986) *Gramatikë historike e gjuhës shqipe*, Tirana: 8 Nëntori.

——— (1988) *Gjuha shqipe dhe historia e saj*, Tirana: Shtëpia Botuese e Librit Universitar.
Hamp, Eric C. (1958) 'Gender shift in Albanian', *Romance Philology* 12 (2): 147–55.
——— (1966) 'The position of Albanian', in Henrik Birnbaum and Jaan Puhvel (eds), *Ancient Indo-European Dialects*, Berkeley and Los Angeles: University of California Press, pp. 97–121.
——— (1969) vol. II, *Istoria limbii rom*â*ne*, Bucharest: Academia Republicii Socialiste România.
Jokl, Norbert (1935–6) 'Slaven und Albaner', *Slavia* (Praga) 13 (2–3): 281–325; 13 (4): 609–45.
Katičić, Radoslav (1976) *Ancient Languages of the Balkans*, The Hague and Paris: Mouton.
Matranga, Luca (1592) *La 'Dottrina cristiana' albanese di Luca Matranga*, ed. Matteo Sciambra, Vatican City: Bibl. Apostol., 1964.
Mayrhofer, Manfred (1986) *Indogermanische Grammatik*, vol. I, Heidelberg: Winter.
Meyer, Gustav (1888) 'Die lateinischen Elemente im Albanesischen', in G. Gröber (ed.), *Grundriss der romanischen Philologie*, Strasburg, pp. 804–30.
——— (1891) *Etymologisches Wörterbuch der albanesischen Sprache*, Strasburg: Trübner.
——— (1892) *Albanesische Studien*, vol. III, Vienna: Holzhausen.
Paul, Hermann (1959) *Deutsche Grammatik*, vol. I, 6th edn, Halle (Saale): VEB Max Verlag.
Pedersen, H. (1894) 'Bidrag til albanesiske Sproghistorie.' In *Festkskrift til Vilhelm Thomsen*, Copenhagen: Gyldendal, pp. 246–57.
Pedersen, Holger (1900) 'Die Gutturale im Albanesischen', *Zeitschrift für vergleichende Sprachforschung* 36: 277–341.
Pisani, Vittore (1961) *Glottologia indoeuropea*, Turin: Rosenberg & Sellier.
Rix, Helmut (1976) *Historische Grammatik des Griechischen*, Darmstadt: Wissenschaftliche Buchgesellschaft.
Sala, Marius (1970) *Contribu*ţ*ii la fonetica istoric*ă *a limbii rom*â*ne*, Bucharest: Editura Academiei Republicii Socialiste România.
Sandfeld, Kristian (1930) *Linguistique balkanique. Problèmes et résultats*, Paris: Champion.
Seliščev, A. M. (1931) *Slavjanskoe naselenie v Albanii*, Sofia: Izdanie Makedonskogo Naučnogo Instituta.
Svane, Gunnar (1992) *Slavische Lehnwörter im Albanischen*, Aarhus: University Press.
Szemerényi, Oswald (1980) *Einführung in die vergleichende Sprachwissenschaft*, Darmstadt: Wissenschaftliche Buchgesellschaft.
Wackernagel, Jakob (1892) 'Über ein Gesetz der indogermanischen Wortstellung', *Indogermanische Forschungen* I: 333–435.
Watkins, Calvert (1969) *Indogermanische Grammatik*, ed. Jerzy Kuryłowicz, vol. III, *Formenlehre*, Heidelberg: Winter.
Xhuvani, A. and Çabej, E. (1956) 'Prapastetesat e gjuhës shqipe', *Buletin për Shkencat Shoqërore*, 1956 (4): 66–103.
——— (1962) *Prapashtesat e gjuhës shqipe*, Tirana: Universiteti Shtetëror i Tiranës, Instituti i Historisë dhe i Gjuhësisë.

Index